GUIDE TO FINANCIAL ANALYSIS

McGraw-Hill Finance Guide Series

CONSULTING EDITOR:

Charles A. D'Ambrosio, *University of Washington*

Bowlin, Martin, and Scott: Guide to Financial Analysis
Farrell: Guide to Portfolio Management
Riley and Montgomery: Guide to Computer Assisted Investment Analysis
Smith: Guide to Working Capital Management

GUIDE TO FINANCIAL ANALYSIS

SECOND EDITION

Oswald D. Bowlin
Texas Tech University

John D. Martin
University of Texas–Austin

David F. Scott, Jr.
University of Central Florida

McGRAW-HILL PUBLISHING COMPANY

New York   St. Louis   San Francisco   Auckland   Bogotá
Caracas   Hamburg   Lisbon   London   Madrid
Mexico   Milan   Montreal   New Delhi   Oklahoma City   Paris
San Juan   São Paulo   Singapore   Sydney   Tokyo   Toronto

This book was set in Times Roman by Publication Services.
The editor was Suzanne BeDell;
the production supervisor was Janelle S. Travers.
The cover was designed by Karen Quigley.
Project supervision was done by Publication Services.
R. R. Donnelley & Sons Company was printer and binder.

GUIDE TO FINANCIAL ANALYSIS

1 2 3 4 5 6 7 8 9 0 DOC DOC 8 9 4 3 2 1 0 9

ISBN   0-07-006805-4

Library of Congress Cataloging-in-Publication Data

Bowlin, Oswald D. (Oswald Doniece, date.)
    Guide to financial analysis / Oswald D. Bowlin, John D. Martin,
  David F. Scott.—2nd ed.
      p.   cm.
    Includes bibliographical references.
    ISBN 0-07-006805-4
    1. Business enterprises—Finance.   2. Corporations—Finance.
  I. Martin, John D., (date). II. Scott, David F., (date).
  III. Title.
  HG4011.B655 1990
  658.15—dc20   89-28400

To the memory of our parents:

Elnie B. Bowlin and Oswald L. Bowlin

Delia G. Martin and J. B. Martin

Anita M. Scott and David F. Scott, Sr.

CONTENTS

PREFACE

The fundamental premise of this book is that competent financial management of a business firm requires the use of the most up-to-date analytical tools and the assessment of the normative value of quantitative results in light of prevailing economic and other environmental factors. There are several implications of this premise for a book such as the *Guide to Financial Analysis*. First, the subject matter should focus primarily on practical decision making. Second, the techniques of financial analysis presented should encompass the latest developments in the field, to the extent that these developments can be applied to real-world problems. Finally, qualitative factors that can influence the financial decision should be carefully examined and, if deemed appropriate, allowed to modify or change the recommended action by the firm. The authors have attempted to follow through on these implications.

This second edition is designed as a textbook for any type of course in which solving financial problems or cases is of major concern. Both the text explanations and the illustrations deal with firms of different sizes—large, small, and in-between. The expanded number of problems at the end of the chapters provides the student with an opportunity to apply the analytical techniques in a decision-making framework. In addition, the book can be used effectively with a casebook.

The revision is a major rewrite of the first edition. In addition to the usual updating of subject matter presented previously, the number of topics covered has been substantially increased. Entirely new chapters include 8, 9, and 10, which deal with working capital problems and policies. The use of computer spreadsheets is discussed in Chapter 2 and at other points throughout the text. Solving some of the end-of-chapter problems requires sensitivity analysis. The use of spreadsheets is recommended in finding the solutions, and this fact is so noted at the beginning of the relevant problems.

Chapter appendixes have been added for those who are interested in digging deeper into some of the topics:

Appendix 3A: Analyzing Forecast Accuracy
Appendix 4A: Summing a Geometric Progression
Appendix 6A: Interest Rate Risk
Appendix 6B: Evaluating Option Components of Capital Expenditures
Appendix 11A: Debt Refunding

Chapter 10 in the first edition, "Using Financial Models" has been dropped, and part of the material refined and included with other topics in the revision. All of the other chapters in the first edition have been updated and, in some instances, substantially expanded. For example, systematic risk is now covered in considerable depth in Chapter 6, and the concept is used extensively in later chapters. Appendix 5A, "Federal Taxation of Business Income," has been almost entirely rewritten by professionals in the tax field in order to explain the major aspects of current tax law that are important in financial decision making.

Although the subject matter of the book focuses primarily on solving financial problems, the theoretical base for each major topic is presented in a straight forward manner. Complex theoretical models are avoided, however. The presentation of each analytical technique begins with the basics and then extends to whatever level is necessary to solve practical problems in the most reliable and efficient manner. Although preparation requirements on the part of the reader are minimal, a basic understanding of college algebra and the material normally covered in the first accounting course at the college level will be helpful.

The chapters have not been partitioned into parts within the text. The following chapter grouping and related description provide an overview of the subject matter.

Chapters	Description of contents
1	Introduction: the nature of financial management and decisions
2–3	Financial analysis, forecasting, and planning
4	Valuation: the foundation of financial decision making
5–6	Capital budgeting decisions: evaluation techniques and impact of risk
7	The required rate of return on new investments
8–10	Working capital decisions
11	The financing decision: choosing both the length and the type of financing
12	The dividend decision

The academic field of finance has been highly dynamic during the past 35 years or so—since the publication of the Markowitz paper "Portfolio Selection" in 1952 and the Modigliani-Miller paper "The Cost of Capital, Corporation Finance, and the Theory of Investment" in 1958. Many new financial concepts and approaches to financial decision making have appeared in the literature, and the trend seems to be accelerating. As noted earlier, we have attempted to cover the most up-to-date techniques, so long as they can be applied in solving realistic problems of financial managers. In those areas where new ideas and theories have yet to produce useful application techniques, the potential for the future is noted. Nevertheless, we have attempted to be brief as well as complete.

Various versions of most of the chapters in the book have been used in our classes. Thanks go to those students who have made *constructive* comments. We especially appreciate the individuals who have read one or more of the chapters and have made detailed comments. The latter group includes Dwight Anderson, David

Bowlin, William Dukes, Andrew Fields, Sharon Graham, Thomas Hamilton, Nancy Jay, Ben Nunnaley, Bill Petty, Ernest Swift, John Thatcher, and Allan Twark. Special thanks go to Charles D'Ambrosio, who has been extremely helpful in the writing of both editions. We also express our appreciation to the editors at McGraw-Hill who have provided both encouragement and coordination for the endeavor; these include in particular Suzanne BeDell, Catherine Woods, and at an early point, Scott Stratford. Finally, the patience and understanding of our families during the writing period deserve a very special tribute.

Oswald D. Bowlin

John D. Martin

David F. Scott, Jr.

1

FINANCIAL MANAGEMENT

Financial management is becoming more complex as well as more crucial to the growth and prosperity of business firms. Fortunately, the increase in complexity and importance of this managerial area has been accompanied by significant improvements in the techniques, or tools, available for making decisions. The objective of this book is to provide a concise explanation of practical techniques of analysis that can be used by financial decision makers. In this first chapter we are concerned primarily with the nature of the financial management function itself and the setting in which financial decisions are made.

FINANCIAL DECISIONS

The financial management of a business enterprise involves (1) analyzing the financial problems with which the firm is faced and deciding which course of action should be taken, and (2) organizing and administering the financial activities of the firm. This book deals with the first of these duties, which we refer to as making *financial decisions*. In this section, the basic types of financial problems encountered in managing a business are reviewed.

The first of these problems concerns how the firm should finance the assets that it needs to conduct its operations. The important elements to consider in making financing decisions include the length of time the assets will be needed, the nature and riskiness of the business operation, the capital structure (debt-equity mix) desired for the firm by management, and the cost of alternative methods of financing.

The second type of financial decision concerns where funds should be invested in the firm. The important factors here include the level of current assets (cash, accounts receivable, and inventories) necessary for day-to-day operations and the "profitability," or worth to the firm, of opportunities available for fixed asset investments.

Finally, the third type of financial decision is concerned with the owners' withdrawal of profits, or the dividends if the firm is a corporation. The dividend and financing decisions are related, since the payment of dividends reduces the amount of the firm's earnings that are available to finance its investments. However, the payment of dividends often requires special considerations by management, such as the effect of the dividends themselves on the value of the owners' investment. For this reason the question surrounding the payment of dividends is considered the third major type of financial decision.

Making "good" financial decisions requires an ability to identify financial problems and analyze the effect of alternative courses of action on the owners of the firm. This book deals with analytical techniques that can be used in making these decisions.

THE FINANCIAL MANAGER

The financial manager is responsible for identifying financial problems, analyzing the alternative courses of action available to the firm, and, in some cases, making the final decision as to which course of action should be taken. When the problem is considered to be of major importance, however, the financial manager usually will only recommend a course of action to top management. In addition, the financial manager normally has the responsibility for the implementation of management decisions as well as the administration of the firm's day-to-day financial activities. The administrative duties primarily include the supervision of cash flows into and out of the firm. The financial manager is often a part of top management and, as such, is involved in all the firm's major decisions.

The nature of the financial manager's position varies with the nature of the business itself and its administrative organization. In small firms, a single individual often manages all of the affairs of the firm, including its financial activities. On the other hand, the chief financial manager in many corporations is either the treasurer or the comptroller. In large corporations, the chief financial officer is usually a vice president who may also be chairman of a finance committee, the latter group actually being the top financial management of the firm. However, many financial decisions in corporations will be made at lower administrative levels, for example, at the division level.

The only generalization that can be made concerning the nature of the financial manager is that usually the position either is a part of the top management of the firm or reports directly to top management. This fact indicates the importance of the finance function.[1] Regardless of the firm's organizational format, the financial manager has

---

[1] The importance of the finance function in large corporations is discussed in an article published in *Fortune* magazine in 1976. The article reported that 25.3 percent of the chief executive officers of the nation's largest corporations had a main career emphasis on finance. Further, this career path appears to be growing in importance in recent years. See C. G. Burck, "A Group Profile of the Fortune 500 Chief Executive," *Fortune*, May 1976, pp. 173ff.

the responsibility for analyzing financial problems, making final decisions in some cases, and recommending decisions to top management in other cases.

In this book, the financial manager is considered either an individual or group of individuals (such as a finance committee) responsible for the three basic finance functions described earlier. We will not be concerned further with the position of the financial manager within the organizational hierarchy of the firm. Rather, our attention will focus on the analytical processes that should be used in choosing among alternative courses of action. Thus, we are concerned with how financial decisions should be made, not with who makes them. The analytical processes for making financial decisions should be the same in any case.

THE OBJECTIVE OF FINANCIAL MANAGEMENT

We have discussed the nature of financial decisions and of the financial manager. The question we now address concerns what the financial manager is ultimately trying to do. What is, or should be, the fundamental objective(s) in making financial decisions? In other words, what does successful financial management accomplish?

The reader has probably heard or read statements by the managers of companies indicating all sorts of impressive sounding objectives. These statements typically either imply or declare that the firm should act and is acting in the best interests of the owners, or the stockholders if the firm is a corporation. The meaning of the term *best interests of the owners* in these pronouncements is rather vague, but it is generally used to mean increasing profits or reducing losses. A question arises at this point: Is the owner of a business always better off if all decisions are based on the objective of maximizing the dollar profits (the net income) of the firm? The answer is no. For example, will the owners be better off if the firm spends $1 million (assuming the money can somehow be obtained) to increase net income by $1? This type of action would appear to be a terrible waste of resources, because the rate of return on the $1 million is very low. Thus, maximizing dollar profits breaks down as a specific objective in making this type of financial decision.

Next, consider maximizing the rate of return earned on investment as the objective of the firm. Assume that a new firm is particularly lucky and is earning a rate of return of 40 percent on its total assets. Does this mean that an investment opportunity that promises a return of 35 percent with little risk should be rejected? This could occur if the firm's objective is to maximize the rate of return earned on its assets. The 35 percent return on the new investment, when averaged in with the 40 percent return on the firm's other assets, would lower the firm's overall rate of return on investment. However, common sense tells us that the new investment should be accepted (1) if funds are available to the firm that cost less than 35 percent and (2) if the firm cannot obtain more than a 35 percent return with the same risk by investing in another project.

The preceding discussion indicates that neither maximizing dollar profits nor maximizing the expected rate of return of the firm as a whole is always consistent with the objective of making financial decisions that are in the best interests of the firm's owners. Obviously, the firm would like to increase its dollar profits as well as its rate of return if everything else is the same. But, as just shown, these objectives cannot be used as the ultimate objective of the firm without considering other factors. Consider next the nature of the decision objective or criterion that should be used by the financial manager.

Requirements for a Decision Criterion

Common sense suggests that a *decision criterion* (an objective for financial decision making) should have the following characteristics:

   1 It should be based on the anticipated benefits to the present owners of the firm.
   2 It should be reasonable, clear, and precise.
   3 It should be applicable to all types of financial decisions, including the financing, investment, and earnings distribution (dividend) decisions.

Financial decisions can benefit the owners of a firm by increasing their wealth. The way to increase the owners' wealth is to increase the market value of their *equity* (i.e., their investment) in the firm. Thus, the decision criterion used in this book is maximizing the market value of the owners' equity. This means that the optimum choice among all possible alternatives is the one that will increase the value of the owners' equity the most. Although the majority of the principles presented can be applied equally well to proprietorships and partnerships, for simplicity of exposition the discussion will usually be directed toward the corporate form of organization. Applying our decision criterion to a corporation means that all decisions should seek to maximize the market value of a share of the common stock of the company.

Application of Maximizing Value to Firms Not Having an Observable Market Price

The objective of maximizing the market value of the owners' equity can be difficult to implement if no observable market value exists. Consider, for example, a firm whose stock has not been traded and therefore does not have an active market or an observable market price. How does a decision maker identify the course(s) of action that will most likely maximize the market value of the owners' equity in this case? The answer lies in the determinants of the value of any earning asset. There are two such determinants: expected return and the risk associated with the return. (We will examine these concepts in Chapters 4, 5, and 6.) Buyers and sellers of an asset base their investment decisions on the expected return and risk from investing in the asset. Thus, the decision maker in a firm whose owners' equity does not have an active market can attempt to make his or her decisions so as to optimize the expected return and risk of the equity. *Optimization*, in this case, means balancing risk and return in an attempt to maximize what the decision maker believes would be the market price of the owners' equity, if it were traded in the market.

   Exceptions to the Rule.   An example where maximizing equity value does not apply is in a firm that has only one or a limited number of owners who may agree to take high risks in the hope that they will come out better in the long run. These individuals are more risk-aggressive than the average investor in the market. Thus, the action taken by this type of firm may actually lower the current market value of the firm because of the high risks assumed. In the 1980s this situation became increasingly common through use of the financing mechanism known as the "leveraged buyout" or LBO. LBO firms typically operate with higher levels of debt and, therefore, with lower common equity bases than more widely held companies. The high debt ratios and strained cash flow coverage relationships displayed by most LBO firms tend to depress the current market value of their equity.[2] However, if the firm is lucky and the course of action taken by the owners proves fruitful, the market value of the equity may be much greater in the long run than it would have been otherwise. It is true that in this situation the principle of maximizing current equity value breaks down. However, note that even in this case, the elements of risk and expected return should be considered by the decision maker. The relationship between the two elements is being optimized from the present owners' point of view, although other investors may not agree. The owners have every right to make decisions in this manner if they are in general agreement. However, they should be aware of the risks involved and willing to assume them.

Finally, maximizing share value does not apply when the firm has a guiding objective other than maximizing the financial benefits to the owners. For example, a firm may have charitable or social objectives that have first priority. Again, objectives of this type are perfectly acceptable, so long as they are legal and all the present owners agree to them. However, even in these cases, analyzing courses of action the firm might take from the point of view of maximizing share value may be useful. The decision maker can then determine the financial benefits the owners have to give up as a result of their company's pursuing other goals. In some cases, this information may indicate that the firm should seek to maximize share value and that the owners should engage in their charitable or social activities in some other manner.

Conclusion

The decision criterion used in this book will be maximizing the market value of the owners' equity. Applied to a corporation, the decision criterion is maximization of the market value of a share of the firm's common stock. As a general rule, this criterion is reasonably precise, and, as we will see in subsequent chapters, it can be applied to financing, investment, and dividend decisions. Empirical evidence indicates that financial management decisions, at least in large corporations, usually seek to maximize the share price of the firm's common stock.[3]

VALUATION IN AN EFFICIENT MARKET

Maximizing the share price of its common stock is the appropriate objective of financial decisions of a corporation only if the forces of supply and demand are

[2] See Christopher Farrell, "Learning to Live With Leverage," *Business Week*, November 7, 1988, pp. 138–143.

[3] See W. G. Lewellen, "Management and Ownership in the Large Firm," *Journal of Finance*, vol. 24, May 1969, pp. 299–322.

allowed to operate freely in the market so that stock prices are determined in an orderly, consistent, and nondiscriminatory manner. Further, stock prices should reflect all available information that has any relevance to or implication for the return and risk associated with investing in the stocks. This type of stock market is called *efficient*. Most research studies published in recent years indicate that capital (both stock and bond) markets in the United States are reasonably efficient.[4]

Implications of Efficient Capital Markets

If capital markets are efficient, relevant new information will be reflected very quickly in security (stock and bond) prices as it becomes available. Furthermore, new information comes to the market in a random fashion, so that no one will be able to predict either when it occurs or whether the next bit of information will be good or bad news.[5] There are two important implications of a market that is efficient in this sense. First, an investor will have no logical reason to expect to earn a higher-than-average return on security investments of a given level of risk. This does not mean that the investor *can not* or *will not* earn a higher-than-average return, but only that such an outcome should *not be expected*. The investor may actually earn a higher-than-average return, but also may earn less than the average. Since there is a 50 percent chance of making more than the average and a 50 percent chance of making less, all the investor should expect to make is an average return for the risk class of the security in which the investment has been made.

Second, market efficiency means that the rate of return an investor should expect on a security is a function of the riskless rate of interest (the best example of which is the interest rate on the shortest-term securities issued by the U.S. government) and the amount of risk associated with the security. Although the precise relationship is

---

[4] This statement is an interpretation by the present authors of the literature concerned with market efficency. Strictly speaking, most of the research studies have reported little or no evidence of inefficiency.

For a review of the empirical research dealing with the capital markets' efficiency before 1970, see E. F. Fama, "Efficient Capital Markets: A Review of Theory and Empirical Work," *Journal of Finance*, vol. 25, May 1970. pp. 383–417.

A useful and pleasant overview of many theoretical aspects of the market efficiency concept appears in Stephen A. Ross, "The Current Status of the Capital Asset Pricing Model (CAPM)," *Journal of Finance*, vol. 33, June 1978, pp. 885–901. In this 1978 piece, Professor Ross provides an early description of an asset pricing model that has generated much research and debate in the 1980s—"arbitrage pricing theory" (APT). APT is presented in much detail and rigor in Stephen A. Ross, "The Arbitrage Theory of Capital Asset Pricing," *Journal of Economic Theory*, vol. 13, December 1976, pp. 341–360. One of the best, workable descriptions of APT around is Dorothy H. Bower, Richard S. Bower and Dennis E. Logue, "A Primer on Arbitrage Pricing Theory," *The Revolution in Corporate Finance*, edited by Joel M. Stern and Donald H. Chew, Jr., New York: Basil Blackwell, 1986, pp. 69–77.

[5] This description of the manner in which information hits the market presumes that security trading is a "fair game." From recent history we know this is not always the case. On November 14, 1986, the Securities and Exchange Commission (SEC) announced that well-known investor, speculator, and arbitrageur Ivan F. Boesky admitted to illegal inside trading. Boesky's agreement to cooperate with the federal government cost him $100 million and a criminal (jail) sentence. Other cases and charges related to the Boesky incident have continued into 1989. On April 26, 1989, a federal judge refused to reduce Boesky's three-year sentence.

Two concise and readable overviews of the insider trading problems are: "Wall Street Enters the Age of the Supergrass," *The Economist*, November 22–28, 1986, pp. 77–78 and "Going After the Crooks," *Time*, December 1, 1986, pp. 48–51.

not always clear, expected return should increase with an increase in risk. Of course, some high-risk securities may actually earn less and some may even prove to be losers, but on the average, the expected return should be higher for an investor who assumes higher risk. The reverse is also true: Expected return should decrease as risk decreases.

An expression of the general nature of the relationship between the riskless rate of interest, risk, and the expected return on a security is given in Figure 1-1. Note that if the security were riskless, the expected return from investing in it would be the riskless rate of interest *i*. The upward slope of the line in the chart indicates that the expected return will be higher at higher levels of risk.

Expected and Required Returns Compared.   In the preceding discussion we have referred to the relationship between the risk associated with a security and the return the investor should expect to receive. Expected return is also related to the return that investors *require* on an investment. Obviously, the expected return must be at least as great as the return required by the investor who purchases the security. Since investors generally require higher return for higher risk, the market price of a high-risk security will have to adjust so that the expected return will be high. Otherwise, no security transactions would ever occur. Note, however, that unforeseen events can cause a wide discrepancy between expected and *realized* returns. Thus, the relationship between risk and expected return appears to be much closer than the relationship between risk and realized returns.

Causes of Efficiency.   What causes a market to be efficient in the sense defined? The final answer to this question has not been provided by researchers. In general,

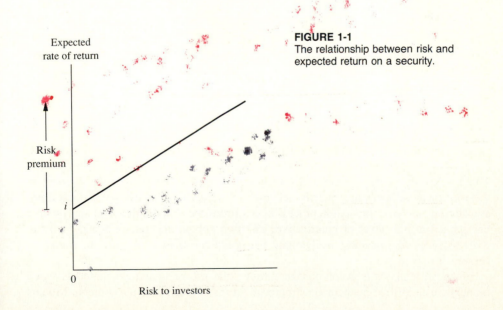

FIGURE 1-1
The relationship between risk and expected return on a security.

however, it appears that the existence of many buyers and many sellers with access to public information tends to promote efficiency. Thus, the markets for securities traded on the organized securities exchanges tend to be efficient.

Importance of Efficiency.   Market efficiency is important to business firms and investors. Both will benefit on the whole because the market will perform its function in a less discriminatory and capricious manner than would otherwise be the case. Decisions made by management will be reflected very quickly in the price of the company's stock when the information becomes available to investors. Good decisions (those whose results are expected to be favorable to the firm) will result in a higher stock price, whereas poor decisions will cause the price to decline.

Economic Value.   The term *economic value* refers to the market value of an earning asset (an asset that promises a return for its owner) in an efficient market. If a stock or any other type of earning asset is not actively traded in the market, the price at which it can be sold may differ considerably from its economic value; thus, the market in this case may not be efficient. This possibility provides a good reason why a manager should benefit from learning the tools of financial analysis. The effect of financial decisions on the economic value of the firm and its equity will be thoroughly examined in this book.

Accounting Value.   The term *accounting value* refers to the value at which the assets of the firm are carried on the balance sheet. Since inventories and fixed assets are normally carried at their original cost to the firm (less accumulated depreciation in the case of fixed assets), accounting values and economic values will often differ considerably. For example, during periods of rising prices, the economic value of inventories and fixed assets stated in current dollars will usually increase. However, since the historical cost of the assets will not be affected by price increases after their purchase by the firm, their economic value will exceed their accounting value. This result will also mean that the economic value of the firm as a whole will be greater than the firm's total accounting value during these periods. Accounting values will be discussed in greater depth in Chapter 2.

SPREADSHEETS IN FINANCIAL ANALYSIS

Along with word processing, the requirements of financial analysis have been most responsible for the proliferation of personal computers in the business environment. The availability of easy-to-use software has generated a significant improvement in the way financial analysts perform their jobs. Not only has the error-prone and time-consuming manual computation process been eliminated, but the financial analyst also has gained a high level of control over his own computing requirements. In many circumstances, the business analyst and the computer analyst can now be the same person.

Financial analysis is accomplished through the use of quantitative models; such models are simplified mathematical representations of real world phenomena. Models are simplified in the sense that they specify the relationships among variables that *adequately* describe or predict the real world system being studied. Some of the factors in the real world system may be unknown, unmeasurable, or unimportant. These factors can be omitted if the other factors in the model fairly represent the relationships under analysis.

Financial models are typically either descriptive or predictive.[6] Descriptive models simply show existing relationships and may be thought of as historical in nature. Last year's income statement is a descriptive model. Predictive models are constructs of variables that provide insights into future relationships. Pro forma financial statements are predictive models. Financial planning involves both types of models. Descriptive models are frequently used to discover the elements that affected prior results. These elements, along with any others that are judged to have significant future impact, are included in the predictive model.

Computer-based financial modeling has greatly enhanced the productivity of the financial analyst. Main frame and time-sharing computer software have been available much longer than the personal computer, but system complexity and learning curves resulted in a single or, at best, a few internal experts per company. Financial software for the personal computer has provided every analyst with access to the tools necessary to accomplish most of his or her tasks.

Most significant among personal computer software was the introduction of electronic spreadsheets. While the available spreadsheets are numerous, all have similar features. The basic format of the spreadsheet is the matrix, or a grid of columns and rows. Words, numbers or formulas can be placed in each cell of the matrix.

The use of formulas, along with the full spreadsheet recalculation feature, has made the spreadsheet an important tool in many areas of financial analysis. A formula can use the content of other cells in the worksheet as input to its calculation. This feature permits the assumptions of the model to be entered once and to be referenced by all computations requiring the data. Because financial analysis requires the estimation of many uncertain economic, market, and firm-specific variables, decision making can be facilitated by varying each factor along the continuum of feasible outcomes. This sensitivity analysis can be accomplished by changing the model assumptions (i.e., allow one variable to change) and recalculating the worksheet for each new analysis.

Spreadsheets can be used for a wide variety of financial problems. Perhaps the most obvious is the recording and reporting of actual financial data, such as income statements and balance sheets. Once the data are available, financial ratios are easily calculated. Predictive models with formats similar to financial statements, such as cash budgets and pro forma statements, are also prime spreadsheet candidates. Chapters 2 and 3 discuss these concepts.

Most spreadsheet software packages include frequently used mathematical functions. From the finance realm, present value, future value, internal rate of return,

---

[6] Some financial and economic models are also referred to as "normative." These present the relationships inherent to a system in a format that is logical to the analyst. They describe the way things "ought" to behave. The Gordon dividend valuation model described in Chapter 7 is an example of a normative model. Briefly, the Gordon model suggests that the value of a share of common stock *should* be equal to the discounted value of all future cash dividends expected by investors.

and some depreciation methods are generally included. Cash flow and investment evaluations are easily accomplished once the data required by the function are available. The output of these functions is only as reasonable as the input. Consequently, these are focal areas for sensitivity analysis as well. These capital budgeting methods are presented in Chapters 5 and 6.

Risk assessment (see Chapter 6) is another important task in financial analysis; spreadsheets can provide some fundamental statistical measures in this area. Most spreadsheets compute means, variances, standard deviations, minimum and maximum values, and basic multiple regression statistics. It should be kept in mind, however, that spreadsheets are not full statistical software packages and flexibility and full complements of output data for model evaluation are generally not available. If the task fits the documentation description, spreadsheets are a valuable resource in completing capital budgeting, cost of capital, and portfolio analysis tasks. All of these decision areas are studied in the text.

If the spreadsheet has a random number generator, simulations of uncertainties can be performed. Because there are no standard situations for which simulation is used, spreadsheets do not normally provide preprogrammed simulation functions. A moderate amount of experience with spreadsheets is sufficient to set up simulations that will be useful in working capital management (Chapters 8, 9, and 10), capital budgeting (Chapters 5 and 6) and long-range financial planning (Chapters 11 and 12).

Spreadsheets are a major focus because of their flexibility and general importance to financial analysts. One area that merits identification is the problem of constrained optimization. Software for mathematical programming techniques, such as linear, nonlinear, integer, and goal programming, are available to solve the problems of allocating limited resources among alternative uses. The procedure requires specification of a stated objective, such as profit maximization or cost minimization. It is equally important to note, however, that almost any financial specialization has personal computer software available on the market.

OUTLINE OF THE BOOK

This book consists of 12 chapters and four separate appendixes. In addition, five of the chapters include appendixes. A brief description of each chapter and appendix is given in the following outline.

Chapter 1—Financial Management: An overview of the subject matter of financial management and the environment in which financial decisions are made. Using models and spreadsheets in financial analysis is introduced.

Chapter 2—Financial Analysis: A description of the more important ratios used in financial analysis. Examples of the application of the ratios are also given.

Chapter 3—Financial Forecasting, Planning, and Control: An explanation of the techniques used in forecasting a company's needs for funds and the planning for obtaining the funds. The appendix to the chapter explains how linear regression coefficients can be calculated.

Chapter 4—Valuation: An explanation of the techniques used in valuing earning assets. Part of the chapter deals specifically with the valuation of stocks and bonds of corporations. The compound sum of $1 and the compound sum of an annuity are explained in the appendix at the end of the chapter. Contingent claims analysis is discussed.

Chapter 5—Capital Budgeting Techniques: An explanation of the basic techniques used in making decisions for investments in long-term assets of a firm. Appendixes to the chapter include discussions of corporate income taxes and the effect of accelerated depreciation.

Chapter 6—The Effect and Measurement of Risk of New Investments: An explanation of how risk can be accounted for in making investment decisions by a firm. Continuous probability distributions are considered in the appendix to the chapter.

Chapter 7—Estimating the Required Rate of Return on Investment Proposals: An explanation of how minimum acceptable rates of return on new investments are established by a firm. This topic is sometimes referred to as *cost of capital*.

Chapter 8—Managing Cash and Marketable Securities: A description and analysis of cash management objectives, decisions, and systems. Collection and disbursement procedures are examined. Designing the firm's marketable securities portfolio is also addressed. Securities popular with corporate treasurers for inclusion in the liquid asset portfolio are described. Yield structures are also studied.

Chapter 9—Credit and Inventory Management: An examination of responsible accounts receivable and inventory procedures and policy. The discussion relates these areas of working capital policy to corporate profitability and, hence, value.

Chapter 10—Credit Policy Decisions: Discusses the relationship between short-term credit decisions and corporate performance.

Chapter 11—Determining the Financing Mix: An examination of the factors influencing the long-term financing decisions of the firm. In addition, the very useful tool of break-even analysis is discussed at this point.

Chapter 12—Dividend Policy: An examination of dividend policies of corporations and the effects of these policies on the value of a share of common stock.

Appendix A—Present Value and Future Value Tables: Tables including values frequently used in making financial decisions. The discussions in Chapters 4–6 make extensive use of these tables.

Appendix B—Cumulative Normal Distribution

Appendix C—Answers to Selected Study Problems

Appendix D—Glossary: Brief definitions of the technical terms used in the text.

REFERENCES

Branch, Ben: "Corporate Objectives and Market Performance," *Financial Management*, vol. 2 (Summer 1973), pp. 24–29.

Burck, C. G.: "A Group Profile of the Fortune 500 Chief Executive," *Fortune* (May 1976), pp. 173ff.

"The Changing World of Corporate Finance," *Dun's Business Month*, vol. 119 (June 1982), pp. 92–93.

Cochran, Philip L., and Robert A. Wood: "Corporate Social Responsibility and Financial Performance," *Academy of Management Journal*, vol. 27 (March 1984), pp. 42–56.

Cornell, Bradford, and Alan C. Shapiro: "Corporate Stakeholders and Corporate Finance," *Financial Management*, vol. 16 (Spring 1987), pp. 5–14.

Donaldson, Gordon: "Financial Goals: Management versus Stockholders," *Harvard Business Review*, vol. 41 (May-June 1963), pp. 116–129.

Fama, E. F.: "Efficient Capital Markets: A Review of Theory and Empirical Evidence," *Journal of Finance*, vol. 25 (May 1970), pp. 383–417.

Findlay, Chapman M., and G. A. Whitmore: "Beyond Shareholder Wealth Maximization," *Financial Management*, vol. 3 (Winter 1974), pp. 25–35.

Fruhan, William E.: "Corporate Raiders: Head 'em Off at the Value Gap," *Harvard Business Review*, vol. 66 (July-August 1988), pp. 63–68.

Gonedes, Nicholas J.: "The Capital Market, The Market for Information, and External Accounting," *Journal of Finance*, vol. 31 (May 1976), pp. 611–630.

Greenberg, Edward, William J. Marshall, and Jess B. Yawitz: "Firm Behavior under Conditions of Uncertainty and the Theory of Finance," *Quarterly Review of Economics and Business*, vol. 23 (Summer 1983), pp. 6–22.

Grundfest, Joseph A.: "The New Technology of Finance," *Financial Executive*, vol. 3 (September-October 1987), pp. 44–47.

Harkins, Edwin P.: *Organizing and Managing the Corporate Financial Function*, Studies in Business Policy, no. 129 (New York: National Industrial Conference Board, 1969).

Hill, Lawrence W.: "The Growth of the Corporate Finance Function," *Financial Executive*, vol. 44 (July 1976), pp. 38–43.

Lewellen, Wilbur G.: "Management and Ownership in the Large Firm," *Journal of Finance*, vol. 24 (May 1969), pp. 299–322.

Jensen, Frederick H.: "Recent Developments in Corporate Finance," *Federal Reserve Bulletin*, vol. 72 (November 1986), pp. 745–756.

Johnson, Eric, and Elliott Kushell: "Company Profitability and Health: A Long-Term Perspective," *Advanced Management Journal*, vol. 50 (Winter 1985), pp. 14–16.

Malik, Z. A., and S. Basu: "Formal Integrated Long-Range Planning: Its Impact on Financial Risk Decisions," *Business Horizons*, vol. 29 (March-April 1986), pp. 80–82.

Muir, Tom: "Basic Corporate Financing: Regaining Perspective," *Canadian Banker*, vol. 91 (June 1984), pp. 46–51.

Scanlon, John J.: "Bell System Financial Policies," *Financial Management*, vol. 1 (Summer 1972), pp. 16–26.

Sturdivant, Frederick D., James L. Ginter, and Alan G. Sawyer: "Managers' Conservatism and Corporate Performance," *Strategic Management Journal*, vol. 6 (January-March 1985), pp. 17–38.

Summers, Lawrence H.: "On Economics and Finance," *Journal of Finance*, vol. 40 (July 1985), pp. 633–635.

"Topsy-turvy: A Survey of Corporate Finance," *The Economist*, vol. 299 (June 7, 1986), pp. 1–38.

West, R. R.: "Two Kinds of Market Efficiency," *Financial Analysts Journal*, vol. 31 (November-December 1975), pp. 30–34.

Weston, J. Fred: *The Scope and Methodology of Finance* (Englewood Cliffs, N.J.: Prentice-Hall, Inc., 1966).

2

FINANCIAL ANALYSIS

In general, financial analysis provides a method for assessing the financial strengths and weaknesses of the firm using information found in its financial statements. Such an analysis can be performed by analysts who work for the firm (an internal analysis) or by outsiders; an example would be credit analysis for a financial institution that is considering the extension of credit to the firm being analyzed. The objective of such an analysis is to gain an understanding of the firm's current financial condition, which, in turn, can serve as the basis for decision making. If the analyst is a loan officer of a bank from whom the firm has requested a loan, then the decision would relate to whether or not to extend the loan and, if extended, what terms to offer. If the analyst is an employee of the firm, the objective of the analysis may relate to an assessment of the relative performance of the operating divisions of the firm or to an evaluation of whether to use debt or equity funds to finance a planned plant expansion.

Financial analysis utilizes the information contained in the firm's financial statements (the balance sheet and income statement, supplemented by the statement of cash flows); the primary tools of financial analysis are financial ratios. This chapter consists of a brief review of the form and content of the firm's financial statements, a definition and discussion of a set of commonly used financial ratios, a discussion of an integrated model for analyzing financial performance, an analysis of the use of financial ratios to predict corporate failures, and a survey of the empirical evidence regarding the stability of financial ratio patterns through time.

A BRIEF REVIEW OF THE FIRM'S FINANCIAL STATEMENTS

Corporate and noncorporate business enterprises report their financial position and performance through the use of two basic financial statements, the **Balance Sheet** and the **Income Statement**. In accordance with generally accepted accounting practice (FASB 95) these two statements are supplemented by the **Statement of Cash Flow**. In addition we will discuss the **Statement of Changes in Financial Position** or **Source and Use of Funds Statement**, which has long been used as a means for evaluating changes in a firm's financial well-being. The concepts and principles that underlie the preparation of these statements constitute much of the subject matter of the discipline of accounting. Thus, in our discussion of these statements we will of necessity provide a limited overview of these principles.

The Balance Sheet

The balance sheet presents an enumeration of a firm's resources (assets) along with its liabilities (debts) and owner's equity on a given date or at a point in time. Thus, the balance sheet is like a "snapshot" of the firm. The balance sheet is characterized by the basic accounting equation, that is,

$$\text{Assets} = \text{Liabilities} + \text{Owner's equity}$$

That is, the sum of the firm's assets (current and long-term) must equal the sum of the firm's liabilities (current and long-term) plus its owners' equity.

Table 2-1 contains a glossary of terms frequently encountered in reading and analyzing a firm's balance sheet. If it has been a while since you have seen these terms, a quick review of the table will prove very helpful in understanding the pages that follow.

Table 2-2 contains the balance sheets for the Peterson Bottling Company (PBC) for December 31, 1988, and December 31, 1989. Total assets for 1989 equal $11,681,738, consisting of $4,533,828 in current assets and $7,147,910 in property, plant, and equipment. These assets are financed by $3,101,050 in current liabilities, $3,055,639 in long-term debt, and $5,525,049 in owner-supplied funds.

Limitations of the Balance Sheet.   Although the balance sheet may be prepared in full compliance with generally accepted accounting practice (GAAP)[1], the analyst should be aware of some inherent limitations of the statement as a tool for financial analysis. Some of the more important limitations include the following:

1 The balance sheet does not reflect current market value.[2] The accounting profession in this country has adopted the "historical cost" principle for valuing assets.

---

[1] The sources of accounting principles are many; however, the main contributors certainly have been the Opinions of the Accounting Principles Board (APB), which was created by the American Institute of Certified Public Accountants (AICPA), and since 1973, the Financial Accounting Standards of the Financial Accounting Standards Board (FASB).

[2] The Securities and Exchange Commission (SEC) now requires that all firms having inventory plus gross property, plant, and equipment totaling at least $100 million and constituting at least 10 percent of total assets report replacement cost information in their 10K disclosures. Specifically, qualifying firms are required to include in their disclosures (1) current replacement cost of inventories and replacement cost of productive capacity, and (2) replacement cost analysis of cost and expenses for the two most recent years. See SEC Accounting Series Release (ASR) 190, March 1976, and Implementation Guide: Staff Accounting Bulletin (SAB) 7. The issue of replacement cost accounting was reviewed on July 1, 1978.

TABLE 2-1
GLOSSARY OF BALANCE SHEET TERMS

Accumulated depreciation. The sum of depreciation charges on an asset since its acquisition. This total is deducted from gross fixed assets to compute net fixed assets. This balance-sheet entry is sometimes referred to as the *reserve for depreciation, accrued depreciation,* or the *allowance for depreciation.*

Authorized capital stock. The total number of shares of stock the firm can issue, as specified in the articles of incorporation.

Balance sheet. A statement of financial position on a particular date. The balance-sheet equation is as follows: Total assets = total liabilities + owners' equity.

Bond. A long-term debt instrument carried on the balance sheet at its par value (usually $1,000 per bond), which is payable at maturity. The coupon rate on the bond is the percent of the bond's face value payable in interest each year. Bonds usually pay interest semi-annually.

Book value. The net amount of an asset shown in the accounts of a firm. When referring to an entire firm, the term relates to the excess of total assets over total liabilities (also referred to as *owner's equity* and *net worth*).

Capital. Sometimes used to mean the total assets of a firm and at other times used to refer to the owners' equity alone.

Capitalization. Stockholders' equity plus the par value of outstanding bonds.

Capital stock. All shares of outstanding common and preferred stock.

Capital structure. The relative composition of the firm's liabilities (often short-term liabilities are omitted from consideration), preferred stockholders' equity, and common equity.

Commercial paper. A short-term, unsecured promissory note issued by the most creditworthy corporate borrowers.

Common stock. The stock interests of the residual owners of the firm. These owners have claim to earnings and asset values remaining after satisfying the claims of all creditors and preferred stockholders.

Convertible preferred stock. Preferred stock that can be exchanged by the owner for a specific number of shares of common stock.

Current assets. Those assets that are normally converted into cash within the operating cycle of the firm (normally a period of one year or less). Such items as cash, accounts receivable, marketable securities, prepaid expenses, and inventories are frequently found among a firm's current assets.

Current liabilities. Those liabilities or debts of the firm that must be paid within the normal operating cycle of the firm (usually less than one year). Items generally found under a firm's current liabilities are accounts and notes payable, income taxes payable, and wages and salaries payable.

Debenture bond. A bond that is not secured by any collateral (contrast with a mortgage bond).

Equity financing. Raising funds through the sale of common or preferred stock.

Fixed assets. Buildings, equipment, and land. These assets share the common characteristic that they are not completely converted into cash within a single operating cycle of the firm.

Footnotes. Statements by management disclosing information not found in the body of the firm's financial statements.

Goodwill. An asset entry included in the balance sheet to reflect the excess over fair market value paid for the assets of an acquired firm.

Intangible asset. An asset that lacks physical substance, such as goodwill or a patent.

Inventory. The balance in an asset account such as raw materials, work in process, or finished goods.

Lease. A contract requiring payments by the user (lessee) to its owner (lessor) for the use of an asset. Leases can be either operating (cancelable) or financial (noncancelable). In accordance with Financial Accounting Standards Board Statement 13, most financial lease agreements entered into after January 1, 1977, must be included in the assets and liabilities of the lessee's balance sheet. The right of the lessee to use the asset is represented by an intangible asset called a *leasehold.*

TABLE 2-1
(*continued*)

Liability. An obligation to pay a specified amount to a creditor in return for some benefit.

Liquid assets. Those assets of the firm that can be easily converted into cash with little or no loss in value. Generally included are cash, marketable securities, and sometimes accounts receivable.

Long-term debt. All liabilities of the firm that are not due and payable in one year or less. Examples of the various types of long-term debt are installment notes, equipment loans, and bonds.

Marketable securities. The securities (bonds and stocks) of other firms and governments held by a firm.

Mortgage bonds. Bonds secured by a lien on real property.

Owners' equity. Total assets minus total liabilities, sometimes referred to as *net worth.*

Paid-in-capital. The amount in excess of par value paid for the capital stock of the firm when it was sold. For example, if a share of stock with a $1 par value is sold by a firm for $10, the common-stock account will be increased by $1 and paid-in-capital will rise by $9.

Participating preferred stock. Preferred stock with rights to dividends in excess of the stated dividend. Thus, the preferred shareholders "participate" in dividends paid to the common shareholders.

Par value. The face value, or stated value, of a security.

Patent. The legal rights to the benefits of an invention.

Preferred stock. The capital stock of the owners of the firm whose claim on the assets and income is secondary to that of bondholders but is superior to (has a higher priority than) the claim of the stockholders.

Refunding bond issue. A bond issue whose proceeds are used to retire an outstanding bond issue.

Retained earnings. The sum of a firm's net income over its life less all cash dividends and adjustments for stock dividends.

Sinking fund. Provision for the periodic retirement of long-term-debt obligations before their maturity. Payments into a sinking fund are usually made with cash. However, since these payments constitute principal payments, they are not tax-deductible.

This means that balance sheet totals for assets represent their historical cost of purchase (net of depreciation for long-term assets) and, correspondingly, liabilities and owners' equity reflect historical figures and not current market values.

√2 Certain account balances must be based upon estimates.[3] Examples include accounts receivable, which reflects the firm's estimate as to the collectability of those accounts; inventories, which are based on the firm's estimate of their salability; and long-term assets whose balance sheet value reflects historical cost less depreciation.[4]

---

[3] In "Opinion 20" the Accounting Principles Board states that preparing financial statements requires estimating the effects of future events. Examples of items for which estimates are necessary are uncollectable receivables, inventory obsolescence, service lives and salvage values of depreciable assets, warranty cost, periods benefited by a defined cost, and recoverable mineral reserves. Since future events cannot be perceived with certainty, estimating requires the exercise of judgment. The implication here is that no reference guidelines can be constructed regarding these estimates; thus, subjectivity enters into determining the affected accounts.

[4] The Internal Revenue Service has set forth asset depreciation range (useful life) guidelines to be used under the Asset Depreciation Range (ADR) election in computing depreciation for tax purposes. Furthermore, these guidelines are often used to compute depreciation for financial statement purposes. See Section 167(m)(1) of the Internal Revenue Code.

TABLE 2-2
Peterson Bottling Corporation
Condensed Balance Sheets
Years Ending December 31

Assets

	1989	1988
Current assets		
Cash	$ 1,349,524	$ 1,563,424
Accounts receivable	1,438,929	1,628,782
Inventories	1,397,248	1,414,104
Prepaid expenses	348,127	179,213
Total current assets	4,533,828	4,785,523
Property, plant, and equipment		
Land	$ 712,614	$ 712,614
Buildings	6,781,823	6,001,264
Machinery, equipment, and furniture	6,617,295	6,035,884
Transportation equipment	528,291	528,291
Total property, plant, and equipment	14,640,023	13,278,053
Less: Accumulated depreciation	(7,492,113)	(6,842,113)
Net property, plant, and equipment	7,147,910	6,435,940
Total assets	$11,681,738	$11,221,463

Liabilities and Stockholders' Equity

	1989	1988
Liabilities		
Long-term notes payable (current portion)	$ 218,468	$ 212,111
Accounts payable	2,317,242	2,817,175
Other liabilities and accrued expenses:		
Accrued wages	151,212	154,188
Accrued taxes	77,736	81,391
Accrued interest	164,880	173,125
Accrued expenses (other)	171,512	167,612
Total current liabilities	3,101,050	3,605,602
Long-term debt (net of current portion)[a]	3,055,639	2,508,477
Stockholders' equity		
Capital stock (authorized 2,000,000 shares, par value $0.10 a share; issued and outstanding 800,000 shares)	80,000	80,000
Capital paid in excess of par value	560,000	560,000
Retained earnings	4,885,049	4,467,384
Total liabilities and stockholders' equity	$11,681,738	$11,221,463

[a] The long-term debt consists of a $2,290,009 note carrying an interest rate of 9.6 percent per annum, with $218,486 due on March 1 of each of the next 10 years and the remaining balance due on March 1, 1999. Also included in the long-term debt is a 5-year note in the amount of $765,630, requiring interest payable at a rate of 12 percent per annum with the principal due at maturity.

3 The depreciation of long-term assets is accepted practice; however, appreciation or enhancement in asset values is generally ignored. This is of particular significance for firms holding large investments in appreciable assets such as land, timberlands, and mining properties.

4 Many items are omitted from the balance sheet even though they have financial value. This occurs because of the extreme difficulties encountered in trying to objectively place a value on such items. The most obvious example of such an asset is the human resources of the firm (i.e., the firm's management team and employee workforce).[5]

The analyst frequently can do nothing to adjust or restate the balance sheet to account for its limitations. However, simply being aware of them serves as the basis for "tempering" the analysis to reflect the impact of any suspected shortcomings of the reported figures.

Income Statement

The income statement measures the net results of the firm's operations over a specified time interval such as a month, quarter, or year. The income statement (sometimes referred to as a profit and loss statement) is compiled on an *accrual* basis, which means that an attempt is made to match the firm's revenues from the period's operations with the expenses incurred in generating those revenues. An important implication of the accrual method is that these revenues and expenses generally do not represent actual cash flows for the period. This means that computed net income for the period will not equal the actual cash provided by the firm's operations.

Table 2-3 contains a glossary of income-statement terminology, followed in Table 2-4 by the income statements of PBC for the years ending December 31, 1988, and December 31, 1989. Note that the income statement measures the cumulated revenues recognized by the firm as having been earned and the associated expenses incurred in generating those revenues. The balance sheet, on the other hand, reflects the book values of the firm's assets, liabilities, and owners' equity accounts as of a particular date.

A brief review of PBC's income statement for the year ended December 31, 1989, reveals the following: The firm earned $417,665 after taxes based upon sales of $22,703,229. Once again we should be reminded that PBC's cash flow for the period may have been larger or smaller than the reported net income, since not all cash flows are reported in the income statement. For example, the firm may have purchased machinery and equipment during 1989. Since these items will be expected to generate revenues over several years, the full cost of these purchases will not be included in the firm's expenses for 1989 but will, instead, be amortized over the useful life of the equipment.

---

[5] The subject of human resource accounting has received increased attention in recent years. For an overview of the subject, see Edwin H. Caplan and Stephen Landekich, *Human Resource Accounting: Past, Present and Future* (New York: National Association of Accountants, 1974); Eric Flamholtz, *Human Resource Accounting* (New York: Dickerson Publishing Company, Inc., 1974).

The Statement of Cash Flows and Statement of Changes in Financial Position

In 1971 the Accounting Principles Board made the Statement or Changes in Financial Position (generally referred to as the *Source and Use of Funds Statement* in the finance literature) a required component of the firm's published corporate reports. However,

TABLE 2-3
GLOSSARY OF INCOME STATEMENT TERMS

Accelerated depreciation. A term encompassing any method for computing depreciation expense wherein the charges decrease with time. Examples of accelerated methods are *sum-of-the years'-digits* and *double-declining balance*. These methods can be contrasted with *straight-line depreciation*, which is not an accelerated method.

Accrual basis of accounting. The method of recognizing revenues when the earning process is virtually complete and when an exchange transaction has occurred, and recognizing expenses as they are incurred in generating those revenues. Thus, revenues and expenses recognized under the accrual basis of accounting are independent of the time when cash is received or expenditures are made. This contrasts with the cash basis of accounting, wherein revenues and expenses are recognized when a cash flow actually occurs.

Administrative expense. An expense category used to report expenses incurred by the firm but not allocated to specific activities such as manufacturing or selling.

Amortizing. The procedure followed in allocating the cost of long-lived assets to the periods in which the benefits are derived. For fixed assets the amortization is called *depreciation expense*, whereas it is called *depletion expense* for wasting assets (natural resources).

Bad-debt expense. An adjustment to income and accounts receivable reflecting the value of uncollectible accounts.

Capital gain. The excess of the proceeds from the sale of a capital asset over its cost. Tax treatment may be different from that of ordinary income depending on the length of time the asset was held.

Cash basis of accounting. See Accrual basis of accounting.

Cash flow. The excess (or deficiency) of cash receipts compared with cash disbursement for a given period of time. This is sometimes referred to as net cash flow.

Composite depreciation. A depreciation expense computed for a group of assets, which may be very dissimilar in terms of their function and useful lives.

Cost of goods manufactured. The total costs allocated to the production of completed products during the period.

Cost of goods sold. Beginning inventory plus purchases for the period less ending inventory. (See **FIFO** and **LIFO**.)

Declining-balance depreciation. A method for computing depreciation expense by multiplying the asset's book value at the start of the period by a constant percentage $[1-(S/A)^{1/N}]$, where N represents the depreciable life of the asset, S is the asset's salvage value, and A is its acquisition cost. (See double-declining-balance depreciation.)

Depreciable cost. The total amount that can be charged against income in the form of depreciation expense over the life of an asset. It is generally equal to acquisition cost less salvage value.

Depreciable Life. The period of time over which an asset is depreciated.

Depreciation. Amortization of the depreciable cost of plant, property, and equipment over the periods during which their benefits are derived. Referred to under the current tax code as *Annual Cost Recovery*.

Dividend. A distribution of earnings to the owners of a corporation, usually either in the form of cash payment (cash dividend) or shares of stock (stock dividend).

TABLE 2-3

GLOSSARY OF INCOME STATEMENT TERMS

(*continued*)

Double-declining-balance depreciation. A method for computing declining-balance depreciation expense in which the constant percentage is equal to $2/N$, where N represents the depreciable life of the asset. For example, the annual depreciation expense on a $1,000 asset with a salvage value of 0 and a four-year depreciable life is found below:

Period	Book value	×	Double-declining rate	=	Depreciation expense
0	$1,000.00		0.5		$500.00
1	500.00		0.5		250.00
2	250.00		0.5		125.00
3	125.00		0.5		67.50
4	67.50		0.5		

Earnings. A synonym for net income or net profit after taxes.

Earnings per share. Net income after taxes available to the common stockholders (after preferred dividends) divided by the number of outstanding common shares.

EAT. Earnings after taxes. Other terms often used with the same meaning are *net income, net profit,* and *earnings*.

EBIT. Earnings before interest and taxes. This is a commonly used synonym for *net operating income*.

EBT. Earnings before taxes. The term is often used to define *income before taxes* or *taxable income*.

Extraordinary item. A revenue or expense item which is both unusual in nature and infrequent in occurrence. Such items and their tax effects are separated from ordinary income in the income statement.

FIFO. A method for determining the inventory cost to be assigned to cost of goods sold, whereby the cost of the oldest items of inventory are assigned to the period's cost of goods sold (*first in, first out*). Consequently, ending inventories consist of the cost of the *most recent* inventory purchases.

GAAP. Generally accepted accounting principles, as defined by the pronouncements of the Accounting Principles Board (APB) and Financial Accounting Standards Board (FASB).

Gross margin. The excess of net sales over cost of goods sold.

Income. The excess of net revenues (expenses) over expenses (revenues) for a period. Other terms used as synonyms include net earnings and net profits.

Income statement. The statement of profit or loss for the period, composed of net revenues less expenses for the period. (See accrual basis of accounting.)

Income tax. An annual expense incurred by the firm, based upon income and paid to a government entity.

Installment sales method. A method for recognizing revenues and expenses for the period that involves only a fraction of the period's sales actually collected during the period.

Investment tax credit. A reduction in a firm's income tax liabilities related to the acquisition of new plant and equipment.

LIFO. A method for determining the inventory cost assigned to cost of goods sold whereby the cost of the most recent purchases of inventory are assigned to the period's cost of goods sold (*last in, first out*). Ending inventories thus contain the cost of the *oldest* items of inventory. In a period of rising prices, LIFO results in a higher cost of goods sold, lower taxable earnings, and

TABLE 2-3
(*continued*)

consequently a lower tax liability than *FIFO*. In a period of declining prices, given the tax advantage of LIFO in inflationary periods, a choice may have to be made in accordance with which method produces the lower tax liability. However, the Internal Revenue Service does not allow frequent changes in inventory policy. Once a policy has been adopted, it may not be changed without the commissioner's consent. Furthermore, changing the inventory costing method solely for the purpose of reducing taxes is not accepted by the Internal Revenue Service. Instead, the taxpayer must show that the new method more closely matches revenues with cost of goods sold. See Regulation 1.471–2 of the Internal Revenue Code for a more detailed discussion.

Line of business reporting. A method of accounting whereby income is reported by segments of a firm's business generally in accordance with product lines.

Matching principle. The method used in the accrual basis of accounting to recognize expenses as being incurred in the period in which they contribute to revenues. Thus, expenses follow revenues in accordance with this principle.

Net sales. Gross sales less returns, allowances, and cash discounts taken by customers.

Paper profit. A gain which has not been realized through a transaction.

Profit-and-loss statement. Another name for the *income statement*.

Profit center. A segment of a firm that is responsible for its own revenues and expenses.

Revenue. A dollar value of a service rendered by a firm, which may or may not correspond to a cash flow in the period in which the revenue is recognized.

Stock dividend. A dividend that results in a transfer of retained earnings to the capital-stock and paid-in-capital accounts. This contrasts with a *cash dividend*. (See *dividend*.)

TABLE 2-4
Peterson Bottling Corporation
Condensed Income Statements
Years Ending December 31

	1989	1988
Sales (net)	$22,703,229	$21,418,202
Cost of goods sold	15,208,914	14,234,814
Gross profit	7,494,315	7,183,388
Operating expenses:		
Selling	4,140,600	3,983,762
Delivery	1,135,159	920,916
General and administrative[a]	1,211,736	1,212,645
Total operating expenses	6,487,495	6,117,323
Operating income	1,006,820	1,066,065
Interest expense	310,711	296,600
Income before taxes	696,109	769,465
Income taxes (40%)	278,444	307,786
Net income	$ 417,665	$ 461,679

[a] This includes depreciation expense of $577,000 for 1988 and $650,000 for 1989. Long-term leases in effect December 31, 1988, had annual rental fees of $102,300. Lease payments for the next 5 years (1988–1992) under existing leases are equal to $102,300 per year.

this statement of generally accepted accounting practice (sometimes referred to simply as *GAAP*) was superseded by Financial Accounting Standards Board (*FASB*) Standard 95 in November 1987. This standard states that for fiscal years ending after July 15, 1988, a firm's financial statements will include a *Statement of Cash Flows*. We will discuss both the Source and Use of Funds Statement and the newer Statement of Cash Flows in the pages that follow so that the similarities in the two statements can be assessed.

The Statement of Changes in Financial Position or Sources and Uses of Funds. This statement provides information concerning "where the firm obtained funds" (i.e., cash) and "how those funds were dispersed" for a past statement period. The value of this information to the analyst comes from the ease with which the firm's primary sources and uses of funds for the period can be identified. The statement itself can be constructed from the firm's balance sheets for the beginning and end of the period being analyzed plus the firm's income statement for the period of interest. Thus, the source and use of a funds statement simply places information already available from the income statement and the firm's past balance sheets into a more readily useful format.

Very briefly, sources of funds result from the sale of current or fixed assets, the incurrence of short- or long-term debt obligations (issuing bonds or notes), the sale of common or preferred shares, and from the retention of the firm's profits. Correspondingly, uses of funds result from the purchase of current or fixed assets, repayment of short- or long-term debt, repurchase of common or preferred stock, payment of common and preferred dividends, and losses from the firm's operations.

Often the analyst will be asked to analyze unaudited or interim financial statements. This frequently will mean that only the balance sheet and income statement will be available. In this circumstance the analyst may want to prepare a source and use of funds statement as a part of the analysis. The first step involved in preparation of this statement is computation of balance sheet changes for the year for which the statement is being prepared. Table 2-5 contains these calculations for PBC covering the year 1989. Using these balance sheet changes and the income statement for the same year found in Table 2-4, we construct the statement of sources and uses of funds found in Table 2-6. Summarizing the information found in that statement, we observe the following: PBC's primary sources of funds for 1989 consisted of income from its operations (i.e., net income plus depreciation), a reduction in accounts receivable, and the issuance of long-term debt. The firm's principal uses of funds consisted of purchases of building and equipment and a decrease in accounts payable.

The Statement of Cash Flows. In defining the format for the Statement of Cash Flow, the Financial Accounting Standards Board sought to resolve some of the confusion that arises out of the use of cash flow terminology in corporate practice. Specifically, this statement seeks to explain the changes in cash plus cash equivalents rather than ambiguous terms such as *funds*.[6]

---

[6] Cash equivalents are defined as short-term, highly liquid investments that are readily convertible into known amounts of cash and are so near to their maturity that they pose an insignificant risk of changes in value because of changes in interest rates.

TABLE 2-5
Peterson Bottling Corporation
Statement of Balance Sheet Changes
Years Ended December 31

Assets

	1989	1988	Changes
Current assets			
Cash	$ 1,349,524	$ 1,563,424	$ (213,900)
Accounts receivable	1,438,929	1,628,782	(189,853)
Inventories	1,397,248	1,414,104	(16,856)
Prepaid expenses..........................	348,127	179,213	168,914
Total current assets	4,533,828	4,785,523	(251,695)
Property, plant, and equipment			
Land	$ 712,614	$ 712,614	$ 0
Buildings	6,781,823	6,001,264	780,559
Machinery, equipment, and furniture	6,617,295	6,085,884	581,411
Transportation equipment	528,291	528,291	0
Total property, plant, and equipment	14,640,023	13,278,053	1,361,970
Less: Accumulated depreciation	(7,492,113)	(6,842,113)	(650,000)
Net property, plant, and equipment	7,147,910	6,435,940	711,970
Total assets.............................	$11,681,738	$11,221,463	$ 460,275

Liabilities and Stockholders' Equity

	1989	1988	Changes
Liabilities			
Notes payable (current portion)	$ 218,468	$ 212,111	$ 6,357
Accounts payable	2,317,242	2,817,175	(499,933)
Other liabilities and accrued expenses			
Accrued wages	151,212	154,188	(2,976)
Accrued taxes	77,736	81,391	(3,655)
Accrued interest	164,880	173,125	(8,245)
Accrued expenses (other)	171,512	167,612	3,900
Total current liabilities	3,101,050	3,605,602	(504,552)
Long-term debt (net of current portion)	3,055,639	2,508,477	547,162
Stockholders' equity			
Capital stock (authorized 2,000,000 shares, par value $0.10 a share; issued and outstanding 8,000,000 shares)	80,000	80,000	0
Capital paid in excess of par value	560,000	560,000	0
Retained earnings	4,885,049	4,467,384	417,665
Total liabilities and stockholders' equity	$11,681,738	$11,221,463	$ 460,275

The basic form of the statement of cash flow for the Peterson Bottling Company is illustrated in Table 2-7. The statement content is equivalent to the statement of sources and uses of funds discussed earlier, since we chose the cash basis for defining that statement. The only differences relate to the format of the cash flow statement, which separates sources and uses of cash into five categories—operating activities, investment activities, financing activities, foreign exchange effects, and the change

TABLE 2-6
Peterson Bottling Corporation
Statement of Sources and Uses of Funds
For the Year Ending December 31, 1989

Sources	Amount	Percent
Funds provided by operations:		
Net income	$ 417,665	20.42
Depreciation	650,000	31.77
	1,067,665	52.19
Decrease in accounts receivable	189,853	9.28
Decrease in inventories	16,856	0.82
Increase in notes payable	6,357	0.31
Increase in other accrued expenses	3,900	0.19
Increase in long-term debt	547,162	26.75
Decrease in cash	213,900	10.45
	$2,045,693	100.00%

Uses of funds	Amount	Percent
Increase in prepaid expenses	$ 168,914	8.26
Purchase of buildings	780,559	38.16
Purchase of machinery, equipment, and furniture	581,411	28.42
Decrease in accounts payable	499,933	24.44
Decrease in accrued wages	2,976	0.15
Decrease in accrued taxes payable	3,655	0.17
Decrease in accrued interest	8,245	0.40
	$2,045,693	100.00%

in cash plus cash equivalents—and the focus of the statement on cash plus cash equivalents. A review of Peterson's Statement of Cash Flows for 1989 indicates that the firm realized a positive cash flow from its operating and financing activities that was $213,900 less than the cash outflow experienced from investing in plant, machinery, and equipment.

FINANCIAL STATEMENT ANALYSIS

In this section of the chapter we will discuss three types of analysis that can be used to gain information from a firm's financial statements. All three are based upon financial ratios, so we will discuss this general form of financial statement analysis first. The second and third forms of analysis relate to the the "format" or "template" used to direct the computation and analysis of a particular set of financial ratios. These latter two forms of analysis consist of **common size financial statements** and **performance analysis.**

Financial Ratios

Financial ratios provide the analyst with a very useful tool for gleaning information from a firm's financial statements. The particular ratio or ratios selected for use by the

TABLE 2-7
Peterson Bottling Corporation
Statement of Cash Flows
For the Year Ending December 31, 1989

A. Cash flows from **operating** activities

Net income (from the statement of income)	$417,665	
Add (deduct) to reconcile net income to net cash flow		
Decrease in accounts receivable	189,853	
Decrease in inventories	16,856	
Increase in other accrued expenses	3,900	
Depreciation expense	650,000	
Increase in prepaid expenses	(168,914)	
Decrease in accounts payable	(499,933)	
Decrease in accrued wages	(2,976)	
Decrease in accrued taxes payable	(3,655)	
Net cash inflow from operating activities		$602,796

B. Cash flows from **investing** activities

Cash inflows		
Cash outflows		
Purchase of buildings	($780,559)	
Purchase of machinery, equipment and furniture	(581,411)	
Net cash outflow from investment activities		($1,361,970)

C. Cash flows from **financing** activities

Cash inflows		
Increase in notes payable	$6,357	
Increase in long-term debt	547,162	
Cash outflows		
Decrease in accrued interest	($8,245)	
Net cash inflow from financing activities		$545,274

D. Effect of foreign exchange rates 0

E. Net increase (decrease) in cash during the period . . . . ($213,900)

Cash balance at the beginning of the period	$1,563,424	
Cash balance at the end of the period	1,349,524	

analyst depends upon the reason for performing the analysis. For example, a commercial loan officer analyzing a loan application would be interested in determining the ability of the applicant to repay the loan when due. In this case, the analyst would be concerned with the level of cash flow of the firm in relation to its existing and proposed levels of interest and principal payments. There exist an almost limitless number of conceivable financial ratios that can be devised. To give order to our discussion of these ratios, we will use the traditional four categories of ratios: liquidity, efficiency, leverage, and profitability.

Liquidity Ratios. Liquidity ratios are used to indicate the ability of the subject firm to pay its bills on time. We will use the financial statements of PBC to demonstrate the calculation of two such ratios. The first is the **current ratio**. PBC's 1989 current ratio is calculated as follows:

$$\text{Current ratio} = \text{Current assets} \div \text{Current liabilites}$$
$$= \$4,533,828 \div \$3,101,050 = 1.46 \text{ times}$$

The second measure of firm liquidity is the **acid-test ratio**, which is a modified version of the current ratio that is:

$$\text{Acid-test ratio} = \text{Current assets} - \text{Inventories} \div \text{Current liabilities}$$
$$= \$3,136,580 \div \$3,101,050 = 1.01$$

The removal of inventories from current assets provides a slightly more refined measure of firm liquidity, in that inventories are frequently the least liquid of the firm's current assets. In PBC's case the current ratio indicates that the firm has approximately one and a half times more current assets than it does current debt; however, when we eliminate inventories, the firm's remaining current assets are approximately equal to its current liabilities. Of course, some of the firm's inventories would be convertible into cash to help meet payment of the firm's current liabilities, should such a dire circumstance arise. Thus, the fact that PBC's acid-test ratio is close to 1 is not necessarily cause for alarm.

At this point, we should comment as to how financial ratios should be used in performing a financial analysis. As we mentioned earlier, ratios are simply tools for gleaning information. They may offer information in an absolute sense, as was the case with the acid-test ratio, where a ratio equal to one indicates solvency. In addition, ratios can be analyzed in a relative sense, where we compare the ratios for the firm being analyzed with "target" ratios or norms. These ratio targets can be determined from looking at similar ratios of other firms or by looking at the same ratio for the firm being analyzed, but from an earlier period. One important source of ratio standards or norms is industry average ratios. There are several sources of these averages, but two deserve particular mention. These are Dun and Bradstreet, and Robert Morris Associates. (Dunn and Bradstreet, *Key Business Ratios*, (New York: updated annually), and Robert Morris Associates, *Annual Statement Studies*, (Philadelphia: updated annually).

Efficiency Ratios.   Efficiency ratios measure the effectiveness with which a firm is utilizing its assets to generate sales. A very efficient firm, then, is one that utilizes its investment in assets to generate the largest possible level of sales revenues. We will consider four measures of asset utilization efficiency: the receivables turnover ratio, inventory turnover ratio, fixed asset turnover ratio, and total asset turnover ratio.

The **receivables turnover ratio** reflects the number of times the firm collects it accounts receivables per year and is calculated as follows:

$$\text{Receivables turnover ratio} = \text{Annual credit sales} \div \text{Accounts receivable}$$
$$= \$22,703,229 \div \$1,438,929 = 15.8 \text{ times}$$

Thus, PBC turns its receivables roughly 16 times per year, or about every 23 days (365 ÷ 15.8). This latter figure is referred to as the average collection period and is also used as a measure of the effectiveness with which a firm is using its investment in accounts receivable to generate sales.

The efficiency with which a firm is managing its inventories is indicated by its **inventory turnover ratio** which is calculated as follows:

$$\text{Inventory turnover} = \text{Cost of goods sold} \div \text{Inventories}$$
$$= \$15,208,914 \div \$1,397,248 = 10.9 \text{ times}$$

Thus PBC is turning its inventory over 10.9 times per year, or about every 34 days (365/10.9).

The last two efficiency ratios we define relate to aggregates of assets. The first is the **fixed asset turnover ratio** and the second is the **total asset turnover ratio**. PBC's fixed asset turnover ratio is calculated as follows:

$$\text{Fixed asset turnover} = \text{Sales} \div \text{Fixed assets}$$
$$= \$22,703,229 \div \$7,147,910 = 3.18 \text{ times}$$

The total asset turnover ratio is calculated in a similar fashion, as follows:

$$\text{Total asset turnover} = \text{Sales} \div \text{Total assets}$$
$$= \$22,703,229 \div \$11,681,738 = 1.943 \text{ times}$$

Thus PBC has a relatively high volume of sales relative to its total investment in assets (roughly two times in fact). However, without information concerning what the norm is for the bottling industry it is not clear how well PBC's ratio compares in a relative sense.

Leverage Ratios. Leverage ratios are used to indicate the extent to which a firm has financed its assets with non-owner sources of funds (i.e., has made use of financial leverage). We will discuss leverage ratios in terms of two categories: balance sheet–based ratios and coverage ratios. Balance sheet–based ratios simply portray the proportion of a firm's assets financed by a particular source of funds (e.g., common equity or long-term debt), while coverage ratios reflect the ability of the firm's earnings to cover its fixed finance payments. We will offer three balance sheet–based leverage ratios: the debt ratio, common equity ratio, and the long-term debt ratio.

The **debt ratio** is calculated as follows:

(on Debt)

$$\text{Debt ratio} = \text{Total liabilities} \div \text{Total assets}$$
$$= \$6,156,689 \div \$11,681,738 = .53 \text{ or } 53 \text{ percent}$$

Thus, PBC has financed over half its assets by borrowing. The **common equity ratio** (**CER**) is a slight refinement of the debt ratio in that it provides a measure of financial leverage that reflects the use of debt and preferred stock financing (should the firm have any). The common equity ratio is calculated as follows:

$$\text{Common equity ratio} = \text{Common equity} \div \text{Total assets}$$
$$= \$5,525,049 \div \$11,681,738 = .47 \text{ or } 47 \text{ percent}$$

In this particular case (PBC) there was no preferred stock financing, so the debt ratio and the common equity ratios are "complements." That is, the sum of these two leverage ratios is unity. However, should there have been preferred equity financing the common equity ratio would have been less than 47 percent and the debt ratio would have remained the same. Thus, the common equity ratio reflects the use of both debt financing and preferred stock financing.

The final balance sheet–based leverage ratio we consider is the **long-term debt ratio**, which is calculated as follows:

$$\text{Long-term debt ratio} = \text{Long-term debt} \div \text{Total assets}$$
$$= \$3,055,639 \div \$11,681,738 = .26 \text{ or } 26 \text{ percent}$$

Here we are interested in measuring the relative proportion of the firm's assets "funded" by long-term or permanent debt. Notice that since PBC has financed 53 percent of its assets by borrowing and 26 percent by using long-term debt, then it must have used 27 percent short-term or current debt to finance its assets.

We will introduce two coverage ratios: the times interest earned ratio and the fixed charge coverage ratio. The **times interest earned ratio** is calculated for PBC as follows:

$$\text{Times interest earned} = \text{Net operating income} \div \text{Interest expense}$$
$$= \$1,006,820 \div \$310,711 = 3.24 \text{ times}$$

The **fixed charge coverage ratio** is actually a refined version of the times interest earned ratio, in that it includes consideration for rental payments and principal payments on debt. The ratio is calculated as follows:

$$\text{Fixed charge coverage ratio} =$$
$$\frac{\text{Net operating income} + \text{Rental payments}}{\text{Interest expense} + \text{Rental payments} + \text{Principal payments}/1 - \text{Tax rate}}$$

$$= \frac{\$1,006,820 + 102,300}{(\$310,711 + 102,300 + 218,468)/(1 - .40)}$$
$$= 1.43 \text{ times}$$

Thus, after considering rental payments, interest, and before-tax principal payments, PBC's earnings for 1989 cover its fixed charges 1.43 times.

Profitability Ratios.   Profitability ratios serve as overall measures of the effectiveness of the firm's management. These ratios can be conveniently segmeneted into two groups: profitability in relation to sales or "profit margin" ratios and profits in relation to investment. We will discuss three profit margin ratios and two profit in relation to investment ratios.

The first profit margin ratio we consider is the **gross profit margin**, which for PBC is calculated as follows:

$$\text{Gross profit margin} = \text{Gross profit} \div \text{Sales}$$
$$= \$7,494,315 \div \$22,703,229$$
$$= 0.33 \text{ or } 33 \text{ percent}$$

Thus two-thirds of PBC's sales revenues go toward paying for cost of goods sold. The next profit margin ratio is the **operating income margin**, which is calculated as follows:

$$\text{Operating income margin} = \text{Net operating income} \div \text{Sales}$$
$$= \$1,006,820 \div \$22,703,229$$
$$= 0.044 \text{ or } 4.4 \text{ percent}$$

Obviously operating expenses are a very significant part of PBC's expenses, since the firm has but 4.4 percent of its sales left after deduction of cost of goods sold (67 percent) and operating expenses. The final profit margin we calculate is the **net profit margin**:

$$\text{Net profit margin} = \text{Net income} \div \text{Sales}$$
$$= \$417,665 \div \$22,703,229$$
$$= 0.018 \text{ or } 1.8 \text{ percent}$$

Here we see that after all expenses are paid, including interest and taxes, the firm earns 1.8 percent of each sales dollar in profits. As we will see in the next set of profitability ratios, this very small profit on each sales dollar can result in a reasonable return on invested capital.

The first profitability in relation to investment ratio we consider is the **operating income return on investment** or **return on investment (ROI)**:

$$\text{Return on investment (ROI)}: = \text{Net operating income} \div \text{Total assets}$$
$$= \$1,006,820 \div \$11,681,738$$
$$= 0.086 \text{ or } 8.6 \text{ percent}$$

On a before interest and tax basis, the management of PBC produced an 8.6 percent return on the total investment of the firm. This number is the appropriate basis for assessing the effectiveness of the operating management of PBC, since those managers do not have direct control over the method of financing selected by the firm. To assess the effectiveness of the management with respect to both its operating and financing decisions, we calculate the **return on common equity (ROCE)**.

$$\text{Return on common equity} = \text{Net income available to common} \div \text{Common equity}$$

$$= \frac{\$417,665}{\$80,000 + 560,000 + 4,885,049}$$

$$= 0.076 \text{ or } 7.6 \text{ percent}$$

Thus, after all expenses, the firm's management earned a return of 7.6 percent on the investment of the common shareholders during 1989. Whether this is good or bad can only be determined by comparing the return earned by PBC with that of other firms. We will return to a discussion of this issue when we consider performance analysis.

Common size statements provide a quick and effective method for developing a system of useful financial ratios. We simply divide every entry in the balance sheet by total assets and every entry in the income statement by total sales. Table 2-8 contains the 1989 common size statements for PBC. Note that we have defined a ratio for each entry in the balance sheet and income statement. It should also be noted that the Robert Morris and Associates industry average ratio data also contain common size statements that can, in turn, be used to provide target ratios.

Performance Analysis

Here we analyze the financial relationships that exist among a firm's operating performance, its use of financial leverage, and its share value. Thus, performance analysis as it is discussed here is a very general tool for evaluating the overall performance of a firm. It should be noted that, though the model used here is a "simplification" of reality, it provides a very useful framework for evaluating the determinants of financial performance. We begin our discussion with a review of some key financial ratios and then extend this analysis to the evaluation of equity value. Since the development of the model used to evaluate performance involves some algebraic manipulations of financial ratios we will follow the convention of numbering key equations so that they can be easily referenced.

In this section we will suggest the use of two ratios as the basis for analyzing the financial performance of a firm. Either one or both ratios can be used depending upon the objective of the analyis. Specifically, there are two fundamental reasons for analyzing financial performance. The first relates to the desire to assess the performance of the firm's operating management. Here we base our analysis on a measure of the firm's return on investment, which reflects only those attributes of the firm's performance which are actually *under the control* of the firm's operating management. We exclude from the analysis any implications of the firm's financing decisions. The basic measure of performance we analyze here is the Return on Investment Before Interest and Taxes or simply return on investment (ROI). The second basic reason for analyzing a firm's financial performance relates to a desire

TABLE 2-8
Peterson Bottling Corporation
Common-Size Balance Sheet
For the Year Ending December 31, 1989

Assets

	1989	Percent of total assets
Current assets		
Cash	$ 1,349,524	11.55
Accounts receivable	1,438,929	12.31
Inventories	1,397,248	11.96
Prepaid expenses	348,127	2.98
Total current assets	4,533,828	38.80
Property, plant, and equipment		
Land	$ 712,614	6.10
Buildings	6,781,823	58.05
Machinery, equipment and furniture	6,617,295	56.65
Transportation equipment	528,291	4.52
Total property, plant, and equipment	14,640,023	125.32
Less: Accumulated depreciation	(7,492,113)	(64.13)
Net property, plant, and equipment	7,147,910	61.19
Total assets	$11,681,738	100.00

Liabilities and Stockholders' Equity

	1989	Percent of total assets
Liabilities		
Notes payable (current portion)	$ 218,468	1.87
Accounts payable	2,317,242	19.84
Other liabilities and accrued expenses:		
Accrued wages	151,212	1.29
Accrued taxes	77,736	0.67
Accrued interest	164,880	1.41
Accrued expenses (other)	171,512	1.47
Total current liabilities	3,101,050	26.55
Long-term debt (net of current portion)	3,055,639	26.16
Stockholders' equity		
Capital stock (authorized 2,000,000 shares, par value $0.10 a share; issued and outstanding 800,000 shares)	80,000	0.68
Capital paid in excess of par value	560,000	4.79
Retained earnings	4,885,049	41.82
Total liabilities and stockholders' equity	$11,681,738	100.00%

TABLE 2-8 (*continued*)
Peterson Bottling Corporation
Common-Size Income Statement
For the Year Ending December 31, 1989

	1989	Percent of sales
Sales (net)	$22,703,229	100.00
Cost of goods sold	15,208,914	66.99
Gross profit	7,494,315	33.00
Operating expenses:		
Selling	4,140,600	18.23
Delivery	1,135,159	4.99
General and administrative	1,211,736	5.33
Total operating expenses	6,487,495	28.57
Operating income	1,006,820	4.43
Interest expense	310,711	1.36
Income before taxes	696,109	3.06
Income taxes	278,444	1.23
Net income	417,665	1.84

to assess the firm's performance from the owner or stockholder's point of view. In this case we do want to consider *both* the firm's operating performance *and* the impact of the firm's financing decisions. The measure of performance used here is the return on common equity (ROCE). In both instances we will seek to deconstruct the performance measure into meaningful components, which in turn can be used to evaluate the firm's performance.

Analyzing Operating Effectiveness.   A firm's operating management is responsible for the efficient use of the firm's assets. Therefore, when we evaluate their performance we should consider only those revenues and expenses that are directly attributable to investments that are under their control. This means that operating profits or EBIT is *the bottom line* for the firm's operating management. Furthermore, since the operating management has control over the total investment of the firm, we use total assets as our measure of total investment. It will be recalled that Return on Investment or ROI is defined as follows:

$$\text{ROI} = \frac{\text{EBIT}}{\text{assets}} \quad \Rightarrow \quad ROI = \frac{EAT}{TA} \tag{2-1}$$

To illustrate the use of the ROI performance measure we will compare the operating performance of PBC and the Clawson Beverage Company (CBC). Table 2-9 contains CBC's abbreviated financial statements for 1989. Earlier we found that for 1989 the ROI for PBC was 8.6 percent. This compares with 9.4 percent for CBC. To further understand the determinants of the ROI measure, and consequently the reasons that

PBC and CBC ratios differ, we will "reformulate" the metric through some basic algebraic rearrangements as follows: First, multipying ROI in (2-1) by the ratio Sales/Sales and rearranging terms produces the following result:

$$\text{ROI} = \underset{\text{OPM}}{\underbrace{\frac{\text{EBIT}}{\text{sales}}}} \cdot \underset{\text{TATO}}{\underbrace{\frac{\text{sales}}{\text{assets}}}}$$

where **OPM** is the **Operating Profit Margin** and **TATO** is **Total Asset Turnover**. Further, noting that EBIT equals Gross Profit (GP) less Operating Expenses (OE) we can further decompose ROI as follows:

$$\text{ROI} = \left(\underset{\text{GPM}}{\underbrace{\frac{\text{GP}}{\text{sales}}}} - \underset{\text{OER}}{\underbrace{\frac{\text{OE}}{\text{sales}}}} \right) \underset{\text{TATO}}{\underbrace{\left(\frac{\text{sales}}{\text{assets}} \right)}} \tag{2-2}$$

We have not changed the definition of ROI at all, but we have deconstructed it into terms that will help us further evaluate a firm's operating performance. Specifically, in equation (2-2) we see that one dimension of the firm's operating performance is related to how well it has controlled its cost of goods sold in combination with its pricing policies, which in turn determine the **Gross Profit Margin (GPM)**. A second determinant of ROI is related to the level of operating expenses relative to sales (the

TABLE 2-9
Abbreviated Financial Statements for
Clawson Beverage Co.
Income Statement for the Year
Ending December 31, 1989

Sales	$25,000,000
Cost of goods	(17,000,000)
Gross profit	8,000,000
Operating expenses	(6,750,000)
EBIT	1,250,000
Interest expense	(541,667)
EBT	708,333
Taxes	283,333
Net income	$ 425,000

Balance Sheet
December 31, 1989

Assets	$13,297,872	Liabilities	$ 5,971,221
		Owners' equity	7,326,651
		Total	$13,297,872

Operating Expense Ratio [OER]). Finally, ROI reflects the sheer size of the firm's asset investment relative to the sales the firm generates, which in turn is reflected in the **Total Asset Turnover Ratio**. Using our PBC example these component ratios for 1989 appear as follows:

$$\text{ROI} = (0.33 - 0.286)(1.943) = 0.086$$

Similarly, comparable ratios for CDC are as follows:

$$\text{ROI} = (0.32 - 0.27)(1.88) = 0.094$$

Comparing the component ratios of ROI for PBC with those of CBC helps explain the difference in ROI we observed earlier. Specifically, PBC had a slightly higher gross profit margin, a higher operating expense ratio, and a higher total asset turnover than CBC. Therefore, although PBC had a substantially higher asset turnover ratio and a slightly higher gross profit margin, its higher operating expense ratio more than offsets both those favorable factors and explains the difference in the two firms' ROIs.

Analyzing the Owner's Return. When we analyze a firm's performance from the perspective of the common stockholder, we select as the focal point of our analysis an earnings figure that reflects the returns to the stockholders—Net Income after Taxes less Preferred Dividends—and then we select an investment base that reflects the investment of the common stockholders (Common Equity). In short, we use the return on common equity as the basis for our analysis, that is:

$$\text{ROCE} = \frac{\text{NI} - \text{PD}}{\text{equity}} \tag{2-3}$$

where *PD* represents preferred stock dividends. Interestingly we observe that in 1989 PBC actually offered a higher return to its common shareholders than CBC even though its ROI was lower. PBC's ROCE was 7.6 percent for 1989, and for the same period CBC's ROCE was 5.8 percent. To understand why this difference occurred we can again deconstruct this performance metric into its basic determinants using some algebraic manipulations. First, if we multiply the right hand side of (2-3) by the ratio of Sales/Sales and then multiply it by the ratio of Assets/Assets we can rearrange terms to obtain the following result:

$$\begin{aligned}
\text{ROCE} &= \left(\frac{\text{NI}}{\text{sales}} - \frac{\text{PD}}{\text{sales}} \right) \frac{\text{sales}}{\text{assets}} \cdot \frac{\text{assets}}{\text{equity}} \\
&= \left(\text{NPM} - \frac{\text{PD}}{\text{sales}} \right) \text{TATO} \cdot \frac{1}{\text{CER}}
\end{aligned} \tag{2-4}$$

Note that the ROCE ratio is now equal to the product of the firm's net profit margin less the ratio of preferred dividends to sales × total asset turnover × and the inverse of the common equity ratio. Thus, the rate of return earned on the common stockholder's investment is increased whenever (other things remaining the same) the firm is able to increase its net profit margin or total asset turnover, or reduce its common equity ratio. Calculating PBC's ROCE using (2-4) we find the following:

$$ROCE = (0.0184)(1.943)(2.114) = 0.076$$

When we calculatae CBC'c ROCE we obtain:

$$ROCE = (0.017)(1.88)(1.815) = 0.058$$

Comparing the components of ROCE for the two firms we observe that the primary reason for PBC's higher ROCE derives from its slightly higher net profit margin and superior asset turnover, in conjunction with a much higher use of financial leverage. With respect to the latter, PBC's common equity to total asset ratio was 0.469 (1/2.114), whereas CBC's corresponding ratio is only 0.55 (1/1.815). Thus, PBC financed approximately 53 percent of its assets by borrowing, while CBC has financed only 45 percent in this way.

FINANCIAL PERFORMANCE AND THE CREATION OF SHAREHOLDER WEALTH

Our objective in this discussion is to link the rate of return earned on a firm's common equity with the value of its shares of common stock. This task is not a trivial one. In Chapter 13 we will discuss the linkage between the rate of return earned on the common stockholder's equity and stock price in detail. There we learn that this relationship is a complex one, which is only partially understood. Roll (1988), in his 1987 presidential address to the American Finance Association, lamented the fact that finance scholars have not been able to explain a very large portion of the variance in stock returns. However, we do know enough to make some meaningful generalizations. For example, the rate of return earned on a firm's common equity is, by definition, the rate that the firm earns on the funds invested in the firm by its owners. Thus, when the firm retains a part of its earnings and reinvests them in the firm, it does so in the expectation that the rate of return it will earn (the ROCE) will exceed the rate of return required by its owners (i.e., the cost of equity capital, k_e). Specifically, the value of the firm's equity, E, will respond to a retention of earnings in the following manner:

If ROCE $> k_e$	E will increase
If ROCE $= k_e$	E will not change
If ROCE $< k_e$	E will decrease

To illustrate this important relationship consider the example of the Apex Manufacturing Company: Apex has a current book value of equity equal to $1000, and follows a policy of paying out 40 percent of its aftertax earnings in common dividends. The firm faces a unique investment opportunity that will allow it to earn a return on its common equity of 25 percent over the next 10 years while its cost of equity capital is only 15 percent. The size of the investment opportunity is sufficient to allow Apex to invest all of its planned earnings retentions to earn the 25 percent rate of return.

In general, we can express the value of a firm's common equity in terms of the present value of future dividend payments, plus the present value of the equity's market value at the time it is sold. That is,

$$E = \sum_{t=1}^{N} \frac{\text{Dividend } (t)}{(1 + k_e)^t} + \frac{E(N)}{(1 + k_e)^N} \tag{2-5}$$

where the assumed holding period is N years and the equity value at the end of the year N is $E(N)$. We can define the dividend for year t as follows:

$$\text{Dividend } (t) = \text{Book } (t - 1) \cdot \text{ROCE} \cdot (1 - b)$$

where Book $(t - 1)$ is the book value of the equity of the firm in year $t - 1$. ROCE was defined earlier, and b is the retention ratio (i.e., the ratio of retained earnings to net profits). Note that both the ROCE and retention ratio are assumed to remain constant for the entire N-year holding period. Neither of these assumptions is necessary to our analysis, but they do simplify matters substantially. For simplicity, we will also assume that the market value of the firm's equity in the Nth year will equal its book value (i.e., $E(N) = \text{Book } (N)$). The book value of the firm's equity at the end of year N (in the setting we have described here) can be defined as follows,

$$\text{Book } (N) = \text{Book } (0) (1 + \text{ROCE} \cdot b)^N$$

where Book (0) is the *original* equity invested in the firm at time zero (i.e., Book $(0) = $ total assets $\cdot$ common equity ratio). Substituting into the general equity valuation model found in equation (2-5) we define the following

$$E = \underbrace{\sum_{t=1}^{N} \frac{\text{Book } (0) (1 + \text{ROCE} \cdot b)^{t-1} \text{ROCE} \cdot (1 - b)}{(1 + k_e)^t}}_{\text{Dividend } (t)}$$

$$+ \underbrace{\frac{\text{Book } (0)(1 + \text{ROCE} \cdot b)^N}{(1 + k_e)^N}}_{\text{Book } (N) = E(N)} \tag{2-6}$$

where $\quad E$ = the current market value of the equity of the firm

N = the holding period used in valuing the equity (we will also assume that N corresponds to the period of time during which ROCE $> k_e$)

Book (t) = the book value of the firm's common equity in year t, which is calculated as follows:

$$\text{Book } (t) = \text{Book } (t - 1) (1 + \text{ROCE} \cdot b)$$
$$= \text{Book } (0)(1 + \text{ROCE} \cdot b)^t$$

Book (N) = the year N book value of the firm's equity (we will assume that this is also equal market value in year N)

b = the retention rate or proportion of earnings retained and reinvested each year of the N year holding period

Table 2-10 contains the elements of the equity valuation model as applied to the Apex Manufacturing Company example. A quick overview of these figures indicates

TABLE 2-10
APEX MANUFACTURING COMPANY—CREATING SHAREHOLDER WEALTH

Example parameters				
Dividend payout rate $(1 - b)$ =	0.60	Cost of equity =		15%
ROCE =	0.25	Beginning book value =		$1,000.00

Year (t)	Net income	Retained earnings	Year-end book value	Dividends + equity value[a]	PV of $1 @ 15%	Present value
1	$250.00	$100.00	$1,100.00	$ 150.00	0.86956522	$130.43
2	275.00	110.00	1,210.00	165.00	0.75614367	124.76
3	302.50	121.00	1,331.00	181.50	0.65751623	119.34
4	332.75	133.10	1,464.10	199.65	0.57175325	114.15
5	366.03	146.41	1,610.51	219.62	0.49717674	109.19
6	402.63	161.05	1,771.56	241.58	0.43232760	104.44
7	442.89	177.16	1,948.72	265.73	0.37593704	99.90
8	487.18	194.87	2,143.59	292.31	0.32690177	95.56
9	535.90	214.36	2,357.95	321.54	0.28426241	91.40
10	589.49	235.79	2,593.74	2,947.43	0.24718471	728.56

Market value of equity (E) =	$1,717.73	
Market to book ratio $[E \div \text{Book}(0)]$ =	1.71773306	

Assumptions:

i Constant dividend payout equal to $(1 - b)$ times earnings.

ii After-tax rate of return earned on reinvested funds equals ROCE for all years 1 through 10.

iii Above normal (i.e., ROCE $> k_e$) returns will continue for 10 years, then ROCE $= k_e$.

[a] For years 1 through 9, these figures are the year end dividend only. For year 10, the corresponding figure represents the sum of the year 10 dividend plus the value of $E(N)$.

that in 10 years Apex will have amassed the income figures found in the second column of Table 2-10, retained 40 percent of these earnings in each year, and reinvested them to earn 25 percent per year (column three). The book value of the firm's equity (assumed to equal its market value) will grow from $1000 to over $2500 by the end of year 10 (column four), the annual dividend cash flows for each year are found in column five, as well as the sum of the year 10 dividend and the year 10 share value. Finally, the present value of the 10 years of dividends plus the year 10 equity value is found at the bottom of the last column (i.e., $1717.73). Thus, the result of following the proposed reinvestment plan over the next 10 years (when the 25 percent ROCE investment opportunity is available) is to create an equity value for Apex of $1717.73, which is 1.71773 times the original book value of Apex's common equity. Note that the $1717.73 equity value is in *present value* terms, such that the impact of the 25 percent investment opportunity in conjunction with the firm's retention (dividend payment) policy and cost of equity capital, is to cause an immediate increase in equity value by $1717.73 − 1000 = $717.73.

There are a number of ways in which the equity valuation model discussed here can be used to illustrate the impact of firm performance and financial policies on equity value. For example, Table 2-11 contains the summary results of similar analyses of the Apex example, where the example is varied to reflect different retention rates and ROCE. This example illustrates the impact of alternative dividend policies on equity value in light of differing assumptions about the ROCE. Note, however, that what is at work here is an analysis of alternative retention/reinvestment policies where no outside equity financing is being considered. That is, if the funds are not retained, then this analysis assumes that investments are not undertaken. Later, when we discuss dividend policy in some detail (Chapter 13), we will learn that in the absence of transactions costs and with competitive capital markets, the firm's management can either retain the necessary funds to finance its profitable investment opportunities (i.e., those investments for which ROCE > k_e) or pay dividends and issue new equity shares with no impact on shareholder wealth. However, where it is costly to issue new stock

TABLE 2-11
APEX MANUFACTURING COMPANY
EQUITY VALUE, ROCE, AND DIVIDEND POLICY[a]

	Dividend Payout (Percent)		
ROCE	0 percent	60 percent	100 percent
10 percent	0.641	0.712	0.749
25 percent	2.302	1.717	1.502
40 percent	7.149	3.261	2.254

[a] The numbers in the body of the table represent the ratio of the present value of the firm's equity—for a given ROCE and dividend payout ratio—divided by the "preinvestment" book value of the equity, (i.e., E/Book(0)).

and investors are not willing to purchase the stock without a substantial discount this type of analysis of dividend policy takes on some relevance.

These results demonstrate the relationship noted earlier with respect to dividend policy and the availability of investment opportunities with returns that exceed the firm's cost of capital. Where k_e is less than the opportunity investment rate for retained earnings (ROCE), equity value is enhanced by retaining all earnings, while the opposite result occurs where k_e is greater than ROCE.

In concluding our discussion of the creation of equity value we recognize once again the simplicity of the assumptions that underlie the Apex example. However the basic implications of the model are correct, and properly indicate the "direction" of the impact of the firm's investment decisions on equity value.

LIMITATIONS OF RATIO ANALYSIS

Financial ratios can provide an invaluable source of information to the analyst; however, they must be used with caution, for ratios calculated from accounting statements can be misleading at times. Specifically, the analyst must be aware of the following major weaknesses of the use of financial ratios:

1. *Firms frequently engage in multiple lines of business.* This means that it can be very difficult to determine an appropriate "peer group" from which to obtain target ratios. This is particularly important when the analyst tries to use industry average ratios as norms.

2. *Industry norms or average ratios reflect a conglomeration of varied accounting practices.* This is particularly important with respect to inventory accounting and fixed asset accounting. For example, if the subject firm used Last-in, First-out inventory accounting in a period of rising prices and the norm for the industry is First-in, First-out, then its inventory turnover will, *ceteris paribus*, be higher than the industry norm.

3. *Published industry norms are not representative samples.* The firms used to calculate industry averages do not represent a scientifically determined sample of the industry. For example, the industry ratios provided by Robert Morris and Associates are compiled from raw data voluntarily submitted by RMA member banks, with the following constraints: (a) the fiscal year-ends of the companies reported may not be April 1 through June 29, and (b) their total assets must be less than $100 million.

4. *Is the average industry ratio a desirable target?* It is not clear that the average ratio for an industry is a desirable target for a firm. Thus, deviation from the industry norm may be desirable in the financial analysis.

5. *Seasonality can influence a firm's computed ratios.* Balance sheet and income statement entries vary throughout the year for many firms whose level of business activity is subject to significant seasonality. This is particularly true of retail firms whose sales are closely tied to the seasons of the year. Thus, for these firms, the analyst must be careful to either adjust his ratio analysis for seasonality (by using average account balances used in calculating ratios using entries for several points in time over the year of interest) or use a ratio norm that itself is not adjusted for seasonality.

6 *What is a "good" ratio?* Ratios can be too high or too low and financial analyses generally do not involve statistical tests of significance. That is, a computed ratio may differ dramatically from an industry norm or target, and the difference may be simply due to wide variation in that particular ratio within the group from which the average was calculated. To deal with this problem, industry average ratios are generally provided with quartile values of the ratio. Thus, the analyst can compare the calculated ratio with the first and third quartiles from the industry. If the calculated ratio falls outside this range, the analyst can reasonbly conclude that the firm's ratio is indeed unusually high or low.

USING RATIOS TO PREDICT CORPORATE BANKRUPTCY

One of the important uses that can be made of financial ratios is the analysis of the likelihood that a firm will fail or become bankrupt. Beaver [1968] and Altman [1968] pioneered the use of modern statistical analysis of financial ratios in the prediction of the likelihood of corporate bankruptcy. Beaver used 14 financial ratios and tested for the differences in these ratios between failed and nonfailed firms. His analysis was "univariate" in that he considered one ratio at a time and did not allow for any interrelationship between the ratios analyzed. Of the ratios considered, the "cash flow to total assets" ratio was the best predictor of failure. In addition, Beaver found that the debt rato and net income to total assets ratio were good predictors.

Altman [1968] provided the first "multivariate" analysis of bankruptcy utilizing financial ratios. He used a tool called *multiple discriminant analysis,* which allowed him to combine several financial ratios into a single predictive equation. The predictive equation looks like a multiple regression equation, and produces a "Z-Score." If the Z-Score for a firm is below 1.8, then the subject firm is considered a prime candidate for bankruptcy. Altman's model appears as follows:

$$Z = 0.012x_1 + 0.014x_2 + 0.033x_3 + 0.006x_4 + 0.999x_5 \qquad (2\text{-}7)$$

where x_1 = working capital/total assets (working capital is assets less current liabilities)

x_2 = retained earnings/total assets

x_3 = earnings before interest and taxes/total assets

x_4 = market value of equity/book value of total debt(market value of equity includes both preferred and common shares, and total debt includes current and long-term liabilities)

x_5 = sales/total assets

The coefficients for each of the x's are determined in such a way as to maximize the predictive power of the function for the sample of firms used to build the function. In addition, when the model is "fitted" you also determine the critical Z-Score. For Altman's model a Z-score less than 1.8 indicates a very high probability of failure, while a Z-score larger than 3 indicates a high probability of nonfailure. Z-scores between 1.8 and 3 fall in the "gray zone" where it is not possible to predict with confidence whether the firm will or will not fail.

To demonstrate the use of the model we will apply it to PBC, using its 1989 financial statements as follows:

$$Z_{PBC} = 0.012(0.735) + 0.014(0.418) + 0.033(0.086) + 0.006(2.60)$$
$$+ 0.999(1.943)$$
$$= 1.97$$

Note that the price of PBC's common stock is $20 share so that the total market value of its equity used in calculating x_4 was $16 million. Now, interpreting PBC's Z-score we find that it is in the gray area, where it is neither clearly a failure candidate nor does it have a high probability of success. It would appear from this analysis that PBC's financial health is at least questionable.

In closing our discussion of Altman's bankruptcy prediction model, we note that it was quite successful in predicting bankrupt firms one statement period prior to their failure. In fact, it was able to successfully classify 90 percent of the firms one statement prior to failure and in subsequent tests has been accurate 80 percent of the time. In a more recent study, Altman (1977) developed a second model that accounts for recent changes in accounting practice—in particular the capitalization of financial lease contracts. This model has proven to be very accurate in predicting corporate failures up to 5 years in advance. There are a number of Failure Prediction Services that offer statistical analyses of the insolvency risk of industrial companies. Four such services are (i) the Z–Score model (Merrill Lynch provides Z-Scores for a wide range of corporations); (ii) the Zeta Model, which is available from Zeta Services, Inc.; (iii) the Gambler's Ruin Model, which is available from Advantage Financial Systems, and (iv) the QES Score, which is available from the Trust Division of the First Union Bank of Charlotte, North Carolina.

STATISTICAL STUDIES OF FINANCIAL RATIOS

In our earlier discussion of financial ratios we used four categories to discuss types of financial ratios: liquidity, efficiency, leverage and profitability. This set of categories serves as a very useful and commonsensical device for surveying financial ratios. However, these categories may or may not actually measure independent dimensions of a firm's financial condition. That is, if efficiency ratios are very highly correlated with profitability ratios, then there may be little need to calculate both of them when analyzing a firm. A number of studies have attempted to study the dimensions of a firm's financial condition. In addition, these studies have tested for the stability of the independent dimensions of a firm's financial health over time. In this section we will briefly review the findings of those studies, for they provide scientific evidence that bears directly on the use of ratios in performing a financial analysis.

Pinches, Mingo, and Caruthers (1973) studied the interrelationships among 48 financial ratios for a sample of 221 industrial films (with Standard Industrial Classification codes from 2000 to 3800). They found that seven groups of financial ratios were present. These groups were identified as follows: (1) return on investment, (2) capital intensiveness, (3) inventory intensiveness, (4) financial leverage, (5) receivables intensity, (6) short-term liquidity, and (7) cash liquidity. Comparing these groups with our four-group classification scheme, we find that all four of our categories are included among the seven; however, the efficiency ratio category is broken up into three categories of intensity ratios related to capital, inventory, and receivables. Further, the profitability ratio category is represented by the return on investment category. These results suggest that the efficiency grouping used in our discussion may include a heterogeneous collection of financial ratios and may not serve as a very useful category for purposes of generalizing about the financial condition of a firm.

In a subsequent study Pinches, Eubank, Mingo, and Caruthers (1975) confirmed the results of the earlier study and further established the stability of these groupings of ratios over four separate time periods. In yet another study Gombola and Ketz (1983) evaluated a set of 58 financial ratios computed for both manufacturing (SIC codes ranging from 2100 through 3800) and retail firms (SIC codes ranging from 5300 through 5900). Their sample included 783 manufacturing firms and 88 retail firms, which all had complete data available for the 10 year period ending with 1980. They identified eight independent categories of financial ratios: (1) return on investment, (2) cash position, (3) financial leverage, (4) receivables intensity, (5) debt structure, (6) cash flow, (7) cash expenditures, and (8) short term liquidity. Six of the eight categories are similar in structure to the Pinches et al. (1973) study. The two exceptions relate to the cash flow and cash expenditures categories, which reflect financial ratios not studied by Pinches and colleagues. Similar results were obtained for the retail sample. Some minor differences were observed related to the presence of a category of ratios containing return on sales, inventory intensiveness, and asset turnover. This particular combination of ratios was not observed for the manufacturing firms. When these ratio groups were tested for time series stability, very similar patterns were observed for each year for which the tests were performed. These studies suggest that the classification of financial ratios into only four groups is probably an over-simplification of reality. In addition, the stability of the groups of independent ratios over time further supports the use of the enlarged set of ratio categories.

CHAPTER SUMMARY

In this chapter we have discussed the basic tools of financial analysis. This discussion included a review of the firm's financial statements and some of the principles underlying their preparation. Furthermore, we discussed the use of financial ratios as a tool for analyzing a firm's financial statements. We have suggested two basic approaches to using financial ratios in performing a financial analysis. These include the common size statement approach and performance analysis.

In closing this chapter we should note that financial analysis is as much art as it is science. The calculation of a set of financial ratios is a relatively easy task. However, combining those ratios into a meaningful analysis of the firm's financial condition can be quite difficult. It is in the latter instance that the financial analyst's pay is earned.

PROBLEMS

2-1 (*Review of Financial Statements*) Assemble an income statement from the following scrambled list of items:

Selling expenses	$ 60,000
Cost of goods sold	850,000
Taxes payable	29,700
Sales (minus returns and allowances)	1,100,000
Administrative expenses	40,000
Depreciation expense	50,000
Net income	60,300
Earnings before taxes	90,000
Interest expense	?

2-2 (*Calculating Firm Earnings per Share*) Using the information from Problem 2-1 and assuming that the firm has 60,000 shares of common stock outstanding, compute the earnings per common share.

2-3 (*Ratio Analysis and Preparation of a Source and Use of Funds Statement*) The balance sheet and income statement for the J. J.'s Equipment Sales Co. are as follows:

J.J's Equipment Sales Co.
Balance Sheets
Years Ending December 31
(In Millions)

	1989	1990		1989	1990
Cash	$ 2	$ 3	Accounts payable	$ 7	$10
Accounts receivable	6	7	Notes payable	4	5
Inventory	14	20	Accrued wages	3	3
Total current assets	22	30	Accrued taxes	2	2
Net plant	40	40	Total current liabilities	16	20
			Long-term debt	20	20
			Common stock ($1 par)	10	10
			Retained earnings	16	20
Total	$62	$70	Total	$62	$70

J.J's Equipment Sales Co.
Income Statement 1990
(In Millions)

Sales		$110
Cost of goods sold	$60	
Selling, general, and administrative expenses	10	
Interest	5	
Depreciation	5	
Total expenses		80
Net income before taxes		30
Taxes		15
Net income		$ 15

a Prepare a statement of sources and uses of funds for the year ending December 31, 1990.

b Assume that you are a commercial banker and that Folley has asked for a six-month loan. The loan is for $1,000,000, and is to be used in financing an expanded inventory for the coming spring. Folley expects record high sales for the spring, resulting from the expectation of good growing conditions and a healthy demand for the area's products (wheat and barley). Compute the following ratios for Folley:

	J.J's 1990	Industry
Current ratio		1.5 times
Acid-test ratio		0.40
Debt ratio		0.60
Inventory turnover ratio[a]		2 times
Average collection period[b]		30 days
Return on investment		40 percent
Return on common equity		15 percent

[a] Use cost of goods sold and ending inventory.
[b] Based on a 360-day year.

c On the basis of your answers to the two preceding parts, should Folley be granted the loan?

d If the median price of Folley's common stock has been $2.00 per share over the past quarter, what is the Altman bankruptcy score for the firm? How does this score aid your analysis of J. J.'s loan request?

2-4 (*Ratio Analysis and Preparation of a Source and Use of Funds Statement*) Harry Smyth, financial vice president of R & R Contractors, Inc., contacted the firm's bank in regard to a short-term loan. The loan was to be used to repay notes payable and to finance current assets. Harry requested a one-year maturity on the loan. Upon receiving the loan request, the bank requested that the firm supply it with complete financial statements for the two previous years. These statements are as follows:

R & R Contractors, Inc.
Balance Sheets
Years Ending December 31

	1989	1990
Cash	$ 18,000	$ 1,000
Accounts receivable	25,000	32,000
Inventories	58,000	91,000
Total current assets	101,000	124,000
Land	40,000	52,000
Buildings and equipment	140,000	200,000
Less: Allowance for depreciation	(56,000)	(76,000)
Total fixed assets	124,000	176,000
Total assets	$225,000	$300,000
Accounts payable	$ 21,000	$ 44,000
Bank notes	34,000	94,000
Total current liabilities	55,000	138,000
Long-term debt	57,500	45,900
Common stock (10,000 shares outstanding)	63,000	63,000
Retained earnings	49,500	53,100
Total liabilities	$225,000	$300,000

R & R Contractors, Inc.
Income Statements
Years Ending December 31

	1989	1990
Sales	$250,000	$320,000
Cost of goods sold	150,000	192,000
Gross profit	100,000	128,000
Operating expenses:		
Fixed cash operating expense	42,000	42,000
Variable operating expense	25,000	32,000
Depreciation	9,000	20,000
Total operating expenses	76,000	94,000
Earnings before interest and taxes	24,000	34,000
Interest	6,000	12,200
Earnings before taxes	18,000	21,800
Taxes	9,000	10,900
Net income	$ 9,000	$ 10,900

a On the basis of the preceding statements, complete the following table:

R & R Contractors, Inc.
Ratio Analysis

	Industry averages	Actual 1989	Actual 1990
Current ratio	1.80 times	1.84	.90
Acid-test ratio	0.70	.78	.24
Average collection period[a]	37 days	36	36
Inventory turnover ratio[a]	2.50 times	2.6	2.1
Debt ratio	58 percent	50%	61%
Long-term-debt-to-total-capitalization ratio	33 percent	25.8%	15%
Times-interest-earned ratio	3.8 times		
Gross profit margin	38 percent	40%	40%
Net profit margin	3.5 percent		
Return on total assets	4.0 percent	10.6%	
Return on common equity	8.2 percent	8%	9.4%

[a] Based on a 360-day year and on end-of-year figures.

b Analyze Mr. Smyth's loan request. Would you grant the loan? Why? Why not?

c Prepare a statement of sources and uses of funds for R & R Contractors, Inc. How does the funds statement supplement your ratio analysis from item b, above? Explain.

d Calculate the Altman bankruptcy score for R & R Contractors. (Note that the trading range of the firm's stock has been from $15.00 to $22.00 during the past year. The median price was $17.00, but the most recent price was $21.00). Does this score aid your analysis? How?

2-5 Use the financial statements for R & R Contractors found in Problem 2-4 to perform a "performance analysis". If the price-earnings ratio for similar firms is 12 to 1, what should the share price of R & R's stock be?

2-6 Altman's Z-score model has been widely used to predict corporate failures. Look at the coefficients of the model and discuss the relative importance of the independent variables.

2-7 The Alton and Bacon companies are competing firms in the publishing industry. The two firms have quite different measures of profitability however. In fact, Alton earns a return on its common equity of 22 percent while Bacon only earns 18 percent. If both firms have identical net profit margins, what is (are) the source(s) of the different measures of return on equity?

2-8 The income statements for the Alton Manufacturing Company are found below. Analyze the historical trend in each of the entries to determine the policies that the firm has chosen to follow:

($000)	19X1	19X2	19X3	19X4	19X5	19X6	19X7
Sales revenues	1,200	1,350	1,500	1,770	1,900	2,300	2,500
Cost of goods sold	800	850	900	1,000	1,100	1,450	1,500
Gross profit	400	500	600	770	800	850	1,000
Operating expenses	100	110	110	120	120	130	130
Interest expense	20	20	20	100	100	100	100
Earnings before tax	280	370	470	550	580	620	770

REFERENCES

Altman, E. I: "Financial Ratios, Discriminant Analysis, and the Prediction of Corporate Bankruptcy," *Journal of Finance*, 23 (1968), pp. 589–609.

Backer, Morton, and Martin Gosman: "The Use of Financial Ratios in Credit Downgrade Decisions," *Financial Management*, (Spring 1980), pp. 53–56.

Beaver, W. H.: "Alternative Accounting Measures as Predictors of Failure," *The Accounting Review*, (January 1968), pp. 113–122.

Bernstein, Leopold: *Financial Statement Analysis: Theory, Application, and Interpretation* (Homewood, Ill.: Richard D. Irwin, 1983).

Chen, K. H., and T. A. Shimerda: "An Empirical Analysis of Useful Financial Ratios," *Financial Management*, vol. 10 (Spring 1981), pp. 51–60.

Collins, R. A.: "An Empirical Comparison of Bankruptcy Prediction Models," *Financial Management*, vol. 9 (Summer 1980), pp. 52–57.

Fraser, Lyn: *Understanding Financial Statements: Through the Maze of a Corporate Annual Report* (Reston, Va.: Reston Publishing, 1985).

Frecka, T., and C. F. Lee: "Generalized Ratio Generation Process and Its Implications," *Journal of Accounting Research*, (Spring 1983), pp. 308–316.

Gombola, M. J., and J. E. Ketz: "Financial Ratio Patterns in Retail and Manufacturing Organizations," *Financial Management*, vol. 11 (Summer 1983), pp. 45–56.

Keiso, D. E., and J. J. Weygandt: *Intermediate Accounting*, (New York: Wiley, 1980).

Kyd, Charles W: "Forecasting Bankruptcy with Z Scores," *Lotus* (September 1985), pp. 43–47.

Orgler, Y. E: *Analytical Methods for Loan Evaluation*, (Lexington, Mass.: Lexington Books, 1975).

Pinches, G., K. S. Mingo, and J. K. Caruthers: "The Stability of Financial Ratio Patterns in Industrial Organizations," *Journal of Finance*, (May 1973), pp. 384–396.

Pinches, G., A. A. Eubank, K. A. Mingo, and J. K. Caruthers: "The Hierarchial Classification of Financial Ratios," *Journal of Business Research*, (October 1975), pp. 295–310.

Roll, R: "R^2," *Journal of Finance* (July 1988), pp. 541–566.

Welsch, Glenn A. and Charles T. Zlatokovich: *Intermediate Accounting*, Eighth Edition (Homewood, Ill.: Richard D. Irwin, 1989).

3

FINANCIAL FORECASTING, PLANNING, AND CONTROL

Financial planning encompasses the firm's efforts to *forecast the firm's future financial needs and prearrange the details of any financial contracts that may be required to meet those needs*. Thus, financial planning entails "present action" to deal with its expectations of the future. For this reason we can think of financial planning as "future-oriented" decision making. The need to plan for a firm's future financing requirements comes from two facts of business life: uncertainty, and the costs of reacting to financing needs when they arise. Very simply, if the future were known there would be no need to be concerned about forecasting its consequences for the firm. Likewise, if the firm cannot save money by prearranging for its potential future financing requirements, then there is little economic motivation for attempting to estimate the consequences of the future for the firm's financing requirements. On the other side of the coin, financial planing is costly, and these costs must be balanced off against the potential savings associated with planning. If a firm engages in financial planning it must either expend the necessary resources to develop its own financial forecasts and plans, or hire outside consultants to do it for them. Thus, each firm must make a decision as to the approach it will take to the financial planning problem (internal or external) and the amount of its resources it will contribute to planning activities. In this chapter we will attempt to describe the basics of the financial planning process that would be used in either case.

Financial planning frequently involves preparation of one or more budgets. For example, the cash budget is the primary element of a short-term financial plan covering a period less than one year. For this reason the terms forecasting and budgeting are sometimes used interchangeably. We will distinguish financial planning and budgeting in a manner similar to that used to distinguish positive and normative economics. That

47

is, a financial forecast can be likened to positive economics in that it is an attempt to forecast or predict "what is" as opposed to "what should be," which is characteristic of a budget. Thus, a financial plan represents the firm's attempt to predict what the future holds (positive), while a budget represents an attempt to direct the firm's financial affairs (normative) in response to its forecast. Budgets, then, can be thought of as an integral component of the financial plan.

Throughout our discussion of the planning and budgeting process the reader should be aware that the personal computer and computer spreadsheet packages such as Lotus 1-2-3® and Excel® (among many others) have had a tremendous impact on the cost of engaging in financial planning. Specifically, the development of personal computers and low cost financial software has dramatically diminished the cost of engaging in financial planning and made it possible now for very small enterprises to engage in extensive planning activities. The major cost of engaging in financial planning today, then, relates to the opportunity cost of the managerial time devoted to the task. We will argue that even this is reduced, however, due to the fact that easy-to-use financial spreadsheet software makes it possible for the financial analyst to do his or her own forecasting and budget construction without the aid of a data processing staff. This means that the financial analyst is free to develop models suited to the particular needs of the task without the need to requisition the support of a centralized data processing staff, which all too frequently his little or no understanding of the particular problem at hand.

The chapter is organized as follows: First we discuss sales forecasting, which lies at the heart of any financial plan. Here we survey three types of forecast models, including subjective models, time series models, and causal models. Next we discuss the preparation of a cash flow estimate using the cash budget based upon the firm's sales forecast. We then discuss the construction of pro forma statements using the percent of sales method and budgeted expense method. Finally, we discuss the use of the "sustainable growth model" for evaluating the "feasibility" of a firm's financial plan.

FORECASTING SALES

The sales forecast provides the starting point for almost every financial plan. Thus the accuracy of this forecast is essential to the accuracy of the remaining elements of the financial plan. The financial analyst will not in general be responsible for the sales forecast, as this forecast is generally prepared by the firm's marketing group or some other planning group. However, given the importance of an accurate sales forecast to the success of the financial plan, the financial analyst should be familiar with sales forecasting methodology. Furthermore, the financial analyst may at times be called upon to either forecast or modify a forecast of firm sales.

A Brief Overview of Sales Forecast Methodology

We will identify three basic groups of forecast methods: subjective, time series, and causal. The forecaster may use all three methodologies or some combination of the three depending upon the particular forecast situation at hand. The **subjective forecast methodology** is actually a whole class of forecast models or techniques which rely on human judgment. They are subjective rather than objective since they do not rely on formal mathematical models whose results can be verified by another forecaster who might use them to predict sales using a given set of data. Instead these methods entail the estimation of sales using the special knowledge or judgment of the individual making the forecast.

There are, however, some "formal" methods for going about the construction of a subjective forecast. We will discuss only one such method here, the **Delphi method**. With this method the forecast is generated through the use of "experts" which may be comprised of the firm's own sales force or members of its planning staff. The Delphi technique has gained particular popularity because it utilizes expert opinion in a manner appealing to many managers. To construct such a forecast, the group of experts is asked to submit individual sales forecasts, with justification for their estimate, to the group leader. The individual group members are not allowed to communicate directly with one another but must do so through the group leader in response to requests for information. The group leader then compiles the individual forecasts and circulates them to the members of the group. The group members are then asked to reevaluate their own forecasts in light of what they have learned from reading the justifications offered for the forecasts of each of the other members of the group. Revised forecasts and justifications are then submitted to the group leader, who continues to process until a consensus is reached or he or she feels no more progress can be made toward achieving one.

Although subjective forecast methods are always valuable where expert opinion is available, these methods are particularly valuable where there is no past data upon which to construct an objective forecast. This situation frequently arises when a new firm is being formed, a new product is being marketed, or a new technology is being utilized. Thus, forecasting the impact of a new technology (such as the microchip or bubble memory) will necessarily involve the use of subjective forecast methods that rely upon expert opinion and judgment.

Time Series Models

This general class of forecast models comprises tools used to exploit past trends to come up with a forecast. Thus, the basic premise underlying the choice of a time series model is "the best estimate of future sales is a continuation of the past trend." We will not demonstrate the use of time series models here but will enumerate some of the more popular types of models. The simplest type of time series model is the **moving average model**. Here the analyst simply forecasts the future using an average of past sales. For example, the analysis might simply add up the four most recent sales figures, divide by four and use this as an estimate of next year's sales. A slightly more sophisticated procedure would involve giving larger weight to the more recent observations; **exponential smoothing** is such a time series forecast model. With this model the weight assigned to each past observation declines in accordance with an exponential function. The number of terms included in the average and the speed with which the exponential function decays are then determined by the analyst. The **Box-Jenkins** forecast methodology is actually a collection of time series models which utilize very sophisticated heuristics, or rules of thumb, to aid the analyst in determining the "best forecast model" for a particular forecast problem. There exists a wide variety of time series forecast software that can be used on personal computers. These software packages allow even the novice user access to very sophisticated forecast methods. Some of these packages are in essence "expert systems," which allow the user to vary the level of user interaction from simply entering the data and allowing the program to make all the model-fitting choices to requiring that all choices be made by the user.

In summary, time series models are quantitative sales forecast methods that attempt to take advantage of any trend in past sales. They can appear to be very "scientific" or mathematically sophisticated when compared with subjective methods or even some types of causal models, which we discuss next. However, the analyst should keep in mind that "accuracy" of a forecast is the objective of the analysis, not the sophistication of the tool used to develop the forecast. In the Appendix 3A to this chapter we present a model for evaluating forecast accuracy that can be applied to any set of forecasts, regardless of their source or the methodology employed in generating them.

Causal Forecast Models

When causal models are used to forecast sales, they attempt to identify the underlying determinants of sales using a formal statistical model. The most commonly used causal sales forecast model is **regression analysis**. Regression analysis is actually a general term used to refer to a number of models that share a similar methodology. **Simple regression analysis** involves the prediction of sales using a single predictor (independent) variable. We will later demonstrate the use of simple regression analysis using time as the independent variable. Any introductory statistics text contains a detailed discussion of the estimation of a simple regression equation. However, it should be noted that most financial spreadsheet software packages available for personal computers include the capability for estimating a simple regression equation and its related statistics. Thus, the analyst must understand the use of such a predictive equation but need not be expert in its estimation. The danger here is that the analyst will not become sufficiently familiar with the technique to use it effectively; having the technical capability needed to estimate a regression equation via the use of a financial spreadsheet program is not a substitute for understanding the tool.

Multiple regression analysis involves the use of several predictor (independent) variables. This type of model is used where the analyst identifies two or more important predictor variables that independently influence the level of a firm's sales. For example, a machine tool manufacturer's sales might be dependent on the level of general economic activity (as measured by gross national product for the economy as a whole), the economic activity in the firm's particular region of the country (as reflected in an index of regional economic activity), and the availability of sufficient plan capacity to meet the projected demand. A multiple regression model might be used to incorporate all these factors into a single forecast of firm sales.

Simultaneous regression equation methods provide sales forecasting methods. This type of model involves the estimation of two or more equations simultaneously. Simultaneous estimation is necessary because of interdependencies that may exist between variables used in the multiple equation models. The need for this type of forecast methodology arises from the complexity of the economic system within which a firm's sales are determined. That is, firm sales are determined simultaneously with many other variables in the context of the whole system of economic relationships. Although this type of forecast methodology is widely used to predict economic aggregates such as gross national product, it is not as well known to sales forecasters. Part of the reason for this is the financial sophistication needed to formulate complex multi-equation systems. Also, it is not at all clear that increased sophistication in forecast methodology leads to superior or even improved forecast accuracy. We will not demonstrate the use of simultaneous equation models in sales forecasting here, but refer the interested reader to any good econometrics text.

Estimating Sales for the Peterson Bottling Company

We will use the Peterson Bottling Company (PBC) example introduced in Chapter 2 to demonstrate the use of two related forecast methodologies: the scatter diagram method and simple regression. The **scatter diagram** method, we discover, is a simplified version of simple regression analysis. It involves estimation of the relationship between firm sales and a single predictor (independent) variable by simply plotting historical values of the two series and sketching a line onto the diagram that "visually" fits the relationship best.

Scatter Diagram Method.   We will demonstrate use of this method by plotting sales for PBC and time. Sales for PBC over the past ten years are presented in Table 3-1. These sales figures are then plotted against time in Figure 3-1 to get a picture of how the firm's sales have been changing over time.

In this example the scatter diagram method is used to determine a trend line for sales with respect to time; the trend line is then used to predict future sales. Note that the predictions made by using this method are solely dependent on the firm's

TABLE 3-1
HISTORICAL SALES FOR PETERSON
BOTTLING CORPORATION (1980–1989)
(IN THOUSANDS)

Year	Sales	Year	Sales
1980	$19,248	1985	$21,250
1981	19,751	1986	20,022
1982	19,753	1987	20,761
1983	19,948	1988	21,418
1984	20,748	1989	22,703

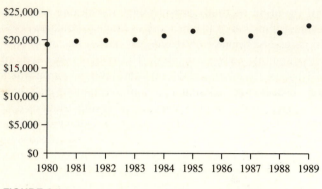

FIGURE 3-1
PBC sales for the years 1980 to 1989 (thousands of dollars).

past sales. The trend lien is determined by simply drawing a straight line through the scatter of points which best fits the observed sales figures.

In Figure 3-2 two trend lines are fitted to the PBC sales data. The first of these trend lines makes use of all ten years of sales data and is labeled AA'. The second trend line, BB', is based on sales for 1986 through 1989 only, since these sales are the most

FIGURE 3-2
Scatter-diagram trend lines for PBC's sales.

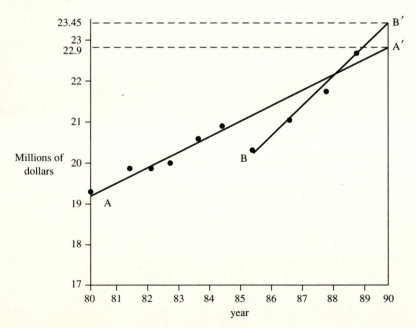

recent and possibly the most relevant in terms of predicting what the firm's future sales are going to be. By the use of the first trend line (AA'), the projection for 1990 sales can be read from the vertical sales axis as being $22,900,000. Using trend line BB', which utilizes the sales for 1986 through 1989, we obtain a very different estimate of 1990 sales: The second estimate is approximately $23,450,000. The AA' and BB' projections may be viewed, respectively, as pessimistic and optimistic forecasts of 1990 sales, since the lower estimate assumes that the sales growth of 1986 through 1989 will *not* continue and the optimistic estimate assumes that it will. At this point the analyst must utilize his or her own judgment in selecting the sales forecast to use in subsequent analyses.

Simple Regression Method.   The regression method represents a "formalization" of the scatter diagram method just discussed, in that we now mathematically fit the trend line to the observed data, rather than use a visual fit. Two regression lines are fitted to the PBC sales data found in Table 3-1. The computations involved in fitting the regression lines are not presented here but can be found in any introductory statistics text. However, we do not have to be able to understand the derivation of the regression lines to understand their use in forecasting future sales.

The trend lines used in the analysis here are linear, that is, straight lines. We must know two things about a trend line to completely describe it mathematically. First, we must determine the intercept term, which is simply the value of the sales variable when the time variable takes on a value of 0. Second, we must find the slope of the regression line, which is the change in sales for each unit change in time. The intercept and slope terms are collectively referred to as the coefficients of the following linear regression equation:

$$\text{Sales}(t) = A + B \cdot \text{Year}(t)$$

where Sales(t) represents firm sales in the year or period t, Year(t) is the corresponding period designation (e.g., 1989), A is the intercept value, and B is the slope term.

The trend equation for PBC's sales computed with the use of all ten years of sales is as follows:

$$\text{Sales}(t) = -563{,}099 + 294.109 \cdot \text{Year}(t) \tag{3-1}$$

To use the preceding trend equation to predict firm sales for 1990, we need only substitute 1990 for Year (t); that is,

$$\begin{aligned}
\text{Sales }(1990) &= -563{,}099 + (294.109)(1990) \\
&= -563{,}099 + 585{,}276.91 \\
&= \$22{,}177.900 \text{ (thousands)}
\end{aligned}$$

Thus, we would predict PBC's 1990 sales to be $22,177,900 on the basis of the observed relationship between sales and time over the past ten years. This prediction compares with $22,900,000 for the scatter diagram method.

A second trend equation can be fitted by using the regression method and the last four years of sales data. The resulting trend equation is found in Equation (3-2):

$$\text{Sales}(t) = -1,707,899 + 870 \cdot \text{Year}(t) \tag{3-2}$$

Substituting 1990 for Year (t) produces a sales estimate of $23,401,000 for 1990. This estimate, as discussed earlier, is based on the assumption that the sales trend of the past four years will continue.

To show the similarity in the two methods discussed to this point, the regression trend lines are plotted in Figure 3-3 for comparison with Figure 3-2. In Figure 3-3 the plotted predictions of firm sales are based on trend Equations (3-1) and (3-2), where we substitute into the appropriate equation for the Year variable, and solve for the corresponding value of sales. These estimates of firm sales are plotted as trend lines CC' and DD'. Note that the predictions for 1990 sales can now be read directly from the graph, where the trend lines intersects a vertical line passing through the year 1990.

Summary Analysis of Sales Predictions. The two forecast methods discussed here rely solely on the firm's historical sales trend. This type of forecast may be the

FIGURE 3-3
Regression trend lines for PBC's sales.

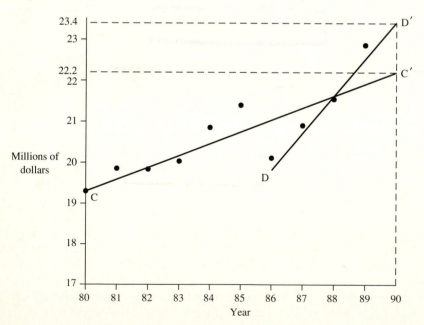

best that the external analyst can do; however, the internal analyst would certainly have access to information other than past sales that could be useful in projecting future sales. Also, it should be noted that we have made no attempt to use anything other than a straight line. Since two trend lines were used, however, we do have some feel for the effect of the changing time pattern of firm sales over the period.

In the preceding pages we discussed the use of simple linear regression equations in predicting firm sales. Analysts should become proficient in the use of these and more complex predictive equations; however, it is not essential that analysts be expert in deriving the models themselves. The low-cost availability of financial spreadsheet software for personal computers capable of solving for the coefficients of regression equations facilitates the use of very sophisticated forecast methodologies by anyone having the desire to use them.

This concludes our brief and rather simplistic look at forecasting techniques. Next, we construct a cash budget and pro forma financial statements based on our estimate of firm sales.

CASH BUDGET

The cash budget represents one of the most useful of all the tools of financial planning in that it provides the basis for analyzing the cash position of the firm at each of any number of intervals over a given planning horizon. Specifically, the cash budget consists of a statement of planned (expected) cash flow, which is the difference in cash receipts and disbursements for a particular interval of time. The budget interval for which cash flow is estimated may be as short as one week or as long as a year. For exposition purposes, in the example that follows, we will prepare a cash budget for PBC spanning the first half of 1990 with intermediate cash-flow calculations based on monthly intervals.

The first step in the preparation of any cash budget involves obtaining an estimate of sales for the budget period. In the preceding section we prepared sales estimates for 1990 which ranged from a low of $22,177,800 to a high of $23,401,000. Lacking more detailed information about next year's expected sales, we adopt for expository purposes a sales estimate of $23,000,000. Actually, the firm analyst may wish to construct three levels of sales. Since the procedure would be the same for any sales estimate, we will limit our discussion to the expected sales level.

Next we project collections from our estimate of future sales. These projections usually reflect the firm's past collection pattern. This past history is useful, however, only when the firm's credit and collection policies are unaltered during the planning period. For example, should the firm decide to offer a cash discount of, say, 2 percent for payment within 10 days after the sale, then, other things remaining the same, first-month collections should increase as a percent of sales. The benefits of making such a change should, of course, be weighted against the lost 2 percent of sales revenues. To complete our projections of cash receipts, we next itemize any external financing that the firm plans to undertake during the budget period. For example, the firm may be planning to enter a long-term loan agreement with an insurance company during the budget period. This would constitute a planned cash receipt, and accordingly must

outflows

be accounted for in the cash budget. Having estimated cash receipts, we now turn to planned cash disbursements for the budget period. Disbursements are a function of when expenses are incurred and the payment habits (plans) of the firm. Cash disbursements can be related to operating expenses, finance charges (interest, rent, etc.), taxes, repayment of debt, payment of cash dividends, and, in general, any activity requiring a cash outlay by the firm. Finally, total disbursements for each budget interval are subtracted from total cash receipts for the corresponding period, to determine the net change in cash position for the period.

Necessary information for the preparation of PBC's monthly cash budget by the first six months of 1990 is found in Table 3-2. The cash flow information contained in Table 3-2 is first converted to a cash basis in a worksheet and then compiled in the cash budget. Table 3-3 contains the worksheet, and Table 3-4 presents the resulting cash budget for PBC spanning the first six months of 1990. The worksheet serves simply as a tool for developing the information needed for the cash budget. For example, PBC's cash receipts from sales do not coincide with the months in which the sales are made, nor do payments for purchases coincide with the months

TABLE 3-2
REVENUE AND EXPENSE INFORMATION FOR PBC's 1990 CASH BUDGET

1 *Sales*—Monthly sales estimates based on the $23,000,000 estimated annual sales and past seasonality in monthly sales are as follows:

	Historical Monthly	
Month	**Percent of annual sales**	**Sales estimates**[a]
January	5	$1,150,000
February	3	690,000
March	4	920,000
April	5	1,150,000
May	7	1,610,000
June	14	2,530,000
July	12	2,760,000
August	13	2,990,000
September	12	2,760,000
October	11	2,530,000
November	9	2,070,000
December	8	$1,840,000

[a] These monthly sales estimates are found by multiplying the relevant percent of annual sales for the month by the estimated $23,000,000 in sales.

2 *Collections*—PBC makes virtually all its sales on credit terms of net 45, which means that the entire invoice is due forty-five days after the sale. Roughly 20 percent of those sales are collected within the sale month, with the remaining 80 percent being collected in the following month. PBC's bad debts are negligible and are, therefore, ignored for purposes of preparing the firm's cash budget.

in which the purchases are actually made. Specifically, during January 1990, PBC expects to have sales of $1,150,000; however, collections for the month will equal 20 percent of January sales, or $230,000, plus 80 percent of December 1988 sales, or $1,452,800, for a total of $1,682,800. Another example involves PBC's purchases, which are made two months in advance of planned sales but paid for three months

TABLE 3-2
(*continued*)

3 *Cost of goods sold*—PBC makes its purchases two months prior to anticipated sales and makes payment ninety days after purchase. Purchases in 1989 were 47.40 percent of sales, and PBC feels that 48 percent is a reasonable estimate of cost of merchandise for 1990. Labor and other expenses included in the cost of goods sold amount to 19.59 percent of sales, with 20 percent of these expenditures coinciding with the month in which the corresponding sales occur and 80 percent in the following month.

4 *Selling and delivery expenses*—These expenses are estimated to maintain the same relationship to sales that existed in 1989. That is, selling expenses will be equal to 14 percent and delivery expenditures equal to 9 percent of anticipated sales. Roughly 25 percent of the selling and delivery expenditures are paid in the month in which the expense is incurred, and the remainder is paid in the following month.

5 *General and Administrative Expenses*—These expenses, unlike selling and delivery expenses, do not vary in a consistent manner with sales. PBC expects that the total of this expense item will not differ substantially from the 1989 level. Depreciation expense for 1989 of $660,000 is included in the estimated annual level of general and administrative expenses of $1,220,000. Since depreciation does not constitute a cash expense, it will not be included in the cash budget. Each month's expense is one-twelfth of the total for the year. With the exception of depreciation, these expenses are paid as follows: 30 percent paid within the month, and 70 percent one month later.

6 *Interest Expense*—PBC interest due during 1989 is as follows:

Debt	Face amount	Interest rate	Interest expense	Due date
Current portion due on long-term debt issued before 1989	$ 218,468	0.096	$ 20,972[a]	3/31/90
Bank loan[b]	200,000	0.120	12,000	6/30/90
Long-term debt (1989)[c]	765,630	0.120	91,876	12/31/90
Long-term debt (old)[d]	2,071,541	0.096	198,868	3/31/90

[a] This represents one year's interest on the current portion of PBC's long-term debt. Both principal and interest are due and payable on March 31, 1990.

[b] This is the requested six-month bank loan and is assumed to be outstanding for the full six months, carrying a 12 percent annual rate of interest. Both interest and principal are assumed to be repaid by June 30, 1990.

[c] This loan was incurred in January 1989 and will not mature until 1993, with annual interest payable at 12 percent on December 31 of every year and no principal due until maturity.

[d] This item reflects the long-term debt of the firm issued before 1989, exclusive of the current portion due in 1990 ($218,468).

7 *Income Taxes*—A quarterly estimated income tax payment of $77,736 is due January 15, 1990, for the fourth quarter of 1989, and estimated taxes of $39,830 are due on April 15, 1990, for the first quarter of 1990.

TABLE 3-3
Peterson Bottling Corporation
Cash Budget Worksheet for the Period
1/1/90–6/30/90

	November	December	January	February
Sales	$2,043,000	$1,816,000	$1,150,000	$ 690,000
Collections:				
Cash (20%)	408,600	363,200	230,000	138,000
One month after the sale (80%)	_____	1,634,000	1,452,800	920,000
Total collections	_____	1,997,600	1,682,800	1,058,000
Payments for purchases:				
Purchases— 47.4% of sales two months in advance	545,100	327,060	436,080	545,100
Cash payments—90 days after purchase			860,784	545,100
Payments for labor expenses:				
Labor expenses— 19.59% of sales	400,224	355,754	225,285	135,171
Cash payments— current month (20%)	80,045	71,151	45,057	27,034
one month later (80%)	_____	320,179	284,603	180,228
Total payments	_____	391,330	329,660	207,262
Payments for selling expenses:				
Selling and delivery expenses (23% of Sales)	469,890	417,680	264,500	158,700
Cash payments— current month (25%)	117,473	104,420	66,125	39,675
one month later (75%)	_____	352,417	313,260	198,375
Total payments	_____	456,837	379,385	238,050

March	April	May	June	July	August
$ 920,000	$1,150,000	$1,610,000	$2,530,000	$2,760,000	$2,990,000
184,000	230,000	322,000	506,000	552,000	598,000
552,000	736,000	920,000	1,288,000	2,024,000	2,208,000
736,000	966,000	1,242,000	1,794,000	2,576,000	2,806,000
763,140	1,199,220	1,130,240	1,417,260		
327,060	436,080	545,100	763,140	1,199,220	1,308,240
180,228	225,285	315,399	495,627	540,684	585,741
36,046	45,057	63,080	99,125	108,137	117,148
108,137	144,182	180,228	252,319	396,502	432,547
144,183	189,239	243,308	351,444	504,639	549,695
211,600	264,500	370,300	581,900	634,800	687,700
52,900	66,125	92,575	145,475	158,700	171,925
119,025	158,700	198,375	277,725	436,425	476,100
171,925	224,825	290,950	423,200	595,125	648,025

TABLE 3-3 (*continued*)
Peterson Bottling Corporation
Cash Budget Worksheet for the Period
1/1/90–6/30/90

	November	December	January	February
Payments for general and administrative expenses:				
General and admin. expenses— $560,000/12	46,667	46,667	46,667	46,667
Cash payments— current month (30%)	14,000	14,000	14,000	14,000
one month later (70%)		32,667	32,667	32,667
Total payments		46,667	46,667	46,667

after purchases. In January 1990, PBC plans to purchase $436,080 worth of materials (0.474 times the March sales of $920,000), which will be paid for in April. However, in January 1990 the company pays for the purchases made back in October 1990 in the amount of 0.474 × $1,816,000 (December sales) = $860,784. This estimate is based on the fact that in 1989 the cost of goods sold equaled 47.4 percent of sales.

Once we have completed our compilation of the firm's cash-flow information for the budget period, the information can then be transferred to the cash budget (see Table 3-4). As we noted earlier, the cash budget consists of three basic components: cash receipts, cash disbursements, and net change in cash for the period. PBC's cash budget indicates, for example, that during January the firm anticipates a net increase in its cash balance of $188,568, resulting from total cash receipts of $1,882,800 and corresponding disbursements of $1,694,232. We see also that PBC anticipates a decrease in cash during the month of March primarily as a result of the interest and principal due in that month ($219,840 + $438,308).

For planning purposes, the analyst can use the cash budget just prepared to examine the firm's cash position for each month within the six-month planning period. In Table 3-5 we prepare a statement of cash position for PBC for the first six months of 1990. PBC's ending cash balance for June 1990 is thus expected to be $1,309,753, which represents a net deterioration in the firm's cash position of $1,309,753 − $1,349,524 = −$39,771. This anticipated deterioration in cash position includes consideration of the planned repayment of the $200,000 bank loan, plus 12 percent interest for the six months the loan was outstanding.

On the basis of PBC's estimates of its operating cash flows for the next six months, it does appear that the firm will be able to repay the requested $200,000 bank loan

March	April	May	June	July	August
46,667	46,667	46,667	46,667	46,667	46,667
14,000	14,000	14,000	14,000	14,000	14,000
32,667	32,667	32,667	32,667	32,667	32,667
46,667	46,667	46,667	46,667	46,667	46,667

by June 30, 1990, as planned. Of course, we have looked at only one set of cash-flow estimates, which may or may not depict accurately the firm's cash flows for the period.

PRO FORMA FINANCIAL STATEMENTS

Pro forma financial statements are simply planned statements of income or financial condition for a future time period. Much of the information required to compile both the pro forma income statement and the pro forma balance sheet can be found in the cash budget just completed. Once again PBC will be used for illustration purposes.

Pro Forma Income Statement

Preparation of the PBC's pro forma income statement for the six-month period ending June 30, 1990, utilizes much of the information found in the firm's cash budget (Table 3-4). Before we begin our discussion, however, we should remember that the income statement is constructed on an accrual and not a cash basis. This means that the income and expense items it contains are those recognized as having occurred during the period covered by the statement even if they have not had an impact on cash flows. For example, all of the firm's sales for the six months ended in June are included in the pro forma income statement as sales revenues, although only 20 percent of those sales are collected in the month of the sale. Similarly, all of the expenses required to generate the sales recognized as having been made during the

TABLE 3-4
Peterson Bottling Corporation
Cash Budget for the Six-Month Period Ending June 30, 1990

	January	February	March	April	May	June
Cash receipts:						
Collections from sales	$1,682,800	$1,058,000	$ 736,000	$ 966,000	$1,242,000	$1,794,000
Proceeds from bank loan	200,000					
Total cash receipts	1,882,800	1,058,000	736,000	966,000	1,242,000	1,794,000
Cash disbursements:						
Payments for purchases	860,784	545,100	327,060	436,080	545,100	763,140
Payments for labor	329,660	207,262	144,183	189,239	243,308	351,444
Payments for selling and delivery expenses	379,385	238,050	171,925	224,825	290,950	423,200
Payments for general and administrative expenses	46,667	46,667	46,667	46,667	46,667	46,667
Interest payments			219,840			12,000
Repayment of debt			218,468			200,000
Quarterly income tax payments	77,736			39,830		
Total disbursements	1,694,232	1,037,079	1,128,143	936,641	1,126,025	1,796,451
Net monthly change	$ 188,568	$ 20,921	$ (392,359)	$ 29,359	$ 115,975	$ (2,451)

TABLE 3-5
Peterson Bottling Corporation
Statement of Monthly Cash Balances for the Six-Month Period Ending June 30, 1990

	January	February	March	April	May	June
Beginning cash balance	$1,349,524[a]	$1,538,092	$1,559,013	$1,166,870	$1,196,229	$1,312,204
Net change for the month[b]	188,568	20,921	(392,143)	29,359	115,975	(2,451)
Ending cash balance	1,538,092	1,559,013	1,166,870	1,196,229	1,312,204	1,309,753

[a] Taken from the end-of-month cash balance for December 1989.
[b] Obtained from the monthly cash budget found in Table 3-4.

period are "matched" with those revenues and included in the statement, even though cash payments may lag behind the incurrence of many of those expenses.

Sales. We begin with an estimate of firm sales for the six-month period, which can simply be taken from the worksheet found in Table 3-3. Thus, for the first six months of 1990, PBC's sales are estimated at $8,050,000.

Cost of goods sold. From the information used in preparing PBC's cash budget, we recall that the cost of goods sold was composed of materials costs, which were equal to 47.4 percent of sales, plus labor costs, which are equal to 19.59 percent of sales. Thus, we can estimate cost of goods sold as 66.99 percent of sales (the sum of 47.4 and 19.59 percent), which, for the first six months of 1990, is $8,050,000 × 0.6699 = $5,392,695.

Selling and delivery expenses. Selling expense was estimated to be 14 percent of sales, and delivery expense to be 9 percent of sales. Thus, for the first six months of 1990, selling expense is estimated to be 0.14 × $8,050,000 = $1,127,000, and delivery expense is expected to equal 0.09 × $8,050,000 = $724,500.

General and administrative expenses. General and administrative expenses, which include depreciation expense, were estimated at $1,220,000 for 1990. Since these expenses are assumed to be relatively constant from month to month, we estimate their six-month total to be one-half this amount, or $610,000.

Interest expense. From Table 3-2 we see that PBC will owe interest for the period on $218,468 in notes payable for three months at 9.6 percent, a $200,000 bank loan for six months at 12 percent, a long-term loan of $765,630 for six months at 12 percent, and $2,071,541 for six months at 12 percent. Thus, the total interest expense for the period is computed as follows.

Loan amount	×	Rate	×	Period	=	Interest expense
$ 218,468		0.096		$1/4$		$ 5,243
200,000		0.120		$1/2$		12,000
765,630		0.120		$1/2$		45,938
2,071,541		0.096		$1/2$		99,434
					Total	$162,615

Income taxes. On the basis of PBC's estimated taxable income for the first six months of 1990 of $33,190, the tax liability for the period is estimated to be $13,276. This figure equals the sum of 40 percent of the firm's taxable income.[1]

Net income. After taxes, PBC expects to earn $19,914 during the first six months of 1990 (see Table 3-6). This six-month-earnings figure compares very unfavorably with 1989 annual earnings, which were $417,665. However, PBC's sales for the first six months of 1990 are only 35 percent of the total projected for 1990 ($8,050,000/23,000,000). Also, PBC's interest expense should be greatly reduced in

[1] The maximum tax rate on corporate income during 1988 was 28 percent. However, this rate has been as high as 52 percent in recent years. Therefore, to simplify matters we use a flat 40 percent tax rate here.

TABLE 3-6
Peterson Bottling Corporation
Pro Forma Income Statement
For the Six-Month Period Ended June 30, 1990

	Amount	Percent of sales
Sales	$8,050,000	100.00%
Cost of goods sold	(5,392,695)	66.99
Gross profit	2,657,305	33.01
Operating expenses		
Selling	(1,127,000)	14.00
Delivery	(724,500)	9.00
General and administrative (0.5 × $1,220,000)	(610,000)	7.50
Total operating expenses	(2,461,500)	30.50
Operating income	195,805	2.40
Interest expense	(162,615)	2.00
Income before taxes	33,190	0.41
Income taxes (0.40 × $33,190)	(13,276)	0.16
Net income	$ 19,914	0.25%

the second half of 1990, since the firm will have repaid over $400,000 in loans during the first half of the year. Finally, PBC's general and administrative expenses will not increase with the sales in the second half of 1990, a fact which will also mean greater second-half profits.[2]

Pro Forma Balance Sheet

The pro forma balance sheet includes predictions for each asset, liability, and equity account for the firm. Thus, we construct PBC's June 30, 1990, pro forma balance sheet by analyzing individually the changes that are expected to take place during the period for each account.

Cash. The general procedure used throughout the construction of the pro forma balance sheet is demonstrated for PBC's ending cash balance as follows.

Cash—Beginning balance	$1,349,524
Plus: Cash receipts	7,678,800
Less: Cash disbursements	(7,718,571)
Ending balance	$1,309,753

Total cash receipts and disbursements are found by summing across all six months in the cash budget found in Table 3-4. Thus, the ending cash for PBC on June 30, 1990, is predicted to be $1,309,753. This figure, it will be recalled, was also computed in Table 3-5 earlier.

---

[2] For example, if general and administrative expense were allocated to the period as a percent of sales, it would be only $429,651 rather than $610,000, since sales for the first six months are only 35 percent of annual sales. This difference would increase the net income for the first six months to $128,123.40.

Accounts receivable. The June 30, 1990, balance for accounts receivable is found as follows.

Accounts receivable—Beginning balance	$1,438,929
Plus: Credit sales for the period	8,050,000
Less: Collections for the period	(7,478,800)
Ending balance	$2,010,129

Since all sales are made under credit terms of net 45, we simply sum sales for the six-month period to get credit sales for the period. Actually, the distinction between credit and cash is inconsequential since we net out total collections (including cash sales) to get the new accounts-receivable balance. Total credit sales can be taken directly from the cash budget worksheet (Table 3-3), and collections can be obtained from either the worksheet or the cash budget (Table 3-4).

Inventories. Ending inventories can be found by adding purchases for the period to the beginning inventory balance and subtracting the cost of merchandise sold.

Inventories—Beginning balance	$1,397,248
Plus: Purchases for the period	5,669,040
Less: Cost of merchandise sold	(3,815,700)
Ending balance	$3,250,588

Purchases for the period are found by summing each month's purchases as found in Table 3-3. The cost of merchandise sold is estimated to be 47.4 percent of the sales for the period.

Prepaid expenses. The only expense for the period which was prepaid during the period was income taxes. Estimated first-quarter taxes of $39,830 were paid on April 15, 1990; however, for the six-month period, the firm's tax liability was only $13,276, as a result of very poor expected second-quarter earnings. Thus, the prepaid expense account as of June 30, 1990, is found as follows.

Prepaid expenses—Beginning balance	$348,127
Plus: First-quarter tax installment	39,830
Less: Six-month tax liability	(13,276)
Ending balance	$374,681

Land. Since land is not expected to be either bought or sold during the period, the end-of-period balance remains unchanged at $712,614.

Property, plant, and equipment. Gross machinery, equipment, and furniture remain unchanged over the period, as does transportation equipment. However, accumulated depreciation increases by an amount equal to the depreciation expense for the period (one-half the annual depreciation expense of $660,000). Thus, the net property, plant, and equipment balance is found as follows.

Net property, plant, and equipment—Beginning balance	$7,147,910
Plus: Purchases of plant and equipment	0
Less: Depreciation expense for the period	(330,000)
Ending balance	$6,817,910

Notes payable. The ending balance for notes payable is found as follows.

Notes payable—Beginning balance	$218,468
Plus: Additional short-term notes incurred	418,468
Less: Payment of notes payable	(418,468)
Ending balance	$218,468

During the period PBC paid all the current portion of its long-term debt, however, a like amount of long-term debt became due one year from the date of payment. Thus, the ending balance was the same as the beginning balance for notes payable. Also, the six-month bank note was incurred and paid during the first six months of 1990.

Accounts payable. Ending accounts payable are found by adding new credit purchases to the beginning balance for the period and subtracting payments for the period.

Accounts payable—Beginning balance	$2,359,430
Plus: Purchases for the period	5,669,040
Less: Payments for the period	(3,477,264)
Ending balance	$4,551,206

Purchases for the period are found by summing the corresponding entries from the cash budget worksheet, and cash payments can be taken from either the worksheet or the cash budget. Since cash payments are subtracted from purchases, we need not be concerned with those purchases that were credit purchases and those that were for cash (if any).

Accrued wages. The ending balance for accrued wages is found as follows.

Accrued wages—Beginning balance	$ 151,212
Plus: Wages and salaries	1,576,995
Less: Cash payments for wages and salaries	(1,465,096)
Ending balance	$ 263,111

Wages and salaries for the period are taken as labor expenses from the cash budget worksheet, and the associated cash payments are as reported in the cash budget.

Accrued taxes. The ending balance for accrued taxes is 0 as a result of the January 15, 1990, payment, which was equal to the outstanding balance of $77,736. The April 15, 1990, installment resulted in an overpayment of taxes for the first half of 1990, thus increasing the prepaid expenses in the current-asset account.

Accrued interest. The ending balance for accrued interest can be found as follows.

Accrued interest—Beginning balance	$164,880
Plus: Interest expense for the period	162,615
Less: Interest paid during the period	(231,840)
Ending balance	$ 95,655

Interest expense for the period is taken from the pro forma income statement, and interest paid is obtained from the cash budget for the period.

Accrued expenses (other). This account serves as a catch-all for those expenses which were incurred but not paid during prior periods, and have not been included in any previous accrued-expense account. The ending balance for June 30, 1990, is computed as follows.

Accrued expenses (other)—Beginning balance	$ 171,512
Plus: Selling and delivery expenses	1,851,500
General and administrative expenses	280,000
Less: Payments for selling and delivery expenses	(1,728,337)
Payments for gen. and admin. expenses	(280,000)
Ending balance	$ 294,675

Long-term debt (net of current portion). The change in long-term debt for the period was the result of the payment of $218,468 on March 31, 1990, and the corresponding transfer to notes payable of an equal amount which is due on March 31, 1990. The ending balance is found as follows.

Long-term debt—Beginning balance	$3,055,639
Plus: Long-term debt incurred during the period	0
Less: Current portion	(218,468)
Ending balance	$2,837,171

Stockholders' equity. The only equity account that was altered during the period is retained earnings since no common stock was either bought (treasury stock) or sold, nor did the firm engage in any stock dividends or stock splits. The appropriate ending balance for retained earnings is found as follows.

Retained earnings—Beginning balance	$4,842,861
Plus: Net income for the period	19,914
Less: Common dividends for the period	(0)
Ending balance	$4,862,775

The resulting pro forma balance sheet is presented in Table 3-7. This statement reflects PBC's planned financial condition as of June 30, 1990. PBC could, for example, perform a financial analysis based on the pro forma statements to determine whether any additional actions should be undertaken during the next six months to improve the firm's end-of-period financial condition. The analysis would proceed along the lines discussed in Chapter 2.

The techniques used to develop pro forma financial statements for PBC represent only one approach among many that are available. We present this analysis simply to demonstrate one method that could be used, and one which requires minimal inputs.

FINANCIAL SPREADSHEETS

A financial spreadsheet is a computer program designed to facilitate a wide range of financial calculations. Very simply, a financial or electronic spreadsheet can be thought of as a grid, or two-dimensional matrix of rows and columns. The analyst "programs" using the spreadsheet package by entering numbers or equations into the cells of the matrix. Equations can be used to relate the value in one cell to one or a number of other cells. For example, the entry in row 10 column 8 could be set equal to the sum of all the entries found in rows 1 through 9 in column 8. Since a wide variety of financial applications can be visualized in terms of calculations involving a two dimensional array, the financial spreadsheet has provided a revolutionary innovation to the financial analyst.

TABLE 3-7
Peterson Bottling Corporation
Pro Forma Balance Sheet
June 30, 1990

Assets

	Amount	Percent of Assets
Current		
Cash	$ 1,309,753	9.52
Accounts receivable	2,010,129	14.60
Inventories	3,250,588	23.62
Prepaid expenses	374,681	2.72
Total current assets	6,945,151	50.46
Property, plant, and equipment		
Land	712,614	5.18
Buildings	6,781,823	49.28
Machinery, equipment, and furniture	6,617,295	48.08
Transportation equipment	528,291	3.84
Total property, plant, and equipment	14,640,023	106.37
Less: Accumulated depreciation	(7,822,113)	(56.83)
Net property, plant, and equipment	6,817,910	49.53
Total assets	$13,763,061	100.00

Liabilities and Stockholders' Equity

	Amount	Percent of Assets
Current		
Notes payable	$ 218,468	1.59
Accounts payable	4,551,206	33.07
Other liabilities and accrued expenses:		
Accrued wages	263,111	1.91
Accrued taxes	0	0.00
Accrued interest	95,655	0.70
Accrued expenses (other)	294,675	2.14
Total current liabilities	5,423,115	39.40
Long-term debt (net of current portion)	2,837,171	20.61
Stockholders' equity		
Capital stock	80,000	0.58
Capital paid in excess of par value	560,000	4.07
Retained earnings	4,862,775	35.53
Total stockholders' equity	5,502,775	40.00
Total liabilities and stockholders' equity	$13,763,061	100.00

The first financial spreadsheet programs were designed for large mainframe computers. One very popular program is IFPS® (Interactive Financial Planning Software, a registered trademark of Execucom, Inc.). However, the advent of the personal computer in the late 70s provided the impetus for unprecedented growth in the use of spreadsheet software. Specifically, the program Visacalc® (a registered trademark of Visacorp) is frequently credited with making the personal computer the phenomenal success it has been. Certainly Visacalc provided a financial spreadsheet package that could be used by analysts with little or no prior computer programming experience. In 1983 Lotus Development Corporation introduced its program Lotus 1-2-3® (a registered trademark of Lotus Development Corporation). This program combined three popular business software programs: spreadsheet, graphics, and database programs. It quickly replaced Visacalc as the sales leader and has enjoyed increasing popularity. The graphics program allowed users to easily plot the results of their spreadsheet programs.

A database management program is simply a computerized filing cabinet. The analyst stores data having some common attribute (such as the purchase and payment records of a customer) into a particular file. Each file consists of a series of records, each record representing, for example, a purchase-payment transaction for a particular customer. The file may contain many records containing different types of information. For example, the first record in the file may be company name, the second record may contain the customer's address, the third record may contain the customer's credit status, and the fourth may be the date of the most recent order. With this type of information about each of a company's customers, the firm can use the database manager to sort its customers by regions of the country or by any other piece of information contained in the customer files.

The growing power and sophistication of personal computers has made it possible to build increasingly more sophisticated financial software packages. For example, integrated software packages are now available that fully integrate spreadsheet, database, graphics, word processing, and communications software. Thus, the analyst can construct a budget, using the spreadsheet program, based on information extracted from the database program; construct graphs from the spreadsheet; and write a report, using the word processing program, that includes tables constructed from the spreadsheet and graphs from the graphics program. If the analyst decides the budget figures in the spreadsheet need modification, all that is necessary to update the entire report is to change these figures in the spreadsheet program. That is, all the changes to the report will be made automatically since the programs are fully integrated. When the final version of the report is ready, the analyst can transmit it to company headquarters located anywhere in the world via the communications program and telephone. The analyst can also use the communications program to gather data from the firm's central computer database and analyze that data locally, using the spreadsheet, database, and graphics programs located on the personal computer. Thus, integrated software programs attempt to combine the essential elements of personal computer use (as we understand them) into a single, easy-to-use package.

CHAPTER SUMMARY

This chapter presents the rudimentary tools of financial forecasting, planning, and control. Our discussion of the tools of sales forecasting involved both scatter diagram and regression methods. The cash budget was discussed as a primary aid to financial planning. Pro forma financial statements were then discussed as a natural extension of the cash budget as an aid in financial planning and control.

We discussed the tools of financial forecasting and planning as natural extensions of the tools of financial analysis discussed in Chapter 2. The usefulness of the tools discussed is by no means limited to the application discussed here. Financial planning, like financial analysis, is both an art and a science. We are necessarily limited here to the scientific aspects of the analysis; however, the imaginative reader can easily visualize many and varied applications for the tools discussed in both Chapters 2 and 3.

QUESTIONS

3-1 Financial planning and budgeting are closely intertwined in the overall planning activities of the firm. Are they one and the same?

3-2 Compare subjective and objective forecast methodologies. When is the use of each methodology appropriate?

3-3 Define causal and time series forecast models.

3-4 What is the basic rationale that underlies the regression method? How is the regression method related to the scatter diagram method of forecasting?

3-5 Discuss the percent of sales method of financial forecasting in terms of the linear equation that characterizes such a forecast.

The following questions pertain to the material found in Appendix 3A:

3-6 Describe the use of the control chart and the prediction-realization diagram in analyzing forecast accuracy. Each of these tools of analysis has its peculiar advantages. Be sure to identify them.

3-7 The mean square error and mean absolute error are two commonly used quantitative measures of forecast accuracy. Define each and contrast the "penalties" associated with forecast errors.

3-8 Verbally describe the decomposition of the mean square forecast error. How would knowledge of its components benefit the analyst?

PROBLEMS

3-1 a Use the scatter diagram method to estimate 1990 sales for the J.P. Mahoney Company. The sales for the preceding five years are as follows:

1989	$14 million
1988	12 million
1987	9 million
1986	10 million
1985	8 million

b What limitations does your forecast have?

3-2 The following data represent the ratios for the Skateboard Manufacturing Industry for 1989:

Common equity ratio	50%
Sales to common equity	4 times
Long-term-debt-ratio	16.67%
Current ratio	1.5 times
Acid-test ratio	0.75
Average collection period	30 days

Pentel Skate Company
Pro Forma Balance Sheet
December 31, 1989

Cash	$	Current debt	$
Accounts receivable		Long-term debt	
Inventory		Total debt	
Total current assets		Common equity	
Fixed assets		Total liabilities and common equity	
Total assets			

a Assuming that Pentel's 1990 expected sales are to be $1.2 million, complete the preceding pro forma balance sheet (round to the nearest thousand).

b What does the use of the financial ratio composites accomplish in this instance?

3-3 The balance sheet of the Hiller Manufacturing Company for December 31, 1989, is as follows:

Hiller Manufacturing Co.
Balance Sheet
December 31,1989

Cash	$ 500,000	Accounts payable	$1,700,000
Accounts receivable	1,520,000	Notes payable	1,100,000
Inventory	1,720,000	Long-term debt	1,600,000
	$3,740,000		
Property, plant,		Common equity	1,200,000
and equipment	3,460,000	Retained earnings	1,600,000
Total assets	$7,200,000	Total liabilities and common equity	$7,200,000

The Treasurer of Hiller Manufacturing wishes to borrow $900,000, the funds from which would be allocated in the following manner:

1 $200,000 to reduce accounts payable;
2 $150,000 to retire current notes payable;
3 $350,000 to expand existing plant facilities;
4 $160,000 to increase inventories;
5 $140,000 to increase cash on hand.

The loan would be repaid in twenty equal installments, beginning one year from the date of the loan.

a Assuming that the loan is obtained, prepare a pro forma balance sheet for Hiller Manufacturing that reflects the use of the loan proceeds described in the preceding list.

b Did the firm's liquidity improve after obtaining the loan and dispensing the proceeds in the preceding manner? Why or why not?

3-4 The Anderson Corporation's projected sales for the first eight months of 1990 are as follows.

January	$180,000	May	$600,000
February	240,000	June	540,000
March	270,000	July	450,000
April	480,000	August	300,000

Of Anderson's sales, 10 percent is for cash, another 60 percent is collected in the month following the sales, and 30 percent is collected in the second month following the sales. November and December sales for 1989 were $440,000 and $350,000, respectively.

Anderson purchases raw materials equal to 60 percent of sales, and it makes its purchases two months in advance of sales. The supplier is paid one month after the purchase. For example, purchases for March sales are made in January and are paid for in February.

In addition, Anderson pays $20,000 per month for rent and $40,000 each month for other expenditures. Each quarter, beginning in March, $45,000 in tax deposits are made.

The company's cash balance on December 31, 1989, was $44,000, and a minimum balance of $30,000 must be maintained at all times. Assume that any short-term financing needed to maintain the minimum cash balance would be paid off in the month following the month of financing.

a Prepare a cash budget for Anderson for the first seven months of 1990.

b Anderson has $400,000 in notes payable due in July that must be paid or renegotiated for an extension. Will the firm be able to pay the notes?

3-5 The Harwell Sales Company is currently engaged in projecting its financing requirements for the next five years. Chris Harwell is the firm's chief financial officer and son of the founder, Christopher Harwell, Sr. After reviewing the firm's performance over the past several years Chris believes that the firm's earnings and asset requirements will be characterized by the following relationships:

Net profit margin = 5%	Return on total assets = 10%
Growth rate in sales = 16% per year	
Dividend payout ratio = 50%	Debt to total assets = 40%

At present the firm's total assets equal $500,000 and its sales equal $1,000,000. Use this information to project Harwell's financing requirements for the next five years.

3-6 Manny Harwell, the younger brother of the chief financial officer of the Harwell Sales Co. from Problem 3-5, questioned the analysis of the firm's future financing requirements. Specifically, Manny does not want the firm to sell any more common stock. If Harwell decides to follow this policy, what impact will it have on the firm's ability to grow over the next five years? Calculate the maximum sales and assets figures for Harwell under the restraint that the firm issue no additional equity.

REFERENCES

Chambers, John C., S.K. Mullick, and D.D. Smith: "How to Choose the Right Forecasting Technique," *Harvard Business Review*, Vol. 49, July-August 1971, pp. 45–74.

Donaldson, G.: *Strategy for Financial Mobility*, Homewood, ILL.: Irwin, 1969.

Donaldson, G.: *Managing Corporate Wealth*, New York: Praeger, 1984.

Francis, Jack C., and D.R. Rowell: "A Simultaneous Equation Model of the Firm for Financial Analysis and Planning," *Financial Management*, Vol. 7, Spring 1978, pp. 29–44.

Gentry, James A., and S.C. Phyrr: "Simulating an EPS Growth Model," *Financial Management*, Vol. 2, Summer, 1973, pp. 68–75.

Gershefski, George W.: "Building a Corporate Financial Model," *Harvard Business Review*, Vol. 47, July-August, 1969, pp. 61–72.

Higgins, Robert C.: "How Much Growth Can a Firm Afford?" *Financial Management*, Vol. 6, Fall 1977, pp. 7–16.

Higgins, Robert C.: "Sustainable Growth under Inflation," *Financial Management*, Vol. 10, Autumn 1981, pp. 36–40.

Kroll, Yoram: "On the Differences Between Accrual Accounting Figures and Cash Flows: The Case of Working Capital," *Financial Management*, Vol. 14, Spring 1985, pp. 75–82.

Lyneis, James M.: "Designing Financial Policies to Deal with Limited Financial Resources, *Financial Management*, Vol. 4, Spring 1975, pp. 13–24.

Merville, Larry J., and L.A. Travis: "Long-Range Financial Planning," *Financial Management*, Vol. 3, Summer 1974, pp. 56–63.

Pan, J., D.R. Nichols, and O.M. Joy: "Sales Forecasting Practices of Large U.S. Industrial Firms," *Financial Management*, Vol. 6, Fall 1977, pp. 72–76.

Pappas, James L., and G.P. Huber: " Probabilistic Short-Term Financial Planning," *Financial Management*, Vol. 2, Autumn 1973, pp. 36–44.

Parker, George G.C., and E. L. Segura: "How to Get a Better Forecast," *Harvard Business Review*, Vol. 49, March-April 1971, pp. 99–109.

Stone, B., and R.A. Wood: "Daily Cash Forecasting: A simple Method for Implementing the Distribution Approach," *Financial Management*, Vol. 6, Fall 1977, pp. 40–50.

Theil, Henri: *Applied Economics Forecasting*, Chicago, 1966.

APPENDIX 3A
Analyzing Forecast Accuracy

Forecast models range in complexity from simple extrapolations of historical time series to complex econometric models. However, they all share a common goal: accurate prediction. In this appendix we will discuss some commonly used tools for analyzing the accuracy of a forecast. These include graphic as well as analytical methods. To illustrate the use of these tools we will make use of the forecast data found in Table 3A-1. These data include the year of the forecast, the predicted sales for the Vidalia Mfg. Co., and the actual sales. Later we will find it convenient to analyze predicted "changes" in the level of sales rather than the "level" of sales.

GRAPHICAL MEASURES OF FORECAST ACCURACY

We will discuss two graphical methods for analyzing forecast accuracy. The first is the **control chart** and the second is the **prediction-realization diagram**. The control chart is illustrated in Figure 3A-1, where the cumulative prediction errors for the Vidalia Mfg. Co. Sales forecast are analyzed. Here we "cumulate" the forecast errors *over time*. If the predictions are consistently too high, as is the case with the Vidalia forecast, then the cumulative prediction errors will drift upward, indicating a need to "adjust" the forecast model. Of course, there is always the possibility that the tendency of the model to over-estimate the actual sales of Vidalia is a chance occurrence. For this reason control charts frequently make use of confidence limits.

TABLE 3A-1
VIDALIA MFG. CO.—SALES FORECAST (000)

Quarter	Predicted change	Actual change	Predicted sales	Actual sales
1	$10.00	$13.00	$110.00	$113.00
2	23.00	23.50	136.00	136.50
3	−14.00	−26.00	122.50	110.50
4	31.00	44.50	141.50	155.00
5	7.00	−9.50	162.00	145.50
6	43.00	65.50	188.50	211.00
7	−25.00	−39.50	186.00	171.50
8	−34.00	−53.00	137.50	118.50
9	15.00	8.50	133.50	127.00
10	33.00	35.50	160.00	162.50
11	−7.00	−15.50	155.50	147.00
12	22.00	16.00	169.00	163.00
13	23.00	32.50	186.00	195.50
14	−12.00	−35.00	183.50	160.50
15	18.00	13.00	178.50	173.50
16	15.00	20.50	188.50	194.00
17	−34.00	−53.00	160.00	141.00
18	44.00	49.00	185.00	190.00
19	−14.00	−32.00	176.00	158.00
20	33.00	47.50	191.00	205.50

For example, if we assume that the forecast errors are normally distributed with standard deviation equal to $10, then the 95 percent confidence limits for the sales forecast are −$20 and $20. Thus, we would attempt to "correct" or alter the forecast model only if the cumulative errors should drift outside these limits. For the Vidalia sales forecast example, this occurs in quarter 8.

FIGURE 3A-1
Control chart for the cumulative sales forecast errors of Vidalia Mfg. Co.

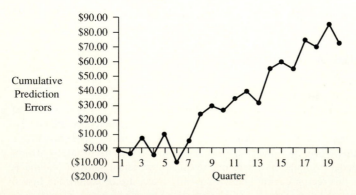

The prediction-realization diagram provides a tool for identifying the *type* of errors that characterize the forecast. For example, using this diagram we can identify whether the predictions vary randomly about the actual values, or if they are consistently higher or lower than the actual figures. In addition, using the prediction-realization diagram, we can identify whether the forecast is prone to making "turning point" errors. That is, when the actual series changes direction (i.e., positive to negative or negative to positive), does the forecast correctly indicate the direction of the change?

Figure 3A-2 contains a prediction-realization diagram for Vidalia Mfg. Co.'s sales forecast. The actual, or realized, values are plotted on the horizontal axis, while the predicted values are plotted on the vertical axis. Should the measurement scales be the same for both predictions and realizations, then a perfect forecast (prediction equals actual) will plot along a 45-degree line that runs through the origin. We will refer to this line as the *line of perfect forecast* (LPF). Note that we have plotted the predicted and actual *changes* in sales rather than the levels of the respective sales numbers. This makes it possible to identify "turning point errors" as those points that lie in quadrants II and IV. In both of the quadrants the predicted and actual change in sales have different signs, indicating a turning point prediction error. Analyzing the Vidalia sales forecast, we observe that the predicted changes are generally of the correct sign (e.g., when sales were predicted to rise, they generally did and vice versa). There was a tendency for the negative predictions to be too negative, and the large positive predictions tended to be too large. We will refer to this phenomenon as "inefficiency" in our later discussion of quantitative measures of forecast accuracy.

QUANTITATIVE MEASURES OF FORECAST ACCURACY

Quantitative measures are helpful in that they summarize the forecast errors in a single metric. To define such a measure of forecast accuracy, we must first determine how prediction errors

FIGURE 3A-2
Prediction-realization diagram for Vidalia Mfg. Co.'s sales forecast.

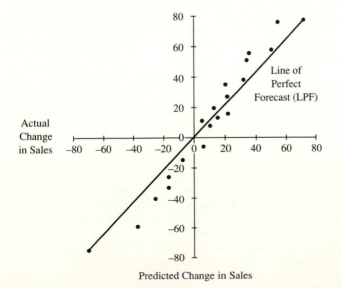

Predicted Change in Sales

are to be measured. We might simply average the difference in predicted and actual values, and use this as a measure of predictive accuracy; however, the positive errors would offset the negative errors if such a measure of overall forecast accuracy were used. One way to avoid this "canceling" problem would be to simply disregard the sign of the prediction error by using the absolute value of the error. In this case the average absolute prediction error, or **mean absolute error (MAE)** could be calculated as follows:

$$\text{MAE} = \sum_{t=1}^{N} \frac{|P_t - A_t|}{N}$$

For the Vidalia sales forecast the MAE is 11.23, indicating that the average absolute error is slightly larger than $11,000. In contrast, the average error was only 3.575, indicating the effects of positive and negative errors "canceling" each other out. Calculations are found in Table 3A-2.

Note that by using the absolute value of the forecast error, we assign no special importance to very large errors. That is, when calculating the average forecast error, an error of 8 is exactly twice as large as an error of 4, and four times as large as an error of 2. However, should large errors be particularly important, then we may want to give them more importance or weight in the summary measure of forecast error. The second quantitative measure of forecast accuracy does just this. This measure is the **Mean Square Error (MSE)**, and it is calculated by averaging the squared forecast errors as follows:

$$\text{MSE} = \sum_{t=1}^{N} \frac{(P_t - A_t)^2}{N}$$

The MSE for the Vidalia sales forecast is 171.84. Note that since this measure is an average *squared* prediction error, it is much larger than the MAE. We can transform MSE back into the same units of measure as the predictions and realizations by taking its square root. This measure, referred to as the **Root Mean Square Error (RMSE)**, equals 13.11 for Vidalia. Recall that we earlier calculated the Mean Absolute Error and found it to be only 11.23. The difference between MAE and RMSE is that the RMSE gives more importance to large forecast errors. A forecast error (i.e., $P_t - A_t$ of 8 enters the calculation of MSE as an 8, whereas it is averaged into the MSE as a 64, which is then averaged with the squares of the remaining forecast errors before taking the square root to calculate the RMSE. To further illustrate, assume that we have a forecast consisting of two predictions having errors of 8 and –8. The MAE for this forecast is simply 8, whereas the RMSE is the square root of $(64 + 64) = 128$, or 11.31. Thus we see the increased importance assigned to large prediction errors by MSE and RMSE, as compared to the MAE.

The relative importance assigned to prediction errors is referred to as the "loss function." In essence, the loss function reflects the relative importance of forecast errors. If the MAE is used, the loss function will consider a forecast error of 8 to be twice as bad as an error of 4. However, with the MAE, an error of 8 is given more than twice the importance of an error of 4, since these errors are squared before summing them and averaging. This attribute of the MAE is neither good nor bad but a simple mathematical result of the way in which the measure of forecast accuracy is calculated. The analyst must assess the relative importance of large versus small errors and then select a loss function which correctly reflects that assessment.

TABLE 3A-2
VIDALIA MFG. CO.—QUANTITATIVE MEASURES OF FORECAST ACCURACY

Time	Predicted change	Actual change	Forecast error	Cumulative error
1	$10.00	$13.00	($3.00)	($3.00)
2	23.00	23.50	−0.50	−3.50
3	−14.00	−26.00	12.00	8.50
4	31.00	44.50	−13.50	−5.00
5	7.00	−9.50	16.50	11.50
6	43.00	65.50	−22.50	−11.00
7	−25.00	−39.50	14.50	3.50
8	−34.00	−53.00	19.00	22.50
9	15.00	8.50	6.50	29.00
10	33.00	35.50	−2.50	26.50
11	−7.00	−15.50	8.50	35.00
12	22.00	16.00	6.00	41.00
13	23.00	32.50	−9.50	31.50
14	−12.00	−35.00	23.00	54.50
15	18.00	13.00	5.00	59.50
16	15.00	20.50	−5.50	54.00
17	−34.00	−53.00	19.00	73.00
18	44.00	49.00	−5.00	68.00
19	−14.00	−32.00	18.00	86.00
20	33.00	47.50	−14.50	71.50
Mean	8.85	5.275	3.575	32.65
Std. dev.	23.81	35.18	12.611	29.06

Measures of forecast accuracy	
Mean absolute error =	11.225
Mean square error (forecast) =	171.837
Root mean square error =	13.108
Mean square error (naive) =	1265.837
Theil's inequality coefficient =	0.135

Mean square error decomposition	
Source of error	**Component of MSE**
Bias	12.780
Inefficiency	115.414
Random	43.642

Both the MAE and MSE offer measures of "absolute" forecast accuracy in that neither provides a standard against which to measure predictive accuracy. Theil [Fig 6] offered one such measure of relative forecast accuracy in **Theil's Inequality Coefficient (TIC)**. This measure is actually the ratio of the MAE of the forecast divided by the MAE of a naive (no-change) forecast. When the forecast is measured in terms of "changes in the variable being forecast" rather than levels, Theil's inequality coefficient is calculated as follows:

$$\text{TIC} = \frac{\sum_{t=1}^{N}(P_t - A_t)^2}{\sum_{t=1}^{N} A_t^2}$$

Note that the MSE for a no-change forecast is simply the average squared realized change in the predicted series(i.e., the average A^2). This results from the fact that P_t is zero by definition for a no-change forecast. For the Vidalia sales forecast example Theil's inequality coefficient is 0.1375. The fact that the coefficient is less than unity indicates that the forecast was superior to a naive forecast of no change. Had the coefficient been greater than 1, we might seriously question the value of the forecast model used, since a no-change forecast provides smaller average squared prediction errors.

We can gain further "quantitative" insight into the sources of forecast error by decomposing the MSE into bias, inefficiency, and random error components. The decomposition of MSE can be accomplished as follows:

$$\text{MSE} = (E[P] - E[A]^2) + (1 - b)^2\sigma_P^2 + (1 - r^2)\sigma_A^2$$

$$\underbrace{\qquad\qquad}_{\text{Bias}} \quad \underbrace{\qquad}_{\text{Inefficiency}} \quad \underbrace{\qquad}_{\text{Random}}$$

where $E[\ ]$ is the expected value operator, b is the slope of a regression line with A the dependent variable and P the independent variable, σ^2 is the variance in the subscripted variable, and r^2 is the coefficient of determination.

Bias in the forecast is reflected in the difference in the means of the predictions and realizations. Thus bias is evidenced by a tendency for the forecast to consistently over- or underpredict. Inefficiency is evidenced in a tendency for the forecast model to over- or under-predict at low levels, and under-or overpredict at high levels of the variable being predicted. An inefficient forecast, then, is one for which a straight line passing through the prediction-realization scatter plot will have a slope that is not equal to 1 (as was the case for the Vidalia sales forecast illustrated in Figure 3A-2). The random error component is simply that portion of the variance in the actual values that *is not* explained by the predictions. Using the Vidalia example, we observe that bias accounts for 12.78 of the total MSE of 171.84, while inefficiency accounts for 115.41, which leaves 43.64 that is attributable to random error. Thus, roughly 7 percent of the forecast's MSE can be attributed to bias, 67 percent is due to inefficiency, and the remaining 26 percent is a result of random prediction error. The Vidalia sales forecast, then, is highly inefficient but is relatively unbiased. Forecast inefficiency is due to the b term in the MSE decomposition being different than one. In Table 3A-2 we observe that the b, or slope, coefficient for the Vidalia sales forecast is 1.45. That is, if we were to fit a straight line equation through the predictions and realizations found in Figure 3A-2, we would find that the slope of the line would be 1.45. This means that when the actual changes in sales for Vidalia were relatively high (and positive), the forecast made predictions that were even higher (i.e., the predictions are above the actual changes in sales for large positive changes in sales). On the other hand, when the actual changes in sales are negative, the predictions are even more negative. Hence, when actual sales go down, the predictions are that they will go down even more.

Systematic forecast errors due to bias and inefficiency can be corrected easily. That is, if we fit a regression model to the actual (A_t) and predicted (P_t) changes in sales of the form

$$A_t = a + bP_t$$

and find that the coefficients of the model (i.e., a and b) are not 0, then we can easily adjust future predictions so that they will not reflect bias ($a = 0$) and inefficiency ($b = 1$). The revised predictions would simply be the right-hand side of the above equation. Thus, instead of using P_t to predict A_t, we would, instead, use $a + bP_t$. However, correcting for random error requires that the underlying forecast model used to produce the predictions (i.e., the P_t) be modified.

CONCLUDING REMARKS

Forecasting is at the very heart of financial planning, for financial planning constitutes the firm's effort to deal with uncertainty in its financial future. However, traditional discussions of financial planning have eschewed discussions of forecast methodology, and have left its discussion to other disciplines of academic endeavor. Although this approach is convenient for those who have the luxury of operating within the confines of the academic ivory tower, it is not terribly realistic for those who must engage in planning for a firm's financial future. Thus, we have endeavored in Chapter 3 to provide a brief overview of forecast tools and in this Appendix to provide an overview of the fundamental tools that can be used to assess forecast accuracy. The tools used to measure forecast accuracy are akin to the tools of analysis used by the production engineer to assess production quality control, and they serve the same basic purpose. That is, forecasting includes the production of information used in determining the firm's financial plans, and it is crucially important that the firm's financial manager be alert to occasions when those predictions get out of control.

4

VALUATION

Financial decision making is based on value comparisons. A machine, building, tract of land, or other asset is purchased by a firm because management believes the asset is worth more than its purchase price. In most cases, deciding upon a bond issue or a stock issue to finance an investment will also depend primarily on which method of financing will result in a higher value of the equity of the present owners. Thus, to function properly, a business manager must understand the concept of value and how to evaluate investments as well as the various types of financing that the firm uses. The purpose of this chapter is threefold. We first examine the concept of valuation and the factors that affect it. Then, we consider the formulas that can be used in the valuation of future cash flows. The last part of the chapter applies the formulas to the valuation of corporate stocks and bonds.

The Concept of Valuation

Valuation is the process of estimating the market value of an object or service. The financial manager of a business is primarily concerned with the valuation of assets which his firm owns or may purchase and the valuation of the various methods of financing which the firm employs or may employ. The focus of this chapter is on the valuation techniques used in estimating the market value of the assets and securities of a firm. We will see in Chapter 5 that the value of an asset to a firm may differ from the asset's market value. The techniques that can be used to value investments in assets from the standpoint of the firm will be presented at that point.

Three factors affect market value: future cash flows, the timing of those flows, and the rate at which the flows are discounted, or time adjusted, back to the present. Let us examine each of these three factors.

The Elements of Value.   If everything else is the same, the greater the amount of the net cash inflows (i.e., total cash inflows minus total cash outflows), the greater the value of the cash-flow stream. This is obvious. But note that the sooner a cash inflow occurs, the more valuable it is, because money has a time value. A dollar received in one year is worth more than a dollar received in two years, because the dollar received in the first year can be invested to earn a return in the second year, an opportunity not available for a dollar received in two years. Therefore, estimating both the size and the timing of the future cash flows of an asset is an essential aspect of the valuation process. For many types of investments, estimating the future cash-flow stream is the most difficult aspect of the process.

The **discount rate** used in the value calculations reflects the value of money over time. For example, if $1 can be invested to earn 10 percent for one year, the investment will be worth $1 + (0.10 \times $1) = (1 + 0.10)($1) = (1.10)($1) = $1.10 at the end of the year. We can also say that the $1.10 expected in one year is worth $1.10/(1.10) = $1 today. The discount rate is the rate of return expected on the investment for one year. Thus, a future cash flow is discounted back to the present to determine its present value, and the rate that should be used in the discounting process is the rate of return that would be expected on an investment of comparable risk made today. The expected rate will be the same as the rate required in the market; the market price of the asset adjusts to make the two equal. The term **opportunity cost** is also used frequently to denote the discount rate. Since the discount rate is a positive rate, the calculated future value of a cash flow will always exceed its present value.

The process of calculating the present value of a future cash flow or the future value of a present cash flow is referred to as **time-adjusting the cash flow**. The impact of the time-adjustment process will be greater the larger the discount rate, and vice versa. For example, if the discount rate is 10 percent, the present value of $1 in one year is $1/1.1 = $0.9091. But if the discount rate is 20 percent, the present value of the $1 is $1.00/1.2 = $0.8333, or approximately $0.076 less than for the 10 percent case.

A risky cash flow is discounted back to the present at a higher rate than a less risky cash flow, because investors require a higher return for taking a greater risk. Measuring the risk in an investment and then estimating the related effect on the risk premium in the discount rate are difficult problems which will be considered in Chapters 6 and 7.

A Graphical Example of Time Value.   The effect of time on present value is expressed in Figure 4-1. The vertical axis of the graph denotes future value and the horizontal axis present value. The diagonal line shown has a negative slope, depicting the fact that reducing cash today by investing it can result in more cash in the future, because of a return on the investment. Thus, money has a time value because it can be invested to earn a return over time. An investor expects to get his original investment back plus a return. In the graph, the diagonal time connects the points for $1 future value and $0.9091 today; this indicates that $0.9091 invested today will be worth $1 in the future. We will see below that the rate of return on the investment is 10 percent. The line also indicates in this case that the investor could invest any amount

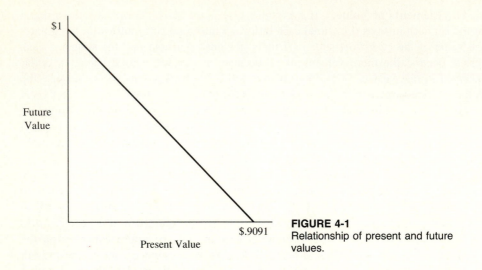

FIGURE 4-1
Relationship of present and future values.

up to $0.9091. The amount of his remaining cash now and the amount expected in the future are indicated by points on the line.

The slope of the line can be determined by dividing the value at the point of intersection on the vertical axis by the value at the point of intersection on the horizontal axis, expressed as a negative number: $1/ - \$0.9091 = -1.1$. The rate of return can then be calculated as: $-(\text{slope} + 1) = -(-1.1 + 1) = 0.1$, or 10 percent.

To summarize the major points covered so far in this chapter, recall that value is defined as the present value of a future cash-flow stream. The stream may have one or more cash flows. The present value is found by discounting the future flow or flows at a discount rate which reflects the riskiness of the stream. Formulas for calculating value under various situations will be covered later. But first, let us take a look at the impact of market conditions on the determination of value.

Market Value in an Efficient Market.   The price at which a product or service sells in a competitive market is determined at the margin. This means that the selling price is the highest known price that any potential buyer in the market will pay at the time and the lowest known price that any potential seller will accept. If the market is efficient, all potential buyers and sellers have knowledge of the prices at which the product or service is selling, and all have an opportunity to make an offer to buy or sell, depending on their choices. Under these conditions, prices will fully reflect all available information of importance to buyers and sellers.

Market prices may change when economic conditions change. However, if the market is efficient, any change in conditions known to anyone becomes known to everyone very quickly, and prices very quickly adjust to reflect the new conditions. Since new information comes into the market randomly, no single market participant or group of market participants will be able to gain consistently at the expense of others.

Fortunately, most business firms operate in reasonably efficient markets in the United States as well as in several other non-Communist countries. However, there are exceptions. Factors such as lack of information, lack of mobility of buyers and sellers, and inability to move products can sometimes cause prices in certain areas to differ considerably from prices in other areas. When these factors are prevalent, the market will not be efficient.

It is important for the economy that all markets be efficient. If they are not, many business firms as well as individuals will suffer, while others obtain unfair benefits. Under these conditions the valuation techniques discussed in this book may not apply. As we noted above, however, markets in the United States are reasonably efficient.

Estimating Market Value

We are now ready to consider the formulas for estimating value in various situations. The general approach stated earlier will continue to apply in all cases: market value is estimated by calculating the present value of a stream of future cash flows. The discount rate used in time-adjusting the future flows back to their present value is the rate of return required in the market on comparable-risk investments. This rate is a function of the risk-free rate at the time and the risk associated with estimating the true cash flows. A cash-flow stream may consist of any number of cash flows—just one, several, or many. We will begin our discussion with the simplest formulas and proceed to the more difficult.

The Basic Formula.   The simplest case for valuation requires the use of the basic valuation equation. In this case, only one cash flow is expected to occur. Equation (4-1) below is an expression of the formula:

$$P = \frac{C_n}{(1 + r)^n} \tag{4-1}$$

where P is the present value, C_n is the cash flow that is expected to occur at the end of period n, and r is the discount rate per period. The expression $(1 + r)^n$ discounts C_n back to the present through n periods at the rate r per period. In some situations, the expected future value of an asset may be considered essentially the same as a cash flow in the valuation of the asset, since it could be sold to obtain cash.

To illustrate the use of equation (4-1), let us estimate the present value of a painting which is expected to be worth $30,000 by the end of five years. If the opportunity cost of funds invested in comparable-risk assets is 14 percent, the present value of the painting can be calculated as follows:

$$P = \frac{\$30,000}{(1.14)^5}$$

$$= \frac{\$30,000}{1.9254}$$

$$= \$15,581.18$$

Present value calculations can be facilitated by the use of calculators, computers, or present value tables. Financial calculators as well as many computer programs allow the analyst to solve for present values directly. Present value tables such as Appendix A-1 at the end of the book provide present value factors which can be multiplied by future cash flows to obtain their present value. A present value factor can be calculated by substituting into equation (4-1) the number 1 for C_n and the appropriate figures for r and n in the denominator. We will refer to the present value factor of a future amount as the present value interest factor. The expression $PVIF_{n,r}$ will refer to the present value interest factor for $1 in the nth period, discounted at the rate of r per period.

The Value of a Series of Cash Flows. Most of the operating assets of a business firm result in a series of cash flows. The total value of this type of asset is the sum of the present values of all cash flows that are expected to occur in the future as a result of owning the asset. The valuation equation is:

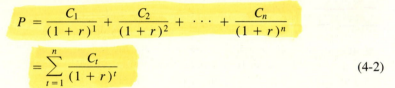

$$P = \frac{C_1}{(1+r)^1} + \frac{C_2}{(1+r)^2} + \cdots + \frac{C_n}{(1+r)^n}$$

$$= \sum_{t=1}^{n} \frac{C_t}{(1+r)^t} \qquad (4\text{-}2)$$

The symbol $\sum_{t=1}^{n}$ means the sum for periods 1 through n. The cash flows do not have to be the same or have the same sign; some may be positive, some negative, and some zero. The principle is still the same; simply determine the present value of each cash flow and sum, retaining all signs.

Table 4-1 presents an example of the calculation of the present value of a stream of cash flows discounted at 12 percent per year. The factors included in column 3

TABLE 4-1
CALCULATION OF THE PRESENT VALUE OF A
STREAM OF CASH FLOWS

(1) Year	(2) Cash flow	(3) Present value factor–12%	(4) Present value
1	$100	0.8929	$ 89.29
2	50	0.7972	39.86
3	235	0.7118	167.27
4	150	0.6355	95.33
5	400	0.5674	226.96
6	150	0.5066	75.99
7	75	0.4523	33.92
8	290	0.4039	117.13
9	375	0.3606	135.23
10	450	0.3320	144.90
	Present value of entire stream:		$1,125.88

can be found in Appendix A-1 at the end of the book or can be computed by the use of a calculator. The present value of the entire cash-flow stream is shown at the bottom of column four to be $1,125.88.

The example in Table 4-1 is intended to help the reader understand the nature of the process of calculating the present value of a stream of uneven cash flows. As a general rule, present value calculations are actually made by the use of a calculator or computer program such as a spreadsheet. In these cases, separate calculations of the present value factors will not be necessary.

Perpetuities. The cash flows in Table 4-1 are uneven. If they had been constant each year, calculation of the present value of the entire stream could have been greatly simplified. The simplest situation is for the stream to extend to infinity, a type of stream called a **perpetuity**. The present value of a perpetuity can be found by simply dividing the cash flow for one period by the discount rate. This is known as capitalizing the cash flow in one period at the discount rate. For example, if the required rate of return is 10 percent, the present value of $100 per year beginning at the end of one year and extending to infinity is:

$$P = \frac{C}{r} \tag{4-3}$$

$$= \frac{\$100}{0.1}$$

$$= \$1,000$$

where *P*, *C*, and *r* retain their previous meanings.

A cash flow stream extending to infinity implies that cash flows will occur forever. Other than land, perhaps, no salable asset in our world will be that productive. However, the formula is often applied to cash flow streams that are expected to last for an indefinitely long period of time in the future. The result is a good approximation because the present value of cash flows that occur in the very distant future is usually close to zero, particularly when the discount rate is relatively high. Thus, if the stream terminates in the very distant future, determining its present value by the use of Equation (4-3) results in approximately the correct answer. To see this, recall the calculation above of the $1,000 present value of a perpetual stream of $100. If the stream is expected to terminate at the end of 100 years rather than infinity, its present value would be $999.93. And for 200 years, the present value would be $1,000 when rounded to the closest cent. The latter two calculations were made with the use of a finance calculator.

Annuities With a Finite Life. A stream of constant cash flows extending for any number of periods is called an **annuity**. Thus, a perpetuity is an annuity for an infinite number of periods. An annuity can have a finite life, however, as in the earlier examples of cash-flow streams of 100 and 200 years, respectively.

The present value of an annuity with a finite life can be calculated by finding the difference in the present values, as of a common point in time, of two perpetual cash-flow streams which differ only in regard to the point in time at which they begin. The result of the calculation is the present value of an annuity extending over the period between the starting points of the two streams. The mathematical process requires four steps. Referring to the dollar amount of the cash flow per period as C and the last year of the annuity as the nth period, the four steps are as follows:

1 Calculate the present value of a perpetuity of C per period for which the initial cash flow occurs at the end of the first period.

2 Calculate the value as of the end of period n of a perpetuity of C per period. The initial cash flow of this perpetuity is assumed to occur at the end of period $n + 1$.

3 Calculate the present value as of time 0 of the perpetuity whose value was determined in step 2. Step 3 involves discounting the value of the perpetuity back n periods to find its value at time 0.

4 Subtract the value calculated in step 3 from the value calculated in step 1.

The procedure is expressed in the following equation:

$$P = \frac{C}{r} - \frac{C}{r} \times \frac{1}{(1 + r)^n}$$

$$= \frac{C}{r} - \frac{C}{r(1 + r)^n} \tag{4-4}$$

To illustrate, let us calculate the present value of a $100 20-year annuity when the required rate of return is 10 percent:

$$P = \frac{\$100}{0.1} - \frac{\$100}{0.1(1.1)^{20}}$$

$$= \$1,000 - \$1,000(0.1486)$$

$$= \$851.40$$

The figure 0.1486 in the second element in the second equation above is the present value interest factor for twenty periods at 10 percent, that is, the $\text{PVIF}_{20,10\%}$, which can be calculated by solving the equation $1/(1.1)^{20}$. The factor can also be obtained from Appendix A-1. The present value of the annuity will be found to be $851.36 if a finance calculator is used to make the calculation. The latter figure is more accurate, because the $851.40 figure was calculated using a PVIF of only four digits to the right of the decimal, whereas the calculator used twelve digits in this case.

Equation (4-4) is often simplified to form the following expression:

$$PV = \frac{C[1 - (1 + r) - n]}{r} \tag{4-4a}$$

Equations (4-4) and (4-4a) are mathematically equivalent.

A finance calculator or computer spreadsheet program will normally be used to solve for the present value of an annuity. Appendix A-2 can also be used. The figures given in the table are the present values of $1 annuities for various periods and rates. These values are referred to as present value annuity factors and will expressed by the notation $\text{PVAF}_{n,r\%}$. Thus, the present value of an n-period annuity at the rate r

percent per period can be expressed as:

$$P = C(\text{PVAF}_{n,r\%}) \qquad (4\text{-}4b)$$

For example, the present value annuity factor for twenty years at 10 percent, $\text{PVAF}_{20,10\%}$, is shown in Appendix A-2 to be 8.5136. Multiplying this factor by the $100 annuity value gives us $851.36 as the value of the annuity. This figure is the same as the one obtained by the use of a calculator.

Discounting More Than Once a Year. Our valuation calculations so far in this chapter have used annual cash flows and discount rates. In some cases, discounting more than once a year will be necessary, since the discount period should be the same as the compound interest period. For example, banks often compound interest quarterly on certificates of deposits. Calculating the present value of the future cash flows from this type of investment will require quarterly discounting.

It is relatively easy to convert a present value formula with annual discounting to a formula applicable to more frequent compounding periods. All that is necessary is to multiply the number of years in the formula by the number of compounding periods in a year, and divide the annual discount rate by the same number of compounding periods.[1] Thus, the present value of a single cash flow is:

$$P = \frac{C_{m \times n}}{[1 + (r/m)]^{m \times n}} \qquad (4\text{-}5)$$

where m is the number of compounding periods in a year and all other symbols have the same meaning as before. According to the equation, the present value is found by discounting $C_{m \times n}$ at the rate r/m for $m \times n$ periods. $C_{m \times n}$ can be interpreted as a cash flow which occurs at the end of $m \times n$ periods; this is the same point in time, of course, as the end of the nth year.

As an example, let us again calculate the present value of the painting referred to previously. Recall that the painting was expected to be worth $30,000 at the end of five years. Its present value was found to be $15,581.18 when the future value was discounted back to the present at 14 percent per year. If semiannual discounting is used, the present value would be calculated as follows:

$$P = \frac{\$30,000}{[1 + (0.14/2)]^{5 \times 2}}$$

$$= \$30,000\,(\text{PVIF}_{10,7\%})$$

$$= \$30,000\,(0.5083)$$

$$= \$15,249.00$$

---

[1] The discount rate for a period less than a year is sometimes calculated by the use of the following equation: $r_p = (1 + r)^{1/m} - 1$, where r_p is the discount rate for a period, r is the annual discount rate, and m is the number of periods in a year. This equation assumes that the cash flow in each period is reinvested at the rate r_p per period. r_p will always be less than r/m in equation (4-5), which follows in the text.

The present value of the painting is thus found to be less if semiannual discounting is used in the calculations. Increasing the number of discounting periods in a year will always reduce the present value of a future cash flow if the discount rate for a period is obtained by dividing the annual rate by the number of periods in a year. On the other hand, increasing the number of compounding periods increases the future value of an investment; in effect, the annual interest rate has been increased.

Now consider a ten-year annuity with annual payments of $100. If the discount rate is 10 percent per year, the present value of the annuity is:

$$P = \sum_{t=1}^{10} \frac{\$100}{(1.1)^t}$$

$$= \$100(6.1446)$$

$$= \$614.46$$

Let us change the annuity so that the $100 total annual payment is received in four quarterly payments of $25 each. Converting both the discount rate and the discount period to a quarterly basis, we get:

$$P = \sum_{t=1}^{40} \frac{\$100/4}{[1 + (0.10/4)^t}$$

$$= \sum_{t=1}^{40} \frac{\$25}{(1.025)^t}$$

$$= \$25(25.1028)$$

$$= \$627.57$$

In this case, the present value of the annuity is increased by converting from an annual basis to a quarterly basis, because $75 of each year's total payment of $100 is received sooner.

Computation of the Time-Adjusted Rate of Return

The concept of valuation is intimately connected with the concept of rate of return. As we have seen, the required rate of return is needed to determine the value of an asset or investment. In many cases, however, the market value of an asset will be known, and an analyst will be interested in estimating the rate of return from investing in the asset. The rate of return is widely used in assessing and comparing the financial benefits from making investments. The factors that affect the calculation of an expected rate of return are discussed in the following section.

The Elements. Determining the expected rate of return on an asset involves finding the discount rate that will equate the present value of the expected future cash flows with the current, known value of the asset. The discount rate that will accomplish this feat is the rate of return. Thus, in this case, the unknown value in the solution equation is the discount rate (i.e., the rate of return), and the known elements are the current value of the asset and the estimated future cash flows. We will solve for the rate of return, first, in situations in which there is only one future cash flow and, second, in situations in which there are multiple cash flows.

Single Cash Flows. As previously stated, the procedure used in determining the rate of return on an asset involves finding the discount rate that will equate the present value of the future cash flow with the known value of the asset. We can do this by solving equation (4-1) or r to get the following equation:

$$r = \left(\frac{C_n}{P}\right)^{1/n} - 1 \tag{4-6}$$

where P is the market price or known present value of the asset, and all other symbols have the same meaning as before.

For example, assume that a city lot which costs $20,000 today is expected to appreciate in value to $30,000 by the end of five years. Due to the benevolence of the city and county governments, no expenditures for taxes or maintenance will be required on the lot. The expected rate of return from investing in the property can be solved for as follows:

$$r = \left(\frac{\$30,000}{\$20,000}\right)^{1/5} - 1$$
$$= 0.0845, \text{ or } 8.45\%$$

When a present value table is used to solve for r, we first need to know the present value interest factor. The factor for our example can be determined by utilizing the following formula:

$$PVIF_{n,r} = \frac{P}{C_n} \tag{4-7}$$

where $PVIF_{n,r}$ is the present value interest factor for n periods and r percent. Substituting the applicable values into the formula we get:

$$PVIF_{i,5} = \frac{\$20,000}{\$30,000}$$
$$= 0.6667$$

We now look in Appendix A-1 for a five-year factor of 0.6667. The figure lies somewhere between the 0.6806 factor for 8 percent and the 0.6449 factor for 9 percent. Thus, the expected rate of return from investing in the lot is between 8 and 9 percent. A finance calculator should be used to find the precise rate.

Multiple Cash Flows.   Calculation of the rate of return when cash flows occur in more than one period in the future is based on the same principle as the single-flow case. The idea is still to find the discount rate that will equate the cost of the asset with the present value of the future cash flows. Thus, we must solve for r in equation (4-2), which is repeated below:

$$P = \sum_{t=1}^{n} \frac{C_t}{(1 + r)^t} \tag{4-2}$$

To illustrate how r can be solved for, assume that a firm invests $100,000 in a mining venture which is expected to return $34,000 after all expenses for each of the next five years and nothing thereafter. What is the expected rate of return on the firm's investment? The answer of 20.76 percent can be obtained quickly by the use of a finance calculator. However, let us examine what is involved in the calculation.

The expected cash flows associated with the investment are given in the second column of Table 4-2. The first step in finding the rate of return is to estimate the discount rate that will equate the present value of the flows with the amount invested. Our initial guess is a discount rate of 20 percent. The present-value factors and the present values of the cash flows discounted at 20 percent per year are shown in the third and fourth columns, respectively. The sum of the present values is given at the bottom of the fourth column. Since the sum is slightly greater than the investment outlay of $100,000, we know that the rate at which we have discounted the future flows is too low. Thus, the rate of return is somewhat larger than 20 percent. If we want greater accuracy, we can try a discount rate of 21 percent. The present-value factors and the present values of the flows at 21 percent are shown in the fifth and sixth columns, respectively. In this case, we see that the $99,487 present value of the inflows shown at the bottom of column 6 is less than $100,000

TABLE 4-2
DETERMINING THE RATE OF RETURN FROM A MINING VENTURE REQUIRING
AN INVESTMENT OF $100,000

(1) Year	(2) Cash flow	(3) Present value factor—20%	(4) Present value (column 2 times column 3)	(5) Present value factor—21%	(6) Present value (column 2 times column 5)
1	$34,000	0.8333	$28,332	0.8265	$28,101
2	34,000	0.6944	23,613	0.6830	23,222
3	34,000	0.5787	19,676	0.5645	19,193
4	34,000	0.4823	16,398	0.4665	15,861
5	34,000	0.4019	13,665	0.3856	13,110
			$101,684		$99,487

investment outlay. Thus, we have discounted the expected cash flows at too high a rate.

The results of the calculations shown in the table indicate that the rate of return on the investment lies somewhere between 20 and 21 percent. We could make a rough estimate of the exact rate. However, use of a finance calculator is easy and a lot more accurate. Recall that the calculator solution was found to be 20.76 percent above.

SUMMARY

The first part of this chapter has been concerned with the mathematical procedures used in calculating the present value of future cash flows and the time-adjusted rate of return. Several additional solved problems which make use of the time-adjustment process are given in the following section. Then, in the later part of the chapter, the techniques will be applied in determining the valuation of corporate securities.

SOLVED PROBLEMS

1 The Small Investment Corporation (SIC) owns 100 shares of the common stock of the Newly Formed Company. The stock is not expected to pay a dividend for at least three years, but estimates indicate that the stock will be worth $10 a share at the end of the third year. If SIC's required rate of return is 10 percent on this type of investment, what is the present value of the firm's 100 shares of Newly Formed's stock? (Note that the total value of the stock at the end of three years is expected to be 100 shares × $10 per share = $1,000.)

Solution

$$P = \$1,000 \times \frac{1}{(1.1)^3}$$
$$= \$1,000(PVIF_{3,10\%})$$
$$= \$1,000(0.7513) = \$751.30$$

2 The ABC Manufacturing Firm is considering the acquisition of a new wood plane which is expected to produce annual cash flows of $1,000, $2,000, and $3,000 at the end of each of the next three years, respectively. What is the present worth of these cash flows if the required rate of return is 8 percent per annum?

Solution

$$P = 1000\frac{1}{(1.08)^1} + 2000\frac{1}{(1.08)^2} + 3000\frac{1}{(1.08)^3} = \$5,022.10$$

3 Mrs. Gould plans to retire at age sixty-five, at which time she will begin to receive a retirement annuity that will pay her $10,000 per year for five years. If the rate of interest is 12 percent, what is the worth of her retirement annuity on her sixty-fourth birthday?

Solution

$$P = \sum_{t=1}^{5} \frac{\$10,000}{(1.12)^t}$$

The calculator solution is $36,048. This value can also be obtained by subtracting the present value of a perpetuity of $10,000 a year, beginning at the end of the sixth year, from the present value of a perpetuity of $10,000 a year, beginning at the end of one year:

$$P = \frac{\$10,000}{0.12} - \frac{\$10,000}{0.12(1.12)^5}$$
$$= \$36,048$$

4 Let us consider again Mrs. Gould and her annuity from Problem Three. What is the value of the annuity to Mrs. Gould now if she has just had her fifty-fourth birthday? the rate of interest is still 12 percent.

The value of the annuity on Mrs. Gould's sixty-fourth birthday was found to be $36,048 in Problem Three. Thus, all that is required to find the present value on her fifty-fourth birthday is to discount the $36,048 back ten years. Using a finance calculator, the present value of $36,048 in ten years, discounted at 12 percent per annum, is $11,606.

The calculation can also be made (although more slowly) by the use of the present value table in Appendix A-1. Determining the appropriate present-value factor for a single sum (i.e., PVIF) from the table, we can solve for P_0 as follows:

Solution

$$P_o = \frac{P_{10}}{(1.12)^{10}}$$
$$= P_{10}[\text{PVIF}_{10,12\%}]$$
$$= \$36,048(0.3220)$$
$$= \$11,607$$

where P_0 and P_{10} are the present values of her annuity today and in ten years, respectively. The preceding calculations indicate that the present value of Mrs. Gould's retirement annuity eleven years before her retirement is $11,607. This figure is slightly different from the calculator solution because of the greater rounding involved in using table values.

Another way to solve this problem is to determine the present value of a $10,000 annuity for fifteen years and then subtract the present value of a $10,000 annuity for ten years; the result is the present value of a five-year ann;uity whose cash flows begin at the end of the eleventh year. Continuing to use a 12 percent interest rate, we get:

$$P_o = \$10,000[\text{PVAF}_{15,12\%}] - \$10,000[\text{PVAF}_{10,12\%}]$$
$$= \$10,000[6.8109 - 5.6502]$$
$$= \$11,607$$

5 The LBS Company has agreed to lease a small truck to a construction firm for an annual rental of $2,314 for six years. Under the terms of the contract, each rental payment is to be made at the end of the year of use. The truck is currently valued on the market at $9,000. Compute the rate of return before income taxes for LBS.

Solution

The objective is to find the discount rate that makes the present value of $2,314 per year for the next six years equal to $9,000. We know that the following equation holds:

$$\$9,000 = \$2,314 \times \text{PVAF for six years at ? percent}$$

Rearranging this equation to solve for $\text{PVAF}_{6,?\%}$ we find:

$$PVAF_{6,?\%} = \frac{\$9,000}{\$2,314} = 3.8894$$

Now, going to Appendix A-2, we search for a six-year factor equal to 3.8894. We find that it is almost the same as the 3.8887 PVAF applicable to a rate of return of 14 percent. The rate of return before income taxes for LBS is therefore very close to 14 percent. Using a finance calculator, the rate will be found to 13.99 percent.

6 Mr. Forsythe has $50,000 and would like to double his money in ten years. What annual rate of return must he earn from investing his capital in order to accomplish his objective?

Solution

The solution requires finding the discount rate that will equate Mr. Forsythe's current savings with the present value of the $100,000 he wants in ten years. This can be done by using equation (4-6) as follows:

$$r = \left(\frac{100,000}{\$50,000}\right)^{1/10} - 1$$
$$= 0.0718, \text{ or } 7.18 \text{ percent}$$

The calculation above assumes that any cash flows received from the investment before the end of the tenth year are reinvested at the 7.18 percent rate.

7 This one is a little different! What annuity cash flow for eight years will produce a present value of $3,000 when discounted at 15 percent?

Solution

In solving this problem, we first substitute the known elements into equation (4-4b) as follows:

$$\$3,000 = C[PVAF_{8,15\%}]$$
$$= C[4.4873]$$

Rearranging the last expression, we can solve for C (the annuity cash flow) as follows:

$$C = \frac{\$3,000}{4.4873}$$
$$= \$668.55$$

THE VALUATION OF CORPORATE SECURITIES AND BUSINESS FIRMS

One of the most important areas to which time-adjustment procedures can be applied is in the valuation of corporate securities. We will consider the valuation of common stock, preferred stock, and bonds separately. Most of the valuation techniques that will be discussed are applicable regardless of whether the securities have an active market or not. The valuation of a security which is not traded in the market, and therefore does not have a known market price, is extremely important to the present owners of the security as well as to potential investors in it.

Business organizations such as sole proprietorships and partnerships, of course, do not issue stocks and bonds. However, the valuation techniques applicable to corporate securities can be adapted to unincorporated businesses. This topic will be considered at the end of the present chapter, where the valuation of a firm as a whole is discussed.

Common Stock

If maximization of the market value of the firm's common stock is the objective in financial decision making, the financial manager should have a clear understanding of the valuation process. The first requirement in the valuation of a common stock is the identification of the factors that affect its value in the market. In general, the factors are the same as for the value of any asset: future cash returns from owning the asset, the timing of those returns, and the discount rate that should be used in determining their present value.

The returns to the stockholder consist of the cash flows obtained from owning the security. These cash flows come from dividends and, in the event that the stock is sold, from the proceeds of the sale. However, if the stock is sold, the price at that time represents the present value of all subsequent dividends. Thus, the current market value is the present value of its future dividends, regardless of any stockholder plans to sell the stock at some future date.

Earnings are important to the value of a common stock. However, the importance of earnings lies in their effect on the cash flows to the stockholder; earnings affect value because of what they imply for future dividends. Over the long run, dividends will be conditioned by the earnings of the firm. For this reason, analysts often base their estimates of a firm's dividends on earnings forecasts. Regardless of how they are estimated, however, dividends affect the value of a firm's common stock, because they are cash flows to stockholders.

Calculation of the Value of a Share of Common Stock. Utilizing the procedures discussed in previous sections, we can estimate the market value of a share of common stock by discounting the expected future dividends at the rate of return required in the market on comparable-risk investments. This calculation can be expressed mathematically by adapting equation (4-2) in the following way:

$$P_o = \frac{DPS_1}{(1 + k_c)^1} + \frac{DPS_2}{(1 + k_c)^2} + \frac{DPS_3}{(1 + k_c)^3} + \cdots + \frac{DPS_n}{(1 + k_c)^n}$$

$$= \sum_{t=1}^{n} \frac{DPS_t}{(1 + k_c)^t} \tag{4-8}$$

where DPS_1, DPS_2, DPS_3, and so on are the dollar dividends expected during their respective years; and k_c is the required annual rate of return on the stock.[2] The subscript o in P_0 indicates that the equation solves for the current price of the stock, which is often referred to as the **price at time zero.**

---

[2] Dividends are usually paid quarterly. Thus, precise accuracy in the valuation formula would require discounting each quarterly dividend back to the present at the required rate of return per quarter. However, this technical adjustment in the valuation process is an overkill in valuing most common stocks because of the uncertainty surrounding estimates of future dividends, particularly quarterly dividends. Thus, we choose to value common stock by discounting the expected total dividends for a year by the required rate of return for the year.

The equation is mathematically sound, but pragmatically, not very useful for purposes of valuing a share of common stock. One reason is that the equation is unwieldy. If n is very large, that is, if dividends are expected to be paid in many future years, and if the dividends are not expected to be constant, a large number of calculations is required to determine the present value. Furthermore, dividends on common stock are not normally expected to remain constant indefinitely. An estimate of the dividend to be received in any particular year in the future, say the eighteenth year, will probably not be very reliable.

But prices of stocks, even with highly unstable dividends, are determined in the market, and discounting expected future dividends is a logical procedure for explaining the valuation process. Fortunately, the valuation calculation can be greatly simplified if future dividends are not expected to grow over time or if they are expected to grow at a constant rate. We will see below that the valuation formula that should be used depends on the expected pattern of future dividends.

Constant Dividends. First, consider the simple but highly unusual case in which a company is not expected to grow, and its dividends are expected to remain constant indefinitely. The price of a share of the company's common stock in this case can be found by simply dividing the expected total dividend for one year by the required rate of return per year. This procedure is often referred to as capitalizing the dividend to determine the present value of the share of stock. For example, assume that a company is expected to pay dividends of $3 a year on each share of its stock and that no change is expected for the future. If the annual rate of return required on the stock is ten percent, its present value can be calculated by adapting equation (4-3) as follows:

$$P_o = \frac{DPS}{k_c} \tag{4-9}$$

$$= \frac{\$3}{0.1}$$

$$= \$30$$

Unstable Dividends. Even if dividends are not expected to grow in the future, they probably will not remain absolutely constant each year. At times the company will have either an excess or a deficiency of cash on hand because of unforeseen events. In this type of situation, dividends paid will often be affected temporarily until cash on hand returns to a more "normal" level. An approximate solution to this problem is found by estimating the normal dividend per period and capitalizing this figure at the required rate of return. However, the variability in expected dividends should be accounted for in the valuation process. There is usually a close relationship between the expected variability in dividends and the risk associated with estimating their future amounts. This risk can be accounted for in the valuation process by including a risk premium in the capitalization rate (the required rate of return), thereby reducing the calculated present value of the stock's future dividends. Ordinarily, the greater the variability expected in future dividends, the greater will be the required return and the lower the present value of the stock. Conversely, the less the variability, the lower the risk and the capitalization rate, and the higher the estimated present value of stock. Chapter 7 will be more specific in explaining how required rates of return are determined.

Growth in Dividends.   Most firms pay out only a portion of their earnings in dividends and reinvest the portion retained. The economic justification for retaining earnings is that the additional investment will increase future earnings and dividends of the firm. The rate of growth will equal the proportion of earnings retained (the **retention rate**) multiplied by the after-tax return the firm earns on the new investment. If the porportion of earnings paid out in dividends (the **dividend payout ratio**) is constant, dividends will grow at the same rate as earnings. Thus, under the conditions depicted, the growth rate in both earnings and dividends can be expressed mathematically as follows:

$$g = br \qquad (4-10)$$

where g is the growth rate, b is the retention rate and r is the after-tax return the firm earns on reinvested earnings. If b and r remain constant over time, earnings and dividends will continue to grow at the rate g.

As an example, assume that the **earnings per share** (EPS) of a firm in year 1 are $5 and **dividends per share** (DPS) are $3. Since the firm's dividend payout ratio is 60 percent, b will be 40 percent. Assume also that the firm expects to earn 12 percent on reinvested earnings; thus, g will be $0.4 \times 0.12 = 0.048$, or 4.8 percent. Earnings per share for year 2 can be estimated as follows:

$$\begin{aligned} EPS_2 &= EPS_1 + g(EPS_1) \qquad (4-11) \\ &= \$5 + 0.048(\$5) \\ &= \$5.24 \end{aligned}$$

where the subscripts refer to years. Note that earnings have grown by $0.24. This figure could also be obtained by multiplying the earnings retained in year 1 by the rate of return earned: $0.4 \times \$5 \times 0.12 = \$0.24$.

Assuming that the dividend payout ratio is expected to remain 60 percent in year 2, *DPS* can be estimated as follows:

$$\begin{aligned} DPS_2 &= DPS_1 + g(DPS_1) \qquad (4-12) \\ &= \$3 + 0.048(\$3) \\ &= \$3.14 \end{aligned}$$

If b and r are expected to remain constant in year 3, the same types of calculations as above will result in EPS$_3$ and DPS$_3$ estimates of $5.49 and $3.29, respectively, when rounded to the nearest cent. Thus, so long as b and r remain constant, earnings and dividends will continue to grow each year at a 4.8 percent rate. We will see below how constantly-growing streams of earnings and dividends can be valued.

Valuation of a Growing Stream of Dividends.   If a company's growth rate in earnings and dividends is expected to remain constant in the future, the basic valuation model, equation (4-8), can be simplified by a mathematical process called "summing a geometric progression" to give the following valuation formula:

$$P_0 = \frac{DPS_1}{k_c - g} \tag{4-13}$$

Note that equation (4-13) solves for the price of the stock at time zero, and the dividend in the equation is the dividend expected at the end of one year. The mathematical procedure used in summing a geometric progression is presented in Appendix 4A at the end of the present chapter. Equation (4-13) is referred to as the **constant growth model.**[3] The formula has attained a position of extreme importance in the field of business finance.

Two requirements are necessary for the constant growth model to be applicable to the valuation of a share of common stock. First, as indicated above, the growth rate in dividends (g) must be expected to remain constant in the future. Second, the expected growth rate must be less than the required rate of return on the stock (k_c). Since the two requirements are reasonably applicable to many firms, the model is widely used in arriving at an estimate of the value of their common stock.

To illustrate the use of the constant growth model, we will consider PepsiCo, Inc. The growth rate in PepsiCo's dividends can be expected to be fairly stable in the future. The company has average risk compared to other firms in the market, and its growth rate should approximate the nominal growth rate of the United States economy over the long run. We will use an expected growth rate of 8 percent for the company's dividends, which are $0.84 annually at the time of this writing.

Given the state of the stock market at the time, we estimate that the required rate of return on PepsiCo's common stock should be between 10 and 11 percent; we will split the middle and use 10.5 percent. Incorporating the preceding information into equation (4-13), the share value of the company's common stock can be calculated as follows:

$$P_0 = \frac{\$0.84}{0.105 - 0.08}$$
$$= \$33.60$$

The $33.60 calculated share value is reasonably close to the $36\frac{1}{8}$ price at which the stock closed on August 2, 1988, the day this example was developed. The reader should be aware of the fact that most estimates will "miss the mark" to some extent.

Expansion vs. True Growth. Recall from our earlier discussion that the rate of growth in earnings per share is equal to the retention rate multiplied by the rate of return earned on reinvested earnings, or as equation (4-10) expresses it: $g = br$. If

---

[3] The model is also referred to as the Gordon-Shapiro model or just the Gordon model. Myron Gordon and Eli Shapiro first presented the model in "Capital Equipment Analysis: The Required Rate of Profit," *Management Science,* Vol. III, Oct. 1956, pp. 102–110. Gordon subsequently popularized it in numerous writings.

stock holders are going to benefit from the firm's retention of earnings, r must exceed k_c. To see why, assume first that $r = k_c$. Equation (4-13) can now be recast to form the following equation:

$$P_0 = \frac{EPS_1(1 - b)}{k_c - bk_c} \tag{4-14}$$

Since $(1 - b)$ is the firm's dividend payout ratio, the numerator in equation (4-14) is the dollar dividend per share in year 1, or DPS_1. Factoring k_c in the denominator results in the following expression:

$$P_0 = \frac{EPS_1(1 - b)}{k_c(1 - b)}$$

$$= \frac{EPS_1}{k_c} \tag{4-15}$$

The result of our algebraic manipulations above indicates that if the return earned on reinvested earning is equal only to the required rate of return, the amount of dividends the firm pays is irrelevant to the determination of the stock price. The price is found simply by dividing EPS by k_c. EPS will increase in year 2 by the amount $bk_c(EPS)$, and P will increase by $bk_c(P_0)$. However, the stock price will not be affected at a given point in time by whether the dividend payout ratio in the future is 0, 50, 100, or any other percent, because the expected value of any earnings retained is exactly equal to value of the dividend foregone.

Illustrations.   As an example, consider a stock with expected $EPS_1 = \$5$ and $r = k_c = 12$ percent. $P_0 = \$5/0.12 = \$41.67$, regardless of the amount of dividends the firm pays now or in the future. However, if the firm pays out 60 percent of earnings and retains 40 percent, the price at the *end* of year 1 will be:

$$P_1 = \frac{(1 + bk_c)(EPS_1)(1 - b)}{k_c - bk_c} \tag{4-16}$$

$$= \frac{(1.048)(\$5.00)(1 - 0.4)}{0.12 - 0.048}$$

$$= \$43.67$$

The numerator in equation (4-16) above is the dividend in year two, since $(1 + bk_c)(EPS_1)$ is the calculation for earning per share in year two, and $(1 - b)$ is the dividend payout ratio. The price of the stock increased from \$41.67 to \$43.67—or 4.8 percent—during year 1 even though the rate of return earned on reinvested earnings was only equal to the required return on the investment.

The case described above is often referred to as simple expansion rather than true growth. In a true growth situation, the firm is expected to earn a higher return on reinvested earnings than the required rate of return in the market on comparable-risk investments, that is, $r > k_c$. Thus, the stockholder will benefit from the firm reinvesting its earnings because the market value of the firm's stock will increase more than the dollar amount of the dividend forgone.

In the example above, the firm earned $5 and retained $2 per share in the first year. If the $2 had been paid out as a dividend, it would have been worth $2 before taxes to the stockholder. But if the firm is able to earn 15 percent on the $2 it retained ($r = 15$ percent), and k_c is still 12 percent, the reinvestment will cause the share price of the common stock to increase more than $2. The growth rate will be $br = 0.4 \times 0.15 = 0.06$ under the conditions now posed.

The increase in the share price of common stock in year 1 resulting from reinvesting the $2 rather than paying it out in dividends, can be calculated with the following equation:

$$\Delta P_1 = \frac{r(RPS_1{}^*)(1-b)}{k_c - g} \tag{4-17}$$

where ΔP_1, is the increase in share price in year one, $RPS_1{}^*$ is the additional retained earnings per share in year one ($2 in our example), and all other symbols have the same meaning as before. Substituting the figures in our example into equation (4-17), we get:

$$\Delta P_1 = \frac{(0.15)(\$2)(1-0.4)}{0.12 - 0.06}$$
$$= \$3.00$$

Thus, the stockholder will benefit in this example by $3 - $2 = $1 if the firm reinvests the $2 rather than paying it out as a dividend. The example is oversimplified somewhat, because the effects of taxes and transaction costs have not been taken into account. However, it does show that stockholders can benefit from the retention of earnings by a firm which has favorable investment opportunities.

Super Growth. We noted earlier that one assumption of the constant growth model presented in equation (4-13) is that the required rate of return, k_c, exceeds the growth rate, g. If not, the model will not produce a positive, finite price. However, the reader may be aware of instances where the earnings and dividends of a firm are growing at a rate which is higher than any reasonable estimate of the required rate of return on the stock in the market. The International Business Machines Corporation (IBM) provides a classic example of this situation. IBM's earnings per share grew at an average annual rate of 20.77 percent from 1954 through 1963. This rate was much higher than required returns on comparable-risk stocks during the period.

If earnings of a firm were expected to grow forever at a rate higher than the required rate of return in the market on comparable-risk investments, the stock would be worth more than the total of all other assets in the economy. Although this is unrealistic, we have already noted that some firms do grow for several years at a rate which exceeds the market's required return on the firm's common stock. How does the market value these super-growth stocks? A logical method of valuing them is, first, to estimate the value of the dividends during the super-growth period and then to combine this figure with the present value of estimated dividends after growth has leveled off to a sustainable rate. The formula can be expressed as follows:

$$P_0 = \sum_{t=1}^{n} \frac{DPS_t}{(1 + k_c)^t} + \frac{DPS_{n+1}}{(k - g)(1 + k_c)^n} \tag{4-18}$$

where the super-growth period occurs during the first n years, and the growth rate is expected to level off to a sustainable rate beginning in year $n + 1$. The second element on the right-hand side of the equation is the value at time zero of the dividends that begin in year $n + 1$. Dividing D_{n+1} by $(k - g)$ determines the value of the stock at the end of year n. This value is then discounted back to time zero by dividing by $(1 + k_c)^n$.

Consider a company whose earnings and dividends have been growing at a 20 percent rate. The rate of growth is expected to continue to be 20 percent for another two years but then to level off to 6 percent indefinitely. If the dividend during the coming year is expected to be $1 and the required rate of return is ten percent, the price of the stock can be estimated as follows:

$$\begin{aligned}
P_0 &= \frac{\$1}{(1.1)^1} + \frac{(1.2)(\$1)}{(1.1)^2} + \frac{(1.2)(\$1)(1.06)}{(0.10 - 0.06)(1.1)^2} \\
&= \$0.91 + \$0.99 + \$26.28 \\
&= \$28.18
\end{aligned}$$

Stocks Paying No Dividends.   The reader may also be familiar with stocks which have value on the market, but which are not paying a dividend currently, and perhaps have never paid one. What is the valuation process for stocks of this type? For a security to have value, it must have the potential to return cash to the investor at some point in time. Thus, even though a stock is not currently paying a dividend, there must be some indication that one will be paid in the future.

In theory, the valuation of such a stock would still require estimating future dividends and then discounting them back to the present. However, the process is not very practical when the amount and timing of the first dividend payment is highly uncertain. In these cases, valuation is usually based on earnings rather than dividends. If $r = k_c$ in this situation, equation (4-15) can be used to estimate the share price of the stock. Another analytical tool which might be used to make the estimate even when r is not equal to k_c is the **price-earnings ratio**, which will be discussed in the following section.

The Price-Earnings Ratio.   The **price-earnings ratio** (P/E) is a widely used valuation concept among practicing financial analysts and investment counselors. We will first describe the P/E and its uses, and then examine the relationship between the ratio and valuation techniques previously discussed.

The P/E for a particular company is obtained by dividing the current price of the company's stock by either the company's earnings per share for the past year or the expected earnings per share for the coming year. The use of expected earnings is more appropriate because the price of the stock reflects what investors believe will happen in the future. The result of the calculation is a price multiple of earnings, which is often used to indicate whether the stock price is either over- or under-priced relative to other stocks which the analyst believes have similar growth prospects and risk. For example, if the P/E of XYZ Company is low relative to the P/E of other companies believed to have approximately the same risk exposure and growth prospects, the analyst may conclude that the stock is underpriced and therefore "a good buy."[4]

For a further illustration of the use of the P/E, assume that an analyst estimates the earnings per share of PepsiCo for the coming year at $2.80. The analyst also determines that the P/E ratios of firms with similar risk and growth prospects (e.g., The Coca-Cola Bottling Company) are currently about 14. The value of the company's common stock would thus be estimated as follows:

$$P_0 = \text{expected EPS} \times \frac{P}{E} \qquad (4\text{-}19)$$
$$= \$2.80 \times 14$$
$$= \$39.20$$

If PepsiCo's common stock is selling at $36\frac{1}{8}$ as indicated earlier, the analyst may conclude that the market is undervaluing the stock.

The implication of an analyst's conclusion that the P/E of a company is either too high or too low is that there is an error in the market's assessment of the stock's (1) future growth in earnings and/or (2) risk. Thus, an analyst who concludes that the stock is a good buy because of its low P/E is pitting his or her judgment against that of the market. If the market is efficient in the sense described earlier, the analyst will be wrong as often as right.

Another use of P/E ratios is in capital market analysis. Market analysts consider the average P/E of all stocks in the market at a given point in time to be indicative of the level of stock prices in general. At the bottom of a bear market (one in which the general level of stock prices is low), most stocks will have a relatively low P/E. Conversely, the P/E of most stocks will be relatively high at the top of a bull market (one in which stock prices are generally high). For example, the P/E of many blue-chip (large, low-risk) companies such as General Foods and American Telephone and Telegraph dropped to 10 or below in the bear markets of 1973–1974 and 1977. On the other hand, the rise in stock prices toward the end of 1985 pulled the P/E of many stocks up to levels well above 10. The P/E of most actively traded stocks have generally remained above 10 through the middle of 1989, despite a sharp, temporary drop as a result of the stock market crash in October, 1987.

P/E and k_c Compared. Let us consider the relationship between the P/E and the required rate of return (k_c) used in the valuation equations discussed earlier. Both the P/E and k_c are affected by the default-free rate of interest (such as the interest rate on U.S. Treasury bonds, which have no risk of default) and the risk associated with

---

[4] If the market is efficient in the sense defined earlier in the chapter, the investor should not expect to obtain a return larger than necessary to compensate for the risk assumed in a stock investment. However, not everyone agrees that the market is always completely efficient.

investing in the stock. Assuming that other factors remain the same, the P/E will fall and k_c will rise if the company's risk is increased. On the other hand, the P/E will rise and k_c will fall if interest rates in general and/or risk declines.

The P/E is affected by one factor that does not affect k_c directly; this factor is the expected growth rate of the company's earnings. Recall that in the valuation equation (4-13), the growth rate was included as a separate element; k_c was affected only by the default-free rate of interest and the risk associated with investing in the stock. But the P/E will be directly affected by the market's assessment of the company's growth prospects. If the company's expected growth rate is high, its P/E will be high, and if its expected growth rate is low, its P/E will be low, assuming that everything else is the same. For example, the P/E of the Hewlett-Packard Company's common stock has long been relatively high; this fact is generally attributed to the firm's growth prospects. On the other hand, General Motors' P/E was less than 6 in the middle of 1988, because of the relatively poor growth prospects of the company.

The use of P/E ratios is popular among finance professionals in valuing common stocks and in advising clients concerning the investment quality of a stock. One apparent reason for this popularity is the relative simplicity in using the ratio. Another reason is because the data inputs for more complex valuation models are often subject to wide error. In these cases, making valuation estimates of common stocks based on the P/E ratio may be more practical and reasonable than estimates based on the more complex models.

The Dividend-Price Ratio or Dividend Yield.   Another important ratio in stock analysis and valuation is the dividend-price ratio, more popularly known as the **dividend yield** (DY) or just yield. The formula is as follows:

$$DY = \frac{\text{Expected annual dividend per share}}{\text{Market price of a share of stock}} \qquad (4\text{-}20)$$

The DY is a type of rate of return figure, where the dollar return included in the numerator is the annual cash flow to the stockholder. It can be used to estimate the value of a stock, given the expected dividends of the company and the DYs of similar companies. Thus, it can be used in conjunction with the P/E to gain additional insights into the valuation process, including investors' attitudes toward the company's dividend policy and use of retained earnings.

Pricing New Stock Issues.   Another use of the price ratios previously discussed is in setting the offering price for an issue of common stock when the stock has not previously been selling in the open market. For example, assume that a company, whose common stock heretofore has not been available to the general public, is coming out with a new issue which is to be sold in the open market. Management expects the earnings per share of the new stock to be about $4 for the coming year, and a 75 percent dividend payout ratio is planned. A study reveals that companies of about the same size and with about the same product mix and growth prospects as our company have a P/E and DY averaging ten times and six percent, respectively. Using these ratios to estimate the share price at which the new issue should be sold, we obtain the following results:

$$\text{Possible issue price} = (\text{expected EPS})\left(\frac{P}{E}\right)$$
$$= (\$4)(10)$$
$$= \$40.00$$
$$\text{Possible issue price} = \text{expected dividends per share}) \div DY$$
$$= 0.75(\$4) \div 0.06$$
$$= \$50.00$$

The preceding calculations indicate that the new stock should be priced somewhere between $40 and $50. However, selling an issue to the public for the first time can be a tricky business; the market is not familiar with the stock and may not be familiar with the company. Furthermore, the market will have to be informed of, and will have to believe in, the earnings estimate and dividend policies of management. For these reasons, the price to the public of a new issue such as the one just described may be set somewhat below $40 in order to provide reasonable assurance that the stock will sell.

Modifying the Share Price.   A company's stock price is affected by the number of shares of the stock that are outstanding. The reason is that, given the total earnings of the firm and the total dividends that are to be paid, the earnings and dividends per share are affected by the number of shares outstanding. In other words, the total earnings and dividends "pies" can be divided into portions of different sizes. Thus a company such as the one discussed in the previous section, which is planning a stock issue for the first time can modify the price at which the stock can be sold by changing the number of shares offered. This may be important when management would like the stock to sell within a range investors appear to prefer at the time. Thus, the company in the last example might increase the number of shares offered so that the stock would sell initially at about $20.

Preferred Stock

The techniques discussed earlier can also be employed to value preferred stock. This type of stock is a hybrid since it usually has characteristics of both a common stock and a bond. Market prices of higher-grade preferred stocks tend to move with bond prices because preferred dividends (like bond interest) are usually limited to a stated amount per year. On the other hand, prices of lower-grade preferred stocks, where payment of the annual dividend is highly uncertain, tend to move with the earnings prospects of the firm.

Preferred-stock valuation is relatively simple in most cases because dividends are constant and expected to continue indefinitely. The valuation formula involves capitalizing (i.e., dividing) the promised dividend for a period by the required rate of return.[5] The promised annual dividend of a preferred stock is either stated on the

---

[5] Recall from our earlier discussion that dividing a constant annual dividend by the required rate of the return on the stock is equivalent to discounting the perpetual stream of dividends back to the present at that rate.

stock certificate or can be found by multiplying the par, or stated, value of the stock by the percentage dividend rate (coupon rate) stated on the certificate.

To illustrate the valuation process, consider General Motors' $5 cumulative preferred stock, which pays $0.9375 per share quarterly. If the required rate of return on the stock in the market is 8.00 percent per year, the market value would be estimated as follows:

$$P_0 = \frac{\$3.75}{0.08}$$
$$= \$46.88$$

Preferred Dividend Yield. The method of calculating the dividend yield on preferred stock is the same as for common; equation (4-20) indicates that the expected annual dividend is divided by the current market price of the stock. Since the dividend rate is generally fixed, the yield will vary inversely to changes in the price. The major factors affecting the price were noted above.

Bonds

As might be expected from our discussion of the valuation of stocks, the market price of a bond is the present value of all cash flows applicable to the bond in the future. The cash flows are the interest payments by the company to the bondholder and the return of the principal (the face value) of the bond to the bondholder at maturity, where maturity is simply the end of life of the bond. The present value is found by discounting the future flows at the required rate of return on the bond.

The usual formula for calculating bond value is as follows.

$$P_0 = \frac{I/m}{(1 + y/m)^1} + \frac{I/m}{(1 + y/m)^2} + \cdots + \frac{I/m}{(1 + y/m)^{mn}} + \frac{\text{Principal}}{(1 + y/m)^{mn}}$$

$$= \sum_{t=1}^{mn} \frac{I/m}{(1 + y/m)^t} + \frac{\text{Principal}}{(1 + y/m)^{mn}} \tag{4-21}$$

where P_0 is the current price of the bond, I is the total cash interest contracted to be paid on the bond in one year, m is the number of times interest is paid in one year, n is the number of years to maturity, and y is the bond's yield, sometimes referred to as the yield to maturity. (Bond yields are discussed below.) If interest is paid semiannually, the length of an interest period is six months. In this event, $k/2$ is the yield for a six-month period, and mn (i.e., $m \times n$) is the total number of six-month periods.

If present-value tables are used, the general formula can be expressed as follows:

$$P_0 = \left(\frac{I}{m}\right)(PVAF) + (Principal)(PVIF) \tag{4-22}$$

where *PVAF* is the present-value factor for a $1 annuity for mn periods at y/m percent per period, and *PVIF* is the present-value interest factor for $1 received at the end of period mn, discounted at y/m percent per period.

We will use as an illustration AT&T's 8.80 debenture bonds. Each of the bonds has a $1,000 face value, 8.80 percent coupon rate of interest, and maturity date of May 15, 2005. Assume for simplicity that the maturity is in exactly sixteen years. As is true for most bonds, interest is paid semiannually. The bondholder will receive $44 at the end of each six-months period for 16 years; hence, there will be a total of 32 interest payments for $44 each. The bondholder will also receive $1,000 at the end of the sixteenth year, that is, at the end of the thirty-second six-months period. The market value of the bonds is estimated by discounting the cash flows over the 32 periods at the yield for a six-months period.

Let us assume that the annual yield on the bonds is 10 percent; thus, the semiannual yield is $10\%/2 = 5\%$. Each of the bonds would be valued as follows:

$$
\begin{aligned}
P_0 &= \frac{\$44}{(1.05)^1} + \frac{\$44}{(1.05)^2} + \cdots + \frac{\$44}{(1.05)^{32}} + \frac{\$1,000}{(1.05)^{32}} \\
&= (\$44)(PVAF_{32,5\%}) + (\$1,000)(PVIF_{32,5\%}) \\
&= (\$44)(15.8027) + (\$1,000)(0.2099) \\
&= \$905.22
\end{aligned}
$$

The quoted market price would probably be $90\frac{1}{2}$, which expresses the price as a percent of par.

Calculation of Bond Yield.   As indicated above, the term **bond yield** refers to a unique type of annual rate of return. It can be calculated by determining the discount rate that will equate the price of the bond with the present value of all contracted cash flows and then, if necessary, converting the discount rate to an annual basis. Contracted cash flows normally include both interest payments and return of the principal amount to the investor at the bond's maturity, as prescribed in the indenture (the bond contract). Equation (4-21) can be used to make the calculation by solving for $y/2$ as a single number. If interest is paid on a bond only once a year, m equals one and $y/m = y$. However, if interest if paid more often, as is the usual case, $y = (y/m) \times m$.

Most finance calculators today have a program for calculating bond yields. However, let us consider what is involved in making the calculation. Recall AT&T's 8.80 debenture bonds discussed earlier. Assume that the market price of a bond is $1,086.25. If the bonds mature in sixteen years, the semiannual yield can be calculated by solving for y/m in equation (4-21):

$$
\$1,086.25 = \sum_{t=1}^{32} \frac{\$44}{(1 + y/m)^t} + \frac{\$1,000}{(1 + y/m)^{mn}}
$$

The result of the calculation of y/m will be approximately 3.92 percent.

The next step is to find the annual yield on the bonds as follows:

$$
\begin{aligned}
y &= 3.92\% \times 2 \\
&= 7.84\%
\end{aligned}
$$

The 7.84 percent figure is the annual yield on the AT&T 8.80s under the stated price and maturity assumptions. The reader should be aware of the fact that the annual yield of a bond is frequently referred to simply as the yield, but as noted earlier, the more elaborate term **yield to maturity** is sometimes used.

Tables have been published which provide the yields on bonds with various prices, coupon rates, and maturity dates. If the analyst knows any three of these elements for a bond, the fourth element can be determined from one of the tables. However, calculators and computers are frequently used to make the calculations today.

Valuation of the Total Equity of a Firm

In our discussion of the valuation of common stock, we focused on the procedure for valuing only one share. This procedure was merely a convenience, however, since the objective of maximizing the value of one share is the equivalent of seeking to maximize the value of all currently outstanding shares, that is, the total value of the existing common stock. Focusing on the value of only one share simply allowed us to use smaller numbers in the calculations.

Nevertheless, in some instances, a decision maker will direct his or her attention toward the total value of the ownership equity of the firm. For example, the owner of a sole proprietorship is obviously concerned primarily with the total value of the equity, because the ownership is not divided into shares. Furthermore, the owners of other types of firms, such as partnerships or even corporations which have a small number of common stockholders, may be able to determine the value of their investment most conveniently by first estimating the total value of the equity.

The principles of valuing the total equity of a business are essentially the same as those we have utilized in the valuation of corporate securities. The net cash flow accruing to the owner(s) in each future period is estimated and then discounted at the required rate of return. The sum of the discounted flows for all future periods is the value of the total ownership equity.

Analysts will sometimes attempt to estimate the total value of a firm and then calculate the value of the equity by subtracting the value of all of the firm's debt from the estimated total value. This procedure is perfectly acceptable so long as total value of the firm has been estimated correctly. However, the discount rate that should be used to time adjust future cash flows in this case should be the required rate of return for the firm as a whole, not the required rate for just one type of security. The required rate of return for the firm as a whole is a weighted average of the required rates on all methods of long-term and permanent financing the firm uses. This subject is discussed in Chapter 7, after we have applied our valuation techniques to investment decisions in the next two chapters.

CHAPTER SUMMARY

This chapter is primarily concerned with the valuation of earning assets, including corporate securities. The topic is of importance to financial managers because most financial decisions have an impact on the value of both the firm as a whole and its owners' equity. Valuation techniques have significantly improved in recent years, and these improved techniques are becomimg more widely used by business firms in making financial decisions.

The essential aspect of valuation is discounting estimated cash flows at the required rate of return to determine their present value. Techniques of valuation were applied to common and preferred stocks and to bonds. A special problem was noted in the case of common stock, because dividends are not usually constant over an extended period of time. The constant growth model was therefore introduced and applied to the valuation of common stock in cases where dividends are expected to grow indefinitely at a constant rate. Another model was presented for the valuation of a stock with dividends growing temporarily at a higher rate than the required rate of return.

Concepts related to value were also discussed and applied in the chapter. In particular, the technique for determining the time-adjusted rate of return was presented. The uses of several important ratios which have market price as one of their elements were also examined. These ratios included the price-earnings ratio and both stock and bond yields. Price ratios are widely used among professional analysts in estimating the value of and returns on securities and other types of assets.

We make extensive use of valuation and other time-adjustment procedures throughout the remainder of this book. In the following chapter, the techniques developed here are shown to be of particular importance in making investment decisions for a firm.

SOLVED PROBLEMS

1 Paul Johnson has been offered one share in a small corporation whose only asset is an office building. He has been told that his share would earn $400 per year forever. All earnings of the company are distributed to the stockholders as dividends. Paul has decided that his required rate of return on this investment is 12 percent. Calculate the maximum price he should pay for the share.

Solution

Since the $400 dividend per year is a perpetual annuity, the following formula should be used in solving this problem:

$$P_0 = \frac{DPS}{k_c}$$

where P_0 is the value of the share, which is the maximum price Paul should pay, and k_c is his required rate of return. Substituting the known elements into the formula we get:

$$P_0 = \frac{\$400}{0.12}$$
$$= \$3,333.33$$

2 The earnings and dividends per share of the BMI Corporation are estimated at $2.20 and $1.80, respectively, for the coming year. Most investment analysts have concluded that the company can indefinitely sustain its present growth rate of 8 percent. The market appears to require a 14 percent rate of return for stocks of the quality of BMI. Estimate the market value, the price-earnings ratio, and the dividend yield of the stock.

Solution

The first objective is to estimate the market value of a stock whose dividends are expected to grow at a constant rate indefinitely. Thus, the constant growth model, equation (4-13), can be used:

$$P_0 = \frac{DPS_1}{(k_c - g)}$$

Solving, we get:

$$P_0 = \frac{\$1.80}{0.14 - 0.08}$$
$$= \$30$$

Assuming that our estimated market value is the actual price at which the stock is selling, we can now calculate the price-earnings ratio as follows:

$$\frac{P}{E} = \frac{P_0}{EPS_1}$$
$$= \frac{\$30}{\$2.20}$$
$$= 13.6$$

The dividend yield is:

$$DY = \frac{DPS}{P_0}$$
$$= \frac{\$1.80}{\$30}$$
$$= 6\%$$

3 The president of the Sterling Electric Company, Mr. Wayland Reese, is considering an investment for his company which he believes will increase the growth rate of per-share earnings of common stock to 18 percent annually for the next two years. Thereafter, the growth rate will decline to its normal level, which is expected to continue indefinitely. Last year the company earned $2 a share and paid a dividend of $1.40, which reflected the company's normal payout ratio. The return on reinvested earnings average is about 14 percent after taxes, and analysts have estimated the required return on the company's common stock at 11 percent.

Estimate the market value of Sterling Electric Company's common stock if the investment is made.

Solution

The "normal" growth rate of EPS is $br = 0.3 \times 0.14 = 0.042$. The approach to valuing the stock is to discount back to time zero the estimated dividend for each of the first two years and the estimated value of the stock at the end of the second year:

$$P_0 = \sum_{t=1}^{n} \frac{DPS_t}{(1 + k_c)^t} + \frac{DPS_{n+1}}{(k_c - g)(1 + k_c)^n}$$

$$= \frac{(\$2.00)(1.18)(0.7)}{(1.11)^1} + \frac{(\$2.00)(1.18)^2(0.7)}{(1.11)^2} + \frac{(\$2)(1.18)^2(1.042)(0.7)}{(0.11 - 0.042)(1.11)^2}$$

$$= \$27.31$$

4 The dividend yield on Commonwealth Edison's $1.90 cumulative preferred stock was 10.41 percent on August 2, 1988. Estimate the price of the stock.

Solution

Since a dividend-paying preferred stock is a perpetuity, the price is estimated by capitalizing the annual dollar dividend at the dividend yield:

$$P_0 = \frac{DPS}{k_p}$$

$$= \frac{\$1.90}{0.1041}$$

$$= \$18.25$$

5 The Bentson Steel Company's 8.5 percent debenture bonds are selling for 88.5, and are due in fifteen years. Interest is paid semiannually. Calculate the yield on the bonds.

Solution

A finance calculator can solve this problem fairly quickly. However, we will again go through the steps involved to facilitate understanding the solution process.

Since the 8.5 percent interest is paid semiannually, the contracted cash flows applicable to a bond are interest payments of $42.50 for thirty periods of six months each and the return of the principal at maturity.

We can solve for the yield for a six-months period (y/m) by using the following formula:

$$\$885 = \$42.50(PVAF_{30,?\%} + \$1,000(PVIF_{30,?\%})$$

where $PVAF_{30,?\%}$ is the present-value annuity factor for a thirty-period annuity at y/m percent, and $PVIF_{30,?\%}$ is the present-value interest factor of $1 received at the end of thirty periods, discounted at y/m percent per period. Our initial estimate is that y/m is five percent. Determining the $PVIF_{30,5\%}$ and the $PVAF_{30,5\%}$ from Appendices A-1 and A-2, respectively, we get the following results:

$$\$885 = \$42.50(15.3725) + \$1,000(0.2314)$$

$$= \$884.73$$

Since the calculated figure of $884.73 is close to the $885 bond price, the six-months yield is approximately five percent. The annual yield on Bentson Steel's bonds is:

$$y = \left(\frac{y}{m}\right) \times m$$

where m is the number of interest payment periods in a year. Solving we get:

$$y = .05 \times 2$$
$$= 0.10, \text{ or } 10\%$$

6 Zip Auto Supply Company is considering the purchase of a used pickup truck to make deliveries of automobile parts. Mr. Zip has estimated that the contemplated delivery service would increase the company's net cash inflows after taxes by $100 a month during the remaining five years of the estimated life of the truck. He also estimates that the salvage value of the truck would be $100 at the end of the five years. Assuming that Mr. Zip requires a rate of return of one percent per month on this possible investment, calculate the maximum amount he should pay for the truck.

Solution

The maximum amount Mr. Zip should pay is the value of the truck to him if he owned it. Thus, the solution to the problem is the present value of all net cash inflows. Net cash inflows from operating the truck are estimated at $100 for sixty months (five years). The estimated salvage value at the end of the sixtieth month is also a cash inflow. Solving, we get:

$$P_0 = \$100(PVAF_{60,1\%}) + \$100(PVIF_{60,1\%})$$
$$= \$100(44.9550) + \$100(0.5504)$$
$$= \$4,550.54$$

PROBLEMS

4-1 Sunshine Farms, Inc. owns a small tract of timberland. The company has contracted to sell the timber over the next three years for $5,000, $7,000, and $10,000, respectively. What is the present value (before taxes) of the contract to Sunshine Farms if the required rate of return is 10 percent per year?

4-2 Refer again to Problem 4-1 above. Assume now, however, that contracted timber sales follow the reverse of the sequence given. That is, contracted sales are $10,000, $7,000, and $5,000 over the next three years. The required rate of return (before taxes) is 10 percent, the same as before.

a Calculate the present value (before taxes) of the contract to Sunshine Farms.

b Explain any difference in your answers to Problems 4-1 and 4-2a.

4-3 Panaramic, Inc., is expected to pay dividends on its common stock as follows:

$2 per share in each of next three years,
$3 per share in years four and five, and
$4 per share each year thereafter.

Estimate the market value of a share of Panaramic's stock if the required rate of return is 15 percent.

4-4 The Grandeur Investment Company has decided to build a fifty-unit apartment complex. The planning and construction will require two years, during which time no income will be received. Management has estimated that, beginning in the third year, net cash inflows after all expenses and taxes will be $150,000 annually for thirty years. Since the land will be leased and net salvage value is expected to be 0, no additional cash flows are expected at the end of the useful life of the apartment building.

a Calculate the present value of the net cash inflows of the complex, assuming that Grandeur Investment requires a 14 percent rate of return on the project.

b What is the maximum amount that the company should pay for the construction and apartment furnishings? Explain.

4-5 The Christopher Marine Company plans to spend $120,000 in the retooling necessary to change the design of one of the inboard motor boats the company manufactures. The design change is expected to increase the net cash inflows of the company, after all expenses and taxes, by $40,000 a year for five years. Calculate the expected rate of return on the investment in the design change.

4-6 An investment of $100,000 is expected to return $40,000, $50,000, and $60,000 over the next three years. Calculate the expected rate of return on the investment.

4-7 An analyst estimates the earnings per common share of the General Electric Company at $4.10 for the forthcoming year. He believes that the annual growth rate of the company's earnings will average 8 percent and that the required rate of return on the common stock should be 10 percent. The company pays out approximately 40 percent of its earnings in dividends. Using the analyst's estimates, complete each of the following for General Electric's common stock:

a Market value of a share p. 101, 108

b Price-earnings ratio - p. 100

c Dividend yield - p. 102

See p. 101

4-8 (This problem is difficult.) An analyst estimates that the earnings of the Raytron Electronics Corporation will grow at the annual rate of 25 percent over the next three years. However, he believes that the growth rate will then decline to a rate which the company can maintain indefinitely. Earnings are estimated at $5 per share for the coming year. The company is expected to pay a $1 dividend per share in each of the next three years, and thereafter to pay out 30 percent of earnings in dividends. The average rate of return on reinvested earnings is expected to be 12.00 percent after taxes, beginning with the earnings retained in the third year and continuing at that rate indefinitely. Note that the dollar returns on the reinvested earnings of any year begins in the following year. The analyst believes that the required rate of return on the stock should be 11 percent. Raytron has an all equity capital structure.

a Estimate the current market price of a share of Raytron Electronic's common stock.

b Estimate the market price of the stock at the end of one year.

c What is the expected growth rate of the stock price during the coming year? Explain.

4-9 Last year, the S&S Corporation sold a preferred stock issue in the open market. The stock had a par value of $100 and a coupon rate of 10 percent. The stock was sold at a price which resulted in a yield to investors of 9 percent.

a Estimate the price at which the preferred stock was sold. p. 102 - 103

b The price of the stock recently declined to $90 per share. Estimate the dividend yield on the stock at this time.

c Explain the factors that could have caused the stock to decline in price.

4-10 The Duke Power Company's 9.75 percent First and Refunding Bonds pay interest semiannually and are due in May 2004. Estimate the yield on the bonds in May 1991, if they are selling at 92.5 ($925 for a bond with a face value of $1,000).

4-11 (This problem can be solved most efficiently by the use of a programmable calculator or by a computer spreadsheet program.)

The American Fuels Corporation (AFC) earned $2.40 a share last year.

a Estimate the price of AFC'c common stock under the following conditions:

The rate of return earned on investments is 10 percent.

The required rate of return is 12 percent.

The divident payout ratio is: (1) 40 percent, (2) 50 percent, (3) 60 percent, (4) 70 percent.

b Estimate the price of the stock under each of the following conditions:

The rate of return earned on investments is 15 percent.

The required rate of return is 12 percent.

The divided payout ratio is: (1) 40 percent, (2) 50 percent, (3) 60 percent, (4) 70 percent.

c Estimate the price of the stock under each of the following conditions:

The rate of return earned on investments is 12 percent.

The required rate of return is 12 percent.

The dividend payout ratio is: (1) 40 percent, (2) 50 percent, (3) 60 percent, (4) 70 percent.

d What do the results of your calculations indicate in respect to the impact of the firm's investment return on the share price of its common stock? Explain.

REFERENCES

Basu, Sanjoy: "The Informational Content of Price-Earnings Ratios," *Financial Management*, vol. 4, Summer 1975, pp. 53–64.

Bauman, W. Scott: "Investment Returns and Present Values," *Financial Analysts Journal*, vol. 25, November-December 1969, pp. 107–118.

Billingsley, Randall S., Robert E. Lamy, and G. Rodney Thompson: "Valuation of Primary Issue Convertible Bonds," *Journal of Financial Research*, vol. IX, Fall 1986, pp. 251–259.

Black, Fischer: ''A Simple Discounting Rule," *Financial Management*, vol. 17, Summer 1988, pp. 7–11.

Campbell, John Y. and Robert J. Shiller: "Stock Prices, Earnings, and Expected Dividends," *Journal of Finance*, vol. 43, July 1988, pp. 661–676.

Fuller, Russell J., and Chi-Cheng Hsia: "A Simplified Common Stock Valuation Model," *Financial Analysts Journal*, vol. 40, September-October 1984, pp. 49–56.

Gordon, M.J. and L.I. Gould: "Comparison of the DCF and HPR Measures of the Yield on Common Shares," *Financial Management*, vol. 13, Winter 1984, pp. 40–47.

Ibbotson, Roger G., and Rex A. Sinquefield: *Stocks, Bonds, Bills, and Inflation: Historical Returns*, Charlottesville, Va.: Financial Analysts Foundation, 1982.

Kross, William: "The Size Effect is Primarily a Price Effect," *Journal of Financial Research*, vol. VIII, Fall 1985, pp. 169–179.

Levy, Haim and Robert Brooks: "Financial Break-Even Analysis and the Value of the Firm," *Financial Management*. vol. 15, Autumn 1986, pp. 22–26.

Marr, M.W. and G.R. Thompson: "The Pricing of New Convertible Bond Issues," *Financial Management*, vol. 13, Summer 1984, pp. 31-37.

Norgaard, Richard L.: "An Examination of the Yields of Corporate Bonds and Stocks," *Journal of Finance*, vol. 29, September 1974, pp. 1275–1286.

Ofer, Aharon R.: "Investors' Expectations of Earnings Growth, Their Accuracy and Effects on the Structure of Realized Rates of Return," *Journal of Finance*, vol. 30, May 1975, pp. 509–23.

Summers, Lawrence H.: "Does the Stock Market Rationally Reflect Fundamental Values?," *Journal of Finance*, vol. 41, July 1986, pp. 591–601.

APPENDIX 4A
Summing a Geometric Progression

Consider the following equation for the valuation of a common stock whose dividends, *DPS*, are expected to grow at the rate of g per period for n periods, where n is very large and k_c is the required rate of return:

$$P_0 = \frac{DPS_1}{(1 + k_c)^1} + \frac{DPS_1(1 + g)^1}{(1 + k_c)^2} + \frac{DPS_1(1 + g)^2}{(1 + k_c)^3} + \cdots + \frac{DPS_1(1 + g)^{n-1}}{(1 + k_c)^n} \quad \text{(4A-1)}$$

Summing equation (4A-1) requires the following steps:

1 Multiply both sides of the equation by $(1 + k_c)^1/(1 + g)^1$ to form equation (4A-2).
2 Subtract equation (4A-1) from equation (4A-2) to obtain equation (4A-3).
3 Solve the result for P_O and simplify.

The three steps are applied as follows:

Step 1:

$$P_0\left[\frac{(1 + k_c)^1}{(1 + g)^1}\right] = \frac{DPS_1(1 + k_c)^1}{(1 + k_c)^1(1 + g)^1} + \frac{DPS_1(1 + g)^1(1 + k_c)^1}{(1 + k_c)^2(1 + g)^1}$$

$$+ \frac{DPS_1(1 + g)^2(1 + k_c)^1}{(1 + k_c)^3(1 + g)^1} + \cdots + \frac{DPS_1(1 + g)^{n-1}(1 + k_c)^1}{(1 + k_c)^n(1 + g)^1}$$

$$= \frac{DPS_1}{(1 + g)^1} + \frac{DPS_1}{(1 + k_c)^1} + \frac{DPS_1(1 + g)^1}{(1 + k_c)^2} + \cdots + \frac{DPS_1(1 + g)^{n-2}}{(1 + k_c)^{n-1}}$$

$$\text{(4A-2)}$$

Step 2:

$$P_0\left[\frac{(1 + k_c)^1}{(1 + g)^1}\right] = \frac{DPS_1}{(1 + g)^1} + \frac{DPS_1}{(1 + k_c)^1} + \frac{DPS_1(1 + g)^1}{(1 + k_c)^2} + \cdots + \frac{DPS_1(1 + g)^{n-2}}{(1 + k_c)^{n-1}}$$

$$\text{(4A-2)}$$

$$- P_0 = -\frac{DPS_1}{(1 + k_c)^1} - \frac{DPS_1(1 + g)^1}{(1 + k_c)^2} - \frac{DPS_1(1 + g)^2}{(1 + k_c)^3} - \cdots - \frac{DPS_1(1 + g)^{n-1}}{(1 + k_c)^n}$$

$$\text{(4A-1)}$$

$$P_0\left[\frac{(1 + k_c)^1}{(1 + g)^1}\right] - P_0 = \frac{DPS_1}{(1 + g)^1} - \frac{DPS_1(1 + g)^{n-1}}{(1 + k_c)^n} \quad \text{(4A-3)}$$

Step 3:
Now if $k_c > g$ (a requirement) and if n is very large, the last element on the right-hand side of equation (4A-3) is very small (it approaches zero as n approaches infinity) and can be discarded.

Then, factoring P_0 on the left-hand side of the equation:

$$P_0 \left[\frac{(1 + k_c)^1}{(1 + g)^1} - 1 \right] = \frac{DPS_1}{(1 + g)^1}$$

Finally, solving the above equation for P_0, we get the constant growth model presented in the chapter:

$$P_0 = \frac{DPS_1}{k_c - g} \tag{4-13}$$

5

CAPITAL
BUDGETING TECHNIQUES

Investment decisions by business firms require the valuation of all investment opportunities available to the firm whose benefits can be quantified. Projects which are finally accepted by management and which involve a commitment of funds for a year or longer are included in the firm's capital budget for the year. For this reason, decisions concerning proposals of such investments are called capital budgeting decisions.

The benefits of some investment proposals cannot be directly quantified. For example, management may be considering a proposal to build a recreation room for employees. The decision in this case will probably be based on qualitative factors, such as improved management-employee relations, with little specific knowledge of the impact on productivity. However, most investment proposals considered by management will require quantitative estimates of the benefits to be derived from accepting the project. This chapter is concerned with the analytical methods that can be used to evaluate investment proposals of this type. Although new investments may have to be made only infrequently, they often involve a large commitment of funds and set the direction in which the firm will move for many years. Thus, a bad decision can be detrimental to the value of the firm's common stock over a long period of time.

Following a brief overview of the capital budgeting process, the remainder of this chapter is divided into three sections. First, we consider how the cash flows from an investment can be categorized and estimated. The second section explains and compares the analytical techniques that can be used to evaluate investment projects. The impact of limiting the amount of funds made available for investments by the firm is briefly examined in the last section.

The Capital Budgeting Process.   The organizational structure for making capital budgeting decisions differs among firms. In larger corporations, decisions affecting the capital budget are generally made at several management levels. Usually, the highest administrative level will make final decisions when proposed new projects involve commitments of relatively large amounts of funds. At the opposite end of the spectrum, in very small firms, all investment decisions may be made by one person, who also makes many other types of decisions for the business. However, the analytical processes we will discuss are applicable to any type of firm, regardless of its size or organization, so long as the objective is to maximize the value of the owners' equity.

Investment expenditures by a business are often thought of primarily as purchases of fixed assets. However, it is the length of time funds are committed, rather than the type of asset, that is important in identifying investments with which we are concerned. Thus, investments can be made in inventories and receivables when a commitment of funds for a year or longer is involved.

A firm will normally have many investment opportunities available to it, and a number of factors will have to be considered in determining which opportunities, if any, should be accepted. One such factor is the direct financial benefit of each opportunity considered by itself. In addition, the composition of the firm's existing assets and management's desire to change that composition will often be important considerations. Another decision required in capital budgeting is the timing of expenditures associated with the projects that are finally accepted. The latter decision is particularly important because the plan for financing the capital budget must also be developed. There is usually a close interrelationship between investment decisions and other aspects of the firm's financial planning.

THE INVESTMENT CASH FLOWS

It is essential to keep in mind that the only cash flows of concern in evaluating a proposed project are those that would be caused by the project itself, if it is accepted. These cash flows can be divided into three groups: the initial investment outlay; the net cash benefits from the investment; and the future nonoperating cash flows, if any, associated with the project. We will consider each of these three groups in the indicated sequence.

Initial Investment Outlay

An investment usually requires an immediate cash commitment. In the case of an investment in a fixed asset, the cash commitment will probably include the purchase price and, perhaps, transportation and installation costs required in bringing the new asset to its place of use and setting it up for operation. In addition, the use of the asset may necessitate an increase in the firm's working capital. For example, a project which significantly increases the firm's productive capacity may also result in an increase in inventories and perhaps accounts receivable. An increase in working capital involves a commitment of funds, and, if the increase occurs immediately, it is part of the initial outlay required to make the investment.

For an illustration, assume that a small manufacturing firm is considering an addition to its plant. A study commissioned by management has estimated that the addition itself would cost $300,000, and the expected expansion in production and sales would necessitate an immediate investment of $40,000 in raw material inventories. Thus, the initial outlay to make the investment is as follows:

Cost of plant addition	$300,000
Investment in additional inventories	40,000 ← (R.M. INV)
Initial investment outlay	$340,000

Some investments of a firm are to replace existing assets. Estimating the cash flow effects in these cases involves unique computational problems. In the following section, the problem of estimating the initial investment outlay is considered.

Asset Replacements.   The preceding discussion of the initial investment outlay focused on the purchase of an additional asset by the firm. However, investments are often made to replace existing assets which are either worn-out or less efficient than new models. The replacement of an existing asset may result in immediate changes in cash flows in addition to those associated with the investment in the new asset itself. More specifically, the investment outlay will include any changes in cash flows that emanate from the termination of the old asset. ← FINAL

The first step in the determination of the initial investment outlay in a replacement case involves the estimation of all cash flows associated with the new asset, as described earlier. The next step is to estimate the changes in the firm's cash flows that are caused by the retirement of the existing asset. For example, any expenses involved in its removal will add to the initial investment outlay. On the other hand, any salvage value will reduce the outlay. If the market value of the existing asset differs from its book value, the sale of the asset will affect the company's taxes. For example, if the sale nets the firms $2,000 and the book value of the asset is $1,000, the $1,000 difference is a gain and would be taxed at the regular tax rate of the company under tax law prevailing in 1989. Conversely, if the market price of the old asset is $1,000 and its book value is $2,000, the sale will result in a loss to the company. This loss would be tax-deductible in the year in which it occurred only to the extent that it can be used to offset capital gains. In the latter event, the savings would equal the company's regular tax rate multiplied by the amount of the loss, since ordinary income and capital gains are currently taxed at the same rate. The reader is referred to Appendix 5A at the end of this chapter for a discussion of federal taxation of business income.

The third and final step in the calculation of the initial investment outlay for a replacement is to net the cash flows determined in the first two steps. For an illustration of the process of making the estimate, consider the following scenario. The firm discussed earlier is engaged primarily in the manufacture of house paints. In addition to its study of the plant expansion, the firm is considering the replacement

TABLE 5-1
CALCULATION OF THE INITIAL INVESTMENT OUTLAY FOR THE REPLACEMENT
OF A PAINT BLENDER

Purchase price of new blender		$20,000
Less cash inflow from sale of existing blender		(13,000)
Plus: Tax on gain from sale of existing blender:		340
Sale price	$13,000	$ 7,340
Less Book Value	(12,000)	
Excess of sale price over book	$ 1,000	
Times tax rate	× 0.34	
Tax on gain	$340	
Initial investment outlay		

of one of its blending machines with a new, computerized model which has recently come on the market. Data applicable to the estimate of the initial investment are as follows:

Book value of existing blender	$12,000
Market value of existing blender	13,000
Purchase price of new blender	20,000
Income tax rate	34%

The investment outlay for the proposed replacement would be calculated as shown in Table 5-1. In the illustration, the proceeds from the sale of the existing blender reduce the net outlay required to make the investment, whereas the tax on the gain from selling at a price greater than the book value serves to increase the net outlay. The final result is an initial investment outlay of $7,340.

Note that the original cost of the existing blender does not enter into the above calculation. The only elements that affect the initial outlay are cash flows that are caused by the replacement decision. The original cost of the existing machine is a sunk cost because it was incurred in the past and is not affected in any way by decisions made today.

Net Cash Benefits

The net cash benefits of an investment are normally spread over a number of years, and the investment valuation process requires that the benefit be estimated for each year. It is essential to recognize that the only cash flows used in the calculation are those that are caused by the investment. Thus, any accounting allocation of the firm's fixed expenses should not be allowed to affect the estimated net cash benefits when the fixed expenses would be incurred if the investment were not made.

The following format can be used for estimating the net cash benefit per year from an investment, where the symbol Δ refers to a change in the firm's cash flows caused by the investment:

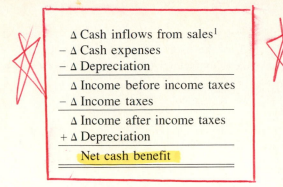

Note that in the calculation of net cash benefit, the change in the company's total depreciation charge which would be caused by the proposed investment (Δ depreciation in the table above) is first subtracted and then added back. It is subtracted in order to determine taxable income. After the additional income tax has been subtracted, the depreciation is then added back to reflect the fact that depreciation per se does not involve a cash flow. It is included in the calculations because it affects income taxes, which do involve a cash flow.

No financial charges are included in the estimation of net cash benefit. The cost of the funds required to make the investment will be included in the analysis at another point.[2] For example, when the value of an investment to a firm is calculated, the required rate of return used to discount the net cash flows will reflect the financing costs.

If cash flows are expected to be constant each year throughout the life of an investment, only one calculation of net cash benefit will be necessary. However, if either sales or costs vary over the life of the investment, a separate estimate of net cash benefit will have to be made for each year in which a change occurs.

The preceding format for the calculation of the annual net cash benefit can be used regardless of whether the benefit is derived from additional sales or from the reduction of expenses. If the investment results in an increase in productive capacity, both sales and expenditures will probably increase. On the other hand, if the investment involves the purchase of a new asset solely for the purpose of reducing costs—for example, a labor-saving machine—cash expenses will decline, but the company's sales may not be affected. The estimated net cash benefits from the investment can still be calculated by the use of the preceding format. In this case, however, the source of the benefits will be a reduction in cash outflows, that is, negative cash expenses. The format shown will produce arithmetically correct results since subtracting a negative number is equivalent to adding a positive number, resulting in an addition to the cash benefit from the investment. The remaining part of the calculation will follow the same procedures as before.

[1] If some sales are on credit, the cash inflows will be derived from cash sales and collections on receivables from past sales. If all sales are on credit, cash inflows will be derived entirely from collections. However, all sales considered in estimating net cash benefits must be caused by the investment under consideration.

[2] Alternatives to this procedure are discussed in John D. Martin, Samuel H. Cox, Jr., and Richard D. MacMinn, *The Theory of Finance: Evidence and Applications*, Chicago: The Dryden Press, 1988, Ch 13.

Illustration of the Asset Expansion Case.   Assume that the following operating data have been estimated for the $300,000 plant expansion being considered by the Home Paint Company, the manufacturer of house paints in the earlier example:

Useful life of the plant addition	30 years
Salvage value at the end of useful life	$30,000
Depreciation rate	Straight-line
Increase in annual cash inflows from sales related to the expansion	$100,000
Increase in annual cash expenses resulting from the expansion	$ 60,000
Income tax rate	34%

Since straight-line depreciation is used in this case, the annual depreciation charge applicable to the expansion is determined by subtracting the estimated salvage value from the cost of the depreciable asset and dividing the result by the number of years of useful life. Thus, depreciation each year will be ($300,000 − $30,000)/30 years = $9,000 for our example. The estimated $40,000 increase in inventories which was included as part of the initial investment outlay discussed earlier is not depreciable for tax purposes.

By using the preceding information, the net cash benefit from the investment in the plant expansion can be calculated as shown in Table 5-2. The result is an estimate of the net cash benefit of $29,460 each year.

Illustration of the Replacement Case.   When the investment is a replacement of an existing asset, the net cash benefit for each year will be determined from the estimated differences in the cash flows from sales and expenses of the old and new assets. The benefit may be caused by an increase in sales and/or a decrease in expenses. In any event, the format presented earlier can be used to determine the benefit.

If the old asset has not been completely depreciated for tax purposes at the time of the replacement, depreciation for the years during which the old asset would be used if not replaced will be the difference in the annual depreciation charges applicable to the two assets. Thus, depreciation in the calculation of the net cash benefits from the replacement decision may be either positive or negative, depending on whether the new asset has larger or smaller annual depreciation charges than the asset which is to be replaced. If the old asset should happen to have the larger depre-

TABLE 5-2
CALCULATION OF THE ESTIMATED
NET CASH BENEFIT PER YEAR FROM
A PLANT EXPANSION

Cash inflows from sales	$100,000
Cash expenses	(60,000)
Depreciation	(9,000)
Income before income taxes	$ 31,000
Income taxes at 34 percent	10,540
Income after income taxes	$ 20,460
Depreciation	9,000
Net cash benefit	$ 29,460

ciation expense, depreciation will be negative and net income before taxes will therefore be increased. On the other hand, if the new asset has the larger depreciation charge per period, depreciation will be positive and net income before taxes will be reduced.

Numerical Example.   Estimating the net cash benefits from the asset replacement being considered by the Home Paint Company may prove helpful to the reader. The initial investment outlay from replacing a blending machine with a new model was found to be $7,340 in Table 5-1. Assume now that the new blender is considerably more efficient than the existing blender, so that the company will be able to increase output and also reduce costs if the replacement is carried out. The existing blender has ten years of useful life remaining, and it is being depreciated on a straight-line basis to a salvage value of 0. The new blender is expected to have a useful life of ten years and will be depreciated on a straight-line basis to a salvage value of 0.

Changes in cash flows from sales and costs related to the replacement are estimated as follows:

	1st Year	Last 9 Years
Increase in cash inflows from sales	$1,000	$3,000
Reduction in operating costs	1,000	2,000

Neither the existing blender nor the proposed replacement has an estimated salvage value, and depreciation in both cases is straight-line. Thus, the annual depreciation charge for the existing blender can be calculated by dividing its book value by the estimated number of years left in its useful life: $12,000/10 years = $1,200. The annual depreciation charge for the new blender can be found by dividing its cost by the number of years in its useful life: $20,000/10 years = $2,000. The difference of $800 in the two depreciation figures is the depreciation change to be used in the estimate of the net cash benefits from an investment in the replacement blender. Since depreciation would be larger for the new model, depreciation is positive and therefore would result in a reduction in taxable income.

The estimated net cash benefits applicable to the replacement proposal are determined in Table 5-3. By following the procedure outlined earlier, the net cash benefit is estimated at $1,592 for the first year and $3,572 for each of the remaining nine years.

Different Types of Depreciation.   Straight-line depreciation was used in the examples above. In most cases, however, firms will use some form of rapid depreciation in order to reduce tax payments in the earlier years of the life of a depreciable asset. Net cash benefits will thereby be increased in the earlier years but reduced in the latter years of the asset's life when depreciation charges are reduced. Since money has a time value, the net effect will be to increase the value of the asset to the company, assuming that the same income tax rates apply in all relevant years. If rapid depreciation will be employed, the net cash benefit from an investment will have to be calculated for each individual year. See Appendix 5A for examples of the treatment of depreciation under tax law prevailing in 1989.

TABLE 5-3
CALCULATION OF THE NET CASH BENEFIT PER YEAR FROM
REPLACING A PAINT BLENDER

	1st year	Each of last 9 years
Cash inflows from sales	$1,000	$3,000
Cash expenses	1,000	2,000
Depreciation	(800)	(800)
Income before taxes	$1,200	$4,200
Income taxes at 34 percent	(408)	(1,428)
Income after taxes	$ 792	$2,772
Depreciation	800	800
Net cash benefit	$1,592	$3,572

TABLE 5-4
FUTURE NONOPERATING CASH FLOWS ASSOCIATED WITH
A PROPOSED PLANT EXPANSION

Type of cash flow	End of thirtieth year
Salvage	$30,000
Release of working-capital commitment	40,000
Total	$70,000

TABLE 5-5
SUMMARY OF ALL CASH FLOWS ASSOCIATED WITH A PROPOSED PLANT
EXPANSION BY THE HOME PAINT COMPANY

Type of cash flow	Time 0[a]	Years 1 to 30	End of year 30
Initial investment outlay	($340,000)		
Net cash benefit		$29,460	
Future nonoperating cash flow			$70,000

[a] Time 0 refers to the beginning of the first year, before any time has expired.

TABLE 5-6
SUMMARY OF ALL CASH FLOWS ASSOCIATED WITH A
PROPOSED REPLACEMENT OF A PAINT BLENDER FOR THE
HOME PAINT COMPANY

Type of cash flow[a]	Time 0[b]	Year 1	Years 2 to 10
Initial investment outlay	(7,340)		
Net cash benefit		$1,592	$3,572

[a] Nonoperating cash flows subsequent to the initial investment outlay
are not expected from this investment.
[b] Time 0 refers to the beginning of the first year, before any time has
expired.

Nonoperating Cash Flows Subsequent To The Initial Investment

The third category of cash flows caused by an investment project are those which occur after the initial investment has been made but which are not derived directly from sales, cost of sales, or operating expenses. These nonoperating cash flows may be caused by (1) the necessity of making additional investment outlays subsequent to the initial outlay and/or (2) the return to the company of part of its investment outlay, generally as a result of a salvage value of an asset. For example, the construction of a new office building by a firm may be expected to require an expenditure of funds at the end of twenty years for a major renovation. Also, at the end of the life of an investment project, there may be a cash inflow from one or more sources. A worn-out machine, for instance, may have a salvage value, even after expenditures required for the removal of the machine have been deducted. Further, if an investment requires an initial commitment of funds to increase the firm's investment in current assets, the termination of the project will release this commitment. The release of the working-capital commitment is equivalent to a cash inflow since funds are made available for other uses.

Consider again the plant expansion being considered by the Home Paint Company. Recall that the salvage value of the plant at the end of its useful life was estimated at $30,000. Note also that at the termination of the project, the working-capital commitment of $40,000 will be released because the project will no longer necessitate the addition to inventories.[3]

Table 5-4 summarizes the nonoperating cash flows subsequent to the initial investment outlay required for the plant expansion. These projections complete the tabulation of the project's cash flows.

Summary

We have categorized the estimated cash flows for a proposed investment into three groups: initial investment outlay, net cash benefits, and nonoperating cash flows which occur after the initial outlay has been made. A summary of all of the cash flows applicable to the Home Paint Company's plant expansion and blender replacement are presented in Tables 5-5 and 5-6, respectively. These estimates provide the basic data necessary for the evaluation processes considered in the next section.

EVALUATION OF INVESTMENT PROPOSALS

A wide variety of analytical techniques are currently used by business firms to evaluate investment proposals. Some of these techniques involve time adjustments of cash flows, whereas others ignore the time value of money entirely. This section will describe the more widely used evaluation procedures. The discussion should provide the reader with the ability to assess the relative merits of procedures which may be familiar but which are not covered here.

---

[3] The firm may continue to need the higher level of inventories indefinitely, but this will be caused by investments other than the plant expansion under consideration, because it will have terminated.

Before we proceed with the discussion of techniques used in the evaluation of investment proposals, the definitions of two important terms—**mutually exclusive investments** and **independent investments**—should be given. If the investment proposals being considered are mutually exclusive, then only one will be accepted. Investing in more than one would be redundant and would not result in additional cash benefits to the firm. Independent investments, on the other hand, are not redundant. The net cash benefits from an independent project will in no way affect the cash benefits of other independent proposals.

For an illustration, assume that an oil company owns a corner lot in the suburb of a city. The company is considering several alternative plans for a service station on the site. Only one of the alternatives will be accepted since more than one building on the lot would be impractical. Thus, investment proposals of this type are mutually exclusive.

Assume now that the oil company is considering opening new service stations in several cities. Since the opening of a station in one city will not affect the benefits to be received from opening stations in other cities, the alternatives are independent. Note that the company may also be considering other independent investments at the same time—for example, a cost reducing process in one of its refineries.

Non-Time-Adjusted Approaches

Payback Period.   The first approach to the evaluation of investments that we will consider is concerned with how quickly the firm will get back its initial investment outlay. The length of time required is referred to as the payback period. The procedure for calculating the payback period is very simple: accumulate the net cash benefit for each year until the sum equals the initial investment outlay. If the net cash benefit is the same each year, the calculation can be made quickly by the use of the following simple formula:

$$\text{Payback period} = \frac{\text{Initial investment}}{\text{Net cash benefit per year}} \qquad (5\text{-}1)$$

For an illustration, assume that the initial outlay for a proposal is $10,000 and that the net cash benefit is estimated at $3,000 per year for the ten-year life of the investment. Calculating, we get:

$$\text{Payback period} = \frac{\$10,000}{\$3,000} = 3\frac{1}{3} \text{ years}$$

If the net cash benefit is not constant each year, estimating the payback period will necessitate the cumulative summing procedure referred to above. The computation of a payback period that includes a fraction of a year implies that the project's cash flows are generated at an even rate throughout that year.

Use of the payback-period approach results in investment projects being accepted or rejected on the basis of their estimated speed in returning the initial cash outlay to the firm. If the investment proposals under consideration are mutually exclusive, the alternative with the shortest payback period will be accepted and all others rejected. In the case of independent investments, all proposals may be accepted that return the initial outlay within a maximum period of time designated by management. Consider the following investment alternatives and their expected payback periods:

Proposals	Expected payback period
A	3.0 years
B	3.5 years
C	4.2 years
D	6.1 years

If the investments are mutually exclusive, Proposal A will be accepted and the others rejected. However, if the proposals are independent, the cut-off point in terms of payback period will have to be designated before the accept-or-reject decisions can be made. If the maximum allowed payback period is five years, for example, A, B, and C will be accepted and D rejected.

Limitations of the Payback Period Approach. The payback period is not a measure of profitability, nor is it a valuation technique. The approach has two obvious weaknesses as an indicator of either profitability or valuation. First, cash flows after the payback period are ignored. For example, consider two investments, each costing $10,000. Investment J has expected net cash benefits of $4,000 for each year during its expected life of three years. Investment K, on the other hand, is expected to have net cash benefits of $3,900 for twenty years. Investment K clearly would be the better investment under any reasonable set of circumstances; however, project J has the shorter payback.

The second weakness in the payback approach is that it does not consider the time value of cash flows, even within the payback period. Consider two investments, each with three-year lives and each costing $10,000. The net cash benefits of investment X are expected to be $4,000, $6,000, and $2,000 for the next three years, respectively, while the net cash benefits for investment Y are expected to be $6,000, $4,000, and $2,000 for the same three years. The payback approach cannot be used to choose between X and Y because both have a payback period of two years. Although the total cash benefits for the two investments are the same, Y is clearly the better alternative. Money has a time value, and the sequence of Y's cash benefits in the first two years is $6,000 and $4,000, whereas the sequence for project X is just the reverse.

Uses by Firms. The payback-period approach appears to be widely used by business firms in making investment decisions. When a decision is based primarily on the payback period, the firm is more concerned with the liquidity of the investment proposal than with its profitability. For example, a firm may be anticipating the need for cash for some purpose in the near future, and this anticipated need may be considered more important than the profitability of immediate investments. The payback approach may be valid in this case if capital costs are expected to rise in the future. However, if the firm is expected to be able to obtain new capital in the future at costs no higher than they are today, the concern for liquidity can be abandoned, since the requisite cash can be raised later by borrowing or issuing equity instruments. This means that the analysis of current investment opportunities should focus on the market value they can create for the firm rather than on their liquidity.

The payback approach is frequently used when the risks associated with investment proposals are high. The longer the time required to return the initial investment, the greater will be the project risk in many cases.[4] This is particularly true if the firm is operating in an industry in which the rate of technological change is high. Thus, management may believe it necessary to hold risks down by selecting investments on the basis of short paybacks. However, making an investment decision based on the payback period alone is inadequate even in this case, since an investment proposal should normally not be approved unless the project is expected to create value for the firm. The payback-period approach is not concerned with value. Recognizing this defect, decision makers sometimes use the payback criterion in conjunction with one of the other techniques described later in the chapter which measure the value that new investments under consideration are expected to generate for the firm. As will be seen, however, the latter techniques alone can take into account the riskiness of investments.

Despite its theoretical weaknesses in investment analysis, the payback-period approach continues to be used by business managers. Its popularity as an analytical technique seems to have declined somewhat in recent years as time-adjusted approaches have become more widely accepted. Before we proceed to a discussion of these latter techniques, however, another non-time-adjusted technique—the average rate of return on investment—will be considered briefly because it, too, is still used by some firms.

Average Rate of Return on Investment. There are several methods of calculating the **average rate of return (AR)** on an investment. One of the most common formulas is as follows:

$$AR = \frac{\text{Average net income}}{\text{Average investment}} \qquad (5\text{-}2)$$

The average investment in the above ratio, is the average net book value of the asset over its life. Net book value is the gross book value less accumulated depreciation.

The numerator of the ratio above is a number determined by accountants rather than a cash flow. Accountants calculate net income by subtracting various expenses from sales. Several of the expense items subtracted do not involve cash flows caused by the investment, for example, depreciation and allocated overhead expenses.

Weaknesses in the AR Method. There are several major weaknesses in the use of the preceding form of the average rate of return in ranking investment proposals. One weakness is the use of net income rather than net cash benefit in the numerator. The real economic benefits of an investment are derived from the effect on the company's cash flows. Net income is a useful accounting figure, but it is directly affected by

---

[4] Risk is usually defined as the variability of returns, which will be considered in Chapter 6. The payback period is clearly not a measure of risk in this sense. Nevertheless, managers of firms often consider the payback period in assessing the risk of a project.

depreciation, which is an allocation over time of the original cost of an asset. Thus, depreciation itself is not a cash-flow item. (Of course, depreciation does affect the company's tax payments, which are cash flows.)

A second weakness in the average rate of return measure is the averaging process used to determine the net income figure in the numerator and the average investment figure in the denominator. The use of an average ignores the time value of money. For example, consider two projects, each requiring an average investment as defined above of $5,000. Project A's expected net income in consecutive years is $400, $600, and $800; and Project B's expected net income in the same sequence of years is $800, $600, and $400. Since the average net income for both projects is $600, the average rate of return for both would be the same: $600/$5,000 = 12 percent. The average-rate-of-return method would rank the two projects equally. Clearly, however, project B would be preferred by management if everything else is the same, because a net income of $800 in the first year and $400 in the third is better than the reverse sequence. An additional distorting factor in this example is that the $5,000 figure for the average investment ignores the timing of the cash outlays required to make the investment.

The example above was a very simple one in which the superiority of Project B is obvious. In more complex cases where the lives of projects are long and net income is highly variable over time, the superiority of one project over another may not be clear without the use of an evaluative tool. The example shows that the average rate of return should not be the tool used when returns are variable over time.

Using average net income in calculating the average rate of return is questionable for another reason. The averaging process ignores the length of the life of the alternatives being evaluated. To illustrate, consider the following projects. One project is expected to have a net income of $1,000 a year for five years, and the other project $1,000 a year for ten years. If the initial investment is the same for both projects, the expected average rate of return will be the same, and no distinction would be made between the two projects by the average-rate-of-return approach. But if everything else is the same, the longer-life project would clearly be the better investment.

As indicated before, there are several methods of calculating the average rate of return on an investment. All of these versions, however, suffer from one or more of the major weaknesses just described.

Conclusions Concerning Non-Time-Adjusted Approaches. Let us generalize our findings to this point. A method of evaluating investment proposals whose benefits can be quantified should satisfy the following requirements:

1 Only those cash flows resulting directly from an investment should be included in its evaluation. Although important for other purposes, the net income figure *per se* should not be included in the evaluation process, because the net income for any given year is affected by cost allocations that may not represent economic flows in that year.

2 The evaluation process should take into consideration the time pattern of cash flows during the life of the project. Since money has a time value, an early cash flow is more valuable than a later cash flow of the same magnitude.

3 The life of an investment project should affect its evaluation. This point is actually part of the preceding one, but it is stated separately here for emphasis.

The payback-period and the average-rate-of-return techniques do not meet the preceding requirements. The reader is encouraged to consider these requirements in relation to non-time-adjusted approaches which may be familiar but which have not been discussed. The objective should be to find a weakness in each procedure—that is, a situation in which the procedure would not rank investments correctly.

Time-Adjusted Approaches

As noted previously, the use of evaluative techniques which take into consideration the timing of cash flows has increased in recent years. Three such techniques will be discussed below: (1) net present value, (2) internal rate of return, and (3) profitability index.

Net Present Value. The **net present value (NPV)** of an investment is the increase in the total value of the firm's common stock that is expected to result from the investment. NPV is determined by subtracting the initial investment outlay from the present value of expected future cash flows. The calculation process requires time adjusting (i.e., discounting) expected cash flows at the rate of return required by management on the new investment. The discount rate should take into account the risk of the project, as will be discussed in Chapters 6 and 7.

The mathematical formula for the calculation of the NPV of an investment is expressed as follows:

$$NPV = \sum_{t=1}^{n} \frac{NCB_t}{(1+k)^t} + \sum_{t=1}^{n} \frac{NOF_t}{(1+k)^t} - I_0 \qquad (5\text{-}3)$$

where NPV is the net present value of the project, n is the last year in which there is a cash flow expected from the project, NCB_t is the expected net cash benefit in year t, NOF_t is the nonoperating cash flow in year t, k is the required rate of return, and I_0 is the initial investment outlay. The formula says that the NPV is the sum of the present values of all net cash benefits plus the sum of the present values of all nonoperating cash flows expected to occur in the future, minus the initial investment outlay. Note that the three elements on the right-hand side of the equality sign in the formula include the three types of cash flows from an investment which were described earlier in the chapter. If any future net cash flows are outflows, their present values will be negative, and the NPV will thereby be reduced. The present value of all expected flows is obtained by discounting at the firm's required rate of return on the project.

Computers and finance calculators can be used to solve for the present value of an investment as well as other time-adjusted statistics that we will be concerned with in this book. Computer spreadsheet programs are particularly useful in solving complex investment problems. The analyst may be required to input (punch in) only the data used in the calculations, and the computer or calculator will then do all of the work. However, finance students and professionals should understand how the calculations are made. For this reason, we will describe the calculation processes in detail in this chapter.

When the NPV method of making capital budgeting decisions is used, the decision rule for independent investments is to accept all proposals whose expected NPV is positive and reject all others. In the case of mutually exclusive proposals, the rule is to accept the single proposal with the largest, positive NPV and reject all others.

Illustration.   For the purpose of illustrating the NPV method, assume that an industrial construction company is considering the purchase of a large backhoe with a complete set of attachments. The project requires an outlay of $250,000, and expected cash benefits are $50,000 a year for ten years. The required rate of return is set at 12 percent by management. Cash flows applicable to the investment are shown in column 2 of Table 5-7. To find the NPV of the investment, the $250,000 cash outlay required immediately must be subtracted from the present value of future net cash benefits; in this example, the project will not incur any nonoperating cash flows after the initial investment. The present value interest factor (PVIF) for each year is presented in column 3, and the products from multiplying the PVIFs by the cash flows in column 2 are given in column 4. Note that the PVIF of 1.000 is applicable to the $250,000 investment since the outlay is made immediately—that is, at time 0. Thus, the present value of the initial investment outlay is ($250,000). The sum of $32,510 shown at the bottom of column 4 is the expected NPV of the project.

Since the expected net cash benefit from the investment is constant each year, the NPV calculation can be greatly simplified by solving for the present value of the annuity cash inflows and then subtracting the initial investment outlay. Finance calculators make the process very easy. An annuity table can also be used to make the calculations. Checking Appendix A-2 at the end of the book, we see that the

TABLE 5-7
CALCULATION OF THE ESTIMATED NET PRESENT VALUE OF A PROPOSED NEW INVESTMENT IN A BACKHOE

1 Year	2 Cash flow	3 Present value factor—12%	4 Present value of cash flows
0	($250,000)	1.0000	($250,000)
1	50,000	0.8929	44,645
2	50,000	0.7972	39,860
3	50,000	0.7118	35,590
4	50,000	0.6355	31,775
5	50,000	0.5674	28,370
6	50,000	0.5066	25,330
7	50,000	0.4523	22,615
8	50,000	0.4039	20,195
9	50,000	0.3606	18,030
10	50,000	0.3220	16,100
			$32,510

present value annuity factor (PVAF) for 10 years at 12 percent is 5.6502. Multiplying the factor by the net cash benefit of $50,000 per year, we get $282,510. Subtracting the $250,000 cost of the investment from the latter figure, the expected NPV of the investment is found to be $32,510, the same result as obtained in Table 5-7. The result indicates that after due consideration of all expected cash inflows and outflows, the backhoe would add about $32,510 to the value of the firm. Thus, the investment proposal should be accepted unless a mutually exclusive proposal with an estimated NPV greater than $32,510 is available.

   A More Complicated Situation. If the cash flows of an investment are not constant over time, the determination of NPV may require year-by-year calculations of present value, as was done in Table 5-7. In some cases, a portion of the cash flows from an investment will form an annuity beginning in some future period. The procedure for solving this type of problem was presented in Chapter 4. The solution can be obtained much more quickly, however, by the use of an advanced calculator.

   For a further illustration, consider the investment problem posed earlier in this chapter, where estimates of the initial investment outlay and net cash benefits from a replacement of a paint blender by the Home Paint Company were discussed. Table 5-6 indicates that the investment outlay was estimated at $7,340, and the net cash benefits at $1,592 for the first year and $3,572 for each of the following nine years. (The project was not expected to have any nonoperating cash flows after the initial investment.) Assuming a required rate of return of 10 percent, the NPV of the project can be calculated as follows:

$$\text{NPV} = \frac{\$1,592}{(1.1)^1} + \frac{1}{(1.1)^1} \sum_{t=1}^{9} \frac{\$3,572}{(1.1)^t} - \$7,340 \qquad (5\text{-}4)$$

   The second element on the right hand side of equation (5-4) is the present value at time 0 of the $3,572 annual cash flows which begin in year 2 and continue through year 10. The expression

$$\sum_{t=1}^{9} \frac{\$3,572}{(1.1)^t}$$

is the value of the nine-year annuity as of the end of year 1. This value is then discounted back to time 0 by multiplying by $1/(1.1)^1$. Calculating the *NPV* by the use of present value factors we get:

$$\begin{aligned}
\text{NPV} &= \$1,592(\text{PVIF}_{1,10\%}) + \$3,572(\text{PVAF}_{9,10\%})(\text{PVIF}_{1,10\%}) - \$7,340 \quad (5\text{-}4a) \\
&= \$1,592(0.9091) + \$3,572(5.759)(0.9091) - \$7,340 \\
&= \$12,809
\end{aligned}$$

   The result indicates that the replacement project would increase the value of the firm by $12,809. Thus, the investment decision should be to accept the project unless there is a mutually exclusive investment available with an estimated NPV greater than $12,809.

The Plant Expansion by Home Paint.   We will complete the discussion of the NPV method by determining whether the Home Paint Company should accept the proposal for the plant expansion discussed earlier in the chapter. The cash flows associated with the investment are summarized in Table 5-5, and we will assume that the company's required rate of return on the project is 12 percent.[5] The formula for the NPV is given in equation (5-3). However, since the only nonoperating cash flows are the $30,000 salvage value of the plant and the release of the $40,000 working capital commitment, equation (5-3) can be simplified to form the following equation:

$$\text{NPV} = \sum_{t=1}^{30} \frac{\$29,460}{(1.12)^t} + \frac{\$70,000}{(1.12)^{30}} - \$340,000$$

Solving by the use of present value factors, we get:

$$\begin{aligned}\text{NPV} &= \$29,460(\text{PVAF}_{30,12\%}) + \$70,000(\text{PVIF}_{30,12\%}) - \$340,000\\ &= \$29,460(8.0552) + \$70,000(0.0334) - \$340,000\\ &= -\$100,356\end{aligned}$$

The negative NPV indicates that management should reject the proposal. Its acceptance would decrease the value of the firm by an estimated $100,356.

Internal Rate of Return.   Calculation of the **internal rate of return (IRR)** is another important approach to the evaluation of investment proposals. This approach also takes into account the time value of money, but the result is a percentage figure rather than a dollar value such as NPV. The calculation of a time-adjusted rate of return was explained in Chapter 4, particularly in Table 4-2 and the related discussion. From the mathematical standpoint, calculation of the IRR of an investment proposal involves exactly the same steps. The objective is to find a discount rate which equates the present value of all future cash flows from the investment with the initial cash outlay. We have categorized the future cash flows into two types: (1) net cash benefits and (2) nonoperating cash flows. Using this categorization, the basic equation for the calculation of the IRR is:

$$I_0 = \sum_{t=1}^{n} \frac{\text{NCB}_t}{(1 + \text{IRR})^t} + \sum_{t=1}^{n} \frac{\text{NOF}_t}{(1 + \text{IRR})^t} \qquad (5\text{-}5)$$

where I_0 is the initial investment, NCB_t is the net cash benefit in period t, and NOF_t is the nonoperating cash flow in period t.

[5]Companies frequently set a higher required rate of return on more risky investment proposals, as will be explained in Chapters 6 and 7. The plant expansion will probably be more risky for Home Paint than the proposal for the replacement of the paint blender.

Def → When the present value of future cash flows equals the initial investment, the NPV will be 0. Thus, the IRR is the discount rate that will result in a NPV calculation of 0 for the investment. This can be expressed by a simple rearrangement of Equation (5-5):

$$NPV = \sum_{t=1}^{n} \frac{NCB_t + NOF_t}{(1 + IRR)^t} - I_0 = 0 \qquad (5\text{-}5a)$$

The *IRR* has to be the same figure in both Equations (5-15) and 5-15a). In the latter equation, the *NCB* and *NOF* are summed for each year. This procedure is necessary when a calculator or computer program is used to solve for the IRR.

Illustration. Consider the investment proposal referred to earlier in which the initial cash outlay for a backhoe was $250,000, and the net cash benefits were estimated at $50,000 a year for ten years. (No nonoperating cash flows after the initial investment were expected for this project.) Calculations using IRR estimates of 14 percent and 16 percent are shown in Table 5-8. Recall that the objective is to find a discount rate which will result in a net present value calculation of 0. Since discount rates of 14 percent and 16 percent result in net present value figures of $10,810 and −$8,335, the IRR appears to be about 15 percent. We could continue to narrow our estimates until a net present value of 0 is found. However, we will not continue to search in the manner described above, since our objective has been merely to show the mathematical process required to find IRR. It is much more efficient to let a computer or calculator do the work for you. If you do, you will find that the IRR for the backhoe project is 15.1 percent.

The Decision Rules. The two rules for making investment decisions by the use of the IRR are (1) to accept all independent investments with an estimated internal

TABLE 5-8
CALCULATION OF THE INTERNAL RATE OF RETURN ON A PROPOSED INVESTMENT IN A BACKHOE

1	2	3	4	5	6
Year	Cash flows	PVIF—14%	Present value of cash flows at 14%	PVIF—16%	Present value of cash flows at 16%
0	($250,000)	1.0000	($250,000)	1.0000	($250,000)
1	50,000	0.8772	43,860	0.8621	43,105
2	50,000	0.7695	38,475	0.7432	37,160
3	50,000	0.6750	33,750	0.6407	32,035
4	50,000	0.5921	29,605	0.5523	27,165
5	50,000	0.5194	25,970	0.4761	23,805
6	50,000	0.4556	22,780	0.4104	20,520
7	50,000	0.3996	19,980	0.3538	17,690
8	50,000	0.3506	17,530	0.3050	15,250
9	50,000	0.3075	15,375	0.2630	13,150
10	50,000	0.2697	13,485	0.2267	11,335
Net present value			$ 10,810		($ 8,335)

rate of return greater than the required rate of return, and (2) if the project proposals being evaluated are mutually exclusive, to accept the proposal with the highest IRR if it is greater than the required rate of return. In this context, assume that the required rate of return for a firm is 10 percent, and investment projects with expected IRRs of 20, 18, 14, and 8 percent have been proposed. If the projects are independent, all would be accepted except the one with the 8 percent expected return, which does not meet the 10 percent minimum acceptance standard. On the other hand, if the projects are mutually exclusive, only the 20 percent proposal would be accepted.

The IRR for the backhoe proposal discussed earlier was found to be 15.1 percent, and the required rate of return was 12 percent. If the construction company needs only one backhoe, the proposal is mutually exclusive. It would be accepted unless another available backhoe requiring the same investment outlay has a higher IRR. If the two alternatives require different investment outlays, a size problem arises, which will be discussed later.

Profitability Index.   Another time-adjusted approach to evaluating investment proposals is provided by the **profitability index (PI)**, sometimes referred to as the **benefit-cost ratio**. Several versions of the PI have been advanced, although the following is probably the most widely used:

$$PI = \frac{\text{Present value of all future cash flows}}{\text{Initial investment outlay}} \qquad (5\text{-}6)$$

$$= \frac{\sum_{t=1}^{n} \text{NCB}_t/(1 + k)^t + \sum_{t=1}^{n} \text{NOF}_t/(1 + k)^t}{I_0} \qquad (5\text{-}6a)$$

where all symbols have the same meaning as before. The numerator of the formula solves for the present value of all future cash flows from the investment, including net cash benefits and nonoperating cash flows. Future flows are time-adjusted, summed, and then divided by the initial investment outlay to determine the PI. The decision rules for use of the PI are: (1) accept all independent proposals with an index value greater than 1, and (2) accept the single mutually exclusive proposal with the highest index value greater than 1. If a proposed investment in either category does not meet the indicated acceptance criterion, it should be rejected.

Assuming a 12 percent return, the PI for the backhoe proposal is:

$$PI = \frac{\sum_{t=1}^{10} \$50,000/(1.12)^t}{\$250,000}$$

$$= \frac{\$282,511}{\$250,000}$$

$$= 1.13$$

The project should be accepted unless another backhoe requiring the same investment, but with a higher PI is available. If two backhoes requiring different investment outlays are available, we again run into a size problem. As indicated previously, size problems are considered later.

Each of the three time-adjusted approaches we have discussed considers only cash flows in the evaluation process, and each of the approaches takes into account the time pattern of the cash flows and the length of life of each project. Will the three approaches always provide the same answer for the analyst? The answer to this question is discussed in the following section.

Comparison of the Time-Adjusted Approaches.   Except under special circumstances which will be described later, the three time-adjusted approaches we have examined will provide the same indication as to whether an investment considered by itself should be accepted or rejected. The accept-or-reject rules are summarized in the following table:

	Accept	Reject
NPV	>0	<0
IRR	$>k$	$<k$
PI	>1	<1

where k is the required rate of return, the symbol $>$ means "greater than," and the symbol $<$ means "less than." Note that the table does not refer to the possibilities that NPV $= 0$, IRR $= k$, and PI $= 1$. If these possibilities occur, the worth of the investment project to the firm would be neither positive nor negative, and management would be indifferent to the project from a purely quantitative standpoint.

The consistency of the NPV, IRR, and PI as indicators of whether independent investment proposals should be accepted or rejected is the result of the following factors:

1 If the NPV is positive, the IRR will always be greater than k, and the PI will always be greater than 1.
2 If the NPV is negative, the IRR will always be less than k, and the PI will always be less than 1.
3 If the NPV is equal to 0, the IRR will always be equal to k, and the PI will always be exactly 1.

An investment proposal for which 1 above applies should be accepted if it is the only project being considered or if it is being considered along with other independent projects. Under these circumstances, an analyst could use either the NPV, the IRR, or the PI in making the investment decision since the three approaches will provide the same accept-or-reject signal. However, a problem can arise in the ranking of mutually exclusive proposals. The three time-adjusted approaches can result in different rankings of mutually exclusive proposals under the following situations:

1 The sizes of the investment projects differ.
2 The time patterns of the net cash benefits of the projects differ. For example, one project might have large cash flows early in its life and smaller cash flows later, while the reverse is true for another project.

3 After a positive net cash benefit in at least one year, the net cash flows of a project are expected to be negative in one or more years.

We will consider below the reasons why each of these conditions may lead to different rankings by the three time-adjusted approaches.

Size Differences in Investment Projects.   Consider the two investment proposals whose expected cash flows are shown in Table 5-9. The required rate of return is assumed to be 12 percent for both projects.

If the two projects are independent, both would be accepted because the NPV is positive, the IRR is greater than the required rate of return of 12 percent, and the PI is greater than 1 for both projects. However, what if the two projects are mutually exclusive, and thus, only one is to be accepted? The capital budgeting approaches give different signals as to which project is better; project A has the higher IRR and PI, but project B has the higher NPV. Which approach should be used in this case and why? In general the net present value method should be used when the investment proposals being considered are mutually exclusive. The reason is that NPV is the total dollar value of a project to the firm. Both the IRR and the PI ignore the effect of the size of the investment. Even though the IRR and PI of project B are less per dollar invested than for project A, the fact that B involves an investment of many more dollars results in more total value for the firm and, therefore, for the common stock.

Differences in Time Patterns of Cash Flows.   A second factor that can result in different rankings by the three capital budgeting approaches is a difference in cash-flow patterns for the investment projects being evaluated. As an example, consider the data applicable to the two projects shown in Table 5-10. The required rate of return is assumed to be 10 percent for both projects, and both involve initial investment outlays of $10,000. Project C's net cash benefits start relatively low and increase for three years, whereas D's remain constant throughout its five-year life. The figures at the bottom of the table show that project C has the higher NPV and profitability index, but the lower IRR. Once again the three approaches give different rankings of investments, which will lead to different decisions if the two investments are mutually exclusive.

What has caused the difference in ranking in this case?   The answer lies in the fact that the most distant (farther in the future) cash flows have a relatively greater impact on the present value of a cash-flow stream, the lower the discount

TABLE 5-9
NET PRESENT VALUES, INTERNAL RATES OF RETURN AND PROFITABILITY
INDEXES OF TWO INVESTMENT PROJECTS OF DIFFERENT SIZES

1 Project	2 Initial outlay	3 Cash flows years 1–10	4 NPV at 12%	5 IRR	6 PI
A	$100,000	$20,000	$13,004	15.1%	1.13
B	140,000	27,500	15,381	14.6	1.11

TABLE 5-10
EFFECT OF THE TIME PATTERN
OF CASH FLOWS

Year	Project C	Project D
0	($10,000)	($10,000)
1	1,000	3,300
2	2,000	3,300
3	5,000	3,300
4	5,000	3,300
5	5,000	3,300
NPV at 10%	$2,838	$2,510
IRR	18.3%	19.4%
PI	1.28	1.25

rate used in making the time adjustments. The discount rate that should be used is the rate of return expected from reinvesting the future flows of the investment. This rate is often referred to as the reinvestment rate. The net present value and profitability indexes approaches are based on the assumption that the reinvestment rate is equal to the required rate of return. On the other hand, the internal rate of return method assumes that the reinvestment rate is equal to the IRR itself. Thus, since the 10 percent required rate of return is relatively low compared to the internal rates of return of the two projects, the larger cash flows of project C in years 3 through 5 have a greater impact on the net present value and profitability index rankings than on the internal rate of return ranking. The impact in this case is sufficient to cause a difference in the rankings of the two projects.

Figure 5-1 illustrates the point further. The net present values of projects C and D are plotted on the graph for discount rates between 10 and 20 percent. Note that if the

FIGURE 5-1
Effect of the Discount Rate on Net Present Value.

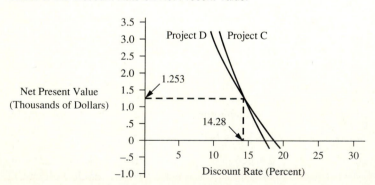

discount rate is 14.28 percent, the net present value of both projects if $1,253. The net present value of project C is greater than the net present value of project D for discount rates less than 14.28 percent. For discount rates higher than 14.28 percent, the net present value of project D is larger. Thus, C has a greater net present value than D if the required rate of return for the two projects is 10 percent.

As we have seen, the internal rate of return of a project is the discount rate that makes the net present value of all cash flows equal to zero. The internal rates of return of projects C and D are depicted in Figure 5-1 at the points where the two curves shown intersect the horizontal axis. The two points are at 18.3 percent and 19.4 percent for C and D, respectively.

The discussion above has shown that differences in the time patterns of cash flows of investment projects can result in different rankings by the net present value, internal rate of return, and profitability index methods of making capital budgeting decisions. Which of the three methods provide the correct ranking? The choice between the net present value or the profitability index approaches and the internal rate of return approach depends on which discount rate—the required rate of return or the internal rate of return—is most appropriate. This will depend on the expected rate of return earned from reinvesting the future cash flows from the investment. Recall that the IRR method is based on the assumption that the cash flows will be reinvested at a rate equal to the IRR. On the other hand, the NPV method assumes that the reinvestment rate will be the required rate of return on the project. Most analysts believe that the assumption of the NPV method is better in most cases, because competition will force the reinvestment rate down to the required rate. For this reason, the ranking indicated by the net present value and profitability index methods should be considered better than the ranking indicated by the internal rate of return method. Recall, however, that only the net present value method accounts for size differences in investments.

Multiple Rates of Return.   Under certain conditions, the internal rate of return method is not appropriate even when all of the investment proposals are independent, or if only one proposal is being considered. These conditions are the special circumstances alluded to at the beginning of our comparisons of the three time-adjusted methods. Such a condition can occur when the mathematical signs applicable to the net cash flows of a project are reversed more than once. Most investment projects involve a cash outflow at the time of the initial outlay, followed by net cash inflows in all future years of the life of the project. The sign applicable to all of the cash flows is reversed only once; it is negative for the initial investment and positive for all subsequent cash flows. However, a project can have more than one sign reversal. For example, the initial investment outlay may be followed by positive cash flows in one or more periods, which in turn are followed by negative cash flows in one or more periods. This type of situation can cause a single project to have more than one IRR.

To illustrate, assume that a lumber company has the opportunity to purchase the timber on a tract of land for $10,000. Management estimates that the timber can be cut, sawed to its specifications, and sold in one year with a net cash benefit for the year of $30,000. However, the present owner of the timber tract will require the company to clean up the land and set out new seedlings after the timber has been harvested. Management of the lumber company estimates that this could be done in the second year at a net cost of $22,000. The cash flows from the investment can be summarized as follows:

Year	Cash Flow
0	($10,000)
1	30,000
2	($22,000)

Two discount rates make the net present value of this project zero: 27.64 percent and 72.36 percent. The project thus has two internal rates of return. Since both are correct from a mathematical standpoint, the internal rate of return should not be used to make the investment decision in this case.

The usefulness of the net present value approach is not affected by the sign problem. Assume that management sets a required rate of return of 12 percent on the investment proposal. Using PVIFs for 12 percent:

$$\text{NPV} = -\$10,000 + (0.8929)\$30,000 + (0.7972)\$22,000 = -\$753$$

Thus, the project would reduce the value of the company in spite of the fact that both of the IRRs are far above the required rate of return. Clearly, the investment proposal should be rejected.

Three sign reversals in the net cash flows of a project can result in three calculated IRRs. More reversals can result in even more IRRs. The conclusion is clear: the IRR method should not be used when more than one sign reversal is expected to occur in the cash flow stream of a proposed investment.

Final Assessment. Our comparison of the three time-adjusted methods of making capital budgeting decisions has shown that, under certain conditions, the IRR and PI methods will not rank investment proposals in a manner which is consistent with the objective of maximizing the share price of common stock. Ranking proposals is important when they are mutually exclusive, because only the highest-ranked proposal will be accepted, assuming it meets the minimum accept-reject standard. In particular, the IRR method can break down in this regard when proposed projects differ as to the amount of investment outlay required and when the time patterns of the cash flows of the project differ. In addition, multiple rates of return can be obtained from projects whose cash flows have more than one sign reversal. The profitability index method can also cause erroneous ranking when project sizes differ.

Our decision is that only the net present value method should be used in making decisions concerning mutually exclusive investments. Any of the three methods can normally be used when the proposals under consideration are independent; the one exception is that the IRR should be avoided any time a project is expected to have more than one sign reversal in its cash flow stream. Because of the superiority of NPV, our subsequent discussions of investment analysis and decisions will utilize that method primarily.

The Problem of Unequal Lives of Investments. So far, we have considered investment decisions involving only choices among projects with the same length of life. But project lives may differ. Will this affect our decision? The answer is that it should not if the proposals are independent, since any investment with a positive NPV will increase the price of the firm's common stock regardless of the decisions concerning the other proposals. However, a problem arises if the investment proposals being considered are mutually exclusive.

Assume that the management of a company has decided to purchase a new copier for its purchasing department. The alternatives have been narrowed down to two models, model X costing $15,000 and model Y costing only $8,000. The net cash benefits from X are estimated at $5,000 a year for five years, whereas the benefits from Y are estimated at $4,500 a year for three years. Management has decided not to count on any salvage value for either model, because of the high obsolescence rate for such equipment. The required rate of return for a new copier has been set at 10 percent. Which model should be purchased?

The NPVs for the two copiers are:

$$\text{For model X:} \quad \text{NPV} = \sum_{t=1}^{5} \frac{\$5,000}{(1.10)^t} - \$15,000$$

$$= \$3,954$$

$$\text{For model Y:} \quad \text{NPV} = \sum_{t=1}^{3} \frac{\$4,500}{(1.10)^t} - \$8,000$$

$$= \$3,191$$

Model X has a greater NPV and might appear to be the better buy. It would be, if management does not intend to replace the equipment when it expires. But if this is not the case, the difference in the expected lives of the two copiers should be considered. Model Y would have to be replaced before model X. Assume that projections indicate that another copier, Model Z, could be purchased at the end of three years. Model Z is expected to cost only $4,000 and to result in a net cash benefit of $3,000 a year for two years. If the firm first purchases model Y and then replaces with model Z at the end of three years, the cash flows will be:

Year:	0	1	2	3	4	5
Cash flows:	($8,000)	$4,500	$4,500	$500	$3,000	$3,000

The $500 cash flow in Year 3 is the net of the $4,500 cash inflow from model Y and the 4,000 cash outflow required to purchase model Z. The reader can verify that if the required rate of return remains 10 percent the NPV of purchasing Y and replacing with Z at the end of three years is $4,097. Clearly, the decision in this case should be to purchase model Y now, with the expectation of replacing with Z in three years. This is a different conclusion from that suggested by simply comparing the NPVs of X and Y.

The above example was simplified in that the models Y and Z combination has the same total life expectancy as model X. If X had an expected life of only four years, the correct decision would still not be clear, since its replacement at that time might result in a very large net cash benefit in year 5. We would have to estimate the cash-flow streams for all investment alternatives, including replacements, which ultimately end at a common point in time. At that point, we will have to make the same decision about a new copier, regardless of which investment alternative we choose now.

Cash Flow Equivalents.   The major problem in evaluating investments with unequal lives is estimating the cash flows from future investments required to equalize the length of the cash streams of the alternatives being considered. If no information to the contrary is available, often the most logical approach is to assume that any investment made currently will be replaced when it expires with a like investment, and that this second investment, in turn, will be replaced when it expires with another like investment, and so on indefinitely. As an illustration, consider again the copier investment problem discussed above, but now assume that information concerning model Z is not available. Applying the concept of replacing with like investments, a decision to purchase model X now will result in a series of model X purchases every five years, with an expected net cash benefit of $5,000 per year. We can solve for the constant cash-flow equivalent (CFE) for each five-year period with the following formula:

$$\text{CFE} = \frac{\text{NPV}}{\text{PVAF}_{n,k}} \tag{5-7}$$

where NPV is the net present value of the asset, and $\text{PVAF}_{n,k}$ is the present value annuity factor. The subscript n is the number of years in the life of the project, and the subscript k is the required rate of return. Inserting the values for each element on the right side of equation (5-7), we get for model X:

$$\text{CFE} = \frac{\$3,954}{3.7908} = \$1,043$$

This result means that the net present value of a series of annual cash inflows of $1,043 for five years is the same as the net present value of an investment of $15,000 with an annual net cash benefit of $5,000 for five years. Thus, replacing model X every five years for any number of five-year periods is equivalent to an annual cash inflow of $1,043 for the same total number of years.

We can likewise solve for the cash-flow equivalent of purchasing model Y now and replacing with a like model every three years:

$$\text{CFE} = \frac{\$3,191}{\text{PVAF}_{3,10\%}}$$
$$= \frac{\$3,191}{2.4868}$$
$$= \$1,283$$

This calculation indicates that replacing model Y every three years for any number of three-year periods has the same net present value as an annual cash inflow of $1,283 for the same total period. We can now compare the CFEs of models X and Y to choose between the two alternative investments. Since a constant cash flow stream of $1,283 is preferable to a constant cash flow stream of $1,043, our final decision would be to purchase the model Y copier.

We have gone through the step-by-step procedure for calculating cash flow equivalents in order to see what calculations are involved. Clearly, the use of a finance calculator would be much more efficient. Simply input the number of periods, the required rate of return, and the net present value as the present value into the calculator and press the payment key. The figure in the display will be the cash flow equivalent for the particular investment.

The procedures described above for deciding between investments that have different life expectancies is based on the rather stringent assumption that once we commit to one investment, the firm will continue to replace with like investments for an indefinite period. While this clearly will not always be the case, it is a logical assumption if better information about future opportunities is not available. However, if better information is available, the procedure discussed earlier should be followed.

Joint Projects. In some cases, an investment proposal may be accepted even though it has a negative net present value. This situation can occur when the investment will be necessary in order to invest in another project, perhaps later, which has a positive net present value. Such projects are joint. For example, the purchase of an expensive tool used only infrequently in a manufacturing process may have a negative NPV in terms of the cash flows directly generated by the use of the tool itself. However, having the tool available may allow the company to engage in certain types of financially-beneficial operations that would not otherwise be feasible. Another example is where a company desires to fill out its product line even though some of the items may not have a positive NPV. The fact that the firm has a complete product line may enhance its business image, resulting in greater sales of many of its products.

In theory, joint projects should not provide an exception to the decision rules that have been discussed. If their combined cash flows can be estimated before any commitment has been made, the projects can be considered as a single investment alternative for decision-making purposes. However, the necessary data may not be available at the time the initial investment has to be made. The decision at that point may thus have to be based on qualitative analysis rather than quantitative analysis.

The Inflation Effect

Price inflation was a major problem in the economies of many nations during most of the decade of the seventies and the first part of the decade of the eighties. The effects of inflation can be highly detrimental for a firm because of rising operating and capital costs. In addition, business and financial risks increase, making financing planning more difficult.

Inflation can cause an error in the estimation of the net present value of an investment if the analyst is not consistent in his or her calculations. Consistency requires that both the required rate of return and estimated cash flows of the investment be stated in either "nominal" terms or "real" terms. If nominal terms are used, the required rate of return will be based on current financing rates, which will include an inflation component determined in the market. The required rate of return in this case is not adjusted by the analyst to eliminate the effect of inflation. Estimates of future cash flows will take into account the effect of inflation on dollar sales and costs, and the estimated flows will also not be adjusted to eliminate the inflation effects. On the other hand, if real terms are used, both the required rate of return and the future cash flows will have to be inflation adjusted; that is, they will have to be reduced to eliminate the effect of inflation.

As an example, assume that a firm is considering the purchase of new equipment which is expected to have the following net cash flows:

Year:	0	1	2	3
Cash flow:	($100,000)	$40,000	$44,000	$48,400

The $100,000 outflow at time zero is the initial outlay. The future cash inflows are net cash benefits from the investment that are estimated to increase annually at a 10 percent rate because of inflation. Management sets a 13 percent required return on the equipment purchase, based on the company's current cost of capital. The net present value of the project is:

$$\text{NPV} = \frac{\$40,000}{(1.13)^1} + \frac{\$44,000}{(1.13)^2} + \frac{\$48,400}{(1.13)^3} - \$100,000$$

$$= \$3,400$$

Adjusting for Inflation.   If real terms are used in the investment analysis, both the required rate of return and the future cash flows will have to be adjusted for inflation. The formula for adjusting the required return is:

$$k^* = \frac{1 + k}{1 + i} - 1 \tag{5-8}$$

where k^* is the required rate of return adjusted for inflation, k is the required rate of return based on current capital costs, and i is the expected rate of inflation.

The process for adjusting expected cash flows for inflation requires the following formula:

$$C_t^* = \frac{C_t}{(1 + i)^t} \tag{5-9}$$

where C_t^* is the expected cash flow in year t, adjusted for inflation, C_t is the expected cash flow in year t, with the effect of inflation included, and i is the expected inflation rate per year.

Making the above adjustments for the equipment purchase described above and then solving for the net present value, we get:

$$\text{Required real rate of return} = (1.13 \div 1.10) - 1 = 0.027273$$
$$= 2.7273 \text{ percent}$$
$$\text{First year cash flow in real terms} = \$40,000 \div (1.10)^1 = \$36,363.64$$
$$\text{Second year cash flow in real terms} = \$44,000 \div (1.10)^2 = \$36,363.64$$
$$\text{Third year cash flow in real terms} = \$48,400 \div (1.10)^3 = \$36,363.64$$

The net present value is:

$$\text{NPV} = \frac{\$36,363.64}{(1.027273)^1} + \frac{\$36,363.64}{(1.027273)^2} + \frac{\$36,363.64}{(1.027273)^3} - \$100,000$$
$$= \$3,400$$

The above calculations show that we can get the same NPV using data that are expressed in nominal terms or that have been adjusted for inflation. Regardless of which type of data is used, however, consistency is necessary; either all or none of the data should be inflation adjusted.

CAPITAL RATIONING

Some firms arbitrarily limit the dollar value of their investments in some manner, a policy referred to as capital rationing. For example, a firm might set its required rate of return at an excessively high level. The most common form of capital rationing, however, is limiting investments to those that can be financed by funds generated internally via retained earnings and depreciation. Obtaining funds from external sources such as bond and stock issues is ruled out. To the extent that opportunities with a positive NPV are rejected by this policy, the firm's growth rate will be reduced, and the market value of its common stock will be lower than it would be otherwise.

It is important to realize that the time-adjusted procedures discussed in this chapter take into account the cost of both internal and external capital required to finance the proposed projects. As noted in the previous paragraph, the arbitrary refusal to use external financing is a poor policy from the economic standpoint. External capital may be inconvenient to obtain, but it should be obtained if needed to finance, or help finance, investments with a positive net present value. The stockholders will benefit because of the higher value of their stock.

Capital-budgeting decisions are made more complicated by capital rationing. For example, assume that a firm has decided to limit its investment for the year to those projects that can be financed with internally generated funds, which are expected to be $100,000. The firm is considering the independent projects presented in Table 5-11.

TABLE 5-11
NET PRESENT VALUE DATA FOR THREE INDEPENDENT
PROJECTS

Project	Initial investment outlay	Present value of net cash benefits	Expected net present value of project
X	$70,000	$110,000	$40,000
Y	40,000	70,000	30,000
Z	60,000	80,000	20,000

If the firm accepts project X, neither Y nor Z can be accepted because only $100,000 is expected to be available for investments. However, both Y and Z can be accepted if X is rejected. The firm should invest in Y and Z because the total expected NPV of the two is $50,000, whereas the expected NPV of X is only $40,000. Project X should be rejected under capital rationing despite the fact that it has the highest NPV as a single project.

The preceding case was very simple. Most firms will usually have more than three opportunities available. Another obvious opportunity would be to invest the funds, or part of them, in ninety-day U.S. Treasury bills. An investment of $70,000 in project X in the previous case and the remaining $30,000 in Treasury bills might result in a greater total NPV than investing in Y and Z together.

The situation would be complicated further if the capital-rationing policy will continue in subsequent years. The availability of funds and expected investment opportunities in the future may affect the alternatives that should be accepted in the current year, because investments made in the current year will affect future cash flows and, therefore, the availability of funds to make investments in the future.

The preceding description indicates that investment decisions under capital rationing may require highly sophisticated analysis. Mathematical programming techniques have been developed to solve many of the investment problems caused by capital rationing. However, a description of these techniques is beyond the scope of this text.

The reader should clearly understand that requiring a high rate of return on a project because of high risk is not capital rationing; higher risk should be compensated by a higher expected return. The problem of how risk should be handled in an investment decision is the subject of the next chapter.

CHAPTER SUMMARY

This chapter is concerned with the basic evaluative techniques and related problems in making investment decisions for a firm. Since most of the techniques discussed make use of cash flows, we first considered the three types of flows caused by an investment: initial cash outlay, net cash benefits, and nonoperating cash flows subsequent to the initial investment.

Methods of evaluating investment projects were classified as either time-adjusted or non-time-adjusted. Time-adjusted methods were shown to be better since they take into account the effect of the timing of the cash flows of a project on the value of the firm. The net present value, internal rate of return, and profitability index methods were shown to result in the same decisions when independent investment proposals are being evaluated. However, the net present value method was shown to provide the best results when investment proposals are mutually exclusive. Several problems in applying the time-adjusted techniques were examined. One major problem—the riskiness of investments—will be considered in the following chapter.

SOLVED PROBLEMS

1 Carswell Motors, Inc. is considering a complete renovation of one of its manufacturing plants at an estimated cost of $3,000,000. The remodeling would not affect the remaining life of the facility, which is estimated at ten years. However, the study has determined that the following effects would be likely to occur:

Additional need for working capital	$200,000
Increase in annual sales	800,000
Decrease in annual cost of goods sold	200,000
Increase in annual fixed overhead	400,000
Increase in salvage value of the plant in ten years	100,000

The remodeling cost, less estimated salvage, would be written off on a straight-line basis over the ten-year remaining life of the plant. The company's tax rate is 34 percent, and management has placed a 10 percent required rate of return on the project.

a Estimate the cash flows from the remodeling.
b Calculate the net present value of the investment.
c What decision should the company make?

Solution

a The investment outlay at time zero is:

Cost of remodeling	$3,000,000
Additional working capital required	200,000
Total investment	$3,200,000

The annual net cost benefit is calculated as follows:

Additional sales	$800,000
Plus decrease in cost of goods sold	200,000
Less increase in fixed overhead	(400,000)
Less additional depreciation:	
($3,000,000 − $100,000)/10	(290,000)
Additional income before tax	$310,000
Less additional income tax @ 34%	(105,400)
Additional income after tax	$204,600
Plus additional depreciation	290,000
Net cash benefit	$494,600

Nonoperating cash flows at the end of ten years:

Release of additional working capital	$200,000
Additional salvage of plant	100,000
Total	$300,000

b The net present value (NPV) equals the present value of the net cash benefits plus the present value of the nonoperating cash flows minus the initial investment outlay:

$$NPV = \sum_{t=1}^{10} \frac{\$494,600}{(1.10)^t} + \frac{\$300,000}{(1.10)^{10}} - \$3,200,000$$

$$= \$494,600(PVAF_{10,10\%}) + \$300,000(PVIF_{10,10\%}) - \$3,200,000$$

$$= \$494,600(6.1446) + \$300,000(0.3855) - \$3,200,000$$

$$= -\$45,231$$

c Since the net present value is negative, the renovation proposal should be rejected.

2 The Applejack Electronics Company is considering two alternative methods of marketing one of the company's calculator lines. Alternative A is expected to involve an initial expenditure of $200,000 and to result in a net cash benefit of $40,000 a year. Alternative B is a more elaborate scheme which is expected to require an initial investment of $500,000 and to result in a net cash benefit of $90,000 a year. Whichever method is accepted will remain in effect for an estimated ten years. The required rate of return on both alternatives is 8 percent.

a Estimate the (1) net present value, (2) internal rate of return, and (3) profitability index of the two alternatives.

b What decision should the company make?

Solution

a The three calculations for each of the two alternatives are as follows:

For A:
$$NPV_A = \sum_{t=1}^{10} \frac{\$40,000}{(1.08)^t} - \$200,000$$

$$= \$40,000(PVAF_{10,8}) - \$200,000$$

$$= \$40,000(6.7101) - \$200,000$$

$$= \$68,404$$

The internal rate of return (IRR) is the discount rate which makes the following equation true:

$$\sum_{t=1}^{10} \frac{\$40,000}{(1 + IRR)^t} = \$200,000$$

The solution value of the IRR can be obtained either by the use of a finance calculator or by trial and error. It will be found to be 15.10 percent.

The profitability index (PI) is calculated by dividing the present value of future cash flows by the initial investment:

$$PI = \frac{\sum_{t=1}^{10}(\$40,000)/(1.08)^t}{\$200,000}$$

$$= \frac{\$268,404}{\$200,000}$$

$$= 1.34$$

For B:
$$NPV_B = \sum_{t=1}^{10} = \frac{\$90,000}{(1.08)^t} - \$500,000$$

$$= \$90,000(PVAF_{10,8}) - \$500,000$$

$$= \$90,000(6.7101) - \$500,000$$

$$= \$103,909$$

The equation for the internal rate of return is:

$$\sum_{t=1}^{10} \frac{\$90,000}{(1 + IRR)^t} = \$500,000$$

Solving by the use of a calculator or by trial and error, the IRR for B will be found to be 12.41 percent.

The profitability index for B is:

$$PI = \frac{\sum_{t=1}^{10}(\$90,000)/(1.08)^t}{\$500,000}$$

$$= \frac{\$603,909}{\$500,000}$$

$$= 1.21$$

b Alternative B has the higher net present value and should be accepted, its lower internal rate of return and profitability index notwithstanding.
3 The Mueller Company services drilling rigs in oil fields. A decision has been made to purchase a pickup truck for runs out to well sites. Two models are currently under study. Data applicable to the two models are as follows:

	Model X	Model Y
Cost	$9,500	$13,000
Annual net cash benefit	$2,100	$2,250
Productive life	8 years	12 years
Salvage value, end of life	$500	$800
Required rate of return	11%	11%

Company policy is to replace a vehicle at the end of its life with a similar model. Which truck should Mueller purchase, if either?

Solution

Since the lives of the two trucks differ, their cash flow equivalents should be calculated. The net present values of the trucks are as follows:

$$NPV_x = \sum_{t=1}^{7} \frac{\$2,100}{(1.11)^t} + \frac{\$2,600}{(1.11)^8} - \$9,500$$

$$= \$1,524$$

$$NPV_y = \sum_{t=1}^{11} \frac{\$2,250}{(1.11)^t} + \frac{\$3,050}{(1.11)^{12}} - \$13,000$$

$$= \$1,836$$

Model Y has the higher net present value, but it has the longer life. The cash flow equivalents (CFEs) are calculated as follows:

$$CFE_x = NPV_x \div (PVAF_{8,11\%})$$
$$= \$1,524 \div 5.1461$$
$$= \$296$$
$$CFE_v = NPV_Y \div (PVAF_{12,11\%})$$
$$= \$1,836 \div 6.4924$$
$$= \$283$$

Since a perpetual cash flow stream of $296 a year is more valuable than a perpetual stream of $283 a year, the model X pickup truck should be purchased.

PROBLEMS

5-1 The items in the following list pertain to a proposed investment by a company in a new plant. Indicate the type of cash flow which each item represents, or will affect, by writing the letter *I* if the item will affect the initial investment outlay, *NOF* if it will affect the nonoperating cash flows subsequent to the initial investment, or *NCB* if it will affect the calculation of the net cash benefits.

Item	Type of cash flow
1 Remodeling expenses expected in the tenth year in the life of a project	_____
2 Additional cash sales by the company	_____
3 Reduction of labor costs	_____
4 Cost of constructing the plant	_____
5 Expenditures required to install new machinery	_____
6 Expected salvage value	_____
7 Annual depreciation expense	_____
8 Commitment of funds to additional inventory at time zero	_____
9 Release of funds committed to additional inventory at the end of the life of the plant	_____
10 Income taxes	_____

5-2 The following list of items pertains to a proposed investment by a department store in the construction of a warehouse:

Cost of land	$ 50,000	Annual cash inflow from additional sales	$75,000
Cost of warehouse	$600,000		
Increase in company's inventories	$ 50,000	Annual reduction in inventory storage costs	$175,000
Increase in accounts receivable	$ 20,000	Annual additions to other costs of operations	$ 20,000
Estimated life of warehouse	30 years	Marginal tax rate	34%
Estimated salvage value of warehouse at the end of 30 years	$ 15,000	Required rate of return	12%
Depreciation method	Straight-line		
Estimated value of the land at the end of 30 years	$ 50,000		

a Determine each of the following items for the proposed investment: (1) initial investment outlay, (2) nonoperating cash flows subsequent to the initial investment, and (3) annual net cash benefit.

b Calculate each of the following: (1) payback period, (2) net present value, (3) internal rate of return, and (4) profitability index.

c Should the department store construct the warehouse? Why or why not?

5-3 Mr. Stanley Pharr, assistant treasurer of the United Appliance Manufacturing Corporation, has been charged with evaluating two proposals for an automatic conveyor to be used in the company's assembly lines. Neither conveyor would affect sales, but both would reduce labor and other costs incurred in handling small appliances. However, the purchase price and operating efficiency of the two alternatives differ considerably. Mr. Pharr has completed the initial phase of his investigation, which included the compilation of the facts and figures necessary to begin his analysis of the two mutually exclusive proposals. The data are as follows:

	Conveyor A	Conveyor B
Purchase price	$12,000	$14,000
Installation cost	$2,000	$2,000
Annual reduction in costs	$3,000	$4,000
Life of conveyor	20 years	20 years
Salvage value minus removal costs	0	0
Depreciation method	SL	SL

The company's marginal tax rate on income is 34 percent. Management normally sets a required rate of return of 11 percent on this type of investment.

a Calculate (1) the net present value, (2) the internal rate of return, and (3) the profitability index of each investment proposal.

b Should either or both proposals be accepted? Why or why not?

5-4 The Jonestown Brick Company is considering the purchase of a small tractor with a forklift for use in loading bricks and concrete blocks. The purchase price would be $8,500. Management expects the tractor to have both a market value and a book value of $2,500 at the end of five years, at which time the company will trade it in for a larger model. Estimated savings in loading costs of bricks and concrete blocks will result in a net cash benefit of $1,000 for the first year; thereafter the net cash benefit should increase $500 annually to $3,000 in the fifth year. Jonestown Brick's required rate of return on this type of investment is 14 percent.

  a Calculate (1) the net present value, (2) the internal rate of return, and (3) the profitability index from investing in the tractor.

  b Should the investment be made? Why or why not?

5-5 The XYZ Company is considering three mutually exclusive investment proposals. Expected net cash flows are as follows:

Year	Project A	Project B	Project C
0	($10,000)	($10,000)	($50,000)
1	6,000	1,000	2,000
2	6,000	9,000	30,000
3	6,000	10,000	50,000

  The required rate of return on all three projects is set at 10 percent.

  a Compute (1) the net present value, (2) the internal rate of return and (3) the profitability index of each project.

  b Explain the reasons for any differences in project rankings by the three capital budgeting techniques.

  c Which proposal(s), if any, should the company accept? Why?

5-6 A & G Metal Fabricating Corporation is considering the replacement of one of its metal-stamping machines. The existing machine, which originally cost $51,000 five years ago, has a book value of $41,000 and an expected remaining life of twenty years. The company could sell the machine immediately for approximately $45,000, but its salvage value at the end of twenty years is estimated at only $1,000.

The new model which is currently available on the market would cost $60,000. It is considerably more powerful than the old machine. If the replacement proposal is accepted, A & G will be able to take on more jobs as well as bid for larger ones, which are often relatively more profitable. Forecasts indicate that the investment would result in increases in annual sales and cash expenses of $100,000 and $90,000, respectively. However, the company would have to increase working capital by $10,000 in order to support the added sales. The new machine would have an estimated useful life of twenty years and a salvage value of $2,000.

The firm uses straight-line depreciation and its marginal tax rate is 34 percent. Mr. Leslie Anderson, the President of A & G, has established a required rate of return of 10 percent for the project.

  a Estimate (1) the initial investment outlay, (2) the nonoperating cash flows subsequent to the initial investment, and (3) the annual net cash benefit of the proposed replacement.

  b Do you agree with the required rate of return of 10 percent set by Mr. Anderson for the project? Explain.

c Should the internal rate of return, the net present value, or the profitability index be used in making the investment decision. Why?

d Do you believe the investment proposal should be accepted? Why or why not?

e Does the information provided for this problem indicate that A & G is in a capital-rationing situation? Explain.

5-7 Lone-Star Feed Lots, Inc., has decided to invest in a mobile feeder to reduce the cost of cattle feeding in its operations. The alternatives have been narrowed down to two models. The following data for the two models have been compiled:

Model	XL 1000	XL 2000
Cost	$21,000	$30,000
Net cash benefit per year	7,000	8,000
Useful life	8 years	10 years
Salvage value (not taxable)	$2,000	$3,000
Required rate of return	14%	14%
Lone-Star's tax rate is 34 percent		

a Estimate the net present value of the two feeders.

b Estimate the cash flow equivalent of the two feeders.

c Under what conditions should the cash flow equivalent be used in making capital budgeting decisions?

d Assuming the conditions you noted in answering question c above apply, which feeder should Lone-Star choose? Explain.

5-8 (This problem is difficult.) Guitteras, Inc., is considering three independent investments, each with an infinite life. Other data for the three projects are as follows:

	A	B	C
Initial outlay	$100,000	$100,000	$100,000
Net cash flow			
Year 1	$20,000	$20,000	$20,000
Annual growth			
Years 2-3	5%	6%	20%
Thereafter	5%	6%	6%
Required return	13%	13%	13%

The above data are based on current dollars; that is, the figures include the impact of expected inflation. Economists have been forecasting an average inflation rate of 5 percent per year over the next decade.

a Calculate the net present value of each project, using current-dollar figures.

b Recast the table at the beginning of the problem using constant-dollar figures; that is, the figures should be deflated to eliminate the impact of expected inflation.

c Calculate the net present value of each project, using the constant-dollar data.

d What do the results of your calculations indicate for calculating the net present value of an investment?

5-9 (This problem can be solved most efficiently by the use of a computer spreadsheet program.) The A. G. Paine Company drills water wells for residences, commercial and industrial firms, farms, and ranches. Management has decided to expand its operations by purchasing a new drilling rig. The alternatives have been narrowed down to models X and Y. The following estimates have been compiled:

	Model X	Model Y
Cost	$200,000	$280,000
Gross revenues in first year of operation	$450,000	$500,000
Variable costs, % of gross revenues	60%	60%
Operating expenses in 1st year	$100,000	$120,000
Depreciation method	SL	SL
Useful life	10 years	10 years
Salvage value in 10 years	$2,000	$5,000
Required return	14%	15%

Paine's marginal tax rate on income is 34 percent. Economists are predicting an inflation rate averaging 4 percent per year over the long run. As a result, management expects gross revenues, variable costs, and operating expenses to grow 4 percent per year in dollar terms.

a Estimate the (1) net present value, (2) internal rate of return, and (3) profitability index of both alternatives.

b Which, if any, of the two alternatives should Paine choose? Explain.

c How would your answer to questions **a** and **b** above be affected if the required rate of return was 14 percent for both models?

d How would your answer to questions **a** and **b** be affected if the required return was 15 percent for both models and gross revenues were only $400,000 for Model X in the first year? Assume gross revenues for Model Y remain $500,000 in the first year.

e Rework question **a**, using constant dollar figures. Compare your results with those obtained in question **a**.

f Do you believe that the assumed effect of inflation on Paine's cash flows is realistic? Explain.

5-10 (This problem can be solved most efficiently by the use of a computer spreadsheet program.)

One analyst has estimated that the sales of the Super G Corporation will grow at the annual rate of 12 percent over the next seven years. The growth rate will then level off to 6 percent indefinitely. Sales were $20.2 million last year. The analyst also compiled the following data for Super G:

Cost of goods sold	65% of sales
Operating expenses	15% of sales
Depreciation	3% of sales
Interest-bearing debt	0
Tax rate on income	34%
Required additional investment to support sales growth	40% of net income

The Consolidated Takeover Company (CTC) is interested in acquiring all of Super G's common stock. The owners of Super G have offered to sell their stock to CTC for $30 million. If the acquisition is completed, CTC does not plan to change Super G's operating and financial policies. A required rate of return of 14 percent is considered appropriate for the investment.

a Calculate the net present value of the acquisition.

b Assume that CTC has been told by another analyst that Super G's stock should be worth approximately $75 million in the market after seven years. Based on this information, calculate (1) the net present value and (2) the internal rate of return on the investment.

c Should CTC accept the offer by Super G's owners? Why or why not?

REFERENCES

Angell, Robert J.: "The Effect of the Tax Reform Act on Capital Investment Decisions," *Financial Management*, vol. 17, Winter 1988, pp. 82–86.

Bierman, Harold, Jr., and Seymour Smidt: *The Capital Budgeting Decision*, 6th ed., New York; Macmillan, 1984.

Brenner, Menachem, and Itzhak Venezia: "The Effects of Inflation and Taxes on Growth Investments and Replacement Policies," *Journal of Finance*, vol. 38, December 1983, pp. 1519–1528.

Brick, Ivan E., and Daniel G. Weaver: "A Comparison of Capital Budgeting Techniques in Identifying Profitable Investments," *Financial Management*, vol. 13, Winter 1984, pp. 29–39.

Cooper, Kerry, and R. Malcolm Richards: "Investing the Alaskan Project Cash Flows: The Sohio Experience," *Financial Management*, vol. 17, Summer 1988, pp. 58–7.

Dorfman, Robert: "The Meaning of Internal Rates of Return," *Journal of Finance*, vol. 36, December 1981, pp. 101–102.

Ezzell, John R., and William A. Kelly, Jr.: "An APV Analysis of Capital Budgeting Under Inflation," *Financial Management*, vol. 13, Autumn 1984, pp. 49–54.

Gordon, M. J., and L. I. Gould: "Comparison of the DCF and HPR Measures of the Yield on Common Shares," *Financial Management*, vol. 13, Winter 1984, pp. 40–47.

Howe, Keith M., and James H. Patterson: "Capital Investment Decisions Under Economies of Scale in Flotation Costs," *Financial Management*, vol. 14, Autumn 1985, pp. 61–69.

Keane, Simon M.: "The Internal Rate of Return and the Reinvestment Fallacy," *Journal of Accounting and Business Studies*, vol. 15, June 1979, pp. 48–55.

Kwan, Clarence C. Y., and Yufei Yuan: "Optimal Sequential Selection in Capital Budgeting: A Shortcut," *Financial Management*, vol. 17, Spring 1988, pp. 54–59.

Logue, Dennis E., and T. Craig Tapley: "Performance Monitoring and the Timing of Cash Flows," *Financial Management*, vol. 14, Autumn 1985, pp. 34–39.

Mehta, Dileep R., Michael D. Curley, and Hung-Gay Fung: "Inflation, Cost of Capital, and Capital Budgeting Procedures," *Financial Management*, vol. 13, Winter 1984, pp. 48–54.

Moore, James S., and Alan K. Reichert: "An Analysis of the Financial Management Techniques Currently Employed by Large U.S. Corporations," *Journal of Business Finance and Accounting*, vol. 10, December 1983, pp. 623–645.

Pinches, George E.: "Myopia, Capital Budgeting and Decision Making," *Financial Management*, vol. 11, Autumn 1982, pp. 6–19.

Pohlman, Randolph A., Emmanuel S. Santiago, and F. Lynn Markel: "Cash Flow Estimation Practices of Large Firms," *Financial Management*, vol. 17, Summer 1988, pp. 71–79.

Quirin, G. David, and John C. Wiginton: *Analyzing Capital Expenditures*, Homewood, Ill.: Richard D. Irwin, 1981.

Rappaport, Alfred, and Robert A. Taggart, Jr.: "Evaluation of Capital Expenditure Proposals Under Inflation," *Financial Management*, vol. 11, Spring 1982, pp. 5–13.

Ross, Marc: "Capital Budgeting Practices of Twelve Large Manufacturers," *Financial Management*, vol. 15, Winter 1986, pp. 15–22.

Sicherman, Neil W., and Richard H. Pettway: "Acquisition of Divested Assets and Shareholders' Wealth," *Journal of Finance*, vol. 42, December 1987, pp. 1261–1273.

Sick, Gordon A.: "A Certainty-Equivalent Approach to Capital Budgeting," *Financial Management*, vol. 15, Winter 1986, pp. 23–32.

Statman, Meir, and David Caldwell: "Applying Behavioral Finance to Capital Budgeting: Project Terminations," *Financial Management*, vol. 16, Winter 1987, pp. 7–15.

Statman, Meir, and Tyzoon T. Tyebjee: "Optimistic Capital Budgeting Forecasts: An Experiment," *Financial Management*, vol. 14, Autumn 1985, pp. 27–33.

APPENDIX 5A
Federal Taxation of Business Income

Rebecca M. Wiseman, CPA
David A. Bowlin, CPA

Income taxes can significantly reduce the net present value of investments. Therefore, the financial decision maker should possess a basic understanding of the calculation of federal income taxes. The state laws pertaining to income taxes will not be discussed in this appendix because of the wide variations in state laws and because not all states have an income tax.

Classifications of Business Income

Prior to the Tax Reform Act of 1986, all business income was considered ordinary income or capital gains. All income is now classified into three groups—active business income, passive income, and portfolio income.

Active business income includes revenues derived from the primary operations of the business and all capital gains created by the sale or conversion of capital and depreciable assets.

Passive income is generally derived from any activity involving a trade or business in which the taxpayer does not materially participate. However, income from rental activities is considered passive regardless of whether or not the taxpayer materially participates.

Portfolio income includes interest, dividends, annuities, and royalties not derived from the ordinary course of a trade or business. Any portfolio income generated in a passive activity is not treated as income from a passive activity and cannot be used to offset passive losses.

Passive Activity Rules

Generally, when the total deductions from passive activities exceed the total income from passive activities, the excess (the passive activity loss) is not allowed to offset any other type of income for that year. The passive activity loss is suspended and carried forward to reduce passive activity income that is generated in future years. Passive activity rules apply to individuals, estates, trusts, and personal service corporations, but they do not apply to regular corporations, except in a modified form for closely held corporations. The modification for closely held corporations provides that passive losses may be used to offset net active business income, but not portfolio income.

Corporate Taxation

The present section is limited to the federal taxation of the corporate entity. The federal taxation of small corporations that wish to be taxed as unincorporated businesses (S Corporations) will be reviewed at the end of this appendix.

Corporate Tax Rates. The federal income tax rates as revised by the Tax Reform Act of 1986 are presented below. The marginal tax rate is graduated from 15 percent on the first $50,000 of income to 34 percent on all income over $75,000. The benefits of the graduated rates are phased out through the imposition of a 5 percent surcharge on taxable income over $100,000, up to a maximum surcharge of $11,750. Thus, a corporation having taxable income of $335,000 or more effectively pays a flat tax calculated at a 34 percent rate.

FEDERAL TAX RATES OF A CORPORATION

Taxable income	Tax rate
$0 to $50,000	15%
$50,001 to $75,000	25%
Over $75,000	34%
$100,000 to $335,000	Surcharge 5%

Illustrations of tax calculations. Corporate taxpayer with taxable income of $80,000:

$$
\begin{array}{rcl}
\$50,000 \times 0.15 &=& \$\,7,500 \\
25,000 \times 0.25 &=& 6,250 \\
5,000 \times 0.34 &=& 1,700 \\
\hline
\$80,000 & & \$15,450
\end{array}
$$

Corporate taxpayer with taxable income of $200,000:

$$
\begin{array}{rcl}
\$\,50,000 \times 0.15 &=& \$\,7,500 \\
25,000 \times 0.25 &=& 6,250 \\
125,000 \times 0.34 &=& 42,500 \\
100,000 \times 0.05 &=& 5,000 \text{ (Surcharge)} \\
\hline
\$200,000 & & \$61,250
\end{array}
$$

Corporate taxpayer with taxable income of $350,000:

$$
\begin{array}{rclcl}
\$\ 50,000 & \times & 0.15 & = & \$\ \ 7,500 \\
25,000 & \times & 0.25 & = & 6,250 \\
275,000 & \times & 0.34 & = & 93,500 \\
250,000 & \times & 0.05 & = & 11,750 \ \text{(Surcharge: limited to \$11,750)} \\
\hline
\$350,000 & & & & \$119,000 \\
\hline
\end{array}
$$

or

$$\$350,000 \times 0.34\% = \$119,000$$

Capital Gains and Losses.   Special rules apply to the computation of gains and losses from the sale or exchange of capital or depreciable assets.

Gain or Loss from Capital Assets.   A capital asset is any property (whether or not connected with a trade or business) except for inventory, depreciable property used in a trade or business, and real property used in a trade or business. Generally, everything you own and use for personal purposes, pleasure, or investment is a capital asset. Examples would include stocks, bonds, and personal residences.

Many companies will have both capital gains and capital losses in the same tax year. Every transaction resulting from the sale or exchange of a capital asset is classified as either a short-term or a long-term capital gain or loss, depending on how long the asset has been held. The required holding period for the classification of a long-term asset is more than one year for assets acquired before June 23, 1984 and after December 31, 1987, and six months if acquired after June 22, 1984 and before January 1, 1988. For example, assume that a company in a given year has the following results:

Active business income	$100,000
Short-term capital gains	3,000
Short-term capital losses	5,000
Long-term capital gains	22,000
Long-term capital losses	10,000

Calculation of Net Capital Gain or Loss.   Every capital transaction will first be classified as either short-term or long-term. Then all short-term gains will be netted against all short-term losses to determine the net short-term capital gain or loss. All long-term gains will be netted against all long-term losses to determine the net long-term capital gain or loss. These two figures are then combined and the resulting figure is the net capital gain or loss.

Illustration:

Short-term capital gains	3,000
Less: Short-term capital losses	(5,000)
Net short-term capital loss	(2,000)
Long-term capital gains	22,000
Less: Long-term capital losses	(10,000)
Net Long-term capital gain	12,000
Net capital gain	$10,000

A net capital gain is included in income in the year of occurrence. But if the corporation's losses exceed gains for an overall capital loss, the capital loss may not offset ordinary income. Instead, the corporation's excess capital loss is subject to capital loss provisions. A corporation may carry back a capital loss to each of the three taxable years preceding the loss year. Any excess can be carried forward five years following the loss year. However, the loss cannot increase or cause a net operating loss in the carryback or carryover year. Regardless of origin, all carrybacks and carryovers are treated as short term capital losses.

Gain or Loss from Depreciable Assets.   The capital gain and loss rules specifically exclude capital gains treatment for sales of depreciable property and real property used in a trade or business. Since the basis of all depreciable assets is systematically reduced by depreciation expense taken as a deduction against ordinary income, all or part of a gain from the sale of these assets may have resulted from excess depreciation taken on it in the past.

Gains on the disposition of depreciable property are first taxed as ordinary income to the extent of all depreciation or amortization deductions claimed on the property (Sec. 1245 and Sec. 1250 recapture rules). The effect is that any sale of depreciable property at a price below its original acquisition price results in recapture of depreciation. A capital gain could only occur if property were to be sold for more than its original cost. For an example, assume the following scenario:

Apple Company sells a machine for $10,000 that originally costs $12,000 and now has accumulated depreciation of $5,000. Book value of the asset is $7,000 ($12,000 − $5,000). The ordinary gain on the sale is calculated:

Sales price	$10,000
Less: book value	7,000
Ordinary gain—considered recapture of depreciation (Sec. 1245)	$ 3,000

The law does contain a special provision (Code Sec. 1231) that will allow capital gains treatment on certain gains and ordinary loss treatment on some losses. These rules are complicated and beyond the scope of this appendix.

Dividends Received Deduction.   A corporation may take a special deduction from gross income for dividends received from investments in the preferred and common stocks of other domestic corporations that are subject to income taxes. The deduction is 70 percent of dividends received if the receiving corporation owns less than 20 percent of the distributing corporation's stock, and 80 percent if 20 percent or more (but less than 80 percent) of the distributing corporation's stock is owned.

For an illustration, assume that a company which is in the 34 percent tax bracket receives $40,000 in dividends during a year from a 30 percent ownership in another domestic corporation. Only 20 percent of the $40,000 (or $8,000) is taxable. The company's tax on the dividends would therefore be $8,000 × 0.34 = $2,720. The effective tax rate on the entire $40,000 in dividends received can be found by dividing the tax liability of $2,720 by the $40,000: $2,720/$40,000 = 6.8 percent. We can also calculate the effective rate by multiplying the proportion of the dividends that are taxable by the company's marginal tax rate of 34 percent: 0.20 × 0.34 = 6.8 percent.

Corporations that do not file a consolidated return are generally allowed to exclude from taxable income all dividends received from members of an affiliated group.

Net Operating Losses.   Corporations are allowed to carry back a net operating loss (NOL) from a trade or business to apply as a deduction against prior income. An NOL is first carried back to the earliest of the three years; if not entirely used to offset income in that year, it is carried to the second year preceding the loss year, and any remaining amount is then carried to the tax year immediately preceding the loss year. If the taxable income for the three years preceding the loss year is not sufficient to absorb the entire loss, it can be carried forward for a maximum of 15 years. A taxpayer may elect to forgo the carryback period. The election must be made by the return filing date and is irrevocable.

Alternative Minimum Tax.   The alternative minimum tax (AMT) helps to ensure that all corporations with economic income in excess of certain allowable exemptions will pay some amount of tax despite their allowable use of certain exclusions, deductions, and credits. The AMT provides a formula for computing tax that, in effect, ignores certain preferential tax treatments that are allowed in figuring the regular corporate tax. By eliminating these preferential deductions and credits, a tax liability can be created for a corporation that would otherwise pay little or nothing.

The tax is figured by first adjusting regular taxable income to eliminate the deductibility of certain items, and then adding back corporate tax preference items. From this amount of income (the alternative minimum taxable income) an exemption amount is subtracted. The maximum amount of this exemption is $40,000. However, it is reduced by $0.25 for every $1 by which the AMT income exceeds $150,000. After subtracting the exemption amount, the remaining income is taxed at a flat rate of 20 percent. The result is the tentative alternative minimum tax. The alternative minimum tax is the amount by which the tentative minimum tax exceeds the corporation's regular tax.

Accumulated Earnings Tax.   Another tax a corporation may be subject to is the accumulated earnings tax. This tax takes on the nature of a penalty. A company may legally retain all or part of its earnings if the retention is needed to finance expansion, provide working capital, or pay off debt. However, the Internal Revenue Code forbids a company from retaining earnings if the purpose of the retention is to allow the stockholders to avoid paying a tax on the dividends that would otherwise be received. In general, a corporation can accumulate up to $250,000 without incurring this penalty. The tax, if imposed, is 27.5 percent of the first $100,000 in excess of the $250,000 allowable amount, and then 38.5 percent of the remainder of the accumulated taxable income.

Other Aspects of Corporate Taxes

Consolidated Returns.   An affiliated group of corporations may elect to be taxed as a single unit, and therefore eliminate intercompany gains and losses. An affiliated group is defined as one or more chains of includible corporations connected through stock ownership with a common parent corporation if 80 percent or more of the voting power of all outstanding stock and 80 percent or more of the value of the outstanding stock of each corporation (except the common parent) is directly owned by one or more of the other corporations. In addition, the common parent is required to directly own at least 80 percent of the voting power and 80 percent of the value of all outstanding stock of at least one of the other corporations.

Whether a consolidated return will be advantageous depends on the facts in each particular case. For example, a consolidated return may result in a tax advantage for the group of corporations if one member of the group has a capital loss and another member has a capital gain. The net capital loss of one offsets the net capital gain of the other. Unless a consolidated return is filed, the loss could not be used in the current tax year. Furthermore, ordinary losses of one corporation from its business operation may offset the profits of another member of the group if a consolidated return is filed.

The disadvantages of filing a consolidated return include the fact that tax credits, the graduated tax rate, the alternative minimum tax credit, and the accumulated earnings credit are shared by a consolidated group of corporations. These tax attributes are allocated equally among members of the group unless they all consent to a different apportionment. The allocation of these various tax attributes can cause tax liabilities that may not have resulted if the corporations had filed separate returns.

Timing of Tax Payments. A corporation is required by law to make quarterly estimates of its income and tax for the entire fiscal year. One fourth of the fiscal year's estimated tax must be paid on or before the fifteenth day of the fourth, sixth, ninth, and twelfth months. If the company's estimates of the year's tax prove to be too low, the shortage must be paid by the fifteenth day of the third month of the following year when the return is filed. Further, if the total amount of income tax paid during the year proves to be less than 90 percent of the tax liability actually incurred, a penalty is imposed on the firm which must be paid when the tax payment shortage is due.

Personal Service Corporations (PSCs). A personal service corporation is a corporation whose stock is owned by doctors, lawyers, accountants, architects, engineers, consultants, or certain other professionals who perform personal services for the corporation. All taxable income of a personal service corporation is taxed at a flat rate of 34 percent, effective for tax years beginning after 1987. Since the individual employee-owners of the corporation are taxed at a maximum tax of 28 percent on their personal returns, the 34 percent flat tax on personal service corporations may cause the owners of a PSC to consider distributing all the corporation's income to take advantage of the lower individual rates currently prevailing.

Taxation of Unincorporated Businesses and S Corporations. The business income of unincorporated businesses (partnerships, proprietorships, and S Corporations) is generally not taxed at the business entity level. Instead, all income is passed through to the partners, proprietors, or stockholders. The proportionate share of the earnings of the business, whether distributed or not, is added to personal income and taxed at the individual level.

For the first time in United States history, the top marginal corporate tax rate (34 percent) exceeds the top marginal individual tax rate (28 percent). There now is no incentive to retain income in a closely held corporation if it can be distributed to owners in some non-dividend manner. Because of this situation, S Corporation elections have become very popular.

There are a number of technical requirements which must be met before S status is granted to a corporation. The owners of the company should consider carefully all these requirements as well as the possible advantages and disadvantages before deciding to elect S Corporation status.

Conclusions

The purpose of this appendix has been to provide the reader with a basic understanding of some of the more important aspects of federal taxation of corporations and other types of business organizations. Tax laws are changed frequently, and the financial manager should keep abreast of these changes. Even so, the tax situation of many firms is so complicated that an expert should be employed to plan the tax result of contemplated transactions and advise the financial manager of the alternatives available under the tax law.

6

THE EFFECT
AND MEASUREMENT
OF RISK
OF NEW INVESTMENTS

The two previous chapters were concerned with the basic analytical techniques used by firms in making investment decisions. Although risk was alluded to on occasion, we did not consider its measurement or specifically how it is accounted for in the decision-making process. We will be more realistic in this chapter. The financial manager is asked continually to make decisions which involve trade-offs between risk and return. Thus, our ultimate objective will be to determine how such trade-offs involved in choosing among investment opportunities can be evaluated.

Risk is sometimes considered to be related primarily to the possibility of "losing." For example, investors in a new business venture are usually faced with the risk that the venture might fail, leaving the owners with very little to show for their investment except the experience. However, the ramifications of the concept are more complex than this example implies. Risk can exist even when there is little or no possibility that earnings will be zero or negative. In particular, it exists anytime there is a possibility that the cash flows from an investment will be less than expected.

We will consider the risk involved in a new investment by the firm from the standpoint of (1) the investment project itself, (2) the firm as a whole, and (3) the owners of the firm. These three standpoints are related, however, since the risk of an investment affects the risk of the firm, which, in turn, affects the risk of the owners. Nevertheless, as we will see, there are significant differences in these viewpoints that can affect decisions made by the firm. Our overriding concern is the risk that affects these decisions.

INVESTMENT RISK OF AN INDIVIDUAL ASSET: PROJECT RISK

For convenience, the risk of an investment considered alone will be referred to as **project risk**. The effects of other investments (existing or proposed) of either the firm or its owners are not of concern in this case. Project risk exists whenever there is a possibility that the realized return on the project will be less than expected. The expected return from an investment is the average return one would expect if the investment were made many times. Therefore, we can say that the expected return is the mean of the probability distribution of all possible returns from the project. Let us consider the attributes of probability distributions applicable to project risk.

Probability Distributions.   In most cases, the amount by which the actual **net cash benefits (NCBs)** from an investment deviate from the expected net cash benefits will depend upon subsequent business conditions. Since there are usually many possible levels of future business activity, typically there will be many possible levels of NCBs. Further, possibilities of earning either more or less than expected will usually exist. All of the possible levels of NCB in any given year, along with their associated probabilities, comprise the probability distribution of the NCB for the year.

The probabilities of earning less than expected are often referred to as the **downside risk** of an investment, and the probabilities of earning more than expected are referred to as the **upside potential.** Downside risk is obviously an undesirable attribute of an investment, whereas upside potential is a desirable attribute. However, most business decision makers are risk-averse; this means that they put heavier weight on downside risk than on upside potential.

A graphical illustration of two probability distributions is given in Figure 6-1. A curve has been drawn in each case by connecting points which represent possible

FIGURE 6-1
Examples of two probability distributions.

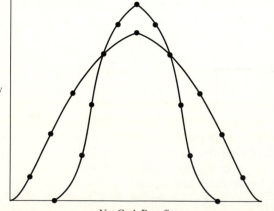

Probability

Net Cash Benefit

amounts of annual net cash benefit from an investment and the probabilities of their occurrence. The curves have been drawn so that the probability distributions can be better visualized.

Project risk is often measured by the total dispersion or total variability in a probability distribution, not just the variability in the distribution depicted by the downside risk. Total variability is perfectly acceptable as a substitute measure of project risk so long as the probability distribution is symmetrical; that is, so long as the shape of the curve depicting the probability distribution is the same on both sides of the midpoint (the expected value if the distribution is symmetrical). The NCBs from most investments tend to be symmetrical.[1]

Causes of Project Risk. The determinants of the risk of a business investment include (1) variations that can occur in the state of the economy, (2) industry characteristics, (3) the nature of the firm, and (4) unique attributes of the investment itself. Although the risks of most investments will be affected to some extent by all four of these factors, the responsiveness of project returns to each factor depends on the circumstances surrounding the particular case. For example, the risk in expanding one of Ford Motor Company's automobile assembly plants is affected primarily by the possible variations in the state of the economy and industry characteristics. Since the company has been manufacturing automobiles for many years and its share of the automobile market is fairly constant from year to year, there is usually little unique or firm risk. On the other hand, the risk in increasing the number of grills in an expensive restaurant emphasizing the evening meal will be more closely associated with the state of the local economy and the nature of the restaurant itself, particularly the competence of the management. The industry in this case is well established and does not change rapidly.

A general economic factor which can have a major impact on the value of an investment by a firm is a change in the level of interest rates in the market. Since the value of most assets varies inversely to changes in interest rates, the possibility of an increase in rates is a risk to an investor. One statistic which is closely related to this interest-rate risk is referred to as "duration," which is a type of weighted average of the time to the expected terminal cash flow of an asset. In general, the greater the duration of an investment, the greater is its interest-rate risk. This topic is covered in Appendix 6A at the end of the present chapter.

Sufficient space is not available in this book to review all of the factors that can impact the risk of an investment project. Various factors will be considered at later points as the occasion arises. However, the concept of operating leverage is of such frequent importance to risk that it should be discussed immediately.

Cash Operating Leverage. A major factor affecting the variability in the NCBs from an investment is the nature of the expenses incurred in operating the asset. The

---

[1]As we will see later in the chapter, investment decisions should not usually be based on project risk as defined here. The more sophisticated type of risk analysis that should be used assumes that investment returns have "normal" probability distributions. Unfortunately, empirical studies have found that distributions of returns tend to have somewhat fatter tails than the normal curve. See E. F. Fama and M. H. Miller: *The Theory of Finance*, Hinsdale, IL: Dryden Press, 1972, pp. 259–260.

higher the fixed expenses relative to the sales revenues from the employment of the asset, the greater will be the change in the NCBs when sales vary. As an illustration, consider Table 6-1. Sales, total expenses and NCB are the same in the first year in both panels of the exhibit. However, the amounts of variable and fixed expenses differ in the two panels. The (a) panel shows the effect on NCB of a 10 percent decrease in sales, assuming that variable costs are 60 percent of sales and fixed costs are $2,000. In this instance, NCB declines $280, or 20 percent, in the second year. The (b) panel shows the effect of the same change in sales if variable costs are 20 percent of sales and fixed costs are $6,000. In this case, NCB declines $560, or 40 percent, in year 2. The greater change in NCB in panel (b) reflects the impact of the higher fixed expenses.

Since the variability in NCBs will be greater in the panel (b) case if sales fluctuate, the dispersion in the probability distribution of NCBs will be greater than for the panel (a) case. However, the extent and timing of future sales fluctuations can not be known with certainty. There is also the possibility that the relationship between sales and expenses will change. For these reasons, the probability distribution will have to be estimated as discussed next.

TABLE 6-1
Impact of Fixed Expenses on the Net Cash Benefits from an Investment[a]

(a)

	Year 1	Year 2
Net sales	$10,000	$9,000
Variable cash expenses	(6,000)	(5,400)
Fixed cash expenses	(2,000)	(2,000)
Income before tax	$ 2,000	1,600
Income tax (30% rate)	(600)	(480)
Net cash benefit	$ 1,400	$ 1,120
Dollar change in net cash benefits		−$280
Percentage change in net cash benefits		−20%

(b)

	Year 1	Year 2
Net sales	$10,000	$ 9,000
Variable cash expenses	(2,000)	(1,800)
Fixed cash expenses	(6,000)	(6,000)
Income before tax	2,000	1,200
Income tax (30% rate)	(600)	(360)
Net cash benefit	$ 1,400	$ 840
Dollar change in net cash benefits		−$560
Percentage change in net cash benefits		−40%

[a] All sales and expenses in this table are assumed to involve immediate cash flows.

Subjective Probability Distributions. The odds of getting a heads from the flip of a fair coin are known to be 0.5, or 50 percent. Further, the odds of getting any particular number from the spin of a roulette wheel, or of drawing the Queen of Spades from a deck of bridge cards, can be determined precisely. The chances of a particular result occurring in any of these three games can be calculated exactly because all of the elements that affect the chances are known and can be defined mathematically. Personal beliefs and intuition are not involved in formulating the probabilities. For these reasons, the probability distribution applicable to the possible results in such games is said to be determined objectively.

The financial analyst will not often be faced with the favorable situation just described in evaluating investments for the firm. The analyst normally will not be able to calculate objectively the probability distribution applicable to the future returns from an investment. Rather, subjective probability distributions must be used in most cases. This type of probability distribution is developed from what the analyst or decision maker believes to be applicable at the time. The analyst must therefore think through the probable effects of the factors that can have an impact on returns. The distribution is then developed from the conclusions reached, and handled in exactly the same manner as if it had been determined objectively.[2]

Project risk can be measured by the use of the subjective probability distributions of the annual NCBs from an investment. Several factors that can affect the cash flows in any given year were discussed earlier. But note also that the annual returns from some projects are affected by returns in previous years. In other cases, the returns may be expected to change over time as the firm's operations and experiences change. Analytical procedures that take these factors into account mathematically will be considered later. Our concern at this point is only with the probability distribution of an investment's NCB in any given year. The first step in the analysis is to pose a subjective probability distribution of the NCB, after carefully considering the factors that can affect both revenues and expenses related to the project during the year. A simple example will be used to illustrate the point.

Illustration. The management of a private golf course is considering the possible expansion of its facilities to include an additional eighteen holes. After a study of all pertinent information available, the conclusion is reached that the probability distribution shown in Table 6-2 should be applicable to the annual cash benefit from the expansion. As the distribution in the table indicates, the realized NCB in any year will be affected by the state of the economy. Five possible levels of NCBs are considered in this hypothetical situation, ranging from −$30,000 to +$110,000. The NCB will be relatively high if economic conditions are good, but relatively low if economic conditions are bad. In this example, the cause of risk is the possibility of an adverse state of the economy. Analysts sometimes replace the latter term with the

---

[2]John J. Curran discusses psychological factors that can lead to errors in assessing the risk of investments in an interesting article in *Fortune* magazine. See "Why Investors Misjudge the Odds," *Fortune: 1989 Investor's Guide*, Fall 1988, pp. 85ff. On p. 97, the author quotes psychologist Amos Tversky's statement that "Research shows that when an expert says he's 90% sure, he's correct only 60% of the time." This reference was suggested by one of the reviewers of the book.

TABLE 6-2

PROBABILITY DISTRIBUTION OF THE ANNUAL NET CASH
BENEFIT FROM EXPANDING A PRIVATE GOLF COURSE

1 State of the economy	2 Probability	3 Net cash benefit
Depression	0.10	−$ 30,000
Recession	0.20	− 10,000
Normal	0.40	40,000
Good	0.20	90,000
Boom	0.10	110,000

Def

somewhat more inclusive term **state of nature**, which takes into account not only the state of the economy, but also the nature of the industry and the attributes of the firm itself. For instance, the ability of the management of our hypothetical golf course to manage the expanded facilities effectively will impact the probability distribution of returns.

The procedure used in developing the probability distribution above was relatively simplistic because the components of NCB were only considered implicitly. A more sophisticated approach to developing a distribution applicable to NCB for a year would be to derive it from probability distributions of sales and expenses. In the next illustration, we will see how this can be accomplished.

A More Complex Case. Assume that a building products distributor (wholesaler) is considering a new facility for warehousing some of the heavier products it sells to retail outlets. The new facility is expected to increase sales because a wider variety of inventories can be maintained, and out-of-stock losses will be reduced. However, both variable and fixed costs will also be increased. An analyst has developed the probability distributions shown in the (a) panel of Table 6-3 for the sales, and two general categories of expenses for a year. Note that the distribution applicable to variable expenses is affected by the sales level, whereas the distribution for fixed expenses is completely independent of sales. Thus, if sales are $100,000, variable expenses will be either $80,000 or $70,000 and fixed expenses either $30,000 or $10,000. But if sales are $140,000, variable expenses will be either $112,000 or $98,000 and fixed expenses will still be either $30,000 or $10,000. A total of eight combinations of sales and expenses, and therefore eight levels of NCB are possible.

The (b) panel of the table shows the probability distribution of the NCB for the year. Each possible level of the NCB is shown in the second column and the associated probability in the first column. The sequence of the elements in the distribution is arranged to show the possible levels of NCB to increase down the column. The probabilities are joint probabilities, obtained by calculating the product of the probabilities of the sales, variable expenses and fixed expenses, respectively, used in obtaining each NCB level. For example, the joint probability of the first level of NCB shown (−$10,000) is obtained by multiplying the .5 probability of $100,000 in sales, times 0.4 probability of $80,000 variable expenses, times the .5 probability of fixed expenses of $30,000 — or .5 × .4 × .5 = .1.

The probability distribution of the NCB shown in panel (b) of Table 6-3 is more difficult to develop than the distribution in the golf course example discussed earlier. However, the more complex example of the situation facing the building products distributor takes more information into account explicitly. For this reason, the latter procedure is preferred if the results obtained from the more thorough calculation procedures is thought to be worth the added development time.

As indicated earlier, different possibilities of sales and costs exist because of the possibilities of different states of nature. Since the state of nature is expected to vary in the future, the NCBs from most investments will also be expected to vary. Thus,

TABLE 6-3
DEVELOPMENT OF A PROBABILITY DISTRIBUTION
OF NET CASH BENEFIT FOR A YEAR

(a)
Component distributions

Sales		Variable costs	
Probability	Amount	Probability	Amount
		------ 0.4	$ 80,000
0.5	$100,000		
		------ 0.6	$ 70,000
		------ 0.6	$112,000
0.5	$140,000		
		------ 0.4	$ 98,000

Fixed costs

Probability	Amount
0.5	$30,000
0.5	$10,000

(b)
Net cash benefit distribution

Probability	Amount
0.10	−$10,000
0.15	−$ 2,000
0.15	$ 0
0.10	$10,000
0.10	$12,000
0.15	$18,000
0.15	$20,000
0.10	$32,000

there is a close relationship between variability or dispersion of possible cash flows and risk. Project risk is often measured by the expected variability in future NCBs, as shown in the following section.

Measurement of Project Risk

The Distribution Mean and Probability.   An important aspect of a probability distribution is its mean, or expected value, calculated by determining the weighted average of all possible outcomes, where the weights are the probabilities of the occurrence of each outcome. This can be expressed in formula form for the NCB for a year as follows:

$$\overline{NCB} = E(NCB) = \sum_{i=1}^{n} p_i(NCB_i) \tag{6-1}$$

where NCB refers to the mean of the probability distribution of the net cash benefit for any given year, which is also the expected value of the NCB, or $E(NCB)$; p_i refers to the probability of the occurrence of the ith value of NCB, and NCB_i refers to the ith possible value of NCB for the year, where i goes from 1 to n. As an example, see Table 6-4, which includes a reproduction of the NCB distribution for a private golf course previously presented in Table 6-2 [p. 166]. The mean of the probability distribution is determined from column 4 figures, and is shown to be $40,000.

Risk can be expressed in terms of probability statements. For example, Table 6-4 shows that there is a 10 percent chance that the NCB will be $-$30,000$, and a 30 percent chance that it will be less than its expected value of $40,000. The 30 percent chance of less than $40,000 is obtained by summing the 10 percent chance of $-$10,000$ and the 20 percent chance of $-$10,000$.

Expressing risk in terms of probability statements can be cumbersome if there are many possible levels of NCB. For this reason, surrogate measures of risk are used in most instances. The **standard deviation**, **variance** and **coefficient of variation** are three such measures discussed below. They are referred to as surrogate measures because they measure variability rather than risk per se. However, as we observed earlier, risk is closely related to variability. The greater the variability of a probability distribution, the greater the risk, and vice versa.

Standard Deviation and Variance.   The standard deviation is expressed as SD and is calculated by the following formula:

$$SD = \sum_{t=1}^{n} [p_i(NCB_i - \overline{NCB})^2]^{1/2} \tag{6-2}$$

where all symbols have the same meaning as defined earlier. The formula indicates that the mean of the probability distribution must be determined first, and then the standard deviation is calculated by (1) squaring the difference between the mean and each possible level of NCB, (2) multiplying each of these squared differences by

TABLE 6-4
THE MEASUREMENT OF RISK IN THE ANNUAL NET CASH BENEFIT FROM EXPANDING A PRIVATE GOLF COURSE

1 State of the economy	2 Probability	3 Net cash benefit	4 $p_i(NCB_i)$ Col. 2 × Col. 3	5 $(NCB_i - \overline{NCB})$ Col. 3 − $40,000	6 $(NCB_i - \overline{NCB})^2$ Col. 5 Squared	7 $p_i(NCB_i - \overline{NCB})^2$ Col. 2 × Col. 6
Depression	0.10	−$ 30,000	−$ 3,000	−$70,000	4,900mm	490mm
Recession	0.20	−$ 10,000	−$ 2,000	−$50,000	2,500mm	500mm
Normal	0.40	$ 40,000	$16,000	–0–	–0–	–0–
Good	0.20	$ 90,000	$18,000	$50,000	2,500mm	500mm
Boom	0.10	$110,000	$11,000	$70,000	4,900mm	490mm
Mean			$40,000			
Variance						1,980mm
Standard deviation						$44,497

169

the probability that the particular level of NCB will occur, (3) summing all of these products to get the variance and, finally, (4) taking the square root of the variance.

An example of the calculations is given in Table 6-4 in which the variance is shown to be 1,980,000,000 and the standard deviation $44,497. (The variance is expressed only as a number; its dimension is technically dollars squared.) The larger the standard deviation and variance, the greater the risk of an investment, and vice versa. In discussing risk, it is more intuitively meaningful to use the standard deviation than the variance since the standard deviation is expressed in dollars. However, the variance is often more convenient to use in mathematical equations.

Coefficient of Variation. Both standard deviation and variance measure risk in terms of the total variability of a probability distribution. In some cases, however, an analyst will be more interested in a measure of the relative risk among projects—which in our example means the variability per dollar of expected NCB. The coefficient of variation (CV) is a measure of relative variation. It can be calculated by dividing the standard deviation by the mean of the probability distribution as expressed in the following formula:

$$CV = \frac{SD}{NCB} \tag{6-3}$$

Applying the formula to the standard deviation calculated in Table 6-4, we get CV = $44,497/$40,000 = 1.11. The higher the coefficient of variation, the higher is the relative risk of the investment, and vice versa.

Continuous Distributions. The probability distributions in Tables 6-2, 6-3, and 6-4 are referred to as discrete, since there is a discrete, or limited, number of possible outcomes with a specific probability given for each possibility. For example, Table 6-4 indicates that there is a 20 percent chance that the NCB from the investment will be exactly $90,000. We have considered discrete distributions as an introduction to the study of risk and its measurement. However, the more powerful analytical tools which will be presented later in the chapter make use of continuous probability distributions. Risk will still be measured by the standard deviation and variance of returns, but the methods of calculating the two statistics are necessarily different from those discussed above.

Figure 6-2 provides a pictorial example of a continuous probability distribution of the NCB for a year from an investment; in this case, the distribution is normal. There is a large variety of possible types or shapes of probability distributions, but the type applicable to many financial problems is approximately normal.[3] This is a fortunate circumstance because normal distributions are relatively easy to use in risk analysis.

---

[3] A normal probability distribution has several attributes. For example, approximately 68 percent of the area under a normal curve (which represents a normal distribution) will be included within the range bounded by the mean of the distribution plus and minus one standard deviation; approximately 95 percent of the area is included within the range bounded by the mean plus and minus two standard deviations; and approximately 99.7 percent is within the range of the mean plus and minus three standard deviations.

For discussion of the applicability of the normality assumption, see Thomas E. Copeland and J. Fred Weston: *Financial Theory and Corporate Policy*, 2nd ed., Boston: Addison-Wesley Publishing Company, 1983, Chapter 6.

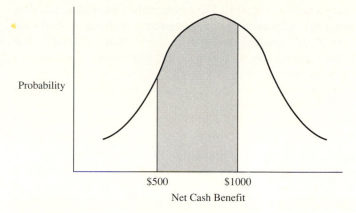

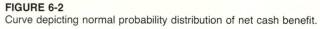

FIGURE 6-2
Curve depicting normal probability distribution of net cash benefit.

When the distribution is continuous, probabilities can be determined for ranges of a variable, but not for specific levels. The probability that the actual NCB will fall somewhere within a given range is the proportion of the total area under the curve which is included in the area above the designated range. In Figure 6-2, the shaded area under the curve indicates the probability that the actual NCB will fall somewhere between $500 and $1,000. The probability is the proportion of the total area under the curve included in the shaded portion. Tables have been published for determining the numerical values of probabilities when the mean and the amount of dispersion (variability) in a continuous distribution have been estimated. See Appendix B at the end of the book.

Risk Measurement When Distributions Are Continuous.   In measuring variability when the probabilities are continuous, the analyst will need to estimate two parameters of the distribution: its mean, or expected value, and its standard deviation. These two parameters can be calculated by the use of calculus if the equation for the curve describing the distribution is known. However, they can be estimated with sufficient accuracy in many cases.

To make the estimates, recall from Footnote 2 that an attribute of a normal distribution is that approximately 99.7 percent of all possibilities are included in the range bounded by the mean plus and minus three standard deviations. Thus, the approximate end point on the upside of the range will be the value (in our case, a possible level of NCB) obtained by adding three standard deviations to the mean of the distribution. The approximate end point on the downside of the range will be the value obtained by subtracting three standard deviations from the mean of the distribution.

The process of estimating the expected value and the standard deviation of the annual NCB from an investment is simplified because of the characteristics of a normal distribution. First, an estimate must be made of the largest and the smallest levels of NCB that could reasonably occur, which are indicated by the approximate end points described in the previous paragraph. The mean of the distribution can then be estimated by determining the midpoint of the range bounded by these two extreme possibilities. The estimate of the standard deviation is determined by dividing the difference between the two extremes by 6, which is the total number of standard deviations between the two extremes.

For an example, assume that the largest and the smallest levels of the NCB that could reasonably occur in a year are estimated at $2,400 and 0, respectively. The midpoint, or mean, of the distribution is ($2,400 + 0)/2 = $1,200. The standard deviation is estimated as ($2,400 − 0)/6 = $400, and the estimated variance is ($400)^2 = 160,000. Finally, the coefficient of variation (CV) can be calculated by dividing the standard deviation by the mean of the distribution: CV = $400/$1,200 = 0.33.

The greater the variability in the probability distribution of returns of a proposed investment, the greater the risk and the less the value of the proposal, other things being the same. Unless otherwise noted, we assume in the remainder of this book that the probability distribution of the net cash benefits from investments is continuous.

Total Project Risk: Risk of the Entire Stream of Cash Flows. Our discussion of risk to this point has focused on the risk of an investment's net cash flow in one year. However, investments always involve expected cash flows at two or more points in time, a net outflow at one point and at least one net inflow at another point. Determination of total project risk requires a summation of the risks of all expected cash flows over time. The summation process is complicated, however, because total project risk is affected by the extent to which the net cash flows are related over time. They may be completely independent from year to year, or they may be perfectly or partially correlated. If everything else is the same, the higher the degree of correlation, the greater will be the risk. We will consider the zero correlation, or independent, case initially.

Cash Flows Independent Over Time. If the net cash flows (NCFs) from an investment are completely independent over time, the probability distribution of the flow in any year will not be affected by the probability distribution applicable to any other year. The following formula can be used to calculate the standard deviation of the NCFs in this case:

$$SD = \left[\sum_{t=0}^{n} \frac{SD_t^2}{(1 + r_f)^{2t}} \right]^{1/2} \tag{6-4}$$

where SD_t^2 is the variance of the NCF in year t and r_f is the risk-free rate of interest. It is important to understand why the risk-free rate is used as the discount rate in the calculation in this case. The reason is that we are measuring risk, and we do not want to affect this measurement by discounting at a risky rate. If we discounted at a risky rate, our estimate of risk would be reduced because of the risk—clearly an absurdity. Thus, the risk-free rate should be used to time-adjust any measurement of future risk.

As an example of the use of Equation (6-4), consider investment J with an expected life of three years. We will assume that the only risky cash flows in this case are the future net cash benefits. The probability distribution of the NCB for each year is considered to be completely independent of the NCBs in other years. Assume that the standard deviations of the annual NCBs have been estimated as $3,000, $6,000 and $4,000 for the three years, respectively. If the risk-free rate of interest is 7 percent, the standard deviation of all of investment J's NCBs can be estimated as follows:

$$SD_j = \left[\frac{(\$3,000)^2}{(1.07)^2} + \frac{(\$6,000)^2}{(1.07)^4} + \frac{(\$4,000)^2}{(1.07)^6} \right]^{1/2}$$
$$= (7,860,949 + 27,464,228 + 10,661,476)^{1/2}$$
$$= \$6,781$$

Cash Flows Perfectly Correlated Over Time.   In this case, the net cash flow in one year is expected to be proportional to the net cash flow in the previous year, and the proportionality is constant for the life of the investment. The formula for calculating the standard deviation of all net cash flows from an investment is as follows:

$$SD = \sum_{t=0}^{n} \frac{SD_t}{(1 + r_f)^t} \tag{6-5}$$

where SD is the standard deviation of all of the net cash flows, and all other symbols have the same meaning as before. The discount rate, r_f, is the risk-free rate for the same reason as in the previous case.

As an illustration, assume that investment k has an expected life of three years, only the future net cash benefits are risky, and the standard deviation of the NCB for each of the three years is the same as for investment J discussed above, that is, $3,000, $6,000 and $4,000, respectively. However, the NCBs of investment K are expected to be perfectly, positively correlated over time. Thus, calculation of the standard deviation of the NCBs of K will make use of equation (6-5). Continuing with the assumption that the risk-free rate is 7 percent, we get:

$$SD_k = \frac{\$3,000}{(1.07)^1} + \frac{\$6,000}{(1.07)^2} + \frac{\$4,000}{(1.07)^3}$$
$$= \$2,804 + \$5,241 + \$3,265$$
$$= \$11,310$$

By comparing the result above with the SD_j of $6,781 calculated in the previous section, we see the effect of perfectly positive correlation on the risk of an investment. All factors were the same in the two cases, except that the NCBs were expected to be completely independent for investment J, but perfectly positively correlated for investment K. The result was a much higher standard deviation for K.

Differences in Correlation in Cash Flows.   As we observed in Chapter 5, the annual cash flows from an investment are derived from sales, various types of expenses, and perhaps, nonoperating cash flows. Some of these component flows may be correlated over time, while others are fixed or vary randomly. In this case, the project's risk can be estimated by combining the standard deviations of the cash flows that are correlated and that are independent. A technique for making this calculation under certain restricted conditions was developed by F. S. Hillier.[4] Because of the technicalities of the calculation, however, we will not pursue the topic further here.

Implications of Project Risk.   As we will see later, much of the project risk can often be diversified away by the firm, as well as by the stockholders acting on their own initiative. Thus, not all of the project risk should affect the decision of whether or not to make the investment. Our coverage of the topic will prove worthwhile, however, because some of the risk will normally remain, irrespective of the amount of diversification. Furthermore, the standard deviation or variance of the return on a project is used in calculating other types of risk measures. In the following section, we will look at the risk of a project from the standpoint of the firm.

INVESTMENT RISK TO THE FIRM: FIRM RISK

The risk which a firm will assume in making a new investment is usually not the same as the risk of the project considered alone. The risk to the firm will depend on the correlation between the returns of the project and those of the firm's other assets.

Correlation in Cash Returns.   The cash returns (NCBs) from a new project are positively correlated over time with the returns from the other assets of the firm, if variations in one of the return streams are accompanied by variations in the same direction in the other stream. For example, consider Figure 6-3(a). The correlation in the two streams of returns is positive because the direction of movement in one stream is always the same as the direction of movement in the other stream. On the other hand, Figure 6-3(b) shows two streams that are negatively correlated, because a change in the return in one of the streams is always accompanied by a change in the opposite direction in the other stream.

Perfectly Positive Correlation.   If the correlation is perfectly positive (i.e., perfect and positive), changes in amount in one of the streams will be accompanied by constant proportional changes in the same direction in the other stream. In other words, the returns in the two streams shown in Figure 6-3(a) have perfectly positive correlation if a change of x percent in one of the streams is always accompanied by a change of bx percent in the other stream, where the coefficient b is a positive constant. To illustrate, assume that b is 0.5. If the more volatile stream decreases by 6 percent (i.e., $x = -6$ percent), the other stream will change by 0.5 times −6 percent, which is a decrease of 3 percent. The proportional relationship between movements in the two streams will always be the same regardless of the directions and sizes of the movements.

---

[4] F. S. Hillier: "The Derivation of Probabilistic Information for the Evaluation of Risky Investments," *Management Science*, Vol. 10, April 1963, pp. 443–457.

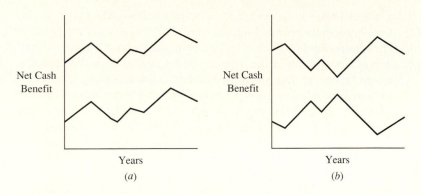

FIGURE 6-3
(a) Positive correlation in two streams of net cash benefits; (b) negative correlation
in two streams of net cash benefits.

Perfectly Negative Correlation.   When the correlation in two streams is perfectly
negative, changes in the returns in one stream will always be accompanied by proportional changes in the returns in the other stream, but in the opposite direction.
More specifically, if the negative correlation in Figure 6-3(b) is perfect, a change
of x percent in the net cash inflow in one stream will always be accompanied by a
change of bx percent in the net cash inflow in the other stream, where the coefficient
b in this case is a negative constant.

No Correlation.   Finally, if the returns in two streams are completely uncorrelat-
ed, there will be no consistent relationship between changes in the returns in the two
streams. In this case, if the return in one stream should change by x percent, the
return in the other stream may remain the same, or it may increase or decrease by
any amount.

The Usual Cases.   The cash flows from an investment which involves an expansion of the existing operations of the firm may be perfectly positively correlated, or
approximately so, with the total cash flows of the firm's other assets. On the other
hand, cash flows from an investment which changes the firm's method of operations
or product mix, probably will not be perfectly positively correlated with the other
cash flows. The correlation for most investments will be positive but less than perfect, which means that their returns and those of the firm's other assets will generally
move in the same direction, but not necessarily always, and not always by the same
proportionate amounts. In some cases, the correlation may be very low, and in rare
instances, even negative.

Implications of the Degree of Correlation.   If the returns of an investment project
are perfectly positively correlated with the returns of other assets of the firm, the
risk of the project by itself will also be the risk assumed by the firm in making the
investment. However, if the correlation is less than perfectly positive, the added risk
to the firm from making the investment will be less than the total risk of the project
by itself. As we will see below, this result comes from the portfolio effect of the
firm's other assets on the risk associated with the new proposal.

The Portfolio Effect Defined. In general, the term **portfolio effect** refers to the tendency of the variability in the returns from one asset or group of assets to be offset by variations in the returns from other assets of the firm. The terms "portfolio effect" and "diversification effect" have the same meaning in the present context. Figures 6-4a, b, and c illustrate this point. The graphs depict a situation in which the expected returns from a proposed investment are negatively correlated with the returns from the other assets of a firm. If the proposal is accepted and the expected returns of the new investment and the firm's other assets are added together, the combined returns will not only be larger, they will also tend to be more stable, as shown in the graphs. Of course, the reason for the stabilizing effect is that the net cash inflows from the investment rise when the net inflows of the other assets decline, and vice versa.

Illustration. For a numerical example, assume that a major new investment being considered by a firm is estimated to have cash returns of $10,000, $20,000, and $10,000 in the next three years, respectively, and that the firm's other returns during the period are estimated at $20,000, $10,000, and $20,000, respectively. If the investment were made, the firm's total cash returns would be estimated at $30,000 in each of the three years in the period. This is a happy situation, since the investment

FIGURE 6-4
Effect of combining negatively correlated net cash benefits: (a) existing assets; (b) new investment; (c) combined cash benefits.

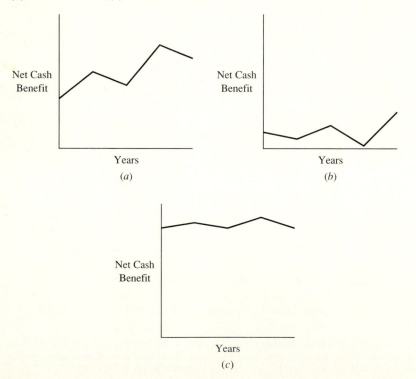

would eliminate the estimated variability in total returns over the period, thereby eliminating the estimated risk of the firm.

The variations in returns from the proposed investment were sufficiently large in the example above to offset completely the variations in the returns from the firm's other assets; thus, the firm's risk would theoretically be eliminated. This is not the usual circumstance, of course, since a new investment normally is much smaller than the total investment by the firm in all of its other assets. Furthermore, the cash flows of most assets tend to vary in the same direction (rather than in the opposite direction, as in the example), although the degree of correlation is sometimes fairly low. The fact remains, however, that variations in the returns from a proposed investment will be at least partially offset by variations in the returns of other assets of the firm if the returns are less than perfectly positively correlated. If so, the portfolio effect will reduce the risk of an investment to a firm below the total risk of the project considered by itself.

The portfolio effect is actually the effect of diversification of a firm's assets on its overall risk exposure. The greater the amount of diversification and the less the degree of correlation in the returns from the various products and services which the firm sells, the lower will be its risk. In the following section, we will be more specific concerning how diversification can reduce variability in returns.

Measurement of Variability in Combined Streams of Cash Flows.   The following equation can be used to calculate the standard deviation of the combined cash flow streams of n assets:

$$\text{SD}_p = \left(\sum_{j=1}^{n} \sum_{k=1}^{n} \text{COR}_{j,k} \text{SD}_j \text{SD}_k \right)^{1/2} \tag{6-6}$$

where SD_p is the standard deviation of the combined cash flows,
$\quad\text{COR}_{j,k}$ is the coefficient of correlation between the cash flows of assets j and k,
$\quad\text{SD}_j$ is the standard deviation of the cash flows of the jth asset, and
$\quad\text{SD}_k$ is the standard deviation of the cash flows of the kth asset.

According to equation (6-6), the standard deviation of the combined cash flows of n assets is the square root of the products of three statistics applicable to all pair combinations of the n cash-flow streams.[5] The three statistics are: the coefficient of

---

[5] The standard deviation of the rates of return of a portfolio of n assets (SD_p) is:

$$\text{SD}_p = \left(\sum_{j=1}^{n} \sum_{k=1}^{n} X_j X_k \text{COR}_{j,k} \text{SD}_j \text{SD}_k \right)^{1/2}$$

where X_j and X_k are scale factors reflecting the proportions of the total portfolio invested in assets j and k, respectively. The SDs in the equation are standard deviations of rates of return. Scale is accounted for in equation (6-6) as a result of expressing SD_j and SD_k in terms of absolute dollar amounts.

correlation between the cash flows of the two assets in each pair and the standard deviation of each of the assets. Since both j and k go from 1 to n in the equation, each cash-flow stream is paired with itself once and with every other cash-flow stream twice. This can be seen from the following matrix of all $COR_{jk}SD_j SD_k$ for a case involving five assets:

$$
\begin{array}{lllll}
COR_{1,1}SD_1SD_1 & COR_{1,2}SD_1SD_2 & COR_{1,3}SD_1SD_3 & COR_{1,4}SD_1SD_4 & COR_{1,5}SD_1SD_5 \\
COR_{2,1}SD_2SD_1 & COR_{2,2}SD_2SD_2 & COR_{2,3}SD_2SD_3 & COR_{2,4}SD_2SD_4 & COR_{2,5}SD_2SD_5 \\
COR_{3,1}SD_3SD_1 & COR_{3,2}SD_3SD_2 & COR_{3,3}SD_3SD_3 & COR_{3,4}SD_3SD_4 & COR_{3,5}SD_3SD_5 \\
COR_{4,1}SD_4SD_1 & COR_{4,2}SD_4SD_2 & COR_{4,3}SD_4SD_3 & COR_{4,4}SD_4SD_4 & COR_{4,5}SD_4SD_5 \\
COR_{5,1}SD_5SD_1 & COR_{5,2}SD_5SD_2 & COR_{5,3}SD_5SD_3 & COR_{5,4}SD_5SD_4 & COR_{5,5}SD_5SD_5
\end{array}
$$

Study of this matrix indicates that there are five pair combinations where $j = k$; these occur along the diagonal from the upper left to the lower right. In these cases, the cash-flow stream is in effect paired with itself. Note that when $j = k$, $Cor_{j,k} SD_j SD_k$ can be reduced to SD_j^2, the variance of the cash-flow stream, because $COR_{j,k} = 1$ and $SD_j = SD_k$.

When j does not equal k, the term $COR_{j,k}SD_j SD_k$ is referred to as the covariance of the jth and kth streams. Since $COR_{j,k}SD_j SD_k = COR_{k,j} SD_k SD_j$ and both expressions appear once in the matrix, there are always two covariance terms for each pair combination in the calculation of the standard deviation of the combined returns of two or more assets. Thus, in the matrix above, there are a total of twenty covariance terms, but these can be combined to give ten terms taking the form: $2COR_{j,k}SD_j SD_k$, where both j and k go from 1 to 5, but j does not equal k.

The Two-Asset Case.   Consider the calculation of the standard deviation for a simple case involving a combination of two cash-flow streams. The equation can be expressed as follows:

$$SD_{j,k} = (SD_j^2 + SD_k^2 + 2COR_{j,k}SD_j SD_k)^{1/2} \tag{6-7}$$

where $SD_{j,k}$ refers to the standard deviation of the combined cash flows of assets j and k, and the other symbols have the same meaning as before. Thus, in the two-asset case, the standard deviation is the square root of the sum of the variances of the cash flows of the two assets plus two times the covariance of the two cash-flow streams.

Study of the Equations (6-6) and (6-7) clearly indicates the importance of correlation for portfolio risk. Recall that the correlation coefficient can vary between $+1$ for perfectly positive correlation and -1 for perfectly negative correlation. The higher the coefficient, that is, the closer it is to $+1$, the higher the standard deviation and, therefore, the greater the risk of a portfolio consisting of the two assets. On the other hand, the lower the correlation, the smaller the standard deviation and risk of the portfolio.

Illustration.   Table 6-5 presents numerical examples of the standard deviations of combined cash flows of two assets, assuming different values of $COR_{j,k}$. The (a)

TABLE 6-5
IMPACT OF COMBINING CASH-FLOW STREAMS ON RISK

(a)

Individual Assets

Asset:	A	B	C	D	E	F	G
Standard deviation:	10,000	10,000	10,000	10,000	10,000	10,000	10,000
Correlation with A:	1.00	1.00	0.70	0.30	0.00	−0.60	−1.00

(b)

Portfolios

Asset combination:	A+B	A+C	A+D	A+E	A+F	A+G
Sum of standard deviations:	20,000	20,000	20,000	20,000	20,000	20,000
Standard deviation of combined streams:	20,000	18,439	16,125	14,142	8,944	−0−

panel in the exhibit includes the standard deviations of the cash flows of each of seven assets and the correlation of each of the streams with that of asset A. The (b) panel shows the sum of the standard deviations of stream A and each of the other streams, respectively. In addition, the standard deviations of the combinations of stream A and each of the other streams is shown in the last row of the exhibit. The standard deviation of the combined streams was calculated by the use of Equation (6-7).

The portfolio effects of the various two-asset combinations can be noted by comparing the two rows of numbers in the (b) panel. When the cash flows of two assets are perfectly positively correlated (e.g., A and B), combining the two assets in a portfolio does not result in any diversification benefits, since the standard deviation of the combined streams is the same as the sum of the standard deviations. However, there are portfolio effects in each of the other combinations. When the correlation coefficient is −0.60 in the illustration, the standard deviation of the portfolio is less than the standard deviation of each of the two component assets. Finally, for portfolio $A + G$, where the correlation is −1, variability is completely eliminated. In this case, the cash flows of the two streams always move in opposite directions and by the same amount.

The Illustration Modified. The reader should note that the standard deviation of a portfolio is a function not only of the correlation among the component assets, but also of the sizes of the standard deviation of the individual assets. For example, if the standard deviation of asset G in Table 6-5 had been $2,000 rather then $10,000, and the correlation with A was still −1, the standard deviation of the portfolio would have been $8,000 rather than 0. In this case, variability is not completely eliminated, although the asset combination still includes substantial portfolio effects since the sum of the standard deviations of the cash flows of the two assets would be $12,000.

A firm investing in an asset is combining the cash flows of two assets—one is the investment project and the other is the firm as a whole without the new investment. The total dollar value of the cash flows of the firm will usually be many times larger than the flows of the proposed project. Thus the impact of the project on the standard deviation of the firm's total cash flows will be less than the impact of combining assets as shown in Table 6-5. Nevertheless, the general relationships shown in the exhibit are still applicable. Of course, given the values of the other variables in equation (6-7), the impact of a new investment on the risk of the firm as a whole will be greater for projects with larger cash flows.

Epitaph. In the following section we will see that, for the most part, stockholders do not have to rely on the firm to diversify because they can diversify their own investment portfolios. In fact, stockholders with a sufficient amount of capital can diversify more completely than a firm, if the latter has to invest a relatively large amount of its capital in only part of its assets. If this is true, then, why have we spent so much effort in examining the portfolio effects of investments by a firm? The reason is that there are two benefits from diversification that may apply to a firm, but which cannot be obtained by the stockholders in diversifying their own portfolios. First, if the diversification will reduce the likelihood of the firm's failure, bankruptcy costs may be avoided. Stockholders as well as the economy as a whole (but not bankruptcy lawyers) will benefit from diversification by the firm in this type of situation; stockholders cannot provide for this benefit in their own portfolios.

Second, in some cases, diversification which results from vertical integration of a firm's productive operations may ensure raw material supplies and/or provide for consumer outlets that would not otherwise be available to the firm. For example, a major reason the Standard Oil Corporation of California acquired the Gulf Oil Corporation in 1984 was to increase oil reserves without having to incur the risk and expense of exploration. Also, automobile manufacturers sometimes invest in the facilities necessary to produce their own parts in an attempt to keep supply lines open. The reduction of risks to the stockholder in these cases cannot be provided by diversifying a privately owned portfolio.

RISK OF A PROJECT TO THE FIRM'S STOCKHOLDERS: SYSTEMATIC RISK

Investments made by a firm impact the risk and return of the firm's common stock. But since investors in securities can diversify their own portfolios, they can diversify away part of the total risk of the firm's investments. With the two exceptions noted at the end of the last section, stockholders can do more easily for themselves what the firm attempts to do by diversifying its assets and operations. This fact implies that well-diversified stockholders do not benefit from the firm diversifying its investments for the purpose of reducing risk, with the two exceptions noted.

Since the investors who dominate the stock market, such as the large financial institutions, typically are highly diversified, they do not require compensation for diversifiable risk. As a result, market prices of stocks adjust to reflect this fact. The implication is that any investor who purchases a common stock should expect to receive a return which includes two components: the risk-free rate of interest and a premium for only undiversifiable risk of owning the stock. The undiversifiable risk is called **systematic** (or **market**) **risk**.

Since stockholders can diversify away diversifiable risk but not systematic risk, finance theory leads to the conclusion that the required rate of return on a proposed investment project by a firm should include a premium for only systematic risk. The latter type of risk is usually measured by the *beta* coefficient, which is often referred to simply as *beta* and denoted symbolically as β. *Beta* is a useful measure of risk, both in theoretical finance and in financial decision making in the real world. The concept is rooted in portfolio theory, which is concerned with the risk-return relationships of asset portfolios. We turn to this topic next.

Portfolio Theory

Risky Portfolios.   Our concern in this section is with the foundation of the modern theory of risk measurement for investment decisions. The beta coefficient is derived from this foundation. The application of beta to investment decisions is considered toward the end of the chapter.

From a practical standpoint, there are an infinite number of risky assets available for investment, and there are an even greater number of combinations of these assets that can be included in an investment portfolio. The entire group of possible combinations is called the **feasible set** of portfolios. It naturally follows that the feasible set of portfolios can result in an infinite number of risk-return possibilities for investors. The dotted area in Figure 6-5 represents all of these risk-return possibilities. Return in the graph is measured by rate of return, rather than simply by cash flows, and risk is measured by the variability in the rate of return. Rate of return is the percentage return on investment, where dollar returns are derived from dividends and changes in the market value of the investment.

Most of the possible portfolios are not important from the financial standpoint, because they are dominated by others in the feasible set in terms of risk and/or return. A dominant portfolio is a member of the feasible set which has the highest expected return for a given risk and the lowest risk for a given expected return. Dominant portfolios in this sense are said to be efficient. The risk-return possibilities of the efficient portfolios are represented by the dark curve along the upper left edge of the feasible set shown in Figure 6-5. The curve is given the rather exotic name of **efficient frontier**.

None of the portfolios along the efficient frontier dominate any of the others along the frontier, since each is efficient. That is, each has the highest expected return for a given risk and the lowest risk for a given expected return. An investor could select a portfolio with a higher expected return along the frontier only by assuming greater

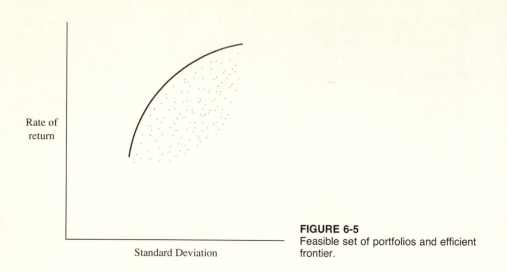

Rate of
return

Standard Deviation

FIGURE 6-5
Feasible set of portfolios and efficient
frontier.

risk. The particular portfolio chosen would depend on the attitude of the investor toward risk and return; the investor would choose the portfolio which provides the greatest total utility (i.e., total satisfaction).

Enter the Risk-free Asset.   Now let us assume that there is a risk-free asset. This assumption is not so outlandish as one might first believe, since short-term Treasury bills (T bills) are almost risk free.[6] An investor could have essentially a risk-free portfolio by investing only in T bills. The investor could also split his portfolio between the risk-free asset and risky assets in various ways. Thus, the risk-return possibilities have now changed from what they were if all assets were risky. The possibilities for the highest return for a given risk and the lowest risk for a given return are now represented by a straight line extending from the return for zero risk through a point which is tangent to the efficient frontier of risky portfolios. This line is known as the **Capital Market Line** (**CML**) and is shown in Figure 6-6.

The CML has now become the efficient frontier because no portfolio will plot above the line. Note that only one portfolio consisting entirely of risky assets is efficient. It is called the **market portfolio** and is labeled *m* in Figure 6-6. All risky assets are in the market portfolio.

Portfolios on the CML are combinations of the risk-free asset and the market portfolio. Investing in *m* obviously cannot mean that the investor buys all of the assets in the market. It simply means that an investment is made in a combination of risky assets which will provide the same risk and return as *m*. Studies have shown that

[6] Investing in T bills involves a small amount of interest-rate and inflation risks.

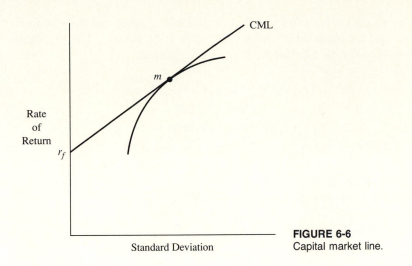

FIGURE 6-6
Capital market line.

this objective can be approximately attained by investing equal amounts in a random selection of eight or more risky assets.

The risk in the market portfolio is entirely systematic risk, since further diversification is not possible. A portfolio consisting of only one or two risky assets will have systematic risk if its returns vary even slightly with the returns on the market portfolio. However, the portfolio with only one or two risky assets will also include a lot of diversifiable risk. Adding randomly selected assets will reduce the latter type of risk. In an efficient portfolio, all of the diversifiable risk will have been diversified away, leaving only systematic risk. The systematic risk of an asset cannot be eliminated or even reduced, although its impact on a portfolio can be reduced by investing in other assets. The total systematic risk of a portfolio is the weighted average of the systematic risks of all assets in the portfolio, where the weights are the proportions of the total value of the portfolio of each of the component assets. More on this later.

Portfolio Return.   The expected return on any portfolio on the CML can be calculated in the following manner:

$$E(r_p) = w_f r_f + (1 - w_f)E(r_m) \tag{6-8}$$

where $E(r_p)$ is the expected return on the portfolio, w_f and $1 - w_f$ are the proportions of the total value of the portfolio derived from the risk-free asset and the market portfolio, respectively, r_f is the risk-free rate of interest, and $E(r_m)$ is the expected return on the market portfolio. Equation 6-8 indicates that the expected return on a portfolio is linearly related to the proportions invested in the market portfolio and the risk-free asset. Thus, decreasing w_f from 0.9 to 0.8 will have the same absolute effect on $E(r_p)$ as decreasing w_f from 0.2 to 0.1. For example, assume that the risk-free rate is 8 percent and the expected return in the market is 14 percent. The expected return on the portfolio for the four values of w_f are as follows

$$W_f = .9: \quad E(r_p) = .9(8\%) + .1(14\%) = \quad 8.6\%$$
$$W_f = .8: \quad E(r_p) = .8(8\%) + .2(14\%) = \quad 9.2\%$$
$$W_f = .2: \quad E(r_p) = .2(8\%) + .8(14\%) = 12.8\%$$
$$W_f = .1: \quad E(r_p) = .1(8\%) + .9(14\%) = 13.4\%$$

In the calculations above, $E(r_p)$ increases by 0.6 of one percent in both instances where W_f decreases by .1, that is, from .9 to .8 and from .2 to .1.

Portfolio Risk.   The risk of portfolios on the CML can be calculated by equation (6-9) below:

$$SD_p = w_f SD_{rf} + (1 - w_f)SD_m \qquad (6\text{-}9)$$

where SD_p is the standard deviation of the portfolio, SD_{rf} is the standard deviation of the risk-free asset, SD_m is the standard deviation of the market portfolio and w_f has the same meaning as before. Since the risk-free asset has no risk, $SD_{rf} = 0$ and $SD_p = (1 - w_f)SD_m$. Thus, the standard deviation of the portfolio is linearly related to $1 - w_f$; a constant absolute change in $(1 - w_f)$ will result in a constant absolute change in SD_p. The CML is a straight line because both the risk and the expected return of efficient portfolios are linearly related to the proportion of the portfolio invested in the market portfolio.

Extension of the CML Beyond *m*.   We have observed that the returns and risks of portfolios represented by points on the CML are simply weighted averages of the returns and risks of the market portfolio and the risk-free asset. This is clear enough for portfolios between r_f and m in Figure 6-6. However, the CML extends beyond (to the right of) m. How can this occur? From a mathematical standpoint, this can occur only if w_f in equations (6-8) and (6-9) is less than zero. This means that rather than investing part of the portfolio in the risk-free asset, the investor borrows at the risk-free rate of interest, and invests the proceeds of the loan in m. (We will discuss the realism of borrowing at the risk-free rate at a later point.)

For example, assume as before that $r_f = 8$ percent and $E(r_m) = 14$ percent. Now assume also that the investor borrows $0.50 for every $1 of his own and invests all funds in m. Calculating the return on the portfolio by the use of equation (6-8), we get:

$$E(r_p) = (-.5).08 + (1 + .5).14$$
$$= .17, \text{ or } 17 \text{ percent}$$

The $-.5$ as the weight applicable to the risk-free rate of interest in the equation above reflects the fact that the investor has borrowed an amount equal to 50 percent of his own funds and must pay the risk-free rate on the loan.

From our earlier discussion using the same figures for $E(R_m)$ and r_f, we found that the $E(r_p)$ increased 0.6 of 1 percent for every 10 percent decrease in w_f and increase in $1 - w_f$. Now note that when w_f is 0 and $1 - w_f$ is 1.0, $E(r_p) = E(r_m) = 14$ percent. In the example above, w_f is $-.5$; thus, $E(r_p)$ should be $.6 \times 5 = 3.0$ percentage points larger than $E(r_m)$, which it is. The result in this example reflects the fact that, if the investor can borrow at the risk-free rate of interest, the CML is a straight line extending beyond m.

We know, however, that even the large financial institutions that dominate the stock market cannot borrow at the risk-free rate of interest. Since borrowing at a higher rate than r_f would cause the return on a portfolio to be less, the slope of the CML should decline somewhat beyond point m. However, empirical studies have not found the CML to decline, which implies that the net borrowing costs of large investors is generally close to the yield on T bills.[7] We will see in the following section what the CML implies for rates of return on assets.

Capital Asset Pricing

Portfolio theory has a direct connection with the pricing of assets and, therefore, with the expected return from investing in them. We are now ready to examine this topic. The first step is to modify our measure of systematic risk so that it applies to individual assets as well as to portfolios. This step makes the theory applicable to investment decisions by business firms.

The Beta Coefficient.   The capital market line applies only to portfolios consisting of various combinations of the market portfolio and the risk-free asset. As we have observed, the only risk of these portfolios is the systematic risk of the market portfolio component. The systematic risk of each of the portfolios as well as that of the individual assets of which the portfolios are composed can be expressed as a proportion of the risk of the market portfolio, SD_m. The proportion applicable to a particular asset is the asset's beta coefficient, which can be calculated as follows:

$$\beta_j = \frac{COR_{j,m} SD_j}{SD_m} \tag{6-10}$$

where β_j is the beta coefficient of the jth asset or portfolio, $COR_{j,m}$ is the coefficient of correlation between the return on j and the return on the market portfolio, SD_j

---

[7] Portfolio theory and its derivative, capital asset pricing theory, have become highly controversial in recent years. Most of the criticism has been specifically directed toward the capital asset pricing model. We will review the principal criticisms at a later point in the chapter.

is the standard deviation of the return on j, and SD_m is the standard deviation of the return on the market portfolio.[8]

Beta is a relative measure of risk; it expresses the systematic risk of an asset or portfolio relative to the risk of the market portfolio. For example, if the beta for an asset is 0.9, variations in the returns on the market portfolio are expected to result in variations in the returns on the asset which are 0.9, or 90 percent, as large as the variations in the market portfolio. The variations in the returns on the asset and on the market portfolio will be in the same direction because the implied sign of the 0.9 beta value is positive. If the beta of the asset had been 1.2, the variability in its returns would have been 0.2 greater than the variability in the market returns. In the unlikely event that beta is negative, the asset returns would vary in a direction opposite to those of the market. Finally, note that the beta for the market portfolio is 1. This result is indicated by Equation (6-10), since SD_j is the same as SD_m in this case, and the correlation coefficient is 1.

The discussion above has shown how the systematic risk of an asset or portfolio is measured. We are now prepared to examine the relationship between beta and the return an investor should expect to obtain from making investments. This topic is considered next.

The Capital Asset Pricing Model.   The expected rate of return on any individual asset or portfolio of assets is a function of the risk-free rate of interest and the systematic risk. Investors require compensation for both of these elements. Using beta as the measure of systematic risk, the following equation can be used to estimate the rate of return on an investment in an asset or portfolio:

$$E(r_j) = r_f + \beta_j[E(r_m) - r_f] \qquad (6\text{-}11)$$

where $E(r_j)$ and $E(r_m)$ are the expected rates of return on asset or portfolio j and on the market portfolio, respectively. r_f is the risk-free rate of interest, and β_j is the beta coefficient of asset or portfolio j.

Equation (6-11) is known as the **capital asset pricing model** (CAPM), one of the most important models in the field of finance. It indicates that the expected rate of return in the market on either an asset or portfolio is composed of the risk-free rate of interest and a premium for systematic risk. If the beta of an asset is less than 1, the expected return is less than the return on the market portfolio. For example, assume that $r_f = 8$ percent, $E(r_m) = 12$ percent and $\beta_j = 0.9$ for asset j. The expected return on j would be:

$$E(r_j) = .08 + .9(.12 - .08)$$
$$= .116, \text{ or } 11.6 \text{ percent}$$

---

[8] The beta coefficient is often referred to in finance literature as equal to the covariance of the asset with the market, divided by the market variance, or $COR_{j,m} SD_j SD_m \div SD_m^2$. The latter expression reduces to Equation (6-10).

On the other hand, if $\beta_j = 1.2$ and everything else is the same as above, the reader can verify that $E(r_j) = 12.8$ percent. Finally, if $\beta_j = 1$, $E(r_j) = 12$ percent, the same as the expected market return.

As we have noted, systematic risk cannot be diversified away. Thus, the risk of an efficient portfolio can be measured by calculating a weighted average of the betas of the individual assets in the portfolio. The return on the portfolio is also a weighted average of the returns on the component assets.

The Security Market Line.   Assume that we calculate several expected rates of return by inserting various beta values in Equation (6-11). We then plot the results on a return/beta graph and draw a line connecting the plotted points. Our graph will look like Figure 6-7. Actually, only two calculations of expected return would have been sufficient, since the line is straight.

The line is labeled SML (for **security market line**) in Figure 6-7. It denotes the risk-return relationship for both individual assets and portfolios. In this particular graph, the SML begins on the Y axis at the point for the risk-free rate and 0 *beta* and then extends on through m and beyond.[9] Drawing the SML as a straight line assumes that investors can both borrow and lend at the risk-free rate of interest. We will consider the effect of dropping this assumption at a later point.

[9] An asset can have a negative beta, in which case, the expected rate of return would be less than the risk-free rate. Thus, the SML can be drawn to continue downward and to the left of the intercept on the Y axis. This relationship is reasonable because an asset with a negative beta will reduce the systematic risk of a portfolio to an even greater extent than a risk-free asset. However, assets which have a negative beta over an extended period of time are rare.

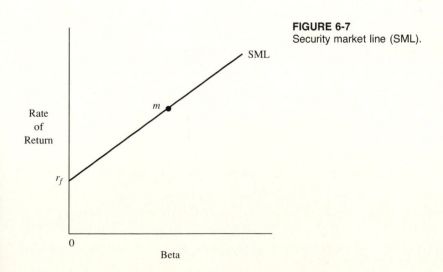

FIGURE 6-7
Security market line (SML).

Implications of the CAPM for Investment Decisions of Firms.   Investors require a rate of return on a new investment that is at least as high as the rate of return expected from making other, comparable-risk investments in the market. Thus, the CAPM can be used by a firm to determine the required rate of return on investment proposals. This rate should be used by the firm as the discount rate to time-adjust estimated cash flows to determine their present value.

We have seen that the security market line is a plot of expected rates of return for different beta values. Thus, the SML also depicts the required rates of return on investments, calculated via the CAPM, for different levels of systematic risk. If the risk-return expectation of a proposed investment lies above the SML, the investment is expected to increase the market value of the firm's common stock. Conversely, if the risk-return point plots below the SML, the investment is expected to decrease the value of the common stock.

The Estimation of Beta.   Beta is a risk measure which reflects how closely the rate of return on an asset varies with the average rate of return in the market, that is, with the rate of return on the market portfolio. Before the CAPM can be used to calculate the required rate of return on a project, the project's beta must be estimated. The first step is to estimate its future cash flows. The cash flows can then be converted to a rate of return form by dividing them by the initial investment outlay required by the project. This step provides the analyst with rate of return figures for future time periods. The final step is to estimate how the future rates of return on the project vary over time with the average rates of return in the market. This problem will be considered in Chapter 7.

In this chapter, we have not considered the effect of financing on the required rate of return on an asset. If a firm uses preferred stock or debt in its financing activities, a financial leverage effect is created which will increase the variability of the returns on investments. The beta value and the required rate of return on each investment is thereby increased. This topic will also be examined in the following chapter.

Criticism of the CAPM.   The CAPM has become a controversial topic in recent years.[10] Specific criticisms have been directed toward the assumptions (1) that the intercept of the SML with the Y axis is at the risk-free rate of interest and (2) that the tradeoff between beta and return is linear. Research has tended to support the conclusion that the intercept is at a point somewhat higher than the risk-free rate.[11] Thus, an asset or portfolio with risk-return attributes represented at the intercept is often referred to as a **zero beta asset** or **portfolio**. On the other hand, the evidence has supported the linearity of the SML.

Probably the most important criticism, however, has been made by Richard Roll,

---

[10] For a review of the tests that have been made of the CAPM, see Diana R. Harrington: *Modern Portfolio Theory, the Capital Asset Pricing Model, and Arbitrage Pricing Theory: A User's Guide*, 2nd. ed., 1987, Englewood Cliffs, N.J.: Prentice-Hall, Chapter 3.

[11] In particular, see Fisher Black: "Capital Market Equilibrium with Restricted Borrowing," *Journal of Business*, Vol. 45, July 1972, pp. 444-455.

who demonstrated that the CAPM cannot be adequately tested empirically, because a market index that is sufficiently comprehensive is not available.[12] Roll's principal criticism was directed toward the practical use of the CAPM, not the theory behind it. He points out that the lack of an all-inclusive market index can cause significant errors in applying the model.

Several models have been suggested as alternatives to the CAPM. The alternative attracting the most attention among academics is the **Arbitrage Pricing Model (APM)** developed by Stephen A. Ross.[13] According to the APM, the risk component in the required rate of return on an investment in a particular asset may be determined by several basic factors, not just the average risk in the market. However, neither Ross nor anyone else has shown conclusively how these factors can be identified correctly. Thus, at this point in time, the APM cannot be used in making practical financial decisions.

Two other alternatives to the CAPM that have been suggested in finance literature are the **option pricing model** and **state preference theory**. The option model has considerable promise as an analytical tool in dealing with certain types of financial problems.[14] However, its applicability to investment decisions of firms is limited at this time. State preference theory requires relatively precise estimates of future states of nature and the effects of these future states on asset returns and individual preferences.[15] For this reason, a practical model based on the theory has not been developed.

Our conclusion is that the alternatives to the CAPM that have appeared in finance literature have limited use for the financial manager in making investment decisions for the firm. Despite the criticisms noted above, the CAPM remains today as the best available tool for this purpose. However, some other model will probably be developed in the future which will prove to be better.

CHAPTER SUMMARY

Our focus in this chapter has been on the nature and measurement of risks associated with investment decisions by business firms. Three types of risk were examined: project risk, firm risk of the project, and the systematic risk of the project. Although

---

[12] Richard Roll: "A Critique of the Asset Pricing Theory Tests," Part 1: "On Past and Potential Testability of the Theory," *Journal of Financial Economics*, Vol. 5, March 1977, pp. 129–176. See also Roll's paper "Performance Evaluation and Benchmark Errors," *Journal of Portfolio Management*, Vol. 6, Summer 1980, pp. 5–12.

[13] S. A. Ross, "The Arbitrage Theory of Capital Asset Pricing," *Journal of Economic Theory*, Vol. 13, December 1976, pp. 341–360.

[14] For a discussion of some of the applications of the model, see Fischer Black and Myron Scholes, "The Pricing of Options and Corporate Liabilities," *The Journal of Political Economy*, Vol. 81, May-June 1973, pp. 637–654.

[15] Jack Hirshleifer developed the basic structure of state preference theory in "Efficient Allocation of Capital in an Uncertain World," *The American Economic Review*, vol. LIV, May 1964, pp. 77–85. For a more recent treatment, see T. E. Copeland and J. F. Weston, *Financial Theory and Corporate Policy*, 2nd ed., 1983, Boston: Addison-Wesley, Chapter 5.

systematic risk is of primary concern in evaluating investment proposals, the examination of the two other types of risk provided building blocks for our study of systematic risk and its impact on investment decisions.

Project risk is the risk of a project considered by itself, with no consideration of the effect of other investments of the firm. This type of risk is the result of the fact that the future cash flows from the investment are not certain—the level of the flows in each period will depend on the state of nature in the period. Since future states of nature are uncertain and often vary from period to period, the cash flows from an investment are best described by a probability distribution. The variability in the cash flows and therefore in the possible returns on the investment is usually measured by the standard deviation or the variance of the cash-flow stream. Since the variability of the cash flows determines the variability of the net present value, the standard deviation or variance of the net present value of the investment project is a measure of its risk.

In most cases, the risk of a project for a firm is less than the project risk, because of the diversification, or portfolio, effects of the firm's other assets. In other words, some of the project risk will be diversified away. Stockholders can usually diversify more efficiently than can the firm, however, because of the dominant impact on the firm of some of its assets, and because firms often invest in similar types of assets with a high degree of correlation in their returns.

The type of risk that is of fundamental importance in the evaluation of investment projects is the systematic risk, which is the risk that cannot be diversified away even by stockholders. Nevertheless, firm risk may affect the investment decision in some cases—when the investment reduces risk in a manner which cannot be replicated by stockholders. For example, if an investment will reduce the likelihood of bankruptcy or of bottlenecks in raw materials or sales, the firm risk of the project should affect the investment decision. The effect of these factors on risk, however, is usually examined qualitatively rather than quantitatively in making investment decisions.

Systematic risk is usually measured by the beta coefficient, which indicates how closely the return on the project will vary with the average return in the market. If an investment has a higher (lower) beta than the market's beta of 1, the systematic risk of the project is higher (lower) than the average risk in the market.

The impact of systematic risk on the required return on a project is accounted for in the capital asset pricing model (CAPM), which expresses return as a function of the risk-free rate and systematic risk. The security market line (SML) is a plot of the various levels of return against various levels of systematic risk. If the expected return of the investment proposal lies above the SML, the investment will be expected to increase the value of the firm's common stock, and vice versa.

We have not considered the effect of a firm's financing of its assets on the investment decision. Thus, we have implicitly assumed that the firm uses only equity financing. Since this is not the usual circumstance, the financing effect must be incorporated in the analytical framework when applicable. We turn to this topic in the following chapter.

SOLVED PROBLEMS

1 The management of John's Sportsware expects sales of the store to rise to a significantly higher level during the next three years, because of a temporary increase in the number of personnel at the local air base. The probability distribution of the additional cash flow in each of the three years is estimated as follows:

Probability	Net cash flow
0.10	$ 5,000
0.20	10,000
0.40	20,000
0.20	30,000
0.10	35,000

The additional sales are expected to be perfectly, positively correlated over the three-year period. On the other hand, the correlation between the added sales and John's regular sales is estimated at only 0.6. The standard deviation of the store's net cash flows has been $10,000 over the past ten years. Treasury bills are currently yielding 6 percent.

a Calculate the standard deviation of the added cash flows over the three-year period.

b Estimate the impact of the new business on John's risk.

Solution

a The first step is to calculate the standard deviation of the cash flow for one year:

Probability	NCB_i	$p_i(NCB_i)$	$(NCB_i - \overline{NCB})$	$(NCB_i - \overline{NCB})^2$	$p(NCB_i - \overline{NCB})^2$
.10	$ 5,000	$ 500	−$15,000	225mm	22.5mm
.20	10,000	2,000	− 10,000	100mm	20.0mm
.40	20,000	8,000	0	0	0
.20	30,000	6,000	10,000	100mm	20.0mm
.10	35,000	3,500	15,000	225mm	22.5mm
Mean		$20,000			
Variance					85.0mm
Standard deviation of cash flow for one year					$9,220

The standard deviation (SD) of the perfectly, positively correlated stream of cash flows is calculated as follows:

$$SD = \sum_{t=1}^{n} \frac{SD_t}{(1 + r_f)^t}$$

$$= \frac{\$9,220}{(1.06)^1} + \frac{\$9,220}{(1.06)^2} + \frac{\$9,220}{(1.06)^3}$$

$$= \$24,645$$

b The following formula should be used to calculate the standard deviation (SD_p) of the store's total cash flows with the added sales:

$$SD_p = (SD_j^2 + SD_k^2 + 2COR_{j,k}SD_j SD_k)^{1/2}$$
$$= [(\$24,645)^2 + (\$10,000)^2 + (2 \times .6 \times \$24,645 \times \$10,000)]^{1/2}$$
$$= \$31,672$$

The calculations above indicate that the risk associated with the expected new business is high. The standard deviation of the store's overall cash flows is expected to increase to $31,672 from $10,000.

2 The composition of Mrs. Massengale's investment portfolio is as follows:

Asset	Total market value	Beta
1	$50,000	0.0
2	10,000	0.9
3	25,000	1.1
4	8,000	1.2
5	7,000	1.7

The yield on 90-day Treasury bills and the average return in the market are expected to be 7 percent and 14 percent, respectively.

a Estimate the beta value of Mrs. Massengale's portfolio.

b Estimate the rate of return on the portfolio.

Solution

a The portfolio *beta* (β_p) is a weighted average of the asset betas:

$$\beta_p = 0.5(0) + 0.1(0.9) + 0.25(1.1) + 0.08(1.2) + 0.07(1.7)$$
$$= 0.58$$

b The expected rate of return on the portfolio (r_p) should be calculated by using the capital asset pricing model:

$$r_p = r_f + \beta_j(r_m - r_f)$$

where the symbols have the same meaning as in the chapter. Calculating, we get

$$r_p = 7\% + 0.58(14\% - 7\%)$$
$$= 11.06\%$$

3 The Aztec Manufacturing Company is researching the possibility of building a new plant. Data applicable to the project and the market are as follows:

Cost of new plant	$10,000,000
Life of plant	30 years
Annual net cash flow	$3,000,000
Correlation of return with market return	0.9
Standard deviation of rate of return on new plant	12%
Standard deviation of average rate of return in the market	10%
Yield on 90-day Treasury bills	5%
Expected average return in market	13%

a Calculate the required rate of return on the new plant.
b Calculate the expected net present value of Aztec's investment in the new plant.

Solution

a The first step is to find the beta value of the investment. In this problem, information is given concerning the standard deviation of the return on both the new plant and the market portfolio. (The return on the market portfolio is the average return in the market.) Thus, the beta can be calculated as follows:

$$\beta_j = \frac{(COR_{j,m}SD_j)}{SD_m}$$

where the symbols have the same meaning as in the chapter. Inserting the appropriate data into the equation, we get

$$\beta_j = \frac{(0.9 \times 12\%)}{10\%}$$
$$= 1.08$$

Using the capital asset pricing model to calculate the required return (k_j) on the new plant, we get

$$k_j = 5\% + 1.08(13\% - 5\%)$$
$$= 13.64\%$$

b Finally, the expected net present value of the plant investment is

$$NPV = \sum_{t=1}^{30} \$3,000,000/(1.1364)^t - \$10,000,000$$
$$= \$11,519,489$$

PROBLEMS

6-1 The Midland Trucking Company is considering two investment proposals. Proposal A is to establish a local hauling service in a town with a population of approximately fifty thousand people. Proposal B is to establish essentially the same type of service in the suburb of a large city with a population of over one million people. The probability distributions of the net cash benefit (NCB) in an average year for the two proposals are as follows:

Proposal A		Proposal B	
Probability	NCB	Probability	NCB
0.05	–0–	0.05	($10,000)
0.20	$ 5,000	0.20	15,000
0.50	20,000	0.50	50,000
0.20	35,000	0.20	85,000
0.05	40,000	0.05	110,000

a Without making any calculations, which proposal do you believe has the greater risk? Why?

b Calculate the following statistics for each of the probability distributions: (1) mean, (2) variance, (3) standard deviation, (4) coefficient of variation.

c Do the results of your calculations in question b indicate the same relative risks of the two opportunities that you found in answering question a? Explain.

d What additional information does the management of Midland Trucking need in order to assess the risks of the investment proposals?

6-2 The probability distributions applicable to the cash flows of project XX in a typical year are as follows: *(PROJECT RISK)*

Probability	Sales	Probability	Variable costs
		0.5	$40,000
0.5	$50,000		
		0.5	$30,000
		0.5	$56,000
0.5	$70,000		
		0.5	$42,000

Probability	Fixed Costs
0.3	$ 5,000
0.4	10,000
0.3	15,000

p.166-167

p.168, p.191

\$350/69

a Calculate the probability distribution of the net cash benefit of project XX.

b Calculate the (1) mean and (2) standard deviation of the probability distribution.

c Do you believe that the standard deviation is a good measure of the project risk in this case? Why or why not?

6-3 A new investment project has an expected net cash benefit of $20,000 per year. The probability distribution of the net cash benefit is assumed to be normal, with a standard deviation of $10,000. The expected life of the project is five years. Treasury bills are currently yielding 6 percent.

a What is the probability that the NCB will be negative in any given year?

b What is the firm risk of the project if the NCBs are perfectly, positively correlated both over time and with respect to the firm's net cash flows without the project? Explain.

c Assume that the NCBs are expected to be completely independent over time. Calculate the standard deviation of the NCBs.

d According to the capital asset pricing model, the required rate of return on a new investment includes a premium only for systematic risk. Keeping this fact in mind, does the degree of correlation in the NCBs over time matter? Why or why not?

e Now assume that the project's NCBs are independent over time, but are perfectly, negatively correlated with the firm's other net cash flows. Estimate the impact of the project on the firm's total risk if the standard deviation of the other cash flows is $100,000.

6-4 The standard deviations of the net cash flows of assets X and Y are $5,000 and $8,000, respectively.

a Calculate the standard deviation of a portfolio consisting of assets X and Y if the correlation in the net cash flows of the two assets is:

(1) 0.0

(2) 0.3

(3) 0.8

(4) 1.0

b Explain the relationships in the results of your calculations.

6-5 Consider the following data for four assets: ~~POST~~ (Piennish)

Asset	Standard deviation
Treasury bills	0
Asset A	$2,000
Asset B	6,000
Asset C	6,000
Asset D	2,000
Asset E	9,000

p. 178

Asset combination	Correlation of net cash benefits
Asset A + Treasury bills	0.0
Assets A + B	+1.0
Assets A + C	+0.5
Assets A + D	−0.4
Assets A + E	−1.0

p.177− p.179

a Rank the above asset combinations in terms of their standard deviations, and explain your results.

b Do any of the portfolios have a standard deviation of zero? Why or why not?

6-6 The following portfolios consist of risky assets only:

Portfolio:	A	B	C	D	E	F	G	H	I	J
Return (percent):	8	10	12	13	15	15	16	19	19	22
Standard deviation (percent):	6	11	10	20	18	26	22	24	32	35

a Plot the return-risk data for each portfolio on a scatter diagram.

b Considering only the information given to this point, which of the portfolios is/are efficient? Explain and state your assumptions.

c Now assume that the risk-free rate is 6 percent. If an investor can borrow and lend at this rate, which of the portfolios consisting entirely of risky assets is/are now efficient? Why?

d Can you identify the portfolio(s) which would be preferable to an investor who is highly risk-aversive? Explain.

6-7 An analyst has made the following estimates:

Standard deviation of the market portfolio	3 percent
Standard deviation of asset j	5 percent
Standard deviation of asset k	8 percent
Correlation of asset j with the market	0.9
Correlation of asset k with the market	0.4

a Estimate the *beta* coefficients for assets j and k.

b Which of the assets has the greater risk (1) in a well-diversified portfolio and (2) in an undiversified portfolio? Explain your reasoning.

6-8 Three friends have decided to pool their resources and go into business. The total funds contributed to the venture consists of $300,000. However, the new venture capitalists have a problem in that they are not certain what type of business they want to start. After a preliminary study, they have narrowed the alternatives down to two, both of which would require the purchase of three assets. Risk-return data for the two alternatives are as follows:

	Conservative alternative				Aggressive alternative		
Asset	Required investment	Expected return	Beta	Asset	Required investment	Expected return	Beta
A	$ 60,000	10 percent	0.8	X	$ 90,000	14 percent	1.0
B	140,000	12 percent	1.0	Y	50,000	20 percent	1.4
C	100,000	15 percent	1.1	Z	160,000	25 percent	1.8

Treasury bills are currently yielding 7 percent, and the average market return is expected to be 13 percent.

a Compute the expected return and beta for both alternatives.

b From the information given, would the expected risk-return point of each alternative lie on the security market line? Why or why not?

6-9 Mr. William Burr plans to construct two separate common stock portfolios, one conservative and the other aggressive. The conservative portfolio is to consist of common stocks with *beta* values less than 1.0. The aggressive portfolio is to consist of common stocks with beta values of 1.0 or higher. The same amount of capital will be invested in each stock, regardless of the portfolio in which it is included.

a Assuming that the standard deviation of the rate of return on the market portfolio is 4 percent, complete the following table for Mr. Burr:

Stock	Standard deviation of return	Correlation with market	Beta	Beta less than 1.0	Beta 1.0 or higher
A	2%	.75			
B	3	.50			
C	4	1.00			
D	5	.05			
E	6	.95			
F	7	−.40			
G	8	−.70			
H	9	−.60			
I	10	−.20			
J	11	−.20			
K	12	.40			
L	13	0.00			
Portfolio beta:				————	————

b Calculate the expected return on each portfolio, assuming 90-day Treasury bills are yielding 7 percent and the average market return is expected to be 14 percent.

6-10 Calculate the beta value for the following efficient portfolios:

a Risk-free asset = 100 percent of portfolio.

b Risk-free asset = 25 percent of portfolio.

c Market portfolio component = 120 percent of investor's own funds invested in a securities portfolio.

6-11 a Using the capital asset pricing model, calculate the required rate of return on an investment project, assuming the yield on ninety-day Treasury bills is 6 percent, the average return in the market is 12 percent, and the beta coefficient of the project is: (1) −0.2, (2) 1, (3) 1.2, (4) 2.0.

b Does your calculation of the required rate of return on the investment proposal assume that the investment would be financed entirely with common equity capital? Explain.

c Under what conditions, if any, should the firm risk of the proposed project, separate and apart from the project's beta, affect the investment decision?

REFERENCES

Beaver, William, and James Manegold: "The Association between Market-Determined and Accounting-Determined Measures of Systematic Risk: Some Further Evidence, " *Journal of Financial and Quantitative Analysis*, vol. X, June 1975, pp. 231–284.

Bey, Roger P.: "Capital Budgeting Decisions When Cash Flows and Project Lives Are Stochastic and Dependent," *Journal of Financial Research*, vol. 6, Fall 1983, pp. 175–187.

Bierman, Harold, Jr., and Seymour Smidt: *The Capital Budgeting Decision*, 6th ed., New York: Macmillan, 1984.

Copeland, Thomas E., and J. Fred Weston: *Financial Theory and Corporate Policy*, 2nd. ed., Reading, Mass.: Addison-Wesley, 1983, Chapter 6.

Harrington, Diana R.: *Modern Portfolio Theory, The Capital Asset Pricing Model and Arbitrage Pricing Theory: A User's Guide*, 2nd. ed., Englewood Cliffs, N.J.:, Prentice-Hall, 1987, Chapter 3.

Pruitt, Stephen W., and Lawrence J. Gitman: "Capital Budgeting Forecast Biases: Evidence From the Fortune 500," *Financial Management*, vol. 16, Spring 1987, pp. 46–51.

Quirin, G. David, and John C. Wiginton: *Analyzing Capital Expenditures*, Homewood, Ill.: Richard D. Irwin, 1981.

Reilly, Frank K., and Rupinder S. Sidhu: "The Many Uses of Bond Duration," *Financial Analysts Journal*, vol. 23, July-August 1980, pp. 58–72.

Schall, Lawrence D., and Gary L. Sundem: "Capital Budgeting Methods and Risk: A Further Analysis," *Financial Management*, vol. 9, Spring 1980, pp. 7–11.

Sharpe, William F.: "A Simplified Model of Portfolio Analysis," *Management Science*, vol. 10, January 1963, pp. 277–293.

Sick, Gordon A: "A Certainty-Equivalent Approach to Capital Budgeting," *Financial Management*, vol. 15, Winter 1986, pp. 23–32.

Statman, Meir, and Tyzoon T. Tyebjee: "Optimistic Capital Budgeting Forecasts," *Financial Management*, vol. 14, Autumn 1985, pp. 27–33.

APPENDIX 6A
Interest Rate Risk

Since the required rate of return, k, on an investment is a function of the risk-free rate of interest and systematic risk, k will vary with interest rate changes in the market. An investment is therefore faced with the risk that interest rates will rise, causing the market value of the investment to decline. This interest-rate risk is included in the systematic risk component of k. In this appendix, we will examine the impact of the factors that affect interest rate risk. These factors are (1) the size of future cash flows, (2) the pattern of the cash flows, and (3) the life of the investment. We initially assume that the required return is unaffected by the life of the investment; that is, the yield curve is flat. The effect of this assumption is considered at a later point.

Cash Flow Size.   The size of the cash flow in each future period will affect the change in the value of an asset when interest rates change. As an example, consider projects A and B in Table 6A-1. Project A has an annuity cash flow of $10,000 per period for 10 periods. The initial required return, k_1, is 10 percent, resulting in a present value of $61,446. Project B has the same characteristics as A, except that B's cash flows are $20,000 per period, which results in a present value of $122,891.

The right-hand side of the exhibit shows the effect of an increase in the level of interest rates. The required rate of return, k_2, on the projects after the increase is shown in column 7 to be 12 percent. The present values of the projects decline to the level shown in column 8. The dollar and percentage changes in the present values are shown in columns 9 and 10, respectively. Note that in this case, the decline in dollar value is much greater for *B*, but the percentage decline is the same for the two projects. This is the result of the relative characteristics of the two projects—they differed only in regard to the amount of cash flow per period.

Investment Life.   The impact of an interest rate change is also affected by the number of periods in which cash flows are expected to occur. This can be seen by comparing projects A and C in Table 6A-1. In this case, the two projects differ only in regard to their length of life;

TABLE 6A-1
IMPACT OF A CHANGE IN THE REQUIRED RATE OF RETURN ON THE VALUE OF INVESTMENT PROJECTS*

1 Project	2 C	3 Years	4 k_1	5 PV_1	6 DUR	7 k_2	8 PV_2	9 $ Change	10 % Change
A	$ 10,000	10	10%	$ 61,446	4.73	12%	$ 56,502	($4,943)	−8.05%
B	$ 20,000	10	10%	$122,891	4.73	12%	$113,004	($9,887)	−8.05%
C	$ 10,000	20	10%	$ 85,136	7.51	12%	$ 74,694	($10,441)	−12.26%
D	$159,374**	1	10%	$ 61,446	10.00	12%	$ 51,314	($10,131)	−16.49%

* Definitions:
C : annuity cash flow in period t, except for project D.
k_1 : initial required rate of return.
k_2 : required rate of return, after interest-rate change.
PV_1 : present value of future cash flows, before interest-rate change.
PV_2 : present value of future cash flows, after interest-rate change.
DUR : duration of the investment.

** Project D has only one future cash flow: $159,374 as of the end of the 10th year.

cash flows are expected to occur in 10 periods for A, but in 20 periods for C. The result of an increase in k from 10 percent to 12 percent is a much greater decline in value for C in both dollar and percentage terms. This is an example of the fact that the value of long-term assets is affected to a much greater extent than the value of short-term assets by changes in interest rates, if long-term rates equal short-term rates both before and after the change. For this reason, the longer the expected life of an asset, the greater will be its interest rate risk.

Pattern of Cash Flows.   In general, the value of an asset will be affected more if most of its cash flows occur toward the end of its life. This relationship can be seen by comparing projects A and D in Table 6A-1. Both projects have the same expected life, the same required return, and initially, the same present value. However, a cash flow is expected to occur for D only at the end of its life; no cash flows are expected in the first nine years. The result of a change in k from 10 percent to 12 percent for both projects is that the value of D declines much more than the value of A in both dollar terms and percentage terms. The implication is that the interest rate risk is much greater for investments whose cash flows are expected in the more distant future. We can therefore say that interest rate risk increases as the proportion of an asset's total cash flows that occur toward the end of the life of the asset increases.

Duration.   The duration of a cash flow stream is a weighted average of the periods in the stream. We will first show how duration is calculated and then investigate its uses.

Consider the following present value equation:

$$PV_0 = \frac{C_1}{(1 + k)^1} + \frac{C_2}{(1 + k)^2} + \cdots + \frac{C_n}{(1 + k)^n} \tag{6A-1}$$

where PV_0 is the present value of cash flows expected in the future, C_t is the cash flow in period t, where t goes from 1 to n, and k is the required rate of return on the investment. The effect of a small change in k and PV_0 can be estimated by taking the derivative of PV_0 with respect to k. The result would be the following equation:

$$\frac{dPV_0}{dk} = -\frac{1}{1 + k} \sum_{t=1}^{n} t\,PV_{0,ct} \tag{6A-2}$$

where $PV_{0,ct}$ is the present value of the cash flow in period t. Dividing Equation (6A-2) by PV_0, we get the percentage change in PV_0 for small changes in k_0:

$$\frac{dPV_0 \div dk}{PV_0} = -\frac{1}{1 + k} \frac{\sum_{t=1}^{n} t\,PV_{0,ct}}{PV_0} \tag{6A-3}$$

The second element on the right-hand side of Equation (6A-3) is called the duration of the cash flow stream. For emphasis, the duration is given the status of a separate equation:

$$DUR = \frac{1C_1/(1 + k)^1 + 2C_2/(1 + k)^2 + \cdots + nC_n/(1 + k)^n}{PV_0} \tag{6A-4}$$

$$= \frac{\sum_{t=1}^{n} t\,C_t/(1 + k)^t}{PV_0} \tag{6A-4a}$$

where DUR symbolizes duration. PV_0 is calculated by equation (6A-1). We see from Equations (6A-4) and (6A-4a) that duration is a weighted sum of the periods during the life of the investment. The weight for period t is

$$\frac{C_t}{PV_0(1 + k)^t}$$

Since the weights will sum to 1, the weighted sum is a weighted average.

As an example, consider project A shown in Table 6A-1. Using the figures shown in the exhibit, the duration of the project before the change in k is:

$$DUR = \frac{1(\$10,000)/(1.1)^1 + 2(\$10,000)/(1.1)^2 + \cdots + 10(\$10,000)/(1.1)^{10}}{\$61,446}$$

$$= 4.73$$

The 4.73 figure we have calculated as project $A's$ duration is shown in column 6 of Table 6A-1. The duration of the other projects discussed earlier are also given in the column.

Duration and Interest Rate Risk.   The importance of duration is indicated by comparing the figures in column 6 of Table 6A-1 with the percentage decreases in the present value of the various projects shown in column 10. Recall that the value decreases were caused by the increase in k from 10 percent to 12 percent, which was assumed to occur because of an increase in interest rates. The comparison shows that the sensitivity of value to interest changes increases as duration increases. Column 10 shows that the percentage change in value increases down the column, except for projects A and B which have the same duration.

An interesting aspect of duration is that it is always less than the life of the investment, except in the case where future cash flows occur only in the last year. Consider project D in Table 6A-1 as an example of the latter case. The difference in the duration and life of an asset increases as the proportion of future flows occurs earlier.

Risk Management.   The liabilities of a firm have an average duration. The firm can manage its interest rate risk by investing in assets of the same dollar amount and the same average duration as the liabilities. Thus, if interest rates increase, the decline in the market value of the firm's assets will be offset by the decline in the market value of its liabilities. If interest rates fall, the increase in the market value of its liabilities will be offset by an increase in the market value of the assets.

A Caution.   In our discussion of interest rate risk and duration, we assumed that the required rate of return was not affected by the life of investment, either before or after an interest rate change in the market. This is not generally the case. Long-term rates are most often, but not always, higher than short-term rates. Furthermore, a change in rates will frequently change the relationship between short-term and long-term rates. This means that our discussion of the impact of a change in the level of interest rates on the relative value of investments with different lives and different patterns of cash flows, described general tendencies and approximations, rather than definite effects. As is usually the case, our study assumed that everything else remained the same. Unfortunately for analysts, everything else is seldom so benign.

APPENDIX 6B:
Evaluating Option Components of Capital Expenditures

A BRIEF INTRODUCTION TO OPTIONS

Options have been in use in various forms for a long time, however it has been only recently that stock options have been traded on an "organized exchange." The Chicago Board of Options Exchange (CBOE) was organized in April 1973 and initially allowed trading of call options on only sixteen widely traded common stocks. Since that time four additional exchanges have begun to offer option trading (AMEX, Philadelphia, Pacific and Midwest). Today, stock options are traded actively on over 400 stocks and more than 10,000 contracts. The CBOE alone has a total dollar value of securities traded which is eclipsed only by the NYSE. In fact, the CBOE *daily* trading volume regularly surpasses options on 10 million shares of stock.

An **option** is a contract that conveys the *right* to buy or sell specified property at a specified price for a specified period of time. The property on which the option contract is written is called the *underlying asset* which for a stock option is shares of stock. The specified price at which the option is exercised is referred to as the *striking price* or *exercise price* of the option, and the period of time over which the option is in effect is the *exercise period*, or term of the contract. The person who creates and offers the contract for sale is called the *option writer* or seller. The other party is called the owner or buyer. When the contract is made the buyer pays cash to the writer for the right to buy or sell at a known price. An important attribute of an option contract is that the owner of the contract has the *right* to buy or sell the underlying asset but has no *obligation* to do so. This lack of obligation to buy or sell provides the distinguishing characteristic of an option contract vis-à-vis *forward* and *futures* contracts, for which there *is* an obligation to execute the contract or, using the terminology of the options literature, *exercise* the contract.

Option contracts come in two forms: call options and put options. A **call option** is a contract which permits the holder to buy an asset during a specified time interval and for a specified price, and requires the option writer to sell. At the time the contract is written both parties agree as to the price at which the purchase can be made, and the time period within which the option can be exercised. A **put option** differs from a call option in that it allows the holder to sell an asset rather than purchase it.

Two categories of option contracts are traditionally discussed, with one differing from the other only in terms of the type of restriction placed on the time when the contract can be exercised. A **European option** contract can be exercised only at the termination of the contract, that is, on its expiration date, whereas an **American option** can be exercised at any time up to and including the exercise date. The American option contract obviously offers the holder greater flexibility, which not only makes the contract more valuable, but makes its valuation more difficult.

To summarize briefly, there are five basic elements which are necessary to characterize or describe an option contract:

1 *The type of option*—Put or Call.

2 *The underlying asset*—the particular common stock, tract of land, or other asset that the owner of the option contract buys or sells if the contract is exercised. We say the option is written on the underlying asset.

3 *The expiration date of the option*—we will designate the maturity date for an option using the symbol T and the current date using t. Hence, an option which expires on date T has $T - t$ days to maturity.

4 *The exercise (or striking) price*—we will use the symbol K to refer to the option's exercise price.

5 *The terms of exercise*—American or European. Here we will couch our initial discussions in terms of European options which, with their single exercise date (T), are easier to value than their American option counterparts.

THE BLACK-SCHOLES OPTION PRICING MODEL[1]

The notation **Call(*P,T,K*)** will be used to identify a call option on a stock with current price P, expiring in T periods and with an exercise price K. The Black-Scholes option pricing equation can be written as follows.

$$\text{Call}(P, T, K) = P(0)[N(d_1)] - K e^{-rT}[N(d_2)] \qquad (6B)$$

where
$$d_1 = \frac{ln(P(0)/K) + [(r + \sigma^2)/2] T}{\sigma\sqrt{T}}$$

$$d_2 = d_1 - \sigma\sqrt{T}$$

$N(d_i)$ = the probability that a deviation less than d_i could occur under the standard normal distribution (i.e., mean zero and standard deviation equal to one)

$e = 2.7183$

$ln\left(\dfrac{P(0)}{K}\right)$ = the natural log of the ratio of the current stock price divided by the exercise price of the option

σ^2 = the variance in the rate of return on the stock, that is, $ln\left(\dfrac{P(t+1)}{P(t)}\right)$

All the remaining terms retain their previous definitions. In case you have not already noticed, the form of this model is *not* intuitively obvious. Do not be concerned, however. We do not need to have the knowledge of the stochastic calculus used in deriving the model to be able to understand its use.[2]

To illustrate the use of the Black-Scholes model consider the following example:

$$P(0) = \$32.00 \qquad K = \$30.00 \qquad T = 0.25 = \frac{90}{360}$$

$$\sigma^2 = 0.16 \qquad r = 12\% \text{ per annum}$$

First we calculate the constants d_1 and d_2 as follows:

$$d_1 = \frac{ln(32/30) + (0.12 + 0.16/2)\,0.25}{0.4\sqrt{0.25}} = 0.57$$

$$d_2 = 0.57 - 0.4\sqrt{0.25} = 0.37$$

[1]This discussion follows that contained in Keown, Martin, Petty, and Scott [forthcoming].
[2]A brief recap of the assumptions underlying the derivation of the Black-Scholes model includes the following assumptions: (i) one plus the rate of return on the underlying stock is distributed lognormally, (ii) both the risk-free rate of interest and variance in the rate of return on the stock are constant throughout the life of the option, (iii) there are no transaction costs or taxes, (iv) the stock pays no dividends, and (v) the option is a European option.

Now, using equation (6B-1) and the table of areas under the standard normal distribution found in Appendix B, we calculate the value of the option as follows:

$$\text{Call}(P, K, T) = \$32(0.7157) - \$30e^{-0.12(0.25)}(0.6443) = \$4.14$$

Thus, the option value is \$4.14 even though the current price is only \$2 greater than the exercise price of \$30. The reason for this difference relates to the potential for an even greater difference, should the stock price rise over the next 90 days. In fact, if the term to maturity of the option had been six months, the value of the option would rise to \$4.70.

It is beyond the scope of our discussion to review the empirical tests that have been performed using the Black-Scholes model.[3] However, we will note that the model performs surprisingly well in light of the somewhat restrictive conditions under which it was derived (no transactions costs, continuous trading and no dividends to name a few.

APPLICATIONS OF OPTION PRICING THEORY TO THE CAPITAL BUDGETING PROBLEM[4]

Capital investments can differ one from the other on a wide variety of dimensions. However, an important source of uniqueness relates to the flexibility that the investment offers the firm. In this context a flexible investment is one which offers the owner a wide variety of applications or uses once it is acquired. Thus the flexibility of an investment incorporates consideration for such things as the opportunity to convert the investment from one application to another (e.g., the ability to change a coal fired electric power plan over to crude oil), or to sell the asset before the end of its useful life, or abandon the investment. We can think of flexibility as simply the presence of "options" which add value to an investment and consequently should be entered into the evaluation of major capital investment decisions. Thus, the evaluation of a capital budgeting problem that involves otpions such as those mentioned here cannot be based solely on the expected cashflows from the project in its intended application. To evaluate a capital budgeting problem which involves one or more options we must calculate an "expanded NPV" which is defined as follows:[5]

$$\text{Expanded NPV} = \text{Static NPV} + \text{Option Premium}$$

Here the NPV calculated using a project's expected cashflows is captured in the concept of **Static NPV** to which we add the value of "managerial flexibility" via an option premium. Kensinger (1987) notes that use of option pricing theory to evaluate the above option premium opens the horizon to consideration of a number of basic problems in capital budgeting. Specifically, an options-based approach to capital budgeting might be used to solve the following problems:

a) Analyze the value of having the option to shut down temporarily, or, in the extreme, abandon the project before the anticipated holding period expires. The abandonment option was

---

[3] For a review of these tests see Chapter 16 of Martin, Cox and MacMinn (1988). In addition, Rubinstein (1985) provides a very extensive set of tests of a wide range of option pricing models.
[4] This section draws upon Martin and Kensinger (1988).
[5] This discussion relies on Trigeorgis and Mason (1987).

analyzed as a European option by Kensinger (1980) and as an American option by Myers and Majd (1983). Examples of the use of option pricing theory to evaluate the shut-down option include papers by McConnell and Siegel (1983), and Mason and Merton (1985), who extend the analysis to consider the expansion and contraction of the size of an investment, as well as the opportunity to extend or contract the life of an investment.

b) Evaluate the option to re-deploy assets to new uses in the business environment as the future unfolds and expectations fail to materialize. This problem can be conceptualized as an option to exchange one commodity or set of commodities for another. Flexibility of use is, in essence, the presence of exchange options, and these options clearly add value to an asset.[6]

c) Analyzing the value of options for future growth that arise out of a given investment. Myers (1977) dichotomizes the value of a firm's equity into two components: the value of assets in place, and the value of growth opportunities. A capital investment can be thought of in exactly the same terms, with those assets possessing superior growth opportunities, other things being the same, having the higher value.[7]

A simple application of option pricing theory can be constructed, using the **abandonment put option**. Consider an investment that requires payment of $100,000 immediately, in return for an anticipated two-year cash flow return. The two annual cash flows have expected values of $60,000 and $50,000, respectively, for years one and two. Discounting the expected cash flows back to the present, using a 10 percent discount rate, produces a NPV of $-\$4,132.24$, indicating that the project should not be undertaken, that is:

$$\text{Static NPV} = \frac{\$60,000}{(1.10)^1} + \frac{\$50,000}{(1.10)^2} - \$100,000 = -\$4,132.24$$

Now consider the impact of having a **put option** for the salvage value of the asset which can be exercised at the end of the first year. In essence, exercising the abandonment put option at the end of Year One requires that the firm forfeit the Year Two cash flow. Consequently, the present value of the expected Year Two cash flow at the end of Year One becomes the exercise price of the option whose payoff is the asset's abandonment value. Thus, the Expanded NPV would equal the following:

$$\text{Expanded NPV} = \text{Put} - \$4,132.24$$

where Put is the value assigned to the abandonment option today. Valuing the abandonment put is made difficult, since active trading in the salvage value of the underlying asset on which it is written is generally not possible. This poses a serious problem for the valuation of the option using a traditional risk-free hedge or spanning type of argument.[8] At the very least, however, by analyzing the project's static NPV and placing it in the Expanded NPV model,

[6] See Kensinger (1987).

[7] As an aside, it is interesting to note that these papers are either working papers, articles in readings books, or have appeared in non-finance journals.

[8] The basic intuition underlying the development of option pricing formulae is as follows: The payoff to the holder of the option is replicated exactly by constructing a portfolio containing both the stock on which the option is written, and risk-free debt. Since the values of both the stock and the risk free debt can be observed, we can calculate the value of the option as a weighted average of these values. The weights used simply reflect those in the "hedge" portfolio which replicates the option payoff. The payoff to the option is said to be "spanned" by the stock and risk-free debt payoffs.

the analyst knows the lower bound on the value of the abandonment Put needed to make the asset's purchase worthwhile. Much remains to be done in developing useful formulae for applying option pricing theory to investments in real/productive assets. At the present time this approach provides a way of *characterizing* the flexibility inherent in various investment alternatives, and focusing managerial efforts on their proper consideration in the capital budgeting process.

REFERENCES

Black, Fisher: "The Pricing of Commodity Contracts," *Journal of Financial Economics*, vol. 9, 1981, pp. 321–46.

Black, Fisher, and Myron Scholes: "The Pricing of Options and Corporate Liabilities," *Journal of Political Economy*, vol. 81, May–June 1973, pp. 637–59.

Bookstaber, Richard: *Option Pricing and Strategies in Investing*, Reading, MA: Addison-Wesley, 1986.

Hayes, R. H., and D. A. Garvin: "Managing as if Tomorrow Mattered," *Harvard Business Review*, vol. 60, May–June 1982.

Kensinger, John: "Adding the Value of Active Management into the Capital Budgeting Equation," *Midland Corporate Finance Journal*, vol. 5, Spring 1987, pp. 31–42.

Kensinger, John: "Project Abandonment as a Put Option: Dealing with the Capital Investment Decision and Operating Risk Using Option Pricing Theory," working paper presented at the Annual Meeting of the Financial Management Association, October 1980.

Keown, Arthur, John D. Martin, J. W. Petty and David F. Scott, Jr.: *Advanced Financial Management*. Englewood Cliffs, NJ: Prentice Hall, forthcoming.

Martin, John D. and John Kensinger: "Some Thoughts in the Evolving Role of Strategy Considerations in the Theory and Practice of Finance," *Managerial Finance*, vol. 14, 1988, pp. 9–15.

Martin, John, Samuel Cox and Richard MacMinn: *The Theory of Finance: Evidence and Applications*. Hinsdale, IL: The Dryden Press, 1988.

Mason, Scott and Robert Merton: "The Role of Contingent Claims Analysis in Corporate Finance," in *Recent Advances in Corporate Finance*. ed. E. Altman and M. Subrahmanyam, Homewood, IL: R. D. Irwin, 1985.

McConnell, John and Dan Siegel: "Investment and the Valuation of Firms When There is an Option to Shut Down," *Northwestern University Working Paper*, June 1983.

Myers, Stewart: "Determinants of Corporate Borrowing," *Journal of Financial Economics*, vol. 5, November 1977, pp. 147–75.

Myers, Stewart: "Finance Theory and Financial Strategy," reprinted in the *Midland Corporate Finance Journal*, vol. 5, Spring 1987, pp. 6–13.

Myers, Stewart and S. Majd: "Calculating Abandonment Value Using Option Pricing Theory," Working Paper, Sloan School of Management, M.I.T., 1983.

Porter, Michael E.: "From Competitive Advantage to Corporate Strategy," *Harvard Business Review*, vol. 65, May–June 1987, pp. 43–59.

Porter, Michael E.: *Competitive Strategy*. New York: The Free Press, 1980.

Porter, Michael E.: *Competitive Advantage: Creating and Sustaining Superior Performance*. New York: The Free Press, 1985.

Rubinstein, Mark: "Nonparametric Tests of Alternative Option Pricing Models Using All Reported Trades and Quotes on the 30 Most Active CBOE Option Classes from August 23, 1976 through August 31, 1978," *Journal of Finance*, vol. 35, June 1985, pp. 455–80.

Shapiro, Alan: "Corporate Strategy and the Capital Budgeting Decision," *Midland Corporate Finance Journal*, vol. 3, Spring 1985, pp. 22–36.

Shapiro, Alan: "Guidelines for Long-Term Corporate Financing Strategy," *Midland Corporate Finance Journal*, vol. 4, Winter 1986, pp. 6–19.

Trigeorgis, Lenos and Scott Mason: "Valuing Managerial Flexibility" *Midland Corporate Finance Journal*, vol. 5, Spring 1987, pp. 14–21.

7

ESTIMATING THE REQUIRED RATE OF RETURN ON INVESTMENT PROPOSALS

Up to this point our discussions of capital expenditure analysis have avoided the problem of determining the proper discount rate to use in the time-adjusted evaluation methods. We have assumed that the required rate of return on a possible investment has been identified by management and, therefore, can be employed in the (1) net present value, (2) internal rate of return, or (3) profitability index methods. The time has arrived for exploring some of the available methodologies which approximate the required returns on proposed expenditures. Accordingly, this chapter deals with assessing the firm's cost-of-capital funds.

The **cost of capital** is a decision criterion to be used by the management of the enterprise. Its basic intent is to provide a defensible answer to this question: What rate of return must an investment promise to deliver in order that the firm's owners will be no better or worse off in a monetary sense if the investment is undertaken? The cost of capital, then, is an aid in determining whether acceptance of a specific project will provide an economic benefit to the firm's owners. A proposed use of corporate funds must earn a rate of return greater than the cost of the funds that the project employs, or the market price of the firm's common stock will be adversely affected. The cost of capital can, therefore, be defined as the minimum rate of return that must be earned on an investment in order to leave the market price of the firm's common stock unchanged.

The analysis of the investment decision in Chapter 5 pointed out that capital expenditures involve outlays of cash in hopes of generating returns that will extend beyond one year. While there is nothing sacred about this one-year cutoff period that distinguishes capital expenditures from operating expenditures, it is a familiar distinction found in industrial practice. It is indicative of a tendency for long-term investments to be financed out of long-term or permanent capital and for short-term investments to be financed out of short-term sources of funds, typically referred to as **current liabilities.** The focus of this chapter is on permanent sources of financing.

The outline of the chapter is as follows:

1 Costs of Individual Sources of Capital
   a The Cost of Long-Term Debt
   b The Cost of Preferred Stock
   c The Cost of Convertible Securities
   d The Cost of Common-Equity Capital
2 More on the Cost of Common-Equity Capital
   a Comparison of the Estimates
   b The Effect of Debt Financing on the Cost of Equity of the Firm
   c The Cost of Equity for an Investment
   d Adjusting the Cost of Equity for Different Capital Structures
3 Deriving a Weighted-Average Cost of Capital
   a Rationale
   b An Example
   c The System of Weights
   d A Solved Problem
4 Setting Required Rates for Risk Categories
5 Cost of Capital for Company Divisions
6 Acquisitions of Other Firms
   a Economic Benefits from Acquisitions
   b Evaluating an Acquisition
7 Chapter Summary

COSTS OF INDIVIDUAL SOURCES OF CAPITAL

The major avenues of long-term financing available to the firm include debt, preferred stock, convertible securities, retained earnings, and new common stock. Methods for approximating the cost of each of these sources of capital will be explained and demonstrated. In this portion of the analysis, each source of funds is evaluated apart from the others.

The Cost of Long-Term Debt

A firm incurs long-term debt by selling bonds to investors who desire to purchase fixed-income securities and retain the position of a creditor rather than an equity investor in the organization. A wide array of bond types can be marketed. These include first mortgage bonds, debentures, and subordinated debentures. While these instruments offer the investor differing claims upon the assets and earnings of the firm which sells them, common elements are present that permit their costs to be estimated. These common elements are (1) an interest payment, (2) a maturity payment, (3) the amortization of any bond discount or premium that arose when the debt was issued, and (4) the net proceeds to the firm from each bond. Several approaches exist for computing the cost of a debt issue. Some are more appropriate under certain circumstances than others.

The Par Value Method. If the net proceeds to the firm from selling one new bond are equal to the maturity value (or par value) of the bond, then the **par value method** is appropriate for approximating the cost of the debt issue. If we let the cost of debt on an after-tax basis be represented by k_d, the par value method calculates the cost as follows:

$$k_d = i(1 - T) \tag{7-1}$$

where i is the interest or coupon rate on the debt issue and T is the firm's marginal income tax rate. In this restricted setting, where the net proceeds from a bond equal its maturity value, i is also the yield to maturity on this instrument.[1]

A Solved Problem. The Blackburn Corporation is going to sell a new issue of twenty-year bonds. The coupon rate on the issue will be 8 percent. The firm will net $1,000 from each bond that is sold. The face value of the bonds is $1,000. The company's marginal income tax rate is 50 percent.[2] What is the cost of this debt issue to the firm?

The cost of the debt issue to the Blackburn Corporation can be determined by applying equation (7-1) to the contractual terms of the issue. The cost of this debt offering (k_d) turns out as follows:

$$k_d = 8.00(1 - 0.50) = 4.00 \text{ percent}$$

Why is 4.00 percent the cost of this twenty-year bond? The answer is most easily understood by thinking of a possible investment that is to be financed by selling a single $1,000 bond. If the $1,000 investment is to earn its cost of capital, it must generate $80 in before-tax income. This additional $80 produced by the project will just cover the incremental interest costs on the new bond, which are also equal to $80, i.e., 8.00 percent of the $1,000 bond.

You might reasonably think that an $80 return on a $1,000 investment should be an 8.00 percent rate of return and not a 4.00 percent return, which was said to be the cost of capital of the bond issue. This matter can be quickly cleared up by pointing out the distinction between before-tax and after-tax returns. The 8.00 percent return on the $1,000 investment is a before-tax return, but after federal income taxes are paid at the presumed rate of 50 percent, the after-tax yield on the investment is reduced to 4.00 percent. Moreover, since the interest costs on debt are deductible for purposes of computing federal income tax burdens, any interest that the firm pays shields an equal number of dollars from being taxed (if the firm faces a 50 percent tax rate).

---

[1] The yield to maturity on a bond is also known as the *bond yield*. *Bond yield* was defined in Chapter 4 and represented there by the variable y. Here $i = y$.

[2] Two simplifying assumptions are followed throughout this chapter: (1) a 50 percent marginal corporate tax rate is used rather than the actual rate, and (2) yields or capital costs are computed on an annual basis as opposed to, say, the semiannual basis representative of most bond issues. Because capital costs are only *estimates* of required returns, nothing of significance is lost by this latter process. Bond tables are, of course, computed on a semiannual basis. If the analyst finds the bond yield in such a collection of tables, the answer will differ slightly from the calculations illustrated in this chapter. Adjustment to an annual basis is discussed in Chapter 4.

Thus, an 8.00 percent before-tax cost of debt is equivalent to a 4.00 percent after-tax cost of debt when the firm's marginal tax rate is 50 percent. Under these conditions the investment returning 4.00 percent after taxes will meet the 4.00 percent cost of the bond issue that financed it. Such an investment would leave unchanged the cash-flow earnings available to the firm's common shareholders. This fact indicates that it has met its minimum acceptable rate of return.

It is possible to express capital costs on either a before- or after-tax basis. The after-tax approach is most commonly employed in industry and in financial research. The logic behind this preference is rather straightforward. You will recall from our study of the investment decision in Chapter 5 that the net cash benefits associated with a possible use of funds were calculated after consideration of income tax payments. If investment returns are stated on an after-tax basis, then capital costs must be expressed on a similar basis. We will continue to follow such a procedure in the remainder of this analysis.

The Yield-to-Maturity Method.   Strictly speaking, we ought to refer to this approach to calculating the cost of debt as the *yield-to-maturity method from the firm's viewpoint*, since the corporation's marginal tax rate will be directly incorporated into the computations. For brevity, however, we will employ the label **yield-to-maturity method**.

Circumstances are often present that tend to render the par value method expressed in equation (7-1) inaccurate. Actually, this occurs any time the net proceeds to the firm from the sale of a new bond differ from its maturity (or par) value. Moreover, the firm may be concerned with measuring the current cost of debt capital on the basis of one of its outstanding bond issues. If the market price of that issue is not equal to the bond's par (or face) value, the par value approach will provide an inaccurate cost estimate. If the bond is sold at a premium or a discount, or if underwriting costs are involved in marketing the issue, the true cost of debt cannot be found by application of equation (7-1).[3] Instead, the bond's cost of capital is better approximated by use of the yield-to-maturity method, expressed as follows:

$$B_p = \sum_{t=1}^{n} \frac{I_t(1 - T)}{(1 + k_d)^t} + \frac{B_m}{(1 + k_d)^n} \tag{7-2}$$

where B_p is the net proceeds to the firm per bond; B_m is the maturity (par) value of the bond, due at the end of n years; I_t is the annual interest payment on the bond made in year t; T is the firm's marginal income tax rate; n is the number of years that the bond will be outstanding; and k_d is the after-tax cost of debt. By observing equation (7-2), we can see that finding the cost of debt by means of the yield-to-maturity method is nothing more than a familiar internal-rate-of-return problem. The rate (k_d) has to be found that will equate the present value of the after-tax interest

---

[3] A bond is said to be *sold at a premium* if the selling price to the investor exceeds its maturity value. It is *sold at a discount* if the selling price is less than the maturity value.

payments plus the bond maturity value with the proceeds received from the sale of the bond. The procedure is illustrated in the next problem.[4]

A Solved Problem.   The Blackburn Corporation is going to offer to the market a $1 million bond issue with a twenty-five-year maturity period. The security will carry an 8 percent coupon and have a $1,000 face value. It will be sold to investors for 96 percent of face value. The underwriting commission on the bond issue will amount to 3 percent of the face value. The company's marginal income tax rate is 50 percent. What is the cost of capital of this debt issue to the Blackburn Corporation?

By drawing upon the facts of this bond issue, the yield-to- maturity expression can be set up as follows, with k_d, the cost of debt, as the only unknown:

$$\$930 = \sum_{t=1}^{25} \frac{\$80(1 - 0.50)}{(1 + k_d)^t} + \frac{\$1,000}{(1 + k_d)^{25}}$$

If you recall our earlier illustrations in Chapters 4 and 5, you know that we must find the approximate value of k_d that will equate the present value of the cash outflows associated with the bond with the $930 net proceeds that the firm will realize from its sale. The procedure is outlined in Table 7-1. Since the Blackburn Corporation will net only $930 from the sale of each bond, the cost of the offering will be more than the 4.00 percent indicated cost that would be obtained by strict application of the par value

---

[4] It is emphasized here and in the remainder of this chapter that the basic procedures for estimating capital costs are the same whether new securities are being issued or existing securities are used to provide the financial data. In the latter instance, the current market price of the existing security is used instead of the net proceeds that would be realized from marketing a new issue. If no flotation costs are suffered by the firm, then this approach must be employed. This rule applies to any form of capital, be it debt, preferred stock, convertibles, or common equity.

TABLE 7-1
BLACKBURN CORPORATION CALCULATION OF THE COST
OF DEBT BY THE YIELD-TO-MATURITY METHOD

Part A: Present value of the bond's cash outflows at 5 percent

$40(PVAF$_{25,5}$) + $1,000(PVIF$_{25,5}$) =
$40(14.094) + $1,000(0.295) =
$563.76 + $295.00 = $858.76

Part B: Present value of the bond's cash outflows at 4 percent

$40(PVAF$_{25,4}$) + $1,000(PVIF$_{25,4}$) =
$40(15.622) + $1,000(0.375) =
$624.88 + $375.00 = $999.88

Part C: Interpolation between 4 and 5 percent

$$\frac{\$999.88 - \$930.00}{\$999.88 - \$858.76} = \frac{\$69.88}{\$141.12} = 0.495$$

Therefore, $k_d \approx 4.495$ percent.

method. In Table 7-1, then, the after-tax value of the interest payments and the face value of the bond are discounted at both 5 and 4 percent. The $930 net proceeds per bond lie between the $858.76 and $999.88 that result from discounting the relevant cash outflows at 5 and 4 percent. The interpolation procedure found in Part C of Table 7-1 demonstrates that the cost of capital of this bond issue is approximately 4.495 percent.

Notice that the particular form of the yield-to-maturity method described by equation (7-2) assumes that the principal value of the bond (B_m) is repaid in one lump sum at the end of the instrument's maturity period. Many bond indentures, though, require sinking-fund payments throughout the life of the issue. These sinking-fund payments provide for the orderly retirement of the principal amount of the bond issue and are not, therefore, tax-deductible. If principal repayment does occur during the life of the issue, then equation (7-3) is a more accurate representation of the cost of capital of the debt obligation.

$$B_p = \sum_{t=1}^{n} \frac{I_t(1-T) + B_t}{(1 + k_d)^t} \tag{7-3}$$

where all the symbols carry the same meanings as in the basic yield-to-maturity equation (7-2), except that B_t is the principal or sinking-fund payment made during year t.

The Yield-To-Maturity Method With Amortization of Bond Discount or Premium.   Our illustration of the yield-to-maturity method for approximating the cost of debt ignored the tax effects that arise from (1) the amortization of any bond discount or premium or (2) the amortization of any bond issue expense. These situations give rise to tax considerations over the life of the issue that affect the firm's tax bill. The amortization of a bond discount and related issue expenses will lower the firm's tax bill since they are tax-deductible. The amortization of a bond premium over the life of the instrument releases a portion of the premium into taxable income each year, so the firm's tax bill will be somewhat higher than in its absence. Since these cash flows are caused by the bond's being sold, they are a part of its cost of capital. We will assume that discounts, premiums, or issue expenses are written off on a straight-line basis over the maturity period of the security. Equation (7-4) allows for these tax effects in the computation of the bond's cost of capital.

$$B_p = \sum_{t=1}^{n} \frac{[I_t(1-T)] - T \cdot (1/n)(B_m - B_p)}{(1 + k_d)^t} + \frac{B_m}{(1 + k_d)^n} \tag{7-4}$$

where all the symbols have the same meanings as in the basic yield-to-maturity equation (7-2). It is the form of the relationship that differs when the tax effect of the premium or discount is considered. Table 7-2 summarizes the direction of such tax effects on the cost of a debt issue.

To illustrate the application of equation (7-4), we can draw upon the problem situation used to demonstrate the basic yield-to- maturity method. Use of that situation

TABLE 7-2
THE COST OF DEBT: TAX EFFECT ARISING FROM
AMORTIZATION OF BOND DISCOUNT OR PREMIUM

Situation	Relationship	Effect on cost of debt
Bond sold at a discount	$B_m - B_p > 0$	Reduction
Bond sold at a premium	$B_m - B_p < 0$	Increase

permits us to write the following equation:

$$\$930 = \sum_{t=1}^{25} \frac{[\$80(1 - 0.50)] - 0.50 \cdot (1/25)(\$1,000 - \$930)}{(1 + k_d)^t} + \frac{\$1,000}{(1 + k_d)^{25}}$$

Since the \$1,000 maturity value of the bond (B_m) exceeds the \$930 net proceeds to the Blackburn Corporation (B_p), the bond is marketed at a discount. Table 7-2 informs us that this circumstance will result in a reduction in the cost of the debt issue. This reduction is relative to the cost derived from the basic yield-to-maturity approach. When the tax effect arising from the amortization of the discount is computed, the equation just stated becomes the following:

$$\$930 = \sum_{t=1}^{25} \frac{\$38.60}{(1 + k_d)^t} + \frac{\$1,000}{(1 + k_d)^{25}}$$

Solving this relationship for k_d, we find that the cost of the debt issue is approximately 4.345 percent. The calculations are displayed in Table 7-3. Note that this figure is less than the 4.495 percent obtained under the basic yield-to-maturity method. We will now discuss one more method for calculating the firm's cost of debt.

The Shortcut Method.   This approach is termed the **shortcut method** or the **approximation method** because it does not explicitly consider the compounding effects associated with the cash outflows required to service the debt commitment. In most instances, however, this technique does provide results adequately (surprisingly) close to those obtained by use of the yield-to-maturity method adjusted for amortization effects. Retaining the notation that we have developed throughout our discussion of the cost of debt, we can express the shortcut method as follows:

$$k_d = \frac{(1 - T)\{I_t + [B_m - B_p/n]\}}{(B_m + B_p)/2} \tag{7-5}$$

Again, we will draw upon the problem situation used to illustrate the yield-to-maturity approach. Recall that the Blackburn Corporation is going to market a \$1,000 face-

TABLE 7-3
BLACKBURN CORPORATION CALCULATION OF THE COST
OF DEBT CONSIDERING AMORTIZATION OF BOND
DISCOUNT OR PREMIUM

Part A: Present value of the bond's cash outflows at 5 percent

$38.60(PVAF$_{25,5}$) + $1,000(PVIF$_{25,5}$) =
$38.60(14.094)   + $1,000(0.295)   =
$544.03   + $295.00   = $839.03

Part B: Present value of the bond's cash outflows at 4 percent

$38.60(PVAF$_{25,4}$) + $1,000(PVIF$_{25,4}$) =
$38.60(15.622)   + $1,000(0.375)   =
$603.01   + $375.00   = $978.01

Part C: Interpolation between 4 and 5 percent

$$\frac{\$978.01 - \$930.00}{\$978.01 - \$839.03} = \frac{\$\ 48.01}{\$138.98} = 0.345$$

Therefore, $k_d \simeq 4.345$ percent.

---

value bond (B_m). The bond will carry an 8 percent interest rate ($I_t = 0.08 \times \$1,000 = \$80$). The bond will be outstanding for 25 years (n) and will net the firm $930 per bond ($B_p$). Blackburn's marginal income tax rate is 50 percent (T). Application of this information to equation (7-5) gives:

$$k_d = \frac{(1 - 0.50)\{\$80 + [(1,000 - 930)/25]\}}{(1,000 + 930)/2}$$

$$= \frac{(0.50)(\$82.80)}{\$965}$$

$$= 4.290 \text{ percent}$$

The shortcut method indicates that the cost of this debt issue to the Blackburn Corporation is 4.290 percent. This is a reasonable approximation to the 4.345 percent that was obtained from application of the yield-to-maturity method adjusted for amortization effects [equation (7-4)].

Five approaches have been presented for estimating the cost of capital of a debt issue. The "proper" one to use depends upon the degree of accuracy demanded by the financial manager and the contractual characteristics of the instrument. The greatest caution must be exercised with use of the par value method [equation (7-1)] because of the very restrictive set of circumstances under which it is accurate.

The Cost of Preferred Stock

Preferred stock carries a claim against the income and assets of the firm prior to that of common stock, but subordinate to that of debt. The claim against income takes the form of a preferred dividend payment. This cash outflow is made at the discretion of the company's board of directors. Legally, bankruptcy proceedings cannot be initiated because a company omits a preferred dividend payment. On the other hand, firms do not market preferred stock with the intention of skipping the associated dividend payments. Doing so makes it very difficult to raise external capital at a later date. Thus, preferred stock can properly be visualized as representing a fixed cash payment that will be honored ahead of any cash dividend payment to common shareholders. Additionally, we will assume that (1) preferred stock is noncallable, (2) it is nonparticipating, (3) it carries no sinking-fund commitment, and (4) that the firm is not in arrears on the dividend payment. Under these conditions, the dividend can be viewed as a level, perpetual payment. This view allows the cost of preferred stock (k_p) to be defined as the rate of return, adjusted for flotation costs, that the investors receive on the preferred shares. **Flotation costs** include fees paid to investment bankers, lawyers, printers, engravers, registration expenses, and any other charges involved in marketing the new security. We can now calculate the cost of preferred stock as follows:

$$k_p = \frac{\text{preferred dividend}}{\text{net proceeds from selling one new share of preferred stock}} = \frac{D_p}{P_{pn}} \quad (7\text{-}6)$$

A Solved Problem.   The Blackburn Corporation is going to sell a new issue of preferred stock. Each preferred share will have a $100 par value. The dividend rate is 9 percent. Because of flotation costs, the firm will net $97.50 per share. The company's marginal income tax rate is 50 percent. What is the cost of this preferred stock issue to the firm?

From equation (7-6) we get:

$$k_p = \frac{D_p}{P_{pn}} = \frac{\$9.00}{\$97.50} = 9.231 \text{ percent}$$

The cost of this preferred stock issue to Blackburn turns out to be 9.231 percent. Notice that the firm's marginal tax rate did not enter into the computations. No adjustment for tax effects is necessary here because preferred dividends are not tax-deductible expenses; rather, they are considered a distribution of income. For this reason, the explicit cost-of-debt capital will be less than preferred-stock capital when the other characteristics of the issues are identical.

The Cost of Convertible Securities

Two major forms of convertible securities are sold by corporations to investors: (1) convertible debt and (2) convertible preferred stock. Up to this point we have discussed various methods for approximating the cost of capital of "straight debt" and "straight preferred stock" as distinct from their convertible forms. Modifications must be made in the previous techniques to accommodate this style of financing.

For purposes of assessing their costs, convertible securities are viewed as delayed-equity financing. This assumes that the convertible security will be a bond or preferred stock for a while, but will become common stock at a later date when converted. By exercising the conversion option, the security owner can convert the bond or preferred stock into a predetermined number of common shares. This ratio of exchange is typically referred to as the **conversion ratio**. A conversion ratio of 20 means that the convertible security can be exchanged for 20 shares of common stock. Suppose the firm sells a convertible bond for its $1,000 face value and the conversion ratio is 20. The effective or conversion price at which common stock will be sold at a later date (i.e., upon conversion) is as follows:

$$\text{Conversion price} = \frac{\text{face value}}{\text{conversion ratio}}$$

$$= \frac{\$1,000}{20} = \$50 \text{ per share}$$

When a convertible security is offered to the public, it will usually be priced so that the conversion price of the security will exceed the prevailing market price of the corresponding common stock. If this were not the case, purchasers of the convertible issue would immediately exchange their security for the common stock. They would, in effect, be buying the common stock at a significant reduction from the current market price. The conversion price, then, tends to be greater than the market price of the firm's common stock when the convertible security is issued.[5]

At a later date, if the fortunes of the company are favorable, the market price of the common stock should rise above the conversion price of the convertible security. When this occurs, the firm can force conversion through exercise of the call privilege. Alternatively, investors on their own initiative may seek to convert. Upon conversion, the investor exchanges his or her creditor or preferred position for that of a residual equity owner. It is as if the principal value of the convertible bond or the par value of the convertible preferred stock is paid off with new shares of common stock. By simply assuming that conversion will take place sometime in the future, the cost of convertible securities can be measured.

Convertible Debt.   The cost of convertible debt (k_{cb}) can be calculated as the discount rate that equates the present value of the after-tax interest payments on the debt plus the conversion value of the instrument with the net proceeds that the firm realizes per security. The **conversion value** of the instrument is equal to the number of shares received upon conversion times the current market price of the common stock. This can be expressed as follows:[6]

---

[5] Infrequently, the conversion price associated with a new convertible bond will be less than the current market price of the related common stock. In these instances the conversion privilege is generally delayed for a specific time period.

[6] A more complicated version of equation (7-7) could be offered that would explicitly recognize the cash-flow effects of amortizing any bond discount or premium, as was explained earlier in regard to equation (7-4). That aspect is purposely ignored here to allow us to focus on the main principles of estimating the capital costs for convertible issues.

$$B_p = \sum_{t=1}^{n} \frac{I_t(1-T)}{(1+k_{cb})^t} + \frac{(CR)(P_n)}{(1+k_{cb})^n} \tag{7-7}$$

where B_p is the net proceeds to the firm per bond; I_t is the annual interest payment on the bond made in year t; T is the firm's marginal income tax rate; n is the investors' holding period on the convertible bond, conversion occurring at the end of year n; P_n is the expected market price of the common stock at the end of year n; CR is the conversion ratio associated with each convertible bond; and k_{cb} is the cost of convertible debt.

From the financial manager's standpoint, two crucial inputs are required to make equation (7-7) operational: (1) a representative holding period (n) must be selected during which the security will not be converted, and (2) the market price of the firm's stock at the end of time period n must be projected. We will assume that both these difficulties can be surmounted. The following problem demonstrates the procedure for finding k_{cb}, the cost of convertible debt.

A Solved Problem. The Blackburn Corporation will market a new convertible bond issue to the investing public. The bond will mature in twenty years. The instrument pays interest at the rate of 7 percent annually. The face value of the bond is $1,000. The sale of each bond will net the company $950. Blackburn's marginal income tax rate is 50 percent. The firm's management believes that a ten-year holding period will be representative of the bond's investors. Blackburn common stock sells today for $42 per share. At the end of the ten-year holding period, the stock is expected to be worth $91 per share. Each convertible bond can be exchanged for twenty common shares at the option of the bond investor. What is the cost of capital of this convertible bond to the Blackburn Corporation?

By applying equation (7-7) to these facts, we get:

$$\$950 = \sum_{t=1}^{10} \frac{\$70.00(1-0.50)}{(1+k_{cb})^t} + \frac{(20)(\$91)}{(1+k_{cb})^{10}}$$

$$= \sum_{t=1}^{10} \frac{\$35.00}{(1+k_{cb})^t} + \frac{\$1,820}{(1+k_{cb})^{10}}$$

Notice that for each of the ten years during which the bond will be outstanding, the investor will receive a $70 annual interest payment. Because this is tax-deductible to the firm, it represents a net outflow of $35 per year. At the end of the tenth year, the investor converts the bond into twenty shares of common stock. The terminal value of the bond is, therefore, $1,820, because each share of stock is forecast to be worth $91 at that point in time. The cost of the convertible bond issue (k_{cb}) is the discount rate that will equate the ten after-tax interest payments of $35 and the terminal value of $1,820 with the $950 net proceeds to the firm. The cost of this convertible bond is found to be 9.568 percent. The final calculations that produce this result are shown in Table 7-4.

TABLE 7-4
BLACKBURN CORPORATION CALCULATION OF THE COST
OF CONVERTIBLE DEBT

Part A: Present value of the bond's cash outflows at 10 percent

$35.00(PVAF$_{10,10}$) + $1,820(PVIF$_{10,10}$) =
$35.00(6.145) + $1,820(0.386) =
$215.08 + $702.52 = $917.60

Part B: Present value of the bond's cash outflows at 9 percent

$35.00(PVAF$_{10,9}$) + $1,820(PVIF$_{10,9}$) =
$35.00(6.418) + $1,820(0.422) =
$224.63 + $768.04 = $992.67

Part C: Interpolation between 9 and 10 percent

$$\frac{\$992.67 - \$950.00}{\$992.67 - \$917.60} = \frac{\$42.67}{\$75.07} = 0.568$$

Therefore, $k_{cb} \approx 9.568$ percent.

Convertible Preferred Stock.   The cost of convertible preferred stock (k_{cp}) can be calculated in a fashion similar to that associated with convertible debt. It is only necessary to keep in mind that the preferred dividend payment made by the firm is *not* deductible for purposes of computing its tax bill. The cost of preferred stock, then, is the discount rate that equates the present value of the cash dividend payments plus the conversion value of the instrument with the net proceeds that the firm realizes per security. Again, the conversion value of the security is equal to the market value of the common shares received upon conversion. In model form we have:

$$P_{pn} = \sum_{t=1}^{n} \frac{D_p}{(1 + k_{cp})^t} + \frac{(CR)(P_n)}{(1 + k_{cp})^n} \tag{7-8}$$

where P_{pn} is the net proceeds to the firm per share; D_p is the annual dividend payment on each convertible preferred share made in year t; n is the investors' holding period on the convertible shares, conversion occurring at the end of year n; P_n is the expected market price of the common stock at the end of year n; CR is the conversion ratio associated with each convertible share; and k_{cp} is the cost of convertible preferred stock.

The mechanical procedure for finding the cost of convertible preferred stock is identical to that illustrated in the previous section for determining the cost of convertible debt. The task is nothing more than an internal-rate-of-return problem in which the proper discount rate, k_{cp} in this case, has to be found. We will continue now with our study of the costs of individual sources of capital. Yet to be examined are methods for assessing the cost of common-equity capital.

The Cost of Common-Equity Capital

Approximating the cost of common-equity capital is a difficult chore. True, investors receive cash returns from their common-stock investments in only two forms: (1)

cash dividends, or (2) capital gains realized upon liquidating their equity holdings. The dividends, though, do not have to be paid by the firm during any given time period. They are not contractual liabilities like the interest payments due on debt obligations. Dividend receipts are, therefore, subject to more uncertainty than interest receipts. Furthermore, equity investors expect that the price of the shares they own will rise over time. Such required stock-price appreciation, or growth, cannot be estimated with certainty. Necessarily, our estimates of common-equity costs are fraught with difficulties not inherent in the measurement techniques associated with other component sources of capital.

Methodologies for computing the cost of common-equity capital abound. We will direct our attention, though, to the two approaches that have the most widespread acceptance by academics and practitioners. More importantly, these models have been implemented in a variety of industrial settings that encompass both regulated and unregulated operating environments. The immediate focus is upon (1) the Gordon perpetual-growth model and (2) the capital-asset pricing model. The structure of each model will permit us to estimate both the firm's cost of retained earnings and its cost of new common stock.

The Gordon Perpetual-Growth Model: The Cost of Retained Earnings. One of the concepts presented in Chapter 4 was the Gordon stock-valuation model.[7] It will be helpful here to review the underpinnings of that methodology.

Common-equity investors are similar to other contributors of corporate capital in that they expect some positive rate of return as compensation for letting the firm have the use of their savings. We refer to this expected return as the investors' **required rate of return**. How can we determine this required rate of return, that is, the cost of common-equity capital? One approach is to forecast (estimate) the cash dividends that investors in the firm's common stock can reasonably expect to receive in the future. Once the prospective dividends have been estimated, the discount rate can be found that will equate the present value of the dividend stream with the current market price of the company's common stock. This discount rate serves as an estimate of the firm's cost of common-equity capital. More specifically, because there are no flotation costs involved in retaining earnings as opposed to raising equity by marketing new common stock, this discount rate is the firm's cost of retentions. The term **retained earnings** is used in this context to refer to the portion of current earnings not paid out in the form of cash dividends. It does *not* refer to the earnings that have been retained over the entire life of the firm.

In equation (7-9) the current market price of the firm's common stock is considered to be equal to the discounted value of all future cash dividends expected by investors.[8]

---

[7] This model first appeared in Myron J. Gordon and Eli Shapiro, "Capital Equipment Analysis: The Required Rate of Profit," *Management Science*, vol. 2, October 1956, pp. 102–110; detailed empirical estimates involving use of the model were presented in Myron J. Gordon, THE INVESTMENT, FINANCING, AND VALUATION OF THE CORPORATION (Homewood, Ill.: Richard D. Irwin, Inc., 1962).

[8] The description of the Gordon perpetual-growth model in Chapter 4 assumed a holding period of *n* years. We then allowed that holding period to become very large. In this discussion we use the largest of holding periods, infinity (∞). The strict mathematical derivation of the perpetual-growth model requires this latter supposition. Pragmatically, it can be thought of as the stock being passed on to one's heirs forever. See the earlier discussion that relates to equation (4-13).

$$P_0 = \frac{D_1}{(1 + k_e)^1} + \frac{D_2}{(1 + k_e)^2} + \frac{D_3}{(1 + k_e)^3} + \cdots + \frac{D_\infty}{(1 + k_e)^\infty}$$

or
$$P_0 = \sum_{t=1}^{\infty} \frac{D_t}{(1 + k_e)^t} \tag{7-9}$$

where P_0 is the current market price of the firm's common stock, D_t is the cash dividend per share expected at the end of each time period t, and k_e is the cost of common-equity capital (retentions).

As we emphasized in our earlier examination of valuation concepts in Chapter 4, it is extremely difficult to estimate what the cash dividend on a particular stock will be several years in the future. This makes literal application of equation (7-9) in an industrial setting a most trying task at best. We can, however, make a simplifying assertion about investor expectations, incorporate it into our method of analysis, and render equation (7-9) more useful in our array of techniques for assessing capital costs. One such possibility involves assuming a constant cash dividend (D_t) over all years of the investment horizon. Assuming that investment horizon to be infinity, we would represent such a case as follows:

$$D_1 = D_2 = D_3 = \cdots = D_\infty$$

It is more likely, however, that the investor will expect the cash dividend receipts on the particular stock to increase over time. He or she may anticipate that each dividend payment will be larger than its predecessor. Such a situation can be represented as follows:

$$D_1 < D_2 < D_3 < \cdots < D_\infty$$

This latter, and more typical, situation assumes that the investor envisions his or her dividend stream to be *growing* over time. By assuming that the dividends are expected to grow at the compound rate of g per year, we can express the share price of the company's common stock (P_o) as follows:

$$P_o = \frac{D_1}{k_e - g} \tag{7-10}$$

where D_1 is the cash dividend per share expected to be paid at the end of year 1, and all other symbols retain their earlier meanings. This is the Gordon perpetual-growth model presented in Chapter 4. When the Gordon valuation model is restated in terms of k_e, the cost of equity capital, we get:

$$k_e = \frac{D_1}{P_o} + g \tag{7-11}$$

where D_1/P_o represents the dividend yield and g represents the rate at which the firm's

(1) stock price, (2) earnings per share, and (3) dividends per share are expected to grow. The return required by the investing marketplace on the firm's common equity, then, can be visualized as follows:

$$\text{required return } (k_e) = \text{dividend yield} \left(\frac{D_1}{P_o}\right)$$
$$+ \text{a representative dividend growth rate } (g)$$

By calculating k_e, we have a workable estimate of the company's cost of retained earnings.

A Solved Problem.   The Blackburn Corporation will earn $4.00 per common share during the coming year. The company follows a dividend policy of paying out 50 percent of each period's earnings in the form of cash dividends. Over the past ten years the firm's earnings, dividends, and stock price have all been growing at about 8 percent per annum. The common stock of Blackburn currently sells for $40 per share. Both security analysts and investors feel that this $40 price represents the "true," or fair, value of Blackburn shares. The investing marketplace also believes that the 8 percent growth rate associated with the firm's key financial variables will continue indefinitely into the future. What is Blackburn Corporation's cost of retained earnings?

From equation (7-11) we get:

$$k_e = \frac{D_1}{P_o} + g = \frac{\$2}{\$40} + 0.08 = 13 \text{ percent}$$

For the Blackburn Corporation, the cost of the retained earnings used to finance a portion of its capital budget is estimated to be 13 percent.

The Gordon Perpetual-Growth Model: The Cost of New Common Stock. The cost of capital of a new issue of common shares will exceed the required rate of return on the firm's retained earnings. Flotation costs incurred on the new issue will cause the net proceeds to the firm per share to be less than the current market price of the shares (P_o). These flotation costs can take any of the following forms:

1 Pricing each share of the new issue below the prevailing market price in order to make it attractive to the investing public. This is typically referred to as *underpricing*.
2 Legal and accounting fees involved in drawing up the related prospectus and registration statement.
3 Engraving and printing costs.
4 Payment for the services of an investment banker.

Since the firm will not obtain an amount equal to P_o for each new share that is sold, equation (7-11) must be altered to reflect this fact. Otherwise, its use in this situation will provide a cost-of-capital estimate that is too low. If we let P_{cn} be the amount per share that the company realizes from selling one additional share of common stock, then equation (7-12) can be employed to estimate the capital cost of such an offering (k_{cn}). The other symbols in the equation have been previously defined.

$$k_{cn} = \frac{D_1}{P_{cn}} + g \qquad (7\text{-}12)$$

Refer back for a moment to the sample problem just solved via equation (7-11). If Blackburn is going to float a common stock issue to raise its needed common equity rather than retain earnings, then equation (7-12) can be used to estimate k_{cn}. Suppose that flotation costs will amount to 15 percent of the current price of the stock (P_o) and that all other aspects of the problem situation remain unchanged. This means that the firm will net $34 per share, or 85 percent of the prevailing $40 market price. The cost of the new common stock issue (k_{cn}) can be computed as follows:

$$k_{cn} = \frac{D_1}{P_{cn}} + g = \frac{\$2}{\$34} + 0.08 = 13.882 \text{ percent}$$

The cost of the new outside common equity for the Blackburn Corporation turns out to be 13.882 percent. We saw that investors require a 13 percent return (k_e) on Blackburn stock. However, this 13 percent return was based on a $40 market price ($P_o$). If additional shares net the firm less than $40 each, then the return must rise on the new common-stock-financed portion of investments in order to provide the required 13 percent return related to the $40 price. Therefore, $k_{cn} > k_e$ and in this sample problem is 13.882 percent. By carrying the calculation of k_{cn} (or any capital source) to three decimal points, we do not imply that the estimate is that accurate. Rather, this is merely a spurious by-product of the technique.

The Capital-Asset Pricing Model: The Cost of Retained Earnings.   An alternative to the Gordon perpetual-growth model for estimating common-equity costs is available. This approach, which will be briefly described, has gained considerable attention in the finance literature over the past 25 years.[9] It is typically called the **capital-asset pricing model** (CAPM)[10] and obviates the need to forecast *directly* the firm's future stream of cash dividends, a basic requirement for application of the Gordon model.

Borrowing from the tenets of the CAPM,[11] we can express the required return on the firm's common equity (k_e) as follows:

[9] An early discussion of the following model is provided by William F. Sharpe, "Capital Asset Prices: A Theory of Market Equilibrium under Conditions of Risk," *Journal of Finance*, vol. 19, September 1964, pp. 425–442.

[10] In Chapter 6, we introduced the concept of systematic risk and its expression through the CAPM (see equation 6-11). Here, we expand upon that discussion and illustrate the use of the CAPM as a method of estimating the firm's cost of common equity(k_e). The present notation is used to blend with the typical cost-of-capital symbols used throughout this chapter.

[11] The technical assumptions that underlie the mathematical derivation of the CAPM are presented in countless places. Among the more readable are Lawrence D. Schall and Charles W. Haley, INTRODUCTION TO FINANCIAL MANAGEMENT, Fourth Edition, (New York: McGraw-Hill Book Company, 1986), pp. 167–177; William F. Sharpe, INVESTMENTS, Third Edition, (Englewood Cliffs, N.J.: Prentice-Hall, Inc., 1985), pp. 158– 173 and David F. Scott, Jr., John D. Martin, J. William Petty, and Arthur J. Keown, BASIC FINANCIAL MANAGEMENT, Fourth Edition, (Englewood Cliffs, N.J.: Prentice Hall, 1988), pp. 391–397 and 443–444.

$$k_e = k_i + (k_m - k_i)\text{Beta}_e \qquad (7\text{-}13)$$

where k_i is the riskless rate of interest (this is typically approximated by using historical returns on some class of U.S. Treasury securities); k_m is the expected rate of return on the **market portfolio**, which can be interpreted as the average rate of return available on all securities in the marketplace (the returns available on a broad-based market index, such as the *Standard & Poor's (S&P) Index* of 500 stocks, is widely used to represent the returns obtainable on the so-called market portfolio); Beta_e is a measure of the responsiveness of the returns available to investors on the firm's common stock in excess of the riskless rate of interest to those available on the market portfolio.

The only mysterious aspect of the preceding equation is the term called *Beta*. Where can an analyst working for a corporation find an estimate of the Beta for the firm's common stock? The answer to this question is relatively simple. The analyst has two choices: (1) calculate the Beta by using the proper mathematical procedure, or (2) use a Beta that has been calculated and published by an investment advisory service.

Calculation of the firm's Beta involves use of the linear regression technique described in Chapter 3. The firm's Beta is nothing more or less than the slope coefficient of a linear regression equation. Recall from Chapter 3 that the general form of the linear regression can be stated as follows:

$$Y = A + BX \qquad (7\text{-}14)$$

Within the realm of the CAPM, the dependent variable (Y) is represented by observations for the rate of return on the firm's stock over some past selected time period. Sixty monthly observations are often used. The rate of return is defined to include both cash dividends received by an investor and changes in the market price of the security. The independent variable (X) is represented by a sample of observations for the rate of return obtainable on the market portfolio of all securities. Usually, the analyst will deduct the risk-free rate (k_i) from both the observations that correspond to returns on the specific stock and the market returns. Thus, we can say that "excess returns" for the security are regressed on the "excess returns" of the market portfolio (e.g., the Standard & Poor's Index). The output of this statistical exercise will provide the analyst with an estimate of the slope coefficient (B) in equation (7-14).[12] This slope of the least-squares regression line can then be used as Beta_e in equation (7-13) to estimate the cost of common equity (retained earnings) for the company. Keep in mind that the use of historical data to estimate Beta presumes that the past is a reasonable model for the future. If it is not, then forecasts must be used for the independent variables in the procedure.

For larger corporations, it is not necessary that an analyst be assigned the task of computing Beta. Several investment advisory services publish Beta information for large numbers of publicly traded securities. As an example, the *Value Line Investment*

---

[12] An excellent illustration of this calculating procedure is contained in J. Fred Weston, "Investment Decisions Using the Capital Asset Pricing Model," *Financial Management*, vol. 2, Spring 1973, pp. 25–33.

TABLE 7-5
SELECTED BETA VALUES*

Industry and firm	Beta value	Industry and firm	Beta value
Steel:		Paper:	
Armco Steel	1.40	Scott Paper	1.15
Bethlehem Steel	1.50	Weyerhaeuser	1.25
Inland Steel	1.35	Petroleum:	
USX	1.00	Chevron	0.95
Food processing:		Exxon	0.80
Borden	1.10	Mobil	0.90
Campbell Soup	1.00	Texaco	0.75
ConAgra	1.20	Computers:	
Kellogg	0.95	Amdahl	1.60
Paper:		Apple	1.35
Georgia Pacific	1.25	Hewlett-Packard	1.20
International Paper	1.30	IBM	0.95

*Source: The Value Line Investment Survey (New York: Arnold Bernhard & Co., Inc., 1989).

Survey contains Betas for several hundred corporations. Table 7-5 contains some selected Beta values for specific firms as reported during 1989 by *Value Line*.

From Table 7-5 we can observe that the Beta value for IBM is 0.95, but it is much larger for Amdahl—1.60. If we feel that these estimates represent "true" Betas, then the responsiveness of rates of return on the common stock of IBM to variations in the rate of return on the market will be considerably less than that experienced on Amdahl common stock.

A Solved Problem. The Blackburn Corporation uses the CAPM to estimate its cost of retained earnings. Blackburn analysts estimate that the default-free rate of return available on U.S. Treasury securities is 6 percent. The expected return on a popular index of stock-market prices is 11 percent. On the basis of holding-period returns over the past five years, the firm has computed its $Beta_e$ to be equal to 1.10. No information is available to cause Blackburn analysts to expect that $Beta_e$ relationship to change in the future. According to the CAPM, what is Blackburn Corporation's cost of retained earnings?

Applying equation (7-14) to this situation gives the following:

$$k_e = k_i + (k_m - k_i)Beta_e$$
$$= 0.06 + (0.11 - 0.06)1.10$$
$$= 11.5 \text{ percent}$$

This technique generates a cost-of-retained-earnings estimate of 11.5 percent for the Blackburn Corporation.

The Capital-Asset Pricing Model: The Cost of New Common Stock. The cost of capital of a new common-stock issue will exceed the cost associated with corporate retentions for the reasons identified in our discussion of the perpetual-growth model. Similarly we must allow for this fact when the CAPM is used to calculate the cost of the common-stock issue. If the flotation costs on the common-stock offering relative to the existing price of the stock are represented by F, then the capital cost of the new equity (k_{cn}) can be represented as follows:

$$k_{cn} = \frac{k_e}{1 - F} \tag{7-15}$$

where k_e is estimated by the CAPM [equation (7-13)]. In the previous solved problem, k_e was estimated to be 11.5 percent. Suppose that a new common-stock issue will net Blackburn Corporation 90 percent of the current market price of its outstanding common stock. Therefore, the flotation factor is 10 percent and F in equation (7-15) is 0.10. Under these conditions the cost of the new common-stock issue is as follows:

$$k_{cn} = \frac{k_e}{1 - F} = \frac{0.115}{1 - 0.1} = 12.78 \text{ percent}$$

Comparison of the Estimates.   The capital-asset pricing model and the Gordon perpetual-growth model provide alternative methods of estimating the cost of equity capital of a firm. Which provides the better estimate? The answer to this question depends on the quality of the inputs used. In using the CAPM, the focus of attention is on the basic ingredients of the required return of investors, that is, on a pure (risk-free) interest rate and the premium required for risk taking. Inputs required in using the model include forecasts of future interest rates, the average (total) return in the market, and an estimate of the beta value, or responsiveness of the return on the firm's equity to changes in the average return in the market. If the analyst has confidence in his or her estimates of these parameter values, he or she should also feel reasonably confident of the cost of equity estimate obtained from using the CAPM.

On the other hand, the perpetual-growth model uses as inputs an estimate of a growing stream of dividends which the company will pay out to common stockholders. The major problems here concern estimating the growth rates and the applicability of the assumption of the model that the growth rate is constant over time. Normally, the growth rate of dividends will *not* be absolutely constant. A major question then is: how much error is produced from assuming that it is. If the firm's earnings are expected to grow at a fairly constant rate and the firm pays out a fairly constant proportion of earnings over a period of, say, five years, the analyst can feel comfortable in using the perpetual-growth model to estimate the cost of equity.

Use of the perpetual-growth model to estimate the cost of equity capital for a new investment which has a *different* level of business risk than that of the firm on average requires an adjustment for the difference. If the new project has the higher (lower) risk, the cost of equity capital estimate will have to be adjusted upward (downward) in some manner to reflect this assertion. No definitive procedure exists for making this necessary adjustment. On the other hand, the beta input used in calculating the cost of equity with the CAPM can be made to account directly for the business risk of the particular project.

As a general rule, both the CAPM and the Gordon perpetual-growth model should be used to make the estimates of the cost of equity for the firm as a whole *and* for specific investments. Since the results of the calculations will almost certainly differ, the analyst will have to use his judgment in choosing between the two estimates, or in weighting the two estimates in some manner. Even though the final result may be a specific figure, the analyst will have to keep in mind that it is only an estimate; the possible error is dependent on the quality of the inputs used in making the calculations.

The Effect of Debt Financing on the Cost of Equity of the Firm.   The element $Beta_e$ in equation (7-13) is affected by two types of systematic risk: systematic business risk and systematic financial risk. Business risk is caused by the problems and vicissitudes of the business operation itself—separate and apart from the financing of the firm. Financial risk is the impact of the firm's financing on the risk of the firm (that is, *added* variability in the firm's cash-flow earnings stream). The impact of this dichotomy of risk on the cost of equity capital is expressed in the following equation:

$$k_e^L = k_e^U + (k_e^U - k_d)(1 - T)\frac{d}{e} \tag{7-16}$$

where k_e^L = the cost of equity capital for the firm
k_e^U = the cost of equity capital if the firm did not use debt financing
k_d = the firm's cost of debt
T = the firm's marginal tax rate on income
d/e = the firm's debt-to-equity ratio

The elements k_e^L and k_e^U in the above equation are often referred to as the costs of levered and unlevered equity capital, respectively. Equation (7-16) indicates that the cost of equity capital when the firm uses debt, k_e^L, is a function of both business and financial risks. Two factors affect k_e^U: the risk-free rate of interest and the systematic business risk of the project. However, when a firm uses debt financing, the cost of equity is increased because of the financial risk in its capital structure. The effect of the financial risk is accounted for in equation (7-16) by the expression.

$$(k_e^U - k_d)(1 - T)\frac{d}{e}$$

The Cost of Equity for an Investment.   Now let us change our focus slightly to consider the cost of equity capital in the required rate of return on a new investment. If the systematic business risk of the investment is assessed to be the same as that of the firm, the cost of equity capital of the firm can be used as the cost of equity capital for the new investment project. This is true regardless of the amount of leverage capital, if any, used by the firm.

When the project's risk differs from the average risk of the firm, however, the beta for the *project* can be estimated by the procedures discussed in Chapter 3. The beta value can then be inserted into equation (7-13) to solve for the cost of equity capital for the project. In the unlikely event that the firm uses only common equity in its long-term financing, the cost of equity for the project is its required rate of return.

In most cases, however, firms use some type of leverage-inducing financing. Determining the cost of equity for an investment in these cases requires that the unlevered cost of equity for the project, k_e^U, be included along with the other required data in equation (7-16) to solve for k_e^L, the levered cost of equity capital for the project.

Adjusting the Cost of Equity for Different Capital Structures   We must be aware of the fact that if the debt-to-equity ratio, d/e, is changed, the cost of debt will be affected. If d/e increases, k_d will increase because of the additional financial risk, and vice versa. This point should be kept in mind any time equation (7-16) is used.

An analyst will sometimes want to "unlever" a company's cost of equity in order to "relever" it for a different capital structure. For example, assume that the Rudd Corporation is considering building a new plant to manufacture a product called elax. Although Rudd has no experience with the product, the Elixir Company's only activity is manufacturing it. However, the two companies differ in regard to the relative amount of debt they use in their financing. They may also differ in regard to their tax rates. Thus, the analyst could "unlever" Elixir's cost of equity and then "relever" it according to Rudd's capital structure and tax rate. If all of the elements of equation (7-16) as applied to Elixir are known except k_e^U, the equation can be rearranged to form the following formula for solving for the unknown statistic:

$$k_e^U = \frac{k_e^L + k_d(1 - T)d/e}{[1 + (1 - T)d/e]} \tag{7-17}$$

The calculated value of k_e^U can then be inserted into equation (7-16) along with the values of the other elements which conform to Rudd's situation. The resulting calculation of k_e^L will provide an estimate of the cost of equity capital for the company's plant.

To illustrate the procedure numerically, assume the following estimates for Rudd and Elixir:

For the Rudd Corporation:

$k_d = 4$ percent
$T = 50$ percent
$d/e = 30/70$

For the Elixir Company:

$k_e^L = 15$ percent
$k_d = 5$ percent
$T = 40$ percent
$d/e = 100$ percent

The Elixir Company's k_e^L can be unlevered by the use of equation (7-17) as follows:

$$k_e^U = \frac{.15 + .05(1 - .4)1}{[1 + (1 - .4)1]}$$

$$= \frac{.18}{1.6}$$

$$= .1125, \text{ or } 11.25 \text{ percent}$$

Relevering k_e^U for Rudd's capital structure, we get

$$k_e^L = .1125 + (.1125 - .04)(1 - .5)\frac{30}{70}$$

$$= 12.8 \text{ percent}$$

Comparing the 15 percent and 12.8 percent estimates of the cost of equity capital for Elixir and the new plant for Rudd, respectively, indicates the impact of the differences in the capital structures and tax rates of the two firms. The financial risk premium in Elixir's cost of equity is $(.1125 - .05)(1 - .4)1 = 3.75$ percent. For Rudd, the risk premium is only $(.1125 - .04)(1 - .5)(30/70) = 1.55$ percent.

DERIVING A WEIGHTED-AVERAGE COST OF CAPITAL

Up to this point we have developed a rather detailed array of computational schemes for the costs of individual sources of capital. Formats for deriving the specific costs of (1) debt, (2) preferred stock, (3) convertible securities, and (4) common equity were presented. Our next step in analyzing the required rate of return on capital expenditures is to combine these individual costs into a composite, or overall, cost of capital. Throughout this discussion, keep in mind that application of a weighted-average cost of capital is strictly valid only if the following two assumptions are met: (1) the investments must be of such a nature that they will not change the riskiness of the firm's traded securities as perceived by the marketplace, and (2) the firm's established financing policies will remain intact if the investments are undertaken. For the broad spectrum of possible corporate investments, these criteria will be satisfied. If they are not, then more complex techniques such as the risk-adjusted required rate of return must be employed.

Rationale

Suppose that your firm is considering the addition of a new wing to your major production facility. A financial analyst has estimated the internal rate of return on this project to be 12 percent. Your company can sell new debt at an effective cost (k_d) of 8 percent. If debt is used to finance the project, then the expected return on the plant addition of 12 percent appears favorable. On the other hand, the same financial analyst has estimated your firm's cost of retained earnings (k_e) to be equal to 14 percent. Adequate funds are available internally to finance the plant expansion. Compared with the cost of retentions, the plant expansion no longer appears to be a prudent investment. Is the plant addition economically favorable if it is financed with debt but unfavorable if it is financed with retentions? This result illustrates the basic fallacy of comparing the expected benefits from a proposed use of corporate funds with the cost of the specific source of funds used to finance it.

We conclude that neither the cost of debt alone nor the cost of retentions alone is the relevant hurdle rate in this simplified example. The firm cannot continue using a given type of funds indefinitely. Continual use of debt financing sooner or later will force the firm into the equity market. Even though a given project may be financed wholly through a bond issue, the true cost of funds to the firm includes the interest cost of the bond issue plus an implicit equity cost, as the firm's capacity to issue further debt has been reduced. Alternatively, if the project is financed with common equity, the firm's capacity to issue debt capital in the future has been increased. Thus, the true cost of capital is a composite cost, reflecting the costs of the permanent sources of funds used by the enterprise.

The composite cost of capital is arrived at by applying a system of weights to the component costs of capital. Pragmatically, this process of weighting the costs of all sources of funds used by the firm keeps the discount rate used in the capital budgeting process from being quite high in some years (when equity is used) and comparatively low in others (when debt is issued). Before we discuss the weighting system that should be employed by the financial officer, it will be useful to illustrate the mechanics of the calculations that result in an estimate of the weighted-average cost of capital.

An Example

A firm has determined that it will invest $1 million next year. The corporation's financial manager has decided to finance 20 percent of the $1 million capital budget by issuing long-term debt, 10 percent by preferred stock, and 70 percent out of the retentions. The after-tax cost of capital for each source of financing has been determined as follows: cost of debt capital, 4 percent; cost of preferred stock, 10 percent; cost of retained earnings, 15 percent. Given this information, we can compute the weighted-average cost of capital used to finance the $1 million budget. This computation is displayed in Table 7-6.

TABLE 7-6
THE WEIGHTED-AVERAGE COST OF CAPITAL

Source of funds	Weights (percentage of financing)	Component costs	Weighted cost
Debt	0.2	4 percent	0.8 percent
Preferred stock	0.1	10 percent	1.0 percent
Retained earnings	0.7	15 percent	10.5 percent
Weighted-average cost of capital			12.3 percent

From this example, we conclude that each investment project accepted into the firm's capital budget should have an expected rate of return in excess of 12.3 percent. Again, this composite cost of funds is to be applied as a screening rate against those projects which will *not* change the firm's riskiness as currently evaluated by the marketplace. A lower rate would be acceptable for risk-reducing projects; a higher screening rate must be applied to projects that would increase the firm's risk exposure.[13]

The System of Weights

We direct our attention now to the second column in Table 7-6. Specifically, what weights should be used to estimate the firm's composite cost of capital? We can offer that it is *inappropriate* to use balance-sheet weights (also called **book-value weights**) in the calculation procedure, and it is *appropriate* to use market-value weights. Even this latter suggestion has to be qualified somewhat, as will be done shortly. First, let us look at Table 7-7, which contains the capital structure of the Blackburn Corporation stated both in book- and market-value terms. Two things are immediately evident from inspecting Table 7-7. First, the capital structure amount under each valuation system is different. It is greater in the case of the market-value approach then with the book-value method. Second, the relative proportions of each major source of funds to the total are also different. That is, the *weights* are different.

The market-value amounts are derived by taking the number of traded securities for each source and multiplying it by the current market price of each security. Thus, the common-equity value is arrived at by taking the number of outstanding common shares and multiplying that total by the current common-stock price. The same procedure is followed for the long-term debt and preferred stock sources. Since the balance-sheet amounts represent historical amounts, they typically bear little resemblance to the market-value amounts. The weights, then, also differ. Obviously, if the weights differ, then the weighted-average cost of capital (k_o) is different for each set of weights used to compute it.

---

[13] Such rates are known as risk-adjusted discount rates.

TABLE 7-7
BLACKBURN CORPORATION CAPITAL STRUCTURE IN BOOK AND MARKET VALUES

Balance-sheet (book) values	Amount	Percent	Market values	Amount	Percent
Long-term debt	$ 2,700,000	27	Long-term debt	$ 2,400,000	20
Preferred stock	1,500,000	15	Preferred stock	1,200,000	10
Common stock	215,760		Common equity	8,400,000	70
Capital surplus	1,566,000				
Retained earnings	4,018,240	58			
Total	$10,000,000	100	Total	$12,000,000	100

If we let w_d, w_p, and w_e represent the weights associated with debt, preferred stock, and common equity, respectively, then the computational process illustrated in Table 7-6 can be expressed as:

$$k_o = k_d w_d + k_p w_p + k_e w_e \qquad (7\text{-}18)$$

Applying the book-value weights in Table 7-7 to the component capital costs observed in Table 7-6 gives us an estimate of the composite cost of capital as follows:

$$k_o = 0.04(0.27) + 0.10(0.15) + 0.15(0.58) = 11.28 \text{ percent}$$

Since the book value of common equity is often less than its market value, the blind application of balance-sheet weights in the calculating process will understate the overall cost of capital. This will lead to suboptimal investing decisions.

But just why is it that market-value weights are preferable to the balance-sheet alternatives? The answer to this question may best be understood by reference to an individual investor. If an investor purchased some common stock five years ago for $10,000 and it is now worth $30,000 in the marketplace, how much does he or she have invested? Clearly, the investor has $30,000 invested since he or she could liquidate the holdings and put the $30,000 (ignoring brokerage fees) in the bank. The $10,000 that was paid for the stock may be considered a sunk cost; it has little or no meaning for current investing decisions. If this same investor wants a 15 percent return on the investment, does he or she want that 15 percent return on the $10,000 sunk cost or on the $30,000 market value of his stockholdings? Being a rational investor, he or she will require the 15 percent return on the current value of his portfolio.

Exactly the same situation faces the corporation in computing the required return on the capital funds that it solicits from investors. The value of the firm's capital investments is represented by the market value of its capital structure. The return of interest to the company's owners and creditors is that based on the market value of its capital investments. Market-value weights, then, and not book-value weights are recommended for use in computing the composite cost of capital.

An additional caveat must be offered. Recall that the objective of measuring a firm's cost of capital is to use it as a decision-making tool in the capital-budgeting process. The cost of capital provides management with a financial standard against which to judge the worthiness of proposed uses of corporate funds. What is of concern is the cost of tomorrow's funds used to finance tomorrow's investments. In finance and economics we say that *marginal* costs are critical, not historical costs. Past financing patterns are of importance only to the extent that they serve as a guide to how funds *may* be raised in the future.

In a similar manner, market-value weights are useful in the estimation of the overall cost of capital only if they truly reflect the manner in which the company will finance its investments over a long period of time. The fact that debt may be issued tomorrow and common equity may be issued one year from tomorrow is not the issue. Over time the weighting system that is employed must accurately represent the proportions in which permanent capital sources are used by the enterprise. If this is not the case, then the real composite cost of capital will differ from that used in the capital budgeting process. This difference would lead to errors in the allocation of corporate capital. Thus, the weights that should be used in computing the average cost of capital should be based on the market values of the various capital inputs that will be used by the firm over the long run. The market- and book-value weights for marginal capital sources, however, are about equal. This means that management's perception of the target proportions in which capital will be employed is the crucial consideration in the determination of the proper weighting system. These target weights are set by seasoned management judgment. A detailed examination of factors that might affect this judgment is the subject of Chapter 11. Our conclusion here is that *target market-value weights* should be used to calculate the weighted-average cost of capital.

A Solved Problem

The intent of this exercise is to analyze a problem situation that will help tie together the major ideas underlying the concept of a composite cost of capital. We will see that more than one average cost of capital can be computed, and that the specific situation will dictate which composite cost should be applied as the proper hurdle rate.

The Problem. The Blackburn Corporation needs to finance next year's capital budget. Asset acquisitions totaling $50 million are planned. Blackburn's financial officers feel that capital costs are lowest if combined in the following target proportions: long-term debt, 20 percent; preferred stock, 10 percent; common equity, 70 percent. Additionally, the current capital structure conforms to the proportions just noted, and all future increments of capital (i.e., every penny) are raised according to those weights. New bonds can be sold at par value and will carry a 10 percent coupon. Preferred stock with a $100 par value can be sold to net the firm $94 per share. The dividend rate on the preferred stock will be 11 percent. Next year the Board of Directors of Blackburn plans to declare a $4.00 cash dividend per common share, and the market seems to be anticipating this proposed action. Primarily on the basis of past performance, the market seems to expect earnings and dividends for Blackburn to grow at an annual rate of 8 percent. The current price of Blackburn common stock is $80.00. New common shares can be sold to net the firm $70.00 a share. Retentions totaling $7 million will be available to finance the expansion partially. Blackburn faces a 50 percent marginal tax rate. Management desires answers to the following questions:

1 How large could the capital budget be without the firm's having to resort to external common-equity financing?
2 What would be the weighted-average cost of capital for the amount of funds identified in the first question?
3 What is the composite cost of capital for the funds used in excess of the amount noted in the first question?
4 What is the cost of capital for the entire $50 million used to finance the capital budget?

The Solution

1 The first question emphasizes the fact that corporate retentions are less expensive for the firm to use than newly issued common stock, because the former do not involve flotation costs. It makes sense, then, to use up retentions before new stock is issued. Because of the desirability of maintaining the target capital-structure weights, the firm will view every penny as if it is raised according to these proportions. Drawing these two notions together means that a capital budget of $10 million would allow the firm to maintain the target weights and not have to sell the expensive new common stock. The $10 million figure is computed in this manner:

$$\frac{\text{Available retained earnings}}{\text{Corresponding target weight}} = \frac{\$7 \text{ million}}{0.7} = \$10 \text{ million}$$

2 Answering the second question requires that the weighted-average cost of capital be computed for the $10 million just identified. First, the component costs of capital are calculated:

$$k_d = i(1 - T) = 0.10(1 = 0.50) = 5.00 \text{ percent}$$

$$k_p = \frac{D_p}{P_{pn}} = \frac{\$11}{\$94} = 11.70 \text{ percent}$$

$$k_e = \frac{D_1}{P_o} + g = \frac{\$4}{\$80} + 0.08 = 0.05 + 0.08 = 13.00 \text{ percent}$$

Then, a worksheet can be set up to compute the composite cost of capital for the first $10 million of funds being used by Blackburn.

Source of funds	Weights	Component costs	Weighted cost
Debt	0.2	5.00 percent	1.00 percent
Preferred stock	0.1	11.70 percent	1.17 percent
Retained earnings	0.7	13.00 percent	9.10 percent
Weighted-average cost of capital			11.27 percent

We see that the composite cost of the first $10 million used to finance Blackburn's capital expenditures is 11.27 percent.

3 Blackburn plans to spend $50 million next year. Now, we assess the cost of funds in excess of $10 million, that is, the next $40 million. The firm could finance only a $10 million expansion without going to the market for additional common equity. In this portion of the exercise, all of the target common-equity weight must be satisfied by means of an external common-equity offering. The cost of the new common-stock issue is given as follows:

$$k_{cn} = \frac{D_1}{P_{cn}} + g = \frac{\$4}{\$70} + 0.08 = 0.0571 + 0.08 = 13.71 \text{ percent}$$

Use of the usual worksheet to calculate the cost of this next $40 million of capital is displayed as follows:

Source of funds	Weights	Component costs	Weighted cost
Debt	0.2	5.00 percent	1.00 percent
Preferred stock	0.1	11.70 percent	1.17 percent
New common stock	0.7	13.71 percent	9.60 percent
Weighted-average cost of capital			11.77 percent

Because the higher-cost common stock is being used to maintain the target common-equity weight, the composite cost of funds has risen from 11.27 percent to 11.77 percent.

4 It would be an unusual management meeting if someone did not inquire about the cost of the entire $50 million being used to finance next year's capital expenditures. We know that $10 million of this amount costs 11.27 percent and that $40 million of the total costs 11.77 percent. The $10 million portion represents 20 percent of the funds raised, and the $40 million portion represents 80 percent of the funds raised. The cost of the entire $50 million ($k_o$) is 11.67 percent. This figure is found in the following manner:

$$k_o = 0.1127(0.2) + 0.1177(0.8) = 11.67 \text{ percent}$$

Some final observations can be made by putting our answers to the preceding four questions into graphic form. This is done in Figure 7-1. Also contained in Figure 7-1 are two investment opportunity schedules, labeled IRR_1 and IRR_2. The investment

FIGURE 7-1
Cost of capital and investment opportunity schedules.

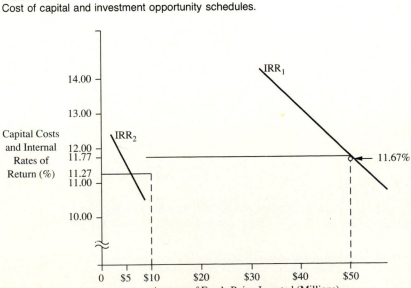

opportunity schedule identified as IRR_1 is consistent with the data in the problem just analyzed. It may be viewed as a line connecting all the individual project's internal rates of return that have been evaluated by Blackburn. Blackburn will reject a project when its expected internal rate of return is less than 11.77 percent, the marginal cost of funds. The intersection of IRR_1 with the weighted-average marginal cost of capital that exists between $10 and $50 million produces a capital budget of $50 million. If the firm had not identified so many potentially favorable projects, then its investment opportunity schedule might be represented by IRR_2. In this case the capital budget would be approximately $6 million in size. Note that the relevant hurdle rate for each project to "beat" in this setting would be 11.27 percent.[14] Now, of what use is the 11.67 percent cost that is representative of the $50 million being used by Blackburn next year? Really, it is of very limited use in the capital-budgeting process. It is an information item about which management will surely inquire, and if the firm had one lumpy $50 million project that it was evaluating, then its cost of funds would be 11.67 percent.

SETTING REQUIRED RATES FOR RISK CATEGORIES

In practice, many business firms establish different required rates of return somewhat arbitrarily for different categories of investments. For example, the rate may be set relatively low for investments that involve replacements of existing assets, somewhat higher for investments that involve an expansion of an existing line of business, and even higher for investments involving new lines of business. This process of risk ranking appears reasonable because business risk is usually lowest for replacements and highest for expansions into new lines.[15] However, the process is inconsistent with the principles we have examined in this chapter unless the betas are always the same for all projects in the same risk category and different from betas of projects in other risk categories. To avoid arbitrariness in the decision making process, the beta value for each project should be estimated, and then used to calculate the required rate of return on the project.

COST OF CAPITAL FOR COMPANY DIVISIONS

If the average systematic business risk of a division is the same as the average systematic business risk of the company as a whole, the costs of capital of the division and the company will be the same. However, if the risks of the division and the company as a whole differ, their costs of capital will also differ. In the latter event, the cost of capital of the division could be calculated by initially considering the division as a separate company.

The first step is to estimate the cost of capital assuming that the division is financed entirely by equity capital. This estimate could be derived from the adjusted cost of

---

[14] Alternatively, each project's net present value could be computed by using 11.27 percent as the discount rate. In this case a given project's net present value would be positive only if its internal rate of return exceeds this 11.27 percent discount rate.

[15] Prospective demand and cost conditions often become more uncertain and unstable for the firm as it expands, particularly if it is expanding into a line of business with which it has no experience.

equity of other (proxy) firms whose sole business is the same as that of the division, provided such firms exist and the necessary information about them is available. If this procedure is not possible, the analyst will have to use firms that have business risks that are *approximately* the same as that of the division.

The effect on the costs of equity or debt financing for proxy companies can be eliminated by the use of equation (7-16). If the unlevered costs of equity of the proxy companies differ, the analyst will have to use his or her judgment in determining which estimate is most applicable under the circumstances.

The next step is to adjust the cost of equity of the division for nonequity financing by the parent company. Theoretically, the systematic business risk of the division should determine the appropriate financing mix applicable to the division. However, a company consisting of more than one division is often able to obtain financial synergisms that would not be available to the division if it were operating as a separate company. For example, income taxes may be reduced by offsetting losses in one division against profits in another division. In addition, if the cash flows of all of the company's divisions are not perfectly positively correlated, the combined cash flows will usually be more stable than those of a single division. The latter effect can reduce the likelihood of incurring the costs associated with bankruptcy. These financial synergisms tend to reduce the cost of nonequity financing of companies with multiple divisions. For this reason, most analysts use the financing mix (i.e., the debt, preferred stock, and common equity proportions) and the costs of nonequity financing of the company as a whole in calculating the cost of capital of a division of a company. The division's (unique) **cost of equity** is then estimated, and finally, the division's cost of capital can be calculated by inserting the appropriate figures into equation (7-18).

The estimate of the division's cost of capital may be useful information for management (e.g., in both intrafirm and interfirm comparisons). However, the estimates should be used as the required rate of return on a new investment only when the investment has the same systematic business risk as the average for the division as a whole. When this is not the case, the required return applicable to the particular project should be estimated.

ACQUISITIONS OF OTHER FIRMS

The acquisition of another firm is a special type of investment—it is special because of the complexity of the possible effects on the operating income of the acquiring firm and because of the multiplicity of possible treatments of the nonequity financing of the acquired company at the time of the acquisition. We will examine this topic by first examining the economic justifications of an acquisition. Then we will consider how an acquisition proposal should be evaluated.

Economic Benefits from Acquisitions

A wide variety of reasons have been given for acquisitions. Some of these reasons have economic merit from the standpoint of the acquiring firm's stockholders, and some do not. In most cases, the purchase price of the acquired firm's common stock will exceed the stock's market price before rumors of the acquisition begin.

Thus, the acquisition will benefit the acquiring firm only if combining the two firms results in either or both operating and financial synergisms. An operating synergism will be obtained if production efficiencies result or if the acquiring firm's supply lines or distribution channels are improved. All of these benefits are often touted in vertical integrations, that is, in combinations of firms operating at different stages of the production of a product. These synergisms doubtless are obtainable in many acquisitions.

Financial synergisms will occur if the acquisition will reduce the likelihood of bankruptcy or if the total taxes paid by the two firms will be reduced because losses of one of the firms can be used to offset the profits of the other. Research studies, however, have been largely inconclusive in regard to the importance of potential bankruptcy costs on the value of a firm.

Another benefit often mentioned in acquisitions is the stabilizing effect on earnings and cash flows. This effect is the result of diversification and was discussed in Chapter 6. Two caveats must be noted in regard to estimating the net benefit from this effect. First, as we have seen, stockholders can obtain diversification benefits much more easily and more completely than can a firm. Thus, this benefit in an acquisition is spurious except to the extent that the likelihood of incurring bankruptcy with all of its attendant costs is reduced. Second, some analysts contend that the stabilizing effect can benefit the firm's bondholders at the expense of the stockholders.[16] According to this point of view, stockholders can lose because of the reduced possibility of earning an exceptionally high return on the common equity. This would cause the market value of the stock to decline. On the other hand, the market price of the bonds will rise because the stabilizing effect on the firm's cash flows will reduce the risk of default on interest and principal payments. This point of view is controversial.[17]

In conclusion, we can say that acquisitions may increase the market value of the common stock of a firm, but they do not always do so, particularly when the price paid for the acquired firm's stock is considerably higher than its market value before the acquisition's impact. Any significant benefits will be the result of operating synergisms. The process for evaluating acquisitions will be considered next.

Evaluating an Acquisition

The evaluation of an acquisition proposal should be based on the same principle as the evaluation of any other investment opportunity: If the net present value is positive, the acquisition would be expected to increase the share price of the acquiring firm's common stock. On the other hand, if the net present value is negative (or zero), the

---

[16] See Robert C. Higgins and Lawrence D. Schall, "Corporate Bankruptcy and Conglomerate Mergers," *Journal of Finance*, 30 (March 1975), 106–111; Dan Galai and Ronald W. Masulis, "The Option Pricing Model and the Risk Factor of Stock," *Journal of Financial Economics*, 3 (January-March 1976), 66–69; E. Han Kim and John J. McConnell, "Corporate Merger and the Co-Insurance of Corporate Debt," *Journal of Finance*, 32 (May 1977), 349–63; and Paul Asquith and E. Han Kim, "The Impact of Merger Bids on the Participating Firms' Security Holders," *Journal of Finance*, 37 (December 1982), 1209–28.

[17] For a different conclusion, see Wilbur G. Lewellen, "A Pure Financial Rationale for the Conglomerate Merger," *Journal of Finance*, 26 (May 1971), 521–37, and Li Way Lee, "Co-insurance and Conglomerate Merger," *Journal of Finance*, 32 (December 1977), 1527–37.

share price would be expected to decrease (or be unaffected). Thus, the evaluation process requires that the purchase price of the acquired firm (the investment outlay) be subtracted from the present value of the incremental, after-tax cash flows from making the investment. The purchase price is usually set well above the market value of the acquired firm in an attempt to ensure that an agreement to the acquisition will be obtained from its stockholders. Because of this fact, the net present value of the investment by the acquiring firm will be negative unless the venture produces significant benefits that are not available to the two firms operating independently.

The purchase price of an acquisition can be paid in any of several ways (e.g., in cash, securities, or a combination of the two). In most cases, the payment is made at least in part by an exchange of the common stocks of the two companies. In these cases, the dollar amount of the purchase price is the market value of the acquiring firm's stock plus the amount of any cash or the market value of any other securities included as a sweetener in the deal.

The incremental, after-tax cash flows will include those of the acquired firm operating as a separate entity plus those related to any synergistic effects resulting from the acquisition. However, financial expenses such as interest expense or preferred dividends should not be subtracted from these incremental cash flows. The format for calculating the net flows is the same as that presented in Chapter 5. The approach to estimating the required return depends on the specific nature of the acquisition. In the simplest case, only the assets of the selling firm are purchased. The required return for this type of acquisition should be calculated in exactly the same way as for a regular investment.

In most acquisitions, however, the acquiring company purchases the acquired company's common stock and assumes its debt. Equation (7-18) can be used to calculate the required return on the investment. But in this case, the weights should be based on the relative market values of the various methods of financing used by the acquired firm; the implicit assumption here is that these financing proportions are used to make the purchase. Estimates of the cost of each method of financing are relatively easy to make since the costs are the costs of the various methods of financing used by the acquired firm.[18] In other words, the acquiring firm's required return on the acquisition is the same as the required return of the acquired firm on investments which do not change its systematic risk.

If the combination of the two firms will significantly reduce the likelihood of incurring bankruptcy costs or bottlenecks in production or selling, the required return should theoretically be reduced. Since the extent of the modification necessary in the latter events is difficult to estimate, many firms simply consider this type of risk reduction separately, as an added benefit of the acquisition. The present value

---

[18] This method of estimating the required return does not take into account any wealth transfer among the acquiring firm's security holders. A wealth transfer will occur, for example, if the market value of the debt rises and the market value of the common stock falls because investors consider the acquisition to be of greater benefit to the bondholders than to stockholders. As discussed earlier in the text, some authors believe this will result from the diversification effects of an acquisition. Such a possibility would obviously make the acquisition less desirable from the standpoint of the stockholders. However, no consensus of opinion has arisen among financial economists concerning the importance of this factor or specifically how it should be accounted for in the acquisition decision.

of the benefit from the risk reduction will probably be fairly small or nonexistent in most cases. Thus, an acquisition can *usually* be justified only if significant synergistic effects are obtained.

CHAPTER SUMMARY

The objective of this chapter was to present a popular framework for the estimation of the cost of capital funds used by the corporation. The cost of capital was treated as a decision tool to be employed in the capital budgeting process. Its purpose is to help management determine whether a specific investment outlay will benefit the firm's owners. We defined the *cost of capital* as the rate of return that must be earned on an investment in order to leave the market price of the firm's common stock unchanged.

Calculation methodologies were presented for the major components of the firm's capital structure. These included several schemes that could be used to estimate the firm's cost of (1) debt, (2) preferred stock, (3) convertible securities, (4) retained earnings, and (5) new common stock. Estimating the costs of retained earnings and new common stock was performed within the tenets of both (1) the Gordon perpetual-growth model, and (2) the capital-asset pricing model (CAPM). Both these popular models were discussed earlier in this text. The Gordon model was examined in Chapter 4, and the CAPM was discussed within the realm of systematic risk in Chapter 6. In addition, the effects of debt financing were examined, focusing on the cost of equity capital for the firm and for individual investors. Procedures for adjusting the cost of equity under different capital structures were outlined.

Next, we ceased to look at the costs of the various sources of funds in isolation and developed the procedure for calculating the weighted-average cost of capital. It is emphasized that historical capital costs have no bearing on this process. Funds raised ten years ago cannot be used to finance next year's plant expansion. Moreover, it is *marginal costs* that are being calculated. The next investment is financed with the next dollar of financial capital. The cost of the marginal dollar being invested is the central feature of this analysis.

Required rates of return vary by risk category. Adjustment methods for projects as well as company divisions were discussed. This chapter concluded with the examination of a special type of investment—acquisition of another firm. Both the economic benefits and the evaluation of acquisitions were presented.

PROBLEMS

7-1 Abbott Electric requires $1.5 million in new capital to expand its business. The new bond issue will have a 20-year maturity, par value of $1000, a coupon rate of 9 percent, and a sinking fund payment of 5 percent annually. Abbott will net $950 from each bond and has a tax rate of 60 percent. What is the cost of the new bond issue?

7-2 The Bombay Corporation is analyzing the sale of $5 million worth of 20-year, 10 percent bonds, with a par value of $1000. Similar-risk debt instruments are currently yielding over 10 percent. To reach the market, Bombay must sell its bonds at a discount price of $960. In addition, the underwriting costs will be 3 percent of the bond value. The bond discount will be amortized on a straight line basis over the life of the issue. Bombay uses a tax rate of 50 percent. What is the cost to Bombay if it issues these bonds?

7-3 Valtech Properties, Inc. will market a $100 par value convertible preferred stock carrying a 10-year maturity date and a 6 percent yield. The company expects to net $90 per share at the initial offering. The firm's analyst expects the holding period to be approximately 8 years. Issue holders can convert preferred stock for common stock at a 1 for 5 ratio. The common stock price in 8 years is expected to be $35. Compute the cost of convertible preferred stock. $(k_{c/s} = 13.85\%)$

7-4 Dyer's common stock has an overall market responsiveness of 1.2 (i.e., beta = 1.2). The riskless rate of return is estimated to be 5 percent with an average market return of 12.5 percent. Underwriting costs on a new issue of common stock will amount to 5 percent of par value. Compute the cost of issuing new common stock.

7-5 The balance sheet for Grossman and Son is as follows:

Assets		Liabilities	
Cash	$ 200	Accounts payable	$ 500
Acc. rec.	300	Accrued taxes due	200
Inventory	600	Long-term debt	800
Plant and equip. net	3,600	Equity	3,200
	$4,700		$4,700

The company has arrived at its optimal financial structure and this is reflected in its book-value weights listed above. The cost of equity to Grossman is 16 percent and its before-tax cost of debt is 11 percent. Grossman's tax rate is 50 percent. Calculate the weighted-average cost of capital. $(k_o = 13.9\%)$ $(p. 229-236)$

7-6 Earhardt Manufacturing has gathered the information below regarding their capital structure and cost of capital:

Source	Book value	Market value	Cost
Debt	$ 9,000,000	$ 7,550,000	4%
Preferred stock	670,000	930,000	9%
Equity	2,705,000	5,400,000	14%
	$12,375,000	$13,880,000	

a Calculate the book-value weighted-average cost of capital.
b Calculate the market-value weighted-average cost of capital.

7-7 After analyzing Earhardt's present capital structure (Problem 7-6 above) and the industry norms, their financial officer decided to change the firm's financial structure to the following:

Debt	40%
Preferred stock	10%
Equity	50%

a What is the weighted-average cost of capital under the new structure?
b Which of the three structures would you use to determine next year's weighted-average cost of capital?

7-8 Three-D, Inc. has common stock selling for $80 a share and expects to pay a dividend of $4. If investors require a 10 percent return, what must Three-D's rate of growth be?

7-9 A portion of the current balance sheet of the Pierce Company is as follows:

Debt (4 percent first-mortgage bonds, issued 5/8/85) $35,000,000
Preferred stock (4.5 percent dividend, issued 11/7/85)   15,000,000
Common equity   50,000,000

The capital structure shown here is considered to be *optimal* by the firm's management and the market. The common stock of the firm is currently selling at $50 a share. Investors expect to receive a $1 dividend this year; over the past 10 to 15 years, the firm's earnings and dividends have increased at an average rate of 6 percent. Retained earnings available to finance in part the upcoming capital investment requirements of the firm are $5 million.

If the firm sells a new common stock, it will net the company $45 a share. New bonds can be sold at par and will carry a 4 percent coupon rate. Preferred stock will have a 5 percent dividend rate and will net the firm $100, or par value, per share. The corporate tax rate is 50 percent. The firm will undertake an asset expansion of $50 million for next year.

a What is the firm's cost of retained earnings?
b What is the cost of new common stock?
c What is the weighted-average cost of capital for $50 million?
d If the Pierce Company invests only $10 million in assets next year, what will be the relevant weighted-average cost of capital for decision making purposes?
e On the basis of the given data, what is the relevant weighted-average cost of capital if the firm's asset expansion exceeds $10 million (i.e., for the $40 million of invested funds between $10 and $50 million)?

7-10 On July 3, the common stock of Famous X Office Copiers sold for $240 per share. This firm's stock is one of the favorites of large institutional investors, and information about the firm and its prospects is widely disseminated. This price was founded upon an expected annual growth rate in key financial variables (e.g., earnings) of 15 percent over a very long time period. By August, however, the national economic climate changed drastically. This change caused investors to adjust downward their estimate of Famous X's future growth to 8 percent. The firm will pay a $6.00 cash dividend next year. A perpetual-growth model appears to be a reasonable way to estimate the true value of this firm's common stock. What should be the price of the firm's common stock after the market adjustment takes place?

7-11 Rick's Wood-Burning Stoves will invest $20 million next year in new assets. Retained earnings and a new bond issue will be used in equal proportions to finance the expansion. Financial analysts estimate the riskless rate of interest to be 6 percent. The expected rate of return on the market portfolio is placed at 9.3 percent. Several financial advisory services have computed the Beta for Rick's and found it to be in the area of 1.50. The new bond issue will net the firm $920 per bond. It will carry a coupon rate of 8.6 percent and have a $1,000 face (par) value. The maturity period is 30 years. The firm uses a 50 percent tax rate in all its analytical procedures. The firm uses the capital-asset pricing model to estimate its common equity costs and the shortcut method to estimate the cost of debt.

a What is the firm's cost of retained earnings?
b What is the cost of the new debt issue?
c What is the estimated composite cost of funds used to finance the asset expansion?

7-12 John Petty Warehousing is going to offer to the market a $5 million bond issue with a twenty-year maturity period. The security will carry a 7.5 percent coupon and have a $1,000 face (par) value. It will be sold to investors for 95 percent of face value. The underwriting commission on the bond issue will amount to 4 percent of the face value. The firm's income tax rate is 50 percent. By employing the yield-to-maturity method, find the cost of capital of this debt issue to John Petty Warehousing.

7-13 Duke's Western Stores will market a convertible bond issue to the investing public. It will mature in 20 years. The security will pay interest at the rate of 9 percent annually. The face (par) value of the bond is $1,000. Duke's will net $960 from the sale of each security. The firm's relevant tax rate is 50 percent. The management of the company believes that an eight-year holding period will be representative of the bond's investors. Duke's common stock sells today for $20 per share. At the end of the eight-year holding period, the stock is expected to be worth $49 per share. Each convertible bond can be exchanged for twenty common shares at the option of the investor. What is the cost of capital of this convertible bond to Duke's Western Stores?

REFERENCES

Alberts, W. W., and S. H. Archer: "Some Evidence on the Effect of Company Size on the Cost of Equity Capital," *Journal of Financial and Quantitative Analysis*, vol. 8, March 1973, pp. 229–245.

Ang, James S., and Tsong-Yue Lai: "Functional Forms of the Capital Asset Pricing Model under Different Market Risk Regimes," *Financial Review*, August 1988, pp. 345–350.

Arditti, Fred D., and Milford S. Tysseland: "Three Ways to Present the Marginal Cost of Capital," *Financial Management*, vol. 2, Summer 1973, pp. 63–67.

Ben-Zion, Uri, and Joseph Yagil: "The PER and the Dividend Growth Models: An Extension," *Financial Review*, vol. 18, September 1983, p. 22.

Bey, Roger P., and J. Markham Collins: "The Relationship between Before- and After-Tax Yields on Financial Assets," *Financial Review*, August 1988, pp. 313–331.

Bhandari, Loxmi Chand: "Debt/Equity Ratio and Expected Common Stock Returns: Empirical Evidence," *Journal of Finance*, vol. 43, June 1988, pp. 507–528.

Billingsley, Randall S., Robert E. Lamy, and G. Rodney Thompson: "The Choice Among Debt, Equity, and Convertible Bonds," *Journal of Financial Research*, vol. 11, Spring 1988, pp. 43–55.

Brennan, Michael J.: "A New Look at the Weighted Average Cost of Capital," *Journal of Business Finance*, vol. 1, no. 1, 1973, pp. 24–30.

Brigham, Eugene F., and Roy L. Crum: "On the Use of the CAPM in Public Utility Rate Cases," *Financial Management*, vol. 6, Summer 1977, pp. 7–15.

Chambers, D. R., Robert S. Harris, and John J. Pringle: "Treatment of Financing Mix in Analyzing Investment Opportunities," *Financial Management*, vol. 11, Summer 1982, pp. 24–41.

Downs, Thomas W.: "The User Cost and Capital Budgeting," *Financial Review*, vol. 21, May 1986, pp. 277–287.

Durand, David: "Comprehensiveness in Capital Budgeting," *Financial Management*, vol. 10, Winter 1981, pp. 7–13.

Fisher, Lawrence, and Jules H. Kamin: "Forecasting Systematic Risk: Estimates of "Raw" Beta that Take Account of the Tendency of Beta to Change and the Heteroskedasticity of Residual Returns," *Journal of Financial and Quantitative Analysis*, vol. 20, June 1985, pp. 127–149.

Gehr, Adam K., Jr.: "Financial Structure and Financial Strategy," *Journal of Financial Review*, vol. 7, Spring 1984, pp. 69–80.

Gitman, Lawrence J., and Vincent A. Mercurio: "Cost of Capital Techniques Used by Major U.S. Firms: Survey and Analysis of Fortune's 1000," *Financial Management*, vol. 11, Winter 1982, pp. 21–29.

Gombola, Michael J., and Kenneth P. Nunn, Jr.: "Valuation of the Preferred Stock Sinking Fund Feature: A Time-Series Approach," *Journal of Financial Research*, vol. 11, Spring 1988, pp. 33–42.

Gordon, Myron J., and Paul J. Halpern: "Cost of Capital for a Division of a Firm," *Journal of Finance*, vol. 29, September 1974, pp. 1153–1163.

Gup, Benton E., and Samuel W. Norwood III: "Divisional Cost of Capital: A Practical Approach," *Financial Management*, vol. 11, Spring 1982, pp. 20–24.

Haley, Charles W.: "Taxes, the Cost of Capital, and the Firm's Investment Decisions," *Journal of Finance*, vol. 26, September 1971, pp. 901–917.

Harrington, Diana R.: "Stock Prices, Beta, and Strategic Planning," *Harvard Business Review*, May 1983, pp. 157–164.

Harris, Robert S., and John J. Pringle: "A Note on the Implications of Miller's Argument for Capital Budgeting," *Journal of Financial Research*, Spring 1983, pp. 13–23.

Jaffe, Jeffrey F.: "Inflation, the Interest Rate, and the Required Return on Equity," *Journal of Financial and Quantitative Analysis*, vol. 20, March 1985, pp. 29–44.

Kalay, Avner, and Adam Shimrat: "Firm Value and Seasoned Equity Issues: Price Pressure, Wealth Redistribution, or Negative Information," *Journal of Financial Economics*, vol. 19, September 1987, pp. 109–126.

Kalotay, A. J.: "Sinking Funds and the Realized Cost of Debt," *Financial Management*, vol. 11, Spring 1982, pp. 43–54.

Kane, Alex, Alan J. Marcus, and Robert L. McDonald: "How Big is the Tax Advantage to Debt?" *Journal of Finance*, vol. 39, July 1984, pp. 841–853.

Litzenberger, Robert H.: "Some Observations on Capital Structure and the Impact of Recent Recapitalizations on Share Price," *Journal of Financial and Quantitative Analysis*, vol. 21, March 1986, pp. 59–71.

Lewellen, Wilbur G.: *The Cost of Capital* (Dubuque, Iowa: Kendall-Hunt Publishing Company, 1976).

Lewellen, Wilbur G.: "Some Observations on Risk-Adjusted Discount Rates," *Journal of Finance*, vol. 32, September 1977, pp. 1331–1337.

Malley, Susan L.: "Unfunded Pension Liability and the Cost of Equity Capital," *Financial Review*, vol. 18, May 1983, pp. 133–145.

Marr, M. Wayne, and G. Rodney Thompson: "Pricing Convertible Preferred Stock," *Financial Review*, vol. 18, September 1983, p. 41.

Martin, John D., and David F. Scott, Jr.: "Debt Capacity and the Capital Budgeting Decision," *Financial Management*, vol. 5, Summer 1976, pp. 7–14.

Narayanan, M. P.: "Debt versus Equity under Asymmetric Information," *Journal of Financial and Quantitative Analysis*, vol. 23, March 1988, pp. 39–51.

Petry, Glenn H.: "Empirical Evidence on Cost of Capital Weights," *Financial Management*, vol. 4, Winter 1975, pp. 58–65.

Pettway, Richard H., and Bradford D. Jordon: "Diversification, Double Leverage, and the Cost of Capital," *Journal of Financial Research*, Winter 1982, pp. 289–301.

Scott, David F., Jr., and J. William Petty: "Determining the Cost of Common Equity Capital: The Direct Method," *Journal of Business Research*, vol. 8, March 1980, pp. 89–103.

Solomon, Ezra: "Measuring a Company's Cost of Capital," *Journal of Business*, vol. 27, October 1955, pp. 240–252.

Taylor, Richard W.: "The Valuation of Semiannual Bonds between Interest Payment Dates," *Financial Review*, August 1988, pp. 365–368.

Weston, J. Fred: "Investment Decisions Using the Capital Asset Pricing Model," *Financial Management*, vol. 2, Spring 1973, pp. 25–33.

MANAGING CASH AND MARKETABLE SECURITIES

This chapter focuses on the formulation of financial policies and decisions for the management of cash and marketable securities. Two major areas are explored: (1) techniques available for favorably influencing cash receipts and disbursements patterns, and (2) responsible investment outlets that enable the company to employ excess cash balances in a productive fashion.

It will be helpful to distinguish among some terms. **Cash** is the currency and coin the firm has on hand in petty cash drawers, in cash registers, or in checking accounts at the various commercial banks where its demand deposits are maintained. **Marketable securities** are those security investments the firm can quickly convert into cash balances. Those held by most firms tend to have very short maturity periods— less than one year. Marketable securities are also referred to as **near cash** or **near-cash assets** because they can be quickly turned into cash. Taken together, cash and near cash are known as **liquid assets**.

RATIONALE FOR HOLDING CASH

An appreciation of why and how a firm holds cash requires an accurate conception of how cash flows into and through the firm. Figure 8-1 depicts this process in a typical manufacturing setting. The arrows designate the direction of the flow.

This chapter was prepared with the assistance of Nancy Jay of the University of Central Florida.

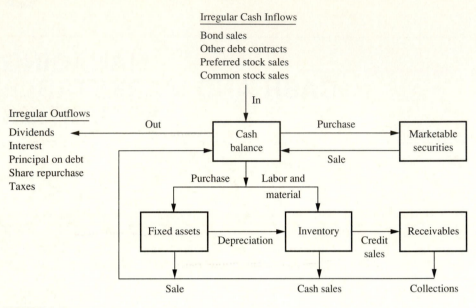

FIGURE 8-1
The cash flow process.

Fluctuations in Cash Holdings

The firm is subject to irregular upswings in its cash holdings from several external sources. Funds can be obtained in the financial markets from the sale of securities, or nonmarketable debt contracts can be entered into with lenders, such as commercial banks. External financing contracts usually involve significant sums of money stemming from a major firm need, such as a plant expansion, and do not occur on a regular basis.

The financial officer responsible for cash management usually controls the transactions that affect the firm's investment in marketable securities. When excess cash becomes available, marketable securities will be bought. A portion of the marketable securities portfolio will be liquidated when the firm is short of cash.

The other *main* sources of cash to the firm stem from internal operations, and occur on a more predictable basis. The largest receipts will generally come from accounts receivable collections, and to a lesser extent from direct cash sales of finished goods. At various times fixed assets will be sold, thereby adding to cash receipts.

Apart from the investment of excess cash in marketable securities, the cash balance will experience reductions for three main reasons: first, withdrawals will be made to (1) pay cash dividends on preferred and common stock; (2) meet interest requirements on debt contracts; (3) pay the principal borrowed from creditors; (4) buy the firm's own shares for use in executive compensation plans, or as an alternative to paying a cash dividend; and (5) pay tax bills. Second, the company's capital expenditure program will designate that fixed assets be acquired at various intervals. Third, inventories will be acquired on a regular basis to ensure a steady flow of finished goods out of the plant.

These influences that constantly affect the firm's cash balance can be related to the classic economic motives for holding cash.

Motives for Cash Demand

In his best-known economic treatise, John Maynard Keynes segmented the firm's demand for cash into three categories: (1) the transactions motive, (2) the precautionary motive, and (3) the speculative motive.[1]

Transactions Motive

Cash held for transactions purposes allows the firm to dispense with needs that arise in the ordinary course of doing business. Note that "ordinary" here is not to be confused with "predictable." In Figure 8-1, transactions balances would be used to meet the *irregular* outflows as well as the planned acquisition of fixed assets and inventories.

The relative amount of transactions cash held will be significantly affected by the industry in which the firm competes. If revenues can be forecast to fall within a tight, rather than wide range of outcomes, then the ratio of cash and near cash to total assets will be less for the firm. Utilities, for example, can forecast cash receipts quite accurately because of stable demand for their services. Computer software firms have a tougher time doing this, as new products are brought to the market at a rapid pace. The demand, then, is difficult to assess in a precise manner.

Precautionary Motive

Precautionary balances are, in practice, a buffer stock of liquid assets. This motive for holding cash relates to the maintenance of balances for possible, but as yet indefinite, needs. In other words "something might happen," and we want to be ready for it.

One of the authors is acquainted with a corporate treasurer who made this statement:

> My management generally shoots from the hip. To be prepared for that I maintain sizable near-cash investments.

Economists describe this type of behavior by the treasurer with the precautionary motive for holding cash (or near-cash).

Cash flow predictability has a material influence on the firm's demand for cash through the precautionary motive as well as the transactions motive. The airline industry is plagued with a high degree of cash flow uncertainty. The weather, rising fuel costs, and frequent strikes by operating personnel make cash forecasting difficult. Because of all the things that *might* happen, the minimum cash balances desired by air carrier managements tend to be large.

---

[1] John Maynard Keynes: *The General Theory of Employment, Interest, and Money*, New York: Harcourt Brace Jovanovich, 1936.

The precautionary motive in practice is met by investment in a portfolio of *liquid assets*. Some actual (positive) rate of return can be earned on the portfolio, compared with a zero rate of return available on cash holdings. In large corporate organizations, funds may flow either into or out of the marketable securities portfolio on a daily basis (Figure 8-1). Be aware that *unused borrowing power* will reduce the need to invest in precautionary balances.

Speculative Motive

Cash is held for speculative purposes to take advantage of future profit-making situations. Construction firms, for instance, will accumlate cash in anticipation of a significant drop in lumber costs. If the price of building supplies does drop, the companies that built up their cash balances stand to profit by purchasing materials in large quantities at the later date. The speculative motive is the *least* important segment of a firm's preference for liquidity. The transactions and precautionary motives account for most of the reasons why a company holds cash balances.

OBJECTIVES AND DECISIONS

The Balance Between Risk and Return

The firm's cash management program must be concerned with minimizing the firm's risk of insolvency. In the context of cash management, the term **insolvency** describes the situation where the firm is unable to meet its maturing liabilities on time. This problem could be solved quite easily by holding large cash balances to pay the bills that come due.

The management of the company's cash position, though, is one of those problem areas where you are criticized if you don't and criticized if you do. The production process will eventually be halted should too little cash be available to pay bills. If excessive cash balances are carried at a zero return, however, the value of the enterprise in the financial marketplace will be suppressed because of the large cost of income forgone. The financial manager must strike an acceptable balance between holding too much cash and too little cash. This is the focal point of the risk-return tradeoff.

The Goals

The risk-return tradeoff can be reduced to two prime goals for the firm's cash management system:

1 Enough cash must be on hand to meet the disbursal needs that arise in the course of doing business.

2 Investment in idle cash balances must be reduced to a minimum.

The activities of management in striving to meet their goals give rise to some typical cash management decisions. The goals are fun to identify; the decisions are the hard part of management activity.

The Decisions

Two conditions would allow the firm to operate for extended periods with cash balances near a level of zero: (1) a completely accurate forecast of net cash flows over the planning horizon, and (2) perfect synchronization of cash receipts and disbursements.

Cash flow forecasting is the initial step in any effective cash management program. This is usually accomplished by the finance function's evaluation of data supplied by the marketing and production functions in the company. The device used to forecast the cash flows over the planning period is the cash budget. The net cash flows identified in the formal cash budget are estimates, subject to considerable variation.

The cash flow process depicted in Figure 8-1 showed that inflows and outflows are *not* synchronized. Some inflows and outflows are irregular; others are more continual. Some finished goods are sold directly for cash, but more likely the sales will be on account. The receivables, then, will have to be collected before a cash inflow is realized. Several suppliers are probably used for raw material purchases, and each may have its own payment date. Further, no law of doing business fixes receivable collections to coincide with raw material payment dates. So the second criterion is not met in actual practice either.

So, the firm must, in practice, invest in some cash balances; certain types of decisions related to the size of those balances dominate the cash management process. The decisions follow from answers to the following questions:

1 What can be done to speed up cash collections and slow down or better control cash outflows?

2 What should be the composition of the marketable securities portfolio?

In the rest of this chapter we direct our attention to these two questions.

COLLECTION AND DISBURSEMENT PROCEDURES

The efficiency of the firm's cash management program can be enhanced by knowledge and use of various procedures aimed at (1) accelerating cash receipts and (2) improving the methods used to disburse cash. The more meaningful opportunity for corporate improvement lies with the cash receipts side, although it would be unwise to ignore opportunities for favorably affecting cash disbursement practices.

Accelerating Cash Receipts

The reduction of "float" lies at the center of several approaches available to speed up cash receipts. *Total float* has four elements as follows:

1 Mail float is caused by the time lapse from the moment a customer mails a remittance check until the firm begins to process it.

2 Processing float is caused by the time required for the firm to process remittance checks before they can be deposited in the bank.

3 Transit float is caused by the time necessary for a deposited check to clear through the commercial banking system and become usable funds to the company.[2]

4 Disbursing float derives from the fact that funds are available in the company's bank account until its payment check has cleared through the banking system.

We use the term "float" in the rest of this discussion to refer to the total of its four elements. Float reduction can yield considerable benefits in terms of returns produced on freed-up balances. As an example, in 1987 Mobil reported total revenues of $56.7 billion. The amount of usable funds that would be released if Mobil could achieve a one-day reduction in float can be approximated by dividing annual revenues (sales) by the number of days in the year. In this case one day's freed-up balances would be

$$\frac{\text{annual revenues}}{\text{days in year}} = \frac{\$56,700,000,000}{365} = \$155,342,466$$

If these released funds, which represent one day's sales of approximately $155.3 million, could be invested to return 8 percent a year, then the annual value of the one-day float reduction would be

$$(\text{sales per day}) \times (\text{assumed yield}) = \$155,342,466 \times 0.08$$
$$= \$12,427,397$$

Notice that effective cash management can yield impressive opportunities for profit improvement. We turn now to specific techniques for reducing float.

The Lock-Box System

The lock-box system is the most widely used commercial banking service for speeding up cash gathering. Such a system accelerates the conversion of receipts into usable funds by reducing both mail and processing float. It is also possible to reduce transit float if lock boxes are located near Federal Reserve Banks and their branches. For large corporations that receive checks from all parts of the country, float reductions of two to four days are possible.

Figure 8-2 illustrates a typical cash collection system for a hypothetical firm. It also shows the origin of mail float, processing float and transit float. In this system the customer places a remittance check in the U.S. mail, which is then delivered to the firm's headquarters. This causes the mail float. At the firm, accounting personnel prepare the checks for local deposit. This causes the processing float. The

---

[2] In the late summer of 1988 commercial banks had to comply with the Expedited Funds Availability Act which was earlier passed by Congress. Financial institutions are required by the Act to establish and publish a permanent funds availability schedule for their customers. Many deposits have "next-day availability," such as U.S. Treasury checks. But variable availability applies to most business customers of commercial banks; the availability is assigned by the bank to the firm's account.

The ability to withdraw funds depends primarily on (1) the length of time the firm has had a transaction account with the bank and (2) whether the check is a local or nonlocal check.

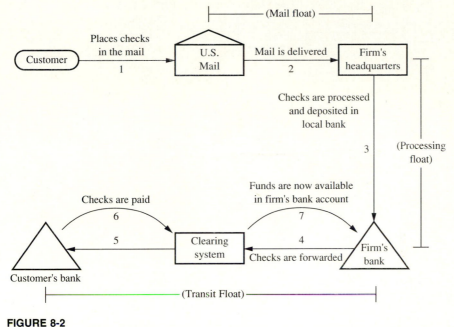

FIGURE 8-2
A typical cash gathering process.

checks are then deposited and forwarded for payment through the commercial bank clearing mechanism. The checks are charged against the customer's own bank account and become "good" funds available to the receiving company. This bank clearing procedure represents transit float.

The lock-box arrangement shown in Figure 8-3 is based on a simple variation of the typical process. The firm's customers are instructed to mail their remittance checks to a numbered Post Office box. The bank that is providing the lock-box service is authorized to open the box, collect the mail, process the checks, and deposit the checks directly into the company's account. Funds deposited in this manner are usually available for company use in one business day or less.

The bank can notify the firm of deposit amounts the same day via some type of telecommunications system. At the conclusion of each day all remittance documents are mailed to the firm. Note that the firm which receives checks from all over the country will have to use several lock boxes to take full advantage of a reduction in mail float.

The two systems described by Figures 8-2 and 8-3 are summarized in Table 8-1. There, the step numbers refer to those shown in Figure 8-2. Furthermore, Table 8-1 assumes that the customer and the firm's headquarters, or its collection center, are located in different cities. This causes the lag of two working days before the firm actually receives the remittance check. We notice at the bottom of Table 8-1 that the installation of the lock-box system can result in funds being credited to the

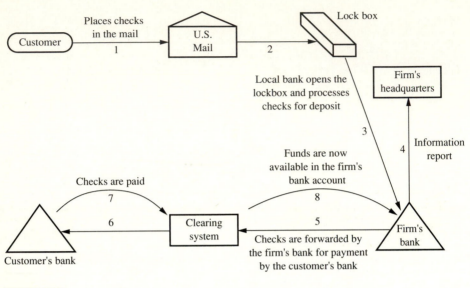

FIGURE 8-3
A simple lock-box arrangement.

firm's bank account a full *four* working days *faster* than is possible under the typical collection system.

We previously calculated the 1987 sales per day for Mobil to be $155.3 million and assumed that firm could invest its excess cash in marketable securities to yield 8 percent annually. If Mobil could speed up its cash collections by four days, the results would be impressive. The gross annual savings to Mobil (apart from operating the lock-box system) would amount to $49.7 million, as follows:

$$\text{(sales per day)} \times \text{(days of float reduction)} \times \text{(assumed yield)}$$
$$\$155,342,466 \times 4 \times 0.08 = \$49,709,589$$

The major benefits of a lock-box arrangement include:

1 Increased working cash. The time required for converting receivables into available funds is reduced.

2 Elimination of clerical functions. The bank takes over the tasks of receiving, endorsing, totaling, and depositing checks.

3 Early knowledge of dishonored checks. Should a customer's check be uncollectible because of lack of funds, it is returned to the firm.

These benefits are not free. Usually the bank levies a charge for each check processed through the system. The benefits derived from the acceleration of receipts must exceed the incremental costs of the lock-box system, or the firm would be better off without it. Later in this chapter we illustrate a method for studying the desirability of a specific cash management service, such as the lock-box arrangement.

TABLE 8-1
COMPARISON OF A TYPICAL CASH-GATHERING PROCESS WITH A SIMPLE LOCK-BOX
ARRANGEMENT

Step numbers	Ordinary system and time		Advantage of lock box
1	Customer writes check and places it in the mail	1 Day	
2	Mail is delivered to firm's headquarters	2 Days	Mail will not have to travel as far. Result: save 1 day
3	Accounting personnel process the checks and deposit them in the firm's local bank	2 Days	Bank personnel prepare checks for deposit. Result: save 2 days
4 and 5	Checks are forwarded for payment through the clearing mechanism	1 Day	As the lock boxes are located near Federal Reserve Banks or branches, transit float can be reduced.
6 and 7	The firm receives notice from its bank that the checks have cleared and the funds are now "good"	1 Day	Result: save 1 day
	Total working days	7	Overall result: Save 4 working days

Other Methods of Accelerating Cash Receipts

The lock-box arrangement can reduce total float by two to four days; for some firms the use of **preauthorized checks** (PACs) can further enhance the conversion of receipts into cash. A PAC resembles the ordinary check, but it does not require the signature of the person on whose account it is being drawn. It is created with the individual's legal authorization. The objective of this system is to reduce *both* mail and processing float and is advantageous when the firm regularly receives a large volume of payments of a fixed amount from the same customers.

For firms that can take advantage of a PAC system, the benefits include these:

1 Highly predictable cash flows.
2 Reduced expenses. Billing and postage costs are eliminated, and clerical processing of customer payments is reduced.

3 Customer preference. Many customers prefer not to be bothered with a regular billing. Here the check is written for the customer.

4 Increased working cash. Mail float and processing float can be dramatically reduced in comparison with other payment processing systems.

To accelerate collections, many companies establish multiple collection centers. This requires many local bank accounts to handle daily deposits. Rather than have funds sitting in multiple bank accounts usually in different geographic regions of the country, most firms will regularly transfer the surplus balances to one or more concentration banks. A **concentration bank** is one where the firm maintains a major disbursing account. Centralizing the firm's pool of cash provides the following benefits:

1 Lower levels of excess cash. Desired cash balance target levels are set for each regional bank. These target levels consider both compensating balance requirements and necessary working levels of cash. Cash in excess of the target levels can be transferred regularly to concentration banks for deployment by the firm's top-level management.

2 Better control. With more cash held in fewer accounts, stricter control over available cash is achieved. The concentration banks can prepare reports that detail corporatewide movements of funds into and out of the central cash pool.

3 More efficient investments in near-cash assets. With information from the firm's cash forecast and available funds supplied by the concentration banks, the firm can quickly transfer cash to the marketable securities portfolio.

Depository transfer checks allow the firm to move funds from local bank accounts to concentration accounts. The depository transfer check itself is an unsigned, nonnegotiable instrument. It is payable only to the bank of deposit for credit to the firm's specific account. An authorization form is filed by the firm with each bank from which it might withdraw funds. This form instructs the bank to pay the depository transfer checks without any signature. The movement of cash through the use of depository transfer checks can operate with a conventional mail system or an automated system. With the **automated depository transfer check system** the mail float involved in moving the transfer document from the local bank to the concentration bank is *eliminated*.

It works like this. A regional data collection center accumulates information by phone throughout the day on the firm's regional deposits. At specified cutoff times the deposit information from all local offices is transmitted to the concentration bank. Funds transferred by use of the automated depository transfer check system can become available for company use in one business day or less.

The fastest way to move cash between banks is by use of **wire transfers**, which elminate transit float. Funds moved in this manner, then, immediately become usable funds to the firm at the receiving bank. Two major communication facilities are used to execute wire transfers. The first is Bank Wire, a private service used by a few hundred major banks in the United States. The second is the Federal Reserve Wire System, popularly called "Fed Wire." Fed Wire is available to member banks of the Federal Reserve System and other banks through their correspondents.

Controlling Cash Outflow

Often-used techniques for improving the firm's management of cash disbursements include zero balance accounts, payable-through drafts, and remote disbursing. The first two offer better control over companywide payments, and as a secondary benefit they *may* increase disbursement float. The last technique, remote disbursing, aims solely to increase disbursement float.

Zero Balance Accounts

Large corporations that operate multiple branches will maintain several bank accounts (in different banks) for the purpose of making timely operating payments. **Zero balance accounts** permit centralized control (at the headquarters level) over cash outflows, while maintaining divisional disbursing authority. Under this system the firm's authorized employees continue to write checks on their individual accounts, but accounts are now *all* located in the same concentration bank. These separate accounts contain no funds at all, thus their appropriate label, "zero balance."

A schematic presentation of a zero balance account disbursing system is shown in Figure 8-4. The firm is assumed to have three operating divisions—each with its

FIGURE 8-4
Zero balance account cash disbursement system (ZBA).

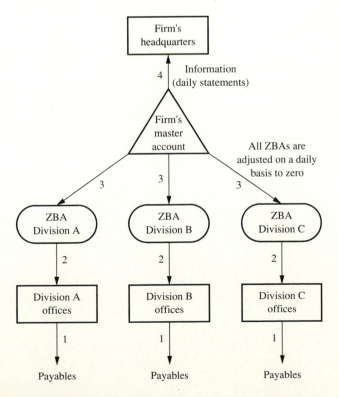

own zero balance account (ZBA). The firm's authorized agents write their payment checks as usual against their specific accounts (Step 1). These checks clear through the banking system in the usual way. On a daily basis checks will be presented to the firm's concentration bank (the drawee bank) for payment. As the checks are paid by the bank, negative (debit) balances will build in the proper disbursing accounts (Step 2). At the end of each day the negative balances will be restored to a zero level by means of credits to the zero balance accounts (Step 3); a corresponding reduction in funds is made against the firm's concentration (master) demand deposit account (also Step 3). Each morning a report is electronically forwarded to corporate headquarters reflecting the balance in the master account as well as the previous day's activity in each zero balance account (Step 4). Using the report, the financial officer in charge of near-cash investments is ready to initiate appropriate transactions.

Managing the cash outflow through use of a zero balance account system offers the following benefits to the firm with many operating units:

1 Centralized control over disbursements, even though payment authority continues to rest with operating units

2 Reduction of management time spent on superficial cash management activities

3 Minimization of excess balances held in outlying accounts

4 Elimination of cash management costs, such as wire transfers to outlying disbursement accounts

5 Availability of funds for company use through an increase in disbursement float. Checks drawn on a more distant concentration bank take more time to clear

Payable-through drafts are legal instruments that have the physical appearance of ordinary checks but are *not* drawn on a bank. Instead, payable-through drafts are drawn on and payment is authorized by the issuing firm against its demand deposit account. Like checks, the drafts are cleared through the banking system and are presented to the issuing firm's bank. The bank serves as a collection point and passes the drafts on to the firm. The corporate issuer usually has to return all drafts it does not wish to cover by the following business day. Drafts that are presented for payment are charged *in total* against the corporate master demand deposit account. Legal payment of the *individual drafts* will still take place after their review and approval by the firm.

The main purpose of using a payable-through draft system is *to provide for effective control over field payments*. Central office control over payments begun by regional units is provided as the drafts are reviewed in advance of final payment.

A few banks will provide the corporate customer with a cash management service specifically designed to extend disbursing float. The firm's concentration bank may have a correspondent relationship with a smaller bank located in a distant city. In that remote city the Federal Reserve System is unable to maintain frequent clearings of checks drawn on local banks. The firm will write the bulk of its payment checks against the account in the distant city. The checks will probably take at least one business day longer to clear, so the firm can "play the float" to its advantage.

A firm must use this technique of remote disbursing with extreme care. If a key supplier of raw materials has to wait an extra day for funds drawn on the distant account, the possibility of incurring ill-will might outweigh the apparent gain from an increase in the disbursing float. As you might guess, the practice of remote disbursing has come under criticism by bank regulatory authorities.

COST/BENEFIT ANALYSIS OF CASH MANAGEMENT SERVICES

A form of breakeven analysis can assist the executive in deciding whether a particular service will benefit the firm. The basic relationship follows:

$$\text{added costs} = \text{added benefits} \qquad (8\text{-}1)$$

When Equation (8-1) holds exactly, then the firm is no better or worse off for having adopted the given service. This procedure is illustrated in terms of the desirability of installing an additional lock box. Equation (8-1) can be restated on a per unit basis as follows:

$$P = (D)(S)(i) \qquad (8\text{-}2)$$

where P = increase in per-check processing cost if the new system is adopted
D = days saved in the collection process
S = average check size in dollars
i = the daily, before-tax opportunity cost (rate of return) of carrying cash

Assume now that check processing cost, P, will rise by $0.20 a check if the lock box is used. The firm has determined that the average check size, S, that will be mailed to the lock-box location will be $1000. If funds are freed by use of the lock box, they will be invested in marketable securities to yield an *annual* before-tax return of 8 percent. Now we determine the reduction in check collection time, D, that is required to justify using the lock box. That level of D is found to be

$$\$0.20 = (D)(\$1000)(0.08 \div 365)$$
$$0.91 \text{ days} = D$$

The lock box is economically beneficial if the firm can reduce float by *more* than 0.91 days. A similar analysis can be used to analyze the other tools of cash management.

MARKETABLE SECURITIES PORTFOLIO STRUCTURE

After designing the firm's cash receipts and payments system, the financial manager faces the task of selecting appropriate financial assets for inclusion in the marketable securities portfolio.

Evaluation Criteria

Certain criteria can provide the financial manager with a useful framework for selecting a proper marketable securities mix. These considerations include evaluation of the (1) financial risk, (2) interest rate risk, (3) liquidity, (4) taxability, and (5) yields among different financial assets. These criteria will be briefly highlighted from the investor's point of view.

Financial Risk

Financial risk is the uncertainty of expected returns from a security attributable to possible changes in the financial capacity of the security issuer to make future payments to the security owner. If the chance of default on the terms of the instrument is high (low), then the financial risk is said to be high (low).

In both financial practice and research, when estimates of risk-free returns are desired, the yields available on Treasury securities are consulted, and the safety of other financial instruments is weighed against them. Because the marketable securities portfolio is designed to provide a return on funds that would otherwise be tied up in idle cash held for transactions or precautionary purposes, the financial officer will not usually be willing to assume much financial risk in the hope of greater return.

Interest Rate Risk

The uncertainty that envelops the expected returns from a financial instrument attributable to changes in interest rates is known as **interest rate risk**. Of particular concern to the corporate treasurer is the price volatility associated with instruments that have long, as opposed to short, terms to maturity.

When the general interest rate rises above the coupon rate of an outstanding financial instrument, the instrument's market price will fall, to bring its yield to maturity in line with what investors could obtain by buying a newly issued security. The price of a security is determined by discounting the annual interest payment and the maturity value over the remaining years to maturity, using the current interest rate as the discount rate.

A longer term instrument is penalized to a greater extent due to its longer time to maturity when rates rise. The market price of a one-year security would be affected less than a two-year security, a 91-day security less than a 182-day security, and so on. Equity securities would exhibit the largest price changes because of their infinite maturity periods. The result in practice is the firm's marketable securities portfolio will tend to be composed of instruments that mature over short periods.

Liquidity

In the present context **liquidity** refers to tranforming a security into cash. Should an unforeseen event require that a significant amount of cash be immediately available, then a sizable portion of the portfolio might have to be sold. The financial manager will want the cash *quickly* and will not want to accept a large *price concession* in order to convert the securities. So the manager will be concerned with (1) the time period needed to sell the security, and (2) the likelihood that the security can be sold at or near its prevailing market price.

Taxability

The tax treatment of the income a firm receives from its security investments does not affect the ultimate mix of the marketable securities portfolio as much as the criteria mentioned earlier. This is because the interest income from *most* instruments suitable for inclusion in the portfolio is taxable at the federal level. Still, the taxability of interest income and capital gains (when the tax code provides for a favorable capital gains rate) is seriously evaluated by some corporate treasurers.

The interest income from **municipal obligations** *only* escapes the federal income tax. Owing to the tax-exempt feature of interest income from state and local government securities, they sell at lower yields to maturity in the market than do securities that pay taxable interest. The after-tax yield on the municipal obligation, however, could be higher than that obtainable from a non-tax-exempt security, depending on the purchasing firm's tax situation.

Yields

The final selection criterion that we mention is a significant one—the yields that are available on the different financial assets. The factors of (1) financial risk, (2) interest rate risk, (3) liquidity, and (4) taxability all influence the available yields on financial instruments. The yield criterion, then, involves a weighing of the risks and benefits inherent in these factors. If a given risk is assumed, such as lack of liquidity, a higher yield may be expected on the instrument lacking the liquidity characteristic.

Table 8-2 summarizes our framework for designing the firm's marketable securities portfolio. The four basic considerations are shown to influence the yields available on securities. The financial manager must focus on the identified risk-return tradeoffs. Coming to grips with these tradeoffs will enable the financial manager to determine the proper marketable securities mix for the company. Next we consider the marketable securities prominent in firms' near-cash portfolios.

MARKETABLE SECURITY ALTERNATIVES

U.S. Treasury Bills

U.S. Treasury bills are the most popular short-term investment vehicle among firms. A Treasury bill is a direct obligation of the United States government sold on a regular

TABLE 8-2
FRAMEWORK OF MARKETABLE SECURITIES PORTFOLIO DESIGN

Considerations $\rightarrow$	Influence $\rightarrow$	Focus upon $\rightarrow$	Determine
Financial risk Interest rate risk Liquidity Taxability	Yields	Risk vs. return preferences	Marketable securities mix

basis by the U.S. Treasury. New Treasury bills are issued in denominations of $10,000, $15,000, $50,000, $100,000, $500,000, and $1,000,000.

At present bills are regularly offered with maturities of 91, 182, and 365 days. The three-month and six-month bills are auctioned weekly by the Treasury, and the one-year bills are offered every four weeks.

Treasury bills are sold on a discount basis; for that reason the investor does not receive an actual interest payment. The return is the difference between the purchase price and the face (par) value of the bill.

The bills are marketed by the Treasury in *bearer* form only. They are purchased, therefore, without the investor's name on them. This makes them easily transferable from one investor to the next. Of prime importance to the corporate treasurer is the fact that a very active secondary market exists for bills. This highly developed secondary market for bills not only makes them extremely liquid, but also allows the firm to buy bills with maturities of a week or even less.

Bills have the full financial backing of the United States government, so they are, for all practical purposes, risk-free. This negligible financial risk and high degree of liquidity makes the yields lower than those obtainable on other marketable securities. The income from Treasury bills is subject to federal income taxes, but *not* to state and local government income taxes.

Federal Agency Securities

Federal agency securities are debt obligations of corporations and agencies that have been created to effect the various lending programs of the United States government. Five such government-sponsored corporations account for the majority of outstanding agency debt. The "big five" agencies are

1 The Federal National Mortgage Association (FNMA). FNMA provides liquidity assistance to the secondary market for mortgages by purchasing mortgages from private financial institutions during periods of tight credit and by selling mortgages when credit is easy.

2 The Federal Home Loan Banks (FHLB). The 12 regional banks in the FHLB system operate as a credit reserve system under the supervision of the Federal Home Loan Bank Board for the benefit of the system's members, all of which engage in home mortgage lending.

3 The Federal Land Banks. The 12 regional banks, owned by almost 300 local Federal Land Bank Associations, arrange loans to persons who are members of the associations and who are engaged in agriculture, provide agricultural services, or own rural homes.

4 The Federal Intermediate Credit Banks. There are 12 of these banks which make loans to and purchase notes originating from loans made to farmers by other financial institutions involved in agricultural lending.

5 The Banks for Cooperatives. The 12 district Banks for Cooperatives make loans to cooperative associations, owned and controlled by farmers, that market farm products, purchase farm supplies, or provide general farm business services.

The "big five" agencies are entirely owned by their member associations or the general public. The agency guarantees the securities it issues, not the federal government as is often assumed. These agencies sell their securities in a variety of denominations, and the entry barrier is not as severe as in the market for Treasury bills. Obligations can at times be purchased with maturities as short as 30 days or as long as 15 years.

Agency debt usually sells on a coupon basis and pays interest to the owner on a semi-annual schedule, although there are exceptions. The secondary market for the agency debt is well developed in the shorter maturity categories—5 years or less—but is not as strong in the longer maturity categories. The income received by the investor in agency debt is subject to taxation at the federal level. Of the "big five" agencies, only the income from FNMA issues is taxed at the state and local level.

The yields available on agency obligations will always exceed those of Treasury securities of similar maturity. This yield differential is attributable to lesser marketability and greater default risk.

Bankers' Acceptances

Bankers' acceptances are one of the least understood instruments suitable for inclusion in the firm's marketable securities portfolio. Their part in United States commerce today is largely concentrated in the financing of foreign transactions. Generally, an acceptance is a draft (order to pay) drawn on a specific bank by an exporter in order to obtain payment for goods shipped to a customer, who maintains an account with that specific bank.

Since acceptances are used to finance the acquisition of goods by one party, the document is not "issued" in specialized denominations; its dollar size is determined by the cost of the goods being purchased. Usual sizes, however, range from $25,000 to $1 million. The maturities on acceptances generally run from 30 to 180 days.

Acceptances, like Treasury bills, are sold on a discount basis and are payable to the bearer of the paper. A secondary market for the acceptances of large banks does exist.

The income from investing in acceptances is fully taxable at federal, state, and local levels. Owing to their greater financial risk and lesser liquidity, acceptances provide investors a yield advantage over Treasury bills and agency obligations.

Negotiable Certificates of Deposit

A **negotiable certificate of deposit**, **CD**, is a marketable receipt for funds that have been deposited in a bank for a fixed time period. The deposited funds earn a fixed rate of interest. These are not to be confused with ordinary passbook savings accounts or nonmarketable time deposits offered by all commercial banks. CDs are offered by major money-center banks.

CDs are offered by key banks in a variety of denominations running from $25,000 to $10,000,000. The original maturities on CDs can range from 1 to 18 months. CDs are not sold at a discount. Rather, when the certificate matures, the owner receives the full amount deposited plus the earned interest.

The secondary market for CDs is well organized but does not operate as smoothly as the aftermarket in Treasuries. CDs are more heterogeneous than Treasury bills. This makes it harder to liquidate large blocks of CDs, because a more specialized investor must be found. The securities dealers who "make" the secondary market in CDs mainly trade in $1 million units. Smaller denominations can be traded but will bring a relatively lower price.

The income received from an investment in CDs is subject to taxation at all government levels. In recent years CD yields have been above those available on bankers' acceptances.

Commercial Paper

Commercial paper refers to short-term, unsecured promissory notes sold by large businesses to raise cash. These are sometimes described in the popular financial press as short-term corporate IOUs. Because they are unsecured, the issuing side of the market is dominated by large corporations, which typically maintain sound credit ratings. The issuing (borrowing) firm can sell the paper to a dealer who will in turn sell it to the investing public; if the firm's reputation is solid, the paper can be sold directly to the ultimate investor.

The denominations in which commercial paper can be bought vary over a wide range. At times paper can be obtained in sizes from $5000 to $5 million, or even more.

Commercial paper can be purchased with maturities that range from three to 270 days. These notes are *generally* sold on a discount basis in bearer form. For practical purposes, there is no active trading in a secondary market for commercial paper, but a specialized (secondary) market does exist. The return on commercial paper is fully taxable to the investor at all levels of government. Because of its lack of marketability, commercial paper in past years consistently provided a yield advantage over other near-cash assets of comparable maturity. Today the yields are approximate to those available on CDs.

Repurchase Agreements

Repurchase agreements (repos) are legal contracts that involve the actual sale of securities by a *borrower* to the *lender*, with a commitment on the part of the borrower to *repurchase* the securities at the contract price plus a stated interest charge. The securities sold to the lender are U.S. government issues or other instruments of the money market such as those described above. The borrower is either a major financial institution or a dealer in U.S. government securities.

Why might the corporation with excess cash prefer to buy repurchase agreements rather than a given marketable security? There are two major reasons. First, the original maturities of the instruments being sold can be adjusted to suit the particular needs of the investing corporation. The second reason is that the contract price of the securities is *fixed* for the duration of the transaction and the corporation that buys a repurchase agreement is protected against market price fluctuations throughout the contract period. This makes it a sound alternative investment for funds that are freed up for only very short periods.

These agreements are usually executed in sizes of $1 million or more. The maturities may be for a specified time period or may have no fixed maturity date. In the latter case either lender or borrower may terminate the contract without advance notice.

The returns the lender receives on repurchase agreements are taxed at all governmental levels. Since the interest rates are set by direct negotiation between lender and borrower, no regular published series of yields is available for direct comparison with the other short-term investments. The rates available on repurchase agreements, however, are closely related to, but generally less than, Treasury bill rates of comparable maturities.

Money Market Mutual Funds

Money market mutual funds, also called liquid-asset funds, sell their shares to raise cash, and by pooling the funds of large numbers of small savers, they can build their liquid-asset portfolios. Many of these funds allow the investor to start an account with as little as $1000. This small initial investment, coupled with the fact that some liquid-asset funds permit subsequent investments in amounts as small as $100, makes this type of outlet for excess cash suited to the small firm. Furthermore, the management of a small enterprise may not be highly versed in the details of short-term investments. By purchasing shares in a liquid-asset fund, the investor is also buying managerial expertise.

Money market funds typically invest in a diversified portfolio of short-term, high-grade debt instruments. Some such funds, however, will accept more interest rate risk in their portfolios and acquire some corporate bonds and notes.

Money market mutual funds offer the investing firm a high degree of liquidity. By redeeming (selling) shares, the investor can obtain cash quickly. The returns earned from owning shares in a money market fund are taxable at all governmental levels. The yields will follow the returns the investor could receive by purchasing the marketable securities directly.

Money Market Deposit Accounts

Congress passed the Depository Institutions Act in 1982. The objective of the act was to enable both banks and thrifts to compete with the fast-growing money market mutual funds. The result was that the Depository Institutions Deregulatory Committee authorized banks and thrifts to offer to investors a new type of account called the **money market deposit account (MMDA)**. The MMDAs became available to the public on December 14, 1982. These accounts differ from the money market fund accounts in significant ways:

1 They carry federal deposit insurance of up to $100,000 per account.

2 They require a minimum balance of $2,500. If the balance falls below the designated $2,500, it earns only the passbook savings rate.

3 Each account is limited to a maximum of six transactions per month, of which only three may be by check. In effect this means the other three transactions must be accomplished by use of preauthorized withdrawals.

The yield on the MMDAs is set individually by each offering bank or thrift institution. The maximum period for which the yield can be guaranteed by the financial institution is one month.

The third characteristic of the MMDAs renders them inappropriate for most businesses as a vehicle for the investment of excess cash. Firms do not want to be restricted on the number of times per month that they can tap their liquid asset reserves.

The Yield Structure—What Returns Can We Get?

The behavior of yields on short-term debt instruments over the 1980–87 period is shown in Table 8-3. An examination of the data in that table permits the following generalizations:

1 The returns from the various instruments are highly correlated in the positive direction over time. That is, the yields tend to rise and fall together.
2 The yields are quite volatile over time. The financial manager, then, cannot plan on any given level of returns prevailing over a long time period.
3 A basic change has occurred in the underlying structure of yields owing to the deregulation of some banking activities. CD rates usually *exceed* the yields available on other common instruments.

The discussion in this chapter on designing the firm's marketable securities portfolio touched upon the essential elements of several near-cash assets. At times it is difficult to sort out the distinguishing features among these short-term investments. To alleviate that problem, Table 8-4 draws together their principal characteristics.

TABLE 8-3
ANNUAL YIELDS ON THREE-MONTH MARKETABLE SECURITIES

Year	T-bills	Agencies	Acceptances	Commercial paper	CDs
1980	11.51	12.09	12.72	12.66	13.07
1981	14.03	15.28	15.32	15.32	15.91
1982	10.69	11.68	11.89	11.89	12.27
1983	8.61	8.95	8.90	8.88	9.07
1984	9.52	10.13	10.14	10.10	10.37
1985	7.47	8.00	7.91	7.95	8.04
1986	5.97	6.49	6.38	6.49	6.50
1987	5.78	6.47	6.75	6.82	7.01

Source: Federal Reserve Statistical Release H.15 (519), "Selected Interest Rates," various issues.

TABLE 8-4
SUMMARY OF MONEY MARKET INSTRUMENTS

Instrument	Denominations	Maturities	Basis	Form	Liquidity	Taxability
U.S. Treasury bills—direct obligations of the U.S. government	$ 10,000 15,000 50,000 100,000 500,000 1,000,000	91 days 182 days 365 days 9-month not presently issued	Discount	Bearer	Excellent secondary market	Exempt from state and local income
Federal agency securities—obligations of cocorporations and agencies created to effect the federal government's lending programs	Wide variation: from $1000 to $1 million	5 days (Farm Credit consolidated system-wide discount notes) to more than 10 years	Discount or coupon; usually on coupon	Bearer or registered	Good for issues of "big five" agencies	Generally exempt at local level; FNMA issues are not
Bankers' acceptances—drafts accepted for future payment by commercial banks	No set size; typically range from $25,000 to $1 million	Predominantly from 30 to 180 days	Discount	Bearer	Good for acceptances of large "money market" banks	Taxed at all levels of government
Negotiable certificates of deposit—marketable receipts for funds deposited in a bank for a fixed time period	$25,000 to $10 million	1 to 18 months	Accrued interest	Bearer or registered; bearer is preferable from liquidity standpoint	Fair to good	Taxed at all levels of government
Commercial paper—short-term unsecured promissory notes	$5000 to $5 million, $1000 and $5000 multiples above the initial offering size are sometimes available	3 to 270 days	Discount	Bearer	Poor; no active secondary market in usual sense	Taxed at all levels of government
Repurchase agreements—legal contracts between a borrower (security seller) and lender (security buyer). The borrower will repurchase at the contract price plus an interest charge	Typical sizes are $500,000 or more	According to terms of contract	Not applicable	Not applicable	Fixed by the agreement; that is, borrower will repurchase	Taxed at all levels of government
Money market mutual funds—holders of diversified portfolios of short-term, high-grade debt instruments	Some require an initial investment as small as $1000	Your shares can be sold at any time	Net asset value	Registered	Good; provided by the fund itself	Taxed at all levels of government

265

CHAPTER SUMMARY

Firms hold cash in order to satisfy transactions, precautionary, and speculative needs for liquidity. Because cash balances provide no direct return, the precautionary motive for investing in cash is met in part by holdings of marketable securities.

Objectives and Decisions

The financial manager must (1) make sure that enough cash is on hand to meet the payment needs that arise in the course of doing business and (2) attempt to reduce the firm's idle cash balances to a minimum.

Collection and Disbursement Procedures

By use of (1) lock-box arrangements, (2) preauthorized checks, (3) special forms of depository transfer checks, and (4) wire transfers, the firm can achieve considerable benefits in terms of float reduction. Lock-box systems and preauthorized checks serve to reduce mail and processing float. Depository transfer checks and wire transfers move funds between banks; they are often used in conjunction with concentration banking. Both the lock-box and preauthorized check systems can be employed as part of the firm's concentration banking setup to speed receipts to regional collection centers.

The firm can delay and favorably affect the control of its cash disbursements through the use of (1) zero balance accounts, (2) payable-through drafts, and (3) remote disbursing. Zero balance accounts allow the company to maintain central-office control over payments while permitting the disbursing authroity to rest with the firm's several divisions. Because key disbursing accounts are located in one major concentration bank, rather than in multiple banks across the country, excess cash balances that tend to build up in the outlying banks are avoided. Payable-through drafts are legal instruments that look like checks but are drawn on and paid by the issuing firm rather than its bank. The bank serves as a collection point for the drafts. The main reason for use of such a system is to provide for effective central-office control over field-authorized payments; it is not used as a major vehicle for extending disbursing float. Remote disbursing, however, is used to increase disbursing float. Remote disbursing refers to the process of writing payment checks on banks located in cities distant from the one where the check is originated.

Before any of these collection and disbursement procedures are initiated by the firm, a careful analysis should be undertaken to see if the expected benefits outweigh the expected costs.

Marketable Securities Portfolio Structure

The factors of (1) financial risk, (2) interest rate risk, (3) liquidity, and (4) taxability affect the yields available on marketable securities. By considering these four factors simultaneously with returns desired from the portfolio, the financial manager can design the mix of near-cash assets most suitable for the firm.

The features of several marketable securities were investigated. Treasury bills and federal agency securities are extremely safe investments. Higher yields are obtainable on bankers' acceptances, CDs, and commercial paper in exchange for greater risk assumption. The firm can hedge against price fluctuations through the use of repurchase agreements. Money market mutual funds, a recent phenomenon of our financial market system, are particularly well suited for the short term investing needs of small firms.

PROBLEMS

8-1 Taylor Gifts has $500,000 in cash available for investment in marketable securities. The transaction costs for the investment are expected to be approximately $20,000.

    a If the annual yield is 9 percent, what recommendations should be made for the purchase of securities if they are held for one month? Two months? Three months? Six months? One Year?

    b What is the required breakeven (or minimum) yield for securities held for 3 months?

8-2 Cole Frozen Foods processes and markets its products nationally, but handles all billings from its home office in Omaha. Omaha First National has offered to operate as a concentration bank for Cole for a flat annual fee of $180,000. An analysis conducted by Omaha First National conclusively shows the elimination of two days of mail float and one day of processing float with the implementation of this process. Cole approximates that it will also save $45,000 a year in clerical costs on its $400 million annual credit sales. Cole already has an established line of credit with this bank with an annual borrowing rate of 15 percent. The value of the float reduction would be applied against this line of credit. Cole uses a 365-day year in financial assessments of this type. Would you recommend that Cole install this concentration banking system?

8-3 What is the value of one day's float reduction to a company with forecasted annual sales of $800 million and an anticipated marketable securities portfolio yield of 9.2 percent. Use a 365-day year for this computation.

8-4 Vicker Chemicals is considering the adoption of a lock-box system to accelerate its cash receipts. The average annual remittances received by Vicker in approximately 5000 checks is $10 million. Minnesota State Bank has offered to expedite checks and documents through the lock-box system for $0.18 per check. Freed up cash from this system can be invested in a near-cash asset portfolio yielding an annual before-tax return of 8 percent. Using a 365-day year:

    a What reduction in check collection time must be accomplished for Vicker to recover the costs associated with this system?

    b How would your answer change in part (a) if a before-tax return of only 4 percent could be obtained from investing the freed cash?

8-5 Kress Software Products markets its computer software packages from its eight regional sales office. All sales are on a credit basis, net 30 days. A recent cash management study conducted by Kress determined that customer payments averaged 3.5 days in the mail. An additional day of processing is required before the checks can be deposited with a local bank. A lock-box system in each region would reduce mail float by 1.5 days and processing float would be eliminated. A reduction of one full day of transit float would also be accomplished. The cost of this system in each region is estimated at $200 per month. Kress averages $5.2 million in sales in each region. Reasonable investment opportunities yielding 8 percent are available for the newly available cash.

a What is Kress's opportunity cost of funds tied up in mailing and processing float? Use a 365-day year.

b What would be the net cost or savings of the lock-box system? Would you recommend that Kress adopt the system?

8-6 Three years ago as the corporate treasurer you purchased a 20-year bond with a coupon rate of 9 percent and a par value of $1000. Interest payments are made annually. Your company now requires cash and you must liquidate this bond. Current yields are 10 percent for instruments in this bond's risk class.

a At what price must you sell your bond, assuming annual compounding?

b What is the gain/loss over the original purchase price?

c Assuming bond characteristics are identical except for maturity, what would the gain/loss have been if the original bond had a five-year maturity period instead of a twenty-year maturity period?

8-7 Princeton Air Conditioning has $6 million in cash available for investment in marketable securities. At least half must be invested at maturity periods of three months or less, but none of the $6 million should be invested in instruments with maturity periods longer than six months. Brokerage fees will be $15,000 to invest the entire $6 million. The current term structure of short-term yields is

Maturity period	Annual yield
One month	8.2%
Two months	8.3%
Three months	8.5%
Four months	8.7%
Five months	8.8%
Six months	9.0%

a What maturities should be purchased with the $6 million to meet the investment restrictions and to maximize before-tax income? What is the income from this investment strategy?

b What would be the profit-maximizing investment if the only restriction is the maturity period limit of six months?

c What is the before-tax income if one-sixth of the $6 million is invested in each maturity period?

8-8 Latham Shoes, Inc., a manufacturer and distributor of sports footwear, currently has no coordinated cash management system. Remittances from customers are mailed to the home office in Philadelphia where they are processed for deposit at a local bank. This process averages four days of mail float and two days for internal processing. Daily collections average $1.5 million with an estimated average check size of $2500. Latham's marketable securities portfolio currently earns 8 percent annually.

The First New England Bank has proposed a cash receipts acceleration system for Latham involving both a lock-box system and concentration banking. This proposal would reduce funds tied up by mail float by two days, and processing float would be eliminated. Funds would be transferred from Latham's five regional banks across the country to First New England twice each business day through an automated depository transfer check system. The depository transfer checks cost $15 each and occur 270 business days each year. The lock-box system will cost $0.20 per check processed.

a How much cash will be freed if Latham adopts the proposed system?
b What is the opportunity cost of maintaining the current setup? (Annual benefits)
c What is the projected annual cost of operating the proposed system?
d Compute the net annual gain/loss associated with the new system. Should Latham adopt it?

REFERENCES

Anderson, Paul F., and R. D. Boyd Harman: "The Management of Excess Corporate Cash," *Financial Executive*, vol. 32, October 1964, pp. 26–30, 51.

Andrews, Horace, and Devdatt Shah: "Managing Short-Term Assets for Long-Term Growth," *FE*, vol. 53, March 1985, pp. 54–56. (Note: *FE* was formerly titled *Financial Executive*)

Archer, Stephen H.: "A Model for the Determination of Firm Cash Balances," *Journal of Financial and Quantitative Analysis*, vol. 1, March 1966, pp. 1–11.

Arnold, Jasper H.: "Banker's Acceptance: A Low-Cost Financing Choice," *Financial Executive*, vol. 48, July 1980, pp. 14–19.

Arthur, William J.: "Cash Flow Yardstick: Here's One Way to Make the Cash Flow Statement More Useful," *FE*, vol. 54, October 1986, pp. 35–40.

Batlin, C. A., and Susan Hinko: "Lockbox Management and Value Maximization," *Financial Management*, vol. 10, Winter 1981, pp. 39–44.

Bennett, Barbara: "Standby Letters of Credit," Federal Reserve Bank of San Francisco, *Weekly Letter*, May 23, 1986, pp. 1–3.

Bonocore, Joseph J.: "Getting a Picture of Cash Management," *Financial Executive*, vol. 48, May 1980, pp. 30–33.

Carraro, Kenneth C., and Daniel L. Thornton: "The Cost of Checkable Deposits in the United States," Federal Reserve Bank of St. Louis, *Review*, vol. 68, April 1986, pp. 19–27.

Carton, Margaret F.: "Credit and the Lockbox: Improving Cash Flow and Internal Control," *Credit & Financial Management*, vol. 88, December 1986, pp. 23–4+.

"Cash Management: The New Art of Wringing More Profit from Corporate Funds," *Business Week*, March 13, 1978, pp. 62–68.

Chastain, Clark E., and Thomas A. Cianciolo: "Strategies in Cash-Flow Management," *Business Horizons*, vol. 29, May–June 1986, pp. 65–73.

Collins, J. Markham, and Alan W. Frankle: "International Cash Practices of Large U.S. Firms," *Journal of Cash Management*, vol. 5, July–August 1985, pp. 42–48.

Cook, Timothy Q., and T. D. Rowe, eds.: *Instruments of the Money Market* (6th ed.), Richmond VA: Federal Reserve Bank of Richmond, 1986.

Davis, Henry A.: "Changing Priorities in Corporate Cash Management," *FE*, vol. 3, January 1987, pp. 18–21.

Desalvo, Alfred: "Cash Management Converts Dollars into Working Assets," *Harvard Business Review*, vol. 50, May–June 1972, pp. 92–100.

Emery, Gary W.: "Some Empirical Evidence on the Properties of Daily Cash Flow," *Financial Management,* vol. 10, Spring 1981, pp. 21–28.

Farrell, Christopher, and Jeffrey M. Laderman: "Wringing More Profits from Idle Corporate Cash," *Business Week*, May 12, 1986, pp. 85–86.

Ferguson, Daniel M.: "Optimize Your Firm's Lockbox Selection System," *Financial Executive*, vol. 51, April 1983, pp. 8–12, 14–15, 18–19.

Ferri, Michael G., and H. Dennis Oberhelman: "A Study of the Management of Money Market Mutual Funds, 1975–1980," *Financial Management*, vol. 10, Autumn 1981, pp. 24–29.

Gitman, Lawrence J., and Mark D. Goodwin: "An Assessment of Marketable Securities Management Practices," *Journal of Financial Research*, vol. 2, Fall 1979, pp. 161–69.

Johnson, James M., David R. Campbell, and Leonard M. Savoie: "Corporate Liquidity: A Comparison of Two Recessions," *Financial Executive*, vol. 51, October 1983, pp. 18–22.

Jones, Charles P., and Jack W. Wilson: "Stocks, Bonds, Paper, and Inflation: 1870–1985," *Journal of Portfolio Management*, vol. 14, Fall 1987, pp. 20–4.

Jones, H. Stanley: "Investing for the Short Haul," *Association Management*, vol. 37, August 1985, pp. 103–4.

Jones, Reginald H: "Face to Face with Cash Management: How One Company Does It," *Financial Executive*, vol. 37, September 1969, pp. 37–39.

Kamath, Ravindra R., Shahriar Khaksari, and Heidi Hylton Meier: "Management of Excess Cash: Practices and Developments," *Financial Management*, vol. 14, Autumn 1985, pp. 70–7.

Kramer, Richard P.: "Corporate Cash: Why Its Meaning Differs Between Treasurers and Controllers," *FE*, vol. 4, January–February 1988, pp. 53–55.

Maier, Steven F., and Larry A. Meeks: "Applications and Models: When Is the Right Time to Do a Lockbox Study?" *Journal of Cash Management*, vol. 6, March–April 1986, pp. 32–34.

Maier, Steven F., and James H. Vander Weide: "A Practical Approach to Short-Run Financial Planning," *Financial Management*, vol. 7, Winter 1978, pp. 10–16.

——. "What Lockbox and Disbursement Models Really Do," *Journal of Finance*, vol. 38, May 1983, pp. 361–71.

Masonson, Leslie N.: "Cash Management Audit: How It Can Uncover Outmoded Practices, Reduce Risk, and Cut Costs," *FE*, vol. 3, February 1987, pp. 30+.

McConoughey, Deborah J.: "Breakeven Analysis for Maturity Decisions in Cash Management," *Journal of Cash Management*, vol. 5, January–February 1985, pp. 18–21.

Miller, Gregory: "Liberating the Cash Manager," *Institutional Investor*, vol. 17, December 1983, pp. 195–6+.

Minster, Tim: "Management of Cashflow," *The CPA Journal*, vol. 56, May 1986, pp. 94–6.

Nauss, Robert M., and Robert E. Markland: "Solving Lock Box Location Problems," *Financial Management*, vol. 8, Spring 1979, pp. 21–27.

Orgler, Yair E., and Yair Tauman: "A Game Theoretic Approach to Collections and Disbursements," *Management Science*, vol. 32, August 1986, pp. 1025–39.

Paustian, Chuck: "Companies Review Lockboxes in Effort to Lower Expenses," *Pensions & Investment Age*, vol. 14, April 14, 1986, pp. 19–20.

Perkins, Daniel M.: "Borrowing Strategies in Foreign Currencies," *Journal of Cash Management*, vol. 6, March–April 1986, pp. 26–30.

Richards, Verlyn D., and Eugene J. Laughlin: "A Cash Conversion Cycle Approach to Liquidity Analysis," *Financial Management*, vol. 9, Spring 1980, pp. 32–38.

Richardson, Ron D.: "Managing Your Company's Cash," *Nation's Business*, vol. 74, November 1986, pp. 52–4.

Rinne, Heikki, Robert A. Wood, and Ned C. Hill: "Reducing Cash Concentration Costs by Anticipatory Forecasting," *Journal of Cash Management*, vol. 6, March–April 1986, pp. 44–50.

Rollins, Cathy L.: "The Hows and Whys of a Lockbox," *Pensions & Investment Age*, vol. 13, July 22, 1985, pp. CM28–CM29+.

Scott, David F., Jr., Laurence J. Moore, Andre Saint-Denis, Edouard Archer, and Bernard W. Taylor III: "Implementation of a Cash Budget Simulator at Air Canada," *Financial Management*, vol. 8, Summer 1979, pp. 46–52.

Searby, Frederick W.: "Use Your Hidden Cash Resources," *Harvard Business Review*, vol. 46, March–April 1968, pp. 71–80.

Segall, Patricia: "Commercial Paper: New Tunes on an Old Instrument," *Journal of Commercial Bank Lending*, vol. 69, April 1987, pp. 16–23.

Senchack, Andrew J., and Don M. Heep: "Auction Profits in the Treasury Bill Market," *Financial Management*, vol. 4, Summer 1975, pp. 45–52,

Sender, Henny: "New Rules for the Yield Game," *Institutional Investor*, vol. 20, December 1986, pp. 235–6+.

Shafer, David L.: "Cash Management: A Cost-Effective Approach," *Journal of Accountancy*, vol. 163, March 1987, p. 114.

Soenen, Luc A.: "The Concept of Cash Flow and Techniques for Speeding Up the Flow of Cash," *Management Decision*, vol. 25, 1987 Management Classics issue, pp. 7–11.

Stone, Bernell K., and Robert A. Wood: "Daily Cash Forecasting: A Simple Method for Implementing the Distribution Approach," *Financial Management*, vol. 6, Fall 1977, pp. 40–50.

Syron, Richard, and Sheila L. Tschinkel: "The Government Securities Market: Playing Field for Repos," Federal Reserve Bank of Atlanta, *Economic Review*, vol. 70, September 1985, pp. 10–19.

Thompson, Ray: "Understanding Cash Flow: A System Dynamics Analysis," *Journal of Small Business Management*, vol. 24, April 1986, pp. 23–30.

Vickson, R. G.: "Simple Optimal Policy for Cash Management: The Average Balanced Requirement Case," *Journal of Financial and Quantitative Analysis*, vol. 20, September 1985, pp. 353–69.

Weiss, Stuart: "Making the Most of the Cash on Hand," *Business Week*, November 3, 1986, p. 112+.

9

CREDIT AND INVENTORY MANAGEMENT

This chapter is concerned with the two least liquid of the firm's current assets: accounts receivable and inventories. The successful management of these two types of assets can be very difficult; financial problems of firms often begin because a large number of customers either pay late or do not pay at all, and/or the level of inventories becomes excessive. We first consider the problems associated with managing the accounts of credit customers, that is, the accounts receivable of the firm. Inventory management will be considered in the second part of the chapter.

CREDIT MANAGEMENT

The purpose of selling on credit is to increase sales and, therefore, the earnings of the firm. However, two major problem areas are created from selling on credit. First, selling on credit involves making decisions concerning the credit classes of customers to whom credit will be extended, and the terms to be offered. These decisions are **investment decisions**, a subject which will be examined in Chapter 10.

The second major problem area is derived from the necessity of administering customer accounts and making collections. Our concern in this section is with the problems and decisions in this area, which is generally referred to as the **management of accounts receivable** or, simply, as credit management. Managing accounts receivable is typically the responsibility of the firm's credit department. Some firms, however, pass this responsibility on by selling their receivables to a third party, such as a bank or a firm which specializes in making such purchases. The sale of receivables in these cases is known as **factoring**.

Since our focus at this point is on the management of customer accounts, we should first consider how decisions are made in respect to credit applications, and the procedures used to collect accounts. The decision-making process in regard to credit applications requires information about the applicant. We review below the sources of this type of information.

Sources of Credit Information.   The data necessary for a credit analysis and decision can be obtained from several sources. The more important of these sources are considered below.

The Company's Past Experience With the Applicant.   This is the most obvious and usually the most convenient source of credit information. If the applicant has purchased on credit from the firm in the past, the company's experience with the account will probably be one of the most important inputs into the decision to either extend or not to extend credit again. If the decision is in the affirmative, the credit limits will still have to be set. Conditions change over time, of course, and the company may feel that new and additional information is needed. This is more likely to be the case if the applicant is asking for more credit than it has received from the firm in the past.

Information Provided By the Applicant.   Credit applicants are usually asked to supply much of the information necessary to judge the merits of their applications. If the applicant is a firm, important financial data are provided in its financial statements. Audited statements provide greater assurance of data accuracy. A ratio analysis of financial data can provide useful information concerning the creditworthiness of an applicant. Although the historical record of profitability and liquidity should be examined carefully, a pro forma analysis of future profitability and liquidity is of greater relevance. The applicant may be asked to provide this pro forma analysis, but the firm which is being asked to grant the credit will have to assess its reliability.

Local Credit Bureaus.   Local credit associations or bureaus provide credit information about local firms as well as individuals. In addition, information can be obtained concerning firms in other localities through data compiled by the National Association of Credit Management. These sources provide information primarily about past payment practices of firms and individuals.

National Credit Agencies.   The best known of these agencies is Dun and Bradstreet, Inc., which publishes credit information concerning thousands of firms located throughout the United States. The primary publication of Dun and Bradstreet is its *Reference Book*. However, on request and for a fee, the agency will provide credit reports dealing with specific firms and individuals, providing the necessary information is available.

Banks.   These institutions will obtain for their depositors credit data concerning firms as well as individuals. The source of this information is normally the credit applicant's bank.

Informal Sources.   A firm may also be able to obtain credit information from other local firms that have done business with the applicant in the past. Credit managers in most communities become acquainted with one another over time and pass credit information around. Although this type of information exchange is highly informal, it can provide reliable data pertinent to the creditworthiness of firms and individuals in the community.

Credit Analysis

After the firm has obtained the necessary data pertinent to a credit application, the next step is the analysis of the data. The thoroughness of the study should depend on the amount of time and effort that can be economically justified, given the prospective profitability of the account. Credit analysis is often informal and unsophisticated in small communities where credit applicants are typically known to the firm. In situations where the number of credit applicants is large and generally unknown to the firm, the analysis will have to be more formal and systematic.

Use of Linear Discriminant Analysis in Credit Scoring.   Numerous methods of credit scoring have been developed to help estimate the creditworthiness of credit applicants. We will consider a method, called **linear discriminant analysis**, that has attracted a great deal of interest among both practicing credit analysts and academics in recent years. The objective is to develop a discriminant function of the following type:

$$Z = a_1X_1 + a_2X_2 + \cdots + a_nX_n \tag{9-1}$$

where Z represents the applicant's credit score
$a_1, \ldots, a_n$ are the coefficients, or weights, given to
the various independent variables
$X_1, \ldots, X_n$ are the independent variables, which are the
factors considered to be important indicators of
credit worthiness

Examples of the Xs, where credit applicants are firms, include the following: current ratio, quick (acid test) ratio, total-debt-to-total-assets ratio, and net operating cash flow to financial charges ratio. The variables for applicants who are individuals might include such factors as: income, the amount of time spent in the last job, and whether the applicant owns a home. The discriminant function can be set up so that a higher credit score indicates a stronger credit rating.

To illustrate graphically the nature of discriminant analysis, assume for simplicity that only two factors are considered in determining the Z score of customer firms applying for credit. These factors are last year's quick ratio, and ratio of net operating cash flow to before-tax financial outlays, which we will refer to hereafter as the **financial coverage ratio.**[1] Assume that the firm studies its past experience with its credit customers vis-à-vis these two ratios. The results are presented in Table 9-1 and plotted in Figure 9-1. In the figure, the squares represent "good" accounts in the sense that balances are typically paid in ninety days or less, and the crosses represent

---

[1] Before-tax financial outlays would be figured as follows:

$$\text{Interest charges} + \left[\frac{\text{sinking funds payments}}{(1 - \text{income tax rate})}\right] + \text{lease payments.}$$

In some types of analyses, before-tax financial outlays might also include: preferred dividend payments/(1 − income tax rate) and, perhaps, common dividend payments/(1 − income tax rate).

TABLE 9-1
ANALYSIS OF ACCOUNTS RECEIVABLE

Customer	Quick ratio	Financial coverage ratio	Classification of account
a	0.41	0.63	Bad
b	0.64	−0.24	Bad
c	0.64	−1.25	Bad
d	0.70	0.98	Bad
e	0.77	3.97	Good
f	0.08	3.74	Bad
g	0.83	0.87	Bad
h	0.88	3.49	Bad
i	0.89	1.05	Bad
j	0.98	2.95	Good
k	1.01	−0.89	Bad
l	1.12	3.29	Good
m	1.22	2.21	Bad
n	1.36	2.34	Good
o	1.42	1.86	Bad
p	1.43	3.74	Good
q	1.52	0.88	Bad
r	1.59	1.08	Good
s	1.63	3.30	Good
t	1.72	−0.12	Bad
u	1.86	3.41	Good
v	1.88	4.53	Good
w	1.92	3.54	Good
x	2.09	2.04	Good
y	2.23	5.86	Good
z	3.51	4.52	Good

"bad" accounts in that balances are typically either not paid, or paid after ninety days. A straight line, representing the discriminant function, has been drawn so as to separate to the extent possible the squares from the crosses. The observations above the line are mostly squares, although there are a couple of crosses. Below the line, the observations are mostly crosses, although there are a couple of squares. These results indicate that the straight line does a fairly good, but not perfect, job of distinguishing between the good and bad accounts. The slope of the discriminant line is −3, and the intercepts on the X and Y axes of the positive quadrant are 6 and 2, respectively. The credit score at all points along the line is 6; thus, a decrease of 1 in the quick ratio is exactly offset by an increase of 3 in the financial coverage ratio along the line. We will see below how discriminant analysis can be used to make a decision concerning a credit application.

Computer programs are available to solve for the values of the coefficients in a discriminant equation. An example of how the coefficients can be calculated by the use of algebra in a very simple case, such as the one being discussed, is given in the Solved Problems at the end of the chapter. In the following section, we assume that one of these approaches has been used to determine the coefficient values.

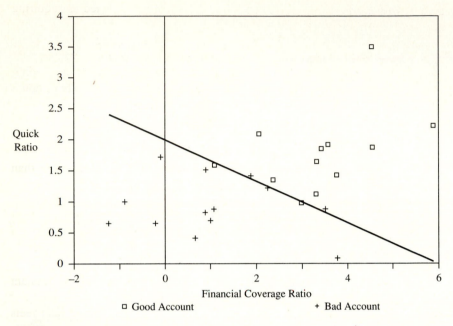

FIGURE 9-1
Analysis of credit accounts.

The Decision. Continuing with the example of the simple, two-variable model, the firm could use the following discriminant function as a basis for making decisions on credit applications:

$$Z = 3X_1 + 1X_2$$

2 VARIABLE → MODEL

where X_1 and X_2 refer to the applicant's quick ratio and financial coverage ratio, respectively. If the applicant's Z score is 6 or higher, credit would be approved, but if the score is less than 6, credit would be disapproved. As indicated earlier, use of 6 as the minimum acceptable Z score does only a fair job of discriminating between good and bad accounts. Using the historical data, two of the accounts would have been disapproved even though they proved to be good accounts, and two other accounts would have been approved that subsequently proved to be bad. Since there are twenty-six observations, the failure rate in the scoring system would have been $4/26 = 15.4$ percent.

A study of Figure 9-1 indicates that the erroneous signals produced by the discriminant function occurred for only marginal accounts, that is, for accounts with Z scores very close to the discriminant line. A study of the data shows that if the firm dropped the cutoff Z score to 5.8 and increased the required score for approval to 6.2, no erroneous signals would have been emitted by the discriminant analysis.

Applicants whose Z scores fall between 5.8 and 6.2 can be designated as requiring more information and study.

The analysis is sufficiently flexible to allow additional constraints on accepting applications. For example, applications by companies with a financial coverage ratio of less than 1.0 or a quick ratio of less than 0.5 may also be classified as needing more information and study, even though the Z score is 6.2 or above. The amount of additional time and money spent in the analysis of accounts should, of course, depend on the likely profitability of the account. The firm should spend to the point at which the marginal costs just equal the marginal benefits.

The two-variable example has been presented only to provide a simple situation to explain the essence of discriminant analysis. In most cases, however, more than two independent variables are necessary for reliability in making credit decisions. Computer programs are available for determining the significant variables (the Xs) as well as their coefficients (the a values) in Equation (9-1). The firm applying for credit will normally have to provide the raw data for determining these statistics, unless the necessary information has been published.

The data applicable to credit analysis will probably change over time as the firm grows and its customers and economic conditions change. Thus, if a discriminant function such as Equation (9-1) is used as a method of credit scoring, the analysis of past credit applications and accounts should be updated whenever management feels that the firm's experience has caused a change in the variables and coefficients of the model.

Collections

Setting the terms of credit does not mean that all credit customers will necessarily live up to their end of the bargain, even if a highly sophisticated credit-scoring scheme is used to facilitate decisions. Indeed, it is a lucky creditor-firm that does not have some slow-pay as well as no-pay customers. The firm attempts to reduce the amount of these undesirable accounts via its collection efforts. Typically, the collection procedure applicable to past-due accounts begins with a series of reminder letters or notices, with more severe language being used in each successive reminder. Finally, if the customer does not pay or make some type of arrangement to pay the account, the creditor firm will send a letter threatening to turn the account over to a collection agency. If the firm is not satisfied with the customer's response to this last letter, the account is usually turned over to the collection agency.

Even though collection procedures may differ in detail among firms, the principle underlying collection policy should always be the same: expend time and money in trying to collect on accounts so long as the marginal benefits exceed the marginal costs. Note, however, that a tough collection policy may not necessarily result in greater marginal benefits than marginal costs for each particular account. Nevertheless, the policy may be beneficial overall because of the effect the policy has on the firm's credit customers as a whole.

Our discussion of credit to this point has focused on the day-to-day administration of credit policy. Chapter 10 will show how the policy should be determined. In the remainder of the present chapter, we examine some of the problems involved in managing inventories.

INVENTORIES

Broadly speaking, inventories pose the same types of problems for the financial manager as other assets: there is an investment problem and a financing problem. The investment problem will be covered in the remaining part of the present chapter and the related financing in Chapter 11. Inventory decisions are complicated in many firms because several different managers may have major inputs in the decision-making process. In manufacturing companies, for example, the production manager will probably be in the best position to determine the amount of raw materials needed and the optimum level of goods-in-process, which often comprise the bulk of the firm's inventories. However, the financial manager will also be involved in making these decisions since investment and financing decisions are necessary. In addition, the marketing manager usually has a significant impact on all inventory decisions, because that person is responsible for making sales forecasts which will affect the overall level of the firm's operations.

Regardless of the nature of the firm and its lines of administrative responsibility, however, the inventory decision should be based on the same principle as other types of investments: the objective is to determine the level of investment that will maximize the share price of the firm's common stock. As we will see, determining the inventory investment that will maximize share price requires an unusual form of analysis, because the focus is on minimization of costs. The objective in the remaining part of this chapter is to (1) examine the nature of the investment problems posed by inventories, and (2) develop the approach that should be used in making inventory decisions.

The Inventory Investment

Most firms carry inventories primarily because purchases, production, and sales do not all occur at the same point in time. Inventories are essential for efficient operations, but they usually do not directly increase the sales of the company.[2] For this reason, inventory decisions are generally based on cost and risk analyses. We will see in subsequent sections how these two types of analyses are employed in making decisions.

Inventories may consist of raw materials, goods-in-process, and finished goods.[3] The factors that affect the level of a firm's inventories include the following:

---

[2] An exception to this statement occurs in situations where displays and stock on shelves cause greater sales. Traditional net present value analysis, which was discussed in Chapters 5 and 6, should be applied in these cases.

[3] Inventories may also include such items as spare parts for the firm's own equipment, and supplies used in company offices. The objective in investing in these inventories should also be to optimize risk and cost; the risk of inadequate supplies must be considered vis-à-vis the cost of maintaining more supplies than will actually be needed. Our main concern in the text, however, is with inventory items that will be included physically in a final product the company sells.

- Type of products sold.
- The nature of the production process.
- The relationship between ordering costs and carrying costs.
- Risk and uncertainty concerning product demand, and the possible delays in having purchase orders filled by suppliers.
- Unusual purchase opportunities.
- Variability in business conditions.
- Inflation.

Each of these factors is discussed below.

Type of Products Sold.   Firms that sell relatively inexpensive, standardized products generally tend to have larger finished-goods inventories. Most wholesale and retail firms fall in this category. The production process for these firms consists primarily of storing goods to be sold, and stocking shelves. For this reason, raw materials and goods-in-process inventories are typically relatively small or nonexistent. However, firms of this type do tend to have high finished-goods inventories.

Firms that manufacture *big-ticket* items, such as commercial aircraft and ocean liners, usually produce only on order. Raw materials and goods-in-process inventories will be very high for these firms. On the other hand, since deliveries to customers are made almost immediately after production is completed, finished goods inventory will typically be relatively small.

Nature of the Production Process.   Inventories of raw materials and goods-in-process will normally increase as the level of operations increases. In addition, the longer the production period, the larger will be the inventory of goods-in-process. A long production period may occur because production requires multiple stages (e.g., in ship building) or simply because production requires the passage of time (e.g., in wine making). Each stage or day in the production period will include semifinished goods. Obviously, the greater the number of stages or days in the process, the larger will be the goods-in-process inventory. A larger raw materials inventory may also be necessary, particularly if raw materials are needed at each stage of production. Finally, because of the time value of money, a longer production period will add more capital costs to the total costs of inventories.

Relationship Between Ordering and Carrying Costs.   The level of a firm's inventories will also be affected by the relationship between the cost of ordering inventory items and the carrying cost of the inventory. Ordering costs include such items as the time and expense involved in filling out and transmitting the purchase order, checking on the order until the goods are received, and checking the goods when they are received. Some of these costs may vary with the order size, but most of them are fairly constant per order. Inventory carrying costs include such items as storage costs, insurance, taxes, and the cost of the funds tied up in inventory. These costs may be expressed in percentage form, but they can be converted to dollars per unit simply by multiplying the percentage figure times the dollar cost per unit. Thus, the dollar amount of carrying costs usually varies with the dollar amount of the firm's inventories.

Since most ordering costs are fairly constant per order, total ordering cost will vary with the number of orders. On the other hand, the amount of inventory, and therefore total amount of carrying costs, will vary inversely with the number of orders. For example, assume that a manufacturing company estimates a total need of 7,200 units of a particular part in its operations for the coming year. The part, which has the code symbols ZJ120, will be used at a constant rate throughout the year. For the moment, we assume that ZJ120 costs $50 per unit, regardless of the amount ordered. Cost per order has been estimated at $30, and annual carrying costs at 15 percent, or 0.15 × $50 = $7.50 per year for each unit maintained in inventory. At one extreme, the company could place a single order (assuming sufficient storage space is available) for the total expected amount of ZJ120 needed for the year. In this case, total ordering costs would be 1 order × $30 cost per order = $30. If the part is used at a constant rate throughout the year, the average inventory of the item would be 7,200 units ordered/2 = 3,600 units. Carrying costs would thus be 3,600 units × $7.50 per unit = $27,000 for the year.

At the other extreme, the company could theoretically place an order each business day. Assuming 360 business days in a year, total ordering costs would be 360 orders × $30 cost per order = $10,800. Since the total amount ordered each day would be 7,200 units needed for the year/360 orders = 20 units, average inventory would be 20/2 = 10 units, and carrying costs for the year would be 10 units × $7.50 = $75.00. The latter calculation assumes constant usage per day during the year.

Since ordering costs and carrying costs vary inversely to each other, the firm has an optimization problem. Figure 9-2 provides a graphical example of the relationships involved. Note that ordering costs decrease, but carrying costs increase, as the quantity ordered increases on the graph. The net effect of these relationships is that the total

FIGURE 9-2
Relationship between order size and inventory costs.

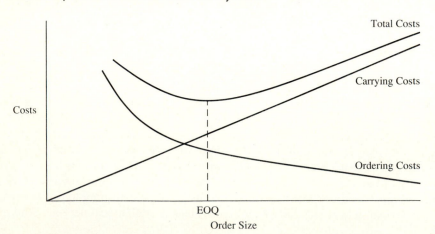

cost curve for inventory decreases at first, but then turns upward as the quantity ordered continues to increase. Management's objective is to determine the order quantity which minimizes total inventory costs. This quantity is denoted as EOQ on the graph. The minimum point on the total cost curve is a function of the relative slopes of the ordering-cost and carrying-cost curves.

   Solving for the EOQ.   To solve for the minimum cost point mathematically, we first state the firm's total inventory costs as a function of both ordering and carrying costs:

$$TC = F\left(\frac{S}{Q}\right) + C\left(\frac{Q}{2}\right) \tag{9-2}$$

where TC represents the total inventory costs for the year
       F is the dollar cost per order (*order-Cost*)
       S is the total amount needed during the year, in units *Sales po-tive period*
       Q is the unit quantity of each order *Quantity ordered*
       C is the dollar carrying cost per unit of average
       inventory during the year.

   The equation for calculating EOQ is derived from taking the derivative of TC with respect to Q, setting the derivative equal to zero and solving for Q.[4] Since this procedure solves for the optimum (i.e., least-cost) amount to order, Q is designated as EOQ and is found to be:

$$EOQ = \left(\frac{2F\,S}{C}\right)^{1/2} \tag{9-3}$$

⊗ See NB for 3/10 Stock out cost!

   The model above can be used when the total planning period is of any length, just so long as the sales rate of the product is constant throughout the period, and carrying costs are expressed in terms of the period length, for example, 5 percent per six months.

---

   [4] The derivative of the total cost in equation (9-2) with respect to the quantity ordered is:

$$\frac{dTC}{dQ} = \frac{2C}{4} - \frac{FS}{Q^2}$$

Since the second derivative of the total cost equation is positive, the equation above can be rearranged to solve for a minimum point on the total cost curve. The procedure is to set the derivative equal to zero and solve for Q as follows:

$$\frac{C}{2} - \frac{FS}{Q^2} = 0$$

$$\frac{C}{2} = \frac{FS}{Q^2}$$

$$Q^2 = \frac{2FS}{C}$$

$$Q = \left(\frac{2FS}{C}\right)^{1/2} = EOQ$$

Substituting the values given in the last section for the appropriate elements in equation (9-3), we get:

$$\text{EOQ} = \left[\frac{2 * \$30 * 7,200)}{\$7.50} \right]^{1/2}$$

$$= \left[\frac{\$432,000}{\$7.50} \right]^{1/2}$$

$$= 240 \text{ units}$$

The above result indicates that each order the firm places should be for 240 units. The total number of orders that will have to be placed for the part during the year under the above conditions is: 7,200 units for the year/240 units per order = 30. Thus, if usage is constant and orders are filled on time, an order should be placed every 12 business days = 360 days in a year/30 orders per year.

When to Order.   If purchase orders could be filled instantaneously, the firm would reorder immediately after running out of an inventory item. Since such efficiency in having orders filled is usually not possible, however, the firm could reorder at the point when the amount of the item remaining in inventory is just sufficient to satisfy the expected amount needed between the date of the order and the date at which the order is expected to be filled. For example, assume that the supplier of part ZJ120 discussed in the previous section normally fills orders in five days. Since expected usage of ZJ120 is: 7,200/360 = 20 units per day, the firm should reorder when its inventory has declined to 100 units. If everything goes as expected, the 100-unit inventory of the item will be depleted in five days, and the reorder will be filled at that point. Such preciseness and certainty in estimating needs for inventory items and in having orders filled will, of course, not generally be the case. In the next section, we will consider what should be done about these problems.

Purchase Discounts.   Firms are often able to obtain inventory items at a cost per unit that declines with the amount ordered. The declining cost per unit in this case is known as a purchase discount, which is usually expressed as a percentage discount from base price. The simple EOQ model expressed in Equation (9-3) cannot be used in this case to determine the optimum amount to order.[5] The most accurate approach to solving this problem requires a level of mathematics that is beyond the scope of this book. However, a practical approach not requiring a high level of mathematics is to calculate the total inventory costs for different order quantities, allowing for purchase discounts that can be obtained, and then designating the amount ordered with the lowest total cost as the EOQ. The calculation error will not be large if the total cost calculations are made for small increments in order quantity. Modern computers, and even calculators, make this requirement fairly easy to meet.

---

[5] This is because a requirement of the simple EOQ model is that all elements in the model be continuous. A purchase discount will result in discrete decreases in unit costs when the quantity ordered is increased.

Risks in Demand and Supply. Since neither the time when orders will be filled nor the demand for the product in which the item is included can always be predicted accurately, the firm should hedge its position by maintaining a safety stock. The amount of safety stock a firm should carry is a function of the following factors: (1) the degree of reliability in forecasting both the need for the item and in getting orders filled, (2) the cost of not having enough of the item, that is, the cost of stockouts, and (3) the carrying cost of the safety stock. The cost of a stockout is the loss of sales and customer goodwill. The less the ability of the firm to predict its needs and the dates when orders will be filled, and the higher the cost of stockouts, the larger should be the level of safety stocks. Conversely, the better the firm's ability to make the necessary predictions and the lower the cost of stockouts, the lower the level of safety stocks that will be necessary.

The importance of safety stocks can be seen from a study of Figure 9-3, in which the firm is assumed to attempt to maintain a safety stock of 100 units of part ZJ120. At time zero, the firm is fully stocked with a total of 340 units of the item; the inventory includes 100 units of safety stock plus 240 units from just having an order filled. If usage is 20 units per day as expected, another 240 units of ZJ120 will have to be ordered after seven days. At that time, 100 units will remain in inventory above the safety-stock level of 100 units. If the reorder is filled in five days, the firm will receive another shipment of 240 units of ZJ120 at the point in time when inventory above the safety-stock level is reduced to 0 units. Total inventory including the safety stock is thereby increased again to 340 units.

FIGURE 9-3
Inventory of part ZJ120 over time.

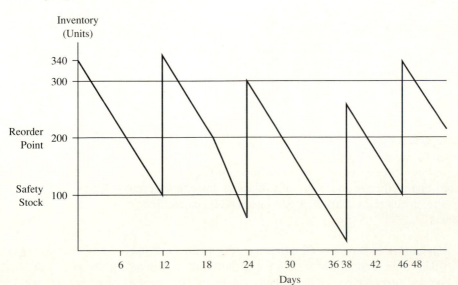

Another order for 240 units will be placed after the nineteenth day in the graph. In this case, however, demand for the product produced by the company picks up unexpectedly, and the usage rate of part ZJ120 increases during the next five days. As a result, inventory is depleted to a total of only 60 units by the time the last order is filled. Note on the graph that receipt of the shipment at the end of the twenty-fourth day will not bring the firm's total inventory back up to 340 units as before, because 40 units of the safety stock have been depleted as a result of the increased usage rate after the last reorder. Inventory is brought up to only 300 units in total. This does not mean that the firm should make a special order or increase the size of its order next time unless the recent increase in the usage rate is expected to continue, which we assume is not the case here. The policy indicated by the EOQ calculation should be continued, and a total of 240 units should be reordered when inventory is reduced to 100 units above the safety-stock level.

After the second order is filled, things go as expected for awhile. The firm again places an order for 240 units when the total inventory is depleted to 200 units, which occurs at the end of day 29 in the graph. In this case, however, the order is filled four days late, on day 38, and the firm's safety stock is reduced to only 20 units—one day's supply. Because of the delay in having the order filled, receipt of the shipment will increase total inventory to only 260 units. In the remaining part of the graph, events occur as expected, in which case, receipt of shipments of ZJ120 will replenish inventory temporarily to 340 units when an order is filled.

In the above example, the safety stock clearly protected the firm against stockouts after the second and third reorders. Determining the amount of safety stock that the firm should attempt to maintain is important, but often very difficult. Increasing the size of the safety stock will reduce the chances of incurring the expense of a stockout. On the other hand, the larger the size of the safety stock, the greater will be inventory carrying costs. Thus, management is faced with the fundamental financial problem of a risk-return tradeoff. The optimum level of safety stock will depend on the nature of the firm and the circumstances. The best teacher in this regard is experience in the firm.

Unusual Opportunities. The EOQ model discussed above assumes that supply conditions are constant. Thus, the terms at which the firm could obtain inventory items were not allowed to change in the calculations. In the real world, of course, this is often not the case—at least not indefinitely. For example, firms sometimes have the opportunity to purchase raw materials or other inventory items at exceptionally favorable prices. Or perhaps, management is convinced that costs are going to rise in the future. In these cases, large purchases of the item or items may provide savings more than sufficient to cover the additional costs of carrying a larger inventory for awhile. Inventories may thus be considerably larger than normal for a temporary period.

Variability in Business Conditions. Consumers inevitably become aware of the fact that some retail firms are not particularly adept at avoiding stockouts. Further, a cursory examination of the balance sheet of corporations also reveals that the inventories of many firms vary widely over time; the variations are often much greater than the variations in general business activity. The implication of these problems is that inventories are sometimes excessive and sometimes deficient. The question arises as to why so many firms appear to be so inadequate in their inventory management. The answer in some cases is that management is poor and inefficient, but this is certainly not always the case. Inventories are particularly difficult to control in some situations and, in others, even the most careful estimate of the amount of inventory needed will be subject to wide error. Two of the principal reasons for these difficulties are discussed below.

Seasonality.   The optimum level of inventories for many firms is highly variable over the course of a year because sales are highly variable. Retail department stores provide an obvious example. In addition, estimating inventory needs is subject to wide error in some industries. The Mattel Corporation provides an extreme example of this problem; inventories of its "Masters of the Universe" line of toys proved vastly excessive during the Christmas season of 1986, when demand almost completely evaporated.

Seasonal demand also causes a problem for firms, particularly manufacturing companies, which operate most efficiently at a constant rate throughout the year. Producing in the most efficient manner will result in seasonal bulges in inventories for these firms. On the other hand, reducing production for periods of slack demand will often result in high startup costs when production has to be increased. In addition, firms following this policy usually have to hire less-efficient labor during busy seasons. Thus, when demand is highly seasonal, management must determine if it is less expensive to incur the carrying costs of higher inventories in order to produce in the most efficient manner. If the decision is to go with level production, inventories will vary during the year.

Cyclical Effects.   Variations in the general level of business activity can also cause major problems in inventory control. Even if changes in economic conditions could be forecast fairly reliably, inventory levels of some firms would vary because of the difficulty in synchronizing changes in production and sales. The major problem, however, is difficulty in forecasting changes in business conditions, and demand for the company's products and services. For example, the management of a firm that has experienced a slackening of demand for a month or even a quarter may be uncertain whether the decline portends a general recession, or is merely a temporary aberration which may be offset by slightly higher demand in the following month or quarter.

The difficulty in forecasting business conditions is indicated by the fact that inventories of most firms tend to be excessive in the early stages of an economic recession. Further, the high level of inventories at that time often adds to the severity of the recession, as firms cut production more than the decline in demand in order to work off some of the fat in inventories. Discounting prices offered to customers is a common practice in these periods, resulting in lower profit margins and a further worsening of business conditions.

How do firms cope with the problems discussed in this section? Obviously, one step is to "keep an ear to the ground" in order to get an idea as early as possible concerning the direction of business activity. In addition, the firm should be prepared to make changes in production, and in ordering inventory items from suppliers as expeditiously as is feasible when the economic picture begins to clear.

Inflation. The above discussion of the effect of changes in business conditions did not include a consideration of the impact of inflation on inventories and their management. Inflation was a major economic problem during the early part of the 1980s. In general, the effect was to increase the carrying value of inventories in current dollars, particularly for those firms which used the first-in, first-out method of inventory valuation. This was amplified by the fact that interest rates and other capital costs were high during the period.

However, there is no strong indication that inflation causes the majority of firms to change the unit quantity carried in inventories. The quantity carried depends upon a number of factors which vary among firms. Inventory carrying costs increase during inflationary periods, but so do ordering costs. In addition, the quantity demanded by customers increases for some firms and decreases for others. The net effect on the EOQ of firms in general is not clear.

CHAPTER SUMMARY

We have dealt with two major topics in this chapter: the management of (1) credit accounts and (2) inventories. The coverage of the first of these topics began with a brief look at the more important sources of information for use in evaluating credit applications. We then turned our attention to the process, or analytical procedure, for making the evaluation. The procedure used by many firms is referred to as credit scoring. The application of discriminant analysis in credit scoring was examined in considerable detail in the chapter. Finally, we briefly reviewed some of the problems involved in collecting accounts receivable. Delinquent accounts include those that are paid late as well as those that are never paid. The fundamental objective of the collection policy and procedures of a firm is to reduce both types of delinquent accounts to the extent possible.

Inventories pose an unusual problem in financial decision making, since they typically do not directly increase the firm's sales. Most of a firm's inventories are necessary because of the nature of the production and selling functions of the firm. In particular, raw materials, goods-in-process, and finished goods inventories result from the fact that the production and selling activities of the firm do not occur at the same time. Thus, decisions concerning the optimum level of inventories as well as when and how much to order is a risk-cost trade-off decision. The specific objective is to minimize cost, given the level of risk the firm is willing to assume.

Minimizing cost, however, does not necessarily mean that inventory levels should be very low. Inventory size affects two types of associated costs in opposite ways. Reducing the inventory level will reduce carrying costs, but order costs will be increased because orders will have to be made more frequently. On the other hand, increasing inventory size will increase carrying cost. The model for calculating the economic order quantity can be used to estimate the optimum amount to order and the frequency of ordering, and therefore, the least-cost size of inventories. Of course, inventory size will still vary between orders.

The optimum level of inventories is affected by the type of products the firm sells and, particularly in the case of manufacturing firms, the nature of the production process. Inventory levels may also be affected by the risk in predicting product demand and the amount of time suppliers take in filling orders. In addition, a firm may significantly increase the size of its inventories for a temporary period if an opportunity arises to purchase certain items at very favorable prices.

However, firms frequently do not maintain optimum levels of inventories for several reasons, the more important of which were discussed in the chapter. One major factor is that changes in demand for a firm's products caused by changes in economic conditions often occur quite unexpectedly. Inventory policy must therefore remain flexible in the order to minimize the adverse affect of these unexpected variations.

SOLVED PROBLEMS

1 Smith Brothers, Inc. employs linear discriminant analysis in rating credit applications. Two ratios of the applicants are used as independent variables: (1) the profitability ratio, defined as the average ratio of net income to total assets over the past three years; and (2) the debt ratio, defined as the ratio of total debt to total assets at the time of the application.

a Develop an equation for estimating the Z score of applicants under the following stipulations:

(1) A Z score of at least 10 is required for an application to be approved.

(2) Only profitability ratios above zero and debt ratios less than 70 percent are considered. All ratios are expressed as numbers representing the percent.

(3) A profitability ratio of 30 percent and a debt ratio of 70 percent will receive a Z score of 10.

(4) A profitability ratio of 5 percent and a debt ratio of zero will receive a Z score of 10.

b Using the equation developed in answering question a above, calculate the Z scores of credit applicants with the following ratios, and indicate the decisions Smith Brothers would make in respect to the applications:

(1) Profitability ratio = 15 percent and debt ratio = 30 percent.

(2) Profitability ratio = 22 percent and debt ratio = 35 percent.

c What is the maximum debt ratio for an application to be approved if the profitability ratio of the applicant is 8 percent?

Solution

a In this case, the discriminant equation takes the following form:

$$Z = a_1 X_1 - a_2 X_2$$

where X_1 and X_2 are the profitability ratio and the debt ratio, respectively. A computer software program can be used to solve for the coefficients in the equation. However, since the problem is very simple in this case, we can use algebra to make the calculations. The a_1 coefficient is solved for by assuming that the debt ratio is zero and the Z score is 10:

$$10 = a_1(5) - a_2(0)$$

Thus,

$$a_1 = \frac{10}{5} = 2$$

We can now solve for a_2 by assuming the profitability ratio is 30 percent, the debt ratio is

70 percent, and the Z score is 10:

$$10 = 2(30) - a_2(70)$$

Thus,
$$a_2 = \frac{(60 - 10)}{70}$$

$$= 0.71, \text{ rounded to two digits}$$

The discriminant equation can now be written as follows:

$$Z = 2X_1 - 0.71X_2$$

b (1) For a profitability ratio of 15 percent and a debt ratio of 30 percent, the Z score is:

$$Z = 2(15) - 0.71(30)$$
$$= 8.70$$

Since the Z score is less than 10, the application would not be approved.
(2) For a profitability ratio of 22 percent and a debt ratio of 35 percent, the Z score is:

$$Z = 2(22) - 0.71(35)$$
$$= 19.15$$

Since the Z score is above 10, the application would be approved.
c Solving for the maximum debt ratio when the profitability ratio is 8 percent, we get:

$$10 = 2(8) - 0.71X_2$$

Thus,
$$X_2 = \frac{(16 - 10)}{0.71}$$

$$= 8.45 \text{ percent}$$

2 The XYZ Corporation uses product X as a component of one of the products the company manufactures and sells. A total of 100,000 units of product X is used at a fairly constant rate throughout the year. Each unit of X costs XYZ $5. Ordering and carrying costs are $20 and 15 percent per year, respectively. Orders are normally filled by the supplier in about ten days. XYZ maintains a safety of 10,000 units.
a Calculate the economic order quantity of product X.
b Calculate the average period between orders.
c Calculate XYZ's total inventory of X on hand at the time of an order.

Solution

a The dollar amount of annual carrying cost per unit (C) must first be calculated by multiplying the cost per unit by the annual percentage rate:

$$C = \$5 \times 0.15$$
$$= \$0.75$$

The EOQ can now be calculated as follows:

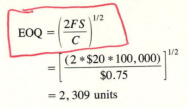

$$EOQ = \left(\frac{2FS}{C}\right)^{1/2}$$
$$= \left[\frac{(2 * \$20 * 100{,}000)}{\$0.75}\right]^{1/2}$$
$$= 2{,}309 \text{ units}$$

b The average period between orders can be found by dividing the amount ordered (i.e., the EOQ if the company orders the optimum quantity) by the average amount used per day:

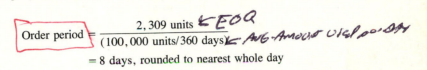

$$\text{Order period} = \frac{2{,}309 \text{ units} \leftarrow EOQ}{(100{,}000 \text{ units}/360 \text{ days}) \leftarrow \text{AVG-Amount used per day}}$$
$$= 8 \text{ days, rounded to nearest whole day}$$

c The inventory of product X at time of order can be found by adding the safety stock to the number of units expected to be used between the time of an order and the time the order *it takes* is filled: *The time which the drawer is filled*

$$\text{Inventory} = 10{,}000 \text{ units} + (\text{usage per day} \times \text{fill time})$$
$$= 10{,}000 \text{ units} + \left[\left(\frac{100{,}000 \text{ units}}{360 \text{ days}}\right) \times 10 \text{ days}\right]$$
$$= 12{,}778 \text{ units}$$

PROBLEMS

9-1 The Winn Department Store uses a linear discriminant function in scoring applications for a Winn credit card. The function is expressed as follows:

$$Z = 2.5X_1 + 0.9X_2 + 2.2X_3$$

where X_1 is the total annual income of the applicant and his/her spouse, if any, expressed in thousands of dollars

X_2 is the number of years the applicant has lived in the metropolitan area since age 21

X_3 is the number of years employed with current employer

A Z score of 65 or above is required for approval of a credit card. The application will be disapproved if the score is less than 60, whereas additional information is required if the score is as high as 60, but less than 65.

a Calculate the Z score of the following applicants and indicate what Winn's decision would be:

Applicant	Income	Years of area residency	Years with current employer
A	$15,000	2	1
B	25,000	3	1
C	18,000	5	5
D	30,000	0	0
E	16,000	20	15

b What problems might Winn have in using the discriminant function to make final decisions concerning credit card applications?

9-2 A list of items which can affect the credit rating of a credit applicant is given below. All applicants are business firms. Explain the likely effect of each item on the credit rating of an applicant.

a Applicant has a high ratio of net worth to total assets.

b Applicant has a high ratio of sales to total assets.

c The average collection period of the applicant's accounts receivable is long.

d The applicant's sales are made primarily to sporting goods stores.

e Most of the applicant's costs of sales vary directly with sales.

9-3 Walton Manufacturing uses linear discriminant analysis in estimating the creditworthiness of certain customer firms. Only two independent variables are used: the profit margin (the ratio of net income to net sales) and the debt ratio (the ratio of total debt to total assets).

a Develop an equation for calculating the Z score of a credit applicant under the following stipulations:

(1) Only firms with profit margins of 1 percent or higher and debt ratios of 75 percent or lower are considered.

(2) A Z score of 100 is required for an application to be approved.

(3) A profit margin of 1 percent and a debt ratio of 0 percent will result in a Z score of 100.

(4) A profit margin of 10 percent and a debt ratio of 75 percent will result in a Z score of 100.

b Graph the equation for the Z score, putting the profit margin on the x axis and the debt ratio on the y axis. (The value at each point on your discriminant line should be 100.)

c Calculate the slope of the discriminant line.

9-4 One year ago, the Stainless Aluminum Corporation (SAC) changed the credit terms offered to customer firms to $n/60$ (i.e., total payment is due in 60 days from invoice date.) Management is pleased with the impact of the credit terms on sales, but is displeased with the number of bad accounts that has resulted. An account which is more than 90 days past due is considered *bad* by the company.

Up to this point, any credit applicant which has had a positive net income on average over the previous three years has been granted credit. However, the management of SAC believes that the two following ratios of credit applicants may provide a better indication of their creditworthiness: (1) the average ratio of current assets to current liabilities over the last five years previous to the application and (2) the average ratio of net income to total assets over the same period. The table below indicates (a) the level of the two ratios of a representative sample of credit customers who meet SAC's current profitability standards and (b) the current status of the accounts:

Applicant	Current assets to current liabilities	Net income to total assets	Status of account
A	3.1	9%	good
B	2.9	10%	good
C	2.6	2%	bad
D	1.8	7%	bad
E	2.1	12%	good
F	0.7	1%	bad
G	2.9	7%	good
H	1.5	8%	good
I	2.1	8%	good
J	2.6	3%	good
K	2.3	10%	good
L	4.5	7%	good
M	0.8	6%	bad
N	1.4	5%	bad
O	2.7	11%	good
P	1.5	14%	good
Q	2.6	9%	good
R	2.5	6%	good
S	1.7	2%	bad
T	1.9	13%	good
U	5.1	6%	good
V	1.9	7%	good
W	0.9	7%	bad
X	2.3	8%	good
Y	2.0	3%	good
Z	2.8	10%	good

a Plot the two ratios for the twenty-six firms on a scatter diagram, and denote by the letter g or b the status of the account for each observation.

b Develop an equation for scoring credit applications submitted to SAC.

c Explain the weaknesses, if any, in the ability of your equation to discriminate between good and bad credit applications.

9-5 The Homewood Sash & Door Company expects to sell 4,000 standard-sized window frames in the coming year. Because of the seasonality of the construction industry, three-fourths of the company's total sales in a year normally occur in the six-month period May-October. Each frame costs Lane $40. Ordering costs run approximately $5 per order, and carrying costs are estimated at $3 per frame per six-month period.

a Estimate the economic order quantity of window frames for Homewood during the May-October period.

b How many orders should be placed during the period?

c How frequently should orders be placed?

d If Homewood maintains a safety stock of 60 frames, what will be the average inventory size during the busy period, if orders are placed in an optimal manner?

9-6 The Waggle Company sells "Waggletes" at a constant rate throughout the year. Sales in the coming year are forecast at 1 million units. The company purchases its Waggletes from a wholesaler at a cost per unit of $8. The economic order quantity has been estimated at 13,000 units. Order costs are $90 per order.

a Calculate the inventory carrying costs (1) in dollars per year and (2) as a percentage of the Waggle Company's average investment in its Wagglete inventory.

b How many orders of Waggletes should the company place in a year?

c Estimate the company's total cost of its Wagglete inventory during a year, assuming that the optimum quantity is always ordered.

9-7 (This problem can be solved most efficiently by the use of a programmable calculator or a computer spreadsheet program.)

The principal products manufactured by the D.C. Sparks Corporation are batteries of various sizes, which are sold directly to automobile supply houses. Demand for Sparks' batteries runs around 1.2 million units a year. The company orders the cases for its batteries at a cost per unit of $10. Order costs are $20 per order, and carrying costs average $2 per unit per year.

a Calculate Sparks' economic order quantity of battery cases.

b The following questions involve a sensitivity analysis of the EOQ to changes in demand, order costs, and carrying costs. In each case, assume the same conditions as in question 9-7a, except for the stated changes in the value of the item indicated.

(1) Annual sales vary from 1.2 million units by the following percentages: (a) +20 percent, (b) +10 percent, (c) −10 percent, and (d) −20 percent.

(2) Order costs vary from $20 per order by the following percentages: (a) +20 percent, (b) +10 percent, (c) −10 percent, and (d) −20 percent.

(3) Carrying costs vary from $2 per unit per year by the following percentages: (a) +20 percent, (b) +10 percent, (c) −10 percent, and (d) −20 percent.

c According to the results of your sensitivity analysis, the EOQ is (1) most sensitive and (2) least sensitive to which changes? Explain in each case.

9-8 (This problem can be solved most efficiently by the use of a computer spreadsheet program.) The Cashways Lighting Company (CLC) expects to sell 1,200 units of a popular model of lighting kit during the coming year. A supplier sells the kits for the following prices:

Dozens of kits	Cost per dozen
1–9	$70
10–19	$68
20–49	$66
50–99	$65
100 or more	$64

Ordering costs average $20 per order, and carrying costs are estimated at an annual rate of 15 percent of average inventory investment.

a Assuming sales are fairly constant throughout the year, calculate each of the following for CLC: (1) EOQ of the lighting kits, (2) optimal number of orders per year, and (3) total costs per year if the optimum quantity is always ordered.

b Due to the fragile nature of the lighting kits and the time required in checking new shipments received, management recently asked the company's head accountant to estimate order costs more specifically. After a careful study, the accountant reported that the order cost of one dozen kits would run approximately $10, and that the cost per order would increase by approximately $1 per additional dozen kits ordered at one time.

Armed with this new information, estimate again the (1) EOQ of the lighting kits, (2) optimal number of orders per year, (3) total costs per year if the optimum quantity is always ordered.

REFERENCES

Barzman, Sol: *Everyday Credit Checking: A Practical Guide*, rev. ed., New York: National Association of Credit Management, 1980.

Bierman, Harold, Jr., Charles P. Bonni, and Warren H. Hausman: *Quantitative Analysis for Business Decisions*, 6th ed., Homewood, IL: Irwin, 1982; Chapters 17–19.

Blackstone, John H., and James F. Cox: "Inventory Management Techniques," *Journal of Small Business Management*, vol. 23, April 1985, pp. 27–33.

Brooks, L. D.: "Risk-Return Criteria and Optimal Inventory Stocks," *Engineering Economist*, vol. 25, Summer 1980, pp. 275–299.

Cristie, George N., and Albert E. Bracuti: *Credit Management*. Lake Success, NY: Credit Research Foundation, 1981.

Eisenbeis, Robert A.: "Pitfalls in the Application of Discriminant Analysis in Business, Finance and Economics," *Journal of Finance*, vol. 32, June 1977, pp. 875–900.

Gentry, James A., and Jesus M. De La Garza: "A Generalized Model for Monitoring Accounts Receivable," *Financial Management*, vol. 14, Winter 1985, pp. 28–38.

Horowitz, Ann R., and Ira Horowitz: "Uncertainty and the Lot-Size Reorder-Point Model," *Decision Sciences*, vol. 18, Fall 1987, pp. 682–686.

Joy, Maurice O., and John O. Tollefson: "On the Financial Applications of Discriminant Analysis," *Journal of Financial and Quantitative Analysis*, vol. 10, December 1975, pp. 723–739.

Kallberg, Jarl G., and Kenneth L. Parkinson: *Current Asset Management: Cash, Credit, and Inventory*, New York: Wiley, 1984.

Kallberg, Jarl G., and Anthony Saunders: "Markov Chain Approaches to the Analysis of Payment Behavior of Retail Credit Customers," *Financial Management*, vol. 12, Summer 1983, pp. 5–14.

Long, Michael S.: "Credit Screening System Selection," *Journal of Financial and Quantitative Analysis*, vol. XI, June 1976, pp. 313–328.

McDaniel, William R.: "The Economic Ordering Quantity and Wealth Maximization," *Financial Review*, vol. 21, November 1986, pp. 527–536.

Mehta, Dillep R.: *Working Capital Management*, Englewood Cliffs, N.J.: Prentice Hall, 1974.

Romano, Patrick L.: "Techniques in Inventory Management and Control," (Survey of Inventory Techniques by the National Association of Accountants), *Management Accounting*, February 1987, p. 46.

Saurs, Dale G.: "Analyzing Inventory Systems," *Management Accounting*, May 1986, pp. 30–36.

Senju, Shizuo, and Seiichi Fujita: "An Applied Procedure for Determining the Economic Lot Sizes of Multiple Products," *Decision Sciences*, vol. 11, July 1980, pp. 503–513.

Smith, Keith V.: *Guide to Working Capital Management*, New York: McGraw-Hill, 1979; Chapter 5.

Standard & Poor's Credit Overview: Corporate and International Ratings, Standard and Poor's Corporation, 1982.

10

CREDIT POLICY DECISIONS

Selling on credit involves an investment by the firm in accounts receivable and generally in other types of assets. The usual purpose of making the investment is to increase sales and, thereby, increase net cash inflows in the future. Thus, credit policy should be guided by the same principle that guides any other investment decision: among the alternatives available, select the investment(s) that are expected to have the greatest net present value for the firm. The level of the investment is controlled in part by selecting (a) the particular customers to whom credit will be extended, (b) the terms of credit offered, and (c) the procedures used in making collections. In addition, external factors such as economic conditions, the demand for the products and services the firm sells, and the amount of competition in the industry affect the level of the firm's credit sales and, therefore, the level of the credit investment.

Chapter 9 examined the problems involved in the day-to-day management of accounts receivable. The primary objective in the present chapter is to develop the procedures for making credit policy decisions. The approach will be to estimate the net present value of the investment required in a proposed change in credit policy. Recall from Chapter 5 that the calculation of the net present value of an investment requires estimates of three basic elements: (1) the investment outlay at time zero, (2) the future cash flows, and (3) the required rate of return, which is used as the discount rate in making time adjustments of future cash flows. Most of our attention in this chapter will focus on estimating the investment outlay and future cash flows. The procedure for estimating the required rate of return was the subject of Chapter 7.

We begin by considering the general principles that should guide the estimation of the investment outlay and future cash flows. Then, numerical examples will be presented for specific policy changes. Toward the end of the chapter, we will examine the impact of different patterns of cash flows that may result from changes in credit policy.

The Investment Required In Offering Credit

A major factor affecting the required investment in offering credit to customers is the increase in accounts receivable that will occur. To understand the nature of the investment, it is first necessary to understand the relationship between credit sales and the amount of accounts receivable the firm has outstanding. The latter problem is considered below.

The Generation of Accounts Receivable.   Estimating the change in accounts receivable caused by a change in credit policy usually begins by estimating the effect on credit sales and the average collection period. By dividing the expected average collection period expressed in days into the number of days in a year, the average receivables turnover is obtained. Using a 360-day year, the equation for the calculation is as follows:

$$RT = \frac{360}{ACP} \tag{10-1}$$

where RT and ACP refer to the receivables turnover and average collection period, respectively. The equation for the calculation of average accounts receivable (AR) is:

$$AR = \frac{CS}{RT} \tag{10-2}$$

where CS refers to the estimated credit sales in a year, and RT is the same as in (10-1).

Equations (10-1) and (10-2) represent average relationships for a given period. If credit sales or the collection period varies over the year, accounts receivable and the firm's related investment will also vary. This problem will be considered at a later point in the chapter.

As indicated above, to estimate the level of receivables generated from the installation of a new credit policy, we must first estimate the annual credit sales and the average collection period. We can then calculate the receivables turnover and finally the expected level of accounts receivable, using equations (10-1) and (10-2) above. However, the level of the firm's investment in accounts receivable depends on the derivation of the credit sales. Part of these sales may be made, albeit perhaps for cash, even if the firm does not install the new credit policy. If the new policy is to be profitable for the firm, however, *additional* sales must occur. The firm's investment will be affected by the relative proportions of these two components of total credit sales. We will first consider the investment resulting from the additional sales.

Impact of Additional Sales.   An increase in sales that results from a change in credit policy can lead to an investment by the firm not only in accounts receivable, but also in other assets, for example, in inventories and fixed assets. We will consider the accounts receivable investment first.

The investment in accounts receivable derived from additional credit sales is not the dollar amount of the receivables. The firm's only commitment of funds in this case is in paying the costs involved in producing the product or service and making the sale, and any additional credit department expenses incurred at the time of the sale.[1] These costs involve cash outlays by the firm and include the costs of goods sold, selling expenses, and administrative expenses.[2] An allowance for bad debts is not part of the investment, however, because the cash flow effects of bad debts occur only after the collection period has transpired. The formula for calculating the investment in receivables applicable to the additional sales can be expressed mathematically as follows:

$$I = AR\left(\frac{CE_u}{CS}\right) \qquad (10\text{-}3)$$

where I is the investment in accounts receivable derived from the additional credit sales

AR represents the accounts receivable derived from the additional credit sales

CE_u/CS is the ratio of up-front cash expenses to credit sales. Up-front expenses are those that are paid before or at the time of the sales. These may include the cost of producing, or otherwise obtaining, the goods to be sold, selling expenses, and credit department expenses incurred at the time of the sale.

Increases in Inventories and Fixed Assets.   Additional credit sales can also lead to an investment by the firm in other assets, for example, in inventories and fixed assets, which may have to be increased to support the higher level of sales. If the firm is operating at full capacity, the additional credit sales will require additional fixed assets immediately. On the other hand, if the firm is operating below full capacity, additional fixed assets may not be necessary at the time of the sales increase. However, if the firm continues to grow, fixed assets will doubtless have to be purchased at some point in the future in order to support the higher level of activity. The additional credit sales reduce the amount of unused capacity, leading to fixed asset purchases sooner than would otherwise be necessary. For this reason, a portion of future asset purchases plus any related freight and installation costs should be considered an investment made necessary by the additional credit sales.

For example, assume that a change in credit policy is expected to lead to an increase in annual credit sales of $2 million. Since the firm is currently operating at less than full capacity, no additions to fixed assets are necessary immediately. However, management expects that the higher level of sales caused by the new credit policy, plus future sales growth caused by other factors, will necessitate a $10 million expansion of the firm's plant in two years. In this case, the additional sales resulting from the change in credit policy is clearly using plant capacity, although the related cash outlays for additional plant space occur two years later. Assume that the total

[1] Additional credit department expenses incurred after the sale, for example, collection expenses, will affect future cash flows, but not the investment.

[2] Income taxes are generally not subtracted, under the assumption that they will not be paid at the time of the sale.

plant expansion is estimated to support a sales level of $20 million. The proportion caused by the credit policy change is estimated by dividing the additional credit sales of $2 million by the $20 million total capacity of the new plant. Thus, 10 percent of the $10 million plant expansion in two years should be considered an investment caused by the change in credit policy. Note that since the $1 million investment is expected to occur in two years, it should be time-adjusted back to the present in the evaluation of the credit policy change. The discount rate used to make the time adjustment should be the required rate of return.

Asset Replacements. Another reason why a change in credit policy may require future investments is that depreciable assets must be replaced in the future if the sales level is to be maintained. Thus, the evaluation of the change in credit policy that results in additional sales extending indefinitely into the future must take into account any future asset replacements necessary to support the increased level of sales. For example, assume that a change in credit policy will increase sales, which in turn will necessitate the purchase of additional equipment at time zero, costing $100,000. Assume also that the equipment is expected to have a productive life of ten years. If the credit policy change is expected to continue indefinitely, the firm will have to replace the equipment about every ten years indefinitely. The present value of these future equipment expenditures, net of any cash-flow effects of disposing of the old asset, should be added to all investments made at time zero, to determine the net investment required by the policy change.

How should the present value of the future replacement expenditures be calculated? Consider the simple case in which each replacement is projected to have a net cost of $100,000. The first step in the calculation process is to estimate the cash flow equivalent of each $100,000 expenditure. To make this estimate, the analyst must calculate a stream of constant cash flows occurring at the end of each of the next ten years, which will have a value of $100,000 at the end of the ten-year period. Assume that the required rate of return is 14 percent. In this case, the annual cash flow equivalent of the $100,000 outlay at the end of ten years can be determined by the use of the following equation:

$$\text{CFE} = \frac{I_n}{(\text{FVAF}_{n,k})} \tag{10-4}$$

where   CFE is the cash flow equivalent

I_n is the investment outlay expected to be made at the end of the nth year

$(\text{FVAF}_{n,k})$ is the future value annuity factor for an n-year annuity and required rate of return of k.

Using either a calculator or a future value table, $(FVAV_{10,14\%})$ will be found to be 19.3373. Inserting the necessary data into equation (10-4), we get:

$$\text{CFE} = \frac{\$100,000}{19.3373}$$

$$= \$5,171$$

The result above indicates that a cash flow of $5,171 at the end of each of ten years will have a value of $100,000 at the end of the tenth year; the cash-flow stream will have the same value at the end of the tenth year as the investment outlay which is expected to be necessary at that time. This calculation process can be continued for any number of ten-year periods. Of course, the result will be the same for each period; the cash flow equivalent will always be $5,171 if the investment outlay is $100,000 and the required rate of return is 14 percent. Thus, a perpetual stream of annual cash flows of $5,171 for our example will have the same value as $100,000 invested every ten years to infinity. By capitalizing the cash flow eqivalent at the required rate of return, we can determine the value of the entire perpetual stream:

$$I_{0,f} = \frac{\$5,171}{0.14}$$
$$= \$36,936$$

where $I_{0,f}$ is the present value of the future investments of $100,000 every ten years to infinity. As indicated above, $I_{0,f}$ is part of the total investment of the firm in changing its credit terms.

Impact of Sales That Would Be Made Irrespective of a Policy Change. For those sales that are expected to be made even without a policy change, the investment effect is solely the result of the change in timing of collections. For example, if the policy change is expected to increase the average collection period on those sales from 45 days to 60 days, the accounts receivable will be outstanding for an average of 15 days longer than if the credit policy is not changed. This delay in receiving payment is an investment by the firm, because capital is committed to the account for an extended period of time, and the total amount of receivables outstanding at any point in time will be increased. The increase in receivables will be proportionate to the increase in the collection period. Continuing with the example above, assume that credit sales were $1,200,000 before the policy change. Since the receivables turnover is reduced from 360/45 = 8 to 360/60 = 6, accounts receivable will increase from $1,200,000/8 = $150,000 to $1,200,000/6 = $200,000. Thus, a 33.3 percent increase in the average collection period results in a 33.3 percent increase in the receivables applicable to credit sales that would be made irrespective of the change in the firm's credit policy.

It is important to recognize that the receivables with which we were concerned in the previous paragraph are derived from sales that are expected to be made even without a change in the firm's credit policy. As indicated, the only effect on the investment is derived from a change in the time when the firm is expected to receive payment for the sale. Thus, the total amount of the additional receivables generated in this case are an investment by the firm, because of the opportunity cost of not receiving this amount earlier. The calculation in this case differs slightly from the calculation of the firm's investment in receivables generated from additional sales. Recall that in the latter case, the firm's investment in the receivables would include only certain cash expenses incurred in generating the credit sales.

Net Cash Benefits

The net cash benefits (NCBs) from either offering credit to a new class of customers or from changing credit terms offered can be determined in the same way as for any investment. The following format can be used to calculate the NCB for a given period, say a year:

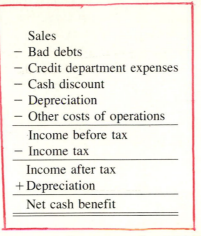

Sales
− Bad debts
− Credit department expenses
− Cash discount
− Depreciation
− Other costs of operations
Income before tax
− Income tax
Income after tax
+ Depreciation
Net cash benefit

All of the items in the cash benefit statement above represent additions caused by the new credit policy. With the exception of the depreciation expense, all of the items also represent cash flows. The statement is sufficiently flexible to allow for any type of operating cash flow, even though some of the items may not apply in a particular case. Each item is briefly examined below.

Sales.   This item represents additions to total firm sales, at invoice prices, that are expected to result from the change in credit policy.

Bad Debts.   This expense consists of the additional bad debts of the firm resulting from the policy change. The ratio of bad debts to credit sales will probably increase if the policy change involves offering credit to customers in a lower credit class. Extending the credit period may also lead to additional bad debts because of increased credit sales, but the bad-debts ratio may or may not increase.

Credit Department Expenses.   Part of these expenses will normally be incurred at about the time of the sale and the remaining part will be incurred later. Relaxing credit terms or extending credit to a lower credit class will usually require increased collection costs. In addition, a change in credit policy may cause other administrative costs to increase. For example, added credit customers may increase bookkeeping and other accounting expenses.

Cash Discounts.   This credit term allows the customer the privilege of reducing his/her payment below invoice price if payment is made on or before a specified date which precedes the end of the credit period. For example, the terms 2/10, *n*/30 signify that credit is granted for a 30-day period after the invoice date, but the customer can reduce his payment by 2 percent below invoice price if he pays in 10 days. The offering of a cash discount to customers is part of the firm's credit policy.

Depreciation.   If the increase in sales requires additional depreciable assets, depreciation will be increased. Note that this is an example of an increase not uniquely caused by a change in credit policy, since a sales increase of the same magnitude caused for any reason will require the same asset addition. Nevertheless, if the change in credit policy causes sales to increase, which in turn necessitates an increase in depreciable assets, the effect on cash flows must be included in estimating net cash benefits. If the investment occurs in later years as discussed earlier, the additional depreciation expenses will apply only to later years.

Other Costs of Operations.   These costs include the additions to the firm's production, selling, and administrative expenses that are expected to result from an increase in sales and which are not included as a separate item on the cash-flow statement. This is another example in which the costs would have been incurred from a sales increase of the same magnitude caused for any reason. Thus, they are not uniquely caused by a change in credit policy. The ratio of these costs to the added sales may be higher than the same ratio at previous, lower levels of sales if the firm is operating at or close to capacity. In the latter event, the firm's efficiency in its operations may be reduced, causing a higher cost ratio and, therefore, lower cash benefits.

After estimating the credit investment and the net cash benefits in future years, the cash benefits must be time-adjusted to determine their present value. The credit investment is then subtracted from the present value figure to determine the net present value of the credit policy change. This problem will be considered next.

The Net Present Calculation.   As we observed in Chapters 6 and 7, the required rate of return on an investment is a function of the level of interest rates prevailing in the market at the time, the risk of the investment, and the types of financing the firm uses. We assume here that the required rate of return has been calculated by the procedures presented in those two chapters. Estimates of the credit investment, net cash benefits in all years, and the required rate of return provide the input values for calculating the net present value of a proposed change in credit policy. We are now ready to apply the principles that have been discussed to specific types of policy changes.

The Evaluation of Credit Policy Proposals: Specifics

We first consider situations in which expected net cash benefits in future years are constant. The effect of variations in the amount of net cash benefits over time will be examined later.

Extending Credit for the First Time to Certain Customers.   The analysis illustrated in this section applies to two situations which are essentially the same in regard to the effect on the firm's credit investment. The first situation is where the firm has been selling only for cash in the past, but is now considering a policy change in which credit will be extended to certain customers. In the second situation, the firm will have been offering credit to some customers, but not to the group being considered.

The Credit Investment. Determining the credit investment in either of the two situations noted above involves three steps. First, an estimate must be made of the amount of accounts receivable that the new proposal will generate. (Under the assumptions of this section, the amount of the additional receivables will be constant over time.) The second step is to calculate the firm's investment in the expected receivables. Finally, an estimate must be made of any additions to inventories and fixed assets that will be required by increased sales. The general principles involved in making all of these estimates have been discussed earlier in the chapter.

To estimate the level of receivables, a forecast must be made of both the credit sales in a year caused by the new policy, and the average collection period. Several factors must be considered in making these forecasts, including the credit rating of the particular class(es) of customers to whom credit will be extended, the terms to be offered, the nature of the product, and conditions in the industry. As an example of the estimates required, assume that a firm is considering extending credit for the first time to customers with a certain credit rating. The terms of credit would be n/30, which means that payment of the full invoice price is due 30 days after the date of the invoice. After careful analysis, the estimates shown in Table 10-1 are compiled.

The receivables turnover is estimated by dividing the number of days in a year by the average collection period: $360/45 = 8.0$. Dividing the expected credit sales by the receivables turnover provides an estimate of the average level of receivables: $\$1,000,000/8.0 = \$125,000$. The \$600,000 reduction in cash sales shown in the exhibit reflects the estimate that 60 percent of total credit sales would be made for cash if the credit were not offered. Thus, the investment applicable to these credit sales is the result of a change in the timing of customer payments. Following the principles discussed earlier in the chapter, the firm's investment in the receivables derived from these sales is 60 percent of total receivables: $0.60(\$125,000) = \$75,000$.

The investment in the receivables derived from the \$400,000 credit sales, which add to total sales, will include only the up-front payments of the applicable credit

TABLE 10-1
PROJECTED EFFECTS OF OFFERING CREDIT TO CERTAIN
CUSTOMERS FOR THE FIRST TIME

Terms	n/30
Credit sales	$1,000,000
Reduction in cash sales	$600,000
Average collection period	45 days
Bad debts (% of credit sales)	2%
Credit department costs, up front (% of credit sales)	1%
Credit department costs, after the sale (% of credit sales)	2%
Other costs of operations* (% of additional total sales)	60%
Additional inventories	$50,000
Additional fixed assets	$200,000
Productive life of fixed assets	10 years
Required rate of return	14%

* Expected to be paid at or before the time of the applicable sale.

department expenses and other costs of operations (1 percent and 60 percent, respectively, of the $400,000 credit sales).[3] Up-front payments are those that are made either at or before the time of the sale. Since the total percentage of these costs to sales is 60 percent plus 1 percent in our example, the investment is: $0.40(\$125,000)(0.61) = \$30,500$.

Table 10-1 indicates that the higher sales level resulting from the policy change will necessitate an increase of $50,000 in inventories and $200,000 in fixed assets. We will assume that the firm expects to replace the fixed assets every ten years, at a cost per replacement of $200,000. Noting that the required rate of return is 14 percent, and following the principles discussed earlier in the chapter, we should estimate the cash flow equivalent of these replacement expenditures by the use of Equation (10-4) presented on page 297:

$$CFE = \frac{\$200,000}{\left(FVAF_{10,14\%}\right)}$$
$$= \frac{\$200,000}{19.3373}$$
$$= \$10,343$$

Capitalizing the cash flow equivalent at the 14 percent required rate of return, we estimate the present value of future replacement expenditures $(I_{0,f})$ to be

$$I_{0,f} = \frac{\$10,343}{0.14}$$
$$= \$73,879$$

The net investment in the credit policy change is the sum of all of the investments discussed above:

From increased receivables resulting from a change in time of customer payments:	$75,000
From receivables applicable to additional total sales:	30,500
From additional inventories:	50,000
From additional fixed assets at time zero:	200,000
From future asset purchases (present value thereof):	73,879
Total investment:	$429,379

To generalize, we can state the equation for estimating the firm's investment caused by extending credit to certain customers for the first time as follows:

$$I_{0,nc} = \left(\frac{CS_a}{RT}\right)\left(\frac{CE_u}{CS}\right) + \left(\frac{CS_c}{RT}\right) + OA_0 + I_{0,f} \qquad (10\text{-}5)$$

where $I_{0,nc}$ is the total investment, valued as of time 0

---

[3] The assumption is made in this example that all of the expenses referred to as "other costs of operations" are paid at or before the time of the applicable sale. In other cases, any of these costs paid after the sale would not be included as part of the investment.

CS_a represents the credit sales that are additions to total sales resulting from the policy change

RT is the receivables turnover

CE_u/CS is the ratio of up-front cash expenses to credit sales

CS_c represents the expected credit sales under the proposed policy that would be cash sales if the credit is not offered

OA_0 represents additions to other assets required at time 0 because of the policy change

I_{0f} is the present value of future asset purchases caused by the policy change

Net Cash Benefits and Net Present Value. The estimate of the annual net cash benefit from the credit investment is calculated in Table 10-2. The calculations are based on the assumption that the fixed assets will be depreciated on a straight-line basis over a ten-year period to a zero salvage, and that the marginal tax rate on income is 30 percent. The result is an estimate of the annual net cash benefit of $83,000. If this benefit is expected to continue for an indefinitely long period of time in the future, the net present value (NPV) can be calculated as follows:

$$NPV = \frac{\$83,000}{0.14} - \$429,379$$
$$= \$592,857 - \$429,379$$
$$= \$163,478$$

Since the net present value is positive, the proposed change in credit policy is expected to be beneficial to the firm. However, other policies may produce even better results. This issue is discussed below.

What-If Analysis. Management will probably want to examine the effects of several possible credit terms before making a final policy decision. Modern spreadsheet programs, such as Lotus 1-2-3, make this relatively easy to accomplish through a

TABLE 10-2
ANNUAL NET CASH BENEFIT FROM OFFERING CREDIT
TO CERTAIN CUSTOMERS FOR THE FIRST TIME

Additional sales	$400,000
− Bad debts	20,000
− Credit department expenses, up front	10,000
− Credit department expenses, after sale	20,000
− Depreciation	20,000
− Other costs of operations	240,000
Income before tax	$90,000
− Income tax	27,000
Income after tax	$63,000
+ Depreciation	20,000
Net cash benefit	$83,000

what-if type of analysis. The process requires the writing of formulas in a computer spreadsheet for the calculation of the total investment, net cash benefits, and net present value for different credit terms that could be offered by the firm. The analyst provides the necessary inputs for the calculations. An illustration of what-if analysis will be presented after we have considered the effect of changing the credit period offered to customers.

Change in the Credit Period.   This modification in credit terms will normally cause a change in credit sales, and perhaps in cash sales. If the modification is to ease credit terms, credit sales should increase, but unfortunately bad debts may increase also. For the reasons discussed earlier, the investment in receivables derived from the additional credit sales will include only the up-front cash expenses related to the sales.

Consider the case where credit terms are changed from $n/30$ to $n/45$, and the average collection period is expected to increase from 45 days to 50 days. Assume that the change is expected to increase annual credit sales to $1.2 million from the $1 million level that would prevail under the old terms. Cash sales are not expected to be affected in this example. The receivables turnover will decline from $360/45 = 8.0$ to $360/50 = 7.2$, and the estimated average level of receivables applicable to the additional credit sales is $200,000/7.2 = $27,778$. Since these receivables are derived from additional sales caused by the new credit terms, the related investment by the firm will include only the up-front cash expenses applicable to the additional sales. Assuming that these expenses are 90 percent of the additional credit sales, the investment will be: $0.90(\$200,000/7.2) = \$25,000$. The change in the firm's investment caused by the increase in the average collection period applicable to the $1,000,000 in credit sales that are expected to be made under either the old or new terms is proportionate to the increase in the collection period. The percentage increase in the collection period is $(50-45)/45 = 11.111$ percent. Under the old terms, the receivables would be $\$1,000,000/8.0 = \$125,000$. Thus, the firm's additional investment in these receivables as a result of the credit policy change is estimated at $0.11111(\$125,000) = \$13,889$.

The same result can be obtained in a different, but equally appropriate manner. First, note that the receivables generated under the new terms from the $1,000,000 in credit sales common to the new and old terms can be estimated as follows: $\$1,000,000/7.2 = \$138,889$. Subtracting the $125,000 receivables under the old terms from this figure gives $13,889.

Thus, for this example in which credit terms are changed from $n/30$ to $n/45$, the total additional investment in receivables is expected to be $\$25,000 + \$13,889 = \$38,889$. Let us now assume that inventories and fixed assets are expected to increase $15,000 and $100,000, respectively, in order to support the higher level of sales. Assume also that the present value of future asset purchases is estimated at $7,847. The firm's total investment would thus be $\$38,889 + \$15,000 + \$100,000 + \$7,847 = \$161,736$.

In summary, we can state the formula for estimating the firm's investment ($I_{0,p}$) caused by extending the credit period as follows:

$$I_{0,p} = \left(\frac{CS_a}{RT}\right)\left(\frac{CE_u}{CS}\right) + (PCP \times AR_o) + OA_0 + I_{0,f} \qquad (10\text{-}6)$$

where CS_a are the expected credit sales that will add to the total sales of the company

   RT is the expected receivables turnover under the new terms

CE_u/CS is the ratio of up-front cash expenses to credit sales

   PCP is the percentage change in the average collection period applicable to sales that are expected irrespective of the change in credit policy

   AR_o are the receivables under the old terms

   OA_0 is the dollar amount of additions at time 0 to assets other than accounts receivable

   $I_{0,f}$ is the present value at time 0 of future asset purchases caused by the change in credit terms.

Net Cash Benefits and Net Present Value.   In order to continue with the example of a change in credit terms from $n/30$ to $n/45$ discussed above, we will assume that depreciation of the additional assets required is $5,000 annually and that the marginal tax rate on income is 30 percent. Since the bad debts ratio is expected to remain at 2 percent, the dollar amount of bad debts is expected to increase by 2 percent of additional credit sales, or $4,000. Recall that additional credit sales are forecast at $200,000 a year and that the ratio of up-front cash expenses to sales is expected to be 90 percent. The cash expenses in the numerator of the ratio in this case include credit department expenses which will be paid at the time of the related sale. Assume now that additional credit department expenses that are expected subsequent to the related sales are 2 percent of additional credit sales. Thus, the ratio of total cash expenses to credit sales would be 92 percent for purposes of estimating net cash benefits. Using these estimates, the annual net cash benefit of $9,900 is calculated in Table 10-3.

We assume for now that the net cash benefit of $9,900 is expected to continue each year indefinitely, and that the required rate of return on the investment in the credit policy change is 14 percent. Recalling that the total investment is estimated at

TABLE 10-3
ANNUAL NET CASH BENEFIT FROM
CHANGING CREDIT TERMS FROM $n/30$
TO $n/45$

Additional sales, all credit	$200,000
− Bad debts	4,000
− Cash expenses	184,000
− Depreciation	5,000
Income before taxes	$ 7,000
− Income taxes	2,100
Income after taxes	$ 4,900
+ Depreciation	5,000
Net cash benefit	$ 9,900

$161,736, the net present value from changing credit terms from $n/30$ to $n/45$ would be:

$$\text{NPV} = \frac{\$9,900}{0.14} - \$161,736$$
$$= -\$91,022$$

Not all policy proposals are good ones! In this case, our estimate of the net present value is negative, clearly indicating that the change should not be made.

Searching for the Optimum Credit Period. A what-if analysis using a computer spreadsheet program can be conducted in an attempt to determine the optimum terms to offer credit customers. An example of the results of this type of analysis is provided in Table 10-4 for changes in credit terms from $n/30$ to $n/15$, $n/45$, and $n/60$. The formulas that have been discussed in this chapter were inserted in the spreadsheet to calculate the required investments, net cash benefit, and net present value for each alternative.

The last row in the exhibit indicates that changing terms to $n/15$ is the only alternative producing a positive net present value in this example. Thus, the what-if analysis indicates that the firm should shorten its credit period to fifteen days. The negative net present values of the $n/45$ and $n/60$ proposals indicate that continuing with the existing policy is better for the firm and its stockholders than offering these terms to customers.

Note in Table 10-4 that shortening the credit period results in signs for the investments, sales, and expenses that are different from those that result from lengthening the credit period. This is expected, because shortening the credit period is in effect tightening credit terms offered to customers. In our example, only tightening terms is expected to increase the value of the firm. In other situations, however, the reverse may be true.

Cash Discount. The term **cash discount** was defined earlier. Even though a credit term such as 2/10 is referred to as a cash discount, payment is actually received several days after the sale. On the other hand, payment for a cash sale is received at the time the sale is made. Cash customers (customers who pay at the time of the sale) will probably also be given any cash discount offered to credit customers. In order to avoid confusion in terminology, we will refer to sales for which the firm receives payment some time after the sale, but no later than the end of the discount period, as **discounted credit sales**. The term **cash sales** will continue to refer to sales for which payment is received by the firm at the time of the sale.

A cash discount has a unique effect on the firm's investment compared to the effect of other credit terms we have considered up to now. A primary objective of the selling firm is to receive payment for credit sales sooner than would otherwise be the case. If this occurs, the firm's investment in the receivables will usually be reduced. Unfortunately for the firm, however, its profit margin will also be reduced because of the discount. Examples of these and related effects will be given in the two following sections.

TABLE 10-4
EVALUATION OF FOUR CREDIT POLICIES

A. Data Inputs

	Existing policy	Possible new policy	Possible new policy	Possible new policy
Credit terms	n/30	n/15	n/45	n/60
Cash sales	$1,000,000	$1,000,000	$1,000,000	$1,000,000
Credit sales	$1,000,000	$900,000	$1,200,000	$1,300,000
Total sales	$2,000,000	$1,900,000	$2,200,000	$2,300,000
Avg collect period	45	20	50	70
Additional expenses:				
Bad debts, (% added credit sales)		1.0%	2.0%	3.0%
Credit dept exps (% added cred sales)				
Up-front		3.0%	4.0%	4.0%
Subsequent		2.0%	2.0%	3.0%
Other exps (% added total sales)		86.0%	86.0%	86.0%
Depreciation type			SL	SL
Depreciation period (yrs)		20	20	20
Salvage value			$0	$0
Tax rate		30.0%	30.0%	30.0%
Required rate of return		14.0%	14.0%	14.0%
Additional inventories		$0	$15,000	$15,000
Additional fixed assets at time zero		($50,000)	$100,000	$110,000

TABLE 10-4
EVALUATION OF FOUR CREDIT POLICIES (*continued*)

A. Data Inputs (*continued*)

	Existing policy	Possible new policy	Possible new policy	Possible new policy
	Calculated Statistics, New Policy			
Avg recs turn, all credit sales		18.00	7.20	5.14
Avg recs outstanding		$50,000	$166,667	$252,778
Increase in average collection period (%)		−55.6%	11.1%	55.6%
Applicable investment; credit sales common to both		($62,500)	$13,889	$69,444
Other add credit sales		($100,000)	$200,000	$300,000
Applicable receivables		($5,556)	$27,778	$58,333
Applicable investment		($5,556)	$25,000	$52,500
Cash flow equivalent to future asset purchases		($549)	$1,099	$1,208
Applicable investment		($3,924)	$7,847	$8,632

B. Calculated Results

Investment

Receivables	($68,056)	$38,889	$121,944
Inventories	0	15,000	15,000
Fix assets	(50,000)	100,000	110,000
PV of future asset purchases	(3,924)	7,847	8,632
Total	($121,979)	$161,736	$255,576

Net Cash Benefit

Add sales	($100,000)	$200,000	$300,000
Less add bad debts	(1,000)	4,000	9,000
Less add credit debt exps	(5,000)	12,000	21,000
Less add other cash exps	(86,000)	172,000	258,000
Less add dep	(2,500)	5,000	5,500
Income before taxes	($5,500)	$7,000	$6,500
Less income taxes	(1,650)	2,100	1,950
Income after taxes	($3,850)	$4,900	$4,550
Plus add dep	(2,500)	5,000	5,500
Net cash benefit	($6,350)	$9,900	$10,050
Net present value	$76,622	($91,022)	($183,791)

The Investment. The approach to estimating the effect on the firm's investment from offering a cash discount is essentially the same, regardless of whether the change in credit terms is an offer of a discount for the first time or an increase in the magnitude of a discount already being offered. As we have observed in other cases, the analyst must distinguish between the receivables applicable to (a) additional credit sales and (b) sales that are expected to occur even if no change is made in credit terms. The firm's investment in each of these two categories of receivables can be estimated in the same general way discussed in previous sections.

Since payments for additional credit sales on which the discount is taken will normally be made between the date of the sale and the last day of the discount period, receivables will thereby be created in which the firm has an investment. For example, let us assume that changing credit terms from $n/30$ to $2/10$, $n/30$ is expected to increase total credit sales by $100,000 at invoice prices and that the related payments by customers are received, on average, on the eighth day after the sale. The receivables turnover on these discounted credit sales will be $360/8 = 45.0$ times a year. Dividing the turnover into the additional credit sales, we get $100,000/45.0 = $2,222$ as the added level of receivables resulting from these sales on average throughout the year. Since the receivables are derived from added sales, the firm's investment is the payment of cash expenses at or before the time of the sale. Thus, if the ratio of these expenses to sales is 80 percent, the firm's investment is $2,222(0.8) = $1,778$. Note that the investment can be calculated in this way even though payments are less than the stated amount of the receivables as a result of the discounts taken by customers. The amount of the discount affects future cash flows and therefore net cash benefits, but it does not affet the method of calculating the investment.

The second way in which a cash discount can affect the level of accounts receivable is the result of collecting within the discount period some of the receivables that would have been collected later under the old terms. This occurs if some of the credit customers under the old terms are expected to take the discount offered under the new terms. The effect on accounts receivable is the result of changing the average collection period applicable to these credit sales.

To illustrate, we continue with the case above in which the firm is considering changing its credit terms from $n/30$ to $2/10$, $n/30$. Assume that credit sales under the existing terms have been running at the annual rate of $500,000, with an average collection period of 45 days. Management estimates that this record will continue in the future if credit terms are not changed. However, if the proposed terms are adopted, it is expected that 30 percent, or $150,000, of these sales will be paid in 8 days on average, because some credit customers under the old terms will take the discount if it is offered. The average collection period for the remaining 70 percent is expected to continue to be 45 days.

The change in the firm's accounts receivable applicable to the $150,000 projected credit sales under the old terms, which are expected to become discounted credit sales under the new terms, is the result of the change in the applicable receivables turnover. The expected effect on receivables will be the difference in the level of receivables under the new and old terms:

$$\left(\frac{\$150,000}{45}\right) - \left(\frac{\$150,000}{8}\right) = -\$15,417$$

The above result indicates that the expected effect is to reduce accounts receivable by $15,417.

The net effect on the accounts receivable investment from changing credit terms in this example is the investment of $1,778 from additional credit sales (which are all discounted credit sales) less the $15,417 from earlier collections of other credit sales. The net amount is $-\$13,639$. However, we will assume that the total amount of additional sales (some of which will be cash sales, as discussed later) will result in an increase in inventories, fixed assets, and the present value of future asset purchases of $5,000, $55,000, and $20,000, respectively. Thus, the firm's total investment from offering the discount is estimated at $-\$13,639 + \$5,000 + \$55,000 + \$20,000 = \$66,361$.

The discussion in this section is summarized by the following equation for the calculation of the investment:

$$I_{0,d} = \left(\frac{CS_a}{RT_d}\right)\left(\frac{CE_u}{CS}\right) + \left[\left(\frac{CS_c}{RT_d}\right) - \left(\frac{CS_c}{RT_e}\right)\right] + OA_0 + I_{0,f} \qquad (10\text{-}7)$$

where

$I_{0,d}$ is the firm's total investment at time 0 in offering a cash discount

CS_a are the additional credit sales exprected from offering the cash discount

CE_u/CS is the ratio of up-front cash expenses to credit sales

CS_c are the credit sales that are expected irrespective of the change in terms, but which will be discounted under the new terms

RT_d is the expected receivables turnover applicable to the discounted credit sales under the new terms

RT_e is the expected receivables turnover under the existing terms

OA_0 are additions to other assets required at time 0 because of the policy change

$I_{0,f}$ is the present value of future asset purchases caused by the policy change →p. 314

The equation above assumes that credit sales which are expected irrespective of the change in terms, and which are not expected to be discounted under the new terms, have the same receivables turnover under either set of terms. Thus, these sales have no impact on the new credit investment. We are now in a position to estimate the net cash benefits from the investment.

Net Cash Benefits. The benefits to the firm from offering a cash discount can come from two sources: the reduction in the firm's investment in accounts receivable as described above and profits from additional sales. However, as was shown, the total investment may increase if additional inventories and/or fixed assets are required. In order for the additional sales to be profitable, they must more than cover the related costs as well as all discounts taken under the new policy.

Let us again examine the case discussed above in which the firm is considering changing its credit terms from *n*/30 to 2/10, *n*/30. The change is expected to add $100,000 to the $500,000 annual credit sales generated under existing terms, with all sales expressed at invoice prices. One additional point of major importance should now be considered. If the firm offers credit customers a cash discount from invoice prices for paying within the discount period, the discount will probably be offered also to cash customers, that is, to customers who pay at the time of the sale. Thus, if the amount of cash sales has been substantial under the old credit terms, the total dollar amount of the cash discount taken under the new terms will be a major cost item. However, this can be offset to some extent by an increase in cash sales that will probably occur as a result of the reduction in the net price (after discount) customers will have to pay.

Continuing with our numerical example, we assume that the change in terms from *n*/30 to 2/10, *n*/30 will increase cash sales form $200,000 to $250,000. Other assumptions include the following:

Additional credit department expenses:	5 percent of additional credit sales up front, plus 10 percent later.
Annual depreciation on $55,000 additional fixed assets:	$3,000
Additional other costs of operations, paid up front:	75 percent of additional total sales.

Using the assumptions noted, the calculation of the annual net cash benefit from offering the discount is shown in Table 10-5. The final step in the valuation is to estimate the overall merit from offering the discount. This problem is considered next.

Net Present Value.   To complete our example, we assume that the required rate of return is 12 percent. The expected net present value (NPV) from offering the discount

TABLE 10-5
Annual Net Cash Benefit from Changing Credit Terms
from *n*/30 to 2/10, *n*/30

Additional cash sales, at invoice	$50,000
+ Additional credit sales, at invoice	$100,000
− Credit department expenses	(15,000)
− Discounts taken on $500,000 sales*	(10,000)
− Depreciation	(3,000)
− Other costs	($112,500)
Profit before tax	$9,500
− Income tax @ 30%	2,850
Profit after tax	$6,650
+ Depreciation	3,000
Net cash benefit	$9,650

* Discounts are expected to be taken on all cash sales, totaling $250,000, plus all discounted credit sales, totaling $250,000. The discounted credit sales are the sum of the $100,000 additional credit sales and 30 percent of the $500,000 credit sales under old terms, which are expected to be paid within the discount period under the new terms.

can then be calculated as follows:

$$NPV = \frac{\$9650}{0.12} - \$66,361$$

$$= \$14,056$$

Net Cash Benefit

Total Investment

Since the NPV is positive, offering the 2 percent discount is expected to increase the value of the firm's common stock.

Combination Changes in Credit Policy.   In our discussion of changes in credit policy to this point, we have focused on changes in only one feature at a time. In many cases, of course, two or more features will be changed simultaneously. For example, the firm may change its terms from $n/30$ to $2/10$, $n/45$. The principle in estimating the net present value in these cases is the same as for the simpler cases. The firm's investment in accounts receivable is estimated by (1) estimating the receivables applicable to (a) additional sales and (b) sales that would be made regardless of whether or not the credit policy is changed; (2) calculating the firm's investment in each of the two categories of receivables; and (3) summing the two investments. Any increase in inventories, fixed assets, or present value of future asset purchases necessitated by the additional sales should be added to this sum to find the firm's total investment. The net cash benefits are then estimated, and the net present value calculated by netting the total investment against the present value of the net cash benefits.

Variations in Cash Flows Over Time

In the discussion of trade credit to this point, we have considered two reasons why future cash flows may not be constant. If the firm has unused productive capacity, a change in credit policy may lead to a future investment in fixed assets because of sales growth. Second, investments in depreciable assets usually require replacement expenditures in the future, if the credit policy change is long-term in nature. But there are also other reasons why the firm's investment or net cash benefits related to a change in credit policy may not remain constant. We will consider two of the more important reasons: seasonal variations, and growth over time.

Seasonal Dating.   Seasonal demand for its products or services may lead the firm to offer credit terms which will smooth out its sales over the year. For example, a cotton seed processor may desire to operate throughout the year even though sales of its customers, retail feed stores and cotton gins, may be concentrated in late winter and early spring. Under these conditions, the processor would have to warehouse the company's output for several months, unless it is able to sell throughout the year to retail outlets. As one feature of its sales promotion, the processor may offer seasonal dating to its customers. Thus, terms of $n/$April 30, that is, payment due next April 30, may be offered.

There are two advantages to seasonal dating from the standpoint of the creditor firm: first, it helps to ensure demand for the firm's products, and second, it reduces inventory carrying costs if production and sales are continuous throughout the year. However, the growth in receivables in certain months involves an increasing investment on the part of the firm. Seasonal dating thus typically gives rise to a variable investment in receivables during the year. The investment increases as accounts receivable build up during some months, and then, when customers pay their accounts, the investment is eliminated. The benefits of seasonal dating are derived from the reduction in inventory costs, any increase in efficiency from level production, and any increase in total sales that the terms are expected to cause. The net present value of the policy for one year can be calculated by time-adjusting all expected cash flows during the year to time zero; the cash flows, of course, are derived from the investment and the cash benefit.

Long-Term Growth in Credit Sales. The effect of offering the same credit terms will probably not remain constant over long periods of time. Growth in units sold as well as in selling prices due to inflation often occur. In this section, we consider the important case in which future growth is expected to remain constant.

Assume that a firm's investment under a proposed credit policy is expected to be $1,000,000 initially and to grow thereafter at the annual rate of 6 percent for an indefinitely long period of time in the future. The constant growth model discussed and used in previous chapters can be adapted to estimate the present value of future investments in this case. The model takes the following form:

$$I_{0,f} = \frac{I_1}{k - g} \tag{10-8}$$

where $I_{0,f}$ is the present value of future investments
I_1 is the additional investment at the end of the first year
k is the required rate of return
g is annual growth rate in the additional investments

Assuming a required rate of return of 10 percent for our example and substituting the necessary data into equation (10-8), the present value of future investments caused by the policy change can be calculated as follows:

$$I_{0,f} = \frac{0.06(\$1,000,000)}{0.1 - 0.06}$$

$$= \$1,500,000 \rightarrow \text{TO BE ADDED TO TOTAL INVESTMENT OR CREDIT POLICY}$$

The result of the calculation above is the present value as of time 0 of expected future investments which begin at the end of the first year. The firm's total investment in the new credit policy is the $1,500,000 plus the $1,000,000 initial investment, or $2,500,000.

If the net cash benefits are expected to grow at a constant rate, the constant growth model can again be used to determine their present value. The net present value of the proposed credit policy can then be calculated in the usual manner by subtracting the present value of the total investment from the present value of the future cash benefits. We will not complete the calculation here since the process should be well known to the student.

CHAPTER SUMMARY

Establishment of a credit policy by a firm requires decisions in regard to the credit terms to be offered and the credit classes of customers to whom the terms will be offered. The decisions should be based on the same criterion as an investment in assets such as land, plant, and equipment. Among all of the alternatives available to the firm, select the terms and credit class(es) which will result in the greatest net present value. The evaluation process requires estimates of (1) the total amount of funds that must be invested, (2) the net cash benefits that will result, the (3) the discount rate that should be used to time adjust future cash flows back to time 0, that is, back to the present.

The greatest difference in making credit policy and fixed asset decisions is in estimating the investment outlays required. Credit policy affects the firm's investment in accounts receivable and often in inventories and fixed assets. Replacements of fixed assets may also be required if the policy change is long term. Another complicating factor in credit policy decisions is that the firm's investment in the additional accounts receivable that will result depends upon whether the additional receivables are generated from additional sales, or from a change in the timing of collections. Receivables generated from additional credit sales involve an investment only in the expenses incurred at or before the time the applicable sale occurs. These expenses may include the costs of producing and selling the product, as well as the expenses of the credit department at the time of the sale. On the other hand, all of the receivables generated from a change in timing of collections are an investment by the firm, because the total amount of the customer's payment is delayed.

The net cash benefits from offering credit for the first time, or from changing credit terms to be more favorable to customers, are derived from the additional sales that are generated. The calculation of net cash benefits is essentially the same as for investments in other types of assets, although a change in credit policy may involve certain unique expenses, such as bad debt expense. In addition, offering a cash discount can reduce the net cash benefits from sales, because customers who take the discount will pay less than invoice price.

Determination of the optimum credit policy will sometime necessitate an evaluation of the effect of tightening credit terms. Offering tougher credit terms to customers will usually result in a reduction in sales and net cash inflows. However, the net present value of the change will be positive if the reduction in investment exceeds the present value of the negative net cash benefits.

SOLVED PROBLEM

The Mom & Pop Grocery currently offers credit terms of n/30 to "local customers who pay their bills in a reasonable amount of time." Mom believes that the store would benefit from extending the same terms to anyone who can provide reliable evidence of a good credit rating. However, Pop contends that any change should be to lengthen the credit period to $n/60$ for local customers. Son John disagrees with both of his parents, since he is of the opinion that accounts receivable require an excessive amount of invested capital. He thus recommends offering credit only to local customers under terms of $1/10$, $n/30$.

Mom and Pop finally agree to hire a consultant to study the problem. The consultant compiles the data given in Table 10-6 under the assumption that the three proposals are mutually exclusive.

1 Estimate the (a) investment, (b) annual net cash benefit, and (c) net present value for each proposal.

2 What decision should Mom & Pop make?

Solution

1 a Since no additional fixed assets are required, the investment for each alternative will be the total capital committed to additional accounts receivable and any additional inventories. The investment in receivables will depend upon the source, whether from a change in sales or from a change in the collection period applicable to sales that are expected to be made even in no policy change occurs. Costs of goods

TABLE 10-6

| | Present policy | Proposal | | |
		Mom's	Pop's	John's
Credit terms	$n/30$	$n//30$	$n/60$	$1/10$, $n/30$
Cash sales	$30,000	$28,000	$30,000	$33,000[a]
Credit sales at invoice,				
Not discounted	$50,000	$70,000	$65,000	$45,000
Discounted	—	—	—	$10,000
Avg collect period,				
Credit sales not discounted	58 days	58 days	65 days	58 days
Discounted credit sales	—	—	—	9 days
Bad debts (% of added credit sales not discounted)	—	3%	2%	—
Added costs of goods sold (% of added total sales)[b]	—	80%	80%	80%
Added other cash expenses (% of added total credit sales)[c]				
Up-front	—	3%	2%	2%
Other	—	4%	3%	3%
Tax rate	15%	15%	15%	15%
Added inventories	—	$1,000	—	—
Required rate of return		16%	15%	15%

[a] Customers who pay cash will receive the 1 percent disount. However, the cash sales figures in the table do not reflect the discount.

[b] Mom & Pop is expected to make payments for costs of goods sold after the applicable sale.

[c] Includes credit handling expenses.

sold are not included in the investment in this problem because the costs are paid after the sale.

Investment required under Mom's proposal: The receivables turnover = 360 days/58 days = 6.2. Up-front cash expenses are given as 3% of credit sales. Inventories are expected to increase by $1,000.

Total credit sales are expected to increase from $50,000 to $70,000, or $20,000. The latter figure is derived from an $18,000 increase in total sales and a $2,000 decrease in cash sales. Equation (10-5) can now be used to estimate the total investment required if Mom's proposal is accepted:

$$
\begin{aligned}
I_{0,nc} &= \left(\frac{CS_a}{RT}\right)\left(\frac{CD_u}{CS}\right) + \left(\frac{CS_c}{RT}\right) + OA_0 + I_{0,f} \\
&= \left(\frac{\$18,000}{6.2}\right)(0.03) + \left(\frac{\$2,000}{6.2}\right) + \$1,000 + 0 \\
&= \$87 + \$323 + \$1,000 \\
&= \$1,410
\end{aligned}
$$

Investment required under Pop's proposal: Credit sales are expected to increase $65,000 - $50,000 = $15,000 with no change in cash sales. The average collection period is expected to increase from 58 days to 65 days; this is a percentage increase of $(65-58)/58 = 0.121$, or 12.1%. The receivables turnover is expected to decrease from 360/58 = 6.2 to 360/65 = 5.5. Up-front cash expenses are estimated at 2% of added credit sales. Using equation (10-6), the investment will be:

$$
\begin{aligned}
I_{0,p} &= \left(\frac{CS_a}{RT}\right)\left(\frac{CE_u}{CS}\right) + (PCP \times AR_o) + OA_0 + I_{0,f} \\
&= \left(\frac{\$15,000}{5.5}\right)(0.02) + 0.121\left(\frac{\$50,000}{6.2}\right) + 0 + 0 \\
&= \$55 + \$976 + 0 + 0 \\
&= \$1,031
\end{aligned}
$$

Investment required under John's proposal:

Receivables turnover under existing terms: $\quad RT_e = \dfrac{360 \text{ days}}{58 \text{ days}} = 6.2$

Receivables turnover for discounted credit sales: $\quad RT_d = \dfrac{360 \text{ days}}{9} = 40$

The investment under John's proposal can be solved for by using equation (10-7):

$$
\begin{aligned}
I_{0,d} &= \left(\frac{CS_a}{RT_d}\right)\left(\frac{CS_u}{CS}\right) + \left[\left(\frac{CS_c}{RT_d}\right) - \left(\frac{CS_c}{RT_e}\right)\right] + OA_0 + I_{0,f} \\
&= \left(\frac{\$5,000}{40}\right)(0.02) + \left[\left(\frac{\$5,000}{40}\right) - \left(\frac{\$5,000}{6.2}\right)\right] + 0 + 0
\end{aligned}
$$

$$= \$3 + [\$125 - \$806]$$
$$= -\$678$$

Thus, John's proposal results is a net decrease in the store's invested capital.

b *Net Cash Benefits*

	Proposal		
	Mom's	Pop's	John's
Added total sales	$18,000	$15,000	$8,000
− Bad debts	600	300	—
− Cost of goods sold	14,400	12,000	6,400
− Other cash expenses			
Up-front	600	300	100[a]
Other	800	450	150[a]
− Discounts taken	—	—	430[b]
Income before taxes	$1,600	$1,950	$920
Income taxes	240	293	138
Net cash benefit	$1,360	$1,657	$782

[a] Under John's proposal, the increase in total credit sales is 5,000.
[b] Under John's proposal, discounts are expected to be taken on $33,000 cash sales and $10,000 credit sales.

Net Present Value

		Mom's	Pop's	John's
Present value of future cash flows	= NCB/k	$8,500	$11,047	$5,213
− Investment		−1,410	−1,031	+678
Net present value		$7,090	$10,016	$5,891

c Since Pop's proposal has the highest net present value, it is the best of the three. The other proposals should be rejected if they are considered by Mom and Pop to be mutually exclusive. However, they almost certainly are not completely mutually exclusive. Thus, the data for various combinations of the three proposals should be estimated and the related net present values calculated. One or more of the combinations may be found to have a higher net present value than Pop's proposal. In this event, the opportunity with the highest net present value should be accepted.

PROBLEMS

10-1   A firm has credit sales of $1 million a year, with an average collection period of 38 days. Estimate the firm's receivables turnover and the amount of receivables outstanding. Indicate any assumptions you make in your calculations.

10-2   Calculate a firm's investment in accounts receivable under the various conditions given below. Assume in each case that the ratio of up-front, cash expenses to credit sales is 75 percent.

    a Credit is offered to customers for the first time. Terms are *n*/30, and the average collection period is 40 days. Credit sales are $1 million a year, but cash sales are not affected.

b Rework Question 1a above, but assume now that cash sales are reduced by $200,000 a year.

c After one year has passed, the firm decides to change its credit terms from $n/30$ to $n/45$. As a result, the average collection period increases from 40 days to 50 days. Credit sales increase from $1 million to $1.2 million, but cash sales are not affected.

10-3 Portsmont Manufacturing, Inc. (PMI) recently changed its credit terms offered to customers from $n/45$ to $n/60$. As a result, credit sales are forecast to be $2.2 million this year, compared to $2.0 million last year. Cash sales are not expected to be affected. However, the average collection period of all receivables is expected to rise to 65 days from 55 days, and bad debts are expected to increase from 1 percent of total credit sales to 1.2 percent. The cash expense-to-sales ratio has been averaging 82 percent, but the ratio is projected to rise to 83 percent on the additional sales. The increased expenses reflected in this ratio do not include the increase in bad debts or the estimated increase in credit department expenses of 0.5 percent of additional credit sales. Annual depreciation applicable to new assets required by the change in credit terms is estimated at $2,500. PMI's marginal tax rate is 34 percent.

a Estimate the net cash benefit per year from the policy change.

b Estimate the maximum investment required by the policy change for the change to be beneficial to the company, assuming a required rate of return of 12 percent.

c What assumption did you make in answering B above concerning the continuity of future cash flows? Justify your assumption.

10-4 The Melton Company is considering offering credit for the first time; terms would be $n/30$. If the decision is to offer the terms, credit sales are expected to run $300,000 annually, with an average collection period of 35 days. Forecasts indicate that cash sales would probably not be affected materially. The ratio of total up-front cash expenses to credit sales is estimated at 80 percent. The additional sales are expected to cause a need for an immediate increase in inventories and fixed assets totaling $150,000. In addition, replacements of fixed assets are projected at $100,000 every 20 years. The treasurer of Melton has estimated the annual net cash benefit from the new credit policy at $30,000. The required rate of return on the investment is 16 percent.

a Estimate Melton's total investment if the new credit terms are offered.

b Calculate the net present value of the investment, and justify any assumptions that you make.

c What decision should the company make in regard to its credit policy?

d Do you believe the forecast that cash sales will not be affected by the new credit policy is credible? Why or why not?

e Assume now that the new credit terms are expected to reduce cash sales by $100,000 per year. As a result, the credit policy change would have the following effects: annual net cash benefit = $20,000, net inventory and fixed asset investment at time 0 = $100,000, and future asset replacements = $60,000 every 25 years. All other effects would be the same as given initially. What decision should the company make in regard to offering credit to customers?

10-5 The Apollo Equipment Company (AEC) has received an order for $1,100,000 worth of equipment from the Western Silver Mining Company (WSMC), AEC's total costs in manufacturing the equipment, handling the order, and processing the account is estimated at $800,000. No increase in fixed assets is anticipated in filling the order.

WSMC is a small company, but it has operated at a profit in each of the last three years. The equipment ordered form AEC would be used in a new silver mine. Tests have shown that the mine has a considerable amount of silver of fairly high grade. However, total costs of mining the silver and transporting it to market for processing are highly uncertain.

The management of AEC believes that there is a 90 percent chance of receiving full payment from WSMC in one year after delivery. If full payment is not received in one year, however, the chances are considered negligible that AEC will ever collect any part of the bill. For this reason, the required rate of return on the order is set at 20 percent.

a How should the probability that WSMC will default on its payment for the new equipment be accounted for in AEC's evaluation of the order?

b Should AEC fill the order? Why or why not?

10-6 A firm which has been offering credit terms of $n/30$ is considering changing the terms to $3/10$, $n/30$. Sales to customers who take the discount are expected to be $10 million at invoice prices, but sales to customers who pay in 45 days (the average collection period under the old terms) are expected to decline from $20 million to $15 million. All customers who take the discount are expected to pay on the tenth day. No change in cash sales is forecast.

The ratio of up-front cash expenses to credit sales is estimated at 80 percent, and subsequent cash expenses are estimated at 10 percent of credit sales. No effects are expected in the dollar amount of bad debts, inventories, or fixed assets. The firm's marginal tax rate is 34 percent, and the required rate of return on investments related to credit offered by the firm is 14 percent.

a Estimate the net present value of the change in credit terms.

b Rework Question 10-6a above, but now assume that inventories and fixed assets will increase by $0.5 million and $3 million respectively. The fixed assets will be depreciated on a straight-line basis to a zero salvage value in twenty years, at which time a replacement expenditure of $3 million will be required. All other changes are expected to be the same as in Question 10-6a.

c Rework Question 10-6b above, but now assume that cash sales are expected to increase from $8 million to $10 million at invoice prices. Customers who pay cash will also receive the discount. The ratio of cash expenses to cash sales is 78 percent. All other factors are expected to be the same as in Question 10-6b.

10-7 The L&H Company has been offering credit terms of $n/60$. However, most of the company's competitors also offer a cash discount to customers who pay early. An estimate of the effects of L&H offering terms of $2/10$, $n/60$ is given below:

	Existing policy	Proposed new policy
Credit terms	$n/60$	$2/10$, $n/60$
Cash sales, @ invoice prices*	$300,000	$350,000
Discounted credit sales		$250,000
Other credit sales	$600,000	$450,000
Average collection period (days):		
Discounted credit sales		8
Other credit sales	45	45
Additional expenses:		
Bad debts (% added credit sales)		—
Credit dept exps (% added cred sales)		
Up-front		5%
Subsequent		10%
Other up-front costs		
(% added total sales)		75%

	Existing policy	Proposed new policy
Depreciation type		SL
Depreciation period (years)		25
Tax rate		34%
Required rate of return		12%
Additional inventories		$10,000
Additional fixed assets (depreciable)		$75,000
Salvage value of fixed assets at the end of 25 years		$0
Asset replacements every 25 years		$75,000

* Payments of cash sales are also discounted by 2% from invoice prices.

Should L&H offer the cash discount? Why or why not?

10-8 (This problem can be solved most efficiently by the use of a computer spreadsheet program.)

The Wayne Equipment Company recently ordered a study of two credit policy proposals:

Proposal 1: To begin offering the firm's regular credit terms to customer firms with average sales between $100,000 and $200,000 during the previous three years. NPV = 25, 9444

Proposal 2: In addition to offering credit to the same customers as Proposal 1, offer the same terms to customer firms with sales between $100,000 and $200,000 during the past year. NPV = 37, 665,833

The study produced the following results:

	Proposal 1	Proposal 2
Terms	n/180	n/180
Added sales (all credit) if proposal is adopted (CSa)	$20,000,000	$30,000,000
Change in cash sales	—	—
Average collection period	200 days	205 days
Bad debts (% of credit sales)	6%	7%
Credit department expenses (% of added credit sales):		
Up-front	5%	5%
Subsequent	10%	11%
Other costs, paid after applicable sale (% of added sales)	40%	40%
Increase in annual depreciation	$300,000	$300,000
Added inventories required	$1,000,000	$1,000,000
Added fixed assets required plus present value of future replacements (OA o + 5 of)	$10,000,000	$10,000,000
Required rate of return	14%	15%

The company's marginal tax rate is 34 percent.

a   Which proposal, if either, should Wayne accept? Why?

b   Assess the sensitivity of Proposal 2 to changes in the average collection period by changing the period to (1) 190 days, (2) 220 days, and (3) 250 days.

10-9 (This problem can be solved most efficiently by the use of a computer spreadsheet program.) A firm is considering offering credit terms to customers for the time. The following forecasts have been compiled for the firm's existing policy of selling only for cash, and for four sets of credit terms that could be offered:

	Existing policy	Proposed policy-1	Proposed policy-2	Proposed policy-3	Proposed policy-4
Credit terms		n/30	n/40	n/50	n/60
Cash sales	$300,000	$200,000	$190,000	$180,000	$175,000
Credit sales		$250,000	$280,000	$295,000	$305,000
Average collection period (days)		40	45	55	65
Additional expenses:					
Bad debts, (% added credit sales)		3.0%	3.1%	3.2%	3.3%
Credit dept exps (% added cred sales)					
Up-front		5.0%	5.0%	5.0%	5.0%
Subsequent		10.0%	10.0%	11.0%	11.0%
Other exps, paid before sale (% of added total sales)		63.0%	63.0%	63.0%	63.0%
Depreciation type		SL	SL	SL	SL
Depreciation period (yrs)		20	20	20	20
Tax rate		34.0%	34.0%	34.0%	34.0%
Required rate of return		12.0%	12.0%	12.5%	13.0%
Additional inventories		$5,000	$5,000	$6,000	$7,000
Additional depreciable assets		$20,000	$20,000	$20,000	$20,000
Salvage value of depreciable assets at end of 20 years		$0	$0	$0	$0
Asset replacements every 20 years		$20,000	$20,000	$20,000	$20,000

a   Calculate the net present value for each set of terms.

b   What terms should the firm offer to its customers? Why?

10-10 (This problem can be solved most efficiently by the use of a computer spreadsheet program.) The management of the Farmington Corporation is convinced that the company's current credit terms of n/60 are excessively generous and have resulted in a high bad-debts ratio. Thus, the credit manager of Farmington, a Ms. Janet Roberts, has been charged with the task of researchng the problem, and reporting her findings and recommendations to the company's Executive committee in one month. Ms. Roberts' study results in the estimates shown on page 323. Should Ms. Roberts recommend a change in the firm's credit terms? Why or why not?

REFERENCES

Atkins, Joseph C. and Yong H. Kim: "Comment and Correction: Opportunity Cost in the Evaluation of Investment in Accounts Receivable," *Financial Management*, Vol. 6, Winter 1977, pp. 71–74.

Ben-Horim, Moshe and Haim Levy: "Management of Accounts Receivable Under Inflation," *Financial Management*, Vol. 12, Spring 1983, pp. 42–48.

Dyl, Edward A.: "Another Look at the Evaluation of Investment in Accounts Receivable," *Financial Management*, Vol. 6, Winter 1977, pp. 67–70.

Emery, Gary W.: "A Pure Financial Explanation for Trade Credit," *Journal of Financial and Quantitative Analysis*, Vol. 19, September 1984, pp. 271–286.

	Existing policy	Alternative 1	Alternative 2	Alternative 3	Alternative 4
Credit terms	n/60	n/45	n/30	n/15	n/10
Cash sales	$5,000,000	$5,000,000	$5,000,000	$5,500,000	$6,000,000
Credit sales	$25,000,000	$24,000,000	$22,000,000	$21,000,000	$20,000,000
Average collection period (days)	75	55	38	20	14
Expenses:					
Bad debts, (% credit sales)	6.0%	5.5%	4.0%	3.0%	3.0%
Credit dept exps (% credit sales)					
Up-front	5.0%	5.0%	5.0%	5.0%	5.0%
Subsequent	15.0%	10.0%	7.0%	5.0%	5.0%
Other exps, paid before sale (% added total sales)	60.0%	60.0%	60.0%	60.0%	60.0%
Depreciation expense (annual)	$750,000	$750,000	$700,000	$700,000	$685,000
Tax rate	30.0%	30.0%	30.0%	30.0%	30.0%
Required rate of return		12.0%	11.5%	11.0%	11.0%
Inventory reduction		$0	$500,000	$500,000	$600,000
Reduction in fixed assets and present value of future replacements		$0	$1,000,000	$1,000,000	$1,300,000

Gentry, James A. and Jesus M. De La Garza: "A Generalized Model for Monitoring Accounts Receivable," *Financial Management*, Vol. 14, Winter 1985, pp. 28–38.

Halloran, John A. and Howard P. Lanser: "The Credit Policy Decision in an Inflationary Environment," *Financial Management*, Vol. 10, Winter 1981, pp. 31–38.

Hill, Ned C. and Kenneth D. Riener: "Determining the Cash Discount in the Firm's Credit Policy," *Financial Management*, Vol. 8, Spring 1979, pp. 68–73.

Kim, Yong H. and Joseph C. Atkins: "Evaluating Investments in Accounts Receivable: A Wealth Maximizing Framework," *Journal of Finance*, Vol. XXXIII, May 1978, pp. 403–412.

Oh, John S.: "Opportunity Cost in the Evaluation of Investment in Accounts Receivable," *Financial Management*, Vol. 5, Summer 1976, pp. 32–36.

Sachdeva, Kanwal S. and Lawrence J. Gitman: "Accounts Receivable Decisions in a Capital Budgeting Framework," *Financial Management*, Vol. 10, Winter 1981, pp. 45–49.

Sartoris, William L. and Ned C. Hill: "Evaluating Credit Policy Alternatives: A Present Value Framework," *Journal of Financial Research*, Vol. IV, Spring 1981, pp. 81–89.

Smith, Janet K.: "Trade Credit and Informational Asymmetry," *Journal of Finance*, Vol. 42, September 1987, pp. 863–872.

Smith, Keith V.: *Guide to Working Capital Management*. New York: McGraw-Hill, 1979; Chapter 5.

Walia, Tinlochan S.: "Explicit and Implicit Cost of Changes in the Level of Accounts Receivable and the Credit Policy Decision of the Firm," *Financial Management*, Vol. 6, Winter 1977, pp. 75–78.

Weston, J. Fred and Pham D. Tuan: "Comment on Analysis of Credit Policy Changes," *Financial Management*, Vol. 9, Winter 1980, pp. 59–63.

11

DETERMINING THE
FINANCING MIX

Earlier in Chapter 7 we discussed the estimation of the firm's cost of capital. In those calculations, the firm's mix of financing sources was assumed to be known. In the current chapter we will discuss two fundamental problems that arise in determining the mix of funds a firm should use. The first of these problems relates to the use of short-term or long-term debt financing. We will refer to this as the **debt maturity financing decision**. The second problem relates to the choice of the mix of long-term debt and equity financing. This latter problem is generally referred to as the **capital structure problem**.

The chapter will be organized as follows: First we will address the concepts of business and financial risk followed by a discussion of operating leverage. A discussion of financial leverage is followed by a review of the concept of total leverage. Then we will discuss the first of the basic financing decisions: the debt maturity decision. The last section contains a discussion of the second major financing question which surrounds the choice among alternative sources of permanent or long-term financing.

BUSINESS RISK AND FINANCIAL RISK

In Chapter 6, *risk* was discussed in terms of the variability associated with expected cash-flow streams. Our attention is now focused on the firm's financing decision rather than on its investment decision. It is useful, then, to separate this total variation in the income stream into variations attributable to (1) the company's exposure to business risk, and (2) its decision to incur financial risk.

The term **business risk** will be used to refer to the relative dispersion (variability) in the firm's expected earnings before interest and taxes (EBIT).[1] Figure 11-1*a* shows a subjectively estimated probability distribution of next year's EBIT for the Polaris Development Corporation. Figure 11-1*b* shows the same type of projection for Polaris's larger competitor, Flagship, Inc. The expected value of EBIT for Polaris is $800,000, with a standard deviation of $200,000. If next year's EBIT for Polaris is one standard deviation higher than the expected $800,000, then the actual EBIT will equal $1,000,000. Flagship's expected EBIT is $1,500,000, and its standard deviation is $200,000. Although the standard deviations in EBIT are the same for both firms, the business risks faced by each firm are not equal. Polaris faces a higher level of business risk than Flagship because it has a larger coefficient of variation (CV) in its EBIT. Figure 11-2 contains these respective CVs and the procedure used to calculate them. Note than Flagship's variation is only 0.13 as compared with a value of 0.25 for Polaris. Business risk is a direct result of the firm's investment decisions. Thus, the firm's asset structure gives rise to both the level and the variability of its operating profits (EBIT).

In contrast, **financial risk** results from the firm's financing decisions. Specifically, financial risk is produced by the use of **financial leverage**, which involves financing a portion of the firm's assets with securities bearing a fixed (limited) rate of return. The use of either debt or preferred stock in the firm's financial structure exposes the common shareholders to financial risk. The decision to use either of these security types will magnify the variability in the firm's EBIT. This additional variability will be embodied in the variability of the earnings available to the residual owner. This, in turn, means that the probability that earnings will not be sufficient to cover fixed interest, principal, and preferred dividend obligations will be increased. Clearly, financial risk takes two forms: (1) an increased variability in earnings per common share, and (2) a higher risk of insolvency.

[1] Where "other income" and "other expenses" are equal to 0, EBIT is equal to net operating income. In the pages that follow, these terms will be used interchangeably.

FIGURE 11-1
Subjective probability distribution of annual EBIT: (*a*) Polaris Development Corporation; (*b*) Flagship, Inc.

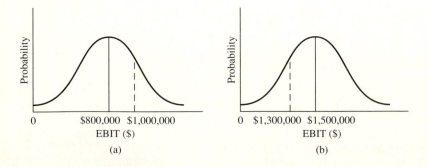

Formula: $CV = \sigma EBIT / \overline{EBIT}$
        where   CV is the coefficient of variation,
               $\sigma EBIT$ is the standard deviation in annual EBIT, and
               $\overline{EBIT}$ is the expected or mean value of annual EBIT

Computations for Polaris and Flagship:

	$\sigma EBIT$	÷	$\overline{EBIT}$	=	CV	
Polaris	$200,000		$ 800,000		0.25	**FIGURE 11-2**
Flagship	200,000		1,500,000		0.13	Calculating the coefficient of variation in EBIT.

The concepts of business and financial risk are closely related to the problem of choosing an appropriate financial structure. This is attributable to the impact of such risks on the variability of the firm's residual earnings stream. In the next two sections we will study techniques that permit a precise assessment of the earnings-stream variability induced by (1) operating leverage, and (2) financial leverage.

THE CONCEPT OF OPERATING LEVERAGE

The business risk of the firm is affected by its use of operating leverage. Operating leverage stems from the incurrence of fixed operating costs. These fixed expenses have the effect of (1) magnifying the variability in EBIT in response to changes in sales and (2) increasing the firm's break-even sales level. Cost-volume-profit analysis provides the necessary foundation for the study of operating leverage.

Break-Even Analysis

Break-even analysis has proved to be a useful tool in a wide array of business settings, encompassing organizations of all sizes. It is based on a set of straightforward assumptions which must be understood by the financial manager or erroneous decisions can result from misapplication.

Objective.   Break-even analysis permits the analyst to determine that quantity of output for which total revenues equal total expenses. The fundamental break-even relationships will be developed by concentrating first on units of output, and then the procedure will be extended to permit direct calculation of the break-even sales level.
We will define **break-even** as that quantity of output, stated in units, that results in an EBIT level equal to 0. Thus, the break-even model enables the financial manager (1) to determine the quantity of output that must be sold to cover all operating costs, as distinct from financial costs, and (2) to calculate the EBIT that will be achieved at various output levels. Our specific interest in break-even analysis relates to its use as a tool for analyzing the financing decision.

Developing the Break-Even Model.   The break-even model becomes operational by separating the production costs of the company into fixed and variable components.

Given a long enough period of time, all costs are variable; thus, break-even analysis is useful in a short-run context, where the concept of fixed costs is relevant.

Fixed Costs.   Fixed costs do not vary in total amount as sales volume or the quantity of output changes over some *relevant* range of output. Thus, total fixed costs are (1) *independent* of the quantity of product produced, and (2) equal to some constant dollar amount. As more units of product are manufactured, total fixed costs are spread over larger quantities of output. The result is that fixed cost per unit of output falls. Specific fixed costs for a manufacturing firm might reasonably include administrative salaries, depreciation, insurance, advertising expenditures, and property taxes.

Variable Costs.   Variable costs are fixed per unit of output, but vary in total as output changes. Thus, if sales rise by 15 percent, then variable costs will likewise rise by 15 percent. Variable costs for a manufacturing firm might include direct labor, direct materials, utility costs related to the production area, freight and packaging costs on products leaving the plant, and sales commissions.

A Word of Caution.   A firm's costs will not all conveniently fall into the fixed and variable categories. Nor does any business principle suggest that a certain cost element always be classified as fixed or variable. This depends on the firm and its specific line of commercial activity.

Also, some costs may be fixed for a while, then rise sharply to a higher level as a higher output is reached, remain fixed, and then rise again with further increases in production. Such costs may be termed either *semivariable* or *semifixed*. To implement the break-even model, then, it is necessary that the manager (1) identify the most relevant output range for planning purposes, and (2) approximate the cost effect of semivariable items over this range by allotting a portion of them to fixed costs and a portion to variable costs.

Sales Revenues and Production Levels.   The remaining key elements of the break-even model are (1) total revenue from sales, and (2) volume of output. **Total revenue** is sales dollars. It is equal to the selling price per unit multiplied by the quantity sold. The **volume of output** refers to the firm's level of operations and may be indicated as a unit quantity or as sales dollars.

Determination of the Break-Even Point.   The break-even point denominated in units of output can be found in several ways. Actually, the break-even model is a mere adaptation of the firm's income statement:

$$\text{Sales} - (\text{total variable costs} + \text{total fixed cost}) = \text{profit} \qquad (11\text{-}1)$$

In terms of units, the income statement shown in Equation (11-1) becomes the break-even model by setting EBIT (profit) equal to 0:

(Sales price per unit) × (units sold)

$$-[(\text{variable cost per unit} \times \text{units sold}) + (\text{total fixed cost})] = \text{EBIT} = \$0 \quad (11\text{-}2)$$

So we aim to find the number of units that must be produced and sold to satisfy Equation (11-2).

Sample Problem. The Polaris Development Corporation manufactures several different products; however, its product mix is rather constant. The firm's management, then, can compute its break-even point by using a "normal" sales price per unit and "normal" variable cost per unit. The selling price used is $20.00, and the variable cost is $12.00. Total fixed costs for the firm are $250,000 per year.

The following notation will be adopted in developing the break-even model: Q is the number of units sold, Q^* is the break-even level of Q, P is the unit sales price, F is total fixed costs anticipated over the planning period, and V is the unit variable cost. Equation (11-2), the break-even model, is repeated as Equation (11-2a), employing the preceding notation. The break-even model is then solved for Q^*, the number of units that have to be sold in order that EBIT will equal $0.

$$(P \cdot Q) - [(V \cdot Q) + F] = \text{EBIT} = \$0 \qquad (11\text{-}2a)$$
$$(P \cdot Q) - (V \cdot Q) - F = \$0$$
$$Q(P - V) = F$$
$$Q^* = \frac{F}{P - V} \qquad (11\text{-}3)$$

Observe that equation (11-3) says we must divide total fixed operating costs (F) by the unit contribution margin (P − V) to obtain the break-even level of output (Q^*).

Using equation (11-3), we can calculate Polaris Development Corporation's break-even point as follows:

$$Q^* = \frac{F}{P - V} = \frac{\$250,000}{\$20 - 12} = 31,250 \text{ units}$$

Sales Break-Even Model. Sales provide a common denominator when a firm has multiple product offerings. Thus, rather than try to deal with an arbitrarily defined unit of measurement for a product mix, the analyst can use total sales dollars. In addition, the outside analyst may not have access to internal unit-cost data. He may, however, be able to obtain the firm's annual reports, from which the firm's total costs can be identified as either fixed or variable. The analyst can then calculate a general break-even point in sales dollars.

The sales break-even model can be found by solving Equation (11-2a) for that level of total revenue at which EBIT equals 0:

$$(P \cdot Q) - [(V \cdot Q) + F] = \text{EBIT} = \$0 \qquad (11\text{-}2a)$$

Substituting S for sales revenue (P · Q), VC for total variable cost (V · Q) and rearranging the terms, we can rewrite Equation (11-2a) as follows:

$$S^* = \frac{F}{1 - VC/S} \qquad (11\text{-}4)$$

where S^* is the break-even sales volume.

Shortcomings. Break-even analysis provides a useful tool in many settings. It is only an indication to managerial action, however, not the ultimate answer. Some drawbacks to using break-even analysis are as follows:

1 The cost-volume-profit relationship is assumed to be linear—that is, variable cost per unit and price per unit are assumed to be the same for all relevant output levels. Over narrow ranges of output, this assumption may be reasonable.

2 A constant production and sales mix is assumed. Shifts in the production and sales mix require that new break-even points be found. This is true except for the rare case in which the variable cost-to-sales ratios are identical for all products.

3 The break-even chart and the break-even computation are static forms of analysis. Adjustments to the firm's cost structure or price structure require that a new break-even point be ascertained.

Operating Leverage

Operating leverage results from the presence of fixed operating costs in the firm's cost structure. We do *not* treat interest as a fixed operating expense. Operating leverage is most easily described in terms of what it does. It is the responsiveness of the firm's EBIT to changes in sales. Consider the income statement for Polaris Development Company shown in Table 11-1. The responsiveness of Polaris's EBIT to sales can be measured by considering the effect of a 10 percent increase in sales on EBIT. The appropriate calculations are found in Table 11-1. Note that the degree of operating leverage (DOL$_s$) is calculated for a given sales or output level (s). It is measured as the ratio of the percent change in EBIT resulting from a given percent change in sales. For Polaris the DOL $_{800,000}$ = 4.57. A 10 percent increase in sales will, therefore, lead to a 45.7 percent increase in EBIT. Correspondingly, a 10 percent drop in sales would cause EBIT to drop by 45.7 percent.

TABLE 11-1
CALCULATING THE DEGREE OF OPERATING LEVERAGE FOR POLARIS DEVELOPMENT COMPANY

Sales	$800,000	$880,000
Less: Variable costs	480,000	528,000
Revenue before fixed cost	$320,000	$352,000
Less: Fixed costs	250,000	250,000
EBIT	$ 70,000	$102,000

$$\text{Degree of operating leverage for sales level } s \text{ (DOL}_s) = \frac{\% \text{ change in EBIT}}{\% \text{ change in sales}}$$

Calculations for Polaris at sales of $800,000:

$$\text{DOL}_{\$800,000} = \frac{\$102,000 - 70,000}{\$70,000} \div \frac{\$880,000 - 800,000}{\$800,000} = \frac{0.457}{0.10} = \underline{4.57}$$

If unit-cost data are available, then DOL$_s$ can be calculated by using the following relationship:

$$DOL_s = \frac{Q(P - V)}{Q(P - V) - F}$$
(11-5)

where Q is the quantity corresponding to the sales volume represented by s, P is the price per unit, V is the variable cost per unit, and F is the total fixed cost. Applying equation (11-5) to the previous Polaris example, we can calculate DOL$_{800,000}$ as follows:

$$DOL_{800,000} = \frac{\$40,000(20 - 12)}{\$40,000(20 - 12) - 250,000} = 4.57$$

If unit cost and price data are unavailable, then equation (11-5) can be easily converted to a total-revenue and total-cost format by substituting S for total sales revenue ($P \times Q$) and VC for total variable cost ($V \times Q$):

$$DOL_s = \frac{S - VC}{(S - VC) - F}$$
(11-6)

Significance. As firm sales move above the break-even point, the degree of operating leverage at each higher sales base declines. The greater the sales level (above the break-even point), the lower will be the degree of operating leverage. This is demonstrated in Table 11-2 for the Polaris Development Corporation. At the break-even sales level for Polaris, the degree of operating leverage is undefined, since the denominator in any of the computational formulas is 0. Clearly, beyond the break-even point of 31,250 units, the degree of operating leverage declines. It will decline at a decreasing rate and approach a value of 1.00. As long as some fixed operating costs are present in the firm's cost structure, however, operating leverage exists and the degree of operating leverage (DOL$_s$) will exceed 1.00.

The greater the firm's degree of operating leverage, the greater its profits (EBIT) will vary with a given percentage change in sales. Operating leverage is a component of a firm's *business risk*. Next, we discuss financial leverage, which gives rise to *financial risk*.

TABLE 11-2
POLARIS DEVELOPMENT CORPORATION
DEGREE OF OPERATING LEVERAGE FOR
DIFFERENT SALES LEVELS

Units produced and sold	Sales dollars	DOL$_s$
31,250	$ 625,000	Undefined
35,000	700,000	9.33
40,000	800,000	4.57
50,000	1,000,000	2.67

FINANCIAL LEVERAGE

Financial leverage occurs when a portion of a firm's assets are financed with securities bearing a fixed rate of return. The objective is to increase the ultimate return flowing to the firm's common-equity investors. We now deal with the responsiveness of the company's earnings per share (EPS) to changes in its EBIT. This relationship can be measured by using the degree of financial leverage for a particular level of EBIT (DFL_{EBIT}). This is defined as follows:

$$DFL_{EBIT} = \frac{percent\ change\ in\ EPS}{percent\ change\ in\ EBIT} \qquad (11\text{-}7)$$

We illustrate DFL_{EBIT} for each of two alternative financing mixes being considered by the Polaris Development Corporation. Information pertinent to each of the financing mixes is contained in Table 11-3. The income-statement data used to illustrate the calculation of DFL_{EBIT} are found in Table 11-4.

Note that the DFL_{EBIT} is equal to 1.0 for all levels of EBIT for which it is defined under plan A, the 100 percent equity financing plan. Hence, a DFL_{EBIT} of 1 signals the absence of financial leverage. However, the DFL_{EBIT} for plan B (60 percent equity) demonstrates vividly the effects of financial leverage. For example, a 45.7 percent increase in EBIT from a level of $70,000 produces a 108 percent increase in EPS. Correspondingly, a similar decrease in EBIT would have resulted in a 108 percent decrease in EPS. Note that the DFL_{EBIT} declines as EBIT increases beyond the level at which EPS equals 0, just as the DOL_s decreased for higher levels of sales.

Instead of taking the time to compute percentage changes in EBIT and EPS, the degree of financial leverage can be found directly as follows:

$$DFL_{EBIT} = \frac{EBIT}{EBIT - I} \qquad (11\text{-}8)$$

See p. 334

TABLE 11-3
ALTERNATIVE FINANCING MIXES FOR THE POLARIS
DEVELOPMENT CORPORATION

		Plan A: 100 percent common equity	
		Total debt	$ 0
		Common equity[a]	1,000,000
Total assets	$1,000,000	Total liabilities and equity	$1,000,000

		Plan B: 60 percent common equity	
		Total debt[b]	$ 400,000
		Common equity[c]	600,000
Total assets	$1,000,000	Total liabilities and equity	$1,000,000

[a] 100,000 shares outstanding with a $10 par value.
[b] Interest cost is 10 percent per annum.
[c] 60,000 shares outstanding.

TABLE 11-4
CALCULATING DFL$_{EBIT}$ FOR POLARIS DEVELOPMENT CORPORATION

	Plan A				Plan B				
EBIT	$0	$40,000	$70,000	$102,000	$0	$40,000	$70,000	$102,000	$204,000
Less: Interest	0	0	0	0	(40,000)	(40,000)	(40,000)	(40,000)	(40,000)
EBT[a]	0	$40,000	$70,000	$102,000	$(40,000)	$ 0	$30,000	$ 62,000	$164,000
Less: Taxes[b]	0	(20,000)	(35,000)	(52,000)	20,000	0	(15,000)	(31,000)	(82,000)
Net Income	0	$20,000	$35,000	$ 52,000	$(20,000)[d]	$ 0	$15,000	$ 31,000	$ 82,000
EPS[c]	$0	$0.20	$0.35	$0.51	$(0.33)	$0	$0.25	$0.52	$1.37
%ΔEPS	Undefined	75%	45.7%		100%	Undefined	108%	163%	
%ΔEBIT	Undefined	75%	45.7%		Undefined	75%	45.7%	100%	
DFL$_{EBIT}$	Undefined	1.0	1.0		Undefined	Undefined	2.36	1.63	

[a] Earnings before taxes, or taxable income.
[b] Taxes are paid at a rate of 50 percent of EBT.
[c] EPS = net income ÷ common shares outstanding.
[d] The positive income tax credit recognizes the tax carry-forward and carry-back provision of the Internal Revenue Code.

333

where I represents the total interest expense incurred on all the firm's contractual debt obligations. If several bonds are outstanding, I is the sum of the interest expense on all of them. If the firm has preferred stock in its financial structure, the dividend payment on such issues must be inflated to a before-tax basis and included in the computation of I.[2] In this latter instance, I is in reality the sum of *all* fixed financing costs.

TOTAL LEVERAGE

Operating leverage causes a given percent change in sales revenues to produce an even greater percent change in EBIT. Financial leverage, in turn, causes changes in EBIT to effect larger variations in both EPS and total earnings available to the common shareholders. Accordingly, combining operating and financial leverage can cause large variations in EPS. This process is depicted in Figure 11-3. It is useful to quantify the effect.

To illustrate, we return to the Polaris Development Corporation data. We assume that Polaris has current sales revenues of $800,000 and utilizes financing plan B. The firm expects a 10 percent increase in sales next year. We wish to analyze the impact of these added sales on EPS.

Table 11-5 contains all the necessary information for assessing the firm's total leverage. We see that a mere 10 percent increase in firm sales produces a 45.7 percent increase in EBIT as a result of the firm's operating leverage. Because of its use of financial leverage, the 45.7 percent increase in EBIT produces a 108 percent increase in EPS. Hence, the firm's degree of total leverage for a given sales level (DTL$_s$) can be defined as follows:

$$DTL_s = \frac{\text{percent change in EPS}}{\text{percent change in sales}} \tag{11-9}$$

[2] Suppose that (1) preferred dividends of $1,000 are paid annually by the firm, and (2) it faces a 40 percent marginal tax rate. How much must the firm earn *before taxes* to make the $1,000 payment out of after-tax earnings? Since preferred dividends are not tax-deductible to the paying company, the answer is $1,000/(1 - 0.40) = $1,666.67.

FIGURE 11-3
Total leverage and the variability in earnings per share.

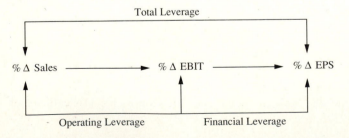

TABLE 11-5
POLARIS DEVELOPMENT CORPORATION TOTAL LEVERAGE ANALYSIS

	Current	Forecast for next year	Key percent changes
Sales	$800,000	$880,000	10 percent
Less: Variable costs	(480,000)	(528,000)	
Revenue before fixed costs	$320,000	$352,000	
Less: Fixed costs	(250,000)	(250,000)	
EBIT	$ 70,000	$102,000	45.7 percent
Less: interest	(40,000)	(40,000)	
EBT[a]	$ 30,000	$ 62,000	
Less: Taxes[b]	(15,000)	(31,000)	
Net income	$ 15,000	$ 31,000	
EPS[c]	$ 0.25	$ 0.52	108 percent

[a] Earnings before taxes, or taxable income.
[b] Taxes are paid at a rate of 50 percent of EBT.
[c] EPS = net income ÷ common shares outstanding.

For the situation depicted in Table 11-5, we find the following:

$$\text{DTL}_{800,000} = \frac{108 \text{ percent}}{10 \text{ percent}} = 10.8$$

For *any* percent change in sales from the existing $800,000 level, EPS will change by 10.8 times that percent change. For example, a 15 percent decrease in sales would produce a 10.8 × 15 percent = 162 percent reduction in EPS. Polaris's EPS are obviously very sensitive to variations in sales from the current $800,000 level.

Just as we were able to use an abbreviated equation for DOL_s and DFL_{EBIT}, we can do the same for DTL_s:

$$\text{DTL}_s = \frac{Q(P - V)}{Q(P - V) - F - I} \qquad (11\text{-}10)$$

where Q is the output quantity in units, P is the price per unit, V is the variable cost per unit, F is the total fixed costs, and I is the total interest expense. Where unit-cost information is unavailable, Equation (11-10a) can be used:

$$\text{DTL}_s = \frac{S - \text{VC}}{S - \text{VC} - F - I} \qquad (11\text{-}10a)$$

where S is the total sales revenue $(P \cdot Q)$, VC is the total variable cost $(V \cdot Q)$, and the remaining symbols retain their prior meanings.

The total risk of variability in EPS that a firm faces can be managed by combining various degrees of operating and financial leverage. Knowledge of these leverage measures assists the financial manager in the determination of the proper level of overall risk to assume. When a high degree of business risk is associated with a specific line of business activity, then a low level of financial risk would minimize additional earnings fluctuations caused by sales alterations. Alternatively, the firm that experiences a low level of fixed operating costs might opt to use a high degree of financial leverage in hopes of increasing earnings per share and the rate of return on the common-equity investment.

THE DEBT MATURITY FINANCING DECISION

The corporate financing decision has traditionally been addressed in terms of the choice among permanent or long-term sources of financing. This emphasis on permanent sources of funds overlooks a crucially important aspect of the firm's financing decisions, namely the maturity structure of the firm's debt financing. In practice, when a need for financing arises, the need may be satisfied using spontaneous, temporary and/or permanent sources of financing as the following list illustrates.

Spontaneous (i) the funding may be provided spontaneously as is the case when purchases of inventory are self-financed through the firm's trade credit terms;

Temporary (ii) the needed funds may be raised by short-term borrowing (e.g., drawing upon a line of credit agreement with a commercial bank);

Permanent (iii) the funds can be raised by arranging for a term loan of one or more years duration with a bank, insurance company or other lender;

(iv) the funding need can be met by issuing long-term debt or bonds;

(v) the necessary funds can be obtained by retaining a portion of the firm's earnings from past investments; or

(vi) the funds can be raised through the sale of equity securities (common or preferred stock).

In this section we will discuss the issues that arise with respect to the choice between short-term debt (temporary financing) and long-term debt (a form of permanent financing). Later we will address the question of the proper mix of long-term debt and owner (equity) financing.

The Advantages and Disadvantages of Short-Term Debt Financing

The Advantages of Short-Term Borrowing. There are two basic advantages which are generally associated with the use of short- as opposed to long-term debt financing. The first is flexibility and the second relates to interest cost. Short-term debt offers a more flexible means of raising needed funds, for it can be increased and decreased with greater ease than bonds. This follows from the fact that bonds are more expensive to issue (involving an investment banker) than short-term debt, and frequently include restrictions and penalties governing their early retirement.[3] Thus, if a firm needs

---

[3] We will discuss some of these restrictions in the Appendix to this chapter where we discuss the bond refunding decision.

financing for a short period of time, it can satisfy those needs more easily with the use of a short-term loan.

The lower cost of short-term financing follows from three factors. First, as we noted above, short-term debt can generally be issued at lower cost than long-term debt. Second, short-term debt can be increased and decreased in response to changing financial requirements, thus forcing the firm to incur financing costs only when funds are actually needed. Finally, the cost of short-term borrowing is generally lower (in percentage terms) than long-term debt. This latter point is reflective of the traditionally upward-sloping term structure of interest rates. For example, the term structure of interest rates facing a given firm might appear as follows:

Loan maturity	Interest rate
3 months	9.20%
6 months	9.25%
1 year	9.50%
3 years	10.00%
5 years	10.65%
10 years	11.25%
30 years	13.00%

These figures are, of course, hypothetical, but they reflect the notion of an upward-sloping set of interest rates for longer maturities.

The Disadvantages of Short-Term Borrowing.   The principal disadvantage associated with short- as opposed to long-term borrowing relates to the increased risk of illiquidity. In a very simplistic sense a firm faces the test of its liquidity every time that a payment of principal or interest comes due. If the firm utilizes short-term debt, then that test comes every time the debt *matures*, which is, by definition, more frequently than is the case with long-term borrowing. Consequently, the lower costs of short-term borrowing must be balanced against the increased risk of illiquidity.

In addition, the interest cost savings associated with short-term borrowing may evaporate if the short-term borrowing rate is higher than the long-term rate (a downward-sloping term structure) and the firm's need for funds turns out to be more permanent than temporary. This situation gives rise to a "risk of illiquidity" versus "cost of financing" tradeoff which we will use to characterize the firm's debt maturity choice problem.

Using the Hedging Principle
to Resolve the Debt Maturity Problem

The **hedging principle** provides a rule of thumb for solving the debt maturity problem. The principle suggests that the decision as to whether to use short- or long-term debt should be made in accordance with the type of asset being financed. Specifically, permanent needs for assets (both current and fixed assets) should be financed with long-term sources of financing, while a temporary need for an asset should be financed using a short-term source of financing.

Figure 11-4 illustrates the use of the hedging principle. In this example the firm's total financing needs are represented by the top line in the figure. These financing needs are composed of an increasing base of permanent assets represented by the top straight line, with a seasonal level of temporary assets superimposed. The hedging principle is followed exactly in this example, in that the firm never uses a temporary source of financing to meet a permanent financing need, and vice versa.

Figures 11-5 and 11-6 contain examples of deviations from the strict hedging principle. In Figure 11-5 a conservative financing strategy is followed whereby the firm uses more permanent financing than is needed to equal its permanent assets.[4] This means that during periods when the firm's temporary needs for financing are the least, the firm actually has more financing than it needs and thus has "financial slack". These slack resources must be invested in short-term marketable securities, since they will eventually be needed when the firm's seasonal needs for temporary financing increase.

The financing plan depicted in Figure 11-6 is an aggressive plan in that the firm continually relies on some level of temporary financing. Thus, even when the firm's financing needs are at their seasonal lows, the firm continues to rely on some level of short-term discretionary borrowing.[5] This plan is aggressive, in the sense that it minimizes the prospects of having idle financial resources (financial slack), which

[4] The shaded region of Figure 11-5 represents the firm's use of permanent plus spontaneous financing which is greater than its permanent asset financing requirements.

[5] The shaded area of Figure 11-6 depicts the firm's continuous reliance on short-term borrowing throughout its planning period.

FIGURE 11-4
The hedging principle.

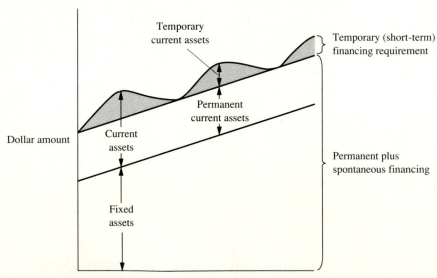

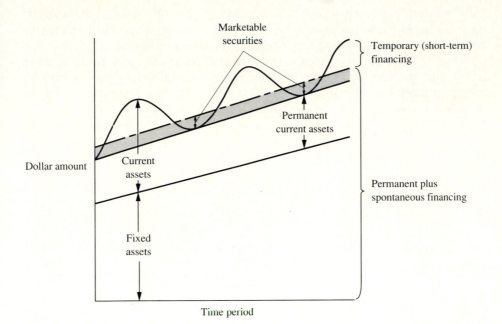

FIGURE 11-5
Conservative financing plan.

FIGURE 11-6
Aggressive financing plan.

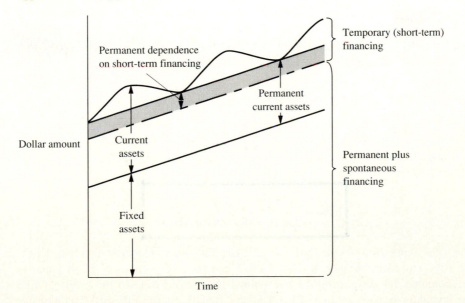

must be invested in low yielding marketable securities. On the other hand, however, this plan forces the firm to face a higher risk of illiquidity since the firm must be continually retiring and raising new funds from short-term sources.

Which of these strategies should a firm follow? In practice, the firm can never follow a perfect hedging strategy since the firm's future financing needs cannot be known with certainty. Thus, a firm will find itself with slack financial resources at times and continuing to rely on short-term borrowing for an extended period at other times. The key point to note here is that by attempting to match the nature (temporary or permanent) of the financing used to the nature of the asset being financed (temporary or permanent), the firm will minimize its risk of illiquidity.

CHOOSING THE APPROPRIATE FINANCING MIX

Selecting the best or optimal mix of financing sources should ideally be done in such a way as to maximize the value of the common shareholder's equity. However, as we noted in the chapter introduction, such an exercise is often technically impossible. Therefore, we suggest that the financial officer concentrate efforts in making financing decisions on the impact of such decisions on (1) the level of EPS, (2) the variability in those EPS, (3) the related risk of insolvency, and (4) the firm's financial condition in the eyes of its creditors.

Impact of the Financing Decision on the Level of EPS

This aspect of a financing decision can be analyzed by using an *EBIT-EPS chart* (or *range of earnings chart*). Very simply, the analyst plots EPS for each of several levels of EBIT corresponding to each alternative financing mix under consideration. The analyst then can use the plotted points to determine which financing mix produces the highest level of EPS at various levels of EBIT.

The relationship between EPS and EBIT is linear, since computing EPS from EBIT does not involve squaring, cubing, or otherwise raising EBIT to any power other than 1. Specifically, the EPS equation can be defined as follows:

$$EPS = \frac{EBIT - I - T(EBIT - I) - P}{\text{number of common shares}} \qquad (11\text{-}11)$$

where T is the firm's marginal tax rate, P is any preferred dividends the firm might owe, and the other symbols have their previous meanings. Equation (11-11) can be rewritten by combining terms and simplifying as follows:

$$EPS = \frac{(EBIT - I)(1 - T) - P}{\text{number of common shares}} \qquad (11\text{-}11a)$$

Using this expression, the analyst can calculate EPS for at least two levels of EBIT. The EPS and corresponding levels of EBIT can then be plotted on graph paper or the computer. By connecting the two points, the analyst can see the levels of EPS corresponding to a wide range of EBIT levels. Recall that the EPS-EBIT relationship

TABLE 11-6
EBIT-EPS DATA FOR POLARIS DEVELOPMENT CORPORATION

	Plan A (100 percent equity)		Plan B (60 Percent equity)	
EBIT	$70,000	$102,000	$70,000	$102,000
EPS	$0.35	$0.51	$0.25	$0.52

is a linear one, such that we need only plot two points to "affix" a plot of the relationship.

Consider the example of financial leverage presented earlier in Table 11-3. Polaris Development Corporation was considering two financing plans. Plan A involved 100 percent equity financing, while plan B was composed of 60 percent equity and 40 percent debt. Two levels of EPS for each alternative are presented in Table 11-6. Figure 11-7 contains the EBIT-EPS chart for Polaris. It appears that for all levels of EBIT higher than $100,000, plan B (60 percent equity) will produce higher EPS than plan A. Hence, if the firm anticipates EBIT levels of $100,000 or more, then its shareholders can expect to benefit from the use of financial leverage in the form of higher EPS.

A Word of Caution.   The main weakness of EBIT-EPS analysis is that it ignores the implicit cost of debt financing. The effect of the specific financing decision on the firm's cost of common-equity capital is not considered in this framework. Investors should be concerned with both the level and the variability of the firm's expected earnings stream. EBIT-EPS analysis dwells upon only the level of the earnings stream

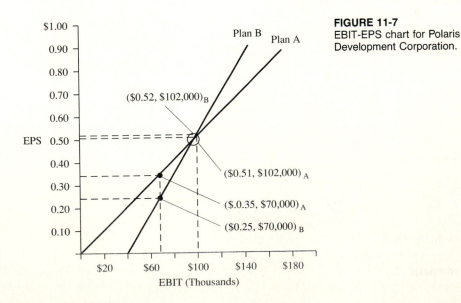

FIGURE 11-7
EBIT-EPS chart for Polaris Development Corporation.

and ignores the related variability in it. It is appropriate, then, to use this type of analysis with other fundamental tools in making prudent financing choices.

Impact of the Financing Decision on the Potential Variability in EPS

The EBIT-EPS chart can be used to evaluate the potential variability in EPS for alternative financing mixes. Consider the example presented in Figure 11-8. Farwell Enterprises is contemplating two financing mix alternatives: (1) 100 percent equity, and (2) 50 percent equity and 50 percent debt. The corresponding EBIT-EPS chart is found in Figure 11-5. Farwell anticipates EBIT will generally fall within the range of $50,000 to $100,000. For the 100 percent equity financing mix, this range of EBIT produces corresponding EPS levels of $0.50 to $1.00 per share. The 50 percent equity financing mix produces EPS of $0.20 to $1.40 for the same levels of EBIT. The analyst could further increase the sophistication of the analysis by assigning probabilities to the levels of EBIT. Next, we will consider a similar methodology in our discussion of the risk of insolvency incumbent to the use of financial leverage.

Impact of the Financing Decision on the Risk of Insolvency

Interest charges, preferred dividends, lease charges, and principal payments all must be paid on time, or the company risks being caught in bankruptcy proceedings. It is also true that dispensing with financing charges on an untimely basis can result in severely restricted business operations.

FIGURE 11-8
EBIT-EPS chart for Farwell Enterprises.

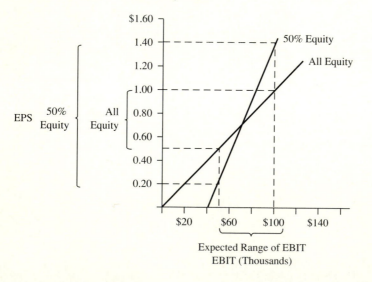

A comprehensive method is available for studying the impact of financing decisions on corporate cash flows and the risk of insolvency. It involves the preparation of several cash budgets under (1) different economic conditions, and (2) different financing mixes.[6] The net cash flows under these different situations can be examined to determine whether the financing requirements expose the firm to an unreasonable degree of insolvency risk.

Donaldson has suggested that the firm's *debt-carrying capacity* (defined in the broad sense here to include preferred dividend payments and lease payments) ought to depend upon the net cash flows that the firm could expect to receive during a recessionary period.[7]

For example, suppose that a recession is expected to last for one year.[8] Further, the end of the year represents the worst portion of the recession. Equation (11-12) defines the cash balance (CB_r) that the firm can expect to have at the end of the recession period:[9]

$$CB_r = CB_0 + (C_s + OR) - (P_a + RM + \cdots + E_n) - FC \qquad (11\text{-}12)$$

where CB_0 is the cash balance at the beginning of the recession, C_s is the collection from sales, OR is other cash receipts, P_a is payroll expenditures, RM is raw material payments, E_n is the last of a long series of expenditures over which management has little control (*nondiscretionary* expenditures), and FC is fixed financial charges associated with a specific capital structure. The net of total cash receipts and nondiscretionary expenditures can be represented by NCF_r. This simplifies Equation (11-12) to

$$CB_r = CB_0 + NCF_r - FC \qquad (11\text{-}13)$$

The inputs to Equation (11-13) come from the firm's cash budget. The variable representing financing costs (FC) can be changed to agree with several alternative financing plans. This allows the analyst to determine whether the net cash balance during the recession (CB_r) might fall below 0.

Suppose that firm policy specifies that $1,000,000 in cash and marketable securities be maintained. This amount is on hand at the start of the recession period. As economic conditions deteriorate, the firm projects that its net cash flows from operations (NCF_r) will be $4,000,000. Assume that the firm currently finances its assets with an unlevered capital structure, so that its cash balance at the worst point of the

---

[6] Cash-budget preparation was discussed in Chapter 3.

[7] See Gordon Donaldson: "New Framework for Corporate Debt Policy," *Harvard Business Review*, vol. 40 (March–April 1962) 117–131; *Corporate Debt Capacity*, Cambridge, MA: Harvard University, 1961; Chap. 7; "Strategy for Financial Emergencies," *Harvard Business Review*, vol. 47 (November–December 1969) 67–79.

[8] The analysis can readily be extended to cover a recessionary period of several years. All that is necessary is to calculate the cash budget over a similar period.

[9] For the most part, the present notation follows that of Donaldson.

recession will be as follows:

$$CB_r = \$1,000,000 + \$4,000,000 - \$0 = \$5,000,000$$

This procedure allows many different situations to be studied.[10] Assume that the same firm is considering a capital-structure change such that annual interest and sinking fund payments will be \$4,600,000. If a recession occurs, the firm's cash balance at the end of the period will be as follows:

$$CB_r = \$1,000,000 + \$4,000,000 - \$4,600,000 = \$400,000$$

The firm ordinarily maintains a liquid-asset balance of \$1,000,000. Hence, the effect of the proposed capital structure shift on the firm's cash balance might seem too risky for management to endure.

Impact of the Financing Decision on the Firm's Creditworthiness

The firm's decisions regarding its financing mix will have an effect on its credit status. This creditworthiness, in turn, affects the cost and availability of credit to the firm. Specifically, creditors often use financial ratios which reflect the use of financial leverage to assess a firm's ability to pay its bills on time. One aspect that should be considered in selecting a financing mix is looking at the firm's leverage ratios in relation to other firms in its industry.

Comparative Leverage Ratios.   In Chapter 2 we studied the usefulness of financial-ratio analysis. Leverage ratios were one of the categories of financial ratios identified in that chapter. In the present setting, the computation of leverage ratios becomes one of the basic tools for analyzing financing decisions.

Two types of leverage ratios must be computed when a financing decision faces a firm. These are known as **balance-sheet leverage ratios** and **coverage ratios**. To calculate the balance-sheet leverage ratios, one must consult the firm's balance sheet. Generally, these measurements compare the firm's use of funds supplied by creditors with its use of those supplied by owners.

Inputs to the coverage ratios *generally* come from the firm's income statement. At times the external analyst may have to consult balance-sheet information to construct some of these needed estimates. On a privately placed debt issue, for example, some fraction of the current portion of the firm's long-term debt may have to be used as an estimate of the issue's sinking fund. Coverage ratios provide estimates of the

---

[10] It is not difficult to improve the usefulness of this sort of analysis by applying the technique of simulation to the generation of the various cash budgets. This facilitates the construction of probability distributions of net cash flows under differing circumstances.

firm's ability to service its financing contracts. High coverage ratios, compared with a standard, imply unused debt capacity.

Industry Practice.   Comparative leverage ratios have more usefulness to the decision maker if they can be compared with some standard. Typically, corporate financial analysts, investment bankers, commercial-bank loan officers, and bond-rating agencies rely upon industry classes from which to compute "normal" ratios. Although industry groupings may actually contain firms whose basic business-risk exposure differs widely, the aforementioned practice seems embedded in U.S. business behavior.[11] From another position, the financial officer should be interested in industry standards because almost everybody else is.

Several studies have been published which indicate that capital-structure ratios vary in a significant manner among industry classes.[12] For example, random samplings of the common-equity ratios of large retail firms seem to differ statistically from those of major steel producers. The major steel producers use financial leverage to a lesser degree than do the large retail organizations. On the whole, firms operating in the same industry tend to exhibit capital structure ratios that cluster around a central value, which we call a *norm*. Business risk will vary from industry to industry. As a consequence, the capital-structure norms will vary from industry to industry.

This is not to say that all companies in the industry will maintain leverage ratios close to the norm. There will always be outliers. For instance, firms that are very profitable may display high coverage ratios and high balance-sheet leverage ratios. The moderately profitable firm, though, may find such a posture unduly risky. It is in this regard that the usefulness of industry-normal leverage ratios is clear. If the firm chooses to deviate in a material manner from the accepted value for the key ratios, then it must have a sound reason for doing so.

THE COST OF FINANCING IN PRACTICE

Professors Blume, Friend and Westerfield of the Wharton School at the University of Pennsylvania surveyed the 100 largest corporations on the New York Stock Exchange to find out what they estimated their cost of capital to be. The results of that survey are reported in Table 11-7.

Of the firms that were surveyed 30 responded, including 10 public utilities and 20 nonfinancial corporations. The figures contained in the exhibit reflect a lower

---

[11] An approach to grouping firms on the basis of several component measures of business risk, as opposed to ordinary industry classes, is reported in John D. Martin, David F. Scott, Jr., and Robert F. Vandell: "Equivalent Risk Classes: A Multidimensional Examination," *Journal of Financial and Quantitative Analysis*, vol. 14 (March 1979), 101–118.

[12] See, for example, Eli Schwartz and J. Richard Aronson: "Some Surrogate Evidence in Support of the Concept of Optimal Financial Structure," *Journal of Finance*, vol. 22 (March 1967) 10–18; David F. Scott, Jr.: "Evidence on the Importance of Financial Structure," *Financial Management*, vol. 1 (Summer 1972) 45–50; David F. Scott, Jr., and John D. Martin: "Industry Influence on Financial Structure," *Financial Management*, vol. 4 (Spring 1975) 67–73.

TABLE 11-7

A SURVEY OF THE AVERAGE COSTS OF CAPITAL AND CUTOFF RATES FOR NEW INVESTMENT

Industries	Before-tax cost-of-debt (%)	After-tax cost (%)				After-tax cutoff rate for plant and equipment investments	
		New common equity	Retained earnings	Debt	Weighted cost	Least risky	Most risky
All industries	12.5%	17.2%	16.6%	6.4%	12.4%	12.9%	19.6%
All industries except public utilities	12.5	17.8	17.0	6.3	13.1	13.1	20.3

Source: Marshall E. Blume, Irwin Friend, and Randolph Westerfield, "Impediments to Capital Formation: Summary Report of a Survey of Nonfinacial Corporations," Working Paper, Wharton School, University of Pennsylvania, 1980, p. 6.

cost of capital for the lower risk utilities. Furthermore, the estimated before-tax cost of debt financing was some five percentage points less than common stock. It is also interesting to note that the estimates of the after-tax average cost of capital is around 12–13 percent while the after-tax cutoff rate for new investments ranges from about 13 to 20 percent. Either these firms are imposing capital rationing in their financing investment decisions, or they are assigning a positive "estimation risk premium" to new investments. That is, the estimated cost of capital is roughly 13 percent but management is not willing to accept projects which offer minimal premiums over this estimated cost, either due to problems associated with estimating the cost of capital, the rate of return on new investments, or both. It is also possible that the cost of capital estimates reflected in Table 11-7 do not reflect high risk projects that the firms consider, but only average risk projects.

CHAPTER SUMMARY

This chapter presented the basic tools which can be used in analyzing a firm's financing decisions. We have discussed two fundamental problems that arise in determining the mix of funds a firm should use. The first of these problems relates to the use of short-term or long-term debt financing. This problem was discussed as the debt maturity financing decision and the guiding paradigm for its analysis was the hedging principle. The second problem related to the choice of the mix of long-term debt and equity financing. This latter problem is generally referred to as the capital structure problem. Financing decisions determine the firm's exposure to financial risk, which, in conjunction with business risk, determines the overall risk of the firm. Operating leverage was identified as a key element of a firm's business-risk exposure. Operating leverage results from the presence of fixed operating expenses in the firm's cost structure. Both break-even analysis and the degree of operating leverage were found to be useful techniques for assessing a firm's operating leverage.

Financial leverage results from the use of sources of financing that require a fixed return, such as debt or preferred stock. We measured the impact of financial leverage on the variability in EPS by using the concept of the degree of financial leverage. Both financial and operating leverage were shown to combine to determine a firm's total leverage. The degree of total leverage was then developed to measure the responsiveness of EPS to changes in firm sales. Each of these leverage concepts provides the basis for understanding the impact of the firm's financing decisions on the level and riskiness of the earnings made available to the owners of the firm.

Although financing decisions should theoretically be made in such a way as to maximize the value of the firm's outstanding common stock, this is most difficult to do directly. Rather, the analyst is forced to rely on an indirect analysis of the financing decision's impact on share value. Specifically, we addressed the impact of the financing decision on (1) the level of the firm's EPS, (2) the volatility in EPS, (3) the risk of insolvency, and (4) the firm's credit status as viewed by its creditors.

PROBLEMS

11-1 Which of the following firms has the greatest business risk:

	Stark	Topper	Watkins	Young
EBIT	$2,000,000	$3,000,000	$40,000,000	$50,000,000
S. D.	400,000	500,000	4,500,000	7,000,000

11-2 Last year Yager Stationery sold pens for $8 with variable cost of $5 and fixed costs of $50,000. How many pens must Yager sell this year to achieve the breakeven level
  a if all figures remain the same?
  b if only fixed costs increase, to $55,000?
  c if only variable costs increase, to $5.30?
  d if only selling price increases, to $8.50?

11-3 Galt Engineering has an average selling price of $2 per unit and variable costs of $1.30 per unit. Fixed costs are $20,000. Four thousand shares of common stock were issued to finance Galt's assets. Galt's major competitor, Holcombe, Inc., operates with identical financial data except that it has 2,000 shares of outstanding common stock and $2,500 of annual interest on its debt obligations. Both firms use a 50% tax rate. At an $80,000 sales level, determine for each firm
  a the degree of operating leverage *p. 330*
  b the degree of financial leverage *p. 332*
  c the degree of total leverage. *p. 334*

11-4 Benton Art Galleries plans an expansion of its facilities. Projections for additional income under two economic conditions are listed below. Benton will finance the entire expansion with a bond issue, leaving their outstanding common stock at 200,000 shares.

	Current	Condition A	Condition B
EBIT	$70,000	$125,000	$150,000
− Interest	20,000	25,000	25,000
EBT	50,000	100,000	125,000
− Taxes	25,000	50,000	62,500
NI	25,000	50,000	62,500

  a Determine the EPS for each net income level.
  b Using the percent change formula, what is the degree of financial leverage for each of the considered economic conditions?

11-5 Starling Meats has a current sales level of $450,000 with variable costs amounting to 70 percent of sales and fixed costs of $50,000. Its capital structure includes debt with annual interest payments of $10,000 and 100,000 shares of common stock. Starling's tax rate is 50%
  a Determine the degree of total leverage.
  b Determine the new EPS if sales:

increased 15%
increased 20%
decreased 5%
decreased 20%

11-6 A firm producing a single product selling for $5 has a variable cost of $3 per unit at the 10,000 unit production level. A 10% operating profit margin (EBIT/Sales) is targeted.

    a What is the maximum amount of fixed cost the firm can carry to meet this target?

    b Assuming a cost structure consistent with a 10,000 unit production level, what is the breakeven quantity?

11-7 The Hobson Manufacturing Company produces and sells one product, the Sempert Butterfly valve. The valve is widely used in the oil industry to control well head gas pressure. Each unit sells for $100, and the firm estimates that its fixed operating expenses equal $50,000, with total variable costs of $60,000, when the firm produces 1,000 valve units.

    a What is the firm's net operating income (EBIT) for 800 units? For 1,800 units?

    b Determine Hobson's break-even level of output in units.

    c What is Hobson's break-even sales level?

    d If Hobson purchases a plating machine for $20,000, it will incur added fixed costs of $10,000 per year, but its variable cost per unit will drop to $57. What will be Hobson's new break-even sales volume?

11-8 Using the information in problem 11-7, calculate Hobson's degree of operating leverage for sales equal to $125,000, $160,000 and $200,000.

11-9 The Hobson Manufacturing Company (from problem 11-7) plans to finance its assets by using $100,000 in debt, carrying a 10 percent rate of interest, and 10,000 shares of common stock with a total value of $100,000. Hobson pays taxes at a rate of 20 percent.

    a For an EBIT of $14,000, what will be Hobson's earnings per share (EPS)? For an EBIT of $78,000?

    b Calculate Hobson's degree of financial leverage for an EBIT of $14,000.

    c What is Hobson's degree of total leverage for a sales level of $320,000?

    d If Hobson's current sales are $320,000 and the firm anticipates a 20 percent decline in sales, what percent drop in EPS should result?

11-10 The Orwell Development Company (ODC) plans to raise an additional $4 million in new capital during the coming year to defray the cost of new capital expenditures. ODC's present financial structure consists of $8 million in 6 percent bonds and 100,000 shares of common stock with a current market price of $50 per share. ODC has three alternative financing plans in mind (assume no retained earnings will be available):

Plan A: 100 percent common stock
Plan B: 50 percent bonds carrying an 8 percent rate of interest
Plan C: 100 percent bonds carrying a 10 percent rate of interest

    a Calculate ODC's EPS for each financing plan for EBIT levels of $1 million and $2 million. ODC pays taxes at a rate of 50 percent. p. 340 (example p. 341)

    b Plot the EBIT-EPS relationship for all three financing plans.

    c On the basis of the information gained in (b), which plan should ODC select?

    d What are the limitations of EBIT-EPS analyses of the financing decision? p 341

11-11 The Orwell Development Company (from problem 11-10) typically maintains a cash balance of $60,000. Further, ODC estimates that during a recessionary period its net cash flow from operations (NCF_r) will be $800,000. Evaluate each of the financing plans discussed in problem 11-10, using Donaldson's debt-capacity model.

REFERENCES

Bowen, Robert M., Lane A. Daley, and Charles C. Huber, Jr.: "Evidence on the Existence and Determinants of Inter-Industry Differences in Leverage," *Financial Management*, vol. 11, Winter 1982, pp. 10–20.

Brigham, Eugene F., and T. Craig Tapley: "Financial Leverage and Use of the Net Present Value Investment Criterion: A Reexamination," *Financial Management*, vol. 14, Summer 1985, pp. 48–52.

Clark, John J., Margaret T. Clark, and Andrew G. Verzilli: "Strategic Planning and Sustainable Growth," *Columbia Journal of World Business*, vol. 20, Fall 1985, p. 51.

Donaldson, Gordon: "Strategy for Financial Emergencies," *Harvard Business Review*, vol. 47, November–December 1969, pp. 67–79.

Donaldson, Gordon: "New Framework for Corporate Debt Policy," *Harvard Business Review*, vol. 40, March–April 1962, pp. 117–131.

Ellis, Charles D.: "New Framework for Analyzing Capital Structure," *Financial Executive*, vol. 37, April 1969, pp. 75–86.

Gahlon, James M., and James A. Gentry: "On the Relationship Between Systematic Risk and the Degrees of Operating and Financial Leverage," *Financial Management*, vol. 11, Summer 1982, pp. 15–23.

Golbe, Devra L., and Barry Schachater: "The Net Present Value Rule and an Algorithm for Maintaining a Constant Debt-Equity Ratio," *Financial Management*, vol. 14, Summer 1985, pp. 53–58.

Greenfield, Robert L., Maury R. Randall, and John C. Woods: "Financial Leverage and Use of the Net Present Value Criterion," *Financial Management*, vol. 12, Autumn 1983, pp. 40–44.

Harris, John M., Jr., Rodney L. Roenfeldt, and Philip L. Cooley: "Evidence of Financial Leverage Clienteles," *Journal of Finance*, vol. 38, September 1983, pp. 1125–1132.

Jaedicke, Robert K., and Alexander A. Robichek: "Cost-Volume-Profit Analysis under Conditions of Uncertainty," *Accounting Review*, vol. 39, October 1964, pp. 917–926.

Joseph, Frederick (Reported by Marvin A. Chatinover): "Why Capital Structure May Never Be the Same Again—And Shouldn't Be," *FE*, vol. 2, October 1986, pp. 24–29.

Kane, Alex, Alan J. Marcus, and Robert L. McDonald: "Debt Policy and the Rate of Return Premium to Leverage," *Journal of Financial and Quantitative Analysis*, vol. 20, December 1985, pp. 479–499.

Martin, John D., David F. Scott, Jr., and Robert F. Vandell: "Equivalent Risk Classes: A Multidimensional Examination," *Journal of Financial and Quantitative Analysis*, vol. 14, March 1979, pp. 101–118.

McConoughey, Deborah J.: "Breakeven Analysis for Maturity Decisions in Cash Management," *Journal of Cash Management*, vol. 5, January–February 1985, pp. 18–21.

Miller, Merton H.: "Debt and Taxes," *Journal of Finance*, vol. 32, May 1977, pp. 261–297.

Piper, Thomas R., and Wolf A. Weinhold: "How Much Debt Is Right for Your Company?" *Harvard Business Review*, vol. 60, July–August 1982, pp. 106–114.

Schwartz, Eli, and J. Richard Aronson: "Some Surrogate Evidence in Support of the Concept of Optimal Capital Structure," *Journal of Finance*, vol. 22, March 1967, pp. 10–18.

Scott, David F., Jr.: "Evidence on the Importance of Financial Structure," *Financial Management*, vol. 1, Summer 1972, pp. 45–50.

Scott, David F., Jr., and Dana J. Johnson: "Financing Policies and Practices in Large Corporations," *Financial Management*, vol. 11, Summer 1982, pp. 51–59.

Scott, David F., Jr., and John D. Martin: "Industry Influence on Financial Structure," *Financial Management*, vol. 4, Spring 1975, pp. 67–73.

Senbet, Lemma A., and Robert A. Taggart, Jr.: "Capital Structure Equilibrium under Market Imperfections and Incompleteness," *Journal of Finance*, vol. 39, March 1984, pp. 93–103.

Shashua, Leon, and Yaaqov Goldschmidt: "Break-even Analysis Under Inflation," *Engineering Economist*, vol. 32, Winter 1987, pp. 79–88.

Taggart, Robert A.: "Corporate Financing: Too Much Debt?" *Financial Analysts Journal*, vol. 41, May–June 1986, pp. 35–42.

Walsh, Francis J., Jr.: *Planning Corporate Capital Structures* (New York: The Conference Board, Inc., 1972).

APPENDIX:
Debt Refunding

All firms that use nonconvertible, long-term debt are eventually faced with paying it off, either at maturity or beforehand. If the funds used to make the payoff come from the sale of another long-term debt issue, the entire operation is known as *debt refunding*, or simply refunding. Firms sometimes refund their debt in order to get rid of a particular feature of the debt contract which management considers undesirable, for example, a covenant which unduly restricts additional debt issues. Most cases of refunding before maturity, however, occur because management desires to take advantage of a decline in interest rates. The latter topic is our principal concern here.

In effect, refunding is an exchange of an outstanding long-term security issue for a new one. In the case of widely held corporate bonds, the exchange is almost always indirect, in that the company sells the new issue and then retires the old one from the proceeds of the sale. As indicated above, in the type of refunding with which we are primarily concerned, the objective is to reduce the interest rate on long-term debt financing.

The procedures for the evaluation of a proposed refunding of a bond issue will be presented in the following section. Both full (complete) and partial refunding will be considered.

Evaluation of Full Debt Refunding.   In a full refunding operation, the new (refunding) bonds have the same future cash flows as the old (refunded) bonds. Thus, both bond issues would have the same risk for the company in the future. The company's risk is affected only to the extent that the refunding operation affects the current amount of cash available for use elsewhere. If the operation is to be beneficial to the firm and its stockholders, the exchange of the new issue for the old one must provide additional cash at the time of the exchange.

Structuring the New Bonds.   In evaluating a refunding operation, we assume that a tax saving is equivalent to a cash inflow, and that the risk associated with changes in tax payments is the same as the risk associated with changes in interest charges. The first step in evaluating a proposed refunding is to determine the structure of the new bonds that will exactly replicate the future cash flows of the old bonds. The process can best be illustrated by an example. Assume that the XYZ Company has a $10 million bond issue outstanding with the following features:

Par	$10,000,000
Coupon rate	10 percent
Maturity	in 20 years
Call price	108
Unamortized discount	$80,000
Unamortized issue expenses	$120,000

We assume that interest is paid annually and that the firm's tax rate is 34 percent. The annual cash outflows of the bonds after taxes for the next 19 years will be as follows:

Interest	$1,000,000
Tax adjustments:	
From interest	(340,000)
From amortization of discount	(1,360)
From amortization of issue expenses	(2,040)
Net cash outflow	$ 656,600

In the cash flow calculations above, the tax savings from amortizing the debt discount and issue expenses were determined by dividing the total amount of each account by the number of years to maturity, and then multiplying the result by the firm's tax rate. For example, the annual tax saving from amortizing the discount was determined as follows: 0.34($80,000/20) = $1,360. Note that if there had been an unamortized premium rather than a discount on the bonds, the amortization would have produced a tax increase for the firm.

The net cash flow of the bonds in the twentieth year would include both the annual cash flow as figured above plus the maturity value of the bonds. Since the maturity value will be the par value of the bonds, the total cash outflow in the twentieth year will be: $656,600 + $10,000,000 = $10,656,600.

Now assume that interest rates have declined to the point that similar bonds with the same risk are currently yielding 8 percent. The market price of a 10 percent, $10 million bond issue of this quality with 20 years to maturity would be $11,963,629, if the market price is not held down because of a lower call price. Let us determine if refunding the bonds would be financially beneficial to the firm and its stockholders. The first step is to determine the structure of a new bond issue which will replicate the future cash flows of the old bonds.

The simplest decision concerns the life of the new bonds; it must be the same as that of the old bonds, that is, 20 years. Another simple decision concerns the par value of the new bond issue. Since its maturity value will be its par value, and since a $10 million maturity value must be added to the other cash outflows in the terminal year, the total par value of the new bonds must be $10 million.

Determination of the appropriate coupon rate for the new bonds requires a little arithmetic. We know that the annual cash outflows from interest and tax adjustments must be $656,600. A complicating factor arises at this point because the annual writeoffs of issue expenses, and any premium or discount, will probably not be the same for the two bond issues. Thus, we must first determine what the annual writeoffs and their tax effects will be for the new bonds. We can then adjust the coupon rate so that the net cash outflows will be the same as those of the old bonds.

If the new bonds have the same cash flows in the future as the old bonds, the new bonds will have an expected market value of $11,963,629. This figure is found by discounting the cash flows back to time zero at an 8 percent rate. Since the par value of the new bonds will be $10 million, the new issue will result in a total premium of $1,963,629. Let us also assume that the underwriters' (investment bankers') spread is expected to be $150,000 and that the firm will incur other expenses of $100,000 from refunding the old issue. The annual tax effects on cash flows from amortizing the bond premium and the two expense items over a 20-year period will be as follows:

Annual tax effects from premium amortization:
0.34($1,963,629/20) = $(33,382)
Annual tax effects from amortization
of underwriters' spread: 0.34($150,000/20) =   2,550
Annual tax effects from amortization
of other issue expenses: 0.34($100,000/20) =   1,700
                                                             $(29,132)

The calculations above indicate that the net effects of the amortizations will be an annual cash outflow of $29,132. Armed with the information we now have available, we can calculate the required coupon rate on the new bonds. Since the net cash outflow on the old bonds is $656,600, the after-tax interest on the new bonds must be $656,600 less the net tax increase of $29,132 from the premium and other expense writeoffs, or $656,600 − $29,132 = $627,468. Dividing the latter figure by 1 minus the tax rate provides the before-tax interest required: $627,468/(1 − 0.34) = $950,709. Finally, the coupon rate on the new bonds will be $950,709 divided by the par value of the bonds: $950,709/$10,000,000 = 9.50709 percent. Given the tax effects of the premium and expense writeoffs, a coupon rate of 9.50709 on a new $10 million bond issue with a twenty-year maturity will produce exactly the same cash flows in the future as the company's outstanding bonds. Thus, the company should refund if the result is additional cash for the firm at the time of the refunding.

Determination of Benefits. The cash outlays at time zero will include the amount paid in calling the old bonds, the issue expenses on the new bonds, the net overlapping interest, and the tax payment required from immediately writing off any unamortized premium on the old bonds. In our example, the old bonds did not have an unamortized premium.

The overlapping interest is the interest paid on the old issue during the period of time both it and the new issue are outstanding concurrently. The reason why both issues will be outstanding concurrently for a short period of time is that the company will not call the old bonds until proceeds of the new issue are assured. This will occur when the underwriting agreement is signed. The call for the old bonds will then be made; usually bondholders are given either thirty or sixty days to turn in their old bonds, during which time the company must pay interest on them. Since interest on the new bonds begins at the time the underwriting agreement is signed, the company pays interest on both issues until the old bonds are turned in. The interest on the old bonds during this overlap period is considered an expense of the refunding.

However, the company will have the proceeds from the sale of the new issue during the overlap period. These funds can be invested in treasury bills during the period at very low or no risk. The return from this investment is netted against the interest the company must pay on the old issue during the overlap period to obtain the net overlapping interest.[1] We assume for our example that the annual yield on treasury bills is 6 percent. Thus, the annual rate of the net overlapping interest is 10 percent minus 6 percent, or 4 percent, although the interest will be incurred only during the overlap period. We will assume the overlap period in our hypothetical refunding example to be one month. The net overlapping interest the firm would have to pay would be: ($10,000,000 × 0.04)/12 months = $33,333.

The cash inflows at time zero include the sale price of the new bonds plus the tax saving from the following items:

  Call premium on the old bonds
  Overlapping interest
  Complete writeoff of any unamortized discount on the old bonds
  Complete writeoff of any unamortized issue expenses on the old bonds

The issue expenses on the new bonds are not tax deductible at time zero; they are written off over the life of the bonds for tax purposes. The cash flows at time zero can now be determined as follows:

Call price on old bonds		($10,800,000)
Issue expenses of new bonds:		
Underwriters' spread	$150,000	
Other	100,000	
Total		(250,000)
Net overlapping interest		(33,333)
Tax adjustments on:		
Call premium	$800,000	
Net overlapping interest	33,333	
Unamortized discount of old bonds	80,000	
Unamortized issue expenses of old bonds . . .	120,000	
Total	$1,033,333	
Total tax savings @ 34% rate		351,333
Sale price of new bond issue		11,963,629
Net benefit		$1,231,629

The above results indicate that the net effect of the refunding will be to increase the firm's cash by $1,231,629. Clearly, the refunding will be financially beneficial to the firm. However, this fact does not necessarily mean that the refunding proposal should be accepted. If interest rates are expected to decline further in the future, management may decide to delay. The question that must be answered before a final decision is made is whether the risk of losing some or all of the currently available benefits from a possible increase in interest rates is worth the chance of additional gains if interest rates decline further in the future.

In our discussion of refunding evaluation to this point, we have been concerned with full, or complete, refunding in which the future cash flows of the new bonds were set equal to the future flows of the old bonds. In many cases, however, a corporation will make the par of

---

[1] Theoretically, the net overlapping interest should be time adjusted back to time zero in the evaluation of refunding. However, since the time adjustment in this case will have very little impact on the net benefit from refunding, it is usually ignored by analysts.

the new issue the same as that of the old, but will set the coupon on the new issue equal, or approximately equal, to the yield to maturity at which the new bonds are sold. The result will be that the future cash flows and market price will be less for the new bonds than for the old. Thus, the operation is only a partial refunding of the old issue, a topic we will consider below.

The Evaluation of Partial Refunding   As indicated above, in this type of refunding, the par values of the new and old bond issues will be the same, and the coupon rate will be set at, or very close to, the yield on the new issue when it is initially sold. The result will be to complicate the evaluation of a proposed refunding because the future cash outlays as well as the market value of the firm's bonds will be reduced.

The evaluation of refunding in this case is essentially a capital budgeting decision. The refunding expenses make up the investment, and the reduction in future cash flows are the net cash benefits. The net present value of the operation is then determined in the usual way, by subtracting the present value of future cash benefits from the investment outlay. If the net present value is positive (negative) the refunding will be expected to increase (decrease) the market value of the firm's common stock.

As an illustration, we will again assume that a company has outstanding a $10,000,000 bond issue with a coupon of 10 percent and a maturity in twenty years. Interest rates have fallen, and the company can replace the old issue with a new one sold to yield 8 percent, if it has a $10,000,000 par value, 8 percent coupon, and 20-year maturity. Note that since the issue will have a coupon rate equal to its yield, it can be sold for a price equal to its par value. The other characteristics of the two bonds are the same as in the previous case and are shown below for the convenience of the reader:

Old bonds:	
Call price	108
Unamortized discount	$80,000
Unamortized issue expenses	$120,000
New bonds:	
Underwriters' spread	$150,000
Other issue expenses	$100,000

We continue to assume annual interest payments, a 34 percent tax rate, and net overlapping interest of $33,333 for one month. The refunding investment will include the net cash outlays that are incurred at time zero to call in the old bonds and sell the new ones:

Call premium of old bonds		$800,000
Net overlapping interest		33,333
Total issue expenses of new bonds		250,000
Tax adjustments on:		
Call premium on old bonds	$800,000	
Net overlapping interest	33,333	
Unamortized discount on old bonds	80,000	
Unamortized issue expenses on old bonds	120,000	
Total deductible	$1,033,333	
Total tax saving @ 34% rate		(351,333)
Net refunding investment		$732,000

The annual net cash benefit will include the net interest saving plus the tax adjustments on the net difference in expense writeoffs on the two issues:

Interest on old bonds	$1,000,000	
Less interest on new bonds	(800,000)	
Interest saving before tax	$200,000	
Interest saving after tax		$132,000
Annual writeoffs on new bonds:		
Underwriters' spread	7,500	
Other issue expenses	5,000	
Total	$12,500	
Annual writeoffs on old bonds:		
Discount	$4,000	
Issue expenses	6,000	
Total	$10,000	
Increase in writeoff	$2,500	
Tax saving from increase in		
writeoff, @ 34% rate		850
Net cash benefit		$132,850

The next step in the evaluation is to determine the present value (PV) of the net cash benefits (NCBs). Although the discount rate that should be used to make the time adjustments is a controversial topic, we believe the yield on the new bonds should be used. Thus, the PV of the NCBs can be calculated as follows:

$$\text{PV of future NCBs} = \sum_{t=1}^{20} \frac{\$132,850}{(1.08)^t}$$

$$= \$1,304,341$$

The final step in the analysis is to calculate the net present value (NPV) from the refunding by subtracting the investment outlay from the present value of the future net cash benefits:

$$\text{NPV} = \$1,304,341 - \$732,000$$

$$= \$572,341$$

Thus, the net present value from the partial refunding is estimated at $572,341. This figure is less than the net benefit in the full refunding example. Although the difference in the net benefits will always depend upon the expenses and other cash flows in the particular case, the benefits from full refunding should be the greater because, in that case, the firm is taking advantage of the decline in interest rates to a greater extent.

One final point should be made in respect to partial refunding. Since the company's interest charges and the market value of its bonds have both been reduced, the capital structure has been changed. In effect, the company is using leverage capital to a lesser extent than before the refunding. The effect of this change may cause the firm's cost of capital to change, although it is difficult to generalize about the direction of the change. If the company's capital structure was optimum before the refunding, the effect of the change in the capital structure will probably be to raise the cost of capital from what it would be otherwise. However, regardless of the effect of the capital structure change, the overall effect of the refunding operation will be to lower the cost of capital because the firm's cost of debt financing will be reduced.

PROBLEMS

1 Seaboard-Western Gas Transmission, Inc., is investigating the possibility of refunding the company's Series A First Mortgage Bonds. Both a partial and a full refunding are being considered. The following data have been compiled in the study:

	Old bonds	New bonds[a]	New bonds[b]
Par value	$20,000,000	$20,000,000	$20,000,000
Coupon rate	12%	9%	11.43619%
Maturity	20 years[c]	20 years	20 years
Issue exps.	$100,000[d]	$130,000	$150,000
Premium	$20,000[d]	0	$4,447,783
Call price	110		
Yield	na	9%	9%

[a] New bonds issued in partial refunding.
[b] New bonds issued in full refunding.
[c] Remaining years to maturity.
[d] Unamortized at date of refunding.

In the event of a call, bondholders have one month to turn in their bonds. The company's tax rate is 34 percent, and 90-day Treasury bills are currently yielding 7 percent.

a Assume that the new bonds are given a 9 percent coupon rate. Estimate the net present value from refunding.

b Now assume that the new bonds are given a 11.43619 percent coupon rate, and that they are sold for $24,447,783. Under these conditions, future cash flows on the new and old bonds would be the same. Estimate the net present value from refunding.

c Should the old bonds be refunded? If so, which type of refunding should be selected? Why?

d Explain the factor(s), if any, that (a) indicate that the old bonds should be refunded now, and (b) may indicate that refunding should be delayed.

REFERENCES

Bowlin, O. D.: "The Refunding Decision: Another Special Case in Capital Budgeting," *Journal of Finance*, vol. 21, March 1966, pp. 55–68.

Gordon, M. J.: "A General Solution to the Buy or Lease Decision: A Pedagogical Note," *Journal of Finance*, vol. 29, March 1974, pp. 245–250.

Mayor, T. H., and K. G. McCoin: "The Rate of Discount in Bond Refunding," *Financial Management*, vol. 3, Autumn 1974, pp. 54–58.

Ofer, A. R., and R. A. Taggart, Jr.: "Bond Refunding: A Clarifying Analysis," *Journal of Finance*, vol. 32, March 1977, pp. 21–30.

Pye, Gordon: "The Value of a Call Option on a Bond," *Journal of Political Economy*, vol. 74, April 1966, pp. 200–205.

Rienner, K. D.: "Financial Structure Effects of Bond Refunding," *Financial Management*, vol. 9, Summer 1980, pp. 18–23.

Yawitz, J. B., and J. A. Anderson: "The Effect of Bond Refunding on Shareholder Wealth," *Journal of Finance*, vol. 32, December 1977, pp. 1738–1746.

12

DIVIDEND POLICY

The dividend policy decision involves the determination of the level of cash dividends which should be distributed to the firm's common stockholders. Since earnings not distributed in dividends are by definition retained in the firm, the dividend policy decision of the firm also impacts the firm's financing decisions. Earlier, in Chapter 1, we noted three traditional policy issues: investment policy, financing policy, and dividend policy. Thus, the subject matter of the present chapter has been accorded a significant role in the study of finance. In many ways, however, the study of dividend policy has been relegated to the lowest priority when compared to investment and financing policy. For one thing, the dividend policy decision can be viewed as a subset of the firm's financial policy (i.e., the amount of a firm's earnings it retains and reinvests will impact its needs for externally raised capital). In addition, there does not exist any satisfactory theory of "why dividend policy matters," in the sense of how its determination impacts firm equity value. In this chapter we will review the pragmatic arguments concerning the relevance of dividend policy to the determination of firm value, as well as some of the theories that have been proposed in this regard. Further, we will survey some of the empirical tests of the impact of dividend policy on firm value, and the controversy which has arisen in this literature.

The chapter is organized as follows: In the first section we provide an overview of the **dividend irrelevance argument** under idealized conditions where there are no taxes or transactions costs. Having established the irrelevance of dividend policy in this idealized world, we are then prepared to discuss the reasons that have been offered for the relevance of dividend policy to the valuation of a firm's common shares in the second section. The third section contains a discussion of three alternative dividend payment strategies. We include here the results of empirical studies that have considered the dividend payment histories of a wide variety of U.S. companies. In the fourth section we consider the dividend payment procedure. Here we consider the institutional arrangements that have been developed to determine who is to receive a firm's quarterly dividend. In the fifth section we discuss two alternatives to the payment of cash dividends: stock dividends and share repurchases. Both these alternatives to cash dividends have been the subject of extensive empirical research, and we review some of the key studies.

THE IRRELEVANCE OF DIVIDEND POLICY

In a world where there are no transactions costs associated with buying and selling securities, there are no taxes, and capital markets are competitive, it is relatively easy to demonstrate that dividend policy does not impact a firm's equity value. We begin by recalling the equation for equity value used in Chapter 6:

$$e_0 = PV[\text{Div}_t] \qquad t = 1, 2, \ldots, \infty \qquad (12\text{-}1)$$

where $PV[\text{Div}_t] = \sum_{t=1}^{\infty} \frac{\text{Div}_t}{(1+k_e)^t}$; k_e is the required rate of return on the firm's equity, and Div_t is the total cash dividend paid to the firm's shareholders in period t. We will use PV[ ] to refer to the present value of the expression in brackets, just to simplify the notation.

For the first year of an all equity-financed firm's operations, the following "cash in equals cash out" relationship must hold:

$$X_1 + NF_1 = \text{Div}_1 + I_1 \qquad (12\text{-}2)$$

where X_1 represents the net cashflow earned in period 1 from the firm's investments in place during period 0; NF_1 represents the new funds requirements for period 1, needed to finance the current period's investments; Div_1 is again the dividend paid in period 1; and I_1 represents the value-maximizing level of investment opportunities facing the firm in period 1, (i.e., given the firm's cost of equity, the optimal level of investment is I_1). Note that we hold the investment decision of the firm fixed in our analysis by assuming that the firm's dividend policy decision will not alter the level of investment made by the firm during the period. In addition, we will hold the financing decision constant by assuming that all new financing is with equity funds, which will leave the firm's (all-equity) financing mix unchanged. Now, for all years subsequent to year 1, the "cash in equals cash out" equation must be modified to contain the "required return" to the new funds raised in the previous period. That is, the right-hand side of (12-2) must now include the required return on NF_{t-1}. Hence we define the following relationship for $t \geq 1$:

$$X_t + NF_t = \text{Div}_t + I_t + (1 + k_e)NF_{t-1} \qquad (12\text{-}3)$$

Solving [12-2] and [12-3] for Div_t, and substituting into [12-1], produces the following equity valuation model:

$$e_0 = PV[X_t - I_t] + PV[NF_t - (1 + k_e)NF_{t-1}] \qquad t = 1, 2, \ldots, \infty \qquad (12\text{-}1a)$$

The second PV term on the right-hand side of (12-1a) can be shown to reduce to $(-NF_0)$, where capital markets are competitive such that the net present value of the firm's financing decisions is zero. To demonstrate this we will write out the second term on the right-hand side of equation (12-1a) where $t = 1$ and 2, i.e.,

$$\frac{NF_1 - NF_0(1 + k_e)}{1 + k_e} + \frac{NF_2 - NF_1(1 + k_e)}{(1 + k_e)^2}$$

Simplifying this expression we find that the terms containing NF_1 disappear, and we are left with an expression containing $-NF_0 + NF_2/(1 + k_e)^2$. If we were to include the third term, the NF_2 term would drop out, and so forth, until the approximate value of the second term in (12-1a) would simply be $-NF_0$. If we substitute this expression into our equity valuation model found in (12-1a) we obtain the following result:

$$e_0 = PV[X_t - I_t] - NF_0 \qquad t = 1, 2, \ldots, \infty \qquad (12\text{-}4)$$

Observe that the value of the firm's equity is defined with no reference to the firm's choice of a dividend payment policy. Equity value is strictly a function of the investment opportunities faced by the firm which, in turn, produce the firm's cashflows, X_t, and give rise to the firm's needs for funds to finance those investments, I_t and NF_0.

In the next section we will endeavor to discover the possible reasons why dividend policy might matter. In so doing we will relax the assumptions we have made here in arguing for the irrelevance of corporate dividend policy.

Factors Influencing Dividend Policy

In the previous section we established the irrelevance of corporate dividend policy under a set of "idealized conditions". With this discussion as background, we are now ready to consider the factors that have been offered as support for the relevance of corporate dividend policy. Our discussion mirrors the treatment accorded this material in the academic literature in that it is basically ad hoc and descriptive. This is not an indictment of that literature, but a commentary on the "state of the art" with respect to the theoretical underpinnings of firm dividend policy.

Investor Preferences for Dividends

Some investors acquire shares of common stock with a desire for current income in the form of cash dividends, while others seek future income in the form of share-price appreciation. The firm determines the form of the proceeds the investor will receive through its dividend policy. For example, if firm A pays out all or a large portion of its earnings in cash dividends, then the desires of those stockholders who prefer current income will be met. If, on the other hand, firm B retains all or a large part of its earnings, then the stockholder's investment in the firm will grow, and, given favorable investment opportunities, so will the value of the firm's common stock. In this instance the desires of those stockholders desiring future income will be met. Does this mean that stockholders who desire current income should not purchase shares of firm B's stock, or that those desiring future income should not purchase firm A's stock? The answer is a qualified no. Stockholders in firm A can take their cash dividends and reinvest them in the firm by purchasing more shares of stock. Similarly, a stockholder in firm B can sell a fraction of shares of stock to produce current income. The investor, therefore, can effectively create his or her own preferred-dividend policy by either purchasing additional shares of stock with dividends received, or selling a portion of the stock owned. However, the ability of the investor to "create" his or her own desired dividend policy is restricted by the existence of brokerage or transaction costs.

Brokerage Fees. When an investor purchases or sells shares of stock, he or she generally requires the services of a stockholder or agent. The broker serves a very useful role in bringing together buyers and sellers. In exchange for services rendered, the broker receives a commission. Thus, each time additional securities are purchased or sold, additional fees are required. As a result, an investor desiring current income would find selling a parcel of stock holdings an expensive way to produce that income, in comparison with buying shares of stock in a dividend-paying firm. Similarly, an investor desiring future income would find reinvesting cash dividends an expensive substitute for acquiring stock of a firm which paid little or no cash dividends.

Thus, the presence of brokerage fees has the effect of restricting the ability of the individual shareholder to "create" a preferred-dividend income pattern. The net result of this factor may well be to create a clientele for a firm's stock whose current versus future-income desires match the dividend policy of the firm. Thus, the existence of brokerage fees, in conjunction with investor preferences for current versus future income, combine to make a firm's dividend policy an important factor in firm valuation.

Personal Taxes. Stockholders' preferences for dividend income is also affected by the tax treatment accorded such income. Specifically, dividend income, and income created by selling shares of stock are treated differently for personal-tax purposes. Prior to the passage of the Tax Reform Act of 1986 dividend income was taxed as ordinary income, whereas capital gains were subjected to only 40 percent of the ordinary tax rate. However, the TRA of 1986 (which became fully effective in January 1988) eliminated the tax rate differential between dividend income and capital gains. One source of tax preference remains, however, and this relates to the fact that capital gains are subjected to taxation only when realized. That is, no capital gains taxes must be paid until the stock on which the gain is realized has been sold. Consequently, "unrealized capital gains" are not taxed and thus there remains a small vestige of the tax preference that capital gains income once enjoyed.[1]

Information Content of Dividend Announcements

Dividend policy gains further importance through the significance that investors attach to announced changes in policy. In Chapter 4 we calculated the value of a firm's common stock as the present value of all expected future dividends. The current dividend paid by a firm often influences investor expectations of future dividends. Thus, a decision by a firm to increase its dividend in one quarter might be construed by investors to mean that the firm will be able to continue to pay the higher level of dividend in the future. Other things remaining the same, this would lead to an upward adjustment in the value of the stock. The point is that the dividend announcements are viewed by investors as a prime source of information concerning the financial well-being of the firm. Dividend announcements serve to confirm or deny rumors concerning the firm's financial health, and therefore these announcements have an impact on the value of the firm's common stock.

Ross (1977) proposed an incentive-signaling model whereby firms use their decisions regarding capital structure and dividend policy to convey information to the investing public. Specifically, the firm was pictured as providing information concerning the firm's future earnings prospects via the setting of its dividend policy. The basic premise here is that the firm's management cannot simply announce its expectations concerning the firm's future earnings prospects, for they have an incentive to paint a very rosy picture and the public may not believe them. Hence, management must turn to the use of signals that cannot be manipulated or imitated by unsuccessful firms. Thus, a glowing earnings report issued by management is more likely to be believed if it is accompanied by an increase in cash dividends. The policy implication of this factor is very simple. Changes in dividend policy should be made only after giving due consideration to the added information that the announced change might impart.

Investment Opportunities and Flotation Costs

The availability of profitable investment opportunities make the retention of earnings a viable alternative to the payment of cash dividends. For example, if, in an extreme case, a firm were to have no investment opportunities earning an expected rate of return higher than the cost of capital, then all of its after-tax net income should be paid out in cash dividends to the firm's common stockholders. Most firms do have acceptable investment alternatives available to them. Thus, a question arises as to whether the firm should pay its earnings out in cash dividends when at least some part of those earnings could be used to finance the equity component of the firm's new investments for the period.

---

[1]For a complete discussion of the remaining tax preference accorded capital gains income see Martin and Blose (1988).

If the firm chooses to pay cash dividends with earnings that could be used to finance worthwhile investments, then it will have to sell new common stock to raise the needed equity funds. The existing common shareholders will not, in the presence of flotation costs, be indifferent between these two alternatives. That is, if cash dividends of $100,000 are paid and the firm has to raise $100,000 through the issuance of common stock, then the existing shareholders as a whole will actually be worse off than if the dividends had not been paid and the earnings retained. The reason relates to the existence of flotation costs. Recall that we assumed no transactions costs for either the firm or investors when we discussed the dividend irrelevance theory earlier.

When a firm sells an issue of common stock, it generally must hire an agent (i.e., an investment banker) to actually sell the issue. The agent receives a fee for services rendered, which, to the issuing firm, constitutes part of the flotation costs. However, when the firm retains earnings, no flotation costs are incurred since the firm does not have to sell new securities. Thus, the firm may have to issue $110,000 in common stock in order to obtain $100,000 in equity funds. In the preceding example the firm's common stockholders receive $100,000 in cash dividends but give up an ownership interest in the firm valued at $110,000.

In summary, the existence of flotation costs in the presence of favorable investment alternatives favors the retention of earnings. At the extreme, the firm might determine its dividend payments solely on the basis of the availability of profitable investment opportunities. This dividend policy (often referred to as the **Residual Theory of Dividend Policy**) would involve paying cash dividends equal to that amount of earnings which cannot be profitably reinvested in the firm.

Consider the situation faced by firm A in Figure 12-1. The firm has four investment projects which it can undertake. These projects are expected to earn rates of return of 14, 12, 10, and 6 percent, respectively. Project 1 involves an investment of $8,000;

FIGURE 12-1
The residual theory of dividend policy.

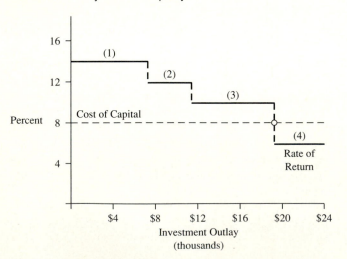

project 2 requires \$4,000; project 3 necessitates an outlay of \$8,000; and finally, project 4 requires an investment of \$4,000. If Firm A's cost of capital is 8 percent, then projects 1, 2, and 3 should be undertaken. These projects involve a total investment of \$20,000. Furthermore, since firm A's optimal financing mix consists of 40 percent debt and 60 percent equity, \$8,000 in new debt capital should be raised as well as \$12,000 in new equity capital. Thus, firm A can profitably retain and invest \$12,000. Should firm A's net income equal \$18,000, then \$12,000 should be reinvested and \$6,000 should be paid in cash dividends. Dividends constitute those residual earnings which cannot be profitably reinvested by the firm while maintaining the firm's target capital structure.

This completes our discussion of the residual theory of dividend policy. This theory considers only the influence on dividend policy of the relative costs of retained earnings versus a new issue of common stock. However, the presence of flotation costs does, in the presence of profitable investment opportunities, lead to a preference by the firm's common stockholders for earnings retention over the payment of cash dividends.

Legal Restrictions

Dividend policy is influenced by legal restrictions surrounding the payment of dividends. This legal environment is very complex and varies from state to state. However, in general, legal restrictions on the payment of dividends take one of three forms. First, firms are generally prohibited from paying dividends while technically insolvent, that is, when liabilities exceed assets. Second, dividends often cannot be paid when they exceed the amount of present and accumulated profits. Where dividends exceed this amount, they involve a liquidation of the owner's investment and must be so identified. In addition, the firm's ability to pay dividends may be restricted through its agreements with creditors. For example, it is not uncommon to find restrictions in a firm's loan agreements as to the amount of cash dividends that can be paid by the firm.

Legal Listing Requirements

There is an important advantage associated with maintaining a history of continuous dividend payments. Various governmental regulatory agencies prepare legal lists of securities in which pension funds, insurance companies, trustees, and others can invest. One of the requirements for inclusion on these lists is very often the continuity of dividend payments. Thus, one factor which should be considered in determining a firm's dividend policy is the effect of the policy on the firm's inclusion on legal lists and the corresponding effect on share value.

Liquidity

Cash flow and net income can differ greatly. That is, a firm might show net income for the year of \$100,000 but have only \$5,000 in cash at the time when dividends are to be paid.[2] Since dividends are paid with cash the firm must possess the requisite cash or liquidity before they can be paid.

Ownership Control

One final factor influencing dividend policy relates to the maintenance of ownership control of the firm. When the firm has a need for equity capital, the existing owners can easily maintain their proportionate control over the firm if earnings are retained. However, if the firm pays cash dividends and issues new common stock, the existing owners must purchase a portion of the firm's new stock issue in order to maintain their existing ownership control. This involves having to pay personal income taxes on their cash dividends, as well as paying brokerage commissions on the purchase of additional shares.[3] Thus, where ownership control is an important consideration, the retention of earnings is favored over dividends.

Comments

In the preceding pages we discussed seven factors which have a potential impact on the firm's dividend policy decision. These factors are summarized in Figure 12-2. Unfortunately, there is no mechanical way of choosing the best dividend-policy.

[2] Since net income is defined on an accrual basis rather than a cash basis, differences between cash flow and net income are to be expected.

[3] This latter statement is correct only when the shares purchased are not part of a new issue. New issues very often do not require the purchaser to pay a brokerage commission. Actually, in those circumstances in which no explicit commission is paid, the commission is buried in the price of the securities.

FIGURE 12-2
Factors influencing the dividend policy decision.

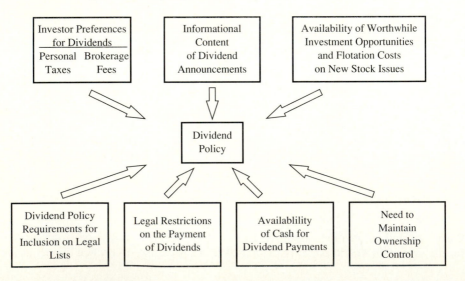

Dividend Payment Strategies

There are many different strategies that a firm may follow in paying dividends. However, there are three basic policies that can be used to describe the practices of most U.S. corporations. These are (1) a stable dollar dividend per share, (2) a low regular dividend with a year-end extra, and (3) a target dividend payout ratio.

Stable Dollar Dividend per Share

Under this policy, dividends are changed only rarely, either when earnings have risen to the point where a larger dividend payment can be sustained or after earnings have fallen to a level where the past dividend payment cannot be continued. Figure 12-3 depicts an example of a stable dividend policy based upon General Telephone and Electric (GTE) Corporation. Note that dividends per share are substantially less than earnings per share. Further, dividends grow steadily while earnings fluctuate from year to year.

There are several advantages to a stable-dollar-dividend policy. First, since investors use dividend announcements as a source of information in formulating their expectations about future dividends, a stable-dividend policy will minimize the possibilities of a dividend reduction, and its corresponding impact on investor expectations and share value. Second, as we discussed earlier, one commonly used requirement for legal lists involves a long history of continuous dividend payments. Still another advantage of the stable-dividend policy relates to the fact that many investors purchase shares of stock for current income. A long history of stable dividends is a very attractive feature to this group of investors.

Low Regular Dividends and Year-End Extras

Many firms that have highly fluctuating earnings simply cannot easily follow the stable-dividend policy just mentioned. In some years firm earnings may be very high,

FIGURE 12-3
Earnings and dividends per share for GTE.

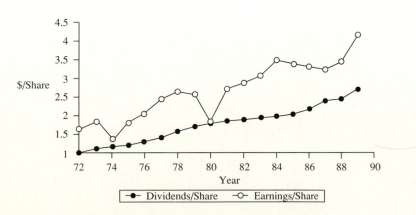

while in others they may even be negative. For these firms any attempt to follow a stable-dividend policy would involve an extremely low dividend. However, when the firm experiences a very good year, the firm can afford a much higher dividend. To obtain some of the benefits of a stable-dollar-dividend policy and still be able to pay higher dividends to the stockholders when earnings permit, many firms follow a policy of paying a very low regular dividend each quarter and a year-end extra. This policy is popular among firms with highly volatile or cyclical earnings. An example is provided in Figure 12-4 involving the dividends paid by General Motors Corporation.

Target Dividend Payout Ratio

The third and final dividend policy we will discuss involves an attempt by the firm to maintain a target dividend payout ratio. The dividend payout ratio is defined as the ratio of dividends per share to earnings per share. This type of dividend payment behavior has been observed in a number of U.S. corporations.[4] Basically, firms that follow such a policy increase (or decrease) dividends only after earnings have risen (or dropped). Dividend payments are usually increased only after the firm feels the new higher level of dividends can be sustained. Conversely, dividend payments are cut only after it is apparent that the previous level of payment cannot be maintained.

This concludes our discussion of alternate dividend-payment strategies. In each, the virtues of payment stability have been emphasized, as well as the information content of changes in dividend policy. The behavior of firms suggests that due consideration should be given to these factors in formulating a dividend policy. In the next section we review some of the empirical evidence concerning the dividend payment practices of U.S. corporations.

---

[4] For example, see J. Lintner, (1956). We review this and other studies of corporate dividend payment practices in a later section of this chapter.

FIGURE 12-4
Earnings and dividends per share for GM Corporation.

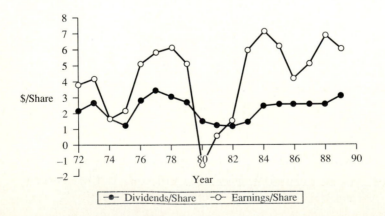

The Empirical Evidence

In his classic study of the dividend payment practices of a sample of 28 U.S. corporations, John Lintner (1956) established the empirical basis for his "stable dividend hypothesis." Lintner began his study by interviewing the top managements of 28 firms, in an effort to discover the determinants of corporate dividend payment practice. From those interviews he noted two key attributes of corporate dividend policy: First, corporate management tended to establish target dividend payouts as a proportion of earnings. In addition, management set its dividend payments so that they adjusted "slowly" over time toward the desired fraction of earnings. From these two observations Lintner hypothesized the following relationship between dividends and earnings:

$$D_t^* = rE_t \qquad (12\text{-}5)$$

where D_t^* is the "target" dividend payment per share for year t; r is the payout ratio (dividends to earnings); and E_t is firm earnings per share in year t. Lintner then hypothesized (based upon the second observation stated above) that firms seek to maintain a stable dividend payout by changing or adapting its dividend payout each year by only a fraction of the change indicated by earnings in conjunction with the target payout ratio. The change in a firm's dividend from year t-1 to t was characterized as follows:

$$D_t - D_{t-1} = a + c(D_t^* - D_{t-1}) \qquad (12\text{-}6)$$

where a is a constant so that even where $D_t^* = D_{t-1}$ there is some positive expected increment to dividends, and c is a constant "speed of adjustment" factor. Substituting (12-5) into (12-6) we obtain the **partial adjustment model** used by Lintner to "explain" the corporate dividend payment practices of U.S. corporations, that is:

$$D_t = a + b_1 E_t + b_2 D_{t-1} + e_t \qquad (12\text{-}7)$$

where $b_1 = cr$, $b_2 = (1 - c)$, and e_t is an error term. Using the period 1915–1951, Lintner estimated (12-7) for the entire period as well as a number of subperiods. The results were quite impressive, explaining over 95 percent of the variation in D_t.

Both Lintner (1956) and Brittain (1964 and 1966) used (12-7) to explain corporate dividend policy, but used "aggregate" data in most of their tests. Fama and Babiak (1968), to the contrary, used firm data, as well as a more extensive set of tests, to evaluate corporate dividend payment practice. They found that the two-variable Lintner partial adjustment model performed well in comparison with the many other models tested. Hence, Lintner's results and consequently the "stable dividend hypothesis" appear to be very robust.

Dividend Payment Procedure

The procedural aspects of the payment of dividends is quite simple. Upon deciding the amount of its dividend for the quarter, the firm's board of directors declares the dividend and specifies a date of record. After this date, people purchasing the stock will not receive the quarterly dividend (they will, however, receive subsequent quarterly dividends). After the date of record, the stock trades ex-dividend, or without the right to the quarterly dividend, until the payment date, when the dividend is actually paid.[5] In theory, the price of the stock should drop by an amount equal to the announced quarterly dividend on the day after the date of record. Very often, however, the drop in price may be wholly or partially offset by the influence of other factors influencing the stock price on that day.

Alternatives to Cash Dividends

There are two commonly used alternatives to the payment of cash dividends. The first involves the use of a stock dividend, whereby shares of stock are issued to the stockholders in lieu of a cash dividend. The second alternative involves the repurchase of a portion of the firm's outstanding shares of common stock. This alternative involves an actual expenditure of cash to purchase shares of the firm's common stock, which then becomes treasury stock.

Stock Dividends

A stock dividend is paid by using shares of the firm's common stock rather than cash. Although the recipients may feel better off after receiving the stock dividend, they are actually no better off than they were prior to its payment.[6] Technically a stock dividend is nothing more than an accounting transfer from retained earnings to the capital stock accounts (common stock and paid-in-capital).

Consider the following example. The ABC Manufacturing Company's balance sheet for December 31, 1988, is found in Table 12-1. ABC decided to make a 20 percent stock dividend, which involved distributing $0.20 \times 10,000$ shares $= 2,000$ shares. Thus, for every five shares of stock owned, a shareholder would receive one new share. Let us assume a fair market value for ABC's stock of $12 a share. The company's balance sheet following the declaration of the stock dividend (January

---

[5] Actually, the stock usually begins trading ex-dividend four or five days prior to the date of record because of the delivery rules of the exchanges.

[6] The stockholders are actually worse off as a result of the payment of the stock dividend, since no value is created by issuing the new shares and the firm must pay for printing up and issuing the new shares.

TABLE 12-1
ABC Manufacturing Company
Balance Sheet December 31, 1988

Total Liabilities	$ 40,000
Common Stock ($2 par, 10,000 shares)	20,000
Paid-in-Capital	30,000
Retained Earnings	100,000
Total Assets $190,000 Total	$190,000

TABLE 12-2
ABC Manufacturing Company
Balance Sheet January 31, 1989

Total Liabilities	$ 40,000
Common stock ($2 par, 12,000 shares)	24,000
Paid-in-Capital	50,000
Retained Earnings	76,000
Total	$190,000

Total Assets $190,000

21, 1989) is contained in Table 12-2. Note that $12 \times 2,000$ shares $= \$24,000$ was transferred from retained earnings account to the common stock ($2,000$ shares $\times$ $2 par value $= \$4,000$) and paid-in-capital ($\$24,000 - \$4,000 = \$20,000$) accounts. Therefore, the stock dividend amounted to nothing more than a transfer of the fair market value of the stock involved in the dividend from retained earnings to the common stock and paid-in-capital accounts. The stockholders neither gained nor lost in the transaction since they now hold six shares of stock for every five they held prior to the stock dividend, and the total value of those six shares equals the previous value of five shares. Very simply, a stock dividend splits the "ownership pie" into more pieces but does not affect the size of the pie.

If the firm's stockholders do not gain anything by receiving stock dividends, then why are they used? There are at least two possible explanations. First, some stockholders may be fooled by a stock dividend in lieu of a cash dividend. In this case the firm effectively substitutes a stock dividend for a cash dividend because of a shortage of cash. Such a shortage may be a result of poor earnings or the existence of favorable investment opportunities which the firm's management has chosen to finance by using current earnings. A second reason for declaring a stock dividend relates to a desire on the part of the firm's management to increase the number of shares of stock so that the stock will trade in a lower price range. This motive follows from the popular belief that a "preferred trading range" exists for a share of common stock. In accordance with this belief, when a stock's price rises above this range, the firm should lower its price. One means of accomplishing this reduction involves the use of a stock dividend.

For example, the ABC Manufacturing Company just discussed had 10,000 shares of stock outstanding prior to the stock dividend, with a total market value of $12 \times 10,000 = \$120,000$. After the 20 percent stock dividend, the total value of the firm's common stock should not change, other things remaining the same. ABC now has 12,000 shares of stock with a total market value of $120,000. Thus, the common-stock price should drop from $12 to $10 per share. In this instance the change in share price was small since the stock dividend was only 20 percent. If there is any positive benefit associated with lowering the price range in which the firm's stock trades, then the price will not drop to the theoretical level of $10. A 100 percent stock dividend would reduce the stock price to one-half its pre-stock-dividend level or $6. Little evidence can be found to support the "preferred trading range" argument.

Fama, Fisher, Jensen, and Roll (1969) studied the stock market reaction to the announcement of stock splits. Splits are similar to stock dividends in that they simply alter the number of shares outstanding without any material impact on the firm's investments. For example, a two for one stock split and a 100 percent stock dividend both results in a doubling of the number of shares outstanding. Fama et. al. observed that stock market value tended to rise prior to the announcement of a stock split but remained relatively stable following the split. Upon closer examination they found that by segmenting their sample into firms that did and did not increase in dividend payout subsequent to the split, a possible explanation for the pre-split announcement increase in stock value was revealed. Specifically, after the split the stock price of those firms having experienced an increase in dividend payout remained stable or even drifted up slightly. However, the subset of firms which did not experience an increase in dividend payout actually experienced a downward drift in their stock price following the split announcement. The authors concluded that the reason for the increase in stock price prior to the split was due to investor anticipation of an increase in the firm's dividend payout, and that there is no evidence to support the notion that a stock split per se leads to an increase in share value.

Stock Repurchase

A second alternative to the payment of cash dividends involves the purchase of a portion of the firm's outstanding common stock. Should a corporation decide to engage in the repurchase of its outstanding common shares the result is to i) reduce the number of shares outstanding, and ii) transfer cash from the corporate coffers to those shareholders who tender their shares. Since a share repurchase is *similar* to the payment of a cash dividend in the latter respect we will consider studies of share repurchase activity in this chapter.

The following example is used to demonstrate the equivalence of a cash dividend and purchase of treasury stock. The A&B Drug Company has 1.2 million shares of common stock outstanding, with a total market value of $14,400,000. The firm has $2,400,000 which it plans to use either to pay a cash dividend or to repurchase its common stock. After the payment of the $2,400,000 cash dividend, the firm's common stock should, other things remaining the same, drop to $14,400,000 − 2,400,000 = $12,000,000 or $10 per share. Thus the shareholders will own shares of stock valued at $10 plus a $2 dividend.

Alternatively, A&B can repurchase 200,000 shares of stock with the $2,400,000, in which case shares are repurchased at the expected market price of $12. Hence, after the repurchase, the market value of A&B's common shares will be $12,000,000/(1,200,000 shares − 200,000 shares) = $12. In this case A&B's remaining shareholders will own shares of stock with a market value of $12. Thus, with the cash dividend option, the stockholders get $2 in cash dividends and the value of their stock is $10. With the treasury stock option, some of A&B's shareholders receive $12 in cash for their stock, while the remaining stockholders are left with shares of stock worth $12 a share.

The purchase of treasury stock is advantageous to the firm's stockholders for two reasons: (1) price appreciation may be taxed at capital gains rates, and taxes are paid only when the stock is actually sold, and (2) the investor has the choice of selling the stock and taking the immediate cash flow, or holding the stock and realizing the price appreciation.

In summary, the purchase of treasury stock offers a viable alternative to a cash dividend. There is, however, the risk that the firm will have to pay too high a price for the treasury stock. In the case of the preceding example, note the effects of purchasing treasury stock whereby the firm has to pay $15 per share. In this instance the $2,400,000 allows the firm to purchase $2,400,000/$15 = 160,000 shares. The share value after the repurchase will be $12,000,000/(1,200,000 − 160,000 shares) = $11.54. Thus, the shareholders realize a price appreciation of only $1.54 in lieu of a $2.00 dividend. Of course, those shareholders who decide to sell their shares to the company will receive $15.00.

Share Repurchase Techniques.   A corporation can repurchase its shares in one of three ways: open market purchases, privately negotiated transactions, or via the use of a "tender offer". Open market transactions simply involve the firm's acquisition of a block of shares from an individual or group of investors desiring to sell. This type of repurchase is frequently associated with a firm's attempts to fend off a unfriendly takeover attempt. Finally, the cash tender offer route involves the firm advertising its willingness to purchase a given quantity of its shares for a set price and within a specified time limit. The empirical research reviewed here relates primarily to the latter form of repurchase activity.

Share Repurchase and Equity Value: The Evidence.   A wide variety of reasons have been offered for firm's engaging in stock repurchase activity. Rather than enumerating them here, however, we will discuss them as they are proposed in the research that we summarize.

The Norgaard and Norgaard (1974) paper is unique among the papers discussed here, in that it did not attempt to assess the market's reaction to the intiation of a tender offer repurchase. Instead, this study sought to determine whether the financial attributes of repurchasing firms differed significantly from non-repurchasing firms. Using a variety of measures of financial condition including such things as the ratio of book value per share to market value per share, payout ratios, return on net worth, and so forth, these authors were able to successfully distinguish between repurchasing and non-repurchasing firms. Using multiple discriminant analysis, the Norgaards concluded that repurchasing firms had below normal expectations for profits caused by either industry circumstances, poor management, or both. They further concluded that firms engaged in repurchases in order to hide their otherwise lackluster performance. Based upon the concluding remarks of this study one might anticipate a negative reaction to the repurchase of a firm's shares in an efficient market. However, as we review the studies of the market's reaction to repurchase activity, we find that the opposite is true.

Stewart (1976) provides one of the early studies of the market reaction to repurchase activity. Segmenting a sample of repurchasing firms by the percentage of shares being acquired (i.e., less than 0.25%, 1.25% to 2.24%, 2.25% to 3.24%, 3.25% to 4.24%, 4.25% to 5.24%, and 5.25% or more), Stewart observed the following: First, the stock market performance of repurchasing firms is generally superior to non-repurchasing firms, although this superiority did not materialize for several years in some cases (e.g., for the largest repurchase group the superior performance was noted only after a period of almost five years). Second, Stewart observed that the intermediate share repurchase group (3.25% − 4.24%) experienced the greatest increase in market value.

Stewart's study is unusual in comparison with the remaining studies of repurchase activity reviewed here in two major respects. First, Stewart looked at long term effects of repurchase spanning several years, whereas subsequent studies have looked at very short term announcement effects occurring within a few days of the announced repurchase. Second, Stewart did not use any "risk adjustment" for equity returns, whereas subsequent studies have used various methods for removing the influence of general market influences on stock returns.

Masulis (1980) provides the first of three major studies of the announcement impact of a tender offer repurchase. He examined the price reaction of common stock, preferred stock, and various categories of nonconvertible securities surrounding an announced repurchase, in an effort to identify the source of the market's reaction. Masulis proposed four possible reasons for a market reaction to a tender offer repurchase :(i) personal tax savings resulting from the differential tax treatment of dividends versus capital gains; (ii) corporate tax shield increases resulting from the use of debt used to finance the repurchase; (iii) wealth transfers across security classes due to changes in the firm's use of financial leverage; and (iv) wealth transfers between tendering and nontendering stockholders.

The first reason for repurchasing a firm's share cited above relates to the fact that the gains due to share repurchase distributions are taxed as capital gains (where the shares tendered were held for the requisite one year holding period), while cash dividends are taxed as ordinary income. Thus, it was hypothesized, the repurchase of a firm's shares should result in a temporary positive price impact reflecting the opportunity to realize capital gains income via the sale of the shares. It should be noted that this argument is contradictory to the Miller and Scholes (1978) tax arbitrage argument. These authors argued that the personal tax differential on dividend and capital gains income is inconsequential where individuals can engage in tax arbitrage by exchanging taxable income for nontaxed income. At this point we simply note that for there to be a market reaction to share repurchase due to personal tax considerations, the Miller-Scholes tax arbitrage scheme must not be functioning as they propose.

According to the second reason for a market reaction to repurchase noted above, the firm's use of debt to finance a repurchase will create greater interest tax savings and (in accordance with the Modigliani and Miller (1963) tax adjusted valuation model discussed in Chapter 4), will lead to an increase in equity value. Thus, it is hypothesized that the market's reaction to repurchase is actually a reaction to the firm's restructuring of its capital structure to include more financial leverage.

The third explanation offered by Masulis suggests that the distribution of cash via share repurchase allows the common shareholders as a group to benefit at the expense of the firm's creditors. The argument goes as follows: Other things being the same, the reduction in the amount of equity capital via a share repurchase makes the debt of the firm more risky. Given no change in the value of the repurchasing corporation's productive assets, the loss in value of the firm's risky debt becomes a gain to the wealth of the nontendering stockholders. Thus, the repurchase of a firm's shares can provide a vehicle whereby the firm's shareholders transfer wealth from the creditors to themselves.

The fourth explanation relates to tender offer premium, and the existence of differential costs of tendering shares among different groups of shareholders. Since the right to tender shares is not transferrable, shareholders who tender capture the entire premium paid at the expense of the nontendering shareholders. If the costs of tendering shares is higher for some groups of shareholders than it is for others, then the wealth impact of the premium for tendered shares will not be shared equally by all shareholders.

Masulis employed a standard cross-sectional event study methodology to the daily returns of 199 repurchasing firms. He found a positive 17% abnormal (i.e., unrelated to firm or market related factors) return over the two-day period, consisting of the day preceding and the announcement day for a tender offer repurchase. In addition he identified evidence of some anticipatory market reaction to the repurchase, indicating some possible insider trading. Unfortunately Masulis was not able to pinpoint the source of the market reaction beyond noting that it was probably due to a combination of the factors reviewed above.

Dann (1981) proposed that, in addition to the factors mentioned by Masulis, the market may react to a share repurchase as a "signal" of new information regarding the firm's future investment and earnings prospects. According to this hypothesis the act of repurchase could signal either good or bad news. That is, repurchase could signal that management (using its superior inside information) believes that the shares are undervalued in the marketplace. Furthermore, the repurchase might signal management's anticipation of a likely takeover attempt, which has been shown to produce substantial gains to the shareholders of the acquired firm. To the contrary, the act of repurchase may simply signal management's conviction that it cannot profitably reinvest the shareholder's funds at acceptable rates of return. This would, in turn, be viewed as bad news. Dann reasons that since management must initiate a repurchase, it will not do so except to signal good news. Thus, he suggests that the repurchase signal is more likely to be positive than negative.

Using an event study methodology very similar to that of Masulis, Dann formed portfolios in event time comprised of the repurchasing firm's common stock, straight debt, straight preferred stock, and convertible preferred stock, respectively. In this way Dann was able to assess whether any wealth transfers accompanied share repurchases. For the common stock portfolio the announcement day portfolio return was 8.95% while the day after return was 6.93%. Note that these are *not* risk adjusted returns but are "raw" daily holding period returns. The average daily return over the fifty-day comparison period ending 11 days prior to the announcement was −0.09%, thus confirming the significance of the market impact of the announced repurchase. The portfolio returns for the announcement day observed for the convertible debt, straight preferred, and convertible preferred securities were all positive, while the return for the straight debt portfolio was negative but very small. Hence, the magnitude of these returns was not sufficient to explain the very large and significant common stock returns. Thus, Dann found no evidence to support the "wealth transfer between debt, preferred, and common stock security holders hypothesis". This result is in contrast with Masulis who suggested that such a wealth transfer could, in part, explain the positive market reaction of the common shares to an announced repurchase.

Further, Dann found no evidence to support the personal tax savings hypothesis. Stock prices were observed to increase permanently subsequent to the repurchase announcement whereas they should only increase temporarily if the benefit to repurchase involves a one time reduction in personal taxes (i.e., a transfer of fully taxed dividends for lower taxed capital gains). Because of the above findings, Dann concluded that the signaling hypothesis was the only plausible explanation for the observed positive market reaction to share repurchase.

In a very comprehensive study Vermaelen (1981) examined the market's reaction to purchases via tender offer, as well as open market transactions. In addition, Vermaelen devised a framework for analyzing the market's pricing of common stocks in relation to tender offer repurchases. The main objective of this study was to determine whether increased legislation was needed to regulate the repurchase phenomenon, since it was believed by some that insiders could manipulate stock prices through repurchase activity at the expense of other holders of the firm's securities.

Vermaelen's tender offer sample consisted of 131 offers by 111 firms over the period 1962–1977. Using an event-study methodology, he found that significant returns were observed on event days -4, -2, -1, 0, and $+1$. Although statistically significant, the event day $+1$ return of 1.08% was deemed practically insignificant. Thus Vermaelen concludes that the market reaction to repurchase is even quicker than reported by previous researchers. Finally, Vermaelen concluded that the information or signaling argument was the most plausible explanation for the market's reaction to tender offer share repurchases.

In summary, studies of share repurchase activity have found that there is a positive market value reaction for the affected firm's common stock which does not result from either personal tax or wealth transfer sources. It would appear that share repurchase is viewed as a signal of positive information to the market regarding its future earnings prospects. Why this particular communication vehicle is used to make such an announcement is not understood and further research is needed before we can fully understand the market's reaction to share repurchase.

CHAPTER SUMMARY

In this chapter we overviewed the firm's dividend-policy decision. Dividend policy relates to the decisions regarding the division of firm earnings between cash payments to the firm's common stockholders, and retention or reinvestment in the firm. Factors influencing the firm's dividend-policy decisions included (1) investor preferences for cash dividends, (2) the information content of dividend announcements and the formulation of investor expectations, (3) the availability of profitable investment opportunities, (4) legal restrictions on the payment of dividends, (5) legal listing requirements regarding a firm's past history of dividend payments, (6) the existence of adequate liquidity, and (7) the maintenance of ownership control.

Three popular dividend payment strategies were discussed: (1) a stable dollar dividend per share, (2) a regular quarterly dividend with a year-end extra, and (3) a target dividend payout ratio. The first policy is the most popular among U.S. corporations with relatively stable earnings. The second strategy is popular among firms with widely fluctuating earnings. The third strategy is observed somewhat less often in practice.

Both stock dividends and the purchase of treasury stock were discussed as alternatives to the payment of cash dividends. Stock dividends were shown to be devoid of value to the recipient stockholders, representing nothing more than an accounting transfer from retained earnings to common-stock account. To the contrary, stock repurchase was shown to provide a viable and potentially desirable alternative to the payment of cash dividends.

PROBLEMS

12-1 In the Spring of 1990, the Amazing Camera Company hopes to fund $4,000,000 in new investments in plant and equipment. The firm has followed a financial policy of involving the maintenance of a 40 percent debt to assets ratio, and also limits its equity funds to those provided internally from firm earnings. The firm plans to continue this financial policy during the coming year. If Amazing's expected earnings for the year total $3,000,000 how much should the firm pay in dividends in accordance with the Residual Theory of Dividend Policy? What if the firm's anticipated earnings were only $2,000,000?

12-2 The Manser Sales Company has 3 million shares of common stock outstanding and is contemplating the payment of a 25 percent stock dividend. The firm's net income for the current year equals $1,500,000 and its price earnings ratio is 10. What is the "theoretical" price for the shares after the stock dividend?

12-3 The financing side of the balance sheet of the Scotty Marketing Company is as follows:

Debt	$ 8,000,000
Common Equity:	
Par ($1.50)	1,500,000
Paid in Capital	4,000,000
Retained Earnings . . .	16,500,000
Total	$30,000,000

a If Scotty engages in a two for one stock split what will be the revised balance sheet for the firm?

b Should Scotty decide to utilize a 100% stock dividend what would be the revised balance sheet for the firm?

12-4 Prepare the revised balance sheet for Scotty (in Problem 12-3) following the payment of a $1.00 per share dividend. If the price of Scotty's shares is $25.00 before payment of the cash dividend, what would you expect the ex-dividend price of one share to be? If instead of paying a $1.00 per share dividend, the firm decided to repurchase $1,500,000 worth of its share in the open market at the current market prices of $25, what would be the ex-purchase share price of the firm's shares? What is the impact of personal taxation on these alternative distribution policies (if any) under the 1988 tax code?

REFERENCES

Barclay, Michael and Clifford Smith, Jr.: "Corporate Payout Policy: Cash Dividends versus Open Market Repurchases," *Journal of Financial Economics*, Vol. 33 1988, pp. 61–82.

Brealey, Richard: "Does Dividend Policy Matter?" *Midland Corporate Finance Journal*, Vol. 19, pp. 17–25.

Brennan, M.: "Taxes, Market Valuation, and Corporate Financial Policy," *National Tax Journal*, Vol. 23, December 1970, pp. 417–27.

Brittain, J. A.: *Corporate Dividend Policy*, Washington, DC: Brookings Institute, 1966.

Dann, Larry Y.: "Common Stock Repurchases," *Journal of Financial Economics*, Vol. 9, 1981, pp. 113–38.

Fama, E. F., and H. Babiak: "Dividend Policy: An Empirical Model," *Journal of American Statistical Association*, Vol. 63, December 1968, pp. 1132–61.

Fama, E. F., L. Fisher, M. Jensen, and R. Roll: "The Adjustment of Stock Prices to New Information," *International Economic Review*, Vol. 10, February 1969, pp. 1–21.

Friend, I., and M. E. Puckett: "Dividends and Stock Prices," *American Economic Review*, Vol. 54, September 1964, pp. 656–82.

Gordon, M. J.: "Dividends, Earnings, and Stock Prices," *Review of Economics and Statistics*, Vol. 54, May 1959, pp. 99–105.

Gordon, M. J.: "Why Corporations Pay Dividends," *Studies in Banking and Finance*, Vol. 5, 1988, pp. 77–96.

Gordon, M. J.: "Optimal Investment and Financing Policy," *Journal of Finance*, Vol. 17, May 1963, pp. 264–72.

Karpoff, Jonathan and Ralph Walking: "Short-Term Trading Around Ex-Dividend Days: Additional Evidence" *Journal of Financial Economics*, Vol. 21, 1988, pp. 291–98.

Laub, P. M.: "On the Informational Content of Dividends," *Journal of Business*, Vol. 49, January 1976, pp. 73–80.

Lee, C. F.: "Functional Form and the Dividend Effect in the Electric Utility Industry," *Journal of Finance*, Vol. 31, December 1976, pp. 1481–86.

Lewellen, Wilbur G., Kenneth L. Stanley, Ronald C. Lease, and Gary G. Schlarbaum: "Some Direct Evidence on the Dividend Clientele Phenomenon," *Journal of Finance*, Vol. 19, December 1978, pp. 1385–99.

Lintner, John: "Distribution of Incomes of Corporations among Dividends, Retained Earnings, and Taxes," *American Economic Review*, Vol. 46, May 1956, pp. 97–113.

Litzenberger, R. H., and K. Ramaswamy: "The Effect of Personal Taxes and Dividends on Capital-Asset Prices: Theory and Empirical Evidence," *Journal of Financial Economics*, Vol. 7, 1979, pp. 163–95.

Marsh, Terry and Robert Merton: "Dividend Behavior for the Aggregate Stock Market," *Journal of Business*, Vol. 60, 1987, pp. 1–40.

Martin, J. D. and L. Blosc: "The Influence of Dividend Taxes on Security Prices Subsequent to the Tax Reform Act of 1986," Working Paper, University of Texas at Austin, 1988.

Masulis, R. W.: "Stock Repurchase by Tender Offer: An Analysis of the Causes of Common Stock Price Changes," *Journal of Finance*, Vol. 35, 1980, pp. 305–21.

Miller, M. H., and F. Modigliani: "Dividend Policy Growth and the Valuation of Shares," *Journal of Business*, 1961, pp. 411–33.

Miller, M. H., and M. S. Scholes: "Dividends and Taxes: Some Empirical Evidence," *Journal of Political Economy*, December 1982, pp. 334–91.

Norgaard, Richard and Corine: "A Critical Examination of Share Repurchase," *Financial Management*, Vol. 3, Spring 1974, pp. 44–50.

Pettit, R.: "Dividend Announcements, Security Performance, and Capital-Market Efficiency," *Journal of Finance*, Vol. 26, September 1972, pp. 993–1007.

Ross, S.: "The Determination of Financial Structure: The Incentive-Signaling Approach," *The Bell Journal of Economics*, Vol. 8, Spring 1977, pp. 23–40.

Stewart, Samuel S., Jr.: "Should a Corporation Repurchase Its Own Stock?" *Journal of Finance*, Vol. 30, June 1976, pp. 911–21.

Vermaelen, Theo.: "Common Stock Repurchases and Market Signaling," *Journal of Financial Economics*, Vol. 9, 1981, pp. 139–83.

PRESENT-VALUE AND FUTURE-VALUE TABLES

TABLE A-1
PRESENT VALUE OF $1

N	0.01	0.02	0.03	0.04	0.05	0.06	0.07	0.08	0.09	0.10
1	0.99010	0.98039	0.97087	0.96154	0.95238	0.94340	0.93458	0.92593	0.91743	0.90909
2	0.98030	0.96117	0.94260	0.92456	0.90703	0.89000	0.87344	0.85734	0.84168	0.82645
3.	0.97059	0.94232	0.91514	0.88900	0.86384	0.83962	0.81630	0.79383	0.77219	0.75132
4	0.96099	0.92385	0.88849	0.85481	0.82271	0.79210	0.76290	0.73503	0.70843	0.68302
5	0.95147	0.90573	0.86261	0.82193	0.78353	0.74726	0.71299	0.68059	0.64993	0.62092
6	0.94205	0.88798	0.83749	0.79032	0.74622	0.70496	0.66635	0.63017	0.59627	0.56448
7	0.93273	0.87056	0.81310	0.75992	0.71069	0.66506	0.62275	0.58349	0.54704	0.51316
8	0.92349	0.85350	0.78941	0.73069	0.67684	0.62742	0.58201	0.54027	0.50187	0.46651
9	0.91435	0.83676	0.76642	0.70259	0.64461	0.59190	0.54394	0.50025	0.46043	0.42410
10	0.90530	0.82035	0.74410	0.67557	0.61392	0.55840	0.50835	0.46320	0.42241	0.38555
11	0.89634	0.80427	0.72243	0.64958	0.58469	0.52679	0.47510	0.42889	0.38754	0.35050
12	0.88746	0.78850	0.70139	0.62460	0.55684	0.49698	0.44402	0.39712	0.35554	0.31863
13	0.87868	0.77304	0.68096	0.60058	0.53033	0.46884	0.41497	0.36770	0.32618	0.28967
14	0.86998	0.75788	0.66113	0.57748	0.50507	0.44231	0.38782	0.34046	0.29925	0.26333
15	0.86137	0.74302	0.64187	0.55527	0.48102	0.41727	0.36245	0.31524	0.27454	0.23940
16	0.85284	0.72846	0.62318	0.53391	0.45812	0.39365	0.33874	0.29189	0.25187	0.21763
17	0.84440	0.71417	0.60502	0.51338	0.43630	0.37137	0.31658	0.27027	0.23108	0.19785
18	0.83604	0.70017	0.58740	0.49363	0.41553	0.35035	0.29587	0.25025	0.21200	0.17986
19	0.82776	0.68644	0.57030	0.47465	0.39574	0.33052	0.27651	0.23171	0.19449	0.16351
20	0.81957	0.67298	0.55369	0.45639	0.37690	0.31181	0.25842	0.21455	0.17843	0.14865
21	0.81145	0.65979	0.53756	0.43884	0.35895	0.29416	0.24152	0.19866	0.16370	0.13513
22	0.80342	0.64685	0.52190	0.42196	0.34186	0.27751	0.22572	0.18394	0.15018	0.12285
23	0.79547	0.63417	0.50670	0.40573	0.32558	0.26180	0.21095	0.17032	0.13778	0.11168
24	0.78759	0.62173	0.49194	0.39013	0.31008	0.24698	0.19715	0.15770	0.12641	0.10153
25	0.77979	0.60954	0.47762	0.37512	0.29531	0.23300	0.18425	0.14602	0.11597	0.09230
26	0.77207	0.59759	0.46370	0.36069	0.28125	0.21982	0.17220	0.13520	0.10640	0.08391
27	0.76443	0.58588	0.45020	0.34682	0.26786	0.20737	0.16093	0.12519	0.09761	0.07628
28	0.75686	0.57439	0.43709	0.33348	0.25510	0.19564	0.15041	0.11592	0.08955	0.06935
29	0.74937	0.56313	0.42436	0.32066	0.24295	0.18456	0.14057	0.10733	0.08216	0.06304
30	0.74195	0.55208	0.41200	0.30832	0.23138	0.17412	0.13137	0.09938	0.07537	0.05731

N	0.11	0.12	0.13	0.14	0.15	0.16	0.17	0.18	0.19	0.20
1	0.90090	0.89286	0.88496	0.87719	0.86957	0.86207	0.85470	0.84746	0.84034	0.83333
2	0.81162	0.79719	0.78315	0.76947	0.75614	0.74316	0.73051	0.71819	0.70617	0.69445
3	0.73119	0.71178	0.69305	0.67497	0.65752	0.64066	0.62437	0.60863	0.59342	0.57870
4	0.65873	0.63552	0.61332	0.59208	0.57175	0.55229	0.53365	0.51579	0.49867	0.48225
5	0.59345	0.56743	0.54276	0.51937	0.49718	0.47611	0.45611	0.43711	0.41905	0.40188
6	0.53464	0.50663	0.48032	0.45559	0.43233	0.41044	0.38984	0.37043	0.35214	0.33490
7	0.48166	0.45235	0.42506	0.39964	0.37594	0.35383	0.33320	0.31393	0.29592	0.27908
8	0.43393	0.40388	0.37616	0.35056	0.32690	0.30503	0.28478	0.26604	0.24867	0.23257
9	0.39093	0.36061	0.33289	0.30751	0.28426	0.26295	0.24341	0.22546	0.20897	0.19381
10	0.35219	0.32197	0.29459	0.26975	0.24719	0.22668	0.20804	0.19107	0.17560	0.16151
11	031729	0.28748	0.26070	0.23662	0.21494	0.19542	0.17781	0.16192	0.14757	0.13459
12	0.28584	0.25668	0.23071	0.20756	0.18691	0.16846	0.15198	0.13722	0.12401	0.11216
13	0.25752	0.22918	0.20417	0.18207	0.16253	0.14523	0.12989	0.11629	0.10421	0.09346
14	0.23200	0.20462	0.18068	0.15971	0.14133	0.12520	0.11102	0.09855	0.08757	0.07789
15	0.20901	0.18270	0.15989	0.14010	0.12290	0.10793	0.09489	0.08352	0.07359	0.06491
16	0.18829	0.16312	0.14150	0.12289	0.10687	0.09304	0.08110	0.07078	0.06184	0.05409
17	0.16963	0.14565	0.12522	0.10780	0.09293	0.08021	0.06932	0.05998	0.05196	0.04507
18	0.15282	0.13004	0.11081	0.09456	0.08081	0.06914	0.05925	0.05083	0.04367	0.03756
19	0.13768	0.11611	0.09807	0.08295	0.07027	0.05961	0.05064	0.04308	0.03670	0.03130
20	0.12404	0.10367	0.08678	0.07276	0.06110	0.05139	0.04328	0.03651	0.03084	0.02608
21	0.11174	0.09256	0.07680	0.06383	0.05313	0.04430	0.03699	0.03094	0.02591	0.02174
22	0.10067	0.08264	0.06796	0.05599	0.04620	0.03819	0.03162	0.02622	0.02178	0.01811
23	0.09069	0.07379	0.06015	0.04911	0.04018	0.03292	0.02702	0.02222	0.01830	0.01510
24	0.08171	0.06588	0.05323	0.04308	0.03493	0.02838	0.02310	0.01883	0.01538	0.01258
25	0.07361	0.05882	0.04710	0.03779	0.03038	0.02447	0.01974	0.01596	0.01292	0.01048
26	0.06631	0.05252	0.04168	0.03315	0.02642	0.02109	0.01687	0.01352	0.01086	0.00874
27	0.05974	0.04689	0.03689	0.02908	0.02297	0.01818	0.01442	0.01146	0.00913	0.00728
28	0.05382	0.04187	0.03265	0.02551	0.01997	0.01567	0.01233	0.00971	0.00767	0.00607
29	0.04849	0.03738	0.02889	0.02238	0.01737	0.01351	0.01053	0.00823	0.00644	0.00506
30	0.04368	0.03338	0.02557	0.01963	0.01510	0.01165	0.00900	0.00698	0.00542	0.00421

TABLE A-1
PRESENT VALUE OF $1 (continued)

N	0.21	0.22	0.23	0.24	0.25	0.26	0.27	0.28	0.29	0.30
1	0.82645	0.81967	0.81301	0.80645	0.80000	0.79365	0.78740	0.78125	0.77519	0.76923
2	0.68301	0.67186	0.66098	0.65036	0.64000	0.62988	0.62000	0.61035	0.60093	0.59172
3	0.56448	0.55071	0.53738	0.52449	0.51200	0.49991	0.48819	0.47684	0.46583	0.45517
4	0.46651	0.45140	0.43690	0.42297	0.40960	0.39675	0.38440	0.37253	0.36111	0.35013
5	0.38555	0.37000	0.35520	0.34111	0.32768	0.31488	0.30268	0.29104	0.27993	0.26933
6	0.31863	0.30328	0.28878	0.27509	0.26214	0.24991	0.23833	0.22737	0.21700	0.20718
7	0.26333	0.24859	0.23478	0.22185	0.20972	0.19834	0.18766	0.17764	0.16822	0.15937
8	0.21763	0.20376	0.19088	0.17891	0.16777	0.15741	0.14777	0.13878	0.13040	0.12259
9	0.17986	0.16702	0.15519	0.14428	0.13422	0.12493	0.11635	0.10842	0.10109	0.09430
10	0.14865	0.13690	0.12617	0.11636	0.10737	0.09915	0.09161	0.08470	0.07836	0.07254
11	0.12285	0.11221	0.10258	0.09383	0.08590	0.07869	0.07214	0.06617	0.06075	0.05580
12	0.10153	0.09198	0.08340	0.07567	0.06872	0.06245	0.05680	0.05170	0.04709	0.04292
13	0.08391	0.07539	0.06780	0.06103	0.05498	0.04957	0.04473	0.04039	0.03650	0.03302
14	0.06934	0.06180	0.05512	0.04922	0.04398	0.03934	0.03522	0.03155	0.02830	0.02540
15	0.05731	0.05065	0.04482	0.03969	0.03518	0.03122	0.02773	0.02465	0.02194	0.01954
16	0.04736	0.04152	0.03644	0.03201	0.02815	0.02478	0.02183	0.01926	0.01700	0.01503
17	0.03914	0.03403	0.02962	0.02581	0.02252	0.01967	0.01719	0.01505	0.01318	0.01156
18	0.03235	0.02790	0.02408	0.02082	0.01801	0.01561	0.01354	0.01176	0.01022	0.00889
19	0.02674	0.02286	0.01958	0.01679	0.01441	0.01239	0.01066	0.00918	0.00792	0.00684
20	0.02210	0.01874	0.01592	0.01354	0.01153	0.00983	0.00839	0.00717	0.00614	0.00526
21	0.01826	0.01536	0.01294	0.01092	0.00922	0.00780	0.00661	0.00561	0.00476	0.00405
22	0.01509	0.01259	0.01052	0.00880	0.00738	0.00619	0.00520	0.00438	0.00369	0.00311
23	0.01247	0.01032	0.00855	0.00710	0.00590	0.00491	0.00410	0.00342	0.00286	0.00240
24	0.01031	0.00846	0.00695	0.00573	0.00472	0.00390	0.00323	0.00267	0.00222	0.00184
25	0.00852	0.00693	0.00565	0.00462	0.00378	0.00310	0.00254	0.00209	0.00172	0.00142
26	0.00704	0.00568	0.00460	0.00372	0.00302	0.00246	0.00200	0.00163	0.00133	0.00109
27	0.00582	0.00466	0.00374	0.00300	0.00242	0.00195	0.00158	0.00127	0.00103	0.00084
28	0.00481	0.00382	0.00304	0.00242	0.00193	0.00155	0.00124	0.00100	0.00080	0.00065
29	0.00397	0.00313	0.00247	0.00195	0.00155	0.00123	0.00098	0.00078	0.00062	0.00050
30	0.00328	0.00257	0.00201	0.00158	0.00124	0.00097	0.00077	0.00061	0.00048	0.00038

N	0.31	0.32	0.33	0.34	0.35	0.36	0.37	0.38	0.39	0.40
1	0.76336	0.75758	0.75188	0.74627	0.74074	0.73529	0.72993	0.72464	0.71942	0.71429
2	0.58272	0.57392	0.56532	0.55692	0.54870	0.54066	0.53279	0.52510	0.51757	0.51020
3	0.44482	0.43479	0.42506	0.41561	0.40644	0.39754	0.38890	0.38051	0.37235	0.36443
4	0.33956	0.32939	0.31959	0.31016	0.30107	0.29231	0.28387	0.27573	0.26788	0.26031
5	0.25921	0.24953	0.24029	0.23146	0.22301	0.21493	0.20720	0.19980	0.19272	0.18593
6	0.19787	0.18904	0.18067	0.17273	0.16520	0.15804	0.15124	0.14479	0.13865	0.13281
7	0.15104	0.14321	0.13584	0.12890	0.12237	0.11621	0.11040	0.10492	0.09975	0.09486
8	0.11530	0.10850	0.10214	0.09620	0.09064	0.08545	0.08058	0.07603	0.07176	0.06776
9	0.08802	0.08219	0.07680	0.07179	0.06714	0.06283	0.05882	0.05509	0.05163	0.04840
10	0.06719	0.06227	0.05774	0.05357	0.04974	0.04620	0.04293	0.03992	0.03714	0.03457
11	0.05129	0.04717	0.04341	0.03998	0.03684	0.03397	0.03134	0.02893	0.02672	0.02469
12	0.03915	0.03574	0.03264	0.02984	0.02729	0.02498	0.02287	0.02096	0.01922	0.01764
13	0.02989	0.02707	0.02454	0.02227	0.02021	0.01837	0.01670	0.01519	0.01383	0.01260
14	0.02281	0.02051	0.01845	0.01662	0.01497	0.01350	0.01219	0.01101	0.00995	0.00900
15	0.01742	0.01554	0.01387	0.01240	0.01109	0.00993	0.00890	0.00798	0.00716	0.00643
16	0.01329	0.01177	0.01043	0.00925	0.00822	0.00730	0.00649	0.00578	0.00515	0.00459
17	0.01015	0.00892	0.00784	0.00691	0.00609	0.00537	0.00474	0.00419	0.00370	0.00328
18	0.00775	0.00676	0.00590	0.00515	0.00451	0.00395	0.00346	0.00304	0.00267	0.00234
19	0.00591	0.00512	0.00443	0.00385	0.00334	0.00290	0.00253	0.00220	0.00192	0.00167
20	0.00451	0.00388	0.00333	0.00287	0.00247	0.00213	0.00184	0.00159	0.00138	0.00120
21	0.00345	0.00294	0.00251	0.00214	0.00183	0.00157	0.00135	0.00115	0.00099	0.00085
22	0.00263	0.00223	0.00188	0.00160	0.00136	0.00115	0.00098	0.00084	0.00071	0.00061
23	0.00201	0.00169	0.00142	0.00119	0.00101	0.00085	0.00072	0.00061	0.00051	0.00044
24	0.00153	0.00128	0.00107	0.00089	0.00074	0.00062	0.00052	0.00044	0.00037	0.00031
25	0.00117	0.00097	0.00080	0.00066	0.00055	0.00046	0.00038	0.00032	0.00027	0.00022
26	0.00089	0.00073	0.00060	0.00050	0.00041	0.00034	0.00028	0.00023	0.00019	0.00016
27	0.00068	0.00056	0.00045	0.00037	0.00030	0.00025	0.00020	0.00017	0.00014	0.00011
28	0.00052	0.00042	0.00034	0.00028	0.00022	0.00018	0.00015	0.00012	0.00010	0.00008
29	0.00040	0.00032	0.00026	0.00021	0.00017	0.00013	0.00011	0.00009	0.00007	0.00006
30	0.00030	0.00024	0.00019	0.00015	0.00012	0.00010	0.00008	0.00006	0.00005	0.00004

TABLE A-2
PRESENT VALUE OF AN ANNUITY OF $1

N	0.01	0.02	0.03	0.04	0.05	0.06	0.07	0.08	0.09	0.10
1	0.99010	0.98039	0.97087	0.96154	0.95238	0.94340	0.93458	0.92593	0.91743	0.90909
2	1.97040	1.94156	1.91347	1.88610	1.85941	1.83339	1.80802	1.78327	1.75911	1.73554
3	2.94099	2.88389	2.82861	2.77509	2.72325	2.67301	2.62432	2.57710	2.53130	2.48685
4	3.90197	3.80773	3.71710	3.62990	3.54596	3.46511	3.38722	3.31213	3.23973	3.16987
5	4.85345	4.71347	4.57971	4.45183	4.32949	4.21237	4.10020	3.99271	3.88966	3.79079
6	5.79550	5.60144	5.41720	5.24214	5.07571	4.91734	4.76655	4.62288	4.48593	4.35527
7	6.72822	6.47201	6.23030	6.00206	5.78639	5.58240	5.38930	5.20638	5.03297	4.86843
8	7.65172	7.32550	7.01971	6.73276	6.46324	6.20981	5.97131	5.74665	5.53484	5.33494
9	8.56607	8.16226	7.78613	7.43535	7.10785	6.80172	6.51525	6.24690	5.99527	5.75904
10	9.47136	8.98262	8.53023	8.11091	7.72177	7.36012	7.02360	6.71009	6.41768	6.14459
11	10.36770	9.78689	9.25266	8.76050	8.30646	7.88691	7.49870	7.13898	6.80522	6.49508
12	11.25516	10.57539	9.95405	9.38510	8.86330	8.38388	7.94271	7.53609	7.16076	6.81372
13	12.13384	11.34843	10.63500	9.98568	9.39363	8.85273	8.35768	7.90380	7.48694	7.10338
14	13.00382	12.10631	11.29613	10.56316	9.89870	9.29503	8.74550	8.24426	7.78619	7.36672
15	13.86518	12.84934	11.93800	11.11843	10.37973	9.71231	9.10795	8.55950	8.06073	7.60611
16	14.71802	13.57779	12.56117	11.65234	10.83784	10.10596	9.44669	8.85140	8.31261	7.82375
17	15.56242	14.29196	13.16620	12.16572	11.27415	10.47733	9.76327	9.12167	8.54368	8.02159
18	16.39845	14.99213	13.75360	12.65935	11.68968	10.82768	10.05914	9.37192	8.75568	8.20145
19	17.22621	15.67858	14.32389	13.13400	12.08542	11.15820	10.33565	9.60363	8.95017	8.36496
20	18.04578	16.35155	14.87758	13.59039	12.46231	11.47001	10.59407	9.81818	9.12861	8.51361
21	18.85722	17.01132	15.41514	14.02923	12.82126	11.76417	10.83559	10.01684	9.29231	8.64874
22	19.66063	17.65817	15.93704	14.45119	13.16312	12.04168	11.06131	10.20078	9.44249	8.77159
23	20.45609	18.29233	16.44373	14.85692	13.48870	12.30348	11.27226	10.37110	9.58028	8.88327
24	21.24367	18.91405	16.93567	15.24705	13.79877	12.55046	11.46941	10.52880	9.70668	8.98480
25	22.02345	19.52359	17.41328	15.62217	14.09408	12.78347	11.65366	10.67482	9.82265	9.07710
26	22.79552	20.12117	17.87698	15.98286	14.37533	13.00328	11.82586	10.81002	9.92905	9.16100
27	23.55994	20.70703	18.32718	16.32968	14.64319	13.21066	11.98679	10.93521	10.02666	9.23728
28	24.31679	21.28142	18.76425	16.66316	14.89829	13.40629	12.13720	11.05113	10.11621	9.30663
29	25.06615	21.84454	19.18860	16.98381	15.14124	13.59085	12.27776	11.15846	10.19837	9.36967
30	25.80809	22.39662	19.60059	17.29213	15.37262	13.76497	12.40913	11.25783	10.27374	9.42698

N	0.11	0.12	0.13	0.14	0.15	0.16	0.17	0.18	0.19	0.20
1	0.90090	0.89286	0.88496	0.87719	0.86957	0.86207	0.85470	0.84746	0.84034	0.83333
2	1.71252	1.69005	1.66810	1.64666	1.62571	1.60523	1.58522	1.56564	1.54650	1.52778
3	2.44372	2.40183	2.36116	2.32163	2.28323	2.24589	2.20959	2.17428	2.13992	2.10648
4	3.10245	3.03735	2.97448	2.91372	2.85498	2.79818	2.74324	2.69007	2.63859	2.58873
5	3.69590	3.60478	3.51724	3.43309	3.35216	3.27430	3.19935	3.12718	3.05764	2.99061
6	4.23054	4.11141	3.99756	3.88868	3.78449	3.68474	3.58919	3.49761	3.40978	3.32551
7	4.71220	4.56376	4.42262	4.28832	4.16043	4.03857	3.92239	3.81154	3.70570	3.60459
8	5.14613	4.96764	4.79879	4.63888	4.48733	4.34359	4.20717	4.07758	3.95437	3.83716
9	5.53706	5.32826	5.13167	4.94639	4.77159	4.60655	4.45058	4.30303	4.16334	4.03097
10	5.88925	5.65023	5.42627	5.21613	5.01878	4.83323	4.65862	4.49410	4.33894	4.19248
11	6.20653	5.93771	5.68697	5.45275	5.23372	5.02865	4.83643	4.65602	4.48651	4.32706
12	6.49237	6.19438	5.91767	5.66031	5.42063	5.19711	4.98841	4.79324	4.61051	4.43922
13	6.74989	6.42356	6.12184	5.84239	5.58316	5.34234	5.11830	4.90953	4.71472	4.53268
14	6.98189	6.62818	6.30252	6.00210	5.72449	5.46753	5.22932	5.00808	4.80228	4.61057
15	7.19089	6.81087	6.46241	6.14220	5.84739	5.57546	5.32421	5.09159	4.87587	4.67548
16	7.37919	6.97400	6.60391	6.26509	5.95425	5.66850	5.40531	5.16237	4.93771	4.72956
17	7.54882	7.11964	6.72913	6.37289	6.04718	5.74871	5.47463	5.22235	4.98967	4.77464
18	7.70164	7.24968	6.83995	6.46745	6.12798	5.81785	5.53387	5.27318	5.03334	4.81220
19	7.83932	7.36579	6.93801	6.55040	6.19825	5.87746	5.58451	5.31626	5.07003	4.84350
20	7.96336	7.46946	7.02479	6.62317	6.25935	5.92885	5.62779	5.35276	5.10087	4.86958
21	8.07510	7.56202	7.10159	6.68699	6.31248	5.97315	5.66478	5.38370	5.12678	4.89132
22	8.17577	7.64466	7.16956	6.74298	6.35868	6.01133	5.69640	5.40992	5.14856	4.90943
23	8.26646	7.71845	7.22970	6.79209	6.39886	6.04425	5.72342	5.43214	5.16685	4.92453
24	8.34817	7.78433	7.28293	6.83517	6.43379	6.07263	5.74652	5.45097	5.18223	4.93711
25	8.42178	7.84315	7.33003	6.87296	6.46417	6.09710	5.76626	5.46692	5.19515	4.94759
26	8.48809	7.89567	7.37172	6.90611	6.49058	6.11819	5.78313	5.48045	5.20601	4.95632
27	8.54784	7.94257	7.40861	6.93519	6.51355	6.13637	5.79755	5.49191	5.21514	4.96360
28	8.60166	7.98444	7.44125	6.96070	6.53353	6.15204	5.80987	5.50162	5.22280	4.96967
29	8.65015	8.02182	7.47014	6.98308	6.55090	6.16556	5.82041	5.50985	5.22925	4.97472
30	8.69383	8.05520	7.49570	7.00270	6.56600	6.17720	5.82941	5.51682	5.23466	4.97894

TABLE A-2
PRESENT VALUE OF AN ANNUITY OF $1 (continued)

N	0.21	0.22	0.23	0.24	0.25	0.26	0.27	0.28	0.29	0.30
1	0.82645	0.81967	0.81301	0.80645	0.80000	0.79365	0.78740	0.78125	0.77519	0.76923
2	1.50946	1.49154	1.47399	1.45682	1.44000	1.42353	1.40740	1.39160	1.37612	1.36095
3	2.07394	2.04224	2.01137	1.98130	1.95200	1.92344	1.89559	1.86844	1.84195	1.81611
4	2.54045	2.49364	2.44827	2.40428	2.36160	2.32019	2.28000	2.24097	2.20306	2.16624
5	2.92599	2.86364	2.80347	2.74539	2.68928	2.63507	2.58267	2.53201	2.48299	2.43557
6	3.24462	3.16692	3.09226	3.02047	2.95142	2.88498	2.82100	2.75938	2.70000	2.64275
7	3.50795	3.41551	3.32704	3.24232	3.16114	3.08332	3.00867	2.93702	2.86821	2.80212
8	3.72558	3.61927	3.51792	3.42122	3.32891	3.24073	3.15643	3.07579	2.99861	2.92471
9	3.90545	3.78629	3.67311	3.56550	3.46312	3.36566	3.27278	3.18421	3.09970	3.01900
10	4.05409	3.92319	3.79927	3.68186	3.57050	3.46481	3.36440	3.26892	3.17806	3.09154
11	4.17694	4.03540	3.90185	3.77569	3.65640	3.54350	3.43653	3.33509	3.23881	3.14734
12	4.27846	4.12738	3.98524	3.85137	3.72511	3.60595	3.49333	3.38679	3.28589	3.19026
13	4.36237	4.20277	4.05304	3.91239	3.78009	3.65552	3.53806	3.42718	3.32240	3.22328
14	4.43171	4.26457	4.10817	3.96161	3.82407	3.69486	3.57328	3.45873	3.35069	3.24868
15	4.48902	4.31522	4.15298	4.00130	3.85925	3.72608	3.60100	3.48339	3.37263	3.26821
16	4.53638	4.35674	4.18942	4.03330	3.88740	3.75086	3.62284	3.50264	3.38963	3.28324
17	4.57553	4.39077	4.21904	4.05911	3.90992	3.77052	3.64003	3.51769	3.40281	3.29480
18	4.60788	4.41867	4.24312	4.07993	3.92793	3.78613	3.65357	3.52944	3.41303	3.30369
19	4.63461	4.44153	4.26270	4.09672	3.94234	3.79852	3.66423	3.53863	3.42095	3.31053
20	4.65671	4.46027	4.27862	4.11026	3.95378	3.80835	3.67262	3.54580	3.42709	3.31579
21	4.67497	4.47564	4.29156	4.12117	3.96309	3.81615	3.67923	3.55141	3.43185	3.31984
22	4.69006	4.48823	4.30208	4.12998	3.97047	3.82234	3.68443	3.55579	3.43554	3.32296
23	4.70253	4.49855	4.31063	4.13708	3.97638	3.82725	3.68853	3.55921	3.43840	3.32535
24	4.71284	4.50701	4.31759	4.14280	3.98110	3.83115	3.69175	3.56188	3.44062	3.32719
25	4.72135	4.51394	4.32324	4.14742	3.98487	3.83425	3.69429	3.56397	3.44234	3.32861
26	4.72839	4.51963	4.32784	4.15115	3.98790	3.83671	3.69629	3.56560	3.44367	3.32970
27	4.73421	4.52428	4.33157	4.15415	3.99031	3.83865	3.69787	3.56687	3.44470	3.33054
28	4.73902	4.52810	4.33461	4.15657	3.99225	3.84020	3.69911	3.56787	3.44550	3.33118
29	4.74300	4.53123	4.33708	4.15852	3.99380	3.84143	3.70008	3.56864	3.44612	3.33168
30	4.74628	4.53380	4.33909	4.16010	3.99503	3.84240	3.70085	3.56925	3.44660	3.33206

N	0.31	0.32	0.33	0.34	0.35	0.36	0.37	0.38	0.39	0.40
1	0.76336	0.75758	0.75188	0.74627	0.74074	0.73529	0.72993	0.72464	0.71942	0.71429
2	1.34608	1.33150	1.31720	1.30319	1.28944	1.27595	1.26272	1.24974	1.23700	1.22449
3	1.79090	1.76629	1.74226	1.71880	1.69588	1.67349	1.65162	1.63025	1.60935	1.58892
4	2.13046	2.09567	2.06185	2.02895	1.99695	1.96580	1.93549	1.90598	1.87723	1.84923
5	2.38966	2.34521	2.30214	2.26041	2.21996	2.18074	2.14269	2.10578	2.06995	2.03516
6	2.58753	2.53425	2.48281	2.43315	2.38516	2.33878	2.29393	2.25057	2.20860	2.16797
7	2.73857	2.67746	2.61866	2.56205	2.50753	2.45498	2.40433	2.35548	2.30834	2.26284
8	2.85387	2.78596	2.72079	2.65825	2.59817	2.54043	2.48491	2.43151	2.38010	2.33060
9	2.94189	2.86815	2.79759	2.73004	2.66531	2.60326	2.54373	2.48660	2.43173	2.37900
10	3.00908	2.93042	2.85533	2.78361	2.71504	2.64945	2.58666	2.52652	2.46887	2.41357
11	3.06036	2.97759	2.89874	2.82359	2.75189	2.68342	2.61800	2.55545	2.49559	2.43826
12	3.09951	3.01332	2.93139	2.85343	2.77917	2.70840	2.64088	2.57642	2.51481	2.45590
13	3.12940	3.04040	2.95593	2.87569	2.79939	2.72676	2.65757	2.59161	2.52864	2.46850
14	3.15222	3.06091	2.97438	2.89231	2.81436	2.74026	2.66976	2.60261	2.53859	2.47750
15	3.16963	3.07644	2.98825	2.90471	2.82545	2.75019	2.67865	2.61059	2.54575	2.48393
16	3.18292	3.08821	2.99869	2.91396	2.83367	2.75749	2.68515	2.61637	2.55090	2.48852
17	3.19307	3.09713	3.00653	2.92087	2.83976	2.76286	2.68989	2.62056	2.55460	2.49180
18	3.20082	3.10388	3.01243	2.92602	2.84426	2.76681	2.69335	2.62359	2.55727	2.49414
19	3.20673	3.10900	3.01686	2.92986	2.84760	2.76971	2.69587	2.62579	2.55918	2.49581
20	3.21125	3.11288	3.02019	2.93273	2.85007	2.77184	2.69771	2.62738	2.56056	2.49701
21	3.21469	3.11582	3.02270	2.93487	2.85191	2.77341	2.69906	2.62854	2.56155	2.49786
22	3.21732	3.11804	3.02458	2.93647	2.85326	2.77457	2.70004	2.62938	2.56227	2.49847
23	3.21933	3.11973	3.02600	2.93766	2.85427	2.77541	2.70075	2.62998	2.56278	2.49891
24	3.22086	3.12100	3.02707	2.93855	2.85501	2.77604	2.70128	2.63042	2.56315	2.49922
25	3.22203	3.12197	3.02787	2.93922	2.85556	2.77649	2.70166	2.63074	2.56341	2.49944
26	3.22292	3.12270	3.02847	2.93971	2.85597	2.77683	2.70194	2.63097	2.56360	2.49960
27	3.22360	3.12326	3.02892	2.94008	2.85627	2.77708	2.70214	2.63113	2.56374	2.49971
28	3.22412	3.12368	3.02926	2.94036	2.85650	2.77726	2.70229	2.63126	2.56384	2.49979
29	3.22452	3.12400	3.02952	2.94056	2.85666	2.77740	2.70240	2.63134	2.56391	2.49985
30	3.22482	3.12424	3.02971	2.94072	2.85679	2.77749	2.70247	2.63141	2.56396	2.49989

TABLE A-3
FUTURE VALUE OF $1

N	0.01	0.02	0.03	0.04	0.05	0.06	0.07	0.08	0.09	0.10
1	1.01000	1.02000	1.03000	1.04000	1.05000	1.06000	1.07000	1.08000	1.09000	1.10000
2	1.02010	1.04040	1.06090	1.08160	1.10250	1.12360	1.14490	1.16640	1.18810	1.21000
3	1.03030	1.06121	1.09272	1.12486	1.15762	1.19101	1.22504	1.25971	1.29502	1.33100
4	1.04060	1.08243	1.12551	1.16986	1.21550	1.26247	1.31079	1.36049	1.41158	1.46410
5	1.05100	1.10408	1.15927	1.21665	1.27628	1.33822	1.40255	1.46932	1.53862	1.61050
6	1.06151	1.12616	1.19405	1.26532	1.34009	1.41851	1.50072	1.58687	1.67709	1.77155
7	1.07213	1.14868	1.22987	1.31593	1.40709	1.50362	1.60577	1.71382	1.82803	1.94870
8	1.08285	1.17165	1.26676	1.36856	1.47744	1.59384	1.71817	1.85092	1.99255	2.14357
9	1.09367	1.19508	1.30476	1.42330	1.55131	1.68946	1.83845	1.99899	2.17187	2.35793
10	1.10461	1.21898	1.34391	1.48024	1.62888	1.79033	1.96714	2.15891	2.36734	2.59372
11	1.11565	1.24336	1.38422	1.53944	1.71032	1.89828	2.10483	2.33162	2.58040	2.85309
12	1.12681	1.26823	1.42575	1.60102	1.79583	2.01217	2.25217	2.51815	2.81263	3.13840
13	1.13807	1.29359	1.46852	1.66506	1.88562	2.13290	2.40982	2.71960	3.06576	3.45223
14	1.14945	1.31946	1.51257	1.73166	1.97990	2.26087	2.57850	2.93717	3.34168	3.79745
15	1.16095	1.34585	1.55795	1.80093	2.07890	2.39652	2.75900	3.17214	3.64243	4.17719
16	1.17255	1.37277	1.60468	1.87296	2.18284	2.54031	2.95212	3.42591	3.97024	4.59491
17	1.18428	1.40022	1.65282	1.94788	2.29198	2.69273	3.15877	3.69998	4.32756	5.05440
18	1.19612	1.42822	1.70241	2.02579	2.40658	2.85429	3.37988	3.99598	4.71704	5.55983
19	1.20808	1.45679	1.75348	2.10683	2.52690	3.02555	3.61647	4.31565	5.14156	6.11581
20	1.22016	1.48592	1.80608	2.19110	2.65324	3.20707	3.86962	4.66090	5.60430	6.72738
21	1.23236	1.51564	1.86026	2.27874	2.78596	3.39950	4.14049	5.03377	6.10868	7.40011
22	1.24468	1.54595	1.91607	2.36989	2.92520	3.60346	4.43032	5.43647	6.65846	8.14012
23	1.25712	1.57687	1.97355	2.46468	3.07145	3.81967	4.74044	5.87138	7.25771	8.95412
24	1.26969	1.60841	2.03275	2.56327	3.22502	4.04884	5.07227	6.34109	7.91090	9.84952
25	1.28239	1.64057	2.09373	2.66580	3.38627	4.29177	5.42732	6.84838	8.62287	10.83447
26	1.29521	1.67338	2.15654	2.77243	3.55558	4.54927	5.80723	7.39624	9.39892	11.91790
27	1.30816	1.70685	2.22124	2.88332	3.73335	4.82222	6.21373	7.98794	10.24481	13.10968
28	1.32124	1.74098	2.28787	2.99865	3.92002	5.11155	6.64868	8.62696	11.16683	14.42064
29	1.33445	1.77580	2.35651	3.11860	4.11602	5.41824	7.11409	9.31712	12.17183	15.86269
30	1.34780	1.81132	2.42720	3.24334	4.32181	5.74332	7.61206	10.06248	13.26729	17.44893

N	0.11	0.12	0.13	0.14	0.15	0.16	0.17	0.18	0.19	0.20
1	1.11000	1.12000	1.13000	1.14000	1.15000	1.16000	1.17000	1.18000	1.19000	1.20000
2	1.23210	1.25440	1.27690	1.29960	1.32250	1.34560	1.36890	1.39240	1.41610	1.44000
3	1.36763	1.40493	1.44289	1.48154	1.52087	1.56089	1.60161	1.64303	1.68516	1.72800
4	1.51807	1.57352	1.63047	1.68895	1.74900	1.81064	1.87388	1.93877	2.00533	2.07360
5	1.68508	1.76234	1.84243	1.92541	2.01135	2.10034	2.19244	2.28775	2.38635	2.48831
6	1.87041	1.97382	2.08194	2.19496	2.31305	2.43639	2.56515	2.69954	2.83975	2.93598
7	2.07615	2.21067	2.35259	2.50225	2.66001	2.82621	3.00122	3.18546	3.37930	3.58317
8	2.30453	2.47596	2.65842	2.85256	3.05901	3.27840	3.51142	3.75883	4.02137	4.29980
9	2.55802	2.77307	3.00401	3.25192	3.51785	3.80295	4.10836	4.43542	4.78542	5.15976
10	2.83940	3.10584	3.39453	3.70718	4.04553	4.41142	4.80678	5.23379	5.69465	6.19171
11	3.15173	3.47853	3.83581	4.22618	4.65236	5.11724	5.62393	6.17587	6.77663	7.43004
12	3.49842	3.89596	4.33447	4.81785	5.35021	5.93600	6.57998	7.28752	8.06419	8.91605
13	3.88325	4.36347	4.89794	5.49234	6.15273	6.88576	7.69858	8.59927	9.59638	10.69925
14	4.31040	4.88708	5.53467	6.26126	7.07564	7.98747	9.00732	10.14712	11.41968	12.83910
15	4.78454	5.47353	6.25416	7.13783	8.13698	9.26546	10.53856	11.97360	13.58941	15.40691
16	5.31084	6.13035	7.06720	8.13711	9.35752	10.74793	12.33010	14.12883	16.17139	18.48827
17	5.89503	6.86599	7.98593	9.27631	10.76114	12.46760	14.42620	16.67201	19.24394	22.18591
18	6.54347	7.68991	9.02409	10.57498	12.37530	14.46241	16.87863	19.67294	22.90027	26.62308
19	7.26325	8.61269	10.19721	12.05546	14.23158	16.77638	19.74799	23.21407	27.25130	31.94768
20	8.06220	9.64621	11.52283	13.74321	16.36630	19.46059	23.10510	27.39256	32.42903	38.33719
21	8.94904	10.80376	13.02079	15.66724	18.82124	22.57428	27.03296	32.32320	38.59053	46.00461
22	9.93343	12.10020	14.71347	17.86063	21.64441	26.18616	31.62852	38.14134	45.92271	55.20549
23	11.02609	13.55221	16.62619	20.36110	24.89105	30.37592	37.00534	45.00676	54.64798	66.24657
24	12.23896	15.17848	18.78758	23.21162	28.62468	35.23607	43.29619	53.10793	65.03199	79.49583
25	13.58523	16.99988	21.22995	26.46124	32.91837	40.87383	50.65649	62.66731	77.38693	95.39497
26	15.07960	19.03986	23.98982	30.16577	37.85609	47.41362	59.26805	73.94736	92.09041	114.47389
27	16.73833	21.32463	27.10846	34.38895	43.53448	54.99976	69.34354	87.25783	109.58749	137.36862
28	18.57954	23.88358	30.63252	39.20335	50.06462	63.79970	81.13185	102.96411	130.40907	164.84224
29	20.62328	26.74960	34.61472	44.69179	57.57428	74.00764	94.92419	121.49756	155.18671	197.81067
30	22.89183	29.95955	39.11458	50.94858	66.21037	85.84883	111.06117	143.36697	184.67207	237.37262

TABLE A-3
FUTURE VALUE OF $1 (continued)

N	0.21	0.22	0.23	0.24	0.25	0.26	0.27	0.28	0.29	0.30
1	1.21000	1.22000	1.23000	1.24000	1.25000	1.26000	1.27000	1.28000	1.29000	1.300
2	1.46410	1.48840	1.51290	1.53760	1.56250	1.58760	1.61290	1.63840	1.66410	1.690
3	1.77156	1.81584	1.86086	1.90662	1.95313	2.00037	2.04838	2.09715	2.14669	2.196
4	2.14358	2.21533	2.28886	2.36421	2.44141	2.52047	2.60144	2.68435	2.76923	2.856
5	2.59373	2.70270	2.81530	2.93162	3.05176	3.17579	3.33383	3.43597	3.57230	3.712
6	3.13841	3.29729	3.46281	3.63520	3.81470	4.00149	4.19586	4.39804	4.60827	4.826
7	3.79747	4.02269	4.25926	4.50765	4.76837	5.04187	5.32873	5.62949	5.94467	6.274
8	4.59493	4.90767	5.23889	5.58948	5.96046	6.35275	6.76749	7.20574	7.66862	8.157
9	5.55986	5.98736	6.44383	6.93096	7.45058	8.00446	8.59470	9.22334	9.89252	10.604
10	6.72743	7.30457	7.92590	8.59438	9.31323	10.08562	10.91526	11.80588	12.76134	13.785
11	8.14018	8.91157	9.74885	10.65703	11.64153	12.70787	13.86238	15.11152	16.46213	17.921
12	9.84960	10.87211	11.99108	13.21471	14.55192	16.01190	17.60519	19.34273	21.23813	23.297
13	11.91801	13.26396	14.74903	16.38623	18.18988	20.17497	22.35860	24.75868	27.39461	30.287
14	14.42077	16.18201	18.14128	20.31891	22.73737	25.42044	28.39539	31.69112	35.33905	39.373
15	17.44911	19.74203	22.31377	25.19543	28.42171	32.02974	36.06212	40.56461	45.58737	51.185
16	21.11340	24.08527	27.44592	31.24232	35.52713	40.35745	45.79887	51.92268	58.80769	66.540
17	25.54720	29.38400	33.75847	38.74046	44.40891	50.85036	58.16454	66.46101	75.86191	86.503
18	30.91206	35.84845	41.52289	48.03815	55.51114	64.07140	73.86690	85.07007	97.86186	112.453
19	37.40356	43.73506	51.07312	59.56726	69.38892	80.72990	93.81345	108.88963	126.24179	146.189
20	45.25826	53.35674	62.81990	73.86339	86.73615	101.71960	119.14299	139.37869	162.85185	190.046
21	54.76244	65.09517	77.26845	91.59058	108.42020	128.16663	151.31152	178.40469	210.07883	247.060
22	66.26247	79.41603	95.04013	113.57222	135.52524	161.48981	192.16548	228.35793	271.00171	321.178
23	80.17751	96.88748	116.89926	140.82947	169.40656	203.47702	244.04999	292.29785	349.59204	417.531
24	97.01466	118.20265	143.78606	174.62848	211.75819	256.38086	309.94833	374.14136	450.97363	542.790
25	117.38765	144.20712	176.85677	216.53968	264.69751	323.03955	393.62769	478.90063	581.75610	705.627
26	142.03886	175.93253	217.53368	268.50830	330.87207	407.02954	499.90674	612.99268	750.46509	917.315
27	171.86688	214.63751	267.56616	332.95020	413.59009	512.85693	634.88110	784.63037	968.09961	1192.508
28	207.95863	261.85742	329.10620	412.85815	516.98755	646.19946	806.29785	1004.32617	1248.84766	1550.259
29	251.62975	319.46582	404.80054	511.94385	646.23413	814.21045	1023.99854	1285.53711	1611.01367	2015.336
30	304.47144	389.74780	497.90405	634.80981	807.79321	1025.90405	1300.47656	1645.48779	2078.20801	2619.936

TABLE A-4
FUTURE VALUE OF AN ANNUITY OF $1

N	0.01	0.02	0.03	0.04	0.05	0.06	0.07	0.08	0.09	0.10
1	1.00000	1.00000	1.00000	1.00000	1.00000	1.00000	1.00000	1.00000	1.00000	1.00000
2	2.01000	2.02000	2.03000	2.04000	2.05000	2.06000	2.07000	2.08000	2.09000	2.10000
3	3.03010	3.06040	3.09090	3.12160	3.15250	3.18360	3.21490	3.24640	3.27810	3.31000
4	4.06039	4.12160	4.18362	4.24646	4.31012	4.37461	4.43994	4.50611	4.57312	4.64099
5	5.10099	5.20403	5.30913	5.41632	5.52562	5.63708	5.75073	5.86660	5.98470	6.10509
6	6.15200	6.30811	6.46840	6.63297	6.80190	6.97530	7.15328	7.33592	7.52331	7.71559
7	7.21351	7.43427	7.66245	7.89828	8.14198	8.39381	8.65400	8.92279	9.20041	9.48714
8	8.28563	8.58295	8.89231	9.21421	9.54907	9.89743	10.25977	10.63661	11.02843	11.43585
9	9.36848	9.75460	10.15907	10.58277	11.02652	11.49127	11.97795	12.48753	13.02098	13.57942
10	10.46215	10.94968	11.46384	12.00608	12.57783	13.18073	13.81639	14.48652	15.19285	15.93735
11	11.56676	12.16867	12.80774	13.48631	14.20671	14.97157	15.78353	16.64543	17.56018	18.53107
12	12.68241	13.41203	14.19197	15.02576	15.91703	16.86984	17.88835	18.97705	20.14056	21.38416
13	13.80922	14.68026	15.61771	16.62677	17.71286	18.88200	20.14052	21.49519	22.95319	24.52254
14	14.94729	15.97385	17.08623	18.29184	19.59848	21.01489	22.55034	24.21478	26.01894	27.97476
15	16.09674	17.29330	18.59879	20.02350	21.57838	23.27576	25.12883	27.15195	29.36061	31.77220
16	17.25769	18.63914	20.15672	21.82442	23.65727	25.67227	27.88782	30.32408	33.00304	35.94939
17	18.43024	20.01190	21.76140	23.69737	25.84010	28.21257	30.83994	33.74998	36.97327	40.54428
18	19.61450	21.41211	23.41422	25.64525	28.13208	30.90529	33.99870	37.44997	41.30083	45.59866
19	20.81061	22.84033	25.11662	27.67104	30.53865	33.75957	37.37857	41.44594	46.01785	51.15849
20	22.01868	24.29712	26.87009	29.77785	33.06555	36.78511	40.99504	45.76158	51.15941	57.27429
21	23.23883	25.78304	28.67616	31.96893	35.71880	39.99217	44.86465	50.42247	56.76370	64.00166
22	24.47118	27.29866	30.53642	34.24767	38.50470	43.39166	49.00514	55.45624	62.87238	71.40176
23	25.71585	28.84460	32.45248	36.61754	41.42989	46.99512	53.43546	60.89270	69.53082	79.54187
24	26.97296	30.42146	34.42603	39.08221	44.50133	50.81477	58.17589	66.76408	76.78853	88.49599
25	28.24265	32.02986	36.45877	41.64548	47.72635	54.86360	63.24815	73.10516	84.69942	98.34550
26	29.52502	33.67043	38.55249	44.31126	51.11261	59.15536	68.67548	79.95354	93.32228	109.17996
27	30.82024	35.34380	40.70903	47.08368	54.66818	63.70462	74.48270	87.34978	102.72119	121.09785
28	32.12839	37.05064	42.93027	49.96700	58.40154	68.52684	80.69643	95.33771	112.96599	134.20752
29	33.44962	38.79163	45.21814	52.96564	62.32155	73.63838	87.34511	103.96466	124.13281	148.62814
30	34.78406	40.56741	47.57465	56.08423	66.43756	79.05661	94.45920	113.28177	136.30464	164.49083

TABLE A-4
FUTURE VALUE OF ANNUITY OF $1 (continued)

N	0.11	0.12	0.13	0.14	0.15	0.16	0.17	0.18	0.19	0.20
1	1.00000	1.00000	1.00000	1.00000	1.00000	1.00000	1.00000	1.00000	1.00000	1.00000
2	2.11000	2.12000	2.13000	2.14000	2.15000	2.16000	2.17000	2.18000	2.19000	2.20000
3	3.34210	3.37440	3.40690	3.43960	3.47250	3.50560	3.53890	3.57240	3.60610	3.64000
4	4.70973	4.77933	4.84979	4.92114	4.99337	5.06649	5.14050	5.21543	5.29125	5.36800
5	6.22779	6.35284	6.48026	6.61009	6.74237	6.87713	7.01438	7.15420	7.29659	7.44159
6	7.91285	8.11518	8.32268	8.53550	8.75372	8.97747	9.20682	9.44195	9.68294	9.92991
7	9.78325	10.08900	10.40462	10.73046	11.06677	11.41386	11.77197	12.14149	12.52269	12.91588
8	11.85940	12.29967	12.75721	13.23271	13.72678	14.24007	14.77319	15.32694	15.90199	16.49904
9	14.16393	14.77563	15.41563	16.08527	16.78578	17.51846	18.28461	19.08577	19.92336	20.79884
10	16.72194	17.54869	18.41963	19.33719	20.30363	21.32141	22.39296	23.52118	24.70877	25.95859
11	19.56134	20.65453	21.81415	23.04437	24.34915	25.73282	27.19974	28.75496	30.40341	32.15028
12	22.71307	24.13306	25.64995	27.27055	29.00150	30.85005	32.82365	34.93082	37.18004	39.58032
13	26.21149	28.02901	29.98441	32.08839	34.35170	36.78604	39.40363	42.21832	45.24422	48.49637
14	30.09473	32.39247	34.88234	37.58073	40.50443	43.67178	47.10219	50.81758	54.84059	59.19562
15	34.40512	37.27954	40.41699	43.84198	47.58005	51.65926	56.10950	60.96469	66.26027	72.03471
16	39.18965	42.75307	46.67114	50.97980	55.71701	60.92471	66.64804	72.93828	79.84967	87.44162
17	44.50049	48.88341	53.73834	59.11690	65.07452	71.67264	78.97813	87.06711	96.02106	105.92989
18	50.39551	55.74939	61.72426	68.39319	75.83566	84.14023	93.40433	103.73912	115.26500	128.11580
19	56.93898	63.43929	70.74834	78.96875	88.21095	98.60263	110.28296	123.41206	138.16527	154.73888
20	64.20222	72.05197	80.94554	91.02361	102.44254	115.37901	130.03094	146.62613	165.41656	186.68655
21	72.26442	81.69818	92.46837	104.76680	118.80884	134.83960	153.13605	174.01869	197.84560	225.02374
22	81.21346	92.50194	105.48915	120.43404	137.63008	157.41388	180.16901	206.34189	236.43613	271.02832
23	91.14688	104.60213	120.20261	138.29466	159.27449	183.60004	211.79753	244.48323	282.35864	326.23364
24	102.17297	118.15433	136.82880	158.65576	184.16554	213.97595	248.80287	289.48999	337.00659	392.47998
25	114.41193	133.33279	155.61638	181.86739	212.79022	249.21202	292.09888	342.59790	402.03760	471.97559
26	127.99715	150.33267	176.84633	208.32863	245.70859	290.08569	342.75537	405.26514	479.42432	567.37036
27	143.07674	169.37253	200.83615	238.49440	283.56445	337.49927	402.02319	479.21240	571.51465	681.84424
28	159.81506	190.69716	227.94461	272.88330	327.09888	392.49902	471.36670	566.47021	681.10205	819.21265
29	178.39461	214.58073	258.57690	312.08643	377.16333	456.29858	552.49854	669.43433	811.51099	984.05469
30	199.01788	241.33034	293.19141	356.77808	434.73755	530.30615	647.42261	790.93188	966.69751	1181.86523

N	0.21	0.22	0.23	0.24	0.25	0.26	0.27	0.28	0.29	0.30
1	1.00000	1.00000	1.00000	1.00000	1.00000	1.00000	1.00000	1.00000	1.00000	1.00000
2	2.21000	2.22000	2.23000	2.24000	2.25000	2.26000	2.27000	2.28000	2.29000	2.30000
3	3.67410	3.70840	3.74290	3.77760	3.81250	3.84760	3.88290	3.91840	3.95410	3.99000
4	5.44565	5.52424	5.60376	5.68422	5.76563	5.84797	5.93128	6.01555	6.10079	6.18699
5	7.58923	7.73957	7.89262	8.04843	8.20703	8.36844	8.53272	8.69990	8.87002	9.04308
6	10.18296	10.44226	10.70792	10.98005	11.25879	11.54422	11.83654	12.13587	12.44232	12.75600
7	13.32137	13.73955	14.17074	14.61525	15.07349	15.54571	16.03239	16.53391	17.05058	17.58278
8	17.11884	17.76224	18.42999	19.12289	19.84186	20.58757	21.36113	22.16339	22.99524	23.85759
9	21.71376	22.66991	23.66887	24.71237	25.80232	26.94032	28.12862	29.36913	30.66385	32.01485
10	27.27362	28.65726	30.11269	31.64333	33.25290	34.94478	36.72331	38.59247	40.55637	42.61926
11	34.00104	35.96182	38.03857	40.23770	42.56612	45.03038	47.63857	50.39835	53.31770	56.40500
12	42.14120	44.87338	47.78741	50.89471	54.20764	57.73824	61.50093	65.50986	69.77983	74.32645
13	51.99080	55.74548	59.77849	64.10942	68.75955	73.75014	79.10612	84.85258	91.01596	97.62431
14	63.90880	69.00943	74.52751	80.49565	86.94943	93.92511	101.46472	109.61127	118.41057	127.91153
15	78.32956	85.19144	92.66879	100.81456	109.68680	119.34555	129.86011	141.30238	153.74962	167.28488
16	95.77867	104.93347	114.98256	126.00999	138.10851	151.37529	165.92223	181.86699	199.33699	218.47018
17	116.89207	129.01874	142.42848	157.25232	173.63564	191.73274	211.72110	233.78967	258.14453	285.01386
18	142.43927	158.40274	176.18695	195.99278	218.04454	242.58310	269.88550	300.25049	334.00635	371.51392
19	173.35133	194.25119	217.70984	244.03093	273.55566	306.65430	343.75439	385.32056	431.86816	483.96777
20	210.75490	237.98625	268.78296	303.59814	342.94458	387.38403	437.56763	494.20996	558.10986	630.15747
21	256.01294	291.34277	331.60278	377.46143	429.68066	489.10352	556.71045	633.58862	720.96167	820.20410
22	310.77539	356.43774	408.87109	469.05200	538.10083	617.27002	708.02197	811.99316	931.04028	1067.26465
23	377.03784	435.85376	503.91113	582.62402	673.62598	778.75977	900.18726	1040.35107	1202.04199	1388.44312
24	457.21533	532.74121	620.81030	723.45337	843.03247	982.23657	1144.23706	1332.64893	1551.63403	1805.97461
25	554.22998	650.94385	764.59619	898.08179	1054.79053	1238.61743	1454.18018	1706.79028	2002.60767	2348.76538
26	671.61743	795.15088	941.45288	1114.62085	1319.48804	1561.65698	1847.80786	2185.69092	2584.36377	3054.39282
27	813.65625	971.08325	1158.98633	1383.12915	1650.36011	1968.68652	2347.71460	2798.68359	3334.82886	3971.70801
28	985.52295	1185.72070	1426.55249	1716.07935	2063.95020	2481.54346	2982.59570	3583.31396	4302.92578	5164.21484
29	1193.48145	1447.57813	1755.65869	2128.93750	2580.93774	3127.74292	3788.89355	4587.63672	5551.77344	6714.47266
30	1445.11108	1767.04395	2160.45923	2640.88135	3227.17188	3941.95337	4812.89063	5873.17188	7162.78516	8729.98548

CUMULATIVE NORMAL DISTRIBUTION

(Area to the Right or Left; One Tail)

$$\Phi(x) = \int_{-\infty}^{x} \frac{1}{\sqrt{2\pi}} e^{-t^2/2} dt$$

χ	.00	.01	.02	.03	.04	.05	.06	.07	.08	.09
.0	.5000	.5040	.5080	.5120	.5160	.5199	.5239	.5279	.5319	.5359
.1	.5398	.5438	.5478	.5517	.5557	.5596	.5636	.5675	.5714	.5753
.2	.5793	.5832	.5871	.5910	.5948	.5987	.6026	.6064	.6103	.6141
.3	.6179	.6217	.6255	.6293	.6331	.6368	.6406	.6443	.6480	.6517
.4	.6554	.6591	.6628	.6664	.6700	.6736	.6772	.6808	.6844	.6879
.5	.6915	.6950	.6985	.7019	.7054	.7088	.7123	.7157	.7190	.7224
.6	.7257	.7291	.7324	.7357	.7389	.7422	.7454	.7486	.7517	.7549
.7	.7580	.7611	.7642	.7673	.7704	.7734	.7764	.7794	.7823	.7852
.8	.7881	.7910	.7939	.7967	.7995	.8023	.8051	.8078	.8106	.8133
.9	.8159	.8186	.8212	.8238	.8264	.8289	.8315	.8340	.8365	.8389
1.0	.8413	.8438	.8461	.8485	.8508	.8531	.8554	.8577	.8599	.8621
1.1	.8643	.8665	.8686	.8708	.8729	.8749	.8770	.8790	.8810	.8830
1.2	.8849	.8869	.8888	.8907	.8925	.8944	.8962	.8980	.8997	.9015
1.3	.9032	.9049	.9066	.9082	.9099	.9115	.9131	.9147	.9162	.9177
1.4	.9192	.9207	.9222	.9236	.9251	.9265	.9279	.9292	.9306	.9319
1.5	.9332	.9345	.9357	.9370	.9382	.9394	.9406	.9418	.9429	.9441
1.6	.9452	.9463	.9474	.9484	.9495	.9505	.9515	.9525	.9535	.9545
1.7	.9554	.9564	.9573	.9582	.9591	.9599	.9608	.9616	.9625	.9633
1.8	.9641	.9649	.9656	.9664	.9671	.9678	.9686	.9693	.9699	.9706
1.9	.9713	.9719	.9726	.9732	.9738	.9744	.9750	.9756	.9761	.9767
2.0	.9772	.9778	.9783	.9788	.9793	.9798	.9803	.9808	.9812	.9817
2.1	.9821	.9826	.9830	.9834	.9838	.9842	.9846	.9850	.9854	.9857
2.2	.9861	.9864	.9868	.9871	.9875	.9878	.9881	.9884	.9887	.9890
2.3	.9893	.9896	.9898	.9901	.9904	.9906	.9909	.9911	.9913	.9916
2.4	.9918	.9920	.9922	.9925	.9927	.9929	.9931	.9932	.9934	.9936
2.5	.9938	.9940	.9941	.9943	.9945	.9946	.9948	.9949	.9951	.9952
2.6	.9953	.9955	.9956	.9957	.9959	.9960	.9961	.9962	.9963	.9964
2.7	.9965	.9966	.9967	.9968	.9969	.9970	.9971	.9972	.9973	.9974
2.8	.9974	.9975	.9976	.9977	.9977	.9978	.9979	.9979	.9980	.9981
2.9	.9981	.9982	.9982	.9983	.9984	.9984	.9985	.9985	.9986	.9986
3.0	.9987	.9987	.9987	.9988	.9988	.9989	.9989	.9989	.9990	.9990
3.1	.9990	.9991	.9991	.9991	.9992	.9992	.9992	.9992	.9993	.9993
3.2	.9993	.9993	.9994	.9994	.9994	.9994	.9994	.9995	.9995	.9995
3.3	.9995	.9995	.9995	.9996	.9996	.9996	.9996	.9996	.9996	.9997
3.4	.9997	.9997	.9997	.9997	.9997	.9997	.9997	.9997	.9997	.9998

Source: Table values are taken from: Alexander M. Mood, Franklin A. Graybill, and Duane C. Boes, *Introduction to the Theory of Statistics,* Third Edition, McGraw-Hill, Inc., 1974, Table 2—Cumulative Normal Distribution.

ANSWERS
TO SELECTED PROBLEMS

2-1 Interest expense = \$10,000

2-3 a Total sources = \$24 million

Total uses = \$23 million

Cash balance increases by \$1 million

2-5 Analysis of the determinants of ROI:

Year	GP/sales	OpExp/sales	Sales/TA	ROI
1989	0.400	0.304	1.111	0.135
1990	0.400	0.294	1.067	0.125

Analysis of the determinants of ROCE:

Year	NI/sales	Sales/assets	Assets/equity	ROCE
1989	0.036	1.111	2.000	0.080
1990	0.034	1.067	2.584	0.094

2-7 Analysis should make use of the following equation:

$$\text{ROCE} = \left(\frac{\text{NI} - \text{preferred dividends}}{\text{sales}} \right)\left(\frac{\text{sales}}{\text{assets}} \right)\left(\frac{\text{assets}}{\text{equity}} \right)$$

3-3 a

Hiller Manufacturing Co.
Pro Forma Balance Sheet
($000)

Cash	640	Accts. Payable	1,500
Receivables	1,520	Notes Payable	950
Inventory	1,880	Current Liabs.	2,450
Current Assets	4,040	Long-Term Debt	2,600
Fixed Assets	3,810	Common Equity	2,800
	7,850		7,850

3-5 New External Financing Requirements ($000):

			Future year		
	1	**2**	**3**	**4**	**5**
Debt	32	37	43	49	57
Equity	44	51	59	68	79
Total	76	88	102	117	136

4-1 $P_0 = \$17,843.30$

4-3 $P_0 = \$21.03$

4-5 $r = 19.86\%$

4-7 a $P_0 = \$82.00$

   b P/E $= 20$

   c DY $= 2\%$

4-9 a $P_0 = \$111$

   b DY $= 11.11\%$

4-11 a (1) $P_0 = \$16.00$

      (3) $P_0 = \$18.00$

   b (1) $P_0 = \$32.00$

      (3) $P_0 = \$24.00$

   c (1) $P_0 = \$20.00$

      (3) $P_0 = \$20.00$

5-1 1 NOF **2** NCB **3** NCB **4** I **5** I **6** NOF **7** NCB **8** I **9** NOF **10** NCB

5-3 a (1) NPV of A $= \$3,663$ NPV of B $= \$7,189$

      (2) IRR of A $= 14.85\%$ IRR of B $= 17.47\%$

      (3) PI of A $= 1.26$ PI of B $= 1.45$

5-5 a

Project	NPV	IRR	PI
A	$ 4,921	36.31%	1.49
B	$ 5,860	33.51%	1.59
C	$14,175	21.35%	1.28

5-7 a NPV of XL1000 $= \$12,174$

      NPV of XL2000 $= \$12,538$

b Cash flow equivalent for XL1000 = $2,624
Cash flow equivalent for XL2000 = $2,404

5-9 a

Model	NPV	IRR	PI
X	$152,831	30.38%	1.76
Y	$ 72,532	21.09%	1.26

6-1 b

Proposal	Mean	Variance	Standard deviation	Coefficient of variation
A	$20,000	130 million	$11,402	.5701
B	$50,000	850 million	$29,155	.5831

6-3 a 2.28% chance of negative NCB in any one year
  b SD = $42,124
  c SD = $18,902
  e SD = $81,098
6-5 a SD_{A+B} = $8,000
  SD_{A+C} = $7,211
  SD_{A+E} = $7,000
  SD_{A+D} = $2,191
  SD_{A+TB} = $2,000
6-7 a Beta of j = 1.5
  Beta of k = 1.067

6-9 a

Stock	Beta
A	0.38
B	0.38
C	1.00
D	0.06
E	1.43
F	−0.70
G	2.80
H	3.04
I	1.25
J	−1.51
K	3.60
L	0.00

  b $E(r)$ of the conservative portfolio = 5.39%
  $E(r)$ of the aggressive portfolio = 22.33%
6-11 a (1) k = 7.2%   (2) k = 12%
  (3) k = 13.2%   (4) k = 18%
7-1 K_d = 6.48%
7-3 K_{cp} = 13.85%
7-5 K_o = 13.9%
7-7 a 9.5%
  b The *new* 40%/10%/50% structure must be used for next year's overall cost of capital.
7-9 a K_e = 8.0%

    b $K_{cn} = 8.2\%$
    c $K_o = 5.53\%$
    d $K_o = 5.45\%$
    e $K_o = 5.55\%$
7-11 a $K_e = 10.95\%$
    b $K_d = 4.62\%$
    c $K_o = 7.785\%$
7-13 $K_{cb} = 4.91\%$

8-1 a

		Recommendation
$ 3,750	$20,000	No
7,500	20,000	No
11,250	20,000	No
22,500	20,000	Yes
45,500	20,000	Yes

    b breakeven yield $= 16\%$
8-3 One day's float reduction $= \$201,644$
8-5 a $41,030
    b Net annual savings $= \$12,712$, so use the lock-box system.
8-7 This is a good one for you to do on your own. But the answer to part (c) is $137,583.

9-1 a

Applicant	Z score
A	41.5
B	67.4
C	60.5
D	75.0
E	91.0

9-3 a $Z = 100M - 12D$
    c Slope $= 75/(10 - 1) = 8.33$
9-5 a EOQ $= 100$ units
    b 30 orders
    c 6 days
    d Average inventory size $= 110$ units
9-7 a EOQ $= 4,899$ units
    b (1) (a) EOQ $= 5,367$ units
        (c) EOQ $= 4,648$ units
      (2) (a) EOQ $= 5,367$ units
        (c) EOQ $= 4,648$ units
      (3) (a) EOQ $= 4,472$ units
        (c) EOQ $= 5,164$ units
10-1 Receivables turnover $= 9.47$
Accounts receivable $= \$105,597$
10-3 a NCB per year $= \$18,406$
    b Maximum investment $=$ present value of future NCBs
                    $= \$153,383$
10-5 a Reduces expected cash flow in one year to $990,000
    b NPV $= \$25,000$
10-7 NPV $= -\$9,794$

10-9 a

Proposed policy	NPV
1	$10,826
2	$14,530
3	−$19,068
4	−$31,685

11-1 Since Stark has the highest coefficient of variation at .20, it has the highest business risk.

11-3 a DOL = 3.5 for both firms

    b DFL for Galt = 1.0

      DFL for Holcombe = 1.45

    c DTL for Galt = 3.5

      DTL for Holcombe = 5.0

11-5 a DTL = 1.8

    b at 15%:   EPS = $0.476

      at 20%:   EPS = 0.51

      at −5%:   EPS = 0.341

      at −20%: EPS = 0.24

11-7 a For 800 units   EBIT = ($18,000)

      For 1,800 units   EBIT = $22,000

    b Breakeven output = 1,250 units

    c Breakeven sales, $S^* = \$125,000$

    d New breakeven sales = $139,535, or $139,600

11-9 a EPS = $0.32 at EBIT of $14,000

      EPS = $5.44 at EBIT of $78,000

    b DFL = 3.5

    c DTL = 1.88

    d 37.6% decline in EPS

11-11 Plan A: CB_r = $380,000

      Plan B: CB_r = $220,000

      Plan C: CB_r = ($20,000)

12-1 If earnings are $3,000,000, dividends will be $600,000.

      If earnings are $2,000,000, no dividends will be paid.

12-3

Scotty Marketing Company
Liabilities and Net Worth

Post Split

Debt	$ 8,000,000
Common equity	
Par ($0.75)	1,500,000
Paid-in-capital	4,000,000
Retained earnings	16,500,000
	$30,000,000

Post-Stock Dividend

Debt	$ 8,000,000
Common equity	
Par ($1.50)	3,000,000
Paid-in-capital	8,000,000
Retained earnings	11,000,000
	$30,000,000

GLOSSARY

accelerated depreciation   Any method of depreciating an asset at a faster rate than under the straight-line method.

accounts receivable turnover   See **receivables turnover**.

acid-test (quick) ratio   A general measure of firm liquidity, calculated as follows:

$$\frac{\text{current assets} - \text{inventories}}{\text{current liabilities}}$$

annuity   A series of constant cash flows occurring for a specified number of periods.

average collection period   The average number of days an account receivable is outstanding. A measure of the liquidity of a firm's accounts receivable, calculated as follows:

$$\frac{\text{number of days in the sales period covered}}{\text{receivables turnover}}$$

bankers' acceptances   A draft (order to pay) drawn on a specific bank by a seller of goods in order to obtain payment for goods that have been shipped (sold) to a customer. The customer maintains an account with that bank.

basic defensive interval   A general measure of firm liquidity, calculated as follows:

$$\frac{\text{total defensive assets}}{\text{projected daily operating expenditures}}$$

beta   A measure of an asset's systematic risk. It relates the variability in the returns on the asset to the variability in the returns on a broad-based portfolio of assets.

break-even analysis   The process of determining the quantity of output for which total revenues equal total expenses.

business risk   The dispersion in the probability distribution of a firm's earnings before interest and taxes; the variability in a firm's earnings before interest and taxes.

capital asset   An asset with a life of more than one year that is not bought and sold in the ordinary course of business.

capital-asset pricing model (CAPM)   A model used to estimate the required, and expected, rate of return on an asset. The model presumes that the required rate of return is equal to the riskless rate of interest plus a risk premium dependent on the asset's systematic risk. It is also used to estimate the cost of equity capital of a firm.

capital budgeting   The process of determining the investments a firm should make. The investments normally have a life of more than one year.

capital gain   The difference between the selling price and the purchase price of a capital asset, when the selling price is the larger of the two.

capital loss   The difference between the selling price and the depreciated book value of an asset, when the selling price is the smaller of the two.

capital market line (CML)   A graph of the relationship between the expected returns on efficient portfolios and the standard deviations of the portfolios; a straight line connecting the risk-return plots of the risk-free asset and the market portfolio.

capital rationing   A policy of placing an arbitrary limit on the amount of investment by a firm.

cash budget   A statement of planned cash receipts and disbursements for a future period.

cash discount   A reduction from invoice price offered to a customer who pays on or before a designated point in time.

cash flow equivalent   A stream of cash flows that has the same value as another asset.

cash flow process   The process of cash generation and disposition in a typical business setting.

coefficient of variation (CV)   A measure of relative variation, calculated by dividing the standard deviation of a probability (or frequency) distribution by the mean of the distribution.

commercial paper   Short-term unsecured promissory notes sold by large businesses in order to raise cash. Unlike most other money market instruments, commercial paper does not have a *highly developed* secondary market.

common-size statement   An income statement with each entry stated as a percentage of sales, or a balance sheet with each entry stated as a percentage of total assets.

compound interest   Interest earned on both principal and accumulated past interest.

concentration bank   A bank where the firm maintains a major disbursing account.

consolidated tax return   An income tax return that combines the income of two or more affiliated firms.

continuous probability distribution   A probability distribution which has an infinite number of possible outcomes or values within any finite range in the distribution.

conversion price   The face value of a convertible security divided by its associated conversion ratio.

conversion ratio   The predetermined number of common shares for which a convertible security may be exchanged.

convertible security   A bond or preferred stock issue that is exchangeable into another form of security (usually common stock) at the investor's option.

correlation   In finance, the relationship of movements in two or more sales, cost, income, or cash-flow streams; the extent to which the streams move together or inversely.

cost of capital   A term often used broadly to refer to the minimum rate of return that must be earned on an investment in order to leave the market price of the firm's common stock unchanged. More specifically, the term refers to the minimum rate of return on investments that have the same systematic risk as the firm as a whole without the investment.

cost of an individual source of capital   The explicit cost of a specific form of financing, such as debt, preferred stock, convertible securities, retained earnings, or common stock. The effect of using one form of financing on the cost of another form is ignored in this computation.

coupon rate   The stated rate of interest on a bond.

credit terms   The terms offered to credit customers, indicating the maximum credit period and the amount of any cash discount.

current ratio   A general measure of liquidity, calculated as follows:

$$\frac{\text{current assets}}{\text{current liabilities}}$$

debt ratio   A leverage ratio, calculated as follows:

$$\frac{\text{total liabilities}}{\text{total assets}}$$

default risk   The uncertainty of expected returns from a security, attributable to possible changes in the financial capacity of the security issuer to make contracted payments to the security owner. Treasury securities are considered to be default-free. Default risk is also referred to as "financial risk" in the context of marketable securities management.

degree of financial leverage   A measure of the relative percentage change in earnings per share (EPS) in response to a given percentage change in earnings before interest and taxes (EBIT).

degree of operating leverage   A measure of the relative percentage change in operating earnings (EBIT) in response to a given percentage change in sales.

degree of total leverage   A measure of the relative percentage change in earnings per share (EPS) in response to a given percentage change in sales.

depository transfer checks   A means for moving funds from local bank accounts to concentration accounts. The depository transfer check itself is an unsigned, nonnegotiable instrument. It is payable only to the bank of deposit for credit to the firm's specific account.

disbursing float   Funds available in the company's bank account until its payment check has cleared through the banking system.

discounting   A mathematical process of time-adjusting a cash flow or a series of cash flows to determine their value at an earlier point in time, usually the present.

discount rate   The rate at which cash flows are time-adjusted; the required rate of return on an investment.

discrete probability distribution   A probability distribution that has a finite number of possible outcomes.

diversification   The act of investing in assets whose returns are less than perfectly positively correlated.

dividend policy   A firm's policy regarding the payment of dividends to its owners.

dividend yield   The ratio of the firm's annual cash dividend to the market price of its common stock.

dominance   The expectation of (1) both higher return and lower risk for one asset than for another, (2) higher return for one asset than for another with the same risk, or (3) lower risk for one asset than for another with the same return.

downside risk   That portion of a probability distribution of the returns on an investment to the left of the mean; the probability of earning less than expected.

economic order quantity (EOQ)   The optimum order quantity of an inventory item; the order quantity that results in the least total cost for the firm.

economic value   The value of an earning asset in an efficient market.

effective annual yield   The promised rate of return on an investment in a bond.

efficient assets (portfolios)   Assets (portfolios) whose risk-return points lie on the efficient frontier.

efficient frontier   The investment projects or asset portfolios that dominate all other investment projects or asset portfolios in a given set on the basis of their return and risk characteristics.

efficient market   A market in which the price of an asset reflects all relevant information available to investors.

EPS   The abbreviation for earnings per share.

equity   The owner's investment in a firm, indicated in the balance sheet of a corporation by the par value of the common stock, paid-in capital, and retained earnings. Preferred stock is considered part of the equity if the preferred stockholders are considered owners.

excess return   The rate of return on an asset above the riskless rate of interest.

federal agency securities   Debt obligations of corporations and agencies created to carry out the lending programs of the U.S. government.

financial assets   Claims for future payment by one economic unit on another.

financial leverage   Financing a portion of the firm's assets with securities bearing a fixed rate of return.

financial risk   The combination of (1) increased variability in earnings per common share, and (2) the higher risk of insolvency induced by the firm's use of financial leverage.

firm risk of a project   The risk of an investment to the investing firm. It will be less than the project risk if there are any portfolio effects within the firm.

fixed costs   Those costs that do not vary with the level of the firm's sales, but remain constant in total over the relevant planning horizon.

flotation costs   The underpricing, legal and accounting fees, engraving and printing costs, and investment banking costs that are incurred by the firm in marketing a new issue of securities.

Gordon (perpetual-growth) model   A mathematical formula for estimating either the cost, or the share price, of common-equity capital, where dividends are presumed to grow at a constant rate.

gross profit margin   A measure of profits in relation to sales, calculated as follows:

$$\frac{\text{gross profit}}{\text{sales}}$$

initial investment outlay   The immediate cash commitment required to undertake an investment.

internal rate of return   The rate of return on an investment, determined by finding the discount rate that will equate the present value of all future cash flows from the investment with the initial investment outlay.

inventory turnover   The number of times inventory is turned over during a specified period of time. A measure of the liquidity of inventory, calculated as follows:

$$\frac{\text{cost of goods sold during the period}}{\text{average inventory during the period}}$$

investment banker   A financial specialist who underwrites and distributes new securities, and advises corporate clients about raising new funds.

leverage ratios   Financial ratios designed to measure the extent to which a firm has financed its assets with nonowner sources of funds.

linear programming   An algorithm for allocating scarce resources involving a linear objective function and a set of linear constraints.

liquidity ratios   Financial ratios designed to measure the ability of the firm to pay its bills on time.

long-term-debt ratio   A measure of financial leverage calculated as follows:

$$\frac{\text{long-term debt}}{\text{total assets}}$$

long-term-debt-to-total-capitalization ratio   A leverage ratio, calculated as follows:

$$\frac{\text{long-term debt}}{\text{long-term debt } + \text{ preferred stock } + \text{ common stockholders' equity}}$$

mail float   Funds tied up during the time that elapses from the moment a customer mails his remittance check until the firm begins to process it.

marginal cost of capital   The cost (expressed as a percentage) of raising additional funds.

marketable securities   Security investments that the firm can quickly convert into cash balances.

market portfolio   The portfolio of all assets in the economy. The stocks in the Standard & Poor's Index of 500 stocks is often used as a proxy for the market portfolio.

market return   The average return on all risky assets in the economy. The Standard & Poor's Index of 500 stock prices is often used as an indicator of the market return.

market value   The price of an asset or service in the market, often estimated by determining the present value of the expected cash flows applicable to the asset or service.

mathematical programming   A term used to describe a wide range of quantitative techniques or algorithms for allocating limited resources.

maturity value   The dollar amount received by a bondholder when the bond contract has been fulfilled. This is also referred to as the *face value* or *par value* of the bond.

model   A simplified representation of a real-world phenomenon; a generalization of reality.

money market   All institutions and procedures that facilitate transactions in short-term debt instruments issued by borrowers with very high credit ratings.

money market mutual funds   Investment companies that purchase a diversified array of short-term, high-grade debt instruments in the money market.

Monte Carlo simulation   A type of simulation using the technique of randomly selecting values from one or more probability distributions for use in a particular run of a simulation study. (See **simulation**.)

negotiable certificates of deposit (CDs)   Marketable receipts for funds deposited in a bank for a fixed period of time. The deposited funds earn a fixed rate of interest.

net cash benefits (NCBs)   The net operating cash flows of an asset, adjusted for taxes; the cash flows of an asset resulting from sales minus cost of goods sold, operating expenses, and income taxes.

net present value (NPV)   The present value of the net cash benefits of an investment minus the initial investment outlay, plus the present value of nonoperating cash flows of the investment subsequent to the initial outlay.

net profit margin   A measure of profits in relation to sales, calculated as follows:

$$\frac{\text{net income after taxes}}{\text{sales}}$$

nonlinear programming   A group of optimization techniques that enable the user to consider nonlinear objective functions.

nonoperating cash flows   Cash flows applicable to an asset, other than those directly associated with operating the asset. They do not include cash flows from sales, cost of goods sold, operating expenses, or taxes.

normal probability distribution   A probability distribution that forms a symmetrical, bell-shaped curve with specifically defined properties. The relationship between the dispersion and the proportion of the distribution is the same for all normal distributions.

operating income rate of return   A measure of profits in relation to investment, calculated as follows:

$$\frac{\text{earnings before interest and taxes}}{\text{total assets}}$$

operating leverage   The presence of fixed operating expenses in the firm's cost structure; the responsiveness of changes in EBIT to changes in sales.

operating profit margin   A measure of profits in relation to sales, calculated as follows:

$$\frac{\text{earnings before interest and taxes}}{\text{sales}}$$

operations research   The application of a scientific approach to management problem solving. The use of quantitative analyses is stressed.

optimal financial structure   The particular mix of sources of financing that minimizes the firm's cost of capital and maximizes the value of the firm.

overall cash-flow coverage ratio   A leverage ratio calculated as follows:

$$\frac{\text{earnings before interest and taxes } + \text{ lease expense } + \text{ depreciation expense}}{\text{interest expense } + \text{ lease expense } + [\text{preferred dividends}/(1 - \text{tax rate})] + [\text{principal payments on debt } (1 - \text{tax rate})]}$$

payable-through draft   A financial instrument that has the physical appearance of an ordinary check, but is not drawn on a bank. A payable-through draft is drawn on and paid by the issuing firm. The bank serves as a collection point and passes the draft on to the firm.

payback period   The length of time required for the cash inflows from an investment to cover the initial investment outlay.

portfolio effect   The tendency of the variability in the returns from one asset or group of assets to be offset by variations in the returns from other assets owned by the firm.

present value   The current worth of the future cash flows of an asset.

present-value annuity factor (PVAF)   The present value of a series of cash flows of $1 per period for a specified number of periods, time-adjusted at a given discount rate.

present-value interest factor (PVIF)   The present value of $1 received at the end of a given future period, time-adjusted at a given discount rate.

price-earnings (P/E) ratio   The market price of a share of common stock divided by the earnings per share for one year.

processing float   Funds tied up during the time required for the firm to process remittance checks before they can be deposited in the bank.

profitability index (PI)   The present value of all expected future cash flows from an investment divided by the initial investment outlay.

profitability ratios   Financial ratios designed to measure how effectively the firm's management controls expenses and turns sales into profits.

pro forma balance sheet   A planned or projected statement of financial condition at a future date.

pro forma income statement   A planned or projected statement of income for a future period.

project risk   The total risk of an investment in an asset; includes both the systematic and the diversifiable risk of the project.

purchase discount   A reduction in the purchase price of a product because of ordering a relatively large quantity.

receivables turnover   The number of times receivables are turned over during a specified period of time, calculated as follows:

$$\frac{\text{total credit sales during the period}}{\text{average level of accounts receivable during the period}}$$

regression method of forecasting   A forecast method involving the use of a regression equation; usually determined by the method of least squares.

repurchase agreements   Legal contracts that involve the sale of short-term securities by a borrower to a lender of funds. The borrower commits to repurchase the securities at a later date at the contract price plus a stated interest charge.

required rate of return   The rate of return required by investors for letting the firm have the use of their funds. It is the minimum acceptable rate of return on new investments by the firm.

residual dividend policy   A dividend policy involving the payment of cash dividends equal to those earnings which the firm cannot reinvest at or above the required rate of return.

return on common equity   A measure of profits in relation to the owner's investment, calculated as follows:

$$\frac{\text{net income available to common stockholders}}{\text{common equity}}$$

return on total assets   A measure of profits in relation to total investment, calculated as follows:

$$\frac{\text{net income after taxes}}{\text{total assets}}$$

risk The dispersion of the possible returns of an investment around their expected value; also, the probability that the returns from an asset will be less than expected.

risk-adjusted discount rate The discount rate used to time-adjust a stream of risky cash flows to determine the present value of the stream; the riskless rate of interest plus the risk premium appropriate to the level of risk associated with the investment.

risk-averse Having a dislike of risk. Investors who are risk-averse will value a probability distribution of the return on an investment at less than the expected value of the distribution.

risk-free asset An asset that does not have any risk of any kind. U.S. Treasury bills are often used as a proxy for a risk-free asset.

risk premium The portion of the required rate of return on an investment necessary to compensate the investor for the risk assumed in making the investment.

scatter diagram method of forecasting A technique of financial forecasting that involves plotting the variable to be forecast against the predictor variable, visually fitting a line to the scatter of points, and then extrapolating the relationship to make predictions.

seasonal dating Tailoring the credit period offered to customers, whose business is seasonal, to fit their ability to pay.

secondary market Transactions in currently outstanding securities. This market is distinguished from the new-issues, or primary, market.

security market line (SML) A graph of the relationship between the expected returns of assets, as well as portfolios, and their beta coefficients. In some cases, the covariances of the returns with the average market return are used in the relation rather than beta coefficients.

simulation Experimentation performed on a system model that has been designed to capture the critical realities of a decision-making situation.

sources-and-uses-of-funds statement A financial statement indicating where a firm obtained funds and how they were used (spent) during a specified time period.

stable dollar dividend policy A policy wherein a firm alters its cash dividend payment only when it feels the new dividend can be sustained in the foreseeable future.

standard deviation A measure of dispersion around the expected value of a probability or frequency distribution; the square root of the variance.

stock dividend The payment of dividends in the form of shares of stock.

sunk cost Any cost that was incurred in the past and is not affected in any way by decisions made today.

systematic risk The portion of the total risk of an investment that is associated with the market as a whole. Systematic risk cannot be diversified away.

target dividend payout ratio A dividend policy wherein the firm seeks to pay out a specified percentage of sustainable earnings.

time adjustment The process of adjusting the value of a cash flow (or stream of cash flows) to reflect its value at another point in time.

times-interest-earned ratio A leverage ratio, calculated as follows:

$$\frac{\text{earnings before interest and taxes}}{\text{annual interest expense}}$$

transit float Funds tied up during the time necessary for a deposited check to clear through the commercial banking system and become usable to the company.

treasury bills Direct, short-term debt obligations of the U.S. government, sold on a regular basis by the U.S. Treasury.

treasury stock Common stock that has been repurchased by the issuing firm.

utility Satisfaction or happiness.

variable costs Those expenses which vary directly with the level of a firm's sales.

variance A measure of dispersion around an expected value; the square of the standard deviation.

weighted-average cost of capital An average of the component costs of the individual sources of capital employed by the firm. The term is sometimes shortened to *average cost of capital* or *cost of capital*.

working capital A concept traditionally defined as a firm's investment in current assets. Net working capital refers to the difference between current assets and current liabilities.

yield One expression of the rate of return on an investment.

yield to maturity A promised rate of return from an investment in a bond, if the bond is held to its maturity.

z-score The result obtained from solving a linear discriminant problem.

INDEX